# *my*Perspectives®

## BRITISH AND WORLD LITERATURE

SAVVAS
LEARNING COMPANY

Savvas Learning Company LLC, 15 East Midland Avenue, Paramus, NJ 07652

Cover: © Sergey Peterman/123RF

Attributions of third-party content appear on page R81, which constitutes an extension of this copyright page.

ISBN-13: 978-1-41-837119-7
ISBN-10: 1-41-837119-X

8 2024

# Welcome!

*myPerspectives™ English Language Arts* is a student-centered learning environment where you will analyze text, cite evidence, and respond critically about your learning. You will take ownership of your learning through goal-setting, reflection, independent text selection, and activities that allow you to collaborate with your peers.

Each unit of study includes selections of different genres—including multimedia—all related to a relevant and meaningful Essential Question. As you read, you will engage in activities that inspire thoughtful discussion and debate with your peers allowing you to formulate, and defend, your own perspectives.

*myPerspectives ELA* offers a variety of ways to interact directly with the text. You can annotate by writing in your print consumable, or you can annotate in your digital Student Edition. In addition, exciting technology allows you to access multimedia directly from your mobile device and communicate using an online discussion board!

We hope you enjoy using *myPerspectives ELA* as you develop the skills required to be successful throughout college and career.

# Authors' Perspectives

*myPerspectives* is informed by a team of respected experts whose experiences working with students and study of instructional best practices have positively impacted education. From the evolving role of the teacher to how students learn in a digital age, our authors bring new ideas, innovations, and strategies that transform teaching and learning in today's competitive and interconnected world.

"The teaching of English needs to focus on engaging a new generation of learners. How do we get them excited about reading and writing? How do we help them to envision themselves as readers and writers? And, how can we make the teaching of English more culturally, socially, and technologically relevant? Throughout the curriculum, we've created spaces that enhance youth voice and participation and that connect the teaching of literature and writing to technological transformations of the digital age."

## Ernest Morrell, Ph.D.

is the Macy professor of English Education at Teachers College, Columbia University, a class of 2014 Fellow of the American Educational Research Association, and the Past-President of the National Council of Teachers of English (NCTE). He is also the Director of Teachers College's Institute for Urban and Minority Education (IUME). He is an award-winning author and in his spare time he coaches youth sports and writes poems and plays. Dr. Morrell has influenced the development of *my*Perspectives in Assessment, Writing & Research, Student Engagement, and Collaborative Learning.

## Elfrieda Hiebert, Ph.D.

is President and CEO of TextProject, a nonprofit that provides resources to support higher reading levels. She is also a research associate at the University of California, Santa Cruz. Dr. Hiebert has worked in the field of early reading acquisition for 45 years, first as a teacher's aide and teacher of primary-level students in California and, subsequently, as a teacher and researcher. Her research addresses how fluency, vocabulary, and knowledge can be fostered through appropriate texts. Dr. Hiebert has influenced the development of *my*Perspectives in Vocabulary, Text Complexity, and Assessment.

"The signature of complex text is challenging vocabulary. In the systems of vocabulary, it's important to provide ways to show how concepts can be made more transparent to students. We provide lessons and activities that develop a strong vocabulary and concept foundation—a foundation that permits students to comprehend increasingly more complex text."

## Kelly Gallagher, M.Ed.

teaches at Magnolia High School in Anaheim, California, where he is in his thirty-first year. He is the former co-director of the South Basin Writing Project at California State University, Long Beach. Mr. Gallagher has influenced the development of *my*Perspectives in Writing, Close Reading, and the Role of Teachers.

"The *my*Perspectives classroom is dynamic. The teacher inspires, models, instructs, facilitates, and advises students as they evolve and grow. When teachers guide students through meaningful learning tasks and then pass them ownership of their own learning, students become engaged and work harder. This is how we make a difference in student achievement—by putting students at the center of their learning and giving them the opportunities to choose, explore, collaborate, and work independently."

"It's critical to give students the opportunity to read a wide range of highly engaging texts and to immerse themselves in exploring powerful ideas and how these ideas are expressed. In *my*Perspectives, we focus on building up students' awareness of how academic language works, which is especially important for English language learners."

## Jim Cummins, Ph.D.

is a Professor Emeritus in the Department of Curriculum, Teaching and Learning of the University of Toronto. His research focuses on literacy development in multilingual school contexts as well as on the potential roles of technology in promoting language and literacy development. In recent years, he has been working actively with teachers to identify ways of increasing the literacy engagement of learners in multilingual school contexts. Dr. Cummins has influenced the development of *my*Perspectives in English Language Learner and English Language Development support.

# UNIT  Forging a Hero

## Warriors and Leaders

### UNIT INTRODUCTION



###  WHOLE-CLASS LEARNING



### SMALL-GROUP LEARNING

## INDEPENDENT LEARNING



These selections can be accessed via the Interactive Student Edition.

PERFORMANCE-BASED ASSESSMENT PREP

## PERFORMANCE-BASED ASSESSMENT



## UNIT REFLECTION



## DIGITAL PERSPECTIVES

- Unit Introduction Videos
- Media Selections/Media Enrichment
- Modeling Videos
- Selection Audio Recordings

Additional digital resources can be found in:

- Interactive Student Edition
- *my*Perspectives+

# UNIT 2 Reflecting on Society

## Argument, Satire, and Reform

### UNIT INTRODUCTION

### WHOLE-CLASS LEARNING

PERFORMANCE TASK



### SMALL-GROUP LEARNING

PERFORMANCE TASK

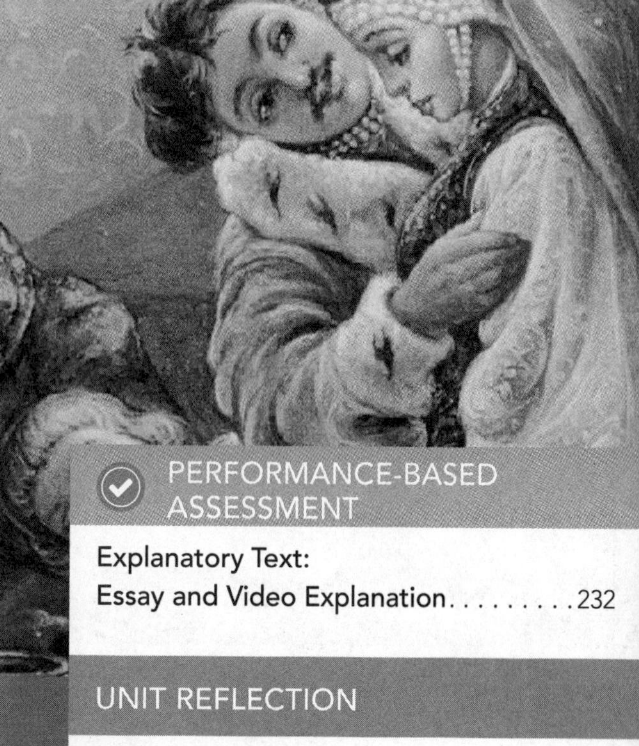

## INDEPENDENT LEARNING



These selections can be accessed via the Interactive Student Edition.

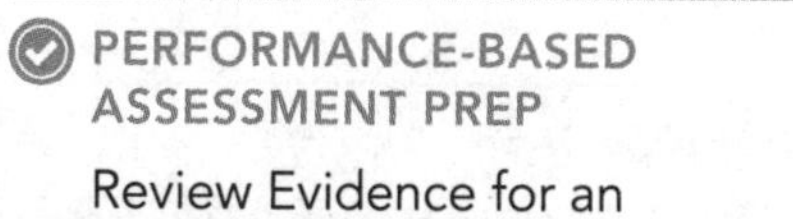

PERFORMANCE-BASED ASSESSMENT PREP



## PERFORMANCE-BASED ASSESSMENT



## UNIT REFLECTION



## DIGITAL PERSPECTIVES

- Unit Introduction Videos
- Media Selections/Media Enrichments
- Modeling Videos
- Selection Audio Recordings

Additional digital resources can be found in:

- Interactive Student Edition
- *my*Perspectives+

# UNIT  3 Facing the Future, Confronting the Past

## Shakespeare Extended Study

### UNIT INTRODUCTION



###  WHOLE-CLASS LEARNING



### SMALL-GROUP LEARNING

ESSENTIAL QUESTION: How do our attitudes toward the past and future shape our actions?

## INDEPENDENT LEARNING



These selections can be accessed via the Interactive Student Edition.

PERFORMANCE-BASED ASSESSMENT PREP

## PERFORMANCE-BASED ASSESSMENT



## UNIT REFLECTION



## DIGITAL PERSPECTIVES

- Unit Introduction Videos
- Media Selections/Media Enrichment
- Modeling Videos
- Selection Audio Recordings

Additional digital resources can be found in:

- Interactive Student Edition
- *my*Perspectives+

# UNIT 4 Seeing Things New

## Visionaries and Skeptics

### UNIT INTRODUCTION

### WHOLE-CLASS LEARNING



### SMALL-GROUP LEARNING

## INDEPENDENT LEARNING



These selections can be accessed via the Interactive Student Edition.

### PERFORMANCE-BASED ASSESSMENT PREP

## PERFORMANCE-BASED ASSESSMENT



## UNIT REFLECTION



## DIGITAL PERSPECTIVES

- Unit Introduction Videos
- Media Selections/Media Enrichment
- Modeling Videos
- Selection Audio Recordings

Additional digital resources can be found in:

- Interactive Student Edition
- *my*Perspectives+

# UNIT  5 Discovering the Self

## Individual, Nature, and Society

### UNIT INTRODUCTION



###  WHOLE-CLASS LEARNING

### SMALL-GROUP LEARNING

## INDEPENDENT LEARNING



These selections can be accessed via the Interactive Student Edition.

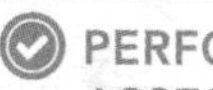

PERFORMANCE-BASED ASSESSMENT PREP

## PERFORMANCE-BASED ASSESSMENT



## UNIT REFLECTION



## DIGITAL PERSPECTIVES

- Unit Introduction Videos
- Media Selections/Media Enrichment
- Modeling Videos
- Selection Audio Recordings

Additional digital resources can be found in:

- Interactive Student Edition
- *my*Perspectives+

# UNIT 6 Finding a Home

## Nation, Exile, and Dominion

### UNIT INTRODUCTION

### WHOLE-CLASS LEARNING



### SMALL-GROUP LEARNING

## INDEPENDENT LEARNING



These selections can be accessed via the Interactive Student Edition.

PERFORMANCE-BASED ASSESSMENT PREP

## PERFORMANCE-BASED ASSESSMENT



## UNIT REFLECTION



## DIGITAL PERSPECTIVES

- Unit Introduction Videos
- Media Selections/Media Enrichment
- Modeling Videos
- Selection Audio Recordings

Additional digital resources can be found in:

- Interactive Student Edition
- *my*Perspectives+

# Standards Overview

The following **English Language Arts** standards will prepare you to succeed in college and your future career. The College and Career Readiness Anchor Standards define what you need to achieve by the end of high school, and the grade-specific Standards define what you need to know by the end of your current grade level.

The following provides an overview of the Standards.

## Standards for Reading

### College and Career Readiness Anchor Standards for Reading

#### Key Ideas and Details

1. Read closely to determine what the text says explicitly and to make logical inferences from it; cite specific textual evidence when writing or speaking to support conclusions drawn from the text.
2. Determine central ideas or themes of a text and analyze their development; summarize the key supporting details and ideas.
3. Analyze how and why individuals, events, and ideas develop and interact over the course of a text.

#### Craft and Structure

4. Interpret words and phrases as they are used in a text, including determining technical, connotative, and figurative meanings, and analyze how specific word choices shape meaning or tone.
5. Analyze the structure of texts, including how specific sentences, paragraphs, and larger portions of the text (e.g., a section, chapter, scene, or stanza) relate to each other and the whole.
6. Assess how point of view or purpose shapes the content and style of a text.

#### Integration of Knowledge and Ideas

7. Integrate and evaluate content presented in diverse formats and media, including visually and quantitatively, as well as in words.
8. Delineate and evaluate the argument and specific claims in a text, including the validity of the reasoning as well as the relevance and sufficiency of the evidence.
9. Analyze how two or more texts address similar themes or topics in order to build knowledge or to compare the approaches the authors take.

#### Range of Reading and Level of Text Complexity

10. Read and comprehend complex literary and informational texts independently and proficiently.

| Grade 12 Reading Standards for Literature |
| --- |
| **Standard** |
| **Key Ideas and Details** |
| Cite strong and thorough textual evidence to support analysis of what the text says explicitly as well as inferences drawn from the text, including determining where the text leaves matters uncertain. |
| Determine two or more themes or central ideas of a text and analyze their development over the course of the text, including how they interact and build on one another to produce a complex account; provide an objective summary of the text. |
| Analyze the impact of the author's choices regarding how to develop and relate elements of a story or drama (e.g., where a story is set, how the action is ordered, how the characters are introduced and developed). |
| **Craft and Structure** |
| Determine the meaning of words and phrases as they are used in the text, including figurative and connotative meanings; analyze the impact of specific word choices on meaning and tone, including words with multiple meanings or language that is particularly fresh, engaging, or beautiful. (Include Shakespeare as well as other authors.) |
| Analyze how an author's choices concerning how to structure specific parts of a text (e.g., the choice of where to begin or end a story, the choice to provide a comedic or tragic resolution) contribute to its overall structure and meaning as well as its aesthetic impact. |
| Analyze a case in which grasping a point of view requires distinguishing what is directly stated in a text from what is really meant (e.g., satire, sarcasm, irony, or understatement). |
| **Integration of Knowledge and Ideas** |
| Analyze multiple interpretations of a story, drama, or poem (e.g., recorded or live production of a play or recorded novel or poetry), evaluating how each version interprets the source text. (Include at least one play by Shakespeare and one play by an American dramatist.) |
| Demonstrate knowledge of eighteenth-, nineteenth- and early-twentieth-century foundational works of American literature, including how two or more texts from the same period treat similar themes or topics. |
| **Range of Reading and Level of Text Complexity** |
| By the end of grade 12, read and comprehend literature, including stories, dramas, and poems, at the high end of the grades 11–CCR text complexity band independently and proficiently. |

# Standards Overview

| Grade 12 Reading Standards for Informational Text |
|---|
| Standard |
| **Key Ideas and Details** |
| Cite strong and thorough textual evidence to support analysis of what the text says explicitly as well as inferences drawn from the text, including determining where the text leaves matters uncertain. |
| Determine two or more central ideas of a text and analyze their development over the course of the text, including how they interact and build on one another to provide a complex analysis; provide an objective summary of the text. |
| Analyze a complex set of ideas or sequence of events and explain how specific individuals, ideas, or events interact and develop over the course of the text. |
| **Craft and Structure** |
| Determine the meaning of words and phrases as they are used in a text, including figurative, connotative, and technical meanings; analyze how an author uses and refines the meaning of a key term or terms over the course of a text (e.g., how Madison defines *faction* in *Federalist* No. 10). |
| Analyze and evaluate the effectiveness of the structure an author uses in his or her exposition or argument, including whether the structure makes points clear, convincing, and engaging. |
| Determine an author's point of view or purpose in a text in which the rhetoric is particularly effective, analyzing how style and content contribute to the power, persuasiveness or beauty of the text. |
| **Integration of Knowledge and Ideas** |
| Integrate and evaluate multiple sources of information presented in different media or formats (e.g., visually, quantitatively) as well as in words in order to address a question or solve a problem. |
| Delineate and evaluate the reasoning in seminal U.S. texts, including the application of constitutional principles and use of legal reasoning (e.g., in U.S. Supreme Court majority opinions and dissents) and the premises, purposes, and arguments in works of public advocacy (e.g., *The Federalist*, presidential addresses). |
| Analyze seventeenth-, eighteenth-, and nineteenth-century foundational U.S. documents of historical and literary significance (including The Declaration of Independence, the Preamble to the Constitution, the Bill of Rights, and Lincoln's Second Inaugural Address) for their themes, purposes, and rhetorical features. |
| **Range of Reading and Level of Text Complexity** |
| By the end of grade 12, read and comprehend literary nonfiction at the high end of the grades 11-CCR text complexity band independently and proficiently. |

# Standards for Writing

| College and Career Readiness Anchor Standards for Writing |
|---|
| **Key Ideas and Details** |
| **1.** Write arguments to support claims in an analysis of substantive topics or texts, using valid reasoning and relevant and sufficient evidence. |
| **2.** Write informative/explanatory texts to examine and convey complex ideas and information clearly and accurately through the effective selection, organization, and analysis of content. |
| **3.** Write narratives to develop real or imagined experiences or events using effective technique, well-chosen details, and well-structured event sequences. |
| **Production and Distribution of Writing** |
| **4.** Produce clear and coherent writing in which the development, organization, and style are appropriate to task, purpose, and audience. |
| **5.** Develop and strengthen writing as needed by planning, revising, editing, rewriting, or trying a new approach. |
| **6.** Use technology, including the Internet, to produce and publish writing and to interact and collaborate with others. |
| **Research to Build and Present Knowledge** |
| **7.** Conduct short as well as more sustained research projects based on focused questions, demonstrating understanding of the subject under investigation. |
| **8.** Gather relevant information from multiple print and digital sources, assess the credibility and accuracy of each source, and integrate the information while avoiding plagiarism. |
| **9.** Draw evidence from literary or informational texts to support analysis, reflection, and research. |
| **Range of Writing** |
| **10.** Write routinely over extended time frames (time for research, reflection, and revision) and shorter time frames (a single sitting or a day or two) for a range of tasks, purposes, and audiences. |

| Grade 12 Writing Standards |
|---|
| **Standard** |
| **Text Types and Purposes** |
| Write arguments to support claims in an analysis of substantive topics or texts, using valid reasoning and relevant and sufficient evidence. |
| Introduce precise, knowledgeable claim(s), establish the significance of the claim(s), distinguish the claim(s) from alternate or opposing claims, and create an organization that logically sequences claim(s), counterclaims, reasons, and evidence. |

# Standards Overview

| Grade 12 Writing Standards |
|---|
| **Standard** |
| **Text Types and Purposes (continued)** |
| Develop claim(s) and counterclaims fairly and thoroughly, supplying the most relevant evidence for each while pointing out the strengths and limitations of both in a manner that anticipates the audience's knowledge level, concerns, values, and possible biases. |
| Use words, phrases, and clauses as well as varied syntax to link the major sections of the text, create cohesion, and clarify the relationships between claim(s) and reasons, between reasons and evidence, and between claim(s) and counterclaims. |
| Establish and maintain a formal style and objective tone while attending to the norms and conventions of the discipline in which they are writing. |
| Provide a concluding statement or section that follows from and supports the argument presented. |
| Write informative/explanatory texts to examine and convey complex ideas, concepts, and information clearly and accurately through the effective selection, organization, and analysis of content. |
| Introduce a topic; organize complex ideas, concepts, and information so that each new element builds on that which precedes it to create a unified whole; include formatting (e.g., headings), graphics (e.g., figures, tables), and multimedia when useful to aiding comprehension. |
| Develop the topic thoroughly by selecting the most significant and relevant facts, extended definitions, concrete details, quotations, or other information and examples appropriate to the audience's knowledge of the topic. |
| Use appropriate and varied transitions and syntax to link the major sections of the text, create cohesion, and clarify the relationships among complex ideas and concepts. |
| Use precise language, domain-specific vocabulary, and techniques such as metaphor, simile, and analogy to manage the complexity of the topic. |
| Establish and maintain a formal style and objective tone while attending to the norms and conventions of the discipline in which they are writing. |
| Provide a concluding statement or section that follows from and supports the information or explanation presented (e.g., articulating implications or the significance of the topic). |
| Write narratives to develop real or imagined experiences or events using effective technique, well-chosen details, and well-structured event sequences. |
| Engage and orient the reader by setting out a problem, situation, or observation and its significance, establishing one or multiple point(s) of view, and introducing a narrator and/or characters; create a smooth progression of experiences or events. |
| Use narrative techniques, such as dialogue, pacing, description, reflection, and multiple plot lines, to develop experiences, events, and/or characters. |

| Grade 12 Writing Standards |
| --- |
| **Standard** |
| **Text Types and Purposes (continued)** |
| Use a variety of techniques to sequence events so that they build on one another to create a coherent whole and build toward a particular tone and outcome (e.g., a sense of mystery, suspense, growth, or resolution). |
| Use precise words and phrases, telling details, and sensory language to convey a vivid picture of the experiences, events, setting, and/or characters. |
| Provide a conclusion that follows from and reflects on what is experienced, observed, or resolved over the course of the narrative. |
| **Production and Distribution of Writing** |
| Produce clear and coherent writing in which the development, organization, and style are appropriate to task, purpose, and audience. (Grade-specific expectations for writing types are defined in standards 1–3 above.) |
| Develop and strengthen writing as needed by planning, revising, editing, rewriting, or trying a new approach, focusing on addressing what is most significant for a specific purpose and audience. (Editing for conventions should demonstrate command of Language standards 1–3 up to and including grades 11–12) |
| Use technology, including the Internet, to produce, publish, and update individual or shared writing products in response to ongoing feedback, including new arguments or information. |
| **Research to Build and Present Knowledge** |
| Conduct short as well as more sustained research projects to answer a question (including a self-generated question) or solve a problem; narrow or broaden the inquiry when appropriate; synthesize multiple sources on the subject, demonstrating understanding of the subject under investigation. |
| Gather relevant information from multiple authoritative print and digital sources, using advanced searches effectively; assess the strengths and limitations of each source in terms of the task, purpose, and audience; integrate information into the text selectively to maintain the flow of ideas, avoiding plagiarism and overreliance on any one source and following a standard format for citation. |
| Draw evidence from literary or informational texts to support analysis, reflection, and research. |
| Apply *grades 11–12 Reading standards* to literature (e.g., "Demonstrate knowledge of eighteenth-, nineteenth- and early-twentieth-century foundational works of American literature, including how two or more texts from the same period treat similar themes or topics"). |
| Apply *grades 11–12 Reading standards* to literary nonfiction (e.g., "Delineate and evaluate the reasoning in seminal U.S. texts, including the application of constitutional principles and use of legal reasoning [e.g., in U.S. Supreme Court Case majority opinions and dissents] and the premises, purposes, and arguments in works of public advocacy [e.g., *The Federalist*, presidential addresses]"). |
| **Range of Writing** |
| Write routinely over extended time frames (time for research, reflection, and revision) and shorter time frames (a single sitting or a day or two) for a range of tasks, purposes, and audiences. |

# Standards Overview

## Standards for Speaking and Listening

**College and Career Readiness**
**Anchor Standards for Speaking and Listening**

### Comprehension and Collaboration

1. Prepare for and participate effectively in a range of conversations and collaborations with diverse partners, building on others' ideas and expressing their own clearly and persuasively.
2. Integrate and evaluate information presented in diverse media and formats, including visually, quantitatively, and orally.
3. Evaluate a speaker's point of view, reasoning, and use of evidence and rhetoric.

### Presentation of Knowledge and Ideas

4. Present information, findings, and supporting evidence such that listeners can follow the line of reasoning and the organization, development, and style are appropriate to task, purpose, and audience.
5. Make strategic use of digital media and visual displays of data to express information and enhance understanding of presentations.
6. Adapt speech to a variety of contexts and communicative tasks, demonstrating command of formal English when indicated or appropriate.

| Grade 12 Standards for Speaking and Listening |
|---|
| Standard |
| **Comprehension and Collaboration** |
| Initiate and participate effectively in a range of collaborative discussions (one-on-one, in groups, and teacher-led) with diverse partners on *grades 11–12 topics, texts, and issues*, building on others' ideas and expressing their own clearly and persuasively. |
| Come to discussions prepared, having read and researched material under study; explicitly draw on that preparation by referring to evidence from texts and other research on the topic or issue to stimulate a thoughtful, well-reasoned exchange of ideas. |
| Work with peers to promote civil, democratic discussions and decision-making, set clear goals and deadlines, and establish individual roles as needed. |
| Propel conversations by posing and responding to questions that probe reasoning and evidence; ensure a hearing for a full range of positions on a topic or issue; clarify, verify, or challenge ideas and conclusions; and promote divergent and creative perspectives. |
| Respond thoughtfully to diverse perspectives; synthesize comments, claims, and evidence made on all sides of an issue; resolve contradictions when possible; and determine what additional information or research is required to deepen the investigation or complete the task. |
| Integrate multiple sources of information presented in diverse formats and media (e.g., visually, quantitatively, orally) in order to make informed decisions and solve problems, evaluating the credibility and accuracy of each source and noting any discrepancies among the data. |
| Evaluate a speaker's point of view, reasoning, and use of evidence and rhetoric, assessing the stance, premises, links among ideas, word choice, points of emphasis, and tone used. |
| **Presentation of Knowledge and Ideas** |
| Present information, findings, and supporting evidence, conveying a clear and distinct perspective, such that listeners can follow the line of reasoning, alternative or opposing perspectives are addressed, and the organization, development, substance, and style are appropriate to purpose, audience, and a range of formal and informal tasks. |
| Make strategic use of digital media (e.g., textual, graphical, audio, visual, and interactive elements) in presentations to enhance understanding of findings, reasoning, and evidence and to add interest. |
| Adapt speech to a variety of contexts and tasks, demonstrating a command of formal English when indicated or appropriate. (See grades 11–12 Language standards 1 and 3 for specific expectations.) |

# Standards Overview

## Standards for Language

| College and Career Readiness Anchor Standards for Language |
|---|
| **Conventions of Standard English**<br>**1.** Demonstrate command of the conventions of standard English grammar and usage when writing or speaking.<br>**2.** Demonstrate command of the conventions of standard English capitalization, punctuation, and spelling when writing. |
| **Knowledge of Language**<br>**3.** Apply knowledge of language to understand how language functions in different contexts, to make effective choices for meaning or style, and to comprehend more fully when reading or listening. |
| **Vocabulary Acquisition and Use**<br>**4.** Determine or clarify the meaning of unknown and multiple-meaning words and phrases by using context clues, analyzing meaningful word parts, and consulting general and specialized reference materials, as appropriate.<br>**5.** Demonstrate understanding of figurative language, word relationships, and nuances in word meanings.<br>**6.** Acquire and use accurately a range of general academic and domain-specific words and phrases sufficient for reading, writing, speaking, and listening at the college and career readiness level; demonstrate independence in gathering vocabulary knowledge when considering a word or phrase important to comprehension or expression. |

| Grade 12 Standards for Language |
|---|
| **Standard** |
| **Conventions of Standard English** |
| Demonstrate command of the conventions of standard English grammar and usage when writing or speaking. |
| Apply the understanding that usage is a matter of convention, can change over time, and is sometimes contested. |
| Resolve issues of complex or contested usage, consulting references (e.g., *Merriam-Webster's Dictionary of English Usage, Garner's Modern American Usage*) as needed. |
| Demonstrate command of the conventions of standard English capitalization, punctuation, and spelling when writing. |
| Observe hyphenation conventions. |
| Spell correctly. |

| Grade 12 Standards for Language |
|---|
| Standard |
| **Knowledge of Language** |
| Apply knowledge of language to understand how language functions in different contexts, to make effective choices for meaning or style, and to comprehend more fully when reading or listening. |
| Vary syntax for effect, consulting references (e.g., Tufte's *Artful Sentences*) for guidance as needed; apply an understanding of syntax to the study of complex texts when reading. |
| **Vocabulary Acquisition and Use** |
| Determine or clarify the meaning of unknown and multiple-meaning words and phrases based on *grades 11–12 reading and content*, choosing flexibly from a range of strategies. |
| Use context (e.g., the overall meaning of a sentence, paragraph, or text; a word's position or function in a sentence) as a clue to the meaning of a word or phrase. |
| Identify and correctly use patterns of word changes that indicate different meanings or parts of speech (e.g., *conceive, conception, conceivable*). |
| Consult general and specialized reference materials (e.g., dictionaries, glossaries, thesauruses), both print and digital, to find the pronunciation of a word or determine or clarify its precise meaning, its part of speech, its etymology, or its standard usage. |
| Verify the preliminary determination of the meaning of a word or phrase (e.g., by checking the inferred meaning in context or in a dictionary). |
| Demonstrate understanding of figurative language, word relationships, and nuances in word meanings. |
| Interpret figures of speech (e.g., hyperbole, paradox) in context and analyze their role in the text. |
| Analyze nuances in the meaning of words with similar denotations. |
| Acquire and use accurately general academic and domain-specific words and phrases, sufficient for reading, writing, speaking, and listening at the college and career readiness level; demonstrate independence in gathering vocabulary knowledge when considering a word or phrase important to comprehension or expression. |

UNIT 4

# Seeing Things New

## Visionaries and Skeptics

How Proust Can Change Your Life

**Discuss It** How is it possible for a favorite book to transform you?

**Write your response before sharing your ideas.**

## UNIT INTRODUCTION

ESSENTIAL QUESTION: **Why are both vision and disillusion necessary?**

LAUNCH TEXT
NARRATIVE MODEL
The Assignment of My Life
*Ruth Gruber*

## WHOLE-CLASS LEARNING

HISTORICAL PERSPECTIVES

*Focus Period: 1625–1798*
A Turbulent Time

ANCHOR TEXT: POETRY COLLECTION 1

A Valediction: Forbidding Mourning

Holy Sonnet 10
*John Donne*

COMPARE

ANCHOR TEXT: NOVEL EXCERPT

*from* Gulliver's Travels
*Jonathan Swift*

MEDIA: FILM | COVER ART

*from* Gulliver's Travels Among the Lilliputians and the Giants
*Georges Méliès*

*Gulliver's Travels* Cover Art

PERFORMANCE TASK

WRITING FOCUS:
Write a Reflective Narrative

## SMALL-GROUP LEARNING

COMPARE

POETRY

To His Coy Mistress
*Andrew Marvell*

POETRY COLLECTION 2

To the Virgins, to Make Much of Time
*Robert Herrick*

Youth's the Season Made for Joys
*John Gay*

POETRY COLLECTION 3

*from the* Divine Comedy: Inferno
*Dante Alighieri, translated by John Ciardi*

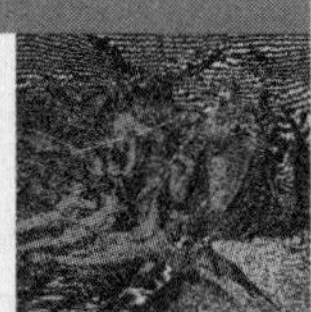

The Second Coming
*W. B. Yeats*

SHORT STORY

Araby
*James Joyce*

POETRY COLLECTION 4

The Explosion
*Philip Larkin*

▸ MEDIA CONNECTION: The Explosion

Old Love
*Francesca Beard*

PERFORMANCE TASK

SPEAKING AND LISTENING FOCUS:
Present a Reflective Narrative

## INDEPENDENT LEARNING

ALLEGORY

*from* The Pilgrim's Progress
*John Bunyan*

POETRY COLLECTION 5

The Lamb

The Tyger

The Chimney Sweeper
*William Blake*

TRANSCRIPT

Sleep
*NOVA scienceNOW, hosted by Neil deGrasse Tyson*

DIARY

*from* The Pillow Book
*Sei Shōnagon, translated by Ivan Morris*

POETRY

Kubla Khan
*Samuel Taylor Coleridge*

PERFORMANCE-BASED ASSESSMENT PREP

Review Notes for a Reflective Narrative

## PERFORMANCE-BASED ASSESSMENT

Narrative: Reflective Narrative and Dramatic Reading

PROMPT:

When can the way we look at things lead to growth—and when can it hold us back?

## Unit Goals

Throughout this unit, you will deepen your perspective on the concepts of vision and disillusion by reading, writing, speaking, listening, and presenting. These goals will help you succeed on the Unit Performance-Based Assessment.

Rate how well you meet these goals right now. You will revisit your ratings later when you reflect on your growth during this unit.

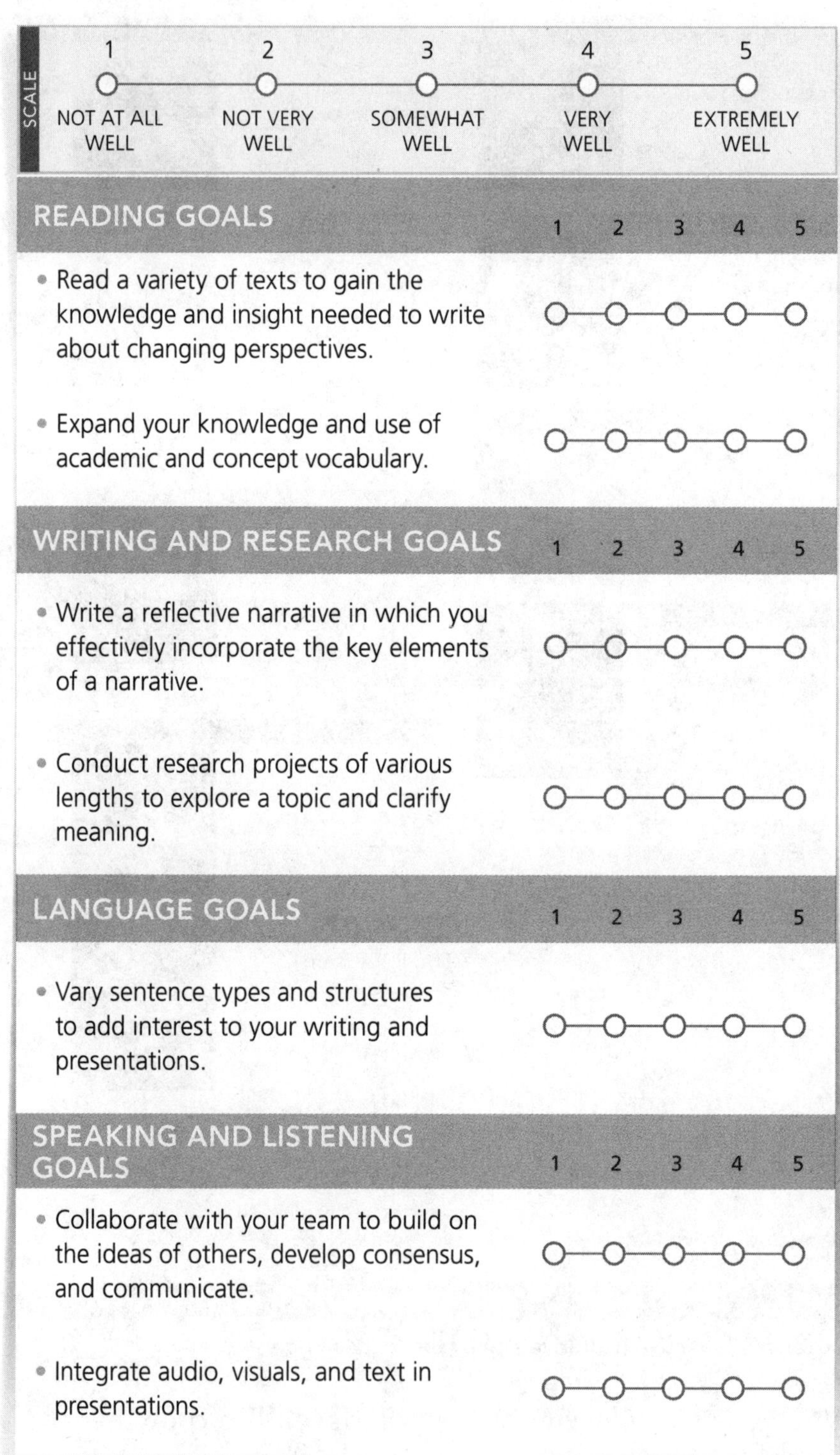

SCALE

| 1 | 2 | 3 | 4 | 5 |
|---|---|---|---|---|
| NOT AT ALL WELL | NOT VERY WELL | SOMEWHAT WELL | VERY WELL | EXTREMELY WELL |

| READING GOALS | 1 | 2 | 3 | 4 | 5 |
|---|---|---|---|---|---|
| • Read a variety of texts to gain the knowledge and insight needed to write about changing perspectives. | O | O | O | O | O |
| • Expand your knowledge and use of academic and concept vocabulary. | O | O | O | O | O |

| WRITING AND RESEARCH GOALS | 1 | 2 | 3 | 4 | 5 |
|---|---|---|---|---|---|
| • Write a reflective narrative in which you effectively incorporate the key elements of a narrative. | O | O | O | O | O |
| • Conduct research projects of various lengths to explore a topic and clarify meaning. | O | O | O | O | O |

| LANGUAGE GOALS | 1 | 2 | 3 | 4 | 5 |
|---|---|---|---|---|---|
| • Vary sentence types and structures to add interest to your writing and presentations. | O | O | O | O | O |

| SPEAKING AND LISTENING GOALS | 1 | 2 | 3 | 4 | 5 |
|---|---|---|---|---|---|
| • Collaborate with your team to build on the ideas of others, develop consensus, and communicate. | O | O | O | O | O |
| • Integrate audio, visuals, and text in presentations. | O | O | O | O | O |

STANDARDS

**Language**

Acquire and use accurately general academic and domain-specific words and phrases, sufficient for reading, writing, speaking, and listening at the college and career readiness level; demonstrate independence in gathering vocabulary knowledge when considering a word or phrase important to comprehension or expression.

## Academic Vocabulary: Narrative

Understanding and using academic terms can help you to read, write, and speak with precision and clarity. Here are five academic words that will be useful to you in this unit as you analyze and write narratives.

**Complete the chart.**

1. Review each word, its root, and the mentor sentences.
2. Use the information and your own knowledge to predict the meaning of each word.
3. For each word, list at least two related words.
4. Refer to a dictionary or other resources if needed.

**FOLLOW THROUGH**
Study the words in this chart, and highlight them or their forms wherever they appear in the unit.

| WORD | MENTOR SENTENCES | PREDICT MEANING | RELATED WORDS |
|---|---|---|---|
| **engender**<br><br>ROOT:<br>***-gen-***<br>"cause" | 1. His years of experience *engender* respect in his students.<br>2. The first snow will always *engender* excitement in young children. | | *generate; genesis* |
| **transformation**<br><br>ROOT:<br>***-form-***<br>"shape" | 1. When my uncle shaved his beard, the *transformation* was astonishing.<br>2. The class marveled at the object's rapid *transformation* from solid to liquid. | | |
| **incorporate**<br><br>ROOT:<br>***-corp-***<br>"body" | 1. The chefs like to *incorporate* local ingredients into their recipes.<br>2. Did the Declaration of Independence *incorporate* ideas from every signer? | | |
| **artifice**<br><br>ROOT:<br>***-art-***<br>"skill" | 1. The actress hides her own personality behind the *artifice* of drama; no one truly knows her.<br>2. Successful entertainers often combine true artistry and skill with *artifice* and showmanship. | | |
| **inexorable**<br><br>ROOT:<br>***-ora-***<br>"plead"; "pray" | 1. Despite our efforts, the *inexorable* tide soon swallowed our sand castle.<br>2. His *inexorable* desire to rule the kingdom led to his rival's quick defeat. | | |

LAUNCH TEXT | NARRATIVE MODEL

This selection is an example of a **reflective narrative,** a type of writing in which an author tells a true story about his or her own life and explores its meaning. You will write in this mode for the Performance-Based Assessment at the end of this unit.

**As you read,** notice how the writer uses dialogue and reflection to develop her story. Mark details that answer this question: How does the writer feel about her experiences?

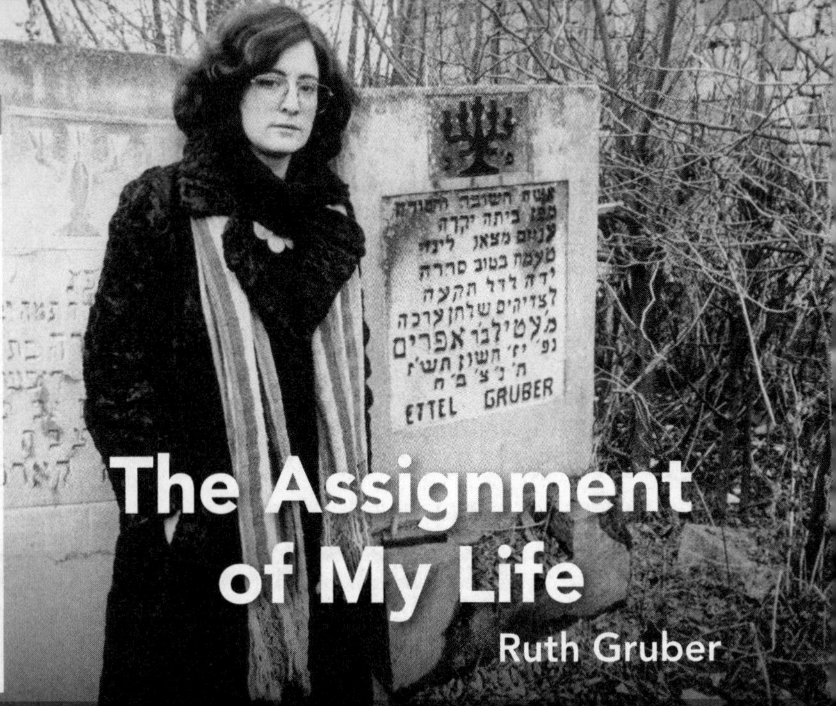


# The Assignment of My Life

Ruth Gruber

NOTES

1 I was born one hundred years ago in Brooklyn's Williamsburg neighborhood, in 1911. I always loved words. In the first grade, I would listen to my beautiful African American teacher read poetry. She was the only teacher I had in elementary school who was not Irish or Jewish, and her soft voice reading poetry was like music. I was mesmerized. Words—written, spoken, waking me in full sentences from my sleep—became the fuel that drove me. That's when I made up my mind that my life would be about writing.

2 As a young girl, I was always restless and in a hurry. I went to NYU and finished in three years. My English professor sent my essays to *The Atlantic, Harper's*, and elsewhere. They all got rejected, but with lovely letters. After NYU, in 1931, just as Hitler was rising to power, I went to Germany for a one-year fellowship at the University of Cologne. My professors encouraged me to get a PhD in writing, but how could I do it in one year? The head of the English department, Professor Herbert Schoffler, said, "It's never been done before, but maybe you can do it." I passed my orals, wrote my thesis on a then relatively unknown British writer named Virginia Woolf—and at twenty years old the *New York Times* called me the youngest PhD in the world.

3 When I came home, there weren't a lot of jobs in journalism, certainly not for young women. I started sending articles and had enough rejections to cover my bedroom walls. If I had ever taken a course in journalism I would have known that you should "write what you know." Eventually I decided to write an article about what I did know, my home of Brooklyn, and the *New York Times* bought it. That was really the beginning of my life.

4 I became a special foreign correspondent for the *New York Herald Tribune*. I reported stories from Alaska, the Soviet Arctic, and elsewhere.

NOTES

5 I left journalism for a period during World War II to take a job as Special Assistant to the Secretary of the Interior, Harold Ickes. In 1944, he assigned me on a secret mission to be an escort for nearly 1,000 Jewish refugees from Italy to the United States aboard a military ship called the *Henry Gibbins*. I was made a simulated general, so that if I was captured by the Nazis, they wouldn't kill me. That was according to the laws of the Geneva Convention.

6 I spent two weeks on this hot, crowded ship; we were hunted by Nazi seaplanes and U-boats. I talked to many of the refugees. I told them they needed to tell me their stories of persecution. Many of them said, "How can we tell you? You're a young woman, and what they did to us was so obscene that you just don't want to know about it." And I, in turn, responded that they were witnesses to history, and they had to help America learn the truth about Hitler's atrocities. So they talked and I listened, and I took down, in longhand, everything they told me.

7 The refugees were brought to and held at a decommissioned military base in Oswego, New York, and decades later, at a 1999 reunion of the refugees in Oswego, several people said, "We know now what happened to many of us former refugees, but we don't know what happened to you." I was 88 at the time of the reunion, and when I looked back at that experience, as well as at more than a half century of journalism, I realized that my involvement with the Oswego refugees was the defining moment of my life.

8 My time on that ship made me aware that as a journalist I would always be both witness and participant; I learned that I must live a story to write it. And I began to live the Oswego story the moment I climbed aboard the *Henry Gibbins* and met the survivors, many still wearing their striped concentration camp pajamas with newspapers wrapped around their bare feet. Because of them and those we lost, I vowed I would fight with every cell in my body to help rescue Jews in danger. After that experience, I would continue to be a journalist, photographer, and book author. But from that moment on, inextricably, my life would be about rescue and survival. ❧

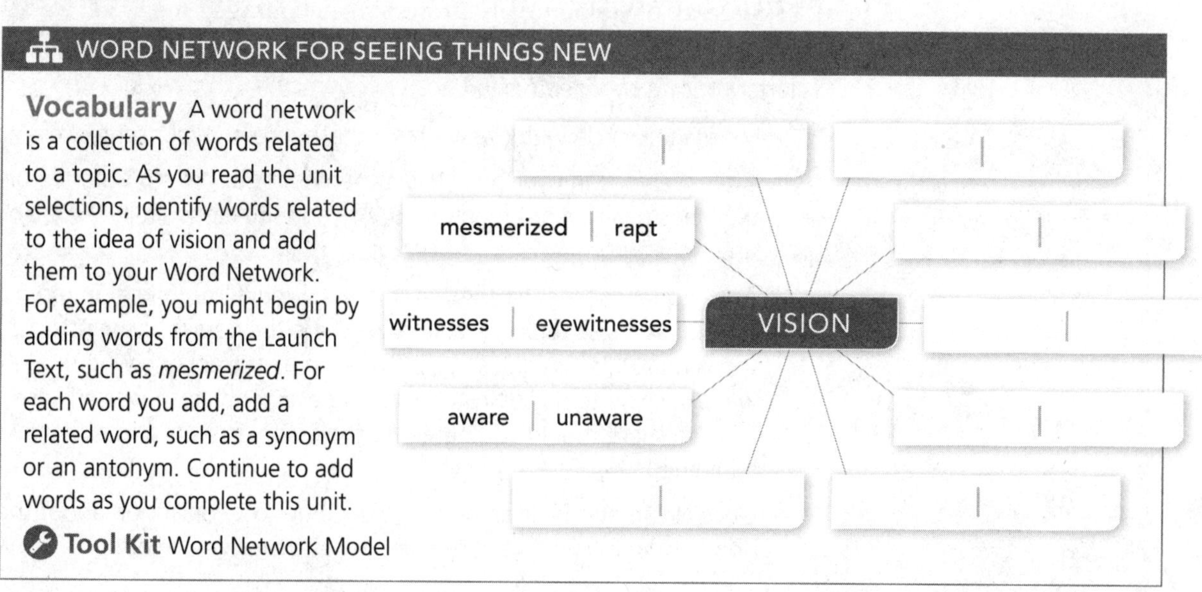


**Vocabulary** A word network is a collection of words related to a topic. As you read the unit selections, identify words related to the idea of vision and add them to your Word Network. For example, you might begin by adding words from the Launch Text, such as *mesmerized*. For each word you add, add a related word, such as a synonym or an antonym. Continue to add words as you complete this unit.

**Tool Kit** Word Network Model

## Summary

Write a summary of "The Assignment of My Life." Remember that a **summary** is a concise, complete, and objective overview of a text. It should contain neither opinion nor analysis.

## Launch Activity

**Story Starter** On an index card, add a sentence to complete this story starter: *My life changed when I . . .*

- Form a talk circle with classmates. In turn, present your sentences.
- After everyone in your circle has presented his or her story starter, discuss the kinds of situations mentioned. Are any situations similar? Are any situations surprising?
- As a group, choose the three stories you would like to hear in more detail. Ask those three classmates to share the details of their stories, speaking for two minutes each. Do not pressure anyone who does not want to share to do so; instead, accept everyone's responses. Those who do share should add details to their story starters and explain what happened.
- Once classmates have shared stories, come to a conclusion about the power of nonfiction narratives and what they reveal about life.

## QuickWrite

Consider class discussions, presentations, the video, and the Launch Text as you think about the prompt. Record your first thoughts here.

PROMPT: **When can the way we look at things lead to growth—and when can it hold us back?**

### EVIDENCE LOG FOR SEEING THINGS NEW

Review your QuickWrite. Summarize your thoughts in one sentence to record in your Evidence Log. Then, record textual details or evidence from "The Assignment of My Life" that supports your position.

After each selection, you will continue to use your Evidence Log to record the evidence you gather and the connections you make. The graphic shows what your Evidence Log looks like.

**Tool Kit**
Evidence Log Model

Title of Text: ________ Date: ________

| CONNECTION TO PROMPT | TEXT EVIDENCE/DETAILS | ADDITIONAL NOTES/IDEAS |
| --- | --- | --- |
| | | |

How does this text change or add to my thinking? Date: ________

ESSENTIAL QUESTION:

# Why are both vision and disillusion necessary?

As you read these selections, work with your whole class to explore how people react when they begin to see the world in a new way.

**From Text to Topic** Great visions have inspired writers, artists, and thinkers throughout history. Yet those visions have sometimes led to bitter disillusion. As you read, you will work with your whole class to explore the concepts of vision and disillusion. The selections you are going to read present insights into visionaries and skeptics.

## Whole-Class Learning Strategies

Throughout your life, in school, in your community, and in your career, you will continue to learn and work in large-group environments.

Review these strategies and the actions you can take to practice them as you work with your whole class. Add ideas of your own for each step. Get ready to use these strategies during Whole-Class Learning.

| STRATEGY | ACTION PLAN |
|---|---|
| Listen actively | • Eliminate distractions. For example, put your cellphone away.<br>• Jot down brief notes on main ideas and points of confusion.<br>• |
| Clarify by asking questions | • If you're confused, other people probably are, too. Ask a question to help your whole class.<br>• Ask follow-up questions as needed; for example, if you do not understand the clarification or if you want to make an additional connection.<br>• |
| Monitor understanding | • Notice what information you already know, and be ready to build on it.<br>• Ask for help if you are struggling.<br>• |
| Interact and share ideas | • Share your ideas and answer questions, even if you are unsure.<br>• Build on the ideas of others by adding details or making a connection.<br>• |

CONTENTS

HISTORICAL PERSPECTIVES

Focus Period: 1625–1798

## A Turbulent Time

The focus period of this unit was a chaotic time in England. Many institutions were overthrown and then later reinstated. Vision and disillusion were natural ingredients in the constantly shifting ideologies of the period.

ANCHOR TEXT: POETRY COLLECTION 1

## A Valediction: Forbidding Mourning

*John Donne*

## Holy Sonnet 10

*John Donne*

Is it possible for love to triumph over death?

COMPARE

ANCHOR TEXT: NOVEL EXCERPT

## *from* Gulliver's Travels

*Jonathan Swift*

What does an outsider see when he walks into a decades-old conflict?

MEDIA: FILM | COVER ART

## *from* Gulliver's Travels Among the Lilliputians and the Giants

*Georges Méliès*

## *Gulliver's Travels* Cover Art

Visions of Lilliput have inspired artists for centuries. What did they see?

PERFORMANCE TASK

WRITING FOCUS

## Write a Reflective Narrative

The Whole-Class readings illustrate the determination it takes to find an inspiring vision and the courage needed to tear that vision apart. After reading, you will write a reflective narrative about the moment when we need to develop a new vision of things.

# A Turbulent Time

## Voices of the Period

"*I tell you we will cut off his head with the crown upon it.*"

—Oliver Cromwell, political leader and later Lord Protector of the Commonwealth of England, to one of the judges at the trial of King Charles I,1648

"*English Society:*

*The great, who live profusely.*

*The rich, who live very plentifully.*

*The middle sort, who live well.*

*The working trades who labor hard but feel no want.*

*The Country people, farmers, etc., who fare indifferently.*

*The poor, that fare hard.*

*The miserable, that really pinch and suffer want.*"

—Daniel Defoe, *London Life*, 1709

"*When in the Course of human events, it becomes necessary for one people to dissolve the political bands which have connected them with another, and to assume among the powers of the earth, the separate and equal station to which the Laws of Nature and of Nature's God entitle them, a decent respect to the opinions of mankind requires that they should declare the causes which impel them to the separation.*"

—from the Declaration of Independence, 1776

## History of the Period

**King Versus Parliament** A proud king, Charles I struggled with Parliament over political and religious authority until, in 1642, civil war broke out. Among the leaders of the Roundheads, the Parliamentary forces, was Oliver Cromwell, a stern general who thought his new model army could bring divine justice to England by defeating the king's forces, the Cavaliers. After six brutal years, King Charles was defeated and tried by his subjects. Condemned to death, he was beheaded in January 1649, a radical act that resulted in hostility throughout Europe.

A dead king does not, however, guarantee a democratic or effective government. Impatient with quarreling parliamentary factions, Cromwell seized power in 1653 and served as Lord Protector of England until his death in 1658.

**Restoring the Monarchy** In 1660, the monarchy was restored when King Charles II returned from exile in France and assumed the throne. Charles died without an heir in 1685, and his brother, a Catholic, became King James II. James had no male heirs, but his daughter, Mary, was a staunch Protestant. So the English, eager for a Protestant king, were willing to wait until Mary could take the throne. But then the aging king had a son.

Nobles, merchants, and other Protestant power brokers would not stand for a Catholic dynasty on the English throne. By this time, Mary had married the Dutch prince William of Orange. In 1688, the

### TIMELINE

1625

**1642:** English Civil War begins.

**1650:** First London coffeehouse opens. As coffee's popularity increases, demand for sugar, grown with slave labor in West Indies, also increases.

**1649:** Charles I is beheaded.

**1653:** Oliver Cromwell becomes Lord Protector.

**1660:** Monarchy is restored after Cromwell's death in 1658.

**1664: North America** Britain seizes New Netherlands.

## Integration of Knowledge and Ideas

**Notebook** If you had lived in England in the 1640s, would you have supported the Cavaliers or the Roundheads? Explain your reasons.

### Cavaliers vs. Roundheads

**Cavaliers**
- Member of the aristocracy
- Long flowing hair and wigs
- Elaborate clothes, plumed hats
- Self-consciously elegant pose
- Pro-Catholic and anti-Puritan
- Believed in divine right of kings

**Roundheads**
- Social class lower than the aristocracy
- Short hair
- Plain dress
- Direct in manner
- Puritan with strict religious beliefs
- Believed in limits to king's rule

English power brokers invited the couple to take the throne as William III and Mary II.

**A Glorious Revolution** This transition was hailed as "The Glorious Revolution." The will of the governed had determined who would rule, but this time without great bloodshed. Soon afterwards a Bill of Rights established in law that only a Protestant could reign in England.

**The Georges** After the deaths of William and Mary, the daughter of James II reigned briefly as Queen Anne. She was succeeded by George I, a German prince from the House of Hanover, who was Anne's closest Protestant relative. George I spoke no English and cared little for his new country, so Parliament soon assumed almost complete control. He was succeeded by his son George II, whose grandson became King George III, the controversial monarch who "lost" the American colonies.

**Revolution in Fields and Factories** Powerful new machinery linked with crop rotation, larger farms, and improved transportation led to an Agricultural Revolution in England. Fewer workers could produce more food, creating a new abundance so that the swelling population of the cities could be fed. This transformation

**1666:** Great Fire of London devastates the city.

**1682: North America** LaSalle claims Louisiana for France.

**1688:** The Glorious Revolution brings William and Mary to the throne.

**1689:** Bill of Rights becomes law.

**1700**

in agriculture was a critical factor in setting the stage for the Industrial Revolution.

The Industrial Revolution, an explosion of manufacturing involving new technology and new energy sources, began in the 1700s. Britain had the necessary ingredients for the rise of industry: a robust population, water power, coal and iron, a government that encouraged growth, and colonies to supply the needed raw materials. British inventions such as the steam engine provided the key to the nation's industrial growth. By the beginning of the nineteenth century, Britain was more heavily industrialized than any country in the world. This led in turn to rapid economic growth and a prosperous country that could support a growing population.

**London Town** The eighteenth-century lexicographer Samuel Johnson once opined that if a man was tired of London, he was tired of life. Since Roman times, London had been the central city of English life. In 1664, the deadly plague struck, and the streets of London were filled with carts carrying dead bodies. Then, in 1666, a great fire broke out, and large areas of London were incinerated. While London was being rebuilt, the construction of turnpikes and canals transformed the countryside, creating new mobility for people outside of the city confines. Still, all roads led to London, especially for the bright and ambitious. By 1750, almost one in ten British citizens lived in London. (At the same time, only one in forty French citizens lived in Paris.) London was the center of government, finance, communications, economics, and fashionable life.

**Revolt of the Colonies** In British eyes, the taxes Parliament began to impose on its American colonies after the Seven Years' War were entirely justified, especially given Britain's defense of the colonies against the French. Americans disagreed, declaring the king a tyrant in the Declaration of Independence. Although both king and parliament were responsible for much that happened, many modern historians believe that America's distance from Great Britain, its growing prosperity, and its increasing sense of a separate regional identity were at the root of the rebellion.

The long war that ended with the Treaty of Paris in 1783 led to Britain's loss of one of the most important and profitable parts of its empire. America became independent but maintained with Britain connections of language, politics, culture, and literature that enriched both countries.

**Liberté, Egalité, Fraternité** The fifth revolution of the period began on July 14, 1789, when the people of Paris stormed the Bastille, a grim prison and hated symbol of royal oppression. Shortly after this, French King Louis XVI was beheaded, and the old order was shattered. Government without kings, already established in America, had now displaced a monarchy in Europe. Many in the upper reaches of British society feared that radical ideas of equality would soon spread to the United Kingdom.

At the end of the American Revolution, when British general Lord Cornwallis led his defeated troops out of Yorktown, the band played a popular tune: "The World Turned Upside Down." It is a fitting theme song for the entire era.

## TIMELINE

1700

**1702:** First daily newspaper begins publication.

**1707:** Great Britain is created by Act of Union.

**1714:** George I becomes King.

**1727: Brazil** First coffee is planted.

**1759: Canada** British troops capture Quebec.

## Literature Selections

**Literature of the Focus Period** A number of the selections in this unit were written during the Focus Period and pertain to the concepts of vision and disillusion.

"A Valediction: Forbidding Mourning," John Donne

"Holy Sonnet 10," John Donne

from *Gulliver's Travels*, Jonathan Swift

"To His Coy Mistress," Andrew Marvell

"To the Virgins, to Make Much of Time," Robert Herrick

"Youth's the Season Made for Joys," John Gay

from *Pilgrim's Progress*, John Bunyan

"The Lamb," William Blake

"The Tyger," William Blake

"The Chimney Sweeper," William Blake

**Connections Across Time** Consideration of the contrasts between vision and disillusion both preceded and continued past the Focus Period. In addition, the observations of the Focus Period have influenced contemporary writers and commentators.

from *Gulliver's Travels Among the Lilliputians and the Giants*, Georges Méliès

from the *Divine Comedy: Inferno*, Dante Alighieri

"The Second Coming," W. B. Yeats

"Araby," James Joyce

"The Explosion," Philip Larkin

"Old Love," Francesca Beard

"Sleep," NOVA scienceNOW

from *The Pillow Book*, Sei Shōnagon

ADDITIONAL FOCUS PERIOD LITERATURE

**Student Edition**

**UNIT 1**
"To Lucasta, on Going to the Wars," Richard Lovelace

**UNIT 3**
"Man's Short Life and Foolish Ambition," Margaret Cavendish, Duchess of Newcastle

**UNIT 5**
"Lines Composed a Few Miles Above Tintern Abbey," William Wordsworth

**UNIT 5**
from *The Prelude,* William Wordsworth

**1763:** Treaty of Paris ends Seven Years' War.

**1775: North America** First battles of the American Revolution are fought.

**1783:** Treaty of Paris ends American Revolution.

**1789: France** French Revolution begins with storming of the Bastille.

**1798**

POETRY COLLECTION 1

# A Valediction: Forbidding Mourning

# Holy Sonnet 10

## Concept Vocabulary

You will encounter the following words as you read "A Valediction: Forbidding Mourning" and "Holy Sonnet 10." Before reading, note how familiar you are with each word. Then, rank the words in order from most familiar (1) to least familiar (6).

| WORD | YOUR RANKING |
|---|---|
| **virtuous** | |
| **profanation** | |
| **laity** | |
| **dreadful** | |
| **delivery** | |
| **eternally** | |

After completing the first read, come back to the concept vocabulary and review your rankings. Mark changes to your original rankings as needed.

## First Read POETRY

Apply these strategies as you conduct your first read. You will have an opportunity to complete the close-read notes after your first read.

NOTICE *who* or *what* is "speaking" the poem and whether the poem tells a story or describes a single moment.

ANNOTATE by marking vocabulary and key passages you want to revisit.

CONNECT ideas within the selection to what you already know and what you've already read.

RESPOND by completing the Comprehension Check.

NOTICE ANNOTATE First Read CONNECT RESPOND

**Tool Kit**
First-Read Guide and Model Annotation

STANDARDS

**Reading Literature**
By the end of grade 12, read and comprehend literature, including stories, dramas, and poems, at the high end of the grades 11–CCR text complexity band independently and proficiently.

About the Poet

## John Donne (1572?–1631)

John Donne's life and poetry fall neatly into two contradictory parts. Wild, young Jack Donne wrote clever love poems read by sophisticated aristocrats. In later life, sober Dr. John Donne, Dean of St. Paul's and the most popular preacher in England, published widely read meditations and sermons. Contradiction and conflict were the stuff of Donne's life; they are also at the heart of his poetic style.

**Religious Conflict** A distant relative of Sir Thomas More, Donne was raised a Catholic. In the England of Queen Elizabeth I, Catholics faced prejudice and restrictive laws. Although Donne studied at Oxford and Cambridge, he never obtained his degree, probably because of his refusal to compromise his Catholicism by swearing an oath acknowledging the supremacy of the king over the church. Later, he abandoned Catholicism and joined the official Church of England. To this day, scholars debate whether Donne experienced a genuine conversion.

**A Secret Marriage** After taking part in two naval expeditions against the Spanish, Donne served as private secretary to one of the queen's highest-ranking officials, Sir Thomas Egerton. Bright, clever, and charming, Donne secretly wed Anne More, his employer's niece, in 1601. Again, some scholars throw doubt on Donne's motives. Some hold that he married for love; others maintain that he hoped his marriage to the daughter of an influential family would promote his career. If Donne counted on this possibility, though, he was sadly mistaken. Because Anne's father disapproved of the union, Donne's marriage temporarily ruined his chance for advancement.

For many years, the devoted couple lived plagued by poverty and illness, in the midst of which Donne still managed to write influential poetry. He eked out a living writing religious tracts and serving as temporary secretary to several aristocrats. Donne finally attained a secure position in 1615 when, at the insistence of King James, he entered the clergy.

**Success** After serving as royal chaplain, Donne became dean of St. Paul's Cathedral in London in 1621, a post he held until his death. He became one of the most popular preachers of his day. No longer the writer of sly or witty passionate verses, he published widely read sermons and religious meditations. Jack Donne's days were over, and John Donne's fame was spreading.

## Background

### The Metaphysical Poets

John Donne was the foremost member of a loosely connected group of writers whose work was described as "metaphysical poetry." Their poetry combined the intellectual with the emotional and offered a departure from the lyrical poetry of the sixteenth century. Metaphysical poems contained remarkable conceits—witty connections between seemingly unrelated things. Conceits were clever and humorous; they made generous use of puns. These metaphors, carried to extremes, startled the reader into paying close attention to the meaning of the poem.

Few practiced this art as well as Donne. His poem "Love's Alchemy" is based on a conceit—that trying to understand the nature of love is like trying to turn base metal into gold. In his poem "The Ecstasy," the conceit compares two lovers to opposing armies:

*As 'twixt two equal armies fate*
*Suspends uncertain victory.*
*Our souls (which to advance their state*
*Were gone out) hung 'twixt her and me.*

Not everyone appreciated this blending of intellect and emotion. The formidable Samuel Johnson wrote of the metaphysical poets that in their poetry "the most heterogeneous ideas are yoked by violence together." Johnson accused them of being crude, yet the ideas expressed by the poets were highly sensitive and insightful.

Samuel Johnson believed that the metaphysical poets were merely interested in demonstrating their vast knowledge. This perception lingered for centuries. The metaphysical poets were not highly regarded until the great twentieth-century poet T. S. Eliot wrote an essay that praised their work, particularly that of John Donne. It was a recognition that was long overdue.

ANCHOR TEXT | POETRY

# A Valediction: Forbidding Mourning

John Donne

As **virtuous** men pass mildly away,
And whisper to their souls to go,
Whilst some of their sad friends do say
The breath goes now, and some say, No;

So let us melt, and make no noise,
No tear-floods, nor sigh-tempests move,
'Twere **profanation** of our joys
To tell the **laity** our love.

Moving of th'earth brings harms and fears,
Men reckon what it did and meant;
But trepidation of the spheres,[1]
Though greater far, is innocent.

Dull sublunary[2] lovers' love
(Whose soul is sense) cannot admit
Absence, because it doth remove
Those things which elemented it.[3]

But we by a love, so much refined,
That our selves know not what it is,
Inter-assurèd of the mind,[4]
Care less, eyes, lips, and hands to miss.

Our two souls therefore, which are one,
Though I must go, endure not yet
A breach, but an expansion,
Like gold to airy thinness beat.

If they be two, they are two so
As stiff twin compasses[5] are two;
Thy soul the fixed foot, makes no show
To move, but doth, If th'other do.

And though it in the center sit,
Yet when the other far doth roam,
It leans, and hearkens after it,
And grows erect, as that comes home.

Such wilt thou be to me, who must
Like th'other foot, obliquely[6] run;
Thy firmness makes my circle just,[7]
And makes me end where I begun.

NOTES

**virtuous** (VUR choo uhs) *adj.* having high moral standards

**profanation** (prof uh NAY shuhn) *n.* act of disrespecting sacred ideas, persons, or things

**laity** (LAY uh tee) *n.* people of religious faith who are not members of the clergy

**CLOSE READ**

**ANNOTATE:** In lines 21–35, mark details related to stillness and other details related to motion.

**QUESTION:** What connection is the speaker making between stillness and motion and the idea of love?

**CONCLUDE:** How do the final two lines of the poem bring together the elements of stillness, motion, and love?

1. **trepidation of the spheres** movements of the stars and planets that are inconsistent with a perfect circular orbit.
2. **sublunary** (SUHB loo nehr ee) *adj.* referring to the region below the moon, considered in early astronomy to be the domain of changeable and perishable things.
3. **Those things . . . elemented it** the basic materials or parts of their love.
4. **Inter-assurèd of the mind** mutually confident of each other's thoughts.
5. **twin compasses** the two legs of a drawing compass.
6. **obliquely** (oh BLEEK lee) *adv.* at an angle; not straight.
7. **just** *adj.* true; perfect.

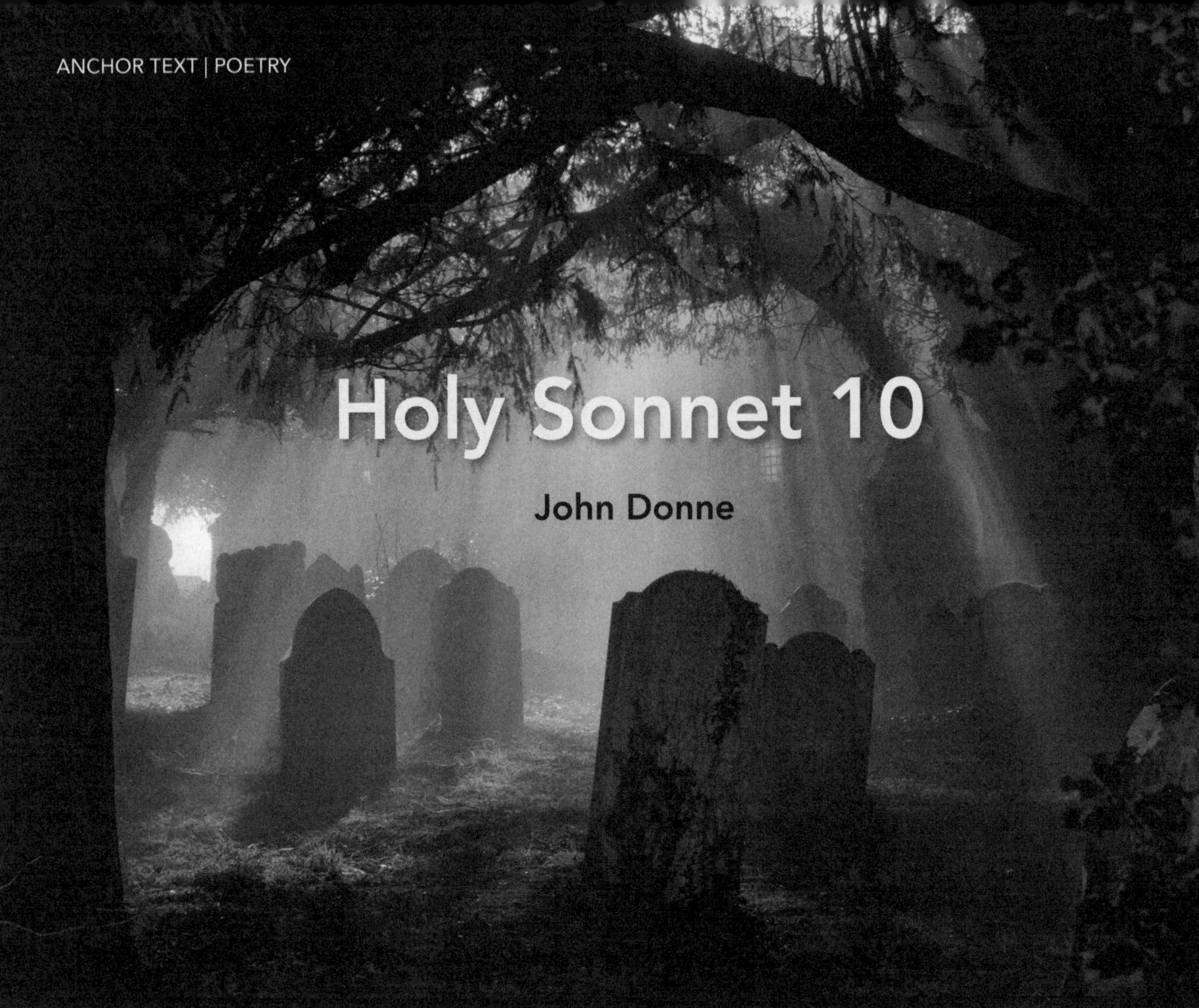

# Holy Sonnet 10

**John Donne**

NOTES

**dreadful** (DREHD fuhl) *adj.* inspiring fear or awe

**delivery** (dih LIHV uhr ee) *n.* giving up or handing over

**eternally** (ih TUR nuh lee) *adv.* lasting forever

Death be not proud, though some have called thee
Mighty and **dreadful**, for thou art not so;
For those whom thou think'st thou dost overthrow,
Die not, poor death, nor yet canst thou kill me.
From rest and sleep, which but thy pictures[1] be,
Much pleasure; then from thee much more must flow,
And soonest our best men with thee do go,
Rest of their bones, and soul's **delivery**.[2]
Thou art slave to fate, chance, kings, and desperate men,
And dost with poison, war, and sickness dwell,
And poppy,[3] or charms can make us sleep as well
And better than thy stroke; why swell'st[4] thou then?
One short sleep past, we wake **eternally**,
And death shall be no more; Death, thou shalt die.

1. **pictures** images.
2. **And . . . delivery** Our best men go with you to rest their bones and find freedom for their souls.
3. **poppy** opium.
4. **swell'st** swell with pride.

## Comprehension Check

**Complete the following items after you finish your first read.**

A VALEDICTION: FORBIDDING MOURNING

1. What disagreement does the first stanza of "A Valediction: Forbidding Mourning" describe?

2. According to the speaker, how should he and his beloved part?

3. According to the speaker, why do the lovers' souls "endure an expansion" rather than a "breach"?

HOLY SONNET 10

1. What does the speaker tell Death in the first two lines of the poem?

2. According to the speaker, what are death's "pictures"?

3. According to the speaker, to what is death a slave?

## RESEARCH

**Research to Clarify** Choose at least one unfamiliar detail from one of the poems. Briefly research that detail. In what way does the information you learned shed light on an aspect of the poem?

POETRY COLLECTION 1

## Close Read the Text

1. This model, from lines 9–12 of "Holy Sonnet 10," shows two sample annotations, along with questions and conclusions. Close read the passage and find another detail to annotate. Then, write a question and your conclusion.

Close Read: ANNOTATE · QUESTION · CONCLUDE

ANNOTATE: The speaker refers to abstract ideas (fate, change, poison, war, and sickness) in human terms.

QUESTION: What effect does the personification have?

CONCLUDE: It places abstract ideas and people on equal terms, which emphasizes the speaker's boldness and Death's weakness.

Thou art slave to fate, chance, kings,
and desperate men,
And dost with poison, war, and
sickness dwell,
And poppy, or charms can make us
sleep as well
And better than thy stroke; why
swell'st thou then?

ANNOTATE: The speaker asks Death a question.

QUESTION: What purpose does this question have?

CONCLUDE: The question is a challenge to Death. The speaker wants to make Death feel inferior.

**Tool Kit**
Close-Read Guide and Model Annotation

2. For more practice, go back into the text, and complete the close-read notes.

3. Revisit a section of the text you found important during your first read. Read this section closely, and **annotate** what you notice. Ask yourself **questions** such as "Why did the author make this choice?" What can you **conclude?**

## Analyze the Text

**CITE TEXTUAL EVIDENCE** to support your answers.

**Notebook** **Respond to these questions.**

1. **Interpret** In "A Valediction: Forbidding Mourning," identify two points at which the speaker transforms the idea of parting into proof of the strength of the couple's love.

2. (a) **Interpret** What two points about sleep does the speaker make in "Holy Sonnet 10"? (b) **Make Inferences** What point about Death does the speaker make with these comparisons?

3. **Compare and Contrast** How does the purpose of "A Valediction: Forbidding Mourning" differ from that of "Holy Sonnet 10"?

4. **Historical Perspectives** Donne's poetry is again admired by scholars after having fallen out of favor earlier. What elements in Donne's poetry may have sparked a renewed interest in his work?

5. **Essential Question:** ***Why are both vision and disillusion necessary?*** What have you learned about vision and disillusion from reading these poems?

**STANDARDS**

**Reading Literature**
• Cite strong and thorough textual evidence to support analysis of what the text says explicitly as well as inferences drawn from the text, including determining where the text leaves matters uncertain.

**Language**
Interpret figures of speech in context and analyze their role in the text.

## Analyze Craft and Structure

**Impact of Word Choice** John Donne and his followers wrote **metaphysical poetry**—poetry characterized by analytical and intellectual displays and concern with metaphysical, or philosophical, issues. Metaphysical poetry includes references to the philosophy, theology, and science of its day, incorporated into both love poetry and religious poetry.

Metaphysical poets use these poetic devices to create witty, intellectual poems:

- A **conceit** is an extended comparison that links objects or ideas not commonly associated with each other.
- A **paradox** is an image or description that appears self-contradictory but instead reveals a deeper truth.
- **Irony** is a surprising contradiction between what is said and what is meant.

### Practice

**CITE TEXTUAL EVIDENCE** to support your answers.

Respond to these questions.

1. (a) What comparison does the speaker make in stanzas 1 and 2 of "A Valediction: Forbidding Mourning"? (b) What is surprising or unusual about this comparison?

2. (a) What comparison does the speaker make in the last three stanzas of "A Valediction: Forbidding Mourning"? (b) How does this comparison help the reader understand the speaker's feelings?

3. What is ironic about the first line of "Holy Sonnet 10"? Explain how the line challenges expectations.

4. Explain the paradox in line 14 of "Holy Sonnet 10." What deeper truth does the speaker reveal with this paradox?

5. Identify another example of one of these literary devices in the two poems and explain how it connects to the overall meaning of the poem.

POETRY COLLECTION 1

# Concept Vocabulary

| virtuous | laity | delivery |
|---|---|---|
| profanation | dreadful | eternally |

**Why These Words?** These concept vocabulary words are used to describe the sacred or spiritual. For example, it is a *profanation* to defile or desecrate a holy book, such as the Bible. On the other hand, it is *virtuous* to do good deeds for others without seeking fame or acknowledgment.

1. How does John Donne use the concept vocabulary to convey his themes more clearly?

2. What other words in the poems connect to this concept?

### Practice

Notebook Respond to these questions.

1. What is an example of a place where you might find the *laity*?
2. How might someone react to something that is *dreadful*?
3. What are the characteristics of a *virtuous* person?
4. Suppose that someone spoke of his *delivery* from danger. What would he mean?
5. What might someone guilty of *profanation* have done?
6. If something lasts *eternally*, when does it end?

WORD NETWORK

Add interesting words related to seeing things new from the texts to your Word Network.

# Word Study

**Latin Suffix: *-ous*** The Latin suffix *-ous* forms adjectives from nouns and means "having," "full of," "made of," or "having to do with." For example, the adjective *virtuous*, which Donne uses to describe certain dying men, means "full of virtue"—that is, "morally good."

In chemistry, the suffix *-ous* combines with various Latin roots to form adjectives indicating which chemical element an object or a substance is made of. For example, the Latin word *ferrum* means "iron." Its root combines with the suffix *-ous* to form the adjective *ferrous*, meaning "made of iron."

1. The Latin word *cuprum* means "copper." Identify an object that is, or may be, *cuprous*.

2. Identify and define two other words, either scientific or nonscientific, that end with the suffix *-ous*. Use a print or online college-level dictionary to check your work.

STANDARDS

**Language**

- Identify and correctly use patterns of word changes that indicate different meanings or parts of speech.
- Consult general and specialized reference materials, both print and digital, to find the pronunciation of a word or determine or clarify its precise meanings, its part of speech, its etymology, or its standard usage.

## Conventions and Style

**Varying Syntax: Periodic Sentences** Writers and poets often vary the **syntax**, or structure, of their sentences to achieve particular effects. For instance, Donne uses periodic sentences to arouse interest and curiosity and to create suspense. A **periodic sentence** is one in which the sense of the independent clause is not complete until the end of the sentence, following all dependent clauses and other modifiers, such as phrases.

Study this periodic sentence from "A Valediction: Forbidding Mourning."

*But we by a love, so much refined,*
*That our selves know not what it is,*
*Inter-assurèd of the mind,*
*Care less, eyes, lips, and hands to miss.* (lines 17–20)

Because Donne interrupts the independent clause (underlined once) with two subordinate clauses (underlined twice)—as well as several phrases—the reader must wait for the final line to discover the sentence's main idea. The effect is the creation of a sense of anticipation, as though time has been stretched out.

Notice that Donne varies his syntax by contrasting periodic sentences with other sentence structures. For example, in lines 33–36, the dependent clauses and modifiers follow the independent clauses. This abrupt switch gives the ideas expressed in these final lines a feeling of immediacy.

### Read It

1. Revisit "A Valediction: Forbidding Mourning," and read these periodic sentences. In each case, mark the two dependent clauses that precede the completion of the main sense of the independent clause.
   a. lines 21–24
   b. lines 29–32

2. **Connect to Style** Take another look at lines 21–24. What effect does Donne's choice to express his ideas using a periodic sentence have on the reader?

### Write It

**Notebook** Write a short paragraph in which you describe Donne's poetic style. Use a combination of independent and dependent clauses, and include at least one periodic sentence.

**CLARIFICATION**
Review the difference between an independent clause and a dependent clause.

- An **independent clause** is a group of words that includes a subject and a verb and can stand alone as a complete sentence.
- A **dependent clause** also includes a subject and a verb, but it cannot stand alone as a complete sentence.

Refer to the Grammar Handbook to learn more about these terms.

**STANDARDS**

**Reading Literature**
Analyze how an author's choices concerning how to structure specific parts of a text contribute to its overall structure and meaning as well as its aesthetic impact.

**Language**
- Demonstrate command of the conventions of standard English grammar and usage when writing or speaking.
- Apply knowledge of language to understand how language functions in different contexts, to make effective choices for meaning or style, and to comprehend more fully when reading or listening.
- Vary syntax for effect, consulting references for guidance as needed; apply an understanding of syntax to the study of complex texts when reading.

POETRY COLLECTION 1

## Writing to Sources

According to Sir Izaak Walton, a John Donne biographer, Donne wrote "A Valediction: Forbidding Mourning" for his beloved wife, Anne Donne, when he prepared to travel with a patron to Europe. Anne was due to give birth and did not want her husband to leave. Imagine John and Anne Donne talking with each other after she has read his poem.

**Assignment**

Write a **narrative scene** presenting the discussion between John and Anne Donne as they consider the issue of his leaving on his journey. Base your narrative on the information in the poem "A Valediction: Forbidding Mourning." Consider the following questions as you develop your narrative:

- What are the speaker's main points in the poem? Is Anne persuaded by them—or does she not accept what the speaker is saying?
- Does the poem work to change Anne's feelings about her husband's departure? If so, why? If not, why not?

Include these elements in your narrative:

- dialogue for both characters
- details and examples drawn from the poem
- a resolution that resolves the conflict between the characters

**Vocabulary and Conventions Connection** In your scene, consider using several of the concept vocabulary words. Also, consider including one or more periodic sentences, to arouse curiosity or to create suspense.

| virtuous | laity | delivery |
|---|---|---|
| profanation | dreadful | eternally |

### Reflect on Your Writing

After you have drafted your narrative scene, answer the following questions.

1. How did writing this scene increase your understanding of the poem?

2. How might you revise your scene to improve it?

3. **Why These Words?** The words you choose make a difference in your writing. Which words helped you bring the scene to life?

STANDARDS

Writing

- Write narratives to develop real or imagined experiences or events using effective technique, well-chosen details, and well-structured event sequences.
- Use narrative techniques, such as dialogue, pacing, description, reflection, and multiple plot lines, to develop experiences, events, and/or characters.
- Provide a conclusion that follows from and reflects on what is experienced, observed, or resolved over the course of the narrative.

# Speaking and Listening

**Assignment**

The work of Anne Bradstreet and Edward Taylor—two early American poets—shares certain qualities, notably the use of conceits and paradoxes, with that of John Donne and other English metaphysical poets. Choose a poem by either Bradstreet or Taylor, and compare it with a poem by John Donne from this collection. Write and present your **comparison of poetry** to the class. Your presentation will have two parts: a recitation of the poems and an analysis you deliver orally. Get started by choosing one of the following poems:

- "Huswifery," by Edward Taylor
- "To My Dear and Loving Husband," by Anne Bradstreet
- "Another (II)" ("As loving hind that [hartless] wants her deer"), by Anne Bradstreet

In your analysis, compare the two poems' subjects, themes, imagery, and uses of conceit or paradox.

1. **Prepare Your Analysis** Compare the poems' subjects, themes, imagery, and uses of conceit or paradox. Then, focus on a few points of comparison, and support your ideas with text evidence. Create a script when you are satisfied with your findings.
2. **Prepare Your Recitation** Practice reading the poems aloud with appropriate pacing and emotional expression.
   - Look up the pronunciation of any unfamiliar words, and practice reading them until your presentation is smooth.
   - Use punctuation to guide your reading. Don't automatically stop at the end of each line. Instead, pause at commas, and stop at periods.
3. **Present and Evaluate** Deliver your presentation to the class. It is up to you whether to begin with the recitation or the analysis. After your presentation, use the presentation evaluation guide to identify what you did well and what could be improved upon.

PRESENTATION EVALUATION GUIDE

**Rate each statement on a scale of 1 (not demonstrated at all) to 5 (demonstrated exceptionally well). Be prepared to defend your rating.**

☐ I read the poems clearly, with appropriate pacing and emotion.

☐ I compared and contrasted a poem by Bradstreet or Taylor with one of Donne's poems, analyzing similarities and differences in the poems' subjects, themes, imagery, and uses of conceit or paradox.

☐ I presented my analysis in an organized way and supported all of my insights with textual evidence.

EVIDENCE LOG

Before moving on to a new selection, go to your Evidence Log and record what you learned from "A Valediction: Forbidden Mourning" and "Holy Sonnet 10."

STANDARDS

**Reading Literature**
Demonstrate knowledge of eighteenth-, nineteenth-, and early twentieth-century foundational works of American literature, including how two or more texts from the same period treat similar themes or topics.

**Speaking and Listening**
Adapt speech to a variety of contexts and tasks, demonstrating a command of formal English when indicated or appropriate.

*from* GULLIVER'S TRAVELS

# *from* Gulliver's Travels

## Concept Vocabulary

You will encounter the following words as you read this excerpt from *Gulliver's Travels*. Before reading, note how familiar you are with each word. Then, rank the words in order from most familiar (1) to least familiar (6).

| WORD | YOUR RANKING |
|---|---|
| proclamation | |
| faction | |
| imperial | |
| dominions | |
| edict | |
| ambassadors | |

After completing your first read, come back to the concept vocabulary and review your rankings. Mark changes to your original rankings as needed.

## First Read FICTION

Apply these strategies as you conduct your first read. You will have an opportunity to complete the close-read notes after your first read.

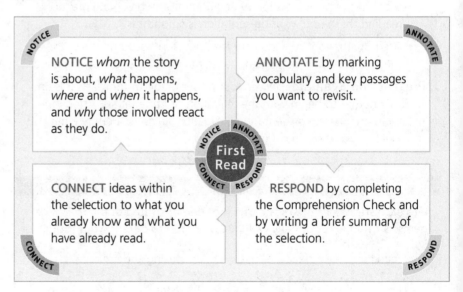

**Tool Kit**
First-Read Guide and Model Annotation

NOTICE *whom* the story is about, *what* happens, *where* and *when* it happens, and *why* those involved react as they do.

ANNOTATE by marking vocabulary and key passages you want to revisit.

CONNECT ideas within the selection to what you already know and what you have already read.

RESPOND by completing the Comprehension Check and by writing a brief summary of the selection.



**STANDARDS**

**Reading Literature**
By the end of grade 12, read and comprehend literature, including stories, dramas, and poems, at the high end of the grades 11–CCR text complexity band independently and proficiently.

About the Author

# Jonathan Swift (1667–1745)

Considered the greatest prose satirist in the English language, Swift is celebrated today for his most famous works, the novel *Gulliver's Travels* and the essay "A Modest Proposal." In his own day, however, Swift was equally well-known as a political pamphleteer and as a religious leader who served for more than thirty years as dean of St. Patrick's Cathedral in Dublin, Ireland.

**Childhood and Early Years** Swift was born in Dublin, Ireland, to English parents. His start was not promising, as his father, a lawyer, had died two months previously. Without any way to make a living, Swift's mother had difficulty providing for her infant son, and they descended into poverty. To complicate the situation, Swift was often sick. Later, he was diagnosed with Ménière's disease, an inner-ear condition that causes dizziness and hearing loss. The disease would afflict Swift during his entire life.

To help her son, Swift's mother sent him to live with his uncle, a successful lawyer. The uncle enrolled Swift in what was likely the best grammar school in Ireland at the time. When he turned 14, Swift entered Trinity College in Dublin, earning his degree five years later. Political unrest in Ireland drove him to England, where his mother found him a job as an assistant to the respected English statesman Sir William Temple. Impressed with Swift's intelligence and work ethic, Temple entrusted him with increasingly more important responsibilities. In 1695, Swift returned to Ireland and became an Anglican priest. In 1699, he found work as a minister to a small congregation near London. For the next decade, Swift ministered, wrote, gardened, and preached. In 1702, he received his Doctor of Divinity degree from Trinity College.

**Satirist** In 1704, Swift released *A Tale of a Tub* and *The Battle of the Books*. The former satirizes excesses in religion and learning; the latter is a satiric comic encounter between ancient and modern literature. Although Swift published these books—as well as much of his writing—anonymously, his authorship was widely known. The satirical writing was out of character for a clergyman, but its brilliance was widely acknowledged, and his fame spread to London.

**Ambition and Achievement** Swift's political allegiance shifted in 1710 when he left the Whig party to join the Tory party, which was favored by Queen Anne. He benefited immediately from this move. As the leading writer for the government, he published some of the most famous and biting political pamphlets of the day.

**The Later Years** After the death of Queen Anne in 1714 and the fall of the Tories from power, Swift's political career in England was over, and he returned to Ireland. Although he failed to achieve his goal of becoming a bishop in the Church of England, Swift remained a staunch defender of the Anglican faith. He took the post of dean at St. Patrick's Cathedral in Dublin, where he wrote *Gulliver's Travels*. His caustic wit continued to burn brightly, as shown in his 1729 essay "A Modest Proposal," a savage satire on starvation in Ireland. Its biting power still shakes up readers, nearly 300 years after its publication.

In 1742, Swift suffered a stroke and lost the ability to speak. On October 19, 1745, he died and was buried in St. Patrick's Cathedral. His death deprived the world of a generous and learned man who despised fanaticism, selfishness, and pride.

# About *Gulliver's Travels*

**The Story Behind *Gulliver's Travels*** The novel had its origin as a humorous assignment from the Scriblerus Club, a group of Swift's sharp-witted literary friends. These writers, who delighted in making fun of literary pretentions, gave Swift the assignment of writing a series of amusing, imaginary journeys because they knew he enjoyed reading travel books.

**Overview of the Novel** Reacting to the violent intolerance displayed by the religious and political figures of his time, Swift ridiculed those whose pride overcame their reason. His novel *Travels into Several Remote Nations of the World, in Four Parts, by Lemuel Gulliver, First a Surgeon, and then a Captain of Several Ships* (commonly called *Gulliver's Travels*) satirizes such intolerance by means of four imaginary voyages of Lemuel Gulliver, the narrator, a well-educated but unimaginative ship's surgeon. The four voyages are:

- Part I: A Voyage to Lilliput
- Part II: A Voyage to Brobdingnag
- Part III: A Voyage to Laputa, Balnibarbi, Luggnagg, Glubbdubdrib, and Japan
- Part IV: A Voyage to the Country of the Houyhnhnms

**Focus on Lilliput** In "A Voyage to Lilliput," Swift created the Lilliputians, who are only six inches tall. He uses the tiny Lilliputians to reduce the importance of people in general and politicians in particular. Focusing on disputes between the Church of England and Roman Catholicism, he called the followers of each Little-endians and Big-endians, respectively. In this section of the novel, Swift also satirizes the religious wars between Protestant England and Catholic France, disguising them as a conflict between Lilliput and Blefuscu.

**An Attack on the Whig Party** On one level, *Gulliver's Travels* is a travel book filled with thrilling and exotic adventures. On another level, however, the novel satirizes how people can be narrow-minded and even cruel. Swift reserved special venom for politicians who belonged to the Whig party.

Why did Swift detest the Whigs? Swift's hostility started when he became involved in English politics on behalf of the Irish church. As the envoy for the Irish bishops, Swift worked to persuade Queen Anne and the Whigs to give some much-needed financial assistance to the Irish church. When they turned Swift down by refusing to help his people, he turned his talents and allegiance to the other main political party, the Tories. Swift's contemporaries would recognize many events in *Gulliver's Travels* as representative of problems in the Whig government. For example, at the end of the excerpt you are about to read, Reldresal, the Lilliputian principal secretary, forces Gulliver to swear his allegiance to the Lilliputian emperor. Swift uses this event to satirize the ridiculous issue the Whigs created over the credentials of the Tory ambassadors who signed the Treaty of Utrecht.

**A Classic Endures** Swift wrote *Gulliver's Travels* to comment on his era, but if that were all the novel were about, it would long ago have vanished into obscurity. The novel was an immediate success—and has never been out of print. Its popularity arises from its insightful portrayal of humanity and of our potential to set aside our differences and achieve some measure of harmony.

from

# Gulliver's Travels

Jonathan Swift

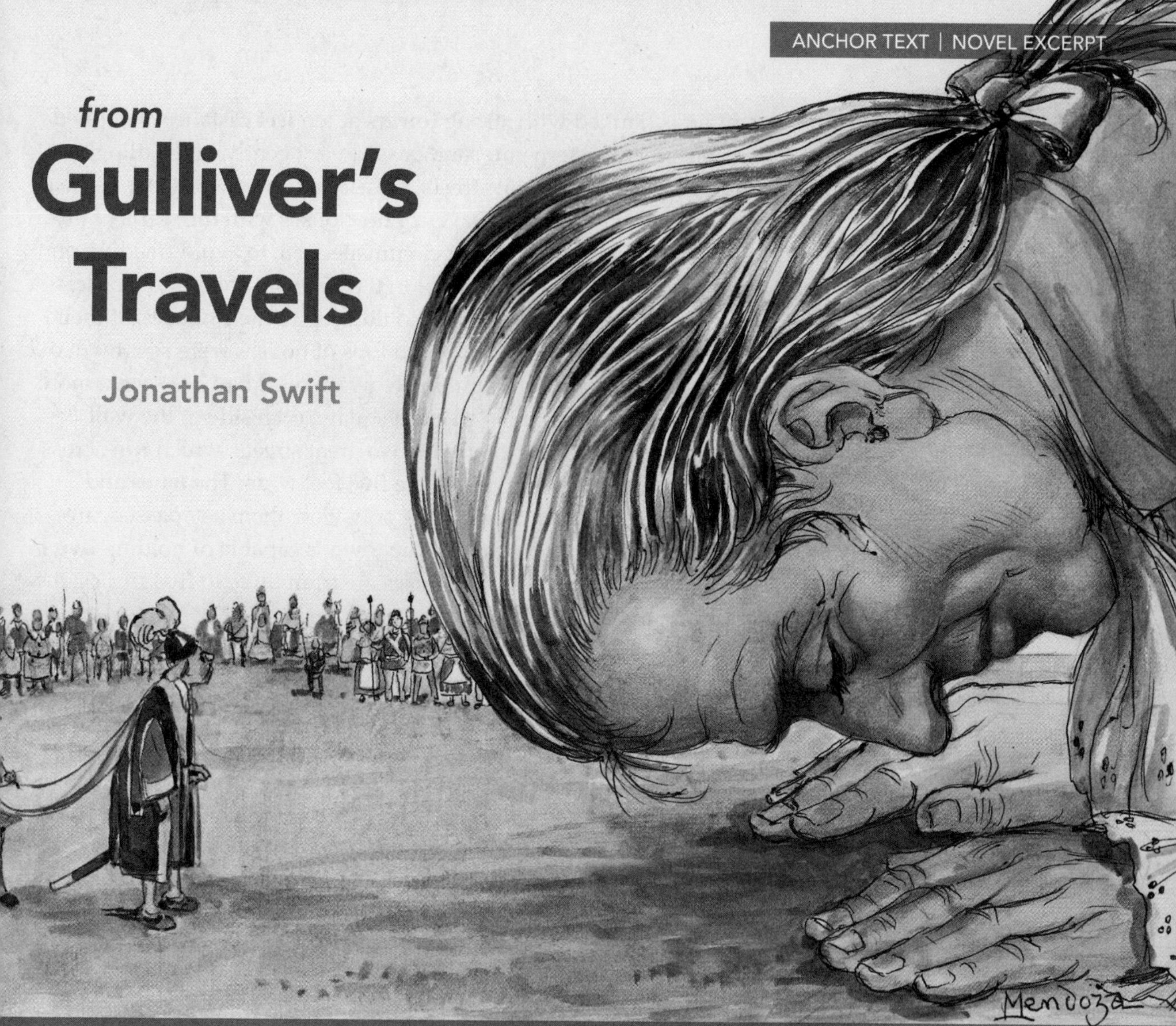


BACKGROUND

Swift's era was marked by religious and political conflicts and intolerance. His novel *Gulliver's Travels* satirizes this intolerance, using fictional characters and countries as analogies. This excerpt begins after Gulliver has been released from captivity by the Lilliputians, a race of people who are only six inches tall.

## Chapter 4

Mildendo, the metropolis of Lilliput, described, together with the emperor's palace. A conversation between the author and a principal secretary, concerning the affairs of that empire. The author's offers to serve the emperor in his wars.

1 The first request I made, after I had obtained my liberty, was, that I might have license to see Mildendo, the metropolis; which the emperor easily granted me, but with a special charge to do no hurt either to the inhabitants or their houses. The people had notice, by **proclamation**, of my design to visit the town. The wall which encompassed it is two feet and a half high, and at least eleven inches broad, so that a coach and horses may be driven very safely round

NOTES

**proclamation** (prok luh MAY shuhn) *n.* something that is proclaimed, or announced officially

NOTES

**CLOSE READ**

**ANNOTATE:** Mark two details in paragraph 1 that describe how Gulliver walks through the town.

**QUESTION:** How does he walk? What picture do these details create in the reader's mind?

**CONCLUDE:** How do these details help you visualize Mildendo and Gulliver?

it; and it is flanked with strong towers at ten feet distance. I stepped over the great western gate, and passed very gently, and sidling, through the two principal streets, only in my short waistcoat, for fear of damaging the roofs and eaves of the houses with the skirts of my coat. I walked with the utmost circumspection, to avoid treading on any stragglers who might remain in the streets, although the orders were very strict, that all people should keep in their houses, at their own peril. The garret windows and tops of houses were so crowded with spectators, that I thought in all my travels I had not seen a more populous place. The city is an exact square, each side of the wall being five hundred feet long. The two great streets, which run across and divide it into four quarters, are five feet wide. The lanes and alleys, which I could not enter, but only view them as I passed, are from twelve to eighteen inches. The town is capable of holding five hundred thousand souls: the houses are from three to five stories: the shops and markets well provided.

2 The emperor's palace is in the center of the city where the two great streets meet. It is enclosed by a wall of two feet high, and twenty feet distance from the buildings. I had his majesty's permission to step over this wall; and, the space being so wide between that and the palace, I could easily view it on every side. The outward court is a square of forty feet, and includes two other courts: in the inmost are the royal apartments, which I was very desirous to see, but found it extremely difficult; for the great gates, from one square into another, were but eighteen inches high, and seven inches wide. Now the buildings of the outer court were at least five feet high, and it was impossible for me to stride over them without infinite damage to the pile, though the walls were strongly built of hewn stone, and four inches thick. At the same time the emperor had a great desire that I should see the magnificence of his palace; but this I was not able to do till three days after, which I spent in cutting down with my knife some of the largest trees in the royal park, about a hundred yards distant from the city. Of these trees I made two stools, each about three feet high, and strong enough to bear my weight. The people having received notice a second time, I went again through the city to the palace with my two stools in my hands. When I came to the side of the outer court, I stood upon one stool, and took the other in my hand; this I lifted over the roof, and gently set it down on the space between the first and second court, which was eight feet wide. I then stepped over the building very conveniently from one stool to the other, and drew up the first after me with a hooked stick. By this contrivance I got into the inmost court; and, lying down upon my side, I applied my face to the windows of the middle stories, which were left open on purpose, and discovered the most splendid apartments that can be imagined. There I saw the empress and the young princes, in their several lodgings, with their chief attendants about them. Her imperial majesty was

pleased to smile very graciously upon me, and gave me out of the window her hand to kiss.

3 But I shall not anticipate the reader with further descriptions of this kind, because I reserve them for a greater work, which is now almost ready for the press; containing a general description of this empire, from its first erection, through a long series of princes; with a particular account of their wars and politics, laws, learning, and religion; their plants and animals; their peculiar manners and customs, with other matters very curious and useful; my chief design at present being only to relate such events and transactions as happened to the public or to myself during a residence of about nine months in that empire.

4 One morning, about a fortnight after I had obtained my liberty, Reldresal, principal secretary (as they style him) for private affairs, came to my house attended only by one servant. He ordered his coach to wait at a distance, and desired I would give him an hour's audience; which I readily consented to, on account of his quality and personal merits, as well as of the many good offices he had done me during my solicitations at court. I offered to lie down that he might the more conveniently reach my ear, but he chose rather to let me hold him in my hand during our conversation. He began with compliments on my liberty; said "he might pretend to some merit in it;" but, however, added, "that if it had not been for the present situation of things at court, perhaps I might not have obtained it so soon. For," said he, "as flourishing a condition as we may appear to be in to foreigners, we labor under two mighty evils: a violent **faction** at home, and the danger of an invasion, by a most potent enemy, from abroad. As to the first, you are to understand, that for about seventy moons past there have been two struggling parties in this empire, under the names of *Tramecksan* and *Slamecksan*, from the high and low heels of their shoes, by which they distinguish themselves. It is alleged, indeed, that the high heels are most agreeable to our ancient constitution; but, however this be, his majesty has determined to make use only of low heels in the administration of the government, and all offices in the gift of the crown, as you cannot but observe; and particularly that his majesty's **imperial** heels are lower at least by a *drurr* than any of his court (*drurr* is a measure about the fourteenth part of an inch). The animosities between these two parties run so high, that they will neither eat, nor drink, nor talk with each other. We compute the *Tramecksan*, or high heels, to exceed us in number; but the power is wholly on our side. We apprehend his imperial highness, the heir to the crown, to have some tendency towards the high heels; at least we can plainly discover that one of his heels is higher than the other, which gives him a hobble in his gait. Now, in the midst of these intestine disquiets, we are threatened with an invasion from the island of Blefuscu,[1] which is the other great

1. **Blefuscu** represents France.

NOTES

**CLOSE READ**

**ANNOTATE:** In paragraph 4, mark details that describe the issue between the two warring parties in Lilliput.

**QUESTION:** Why does Swift present this particular issue as being serious enough to divide the nation?

**CONCLUDE:** What do the details about this critical national issue reveal about Swift's purpose?

**faction** (FAK shuhn) *n.* partisan conflict within an organization or a country; dissension

**imperial** (ihm PEER ee uhl) *adj.* of or related to an empire or emperor; of superior quality

NOTES

**dominions** (duh MIHN yuhnz) *n.* governed territories or countries

**edict** (EE dihkt) *n.* formal order issued by authority

**ambassadors** (am BAS uh duhrz) *n.* special representatives to other countries

empire of the universe, almost as large and powerful as this of his majesty. For as to what we have heard you affirm, that there are other kingdoms and states in the world inhabited by human creatures as large as yourself, our philosophers are in much doubt, and would rather conjecture that you dropped from the moon, or one of the stars; because it is certain, that a hundred mortals of your bulk would in a short time destroy all the fruits and cattle of his majesty's **dominions**: besides, our histories of six thousand moons make no mention of any other regions than the two great empires of Lilliput and Blefuscu. Which two mighty powers have, as I was going to tell you, been engaged in a most obstinate war for six-and-thirty moons past. It began upon the following occasion. It is allowed on all hands, that the primitive way of breaking eggs, before we eat them, was upon the larger end; but his present majesty's grandfather, while he was a boy, going to eat an egg, and breaking it according to the ancient practice, happened to cut one of his fingers. Whereupon the emperor his father published an **edict**, commanding all his subjects, upon great penalties, to break the smaller end of their eggs. The people so highly resented this law, that our histories tell us, there have been six rebellions raised on that account; wherein one emperor lost his life, and another his crown.[2] These civil commotions were constantly fomented by the monarchs of Blefuscu; and when they were quelled, the exiles always fled for refuge to that empire. It is computed that eleven thousand persons have at several times suffered death, rather than submit to break their eggs at the smaller end.

5 Many hundred large volumes have been published upon this controversy: but the books of the Big-endians have been long forbidden, and the whole party rendered incapable by law of holding employments.[3] During the course of these troubles, the emperors of Blefuscu did frequently expostulate[4] by their **ambassadors**, accusing us of making a schism in religion, by offending against a fundamental doctrine of our great prophet Lustrog, in the fifty-fourth chapter of the Blundecral (which is their Alcoran[5]). This, however, is thought to be a mere strain upon the text; for the words are these: "that all true believers break their eggs at the convenient end." And which is the convenient end, seems, in my humble opinion to be left to every man's conscience, or at least in the power of the chief magistrate[6] to determine. Now, the Big-endian exiles have found so much credit in the emperor of Blefuscu's court, and so much private assistance and encouragement from their party here at home, that a bloody war has been carried on between the two empires for six-and-thirty moons,

2. **It is allowed . . . crown** Here, Swift satirizes the dispute in England between the Catholics (Big-endians) and Protestants (Little-endians). King Henry VIII, who "broke" with the Catholic church; King Charles I, who "lost his life;" and King James, who "lost . . . his crown," are each referred to in the passage.
3. **the whole party . . . employments** The Test Act of 1673 prevented Catholics from holding office.
4. **expostulate** (ehk SPOS chuh layt) *v.* reason earnestly with.
5. **Alcoran** Koran, the sacred book of Muslims.
6. **chief magistrate** ruler.

with various success; during which time we have lost forty capital ships, and a much greater number of smaller vessels, together with thirty thousand of our best seamen and soldiers; and the damage received by the enemy is reckoned to be somewhat greater than ours. However, they have now equipped a numerous fleet, and are just preparing to make a descent upon us; and his imperial majesty, placing great confidence in your valor and strength, has commanded me to lay this account of his affairs before you." I desired the secretary to present my humble duty to the emperor; and to let him know, "that I thought it would not become me, who was a foreigner, to interfere with parties; but I was ready, with the hazard of my life, to defend his person and state against all invaders." ❧

NOTES

## Comprehension Check

Complete the following items after you finish your first read.

1. After Gulliver is freed from captivity, what is his first request?

2. How does the empress react when she sees Gulliver looking through her window?

3. What issue leads to the war between the great empires of Lilliput and Blefuscu?

4. What preparations for war has Blefuscu completed?

5. **Notebook** Write a summary of this excerpt from *Gulliver's Travels* to confirm your understanding of the text.

## RESEARCH

**Research to Clarify** Choose at least one unfamiliar detail from the text. Briefly research that detail. In what way does the information you learned shed light on an aspect of the novel excerpt?

**Research to Explore** Learn more about the schism between the Catholic and Anglican churches and the Nonconformists. Briefly research its origin, as well as its impact on events during Swift's day.

from GULLIVER'S TRAVELS

## Close Read the Text

1. This model, from paragraph 4 of the text, shows two sample annotations, along with questions and conclusions. Close read the passage and find another detail to annotate. Then, write a question and your conclusion.

ANNOTATE: The names of the two warring parties end with the same syllable.

QUESTION: Why would Swift have chosen names that have the same endings?

CONCLUDE: Swift is suggesting that the two parties may not be that different.

. . . there have been two struggling parties in this empire, under the names of *Tramecksan* and *Slamecksan,* from the high and low heels of their shoes, by which they distinguish themselves. . . . We compute the Tramecksan, or high heels, to exceed us in number; but the power is wholly on our side.

ANNOTATE: Swift uses formal language in his description.

QUESTION: What effect does Swift's use of this language create?

CONCLUDE: Using formal language to describe a ridiculous situation creates humor.

2. For more practice, go back into the text, and complete the close-read notes.
3. Revisit a section of the text you found important during your first read. Read this section closely, and **annotate** what you notice. Ask yourself **questions** such as "Why did the author make this choice?" What can you **conclude?**

**Tool Kit**
Close-Read Guide and Model Annotation

## Analyze the Text

**CITE TEXTUAL EVIDENCE** to support your answers.

**Notebook** **Respond to these questions.**

1. **Make Inferences** What can you infer about Gulliver's relationship with the Lilliputians, based on the way he walks around their city?
2. **Cause and Effect** Based on what Reldresal says about Gulliver's size, why does the emperor seek Gulliver's aid against Blefuscu?
3. **Connect** What is Swift suggesting about political disputes through the reasons for the conflict between the Big-endians and the Little-endians?
4. **Historical Perspectives** Fearing that the author would be charged with treason, the original publisher of *Gulliver's Travels* censored the novel. Why would the novel have been so controversial in the early 1700s?
5. **Essential Question:** ***Why are both vision and disillusion necessary?*** What have you learned about vision and disillusion by reading this excerpt from *Gulliver's Travels?*

STANDARDS

**Reading Literature**

- Cite strong and thorough textual evidence to support analysis of what the text says explicitly as well as inferences drawn from the text, including determining where the text leaves matters uncertain.
- Analyze a case in which grasping a point of view requires distinguishing what is directly stated in a text from what is really meant.

# Analyze Craft and Structure

**Author's Point of View: Satire** *Gulliver's Travels* is a classic work of **satire**, writing that uses humor to expose and ridicule the faults of individuals, groups, institutions, or humanity in general. Sometimes satirists explicitly state the target of their work. Other times, they hide their true subjects behind other characters or situations to make their points in a certain way or to avoid negative consequences for their criticism. Swift hides his true targets behind fictional people and places. Many satirists, including Swift, make extensive use of the following literary elements:

- **hyperbole,** or exaggeration. For example, it is hyperbolic when someone steps outside on a hot and humid day and says, "It's like a sauna out here!"
- **understatement,** or a statement in which the literal meaning falls short of what is meant. If a runner says she has just gone for a "bit of a jog" after finishing a marathon, she is using understatement.
- **verbal irony,** or a statement that is the opposite of what the speaker actually means or believes. For example, in Shakespeare's *Julius Caesar,* Marc Antony refers to Brutus as "an honorable man," after Brutus has just participated in Caesar's murder.

## Practice

**CITE TEXTUAL EVIDENCE** to support your answers.

Notebook Respond to these questions.

1. Reldresal is sure that Gulliver and his land cannot exist, stating that Gulliver must have "dropped from the moon, or one of the stars." In what way does this statement satirize small-mindedness?
2. (a) What is ironic about calling Lilliput's major city a "metropolis"? (b) How does this irony contribute to Swift's satire?
3. (a) Why does Swift include details about the height of the emperor's heels? (b) What is Swift satirizing here?
4. (a) What elements of hyperbole are present in Gulliver's description of the emperor's palace? (b) How could Reldresal's use of the phrase "in my humble opinion" be viewed as understatement?
5. Reread the following passages from paragraph 4 of the excerpt from *Gulliver's Travels*. Then, explain the difference between the literal meaning of Gulliver's adventures and the satirical meaning Swift intends to convey.
   a. . . . two mighty powers [Lilliput and Blefuscu] have . . . been engaged in a most obstinate war for six-and-thirty moons past.
   b. . . . his present majesty's grandfather, while he was a boy, going to eat an egg, and breaking it according to the ancient practice, happened to cut one of his fingers. Whereupon the emperor his father published an edict, commanding all his subjects, upon great penalties, to break the smaller end of their eggs.

*from* GULLIVER'S TRAVELS

## Concept Vocabulary

| proclamation | imperial | edict |
|---|---|---|
| faction | dominions | ambassadors |

**Why These Words?** These concept vocabulary words all have to do with government and politics. For example, an *ambassador* meets with foreign leaders to foster relationships between nations. In so doing, the ambassador might help eliminate *faction* in either or both nations.

1. In what way does use of the concept vocabulary enable Swift to create the setting and context of his story?

2. What other words in the selection connect to this concept?

### Practice

Notebook **Respond to these questions.**

1. When might a leader issue a *proclamation*?
2. What is an issue an *ambassador* might work to resolve?
3. Describe the mannerisms of an *imperial* ruler.
4. Name some of the countries that were part of Great Britain's *dominions* in the nineteenth century.
5. Who would deliver an *edict*? Why?
6. If there is *faction* within a community, are all community members in complete agreement? Explain.

WORD NETWORK

Add interesting words related to seeing things new from the text to your Word Network.

## Word Study

**Latin Root: *-dict-*** The Latin root *-dict-* means "to say" or "to speak." When combined with the Latin prefix e-, meaning "out," it forms the word *edict*—literally, "something that has been spoken out."

1. The Latin prefix *contra-* means "against." Using this information, write a definition of the word *contradict* that demonstrates your understanding of the root *-dict-*. Check your answer in a print or online college-level dictionary.

2. Identify and define two other words that feature the root *-dict-*. Use a print or online college-level dictionary to check your work.

STANDARDS

**Language**

- Consult general and specialized reference materials, both print and digital, to find the pronunciation of a word or determine or clarify its precise meanings, its part of speech, its etymology, or its standard usage.
- Verify the preliminary determination of the meaning of a word or phrase.

# Conventions and Style

**Participial and Gerund Phrases** Swift and other writers use various types of phrases to convey specific meanings and to add variety to their writing. Two of these types of phrases are participial phrases and gerund phrases.

A **participial phrase** consists of a present or past participle and its objects, complements, or modifiers, all acting together as an *adjective*. A **gerund phrase** consists of a gerund and its objects, complements, or modifiers, all acting together as a *noun*.

This chart shows how participial and gerund phrases function.

**CLARIFICATION**
Be sure not to confuse present participles and gerunds. Although both verb forms end in *-ing*, a participle always acts as an adjective, whereas a gerund always acts as a noun.

| TYPE OF PHRASE | FUNCTION | EXAMPLES |
|---|---|---|
| participial phrase | acts as an adjective—by modifying, or describing, a noun or pronoun | The Lilliputian, frightened by Gulliver's size, scurried away. (modifies the noun *Lilliputian*)<br>Walking quickly, he didn't notice the Lilliputian. (modifies the pronoun *he*) |
| gerund phrase | acts as a noun—for instance, as a subject, a direct or indirect object, a predicate nominative, or the object of a preposition | Gulliver enters the city by climbing over the wall. (object of the preposition *by*)<br>His favorite activity is meeting with Reldresal. (predicate nominative) |

Because participial and gerund phrases are built around verb forms, they help writers combine sentences that express related ideas. When you notice a series of short, choppy sentences in your own writing, consider expressing the ideas of one of the sentences as a participial or gerund phrase instead.

## Read It

1. Read these sentences from the excerpt from *Gulliver's Travels*. Mark and label each participial phrase or gerund phrase. Then, identify its function in the sentence.
   a. I walked with the utmost circumspection, to avoid treading on any stragglers who might remain in the streets. . . .
   b. . . . and, lying down upon my side, I applied my face to the windows of the middle stories, which were left open on purpose. . . .

2. **Connect to Style** Reread the section of paragraph 4 of the excerpt from *Gulliver's Travels* in which the concept vocabulary word *edict* appears. Mark the participial phrase Swift has used to combine these two sentences that express related ideas:

   *Whereupon the emperor his father published an edict. The edict commanded all his subjects, upon great penalties, to break the smaller end of their eggs.*

## Write It

**Notebook** Write a paragraph that uses participial phrases and gerund phrases to describe Gulliver and his adventures in Lilliput.

**STANDARDS**
**Language**
- Demonstrate command of the conventions of standard English grammar and usage when writing or speaking.
- Apply knowledge of language to understand how language functions in different contexts, to make effective choices for meaning or style, and to comprehend more fully when reading or listening.
- Vary syntax for effect, consulting references for guidance as needed; apply an understanding of syntax to the study of complex texts when reading.

*from* GULLIVER'S TRAVELS

## Writing to Sources

As Jonathan Swift demonstrates in *Gulliver's Travels*, satire is a powerful way to comment on the human condition and perhaps even bring about social change. Today, there are countless issues a writer like Swift might satirize.

### Assignment

Write a **satiric narrative** modeled on the excerpt from *Gulliver's Travels*. Use Gulliver as your main character, and place him in a twenty-first century version of Lilliput.

- Choose a social trend, custom, event in the news, or other issue that you feel represents the less-than-reasonable side of humanity in today's world.
- Find a metaphor or analogy, such as Swift's use of heel heights or conflicts over the proper way to break an egg, to capture the absurdity of the element you are satirizing.
- Have a twenty-first century Lilliputian describe the complexities of the issue to your updated version of Gulliver. Make sure the seriousness of the conversation serves to reveal the point of the satire—that the situation is, in reality, foolish, misguided, or even dangerous.
- Incorporate literary elements, including hyperbole, understatement, and verbal irony, to add vividness and humor to your narrative.

Make sure your narrative is consistent with the characters and situations presented in Swift's satire.

**Vocabulary and Conventions Connection** Consider using one or more of the concept vocabulary words in your narrative. Also, consider using participial and gerund phrases to combine sentences expressing related ideas.

| proclamation | imperial | edict |
|---|---|---|
| faction | dominions | ambassadors |

### Reflect on Your Writing

After you have drafted your narrative, answer the following questions.

1. How did writing your own satire strengthen your understanding of the excerpt from *Gulliver's Travels*?
2. What advice would you give to another student writing a satiric narrative?
3. **Why These Words?** The words you choose make a difference in your writing. Which words did you specifically choose to add power or clarity to your narrative?

### STANDARDS

**Writing**

- Write narratives to develop real or imagined experiences or events using effective technique, well-chosen details, and well-structured event sequences
- Use precise words and phrases, telling details, and sensory language to convey a vivid picture of the experiences, events, setting and/or characters.
- Produce clear and coherent writing in which the development, organization, and style are appropriate to task, purpose, and audience.

**Speaking and Listening**

Present information, findings, and supporting evidence, conveying a clear and distinct perspective, such that listeners can follow the line of reasoning, alternative or opposing perspectives are addressed, and the organization, development, substance, and style are appropriate to purpose, audience, and a range of formal and informal tasks.

# Speaking and Listening

**Assignment**

In *Gulliver's Travels,* Lemuel Gulliver narrates some surprising shifts in perspective. Develop and present a **reflective narrative** in which you tell about an event or situation in which you, a friend, or family member saw something from a unique perspective. As you tell your story, draw a conclusion about life or human nature, and connect it to your narrative.

1. **Choose a Topic** Make a list of times you or someone you know saw an event or situation from a unique perspective. Choose the event you can best support with narrative details. Alternatively, you may choose to explore a current perspective on past events.

2. **Write the Narrative** Be sure to develop a beginning, a middle, and an end. Use dialogue that sounds realistic and drives the plot forward. Add details and description to bring your narrative to life. Conclude by drawing a conclusion about life or human nature based on your story.

3. **Prepare and Present Your Narrative** Practice reading the narrative aloud several times, and then present to the class. Strive to do the following:
   - Make eye contact, and vary your volume, tone, and pacing to convey meaning and engage your audience.
   - Use appropriate gestures and body language to emphasize key points.
   - Take care to speak clearly, enunciating each word carefully.

4. **Evaluate the Presentation** As your classmates deliver their narratives, listen attentively. Use an evaluation guide to evaluate their presentations.

EVALUATION GUIDE

**Rate each statement on a scale of 1 (not demonstrated) to 5 (demonstrated)**

☐ The speaker developed an engaging narrative that showed what it is like to see an event from a unique perspective.

☐ The speaker drew a conclusion and connected it to the events told in his or her narrative.

☐ The speaker read the narrative clearly.

☐ The speaker made eye contact with the audience.

☐ The speaker used appropriate gestures and body language to emphasize key points.

EVIDENCE LOG

Before moving on to a new selection, go to your Evidence Log and record what you learned from this excerpt from *Gulliver's Travels.*

from GULLIVER'S TRAVELS

## Comparing Text to Media

In this lesson, you will watch a silent film adaptation of *Gulliver's Travels* and review a gallery of cover art. After your review, you will compare these adaptations to the novel excerpt you read earlier.

• GULLIVER'S TRAVELS (film)
• *GULLIVER'S TRAVELS* COVER ART

# *from* Gulliver's Travels Among the Lilliputians and the Giants

# *Gulliver's Travels* Cover Art

### About the Director

**Georges Méliès** (1861–1938) was born in Paris and received a classical education at the Lycée Louis-le-Grand. As a filmmaker, Méliès is known for his innovative special effects. In his film *A Trip to the Moon* (1902), he hand-painted scenes directly onto the film. In this film and in others, such as *The Impossible Voyage,* characters travel through bizarre landscapes on surreal journeys. For this reason, he is considered a pioneer of science-fiction films.

## Media Vocabulary

These words or concepts will be useful to you as you analyze, discuss, and write about silent films and cover art.

| SILENT FILMS | COVER ART |
|---|---|
| **cinematography:** art and science of filmmaking; involves all the visual aspects of making movies, including choices of lighting, camera angles, camera movement, color, and focus | **cover design:** visual art created by an illustrator, photographer, or graphic artist for the cover of a book or other printed material |
| **superimposition:** placement of one image on top of another to create a new image or effect | **typography:** size and style of type used for books and other printed materials |
| **mime:** theatrical technique of portraying characters and actions wordlessly, using movement only | **realism and stylization:** In art, realism portrays images as they actually appear; stylization presents images that are exaggerated, distorted, or otherwise altered to show an imagined vision. |

## First Review MEDIA: FILM | IMAGE GALLERY

Apply these strategies as you conduct your first review. You will have an opportunity to complete a close review after your first review.

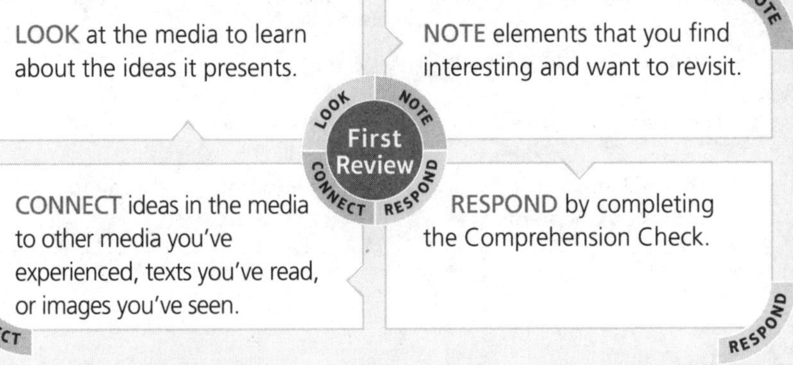

LOOK
LOOK at the media to learn about the ideas it presents.
NOTE
NOTE elements that you find interesting and want to revisit.
First Review
CONNECT
CONNECT ideas in the media to other media you've experienced, texts you've read, or images you've seen.
RESPOND
RESPOND by completing the Comprehension Check.


### STANDARDS

**Reading Literature**

- Analyze multiple interpretations of a story, drama, or poem, evaluating how each version interprets the source text.
- By the end of grade 12, read and comprehend literature, including stories, dramas, and poems, at the high end of the grades 11–CCR text complexity band independently and proficiently.

# *from* Gulliver's Travels Among the Lilliputians and the Giants

Georges Méliès

## BACKGROUNDS

Released in France in 1902, "Gulliver's Travels Among the Lilliputians" was the first cinematic depiction of Jonathan Swift's satiric novel. In addition to directing the film, Georges Méliès also played the part of Gulliver.

NOTES

# *Gulliver's Travels* Cover Art

## BACKGROUND

*Gulliver's Travels* has been illustrated hundreds of times since its first publication. Gulliver's encounter with the Lilliputians is among the most frequently illustrated scenes in literature and has often been used as the cover image for the novel. Here are four examples of cover art featuring Gulliver among the Lilliputians.

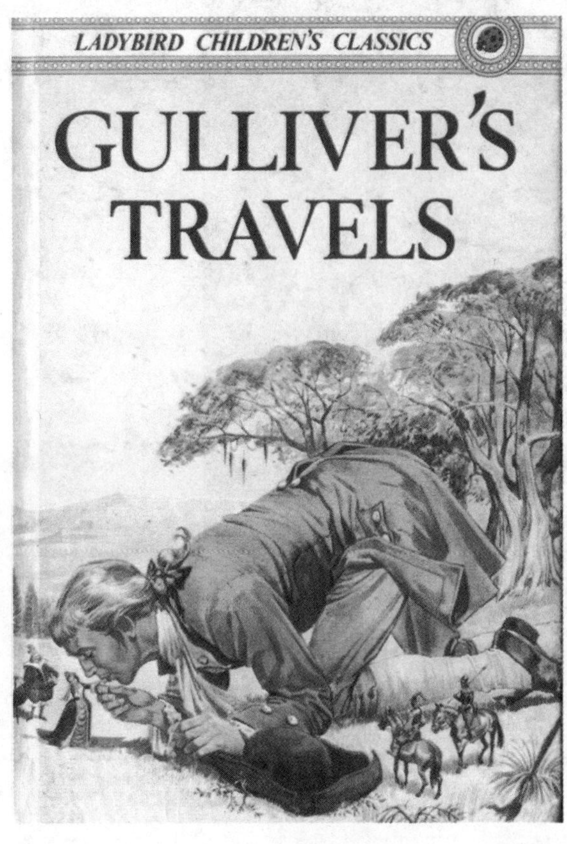


**COVER 1** • Publisher: Ladybird Children's Classics, circa 1970s

NOTES

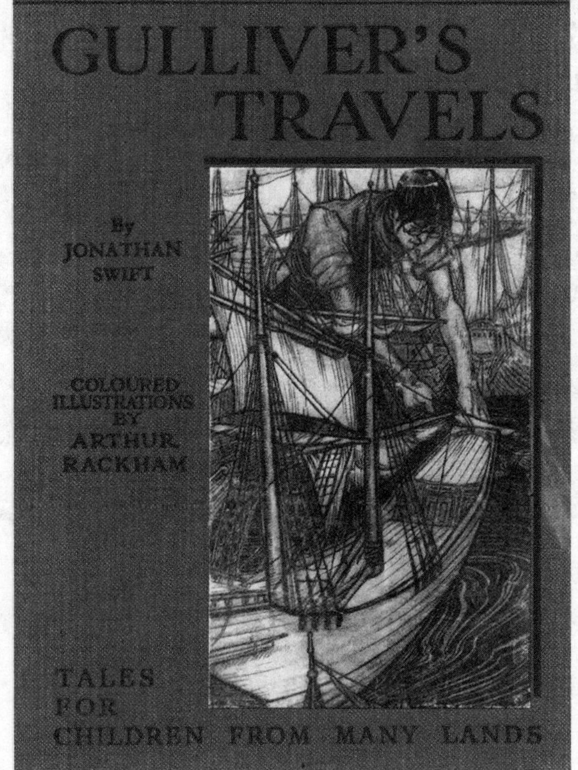


**COVER 2** • Publisher: E. P. Dutton, circa 1910s
Illustrator: Arthur Rackhamw

NOTES

**COVER 3:** Publisher: Librairie Renouard, 1904
Illustrator: Albert Robida
French Edition

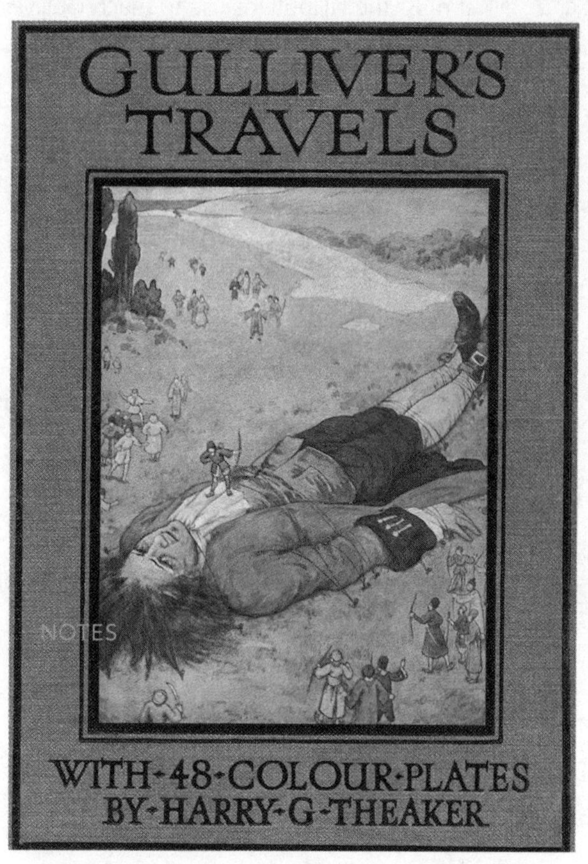


**COVER 4:** Publisher: Ward Lock & Company, 1928
Illustrator: Harry G. Theaker

## Comprehension Check

**Complete the following items after you finish your first review.**

### *from* GULLIVER'S TRAVELS AMONG THE LILLIPUTIANS AND THE GIANTS

**1.** Describe what Gulliver is doing in Lilliput in the first scene of the film.

**2.** What must the Lilliputians use to reach Gulliver's tabletop?

**3.** How does Gulliver put out the fire in the Lilliputian house?

### *GULLIVER'S TRAVELS* COVER ART

**1.** Whom is Gulliver bending down to greet in Cover 1?

**2.** What service does Cover 2 show Gulliver performing for Lilliput in its war with Blefuscu?

**3.** In Cover 3, how does Gulliver's attitude seem to differ from those of the Lilliputians?

**4.** What has happened to Gulliver in Cover 4?

## RESEARCH

**Research to Clarify** Choose at least one unfamiliar detail from one of the selections. Briefly research that detail. In what way does the information you learned shed light on an aspect of the selection?

## Close Review

Review your notes and, if necessary, watch the film and look at the book covers again. Record any new observations that seem important. What **questions** do you have? What can you **conclude**?

*from* GULLIVER'S TRAVELS AMONG THE LILLIPUTIANS AND THE GIANTS | *GULLIVER'S TRAVELS* COVER ART

## Analyze the Media

**CITE TEXTUAL EVIDENCE** to support your answers.

**Notebook** **Respond to these questions.**

1. **(a) Classify** Describe Gulliver in relation to the other characters in the third scene of the film, and explain how they interact. Describe Gulliver in relation to the other characters in the fourth scene, and explain how they interact. **(b) Analyze Cause and Effect** Explain what causes each set of characters to interact in the way they do.

2. **Evaluate** Some, but not all, of the film has been colorized. What is the effect of this technique?

3. **(a) Generalize** Name two or more traits that all of the book covers have in common. **(b) Distinguish** Name at least two significant differences between two or more of the book covers.

4. **Categorize** Rank the book covers in order from most *realistic* to most *stylized*. Explain your rankings.

5. **Essential Question:** ***Why are both vision and disillusion necessary?*** What have you learned about vision and disillusion from these media pieces?

LANGUAGE DEVELOPMENT

## Media Vocabulary

| cinematography | mime | typography |
|---|---|---|
| superimposition | cover design | realism and stylization |

Confirm your understanding of these domain-specific words by using them in a descriptive paragraph about the different versions of Gulliver's story that you have encountered. Try to incorporate at least four of the seven terms.

**STANDARDS**

**Reading Literature**
Analyze multiple interpretations of a story, drama, or poem, evaluating how each version interprets the source text.

**Language**
Acquire and use accurately general academic and domain-specific words and phrases, sufficient for reading, writing, speaking, and listening at the college and career readiness level; demonstrate independence in gathering vocabulary knowledge when considering a word or phrase important to comprehension or expression.

*from* GULLIVER'S TRAVELS

*from* GULLIVER'S TRAVELS AMONG THE LILLIPUTIANS AND THE GIANTS | *GULLIVER'S TRAVELS* COVER ART

## Writing to Compare

You have read an excerpt from Jonathan Swift's *Gulliver's Travels*. You have also watched an excerpt from a silent film adaptation of the novel and a gallery of *Gulliver's Travels* book covers. Now, deepen your understanding of the original text by comparing and analyzing these artistic interpretations of Swift's satire.

### Assignment

**Satire** is writing that uses humor to expose and ridicule the faults of individuals, groups, or humanity in general. Satire often includes the following elements.

- **hyperbole:** the use of exaggeration for comic or emotional effect
- **understatement:** a statement that presents a subject as being less than it really is
- **verbal irony:** a contradiction between what is meant and what is said

Write a **critical evaluation** of the artistic representations of Swift's text. State which representation best captures the qualities—including the satire, tone, and style—of the original. In support of this claim, evaluate each representation's fidelity to the original, with specific reference to one or more elements of satire.

### STANDARDS

**Reading Literature**
Analyze multiple interpretations of a story, drama, or poem, evaluating how each version interprets the source text.

**Writing**
- Write arguments to support claims in an analysis of substantive topics or texts, using valid reasoning and relevant and sufficient evidence.
- Introduce precise, knowledgeable claim(s), establish the significance of the claim(s), distinguish the claim(s) from alternate or opposing claims, and create an organization that logically sequences claim(s), counterclaims, reasons, and evidence.
- Develop claim(s) and counterclaims fairly and thoroughly, supplying the most relevant evidence for each while pointing out the strengths and limitations of both in a manner that anticipates the audience's knowledge level, concerns, values, and possible biases.
- Apply *grades 11–12 Reading standards* to literature.

## Prewriting

**Analyze the Texts** Use the chart to record details that show the presence (or absence) of satiric elements in Swift's text and the artistic interpretations. Make sure to consider the extent to which visual media may show hyperbole, understatement, or irony in nonverbal ways.

| SATIRIC ELEMENT | SWIFT'S TEXT | FILM | COVERS (indicate 1, 2, 3, or 4) |
|---|---|---|---|
| Hyperbole | | | |
| Understatement | | | |
| Irony | | | |

**Notebook** Respond to these questions.

1. Which artistic representation best captures the tone and style of Swift's satire? Explain.

2. What makes the other representations less effective or true to Swift's text?

# Drafting

**Write a Claim** Review your Prewriting notes. Draft a brief statement of your claim, or position. Identify the visual representation you think best captures the spirit and quality of Swift's text, as well as how it does so.

Claim: ______________________________

______________________________

**Consider a Counterclaim** Write a brief statement expressing an opposing position and a reason that supports it.

Counterclaim: ______________________________

______________________________

Address this counterclaim in your essay. Point out that some readers or viewers might have a perception of the works that is different from yours. Provide reasons and evidence that demonstrate why your claim remains more persuasive.

**Organize Ideas and Evidence** Use the chart to clarify your thinking and organize your ideas and evidence.

| Most Effective Representation (mark one): Film / Cover 1 / Cover 2 / Cover 3 / Cover 4 | Least Effective Representation (mark one): Film / Cover 1 / Cover 2 / Cover 3 / Cover 4 |
|---|---|
| Why it is most effective:<br>• Use of Satiric Elements<br><br>• Overall Quality, Tone, Style | Why it is least effective:<br>• Use of Satiric Elements<br><br>• Overall Quality, Tone, Style |

EVIDENCE LOG

Before moving on to a new selection, go to your Evidence Log and record what you've learned from the excerpt from the film *Gulliver's Travels Among the Lilliputians and the Giants* and *Gulliver's Travels* cover art.

**Review, Revise, and Edit**

When you have completed your draft, set it aside for a while. Then, return to it with an editor's eye. Read it to answer these questions: Is the claim clear? Is the evidence sufficient and persuasive? Does the organization carry the reader along, or create obstacles to understanding? Make notes, and indicate where new information is needed. Then, revise, edit, and proofread your draft.

WRITING TO SOURCES

- A VALEDICTION: FORBIDDING MOURNING
- HOLY SONNET 10
- *from* GULLIVER'S TRAVELS
- *from* GULLIVER'S TRAVELS AMONG THE LILLIPUTIANS AND THE GIANTS
- *GULLIVER'S TRAVELS* COVER ART

# Write a Reflective Narrative

You have read two poems that offer new perspectives on love and death. You have also read an excerpt from a novel that presents a satirical view of religion and politics, and you have viewed media selections that were inspired by the novel. Now you will use your understanding of those selections to create a narrative that explores a new way of looking at things.

**Assignment**

Write a brief **reflective narrative** in which you address this question:

**When do we need a new vision of things?**

Start by recalling an incident from your life that presented a difficult challenge. Develop that memory into a narrative, sequencing events so that they reveal how you used that experience to develop and grow and see things differently. In your conclusion, reflect on the meaning of the event. Incorporate one or more of the readings from this unit as a way of illuminating your own experience.

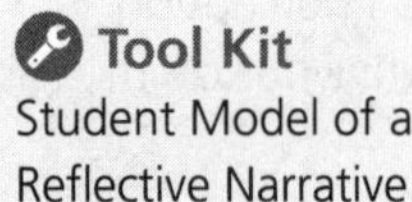

**Tool Kit**
Student Model of a Reflective Narrative

## Elements of a Reflective Narrative

A **reflective narrative** is a first-person story about a real-life experience. Unlike a memoir or autobiography, a reflective narrative typically focuses on one specific incident or event. The writer is the narrator, and the narrator offers thoughtful judgments about the experience he or she relates.

A well-written reflective narrative contains these elements:

- a clear and consistent point of view
- multi-dimensional descriptions of key people
- a smooth sequence of events or experiences
- effective use of dialogue, description, and/or reflection to develop the story
- precise words to clarify experiences
- a conclusion that follows from and reflects on the events in the narrative
- varied sentence types and constructions

**ACADEMIC VOCABULARY**

As you craft your reflective narrative, consider using some of the academic vocabulary you learned in the beginning of the unit.

**engender**
**transformation**
**incorporate**
**artifice**
**inexorable**

**Model Reflective Narrative** For a model of a well-crafted reflective narrative, see the Launch Text, "The Assignment of My Life." Challenge yourself to find all of the elements of an effective reflective narrative in the text. You will have the opportunity to review these elements as you prepare to write your own reflective narrative.

**STANDARDS**

**Writing**

- Write narratives to develop real or imagined experiences or events using effective technique, well-chosen details, and well-structured event sequences.
- Write routinely over extended time frames and shorter time frames for a range of tasks, purposes, and audiences.

# Prewriting / Planning

**Develop Your Narrator** In a reflective narrative about a real-life event, your perspective as a narrator is especially important. Your perspective controls how the reader receives information. As you write about an experience that altered your way of thinking, think of how to describe the person you were then—and how you have changed due to the event. Use this chart to explore ways of looking at the incident you will recount in your narrative.

| | THEN | NOW |
|---|---|---|
| My appearance | | |
| My beliefs | | |
| My interests | | |
| My attitudes | | |

**Gather Evidence from Sources** Although evidence for a reflective narrative comes mostly from personal memories, including specific details makes your narrative come alive for the reader. For example, in the Launch Text, the writer includes specifics of who, when, and where:

> *After NYU, in 1931, just as Hitler was rising to power, I went to Germany for a one-year fellowship at the University of Cologne. My professors encouraged me to get a PhD in writing, but how could I do it in one year? The head of the English department, Professor Herbert Schoffler, said, "It's never been done before, but maybe you can do it."*
>
> —"The Assignment of My Life," Ruth Gruber

If you do not remember specific details, ask someone in your family, look at old photographs and letters, or do some online research to add realism to your writing.

**Connect Across Texts** The prompt asks you to use one or more texts to illuminate your personal experience. Scan the texts to locate a line or lines that speak to your own story or show another way to answer the question in the prompt. Think about where you might use the lines in your narrative.

EVIDENCE LOG

Review your Evidence Log and identify key details you may want to use in your reflective narrative.

STANDARDS

**Writing**

Engage and orient the reader by setting out a problem, situation, or observation and its significance, establishing one or multiple point(s) of view, and introducing a narrator and/ or characters; create a smooth progression of experiences or events.

## Drafting

**Shape Your Writing** It is easy to write about events in order. That is something you have done since childhood. It is harder to "shape" events so that they tell a story worth telling. As the writer Annie Dillard once said, "The writer of any work, and particularly any nonfiction, must decide two crucial points: what to put in and what to leave out."

A reflective narrative is two things in one: the event, and the story that flows from the event. In the Launch Text, the *event* is the narrator's experience on the boat with refugees. The *story* is the change in her life's focus brought on by that event. *Before* the event, she was a journalist. *After* the event, she was a journalist whose life was focused on rescue and survival.

Use this organizer to identify your event and plan the story that surrounds it.

### Reflective Narrative Organizer

My story is:

BEFORE

____________________

____________________

____________________

____________________

EVENT

____________________

____________________

____________________

____________________

AFTER

____________________

____________________

____________________

____________________

**Write a First Draft** Use your organizer to write your first draft. Use specific details to set the scene and to establish your narrative's point of view. Introduce and develop key people in the narrative, as necessary. Add dialogue and description where they help develop your story. Sequence events to build toward a satisfactory conclusion that supports your overarching story.

STANDARDS

**Writing**

- Engage and orient the reader by setting out a problem, situation, or observation and its significance, establishing one or multiple point(s) of view, and introducing a narrator and/or characters; create a smooth progression of experiences or events.
- Use narrative techniques, such as dialogue, pacing, description, reflection, and multiple plot lines, to develop experiences, events, and/or characters.
- Use a variety of techniques to sequence events so that they build on one another to create a coherent whole and build toward a particular tone and outcome.
- Provide a conclusion that follows from and reflects on what is experienced, observed, or resolved over the course of the narrative.

LANGUAGE DEVELOPMENT: STYLE

# Sentence Variety: Varying Syntax

You learned early in your life as a writer not to start every sentence with *I*. Adding variety to sentences helps add liveliness and rhythm to your writing. To do so, you might use **clauses**, groups of words that contain verbs and subjects. You might also use **participial phrases**, which contain verb forms often ending in *-ing* or *-ed*, or **infinitive phrases**, which usually start with the word *to*. Every phrase or clause can convey useful information to your readers.

## Read It

These sentences from the Launch Text use phrases and clauses to convey information.

- *She was the only teacher* ***that I had in elementary school who was not Irish or Jewish****. . . .* (adjective clauses), modifying *teacher* and *school*)
- *Words—written, spoken,* ***waking me in full sentences from my sleep****—became the fuel that drove me.* (participial phrase, modifying *words*)
- ***When I came home****, there weren't a lot of jobs in journalism. . . .* (adverb clause, modifying *were*).
- *. . . I learned* ***that I must live a story to write it****.* (noun clause—direct object; infinitive phrase, modifying *must live*)

TIP

**PUNCTUATION**

Punctuation rules for clauses depend on where the clauses appear in a sentence.

- When you start a sentence with an adverb clause, use a comma between the clause and the rest of the sentence: *Before you leave, see me.*
- When you end a sentence with an adverb clause, no comma is usually needed: *See me before you leave.*

## Write It

As you draft your reflective narrative, look for ways to expand your sentences with phrases and clauses that add specific information. Watch especially for ways to vary sentence beginnings so that your sentences do not all look and sound the same.

| TYPE OF ADDITION | USUALLY BEGINS WITH |
|---|---|
| **adjective clause** | a relative pronoun, such as *that, which, who, whom, whose* |
| **adverb clause** | a subordinating conjunction, such as *after, although, because, before, if, since, unless, until, when, while* |
| **noun clause** | *that, what, whatever, which, whichever, who, whoever, whom, whomever* |
| **infinitive phrase** | *to* (not to be confused with the preposition *to*) |
| **participial phrase** | a verb form that ends in *-ing* or *-ed* |

STANDARDS

**Language**

- Demonstrate command of the conventions of standard English capitalization, punctuation, and spelling when writing.
- Apply knowledge of language to understand how language functions in different contexts, to make effective choices for meaning or style, and to comprehend more fully when reading or listening.
- Vary syntax for effect, consulting references for guidance as needed; apply an understanding of syntax to the study of complex texts when reading.

## MAKING WRITING SOPHISTICATED

**Sequencing Events** We are used to reading stories that proceed from beginning to middle to end in chronological order. However, in a reflective narrative, the order of events may not be that predictable. Because the narrator is looking back at the past from a position in the present, the writer may use a variety of **narrative techniques** to connect events over time.

- **Backstory** is the inclusion of past events that help a reader understand the main event being retold.
- **Flashback** is a movement backward in time from the chronological time of the narrative.
- **Foreshadowing** is hinting about what is to come later on in a narrative.
- **Framing device** is a way of surrounding the main narrative with a secondary narrative, as when a writer starts in the present, looks back in time, and then returns to the present to comment on the past.

### Read It

These examples from the Launch Text show how the writer moves around in time over the course of her narrative.

LAUNCH TEXT

BEFORE: This backstory sets up the scene on the ship with the refugees. It explains how the writer came to be there.

I left journalism for a period during World War II to take a job as Special Assistant to the Secretary of the Interior, Harold Ickes. In 1944, he assigned me on a secret mission to be an escort for nearly 1,000 Jewish refugees from Italy to the United States aboard a military ship called the *Henry Gibbins*. I was made a simulated general, so that if I was captured by the Nazis, they wouldn't kill me. That was according to the laws of the Geneva Convention.

❧

AFTER: Here, the writer clearly is looking back and reflecting on a long-ago experience. She flashes back to the memory of concentration camp survivors.

. . . And I began to live the Oswego story the moment I climbed aboard the *Henry Gibbins* and met the survivors, many still wearing their striped concentration camp pajamas with newspapers wrapped around their bare feet. Because of them and those we lost, I vowed I would fight with every cell in my body to help rescue Jews in danger. After that experience, I would continue to be a journalist, photographer, and book author. But from that moment on, inextricably, my life would be about rescue and survival.

STANDARDS

**Writing**
Use a variety of techniques to sequence events so that they build on one another to create a coherent whole and build toward a particular tone and outcome.

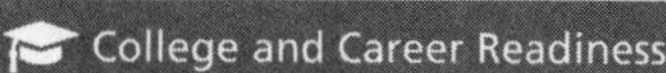


## Write It

Reread the Then-Now chart you completed in Prewriting. Think about how you might use one or more of the techniques listed in the chart to show more clearly how the event you chose changed your point of view and helped you to develop and grow.

| TECHNIQUE | MY IDEAS |
|---|---|
| BACKSTORY<br>Do I need to add more background so that my reader understands when and why the event happened? | |
| FLASHBACK<br>Would a flashback to an earlier event add anything meaningful to my narrative? | |
| FORESHADOWING<br>Can I use a hint about what will happen to stimulate a reader's interest in my narrative? | |
| FRAMING DEVICE<br>If I started and ended my narrative in the present time, would that change be useful? Would that make it easier to show how I have reflected on and learned from the event? | |

**Use Precise Words to Indicate Time** Too many unexplained shifts in time may cause a reader to lose track of the narrative. Be sure to use specific words to indicate when the action takes place. Some examples are listed here. Add other time words and phrases to the chart.

| TIME WORDS AND PHRASES | | | |
|---|---|---|---|
| after that | at first | at that time | by now |
| consequently | earlier | eventually | from that point |
| in the meantime | later on | not long afterward | presently |
| recently | prior to | soon after | thereafter |
| | | | |
| | | | |

# Revising

## Evaluating Your Draft

Use this checklist to evaluate the effectiveness of your first draft. Then, use your evaluation and the instruction on this page to guide your revision.

| FOCUS AND ORGANIZATION | EVIDENCE AND ELABORATION | CONVENTIONS |
|---|---|---|
| ☐ Establishes a clear, consistent point of view and describes key people in detail. | ☐ Uses techniques such as dialogue, description, and reflection to develop the experience being narrated. | ☐ Attends to the norms and conventions of the discipline; varies sentence structure. |
| ☐ Establishes a sequence of events that unfolds smoothly and logically. | ☐ Uses precise words and phrases and specific details to clarify events for the reader. | |
| ☐ Includes a conclusion that reflects on events in the narrative in a satisfying way. | | |

WORD NETWORK

Include interesting words from your Word Network in your reflective narrative.

### Revising for Focus and Organization

**Reflection** Remember that the focus of a reflective narrative is to look back and evaluate an event. Reread your narrative with a critical eye. Can a reader tell how this event changed your perspective? Do you need to add something to your conclusion that stresses the meaning of the event in your life?

### Revising for Evidence and Elaboration

**Characterization** A reflective narrative is about the narrator, but it may revolve around an event that involves others. Consider using techniques of characterization to develop the personas of the narrator and other people in the text.

- In **direct characterization**, you describe the person's behavior and appearance.
- **Indirect characterization** relies on dialogue and the responses of others to show people's personalities.

**Dialogue and Description** Look for ways to add descriptive words and phrases as you set the scene for the event you are retelling. Use vivid sensory details that capture the experience through sights, sounds, tastes, sensations, or smells. Return to the Launch Text to find places where the writer uses dialogue to develop her narrative. Are there places where a person's words or thoughts might help your reader understand your story better?

STANDARDS

**Writing**

- Use narrative techniques, such as dialogue, pacing, description, reflection, and multiple plot lines, to develop experiences, events, and/or characters.
- Use precise words and phrases, telling details, and sensory language to convey a vivid picture of the experiences, events, setting, and/or characters.
- Provide a conclusion that follows from and reflects on what is experienced, observed, or resolved over the course of the narrative.

PEER REVIEW

Exchange papers with a classmate. Use the checklist to evaluate your classmate's narrative and provide supportive feedback.

1. Is the order of events easy to follow?

   ☐ yes ☐ no If no, explain what confused you.

2. Does the narrative reveal how the narrator developed and grew?

   ☐ yes ☐ no If no, tell what you think might be added.

3. Has the narrator reflected on the meaning of the event?

   ☐ yes ☐ no If no, suggest what you might change.

4. What is the strongest part of your classmate's narrative? Why?

## Editing and Proofreading

**Edit for Conventions** Reread your draft for accuracy and consistency. Correct errors in grammar and word usage. Be sure that any shifts in time will be clear to a reader.

**Proofread for Accuracy** Read your draft carefully, looking for errors in spelling and punctuation. Punctuate any introductory adverb clauses correctly.

## Publishing and Presenting

Combine your writing with your classmates' in a classroom literary journal. If possible, store multiple copies in the classroom library. Take the time to read your classmates' work and to think about how your experiences are alike and different.

## Reflecting

Reflect on what you learned by writing your reflective narrative. Does the incident you chose work well as a response to the prompt? Was it difficult to incorporate reflection into your description of an event? Think about what you might do differently the next time you write a reflective narrative.

STANDARDS

**Writing**

Develop and strengthen writing as needed by planning, revising, editing, rewriting, or trying a new approach, focusing on addressing what is most significant for a specific purpose and audience.

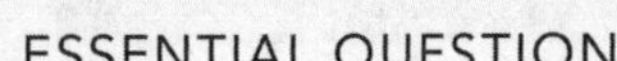

OVERVIEW: SMALL-GROUP LEARNING

ESSENTIAL QUESTION:

# Why are both vision and disillusion necessary?

It requires both humility and courage to give up one's vision. The pain of disillusion, however, often leads to a new—perhaps better—vision. You will read selections that show how people have gained insight through disillusion. You will work in a group to continue your exploration of the concepts of vision and disillusion.

## Small-Group Learning Strategies

Throughout your life, in school, in your community, and in your career, you will continue to develop strategies when you work in teams. Use these strategies during Small-Group learning. Add ideas of our own at each step.

| STRATEGY | ACTION PLAN |
| --- | --- |
| Prepare | • Complete your assignments so that you are prepared for group work.<br>• Take notes on your reading so you can contribute to your group's discussions.<br>• |
| Participate fully | • Make eye contact to signal that you are listening and taking in what is being said.<br>• Use text evidence when making a point.<br>• |
| Support others | • Build off ideas from others in your group.<br>• State the relationship of your points to the points of others—whether you are supporting someone's point, refuting it, or taking the conversation in a new direction.<br>• |
| Clarify | • Paraphrase the ideas of others to ensure that your understanding is correct.<br>• Ask follow-up questions.<br>• |

## CONTENTS

COMPARE

### POETRY

**To His Coy Mistress**
*Andrew Marvell*

Should we live as though we have all the time in the world?

### POETRY COLLECTION 2

**To the Virgins, to Make Much of Time**
*Robert Herrick*

**Youth's the Season Made for Joys** *John Gay*

Should we seize the day and live for the moment?

### POETRY COLLECTION 3

*from the* **Divine Comedy: Inferno**
*Dante Alighieri, translated by John Ciardi*

**The Second Coming** *W. B. Yeats*

Do visions at the edge of the imagination bring insight or despair?

### SHORT STORY

**Araby**
*James Joyce*

A boy's first encounter with love changes how he sees himself and everything else.

### POETRY COLLECTION 4

**The Explosion** *Philip Larkin*

▶ MEDIA CONNECTION: The Explosion

**Old Love** *Francesca Beard*

Do disaster and loss always lead to disillusion?

### PERFORMANCE TASK

SPEAKING AND LISTENING FOCUS

## Present a Reflective Narrative

The Small-Group readings feature people writing about having grand visions and losing them. After reading, your group will plan and deliver a reflective narrative about the ways in which our visions of the world can help us grow or hold us back.

## Working as a Team

1. **Take a Position** In your group, discuss the following question:

   In what ways is growing up a process of finding your own vision?

   As you take turns sharing your positions, be sure to provide reasons for your choice. After all group members have shared, discuss some of the personal attributes that might be required to change the way you look at things.

2. **List Your Rules** As a group, decide on the rules that you will follow as you work together. Samples are provided; add two more of your own. You may add or revise rules based on your experience together.

   - Everyone should participate in group discussions.
   - People should not interrupt.
   - ______________________________
     ______________________________
   - ______________________________
     ______________________________

3. **Apply the Rules** Practice working as a group. Share what you have learned about skeptics and visionaries. Make sure each person in the group contributes. Take notes on and be prepared to share with the class one thing that you heard from another member of your group.

4. **Name Your Group** Choose a name that reflects the unit topic.

   Our group's name: ______________________________

5. **Create a Communication Plan** Decide how you want to communicate with one another. For example, you might use online collaboration tools, email, or instant messaging.

   Our group's decision: ______________________________

   ______________________________

## Making a Schedule

First, find out the due dates for the small-group activities. Then, preview the texts and activities with your group, and make a schedule for completing the tasks.

| SELECTION | ACTIVITIES | DUE DATE |
|---|---|---|
| To His Coy Mistress | | |
| To the Virgins, to Make Much of Time<br>Youth's the Season Made for Joys | | |
| *from the* Divine Comedy: Inferno<br>The Second Coming | | |
| Araby | | |
| The Explosion<br>Old Love | | |

## Working on Group Projects

As your group works together, you'll find it more effective if each person has a specific role. Different projects require different roles. Before beginning a project, discuss the necessary roles, and choose one for each group member. Here are some possible roles; add your own ideas.

**Project Manager:** monitors the schedule and keeps everyone on task
**Researcher:** organizes research activities
**Recorder:** takes notes during group meetings

TO HIS COY MISTRESS

## Comparing Texts

In this lesson, you will read and compare three poems that express a similar theme. First, you will complete the first-read and close-read activities for "To His Coy Mistress." The work you do with your group on this title will help prepare you for your final comparison.

POETRY COLLECTION 2

### About the Poet

**Andrew Marvell** (1621–1678) lived in a troubled time during which King Charles I, who was eventually executed, was feuding with England's Parliament. Marvell's poetic career began with an apprenticeship to the renowned poet John Milton. On his own, Marvell wrote masterful poetry in both a metaphysical and a classical vein. Marvell's work went largely unappreciated until the nineteenth century. Since then, Marvell has been regarded as one of the major poets of his time.

# To His Coy Mistress

## Concept Vocabulary

As you perform your first read, you will encounter the following words.

| sport | languish |
|---|---|

**Context Clues** If these words are unfamiliar, try using various types of **context clues**—other words and phrases that appear nearby in the text—to help you determine their meanings.

**Synonyms:** Some of the hikers chose the most **rigorous**, challenging route to the mountain's summit.

**Elaborating Details:** We listened in silent awe to the cello **virtuoso**, amazed by her technical skill and musicality.

**Contrast of Ideas:** Although Violet had a reputation for being withdrawn and aloof, we always found her to be quite **gregarious**.

Apply your knowledge of context clues and other vocabulary strategies to determine the meanings of unfamiliar words you encounter during your first read.

## First Read POETRY

Apply these strategies as you conduct your first read. You will have an opportunity to complete a close read after your first read.

NOTICE *who* or *what* is "speaking" the poem and whether the poem tells a story or describes a single moment.

ANNOTATE by marking vocabulary and key passages you want to revisit.

CONNECT ideas within the selection to what you already know and what you've already read.

RESPOND by completing the Comprehension Check.

### STANDARDS

**Reading Literature**
By the end of grade 12, read and comprehend literature, including stories, dramas, and poems, at the high end of the grades 11–CCR text complexity band independently and proficiently.

**Language**
- Determine or clarify the meaning of unknown and multiple-meaning words and phrases based on *grades 11–12 reading and content*, choosing flexibly from a range of strategies.
- Use context as a clue to the meaning of a word or phrase.

# To His Coy Mistress

Andrew Marvell

## BACKGROUND

By the seventeenth century, the English language had become enriched with words borrowed from French, Italian, Latin, and Greek. It was more than a tool for basic communication; through it, one could express philosophical ideas, convey abstract theories, and indulge in humorous wordplay. This poem shows the range of this language, from witty puns to fanciful imagery.

NOTES

Had we but world enough, and time,
This coyness lady were no crime.
We would sit down, and think which way
To walk, and pass our long love's day.

NOTES

Thou by the Indian Ganges' side
Should'st rubies find; I by the tide
Of Humber[1] would complain. I would
Love you ten years before the Flood,
And you should if you please refuse
Till the conversion of the Jews.[2]
My vegetable love should grow
Vaster than empires, and more slow;
An hundred years should go to praise
Thine eyes, and on thy forehead gaze;
Two hundred to adore each breast,
But thirty thousand to the rest;
An age at least to every part,
And the last age should show your heart.
For, lady, you deserve this state,[3]
Nor would I love at lower rate.

But at my back I always hear
Time's wingèd chariot hurrying near:
And yonder all before us lie
Deserts of vast eternity.
Thy beauty shall no more be found,
Nor, in thy marble vault, shall sound
My echoing songs; then worms shall try
That long-preserved virginity,
And your quaint honor turn to dust,
And into ashes all my lust:
The grave's a fine and private place,
But none I think do there embrace.

Now therefore, while the youthful hue
Sits on thy skin like morning dew,
And while thy willing soul transpires[4]
At every pore with instant fires,

1. **Humber** river flowing through Hull, Marvell's hometown.
2. **conversion of the Jews** According to Christian tradition, the Jews were to be converted immediately before the Last Judgment.
3. **state** dignity.
4. **transpires** breathes out.

Now let us **sport** us while we may,
And now, like amorous birds of prey,
Rather at once our time devour
Than **languish** in his slow-chapped[5] power.
Let us roll all our strength, and all
Our sweetness, up into one ball,
And tear our pleasures with rough strife
Thorough[6] the iron gates of life:
Thus, though we cannot make our sun
Stand still, yet we will make him run.

5. **slow-chapped** slow-jawed.
6. **Thorough** through.

NOTES

Mark context clues or indicate another strategy you used that helped you determine meaning.

**sport** (spawrt) *V.*

MEANING:

**languish** (LANG gwihsh) *V.*

MEANING:

## Comprehension Check

**Complete the following items after you finish your first read. Review and clarify details with your group.**

**1.** What adjective does the speaker use to describe the behavior and attitude of his mistress?

**2.** Under what circumstances would the speaker be willing to accept his mistress's reluctance?

**3.** What does the speaker always hear at his back?

**4.** What course of action does the speaker propose in the final stanza?

## RESEARCH

**Research to Clarify** Choose at least one unfamiliar detail from the poem. Briefly research that detail. In what way does the information you learned shed light on an aspect of the poem?

**Research to Explore** Briefly research other works by Andrew Marvell. List those works and the source or sources that provided you with this information. You may want to share what you learned with your group.

MAKING MEANING

## Close Read the Text

With your group, revisit sections of the text you marked during your first read. **Annotate** details that you notice. What **questions** do you have? What can you **conclude**?

TO HIS COY MISTRESS

## Analyze the Text

**CITE TEXTUAL EVIDENCE** to support your answers.

**Notebook** Complete the activities.

1. **Review and Clarify** With your group, reread lines 13–18, and identify the speaker's main idea in these lines. Then, reread lines 21–32. How have the speaker's ideas shifted? Is this shift surprising? Why or why not?
2. **Present and Discuss** Now, work with your group to share passages from the poem that you found especially important. Take turns presenting your passages. Discuss what details you noticed, what questions you asked, and what conclusions you reached.
3. **Essential Question:** ***Why are both vision and disillusion necessary?*** What has this poem taught you about either vision or disillusion?

TIP

**CLARIFICATION**

The speaker is the imaginary voice that expresses the ideas in a poem. Often, the speaker sounds like the poet and bears a close resemblance to the poet, but you should not assume that the poet and the speaker are identical. Like the narrator in a work of fiction, the speaker is an assumed voice.

LANGUAGE DEVELOPMENT

## Concept Vocabulary

**sport** **languish**

**Why These Words?** The two concept vocabulary words are related. With your group, determine what the words have in common. Write your ideas, and add another word that fits the category.

### Practice

**Notebook** Confirm your understanding of the concept vocabulary words by rewriting the lines of the poem in which they appear, using contemporary English.

Add interesting words related to seeing things new from the text to your Word Network.

## Word Study

**Notebook** **Changing Usage** Many English words have multiple possible usages. A word's most common usage may change over time. For example, in line 37 of "To His Coy Mistress," Marvell uses the word *sport* as a verb. This usage has grown less common since the seventeenth century, and the word is now primarily used as a noun, meaning "physical activity done for enjoyment."

Revisit the poem, and find these familiar words: *state* (line 19), *try* (line 27), *transpire* (line 35), *instant* (line 36). Infer from context clues how each word is being used, and write a probable definition. Then, use a dictionary or text aids, such as footnotes, to verify the words' meanings.

STANDARDS

**Language**

- Apply the understanding that usage is a matter of convention, can change over time, and is sometimes contested.
- Resolve issues of complex or contested usage, consulting references as needed.
- Consult general and specialized reference materials, both print and online, to find the pronunciation of a word or determine or clarify its precise meaning, its part of speech, its etymology, or its standard usage.
- Verify the preliminary definition of the meaning of a word or phrase.

TO HIS COY MISTRESS

TIP

**GROUP DISCUSSION**

Keep in mind that members of your group might have impressions of the poem's theme that are different from yours. There's no right impression or conclusion, but talking out differing opinions and the reasons for them will help you clarify your thoughts and learn from one another.

STANDARDS

**Reading Literature**

Determine two or more themes or central ideas of a text and analyze their development over the course of the text, including how they interact and build on one another to produce a complex account; provide an objective summary of the text.

**Language**

- Apply the understanding that usage is a matter of convention, can change over time, and is sometimes contested.
- Resolve issues of complex or contested usage, consulting references as needed.
- Apply knowledge of language to understand how language functions in different contexts, to make effective choices for meaning or style, and to comprehend more fully when reading or listening.

# Analyze Craft and Structure

**Development of Theme** A **theme** is a central idea, message, or insight that a literary work reveals. Many literary works contain more than one theme, and those multiple themes are often related. The principal theme of Marvell's "To His Coy Mistress" is *carpe diem*, a Latin phrase typically translated as "seize the day" or "make the most of time." This theme has natural connections to other thematic ideas, such as the fleeting nature of youth or the inevitability of mortality.

To identify themes, look at what a writer says and how it is said. The writer's choice of *how* to say something is referred to as **style.** Two key elements of a writer's style are tone and imagery.

- **Tone:** the attitude the writer expresses toward the subject or the audience; a writer's tone may range from humorous to serious, from conversational to elevated, and so on.
- **Imagery:** descriptive language that re-creates sensory experiences in the reader's mind

Although many literary works may convey the same theme, each does so in its own way. For example, the *carpe diem* theme is common to many other works of literature besides "To His Coy Mistress." However, Marvell conveys this common theme in his own distinctive style, combining serious-sounding yet comically hyperbolic language with fantastical images.

**CITE TEXTUAL EVIDENCE** to support your answers.

## Practice

Work together to complete the chart. Select one passage of two to three lines from each of the poem's three stanzas. Examine the speaker's words, as well as the tone and imagery in each passage. Then, discuss with your group how these elements contribute to the poem's themes.

| PASSAGE | ELEMENT |
|---|---|
| (1st stanza) | what is said: |
| | tone: |
| | imagery: |
| (2nd stanza) | what is said: |
| | tone: |
| | imagery: |
| (3rd stanza) | what is said: |
| | tone: |
| | imagery: |

## Conventions and Style

**Expressing Theme With Verb Mood** The **mood** of a verb conveys the speaker's attitude toward the action or state of being that the verb expresses—for instance, uncertainty or insistence.

This chart shows examples from the poem of four verb moods.

| MOOD | USE | NOTE | EXAMPLE |
|---|---|---|---|
| indicative | make a statement of fact | may be in the past ("it was"), the present ("it is"), or the future ("it will be") tense | *Thy beauty shall no more be found,* (line 25) |
| imperative | issue a request or command | may be in the second-person singular or plural ("Be!") or the first-person plural ("Let's be!") | *Now let us sport us while we may,* (line 37) |
| subjunctive | express a hypothetical, a wish, or a statement contrary to fact | often found in an *if* clause ("if it were") or in a clause whose subject and verb are inverted ("were it") | *Had we but world enough, and time,* (line 1) |
| conditional | show uncertainty or refer to a thing that has not yet happened | expressed with an auxiliary verb such as *could, would,* or *should* ("would be") | *And you should, if you please, refuse* (line 9) |

Writers and poets may use verb mood to support their themes. For instance, in "To His Coy Mistress," Marvell uses a progression of verb moods to help convey the theme of *carpe diem*. In the first stanza (lines 1–20), he uses the subjunctive and conditional moods to express hypothetical "if-then" relationships. These moods match the unreality of his mistress's attitude. Next, in the second stanza (lines 21–32), he switches to the indicative mood to express the speaker's sense of conviction. Then, in the third stanza (lines 33–45), he employs the imperative mood to express the speaker's urgency that he and his mistress must take action.

TIP

**USAGE**

The subjective mood is used less frequently today than it was in the past. Consult a specialized reference book, such as a usage guide, to learn more about this change. Discuss your findings with your group.

### Read It

1. Identify the mood of the underlined verb in each of these sentences.
   a. The speaker wishes that his mistress were receptive to his pleas.
   b. He implores her not to let opportunity pass her by.
   c. "Join me," he thinks, "while we are still young."
2. **Connect to Style** Reread the last two lines of the poem. Identify the verb mood Marvell uses. What is the effect of this final switch?

### Write It

Rewrite the following sentences using the verb mood specified below.

**Indicative:** You are reading the collected works of W. H. Auden.
**Imperative:**

**Conditional:** They might have been able to view the eclipse.
**Indicative:**

**Indicative:** I woke up early and went for a walk.
**Subjunctive/Conditional:**

EVIDENCE LOG

Before moving on to a new selection, go to your log and record what you learned from "To His Coy Mistress."

TO HIS COY MISTRESS

## Comparing Texts

You will now read Poetry Collection 2, which includes "To the Virgins, to Make Much of Time" and "Youth's the Season Made for Joys." First, complete the first-read and close-read activities for Poetry Collection 2. Then, compare the development of the *carpe diem* theme in all three of the poems in this section.

POETRY COLLECTION 2

# To the Virgins, to Make Much of Time

# Youth's the Season Made for Joys

## Concept Vocabulary

As you perform your first read, you will encounter the following words:

**succeed** **prime** **season**

**Context Clues** If these words are unfamiliar to you, try using various types of **context clues** to help you determine their meanings.

**Elaborating Details:** The administrator **abhorred** noise, so he asked people in the office to speak softly.

**Contrast of Ideas:** Although the group's first presentation seemed **banal**, their revised presentation was inspired.

Apply your knowledge of context clues and other vocabulary strategies to determine the meanings of unfamiliar words you encounter during your first read.

## First Read POETRY

Apply these strategies as you conduct your first read. You will have an opportunity to complete a close read after your first read.

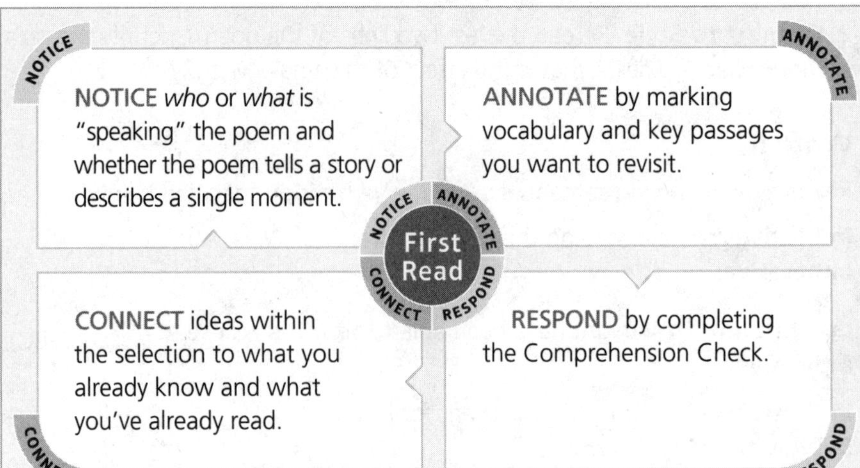
NOTICE
ANNOTATE
NOTICE *who* or *what* is "speaking" the poem and whether the poem tells a story or describes a single moment.
ANNOTATE by marking vocabulary and key passages you want to revisit.
First Read
CONNECT ideas within the selection to what you already know and what you've already read.
RESPOND by completing the Comprehension Check.
CONNECT
RESPOND

**STANDARDS**

**Reading Literature**
By the end of grade 12, read and comprehend literature, including stories, dramas, and poems, at the high end of the grades 11–CCR text complexity band independently and proficiently.

**Language**
- Determine or clarify the meaning of unknown and multiple-meaning words and phrases based on *grades 11–12 reading and content*, choosing flexibly from a range of strategies.
- Use context as a clue to the meaning of a word or phrase.

## About the Poets

**Robert Herrick** (1591–1674) was born into a family of London goldsmiths. Herrick became a parish priest who not only performed churchly duties but also wrote religious verse and musical love poems. Although not politically active, Herrick was evicted from his parish in Devonshire by the Puritans and allowed back only with the Restoration of Charles II. While barred from his church, Herrick returned to his native London, where he continued to write and publish his poetry. Never hugely popular during his lifetime, Herrick's verse was rediscovered during the 19th century. Today, he is regarded as a major seventeenth-century poet.

**John Gay** (1685–1732) was born in Barnstaple, Devon. He was orphaned at a young age and spent most of his childhood with his uncle. After finishing school in Devon, he went to London to seek success. His poetry was well known among London's literary elite and was admired by many literary stars, including Alexander Pope and Jonathan Swift.

## Backgrounds

### To the Virgins, to Make Much of Time

In England during the 1600s, when Robert Herrick wrote this poem, most people married in their mid-twenties, although the minimum legal age was 12 for women and 14 for men. Arranged marriages, while still common, were not universal, and the idea that spouses should love each other was gaining acceptance.

### Youth's the Season Made for Joys

This poem is an excerpt from John Gay's play *The Beggar's Opera*, and was originally set to music. This popular opera was first produced in 1728 and has inspired many imitations and parodies since then. It ran for an unprecedented sixty-two performances and was notorious for supposedly satirizing the prime minister of the era.

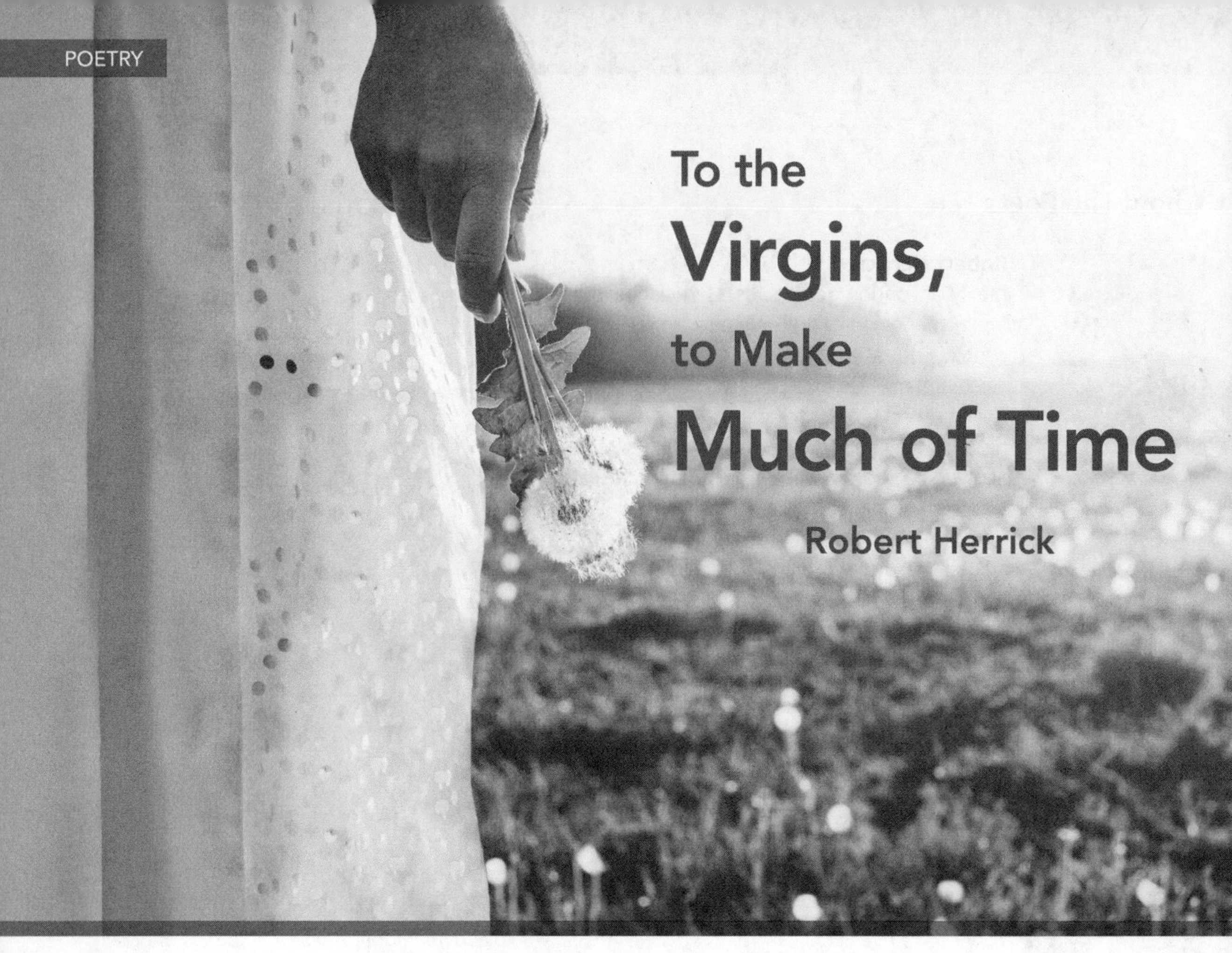

# To the Virgins, to Make Much of Time

**Robert Herrick**

NOTES

Gather ye rosebuds while ye may,
Old time is still a-flying;
And this same flower that smiles today
Tomorrow will be dying.

The glorious lamp of heaven, the sun,
The higher he's a-getting,
The sooner will his race be run,
And nearer he's to setting.

That age is best which is the first,
When youth and blood are warmer;
But being spent, the worse, and worst
Times still **succeed** the former.

Then be not coy, but use your time,
And, while ye may, go marry;
For, having lost but once your **prime**,
You may forever tarry.[1]

Mark context clues or indicate another strategy you used that helped you determine meaning.

**succeed** (suhk SEED) *v.*

MEANING:

**prime** (prym) *n.*

MEANING:

1. **tarry** (TAR ee) *v.* wait or stay longer than intended.

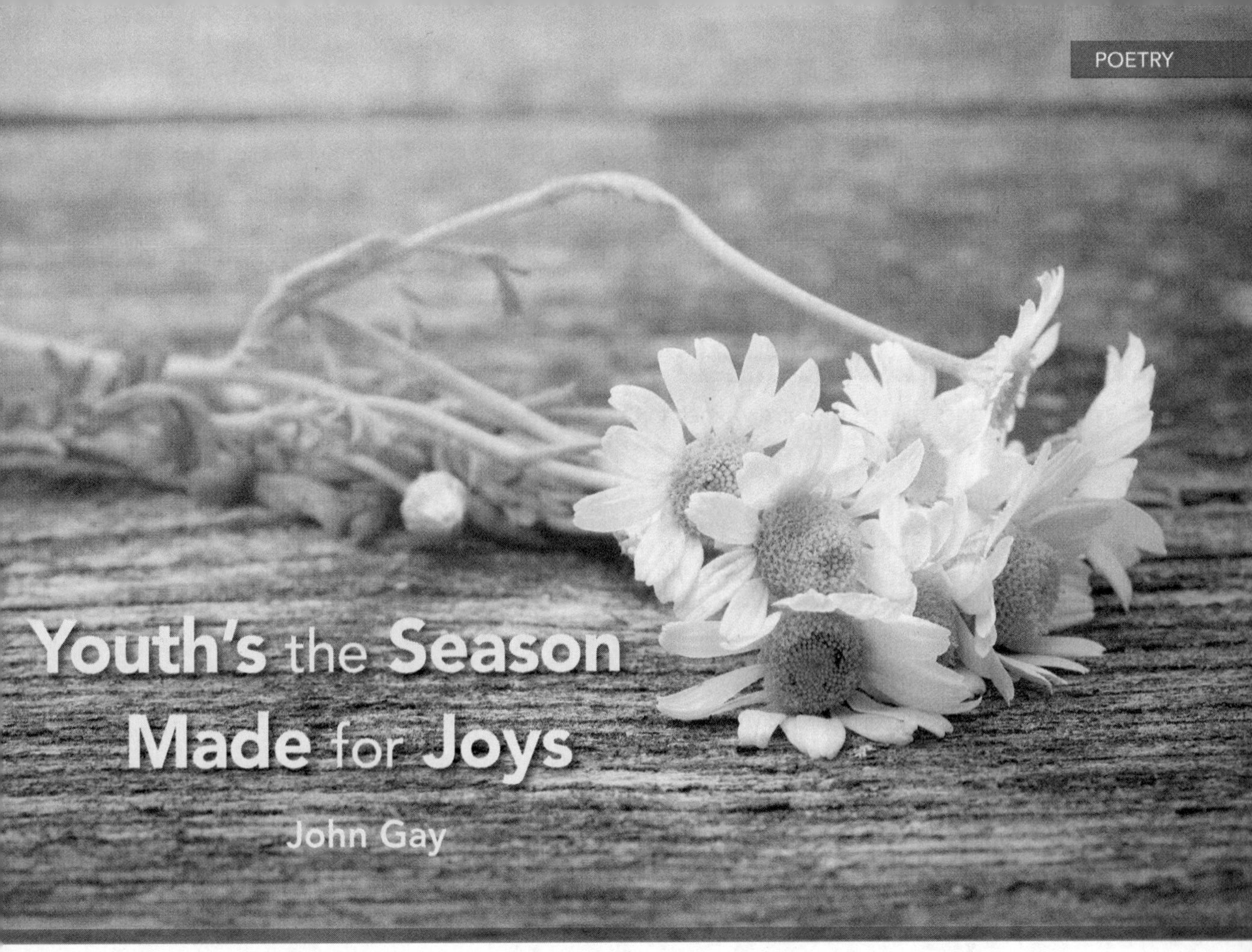

# Youth's the Season Made for Joys

John Gay

Youth's the **season** made for joys,
Love is then our duty;
She alone who that employs,
Well deserves her beauty.
Let's be gay,
While we may,
Beauty's a flower despis'd in decay.

Let us drink and sport today,
Ours is not tomorrow.
Love with youth flies swift away,
Age is nought[1] but sorrow.
Dance and sing,
Time's on the wing,
Life never knows the return of spring.

1. **nought** (nawt) *n.* nothing.

NOTES

Mark context clues or indicate another strategy you used that helped you determine meaning.

**season** (SEE zuhn) *n.*

MEANING:

# Comprehension Check

**Complete the following items after you finish your first read. Review and clarify details with your group.**

TO THE VIRGINS, TO MAKE MUCH OF TIME

**1.** What advice does the speaker give women in the first stanza?

**2.** According to the speaker, which stage of life is the best?

**3.** What warning does the speaker give to women?

YOUTH'S THE SEASON MADE FOR JOYS

**1.** According to the speaker, what is our duty when we are young?

**2.** How does the speaker feel about growing old?

**3.** According to the speaker, what happens to love when youth is gone?

## RESEARCH

**Research to Clarify** Choose at least one unfamiliar detail from one of the poems. Briefly research that detail. In what way does the information you learned shed light on an aspect of the poem?

**Research to Explore** Choose something that interested you from the texts, and formulate a research question. Write your question here.

## Close Read the Text

With your group, revisit sections of the text you marked during your first read. **Annotate** details that you notice. What **questions** do you have? What can you **conclude**?

## Analyze the Text

**CITE TEXTUAL EVIDENCE** to support your answers.

**Notebook** Complete the activities.

1. **Review and Clarify** With your group, reread lines 5–9 of "To the Virgins, to Make Much of Time." Explain the meaning of the lines in your own words. To what do you think the author is comparing the sun?

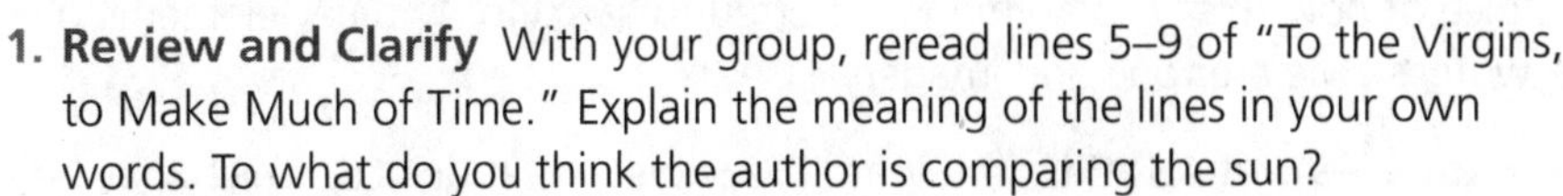

2. **Present and Discuss** Now, work with your group to share the passages from the poems that you found especially important. Take turns presenting your passages. Discuss what details you noticed, what questions you asked, and what conclusions you reached.
3. **Essential Question:** ***Why are both vision and disillusion necessary?*** What have these poems taught you about vision and disillusion?

POETRY COLLECTION 2

TIP

**GROUP DISCUSSION**

Remember that sometimes poems describe one thing that is a metaphor for something else. Consider both literal and figurative meanings as you read.

LANGUAGE DEVELOPMENT

## Concept Vocabulary

**succeed** **prime** **season**

**Why These Words?** The three concept vocabulary words are related. With your group, determine what the words have in common. Write your ideas, and add another word that fits the category.

### Practice

**Notebook** Demonstrate your understanding of the concept vocabulary words by using each one in a sentence.

## Word Study

**Latin Root: *-prim-*** In "To the Virgins, to Make Much of Time," Herrick refers to the *prime* of a woman's life. The word *prime* comes from the Latin root *-prim-*, which means "first." Many English words are derived from this root—for instance, *primary*, meaning "first in order or importance," and *primogeniture*, the name for a social system in which a family's first-born child has the exclusive right of inheritance.

In mathematics, a *prime* number is a number that can only be divided by itself and the number one: Every other number can be formed by multiplying two or more prime numbers together. Using your own words, explain why, in your estimation, these numbers are called *prime*. Verify your answer using an etymological dictionary.

 WORD NETWORK

Add interesting words related to vision from the text to your Word Network.

STANDARDS

**Language**

- Identify and correctly use patterns of word changes that indicate different meanings or parts of speech.
- Consult general and specialized reference materials, both print and digital, to find the pronunciation of a word or determine or clarify its precise meaning, its part of speech, its etymology, or its standard usage.

POETRY COLLECTION 2

## Analyze Craft and Structure

**Development of Theme** A **theme** is a central idea, message, or insight that a literary work reveals. Note that a work may include more than one theme. Herrick's and Gay's poems share a common theme with Andrew Marvell's "To His Coy Mistress": *carpe diem. Carpe diem* is a Latin phrase that is usually translated as "seize the day." This theme has natural connections to other thematic ideas, such as the fleeting nature of youth or the inevitability of mortality.

To identify themes, look at what a writer says and how it is said. The writer's choice of *how* to say something is referred to as **style**. Two key elements of a writer's style are tone and imagery.

- **tone**—a writer's attitude toward the subject or audience, which may be amused, serious, sorrowful, jubilant, and so on.
- **imagery**—descriptive language used to re-create sensory experiences.

**CITE TEXTUAL EVIDENCE** to support your answers.

### Practice

Work individually to complete the chart. When you have finished, discuss your responses with your group.

| | TO THE VIRGINS, TO MAKE MUCH OF TIME | YOUTH'S THE SEASON MADE FOR JOY |
|---|---|---|
| What is the poet's style and tone? | | |
| What images related to the passing of time does the poet use? | | |
| What other images does the poet use? | | |
| What are the themes of the poem? | | |

### STANDARDS

**Reading Literature**

- Determine two or more themes or central ideas of a text and analyze their development over the course of the text, including how they interact and build on one another to produce a complex account; provide an objective summary of the text.
- Analyze how an author's choices concerning how to structure specific parts of a text contribute to its overall structure and meaning as well as its aesthetic impact.

**Language**

- Demonstrate command of the conventions of standard English grammar and usage when writing or speaking.
- Apply knowledge of language to understand how language functions in different contexts, to make effective choices for meaning or style, and to comprehend more fully when reading or listening.
- Vary syntax for effect, consulting references for guidance as needed; apply an understanding of syntax to the study of complex texts when reading.

## Conventions and Style

**Varying Syntax: Balanced Sentences** Poets Robert Herrick and John Gay shared an interest in and respect for ancient Roman poetry. The style of their work, which mimics that of the poets they admired, values these attributes:

- clear, direct expression of ideas
- simple, obvious rhythms—often having a singsong quality
- a graceful or logical form

Characteristic of Herrick' and Gay's work is the use of **balanced sentences**—sentences whose parts have about the same length and parallel structure. **Parallel structure**, or parallelism, is the use of similar grammatical forms to express ideas that are similar or are equal in importance.

The parallel structure of balance sentences makes them well suited to the rhetorical device known as antithesis. **Antithesis** is the placing of two contrasting ideas near each other, in grammatically parallel constructions.

Consider this balanced sentence from lines 5–8 of "To the Virgins, to Make Much of Time."

*The glorious lamp of heaven, the sun,*
*The higher he's a-getting,*
*The sooner will his race be run,*
*And nearer he's to setting.*

The structure of the two underlined groups of words is parallel. Each includes a comparative adjective ending in *-er*, followed by the contraction *he's*, followed by a verb form ending in *-ing*. Herrick uses antithesis in these lines to contrast the rising and falling of the sun in the sky.

**TIP**

**CLARIFICATION**
Writers may use parallelism to emphasize, link, or balance related ideas—or to juxtapose contrasting ones. Poets, in particular, often use parallelism to create a memorable rhythm.

### Read It

1. Work with your group to identify another example of a balanced sentence in either "To the Virgins, to Make Much of Time" or "Youth's the Season Made for Joys." Write down the line numbers of the sentence you identify. Discuss your answers with your group.

2. **Connect to Style** Reread lines 13–16 of "To the Virgins to Make Much of Time." Identify an example of antithesis, and write the two ideas that are being contrasted. Discuss your answers with your group.

### Write It

**Notebook** Write a balanced sentence about reading poetry. Try to include parallelism in the sentence.

TO HIS COY MISTRESS

POETRY COLLECTION 2

## Writing to Compare

You have read three poems that share a common theme. Deepen your understanding of the poems by exploring their thematic nuances and capturing your ideas in writing.

### Assignment

The theme of a poem emerges from the elements of the poem itself, including the writer's unique **style, tone,** and uses of **imagery.** Write a **critical essay,** a type of argument, in which you evaluate the three poems' treatments of a similar theme.

- Note how each writer uses poetic elements to express the *carpe diem* theme and to suggest a secondary theme.
- Make a claim about which poem best develops its themes.
- Articulate the criteria you are using to evaluate the poems. For example, you might base your evaluation on a poem's ability to entertain, its beauty, its novelty, or its depth of insight.

### Prewriting

**Analyze the Texts** With your group, look for similarities and differences in the poems' style, tone, and imagery. Use these questions to guide your discussion:

- What picture of old age does the poem present?
- What idea of death (if any) does the poem present?
- What does the poem suggest about humans' ability to conquer time?

Use the chart to record your notes. Identify phrases or passages that reflect each poetic element. Consider, too, other themes that the poems express.

| | TO HIS COY MISTRESS | TO THE VIRGINS... | YOUTH'S THE SEASON... |
|---|---|---|---|
| Literal Meaning | | | |
| Style/Tone | | | |
| Imagery | | | |
| Secondary Themes | | | |

**Notebook**

Answer the following questions. Cite textual evidence to support your answers.

1. Which poem most effectively expresses the *carpe diem* theme? How?
2. What additional quality lifts this poem above the others?

## Drafting

**State a Claim** Review the notes you took. Then, work independently to write a central claim and supporting ideas.

**Claim:** ______________________________________________

______________________________________________

**Supporting Ideas:** ______________________________________________

______________________________________________

______________________________________________

**Discuss a Writing Plan** As a group, take turns sharing your claims, supporting ideas, and evidence, and giving one another feedback. Use the Discussion Guide to start the conversations.

**Discussion Guide**

**Quality of the Claim**

- Have you considered all aspects of the assignment?
- Is your claim specific and clearly worded?

Notes:

**Quality of Supporting Ideas**

- Does each supporting idea serve a specific purpose?
- Are your supporting ideas precisely worded?

Notes:

**Quality of Evidence**

- Does each piece of evidence speak directly to the claim?
- Is the evidence sufficient? Is anything missing?

Notes:

**Write a Rough Draft** Use your notes to produce a first draft. If you suspect something is not quite right, make a note to yourself in brackets—for example, "[add a transition]." Then, keep writing. You can go back later and resolve any open issues.

## Review, Revise, and Edit

Read your completed draft aloud to your group. Get feedback from by asking questions such as these: *Do you notice anything I should cut or refine? Do any ideas, evidence, or wording seem weak?* Use the feedback to revise your draft. Then, finalize your essay by editing and proofreading it.

Before moving on to a new selection, go to your Evidence Log and record what you learned from "To His Coy Mistress," "To the Virgins, to Make Much of Time," and "Youth's the Season Made for Joys."

**STANDARDS**

**Reading Literature**

Determine two or more themes or central ideas of a text and analyze their development over the course of the text, including how they interact and build on one another to produce a complex account; provide an objective summary of the text.

**Writing**

- Write arguments to support claims in an analysis of substantive topics or texts, using valid reasoning and relevant and sufficient evidence.
- Produce clear and coherent writing in which the development, organization, and style are appropriate to task, purpose, and audience.
- Apply *grades 11–12 Reading standards* to literature.

POETRY COLLECTION 3

# *from the* Divine Comedy: Inferno

# The Second Coming

## Concept Vocabulary

As you perform your first read of the excerpt from the *Divine Comedy: Inferno* and "The Second Coming," you will encounter these words.

| jutted | converged | entwining |
|---|---|---|

**Context Clues** If these words are unfamiliar to you, try using **context clues** to help you determine their meanings. There are various types of context clues that you may encounter as you read.

**Restatement, or Synonyms:** I was **perplexed** about how best to proceed, completely unsure which assignment I should complete first.

**Elaborating Details:** Delia's clothes were **strewn** all over the floor: a pair of pants at the foot of the bed, one sneaker in front of the closet, and the other by the desk.

**Contrast of Ideas:** Fernando had felt at ease about his baseball tryout, so he was **indignant** when he didn't make the team.

Apply your knowledge of context clues and other vocabulary strategies to determine the meanings of unfamiliar words you encounter during your first read.

## First Read POETRY

Apply these strategies as you conduct your first read. You will have an opportunity to complete a close read after your first read.

NOTICE *who* or *what* is "speaking" the poem and whether the poem tells a story or describes a single moment.

ANNOTATE by marking vocabulary and key passages you want to revisit.

CONNECT ideas within the selection to what you already know and what you've already read.

RESPOND by completing the Comprehension Check and by writing a brief summary of the selection.

### STANDARDS

**Reading Literature**

- By the end of grade 12, read and comprehend literature, including stories, dramas, and poems, at the high end of the grades 11–CCR text complexity band independently and proficiently.

**Language**

- Determine or clarify the meaning of unknown and multiple-meaning words and phrases based on *grades 11–12 reading and content*, choosing flexibly from a range of strategies.
- Use context as a clue to the meaning of a word or phrase.

## About the Poets

**Dante Alighieri** (1265–1321), whose visions of hell have haunted readers for centuries, is widely considered one of the greatest poets of western civilization. Dante was born into a poor but noble family in the Italian city of Florence. At the time, Italy was not a unified nation, but a collection of independent city-states. Elected to help run Florence's government, Dante and his party were overthrown in civil warfare that led to exile from his city in 1302. Most of his better-known works were written in exile. Unlike many of the writers of his age, Dante wrote in Italian: *Divine Comedy,* his masterpiece, was written in this language.

**William Butler Yeats** (1865–1939) was born in Dublin, Ireland. He was educated there and in London. His heart lay to the west, though, in County Sligo, where he spent childhood vacations with his grandparents. There, Yeats was immersed in the mythology and legends of Ireland. During his long career, Yeats wrote both poetry and plays. He was awarded the Nobel Prize in Literature in 1923. On his seventieth birthday, Yeats was hailed by his nation as the greatest living Irishman. He continued to write up until a day or two before his death, in France.

## Backgrounds

### *from the* Divine Comedy: Inferno

In this epic poem, Dante documents his imagined visit to Hell, Purgatory, and Heaven in three parts—"Inferno," "Purgatorio," and "Paradiso." Virgil, an ancient Roman poet, guides Dante through the nine circles of Hell on their way to Purgatory. In this excerpt from "Inferno," Virgil and Dante have arrived at the ninth circle, where those guilty of the worst sin—treachery—are found. The selection begins with a translator's note, in which John Ciardi, a noted translator and poet in his own right, offers his interpretation of the canto that follows.

### The Second Coming

Yeats believed that history occurs in two-thousand-year cycles, during which a particular civilization is born, grows, and decays. To him the society of the early twentieth century was decaying and would lead to another sort of rebirth, very different from the birth of Christ. These ideas are vividly expressed in the poem "The Second Coming."

EPIC POETRY

# *from the* Divine Comedy:
# Inferno

Dante Alighieri
translated by John Ciardi

## Translator's Note

NOTES

*"On march the banners of the King,"*[1] *Virgil begins as the Poets face the last depth. He is quoting a medieval hymn, and to it he adds the distortion and perversion of all that lies about him. "On march the banners of the King—of Hell." And there before them, in an infernal parody of Godhead, they see Satan in the distance, his great wings beating like a windmill. It is their beating that is the source of the icy wind of Cocytus,*[2] *the exhalation of all evil.*

*All about him in the ice are strewn the sinners of the last round,* JUDECCA, *named for Judas Iscariot.*[3] *These are the* TREACHEROUS TO THEIR MASTERS. *They lie completely sealed in the ice, twisted and distorted into every conceivable posture. It is impossible to speak to them, and the Poets move on to observe Satan.*

*He is fixed into the ice at the center to which flow all the rivers of guilt; and as he beats his great wings as if to escape, their icy wind only freezes him more surely into the polluted ice. In a grotesque parody of the Trinity, he has three faces, each a different color, and in each mouth he clamps a sinner whom he rips eternally with his teeth.* JUDAS ISCARIOT *is in the central mouth:* BRUTUS *and* CASSIUS[4] *in the mouths on either side.*

*Having seen all, the Poets now climb through the center, grappling hand over hand down the hairy flank of Satan himself—a last supremely symbolic action—and at last, when they have passed the center of all gravity, they emerge from Hell. A long climb from the earth's center to the Mount of Purgatory awaits them, and they push on without rest, ascending along the sides of the river Lethe, till they emerge once more to see the stars of Heaven, just before dawn on Easter Sunday.*

## Canto XXXIV

"On march the banners of the King of Hell,"
    my Master said. "Toward us. Look straight ahead:
    can you make him out at the core of the frozen shell?"
Like a whirling windmill seen afar at twilight,
    or when a mist has risen from the ground—
    just such an engine rose upon my sight
stirring up such a wild and bitter wind
    I cowered for shelter at my Master's back,
    there being no other windbreak I could find.

1. **On . . . King** hymn written in the sixth century by Venantius Fortunatus, Bishop of Poitiers. The original celebrates the Holy Cross and is part of the service for Good Friday, to be sung at the moment of uncovering the cross.
2. **Cocytus** (koh SYT uhs) "river of wailing" (Greek).
3. **Judas Iscariot** (ihs KAIR ee uht) disciple who betrayed Jesus.
4. ***Brutus* and *Cassius*** They took part in a plot to assassinate Julius Caesar.

NOTES

I stood now where the souls of the last class
(with fear my verses tell it) were covered wholly;
they shone below the ice like straws in glass.
Some lie stretched out; others are fixed in place
upright, some on their heads, some on their soles;
another, like a bow, bends foot to face.
When we had gone so far across the ice
that it pleased my Guide to show me the foul creature[5]
which once had worn the grace of Paradise,
he made me stop, and, stepping aside, he said:
"Now see the face of Dis![6] This is the place
where you must arm your soul against all dread."
Do not ask, Reader, how my blood ran cold
and my voice choked up with fear. I cannot write it:
this is a terror that cannot be told.
I did not die, and yet I lost life's breath:
imagine for yourself what I became,
deprived at once of both my life and death.
The Emperor of the Universe of Pain
**jutted** his upper chest above the ice;
and I am closer in size to the great mountain
the Titans[7] make around the central pit,
than they to his arms. Now, starting from this part,
imagine the whole that corresponds to it!
If he was once as beautiful as now
he is hideous, and still turned on his Maker,
well may he be the source of every woe!
With what a sense of awe I saw his head
towering above me! for it had three faces:[8]
one was in front, and it was fiery red;
the other two, as weirdly wonderful,
merged with it from the middle of each shoulder
to the point where all **converged** at the top of the skull;
the right was something between white and bile;
the left was about the color one observes
on those who live along the banks of the Nile.
Under each head two wings rose terribly,
their span proportioned to so gross a bird:
I never saw such sails upon the sea.
They were not feathers—their texture and their form

Mark context clues or indicate another strategy you used that helped you determine meaning.

**jutted** (JUHT ihd) *V.*

MEANING:

**converged** (kuhn VURJD) *V.*

MEANING:

5. **the foul creature** angel-turned-devil Satan, here called Lucifer, the ultimate traitor who rebelled against God.
6. **Dis** (dihs) in Greek mythology, the god of the lower world or the lower world itself. Here, it stands for Lucifer.
7. **Titans** giant deities who were overthrown by Zeus and the Olympian gods of Greece.
8. **three faces** There are many interpretations of these three faces. The common theme in all of them is that the faces are a perversion of the qualities of the Holy Trinity.

were like a bat's wings—and he beat them so
that three winds blew from him in one great storm:
it is these winds that freeze all Cocytus.
He wept from his six eyes, and down three chins
the tears ran mixed with bloody froth and pus.[9]
In every mouth he worked a broken sinner
between his rake-like teeth. Thus he kept three
in eternal pain at his eternal dinner.
For the one in front the biting seemed to play
no part at all compared to the ripping: at times
the whole skin of his back was flayed away.
"That soul that suffers most," explained my Guide,
"is Judas Iscariot, he who kicks his legs
on the fiery chin and has his head inside.
Of the other two, who have their heads thrust forward,
the one who dangles down from the black face
is Brutus: note how he writhes without a word.
And there, with the huge and sinewy arms, is the soul,
of Cassius,—But the night is coming on[10]
and we must go, for we have seen the whole."
Then, as he bade, I clasped his neck, and he,
watching for a moment when the wings
were opened wide, reached over dexterously[11]
and seized the shaggy coat of the king demon;
then grappling matted hair and frozen crusts
from one tuft to another, clambered down.
When we had reached the joint where the great thigh
merges into the swelling of the haunch,
my Guide and Master, straining terribly,
turned his head to where his feet had been
and began to grip the hair as if he were climbing;[12]
so that I thought we moved toward Hell again.
"Hold fast!" my Guide said, and his breath came shrill
with labor and exhaustion. "There is no way
but by such stairs to rise above such evil."
At last he climbed out through an opening
in the central rock, and he seated me on the rim;
then joined me with a nimble backward spring.
I looked up, thinking to see Lucifer
as I had left him, and I saw instead
his legs projecting high into the air.

NOTES

9. **bloody froth and pus** gore of the sinners he chews, which is mixed with his saliva.
10. **the night is coming on** It is now Saturday evening.
11. **dexterously** (DEHKS tuhr uhs lee) *adv.* skillfully.
12. **as if he were climbing** They have passed the center of gravity and so must turn around and start climbing.

NOTES

Now let all those whose dull minds are still vexed
by failure to understand what point it was
I had passed through, judge if I was perplexed.
"Get up. Up on your feet," my Master said.
"The sun already mounts to middle tierce,[13]
and a long road and hard climbing lie ahead."
It was no hall of state we had found there,
but a natural animal pit hollowed from rock
with a broken floor and a close and sunless air.
"Before I tear myself from the Abyss,"
I said when I had risen, "O my Master,
explain to me my error in all this:
where is the ice? and Lucifer—how has he
been turned from top to bottom: and how can the sun
have gone from night to day so suddenly?"
And he to me: "You imagine you are still
on the other side of the center where I grasped
the shaggy flank of the Great Worm of Evil
which bores through the world—you were while I climbed down,
but when I turned myself about, you passed
the point to which all gravities are drawn.
You are under the other hemisphere where you stand;
the sky above us is the half opposed
to that which canopies the great dry land.
Under the midpoint of that other sky
the Man[14] who was born sinless and who lived
beyond all blemish, came to suffer and die.
You have your feet upon a little sphere
which forms the other face of the Judecca.
There it is evening when it is morning here.
And this gross Fiend and Image of all Evil
who made a stairway for us with his hide
is pinched and prisoned in the ice-pack still.
On this side he plunged down from heaven's height,
and the land that spread here once hid in the sea
and fled North to our hemisphere for fright;[15]
And it may be that moved by that same fear,
the one peak[16] that still rises on this side

13. **middle tierce** According to the church's division of the day for prayer, tierce is the period from about six to nine A.M. Middle tierce, therefore, is seven-thirty. In going through the center point, Dante and Virgil have gone from night to day. They have moved ahead twelve hours.
14. **the Man** Jesus, who suffered and died in Jerusalem, which was thought to be the middle of the Earth.
15. **fled North . . . for fright** Dante believed that the Northern Hemisphere was mostly land and the Southern Hemisphere, mostly water. Here, he explains the reason for this state of affairs.
16. **the one peak** Mount of Purgatory.

fled upward leaving this great cavern[17] here."
Down there, beginning at the further bound
of Beelzebub's[18] dim tomb, there is a space
not known by sight, but only by the sound
of a little stream[19] descending through the hollow
it has eroded from the massive stone
in its endlessly **entwining** lazy flow."
My Guide and I crossed over and began
to mount that little known and lightless road
to ascend into the shining world again.
He first, I second, without thought of rest
we climbed the dark until we reached the point
where a round opening brought in sight the blest
and beauteous shining of the Heavenly cars.
And we walked out once more beneath the Stars.[20]

NOTES

Mark context clues or indicate another strategy you used that helped you determine meaning.

**entwining** (ehn TWYN ihng) *adj.*

MEANING:

17. **this great cavern** natural animal pit of line 98. It is also "Beelzebub's dim tomb," line 131.
18. **Beelzebub's** (bee EHL zuh buhbz) Beelzebub, which in Hebrew means "god of flies," was another name for Lucifer or Satan.
19. **a little stream** Lethe (LEE thee); in classical mythology, the river of forgetfulness, from which souls drank before being born. In Dante's symbolism, it flows down from Purgatory, where it has washed away the memory of sin from the souls who are undergoing purification. That memory it delivers to Hell, which draws all sin to itself.
20. **Stars** As part of his total symbolism, Dante ends each of the three divisions of the *Divine Comedy* with this word. Every conclusion of the upward soul is toward the stars, symbols of hope and virtue. It is just before the dawn of Easter Sunday that the Poets emerge—further symbolism.

# The Second Coming

William Butler Yeats

NOTES

Turning and turning in the widening gyre
The falcon cannot hear the falconer;
Things fall apart; the center cannot hold;
Mere anarchy is loosed upon the world,
The blood-dimmed tide is loosed, and everywhere
The ceremony of innocence is drowned;
The best lack all conviction, while the worst
Are full of passionate intensity.[1]
Surely some revelation is at hand;
Surely the Second Coming is at hand.
The Second Coming! Hardly are those words out
When a vast image out of *Spiritus Mundi*[2]
Troubles my sight: somewhere in sands of the desert
A shape with lion body and the head of a man,[3]
A gaze blank and pitiless as the sun,
Is moving its slow thighs, while all about it
Reel shadows of the indignant desert birds.
The darkness drops again; but now I know
That twenty centuries[4] of stony sleep
Were vexed to nightmare by a rocking cradle,[5]
And what rough beast, its hour come round at last,
Slouches towards Bethlehem to be born?

1. **Mere . . . intensity** refers to the Russian Revolution of 1917.
2. ***Spiritus Mundi*** (SPIHR ih tuhs MOON dee) Universal Spirit or Soul, in which the memories of the entire human race are forever preserved.
3. **A . . . man** Sphinx, a monster in Greek mythology that posed a riddle to passing travelers and destroyed those who could not answer it. The answer to the riddle was "man."
4. **twenty centuries** historical cycle preceding the birth of Christ.
5. **rocking cradle** cradle of Jesus Christ.

## Comprehension Check

**Complete the following items after you finish your first read. Review and clarify details with your group.**

*from the* DIVINE COMEDY: INFERNO

1. What is the source of the icy wind of Cocytus?

2. In what substance are the souls of the damned trapped?

3. What torture do Judas Iscariot, Brutus, and Cassius suffer?

4. **Notebook** Demonstrate your understanding of this canto by writing a summary of it.

THE SECOND COMING

1. In the "widening gyre," what is loosed upon the world?

2. According to the speaker, what do the "best" lack and what are the "worst" full of?

3. What vision troubles the speaker's sight?

## RESEARCH

**Research to Clarify** Choose at least one unfamiliar detail from one of the poems. Briefly research that detail. In what way does the information you learned shed light on an aspect of the poem?

POETRY COLLECTION 3

## Close Read the Text

With your group, revisit sections of the text you marked during your first read. **Annotate** details that you notice. What **questions** do you have? What can you **conclude**?

## Analyze the Text

**CITE TEXTUAL EVIDENCE** to support your answers.

**Notebook** Complete the activities.

1. **Review and Clarify** With your group, reread lines 28–54 of the excerpt. What does Satan look like? Why does Dante describe him this way?

2. **Present and Discuss** Now, work with your group to share the passages from the poems that you found especially important. Take turns presenting your passages. Discuss what details you noticed, what questions you asked, and what conclusions you reached.

3. **Essential Question:** *Why are both vision and disillusion necessary?* What have these poems taught you about vision and disillusion?

TIP

**GROUP DISCUSSION**

Discussing your reading with your group can be helpful in clarifying any questions you may have about one or both poems. In your group, talk about each poem line by line to understand it more fully.

LANGUAGE DEVELOPMENT

## Concept Vocabulary

**jutted** **converged** **entwining**

**Why These Words?** The three concept vocabulary words are related. With your group, determine what the words have in common. Write your ideas, and add another word that fits the category.

### Practice

**Notebook** Confirm your understanding of the concept vocabulary words by including them as you write a descriptive paragraph. Then, read your paragraph aloud to your group, but leave out the vocabulary words. Challenge your group to use context clues to guess the missing words.

WORD NETWORK

Add interesting words related to seeing things new from the text to your Word Network.

## Word Study

**Notebook** **Latin Prefix: *con-*** The Latin prefix *con-* means "with" or "together." In the word *converged,* this prefix combines with the Latin root *-ver-*, meaning "to turn," "to bend," or "to move."

1. Write a definition of *converged* that demonstrates how the prefix *con-* contributes to its meaning.

2. Reread lines 1–8 of "The Second Coming." Identify the word that begins with the prefix *con-*. Write the word and its definition. Consult a dictionary if needed.

STANDARDS

**Language**

- Identify and correctly use patterns of word changes that indicate different meanings or parts of speech.
- Consult general and specialized reference materials, both print and digital, to find the pronunciation of a word or determine or clarify its precise meaning, its part of speech, its etymology, or its standard usage.

## Analyze Craft and Structure

**Author's Choices: Symbolism** A **symbol** is a character, a place, an object, or an event that has its own meaning but also represents something larger, usually an abstract idea. A symbol may concentrate a number of associated ideas. For example, the stock symbol of a dove represents peace in many cultures. It may also represent gentleness. In Western culture, the dove's white color further suggests innocence. These multiple associations enrich the dove's symbolic meaning.

Literary symbols can be even more multilayered. Unlike stock symbols, they do not have general, agreed-upon meanings. Instead their meanings are specific to a given work. By analyzing symbols, you can unlock a work's deeper meaning.

### Practice

**CITE TEXTUAL EVIDENCE** to support your answers.

Work independently to complete the chart. Note possible meanings for each symbol listed. Identify another symbolic element from each poem, and explain its meaning. Discuss your responses with your group.

| THE SECOND COMING | *from the* DIVINE COMEDY: INFERNO |
|---|---|
| Symbol: falcon and falconer<br>Meaning: | Symbol: Lucifer's three heads<br>Meaning: |
| Symbol: the gyre<br>Meaning: | Symbol: Judas, Cassius, and Brutus Meaning: |
| Symbol: sphinx/rough beast<br>Meaning: | Symbol: Stars<br>Meaning: |
| Other:<br>Meaning: | Other:<br>Meaning: |

**Notebook** Respond to these questions.

1. Which symbol in the excerpt from "Inferno" do you think is most powerful? Why?

2. What message do you think Yeats is communicating through symbols in "The Second Coming"?

**GROUP DISCUSSION**

Keep in mind that members of your group might have different interpretations of symbols in a text. There is no right interpretation or conclusion, but talking out differing opinions and the reasons for them will help you clarify your thoughts and learn from one another.

**STANDARDS**

**Reading Literature**

- Cite strong and thorough textual evidence to support analysis of what the text says explicitly as well as inferences drawn from the text, including determining where the text leaves matters uncertain.
- Determine the meaning of words and phrases as they are used in the text, including figurative and connotative meanings; analyze the impact of specific word choices on meaning and tone, including words with multiple meanings or language that is particularly fresh, engaging, or beautiful.

POETRY COLLECTION 3

## Conventions and Style

**Rhetorical Devices** Writers often use descriptive or inventive substitutes for simpler names and terms. This technique is called **periphrasis**. Informally, periphrasis could be called "beating around the bush," but writers use this device to make their work more colorful and imaginative. In addition, writers often use **allusion**, which is an unexplained reference to a person, place, event, or other literary passage that will be familiar to readers. Periphrasis and allusion may be used together in a literary work. Note the following examples:

- **Periphrasis:** Dante refers to Satan as "the Emperor of the Universe of Pain," and to Jesus as "the Man who was born sinless."
- **Allusion:** In the lines "I am closer in size to the great mountain / the Titans make around the central pit, / than they to his arms," Dante makes an allusion to the Titans of Greek mythology to express how small he feels.

### Read It

1. In "The Second Coming," how does Yeats use periphrasis to identify the Sphinx?

2. Explain how the periphrasis "endlessly entwining lazy flow" enhances a reader's impression of Lethe in lines 130–135 of the excerpt from "Inferno."

3. To what is Yeats alluding with the word Bethlehem in line 22 of "The Second Coming"?

### Write It

Write a paragraph in which you describe your classroom or another familiar place. Use at least one example of periphrasis and one allusion. Trade your paragraphs with another member of your group, and identify uses of periphrasis and allusion in your partner's work.

STANDARDS

**Reading Literature**

- Analyze the impact of the author's choices regarding how to develop and relate elements of a story or drama.
- Determine the meaning of words and phrases as they are used in the text, including figurative and connotative meanings; analyze the impact of specific word choices on meaning and tone, including words with multiple meanings or language that is particularly fresh, engaging, or beautiful.

**Writing**

Use technology, including the Internet, to produce, publish, and update individual or shared writing products in response to ongoing feedback, including new arguments or information.

**Speaking and Listening**

Make strategic use of digital media in presentations to enhance understanding of findings, reasoning, and evidence and to add interest.

**Language**

Interpret figures of speech in context and analyze their role in the text.

# Research

**Assignment**

With your group, conduct research on the historical context of "Inferno" or "The Second Coming." Present your results to the class in a **presentation with graphics.** Choose from the following options:

- [ ] Using digital tools, create an **illustrated map** showing the important parts and organization of Hell as Dante imagines it in "Inferno." Include the major categories of the sinners and their punishments, as well as the geographical location of the region in relation to the surface of the earth. When you present your map to the class, use it to explain Dante and Virgil's exit from Hell.

- [ ] Yeats wrote "The Second Coming" in January 1919. Using digital tools, create an **annotated timeline** showing major twentieth-century events preceding 1919, including World War I and the Russian Revolution. When you present your findings to the class, comment on the connection between these events and Yeats's poem.

- [ ] Using digital tools, create a **diagram of a vision** showing how Yeats believed that "gyres" influence the progress of history. In your diagram, lay out the ages of history as Yeats conceives them, as well as the forces at work in each. Explain how the images in Yeats's poem can be mapped to your diagram.

**EVIDENCE LOG**

Before moving on to a new selection, go to your Evidence Log and record what you learned from "Inferno" and "The Second Coming."

## Integrate Content and Media

Use an outline to identify media elements for the introduction, body, and conclusion of your presentation. Discuss connections between content and media elements to make sure your choices support and enhance the content of your presentation.

| | CONTENT | MEDIA ELEMENT |
|---|---|---|
| Introduction | | |
| Body | | |
| | | |
| | | |
| Conclusion | | |

## Rehearse and Present

Digitally record your completed presentation, and view it as a group prior to sharing it with the class. This digital rehearsal is your opportunity to make changes to your content and presentation. Each group member should contribute revision ideas to create a presentation that is concise, clear, and effective.

**About the Author**

His innovations in plot, character, and language make **James Joyce** (1882–1941) one of the most challenging and distinguished writers of the twentieth century. Joyce's early efforts were impressive but fairly conventional in approach. In 1922, however, Joyce broke from all known literary forms with his experimental, stream-of-consciousness novel *Ulysses*. Using a variety of radical techniques, *Ulysses* was soon judged to be a true masterpiece, and in many circles, it is regarded as the greatest novel of the twentieth century.

STANDARDS

**Reading Literature**
By the end of grade 12, read and comprehend literature, including stories, dramas, and poems, at the high end of the grades 11–CCR text complexity band independently and proficiently.

**Language**
- Use context as a clue to the meaning of a word or phrase.
- Determine or clarify the meaning of unknown and multiple-meaning words and phrases based on *grades 11–12 reading and content*, choosing flexibly from a range of strategies.
- Verify the preliminary determination of the meaning of a word or phrase.

# Araby

## Concept Vocabulary

As you perform your first read of "Araby," you will encounter these words.

**tedious** **chafed** **intolerable**

**Context Clues** If these words are unfamiliar to you, try using **context clues**—other words and phrases that appear nearby in the text—to help you determine their meanings. There are various types of context clues that you may encounter as you read.

**Contrast of Ideas:** Her **sedulous** study of the problem stood in stark contrast to her friend's careless attention to details.

**Inference:** One cannot survive long in the **gelid** water of the North Sea in winter.

**Definition:** His **vacillation**, or inability to make a decision, frustrated his friends.

Apply your knowledge of context clues and other vocabulary strategies to determine the meanings of unfamiliar words you encounter during your first read. Use a resource such as a dictionary or a thesaurus to verify the meanings you identify.

## First Read FICTION

Apply these strategies as you conduct your first read. You will have an opportunity to complete a close read after your first read.

NOTICE *whom* the story is about, *what* happens, *where* and *when* it happens, and *why* those involved react as they do.

ANNOTATE by marking vocabulary and key passages you want to revisit.

CONNECT ideas within the selection to what you already know and what you've already read.

RESPOND by completing the Comprehension Check and by writing a brief summary of the selection.

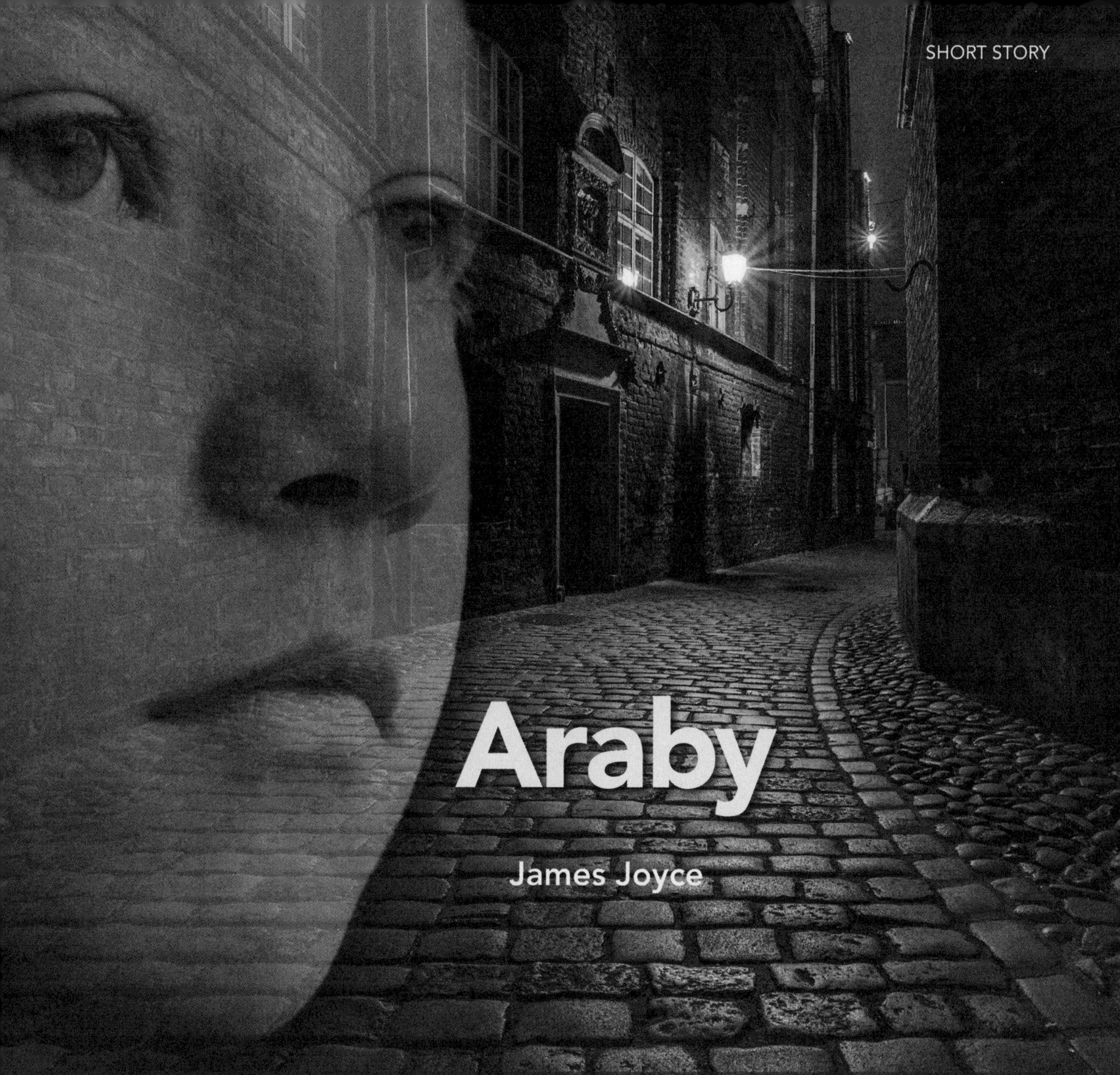

# Araby

James Joyce

## BACKGROUND

Joyce's short story is based on the Araby Bazaar, one of the largest and most memorable public events held in Dublin, Ireland, in the late nineteenth century. More than a quarter of Dublin's population attended the bazaar. It featured elaborate displays, goods for sale, multiple restaurants, tightrope demonstrations, and firework displays.

1 North Richmond Street, being blind,[1] was a quiet street except at the hour when the Christian Brothers' School set the boys free. An uninhabited house of two stories stood at the blind end, detached from its neighbors in a square ground. The other houses of the street, conscious of decent lives within them, gazed at one another with brown imperturbable faces.

NOTES

1. **blind** dead-end.

NOTES

2 The former tenant of our house, a priest, had died in the back drawing room. Air, musty from having been long enclosed, hung in all the rooms, and the waste room behind the kitchen was littered with old useless papers. Among these I found a few paper-covered books, the pages of which were curled and damp: *The Abbot,* by Walter Scott, *The Devout Communicant,* and *The Memoirs of Vidocq.*[2] I liked the last best because its leaves were yellow. The wild garden behind the house contained a central apple tree and a few straggling bushes under one of which I found the late tenant's rusty bicycle pump. He had been a very charitable priest: in his will he had left all his money to institutions and the furniture of his house to his sister.

3 When the short days of winter came, dusk fell before we had well eaten our dinners. When we met in the street the houses had grown somber. The space of sky above us was the color of ever-changing violet and toward it the lamps of the street lifted their feeble lanterns. The cold air stung us and we played till our bodies glowed. Our shouts echoed in the silent street. The career of our play brought us through the dark muddy lanes behind the houses where we ran the gantlet of the rough tribes from the cottages, to the back doors of the dark dripping gardens where odors arose from the ashpits, to the dark odorous stables where a coachman smoothed and combed the horse or shook music from the buckled harness. When we returned to the street, light from the kitchen windows had filled the areas. If my uncle was seen turning the corner we hid in the shadow until we had seen him safely housed. Or if Mangan's sister came out on the doorstep to call her brother in to his tea we watched her from our shadow peer up and down the street. We waited to see whether she would remain or go in and, if she remained, we left our shadow and walked up to Mangan's steps resignedly. She was waiting for us, her figure defined by the light from the half-opened door. Her brother always teased her before he obeyed and I stood by the railings looking at her. Her dress swung as she moved her body, and the soft rope of her hair tossed from side to side.

4 Every morning I lay on the floor in the front parlor watching her door. The blind was pulled down to within an inch of the sash so that I could not be seen. When she came out on the doorstep my heart leaped. I ran to the hall, seized my books, and followed her. I kept her brown figure always in my eye and, when we came near the point at which our ways diverged, I quickened my pace and passed her. This happened morning after morning. I had never spoken to her, except

"When she came out on the doorstep my heart leaped. I ran to the hall, seized my books, and followed her."

2. ***The Abbot . . . Vidocq*** a historical tale, a religious manual, and the remembrances of a French adventurer, respectively.

for a few casual words, and yet her name was like a summons to all my foolish blood.

5 Her image accompanied me even in places the most hostile to romance. On Saturday evenings when my aunt went marketing I had to go to carry some of the parcels. We walked through the flaring streets, jostled by drunken men and bargaining women, amid the curses of laborers, the shrill litanies[3] of shop-boys who stood on guard by the barrels of pigs' cheeks, the nasal chanting of street singers, who sang a *come-all-you* about O'Donovan Rossa,[4] or a ballad about the troubles in our native land. These noises converged in a single sensation of life for me: I imagined that I bore my chalice safely through a throng of foes. Her name sprang to my lips at moments in strange prayers and praises which I myself did not understand. My eyes were often full of tears (I could not tell why) and at times a flood from my heart seemed to pour itself out into my bosom. I thought little of the future. I did not know whether I would ever speak to her or not or, if I spoke to her, how I could tell her of my confused adoration. But my body was like a harp and her words and gestures were like fingers running upon the wires.

6 One evening I went into the back drawing room in which the priest had died. It was a dark rainy evening and there was no sound in the house. Through one of the broken panes I heard the rain impinge upon the earth, the fine incessant needles of water playing in the sodden beds. Some distant lamp or lighted window gleamed below me. I was thankful that I could see so little. All my senses seemed to desire to veil themselves and, feeling that I was about to slip from them, I pressed the palms of my hands together until they trembled, murmuring: "*O love! O love!*" many times.

7 At last she spoke to me. When she addressed the first words to me I was so confused that I did not know what to answer. She asked me was I going to *Araby*. I forget whether I answered yes or no. It would be a splendid bazaar, she said; she would love to go.

8 "And why can't you?" I asked.

9 While she spoke she turned a silver bracelet round and round her wrist. She could not go, she said, because there would be a retreat[5] that week in her convent.[6] Her brother and two other boys were fighting for their caps and I was alone at the railings. She held one of the spikes, bowing her head toward me. The light from the lamp opposite our door caught the white curve of her neck, lit up her hair that rested there and, falling, lit up the hand upon the railing. It fell

NOTES

3. **litanies** (LIHT uhn eez) *n.* prayers in which a congregation repeats a fixed response; repetitive recitations.
4. ***come-all-you* . . . Rossa** opening of a ballad about an Irish hero.
5. **retreat** *n.* period of retirement or seclusion for prayer, religious study, and meditation.
6. **convent** *n.* school run by an order of nuns.

NOTES

Mark context clues or indicate another strategy you used that helped you determine meaning.

**tedious** (TEE dee uhs) *adj.*

MEANING:

**chafed** (chayft) *v.*

MEANING:

over one side of her dress and caught the white border of a petticoat, just visible as she stood at ease.

10 "It's well for you," she said.

11 "If I go," I said, "I will bring you something."

12 What innumerable follies laid waste my waking and sleeping thoughts after that evening! I wished to annihilate the **tedious** intervening days. I **chafed** against the work of school. At night in my bedroom and by day in the classroom her image came between me and the page I strove to read. The syllables of the word *Araby* were called to me through the silence in which my soul luxuriated and cast an Eastern enchantment over me. I asked for leave to go to the bazaar on Saturday night. My aunt was surprised, and hoped it was not some Freemason[7] affair. I answered few questions in class. I watched my master's face pass from amiability to sternness; he hoped I was not beginning to idle. I could not call my wandering thoughts together. I had hardly any patience with the serious work of life which, now that it stood between me and my desire, seemed to me child's play, ugly monotonous child's play.

13 On Saturday morning I reminded my uncle that I wished to go to the bazaar in the evening. He was fussing at the hallstand, looking for the hat-brush, and answered me curtly:

14 "Yes, boy, I know."

15 As he was in the hall I could not go into the front parlor and lie at the window. I felt the house in bad humor and walked slowly toward the school. The air was pitilessly raw and already my heart misgave me.

16 When I came home to dinner my uncle had not yet been home. Still it was early. I sat staring at the clock for some time and, when its ticking began to irritate me, I left the room. I mounted the staircase and gained the upper part of the house. The high cold empty gloomy rooms liberated me and I went from room to room singing. From the front window I saw my companions playing in the street. Their cries reached me weakened and indistinct and, leaning my forehead against the cool glass, I looked over at the dark house where she lived. I may have stood there for an hour, seeing nothing but the brown-clad figure cast by my imagination, touched discreetly by the lamplight at the curved neck, at the hand upon the railings and at the border below the dress.

17 When I came downstairs again I found Mrs. Mercer sitting at the fire. She was an old garrulous woman, a pawnbroker's widow, who collected used stamps for some pious purpose. I had to endure the gossip of the tea table. The meal was prolonged beyond an hour and still my uncle did not come. Mrs. Mercer stood up to go: she was sorry she couldn't wait any longer, but it was after eight o'clock and

7. **Freemason** Free and Accepted Masons, an international secret society.

she did not like to be out late, as the night air was bad for her. When she had gone I began to walk up and down the room, clenching my fists. My aunt said:

18 "I'm afraid you may put off your bazaar for this night of Our Lord."

19 At nine o'clock I heard my uncle's latchkey in the hall door. I heard him talking to himself and heard the hallstand rocking when it had received the weight of his overcoat. I could interpret these signs. When he was midway through his dinner I asked him to give me the money to go to the bazaar. He had forgotten.

20 "The people are in bed and after their first sleep now," he said.

21 I did not smile. My aunt said to him energetically:

22 "Can't you give him the money and let him go? You've kept him late enough as it is."

23 My uncle said he was very sorry he had forgotten. He said he believed in the old saying: *All work and no play makes Jack a dull boy.* He asked me where I was going and, when I told him a second time he asked me did I know *The Arab's Farewell to His Steed.*[8] When I left the kitchen he was about to recite the opening lines of the piece to my aunt.

24 I held a florin[9] tightly in my hand as I strode down Buckingham Street toward the station. The sight of the streets thronged with buyers and glaring with gas recalled to me the purpose of my journey. I took my seat in a third-class carriage of a deserted train. After an **intolerable** delay the train moved out of the station slowly. It crept onward among ruinous houses and over the twinkling river. At Westland Row Station a crowd of people pressed to the carriage doors; but the porters moved them back, saying that it was a special train for the bazaar. I remained alone in the bare carriage. In a few minutes the train drew up beside an improvised wooden platform. I passed out onto the road and saw by the lighted dial of a clock that it was ten minutes to ten. In front of me was a large building which displayed the magical name.

25 I could not find any sixpenny entrance and, fearing that the bazaar would be closed, I passed in quickly through a turnstile, handing a shilling to a weary-looking man. I found myself in a big hall girdled at half its height by a gallery. Nearly all the stalls were closed and the greater part of the hall was in darkness. I recognized a silence like that which pervades a church after a service. I walked into the center of the bazaar timidly. A few people were gathered about the stalls which were still open. Before a curtain, over which the words *Café*

"In front of me was a large building which displayed the magical name."

NOTES

Mark context clues or indicate another strategy you used that helped you determine meaning.

**intolerable** (ihn TOL uhr uh buhl) *adj.*

MEANING:

---

8. ***The Arab's . . . His Steed*** popular nineteenth-century poem.
9. **florin** *n.* British two-shilling coin of the time.

NOTES

*Chantant*[10] were written in colored lamps, two men were counting money on a salver.[11] I listened to the fall of the coins.

26 Remembering with difficulty why I had come, I went over to one of the stalls and examined porcelain vases and flowered tea sets. At the door of the stall a young lady was talking and laughing with two young gentlemen. I remarked their English accents and listened vaguely to their conversation.

27 "O, I never said such a thing!"

28 "O, but you did!"

29 "O, but I didn't!"

30 "Didn't she say that?"

31 "Yes. I heard her."

32 "O, there's a . . . fib!"

33 Observing me, the young lady came over and asked me did I wish to buy anything. The tone of her voice was not encouraging; she seemed to have spoken to me out of a sense of duty. I looked humbly at the great jars that stood like Eastern guards at either side of the dark entrance to the stall and murmured:

34 "No, thank you."

35 The young lady changed the position of one of the vases and went back to the two young men. They began to talk of the same subject. Once or twice the young lady glanced at me over her shoulder.

36 I lingered before her stall, though I knew my stay was useless, to make my interest in her wares seem the more real. Then I turned away slowly and walked down the middle of the bazaar. I allowed the two pennies to fall against the sixpence in my pocket. I heard a voice call from one end of the gallery that the light was out. The upper part of the hall was now completely dark.

37 Gazing up into the darkness I saw myself as a creature driven and derided by vanity; and my eyes burned with anguish and anger. ❧

---

10. ***Café Chantant*** café with musical entertainment.

11. **salver** *n.* tray usually used for the presentation of letters or visiting cards.

## Comprehension Check

**Complete the following items after you finish your first read. Review and clarify details with your group.**

**1.** When and where does the story take place?

**2.** What does the narrator say he does every morning?

**3.** Why is the narrator so distracted in school?

**4.** What does the narrator promise Mangan's sister?

**5.** Why does the narrator have to wait to go to the bazaar?

**6.** **Notebook** Confirm your understanding of the text by writing a summary.

### RESEARCH

**Research to Clarify** Choose at least one unfamiliar detail from the text. Briefly research that detail. In what way does the information you learned shed light on an aspect of the story?

**Research to Explore** Pick something from the text that interests you, and formulate a research question. Write your question here.

ARABY

## Close Read the Text

With your group, revisit the sections of the text you marked during your first read. **Annotate** details that you notice. What **questions** do you have? What can you **conclude**?

## Analyze the Text

**CITE TEXTUAL EVIDENCE** to support your answers.

Complete the activities.

1. **Review and Clarify** With your group, reread paragraph 12. How does the narrator feel as he waits for the day of the bazaar? What is his aim in attending?

2. **Present and Discuss** Now, work with your group to share the passages from the text that you found especially important. Take turns presenting your passages. Discuss what details you noticed, what questions you asked, and what conclusions you reached.

3. **Essential Question:** ***Why are both vision and disillusion necessary?*** What has this story taught you about vision and disillusion?

TIP

**GROUP DISCUSSION**

The main characters in "Araby" are not named. While discussing the text, use descriptive language to be clear about whom you are speaking.

LANGUAGE DEVELOPMENT

## Concept Vocabulary

**tedious** **chafed** **intolerable**

**Why These Words?** The three concept vocabulary words are related. With your group, discuss the words, and determine what they have in common. Write your ideas, and add another word that fits the category.

### Practice

**Notebook** Confirm your understanding of these words by using them in sentences. Include context clues that hint at each word's meaning.

## Word Study

**Notebook** **Word Families** A word family is a group of words that are all formed from the same base word. For instance, the words *avoid*, *avoidance*, and *unavoidable* are all part of the same word family.

Like most words, *intolerable* is part of a word family. Write the base word from which it is formed, as well as the base word's definition. Then, drawing from your knowledge of prefixes and suffixes, use each of these members of the same word family in a sentence: *intolerance*, *tolerable*, *toleration*.

**WORD NETWORK**

Add interesting words related to seeing things new from the text to your Word Network.

**STANDARDS**

**Reading Literature**
- Cite strong and thorough textual evidence to support analysis of what the text says explicitly as well as inferences drawn from the text, including determining where the text leaves matters uncertain.
- Analyze how an author's choices concerning how to structure specific parts of a text contribute to its overall structure and meaning as well as its aesthetic impact.
- Identify and correctly use patterns of word changes that indicate different meanings or parts of speech.

**Language**
- Demonstrate understanding of figurative language, word relationships, and nuances in word meanings.

# Analyze Craft and Structure

**Author's Choices: Narrative Structure** An **epiphany** is a sudden revelation or flash of insight. Characters may have epiphanies about themselves, other characters, or an aspect of life. In modern literature, authors often use epiphany in place of a true resolution to a conflict. The flash of insight may change a character's understanding, but the conflict may persist.

Because epiphanies reveal a character's deepest feelings, they can be heightened by the use of first-person narration. In **first-person narration**, the narrator tells the reader directly about his or her experiences. This suggests that the narrator explains all there is to know, but that is not the case in Joyce's work. Instead, Joyce suggests meaning but does not fully articulate it. The reader must make **inferences**, or educated guesses guided by textual evidence, to build an interpretation of the story and to understand the narrator's epiphany.

**GROUP DISCUSSION**

Keep in mind that members of your group will have different interpretations of the text. There's no right impression or conclusion, but talking out differing opinions and the reasons for them will help you clarify your thoughts and learn from one another.

## Practice

**CITE TEXTUAL EVIDENCE** to support your answers.

1. Work with your group to complete the chart. Describe the inferences that you can draw from each passage—the meanings the details suggest.

| PASSAGE | INFERENCE |
|---|---|
| *These noises converged in a single sensation of life for me: I imagined that I bore my chalice safely through a throng of foes. Her name sprang to my lips at moments in strange prayers and praises which I myself did not understand.* (paragraph 5) | |
| *The syllables of the word Araby were called to me through the silence in which my soul luxuriated and cast an Eastern enchantment over me.* (paragraph 12) | |
| *Nearly all the stalls were closed and the greater part of the hall was in darkness. I recognized a silence like that which pervades a church after a service.* (paragraph 25) | |

2. **(a)** Where in "Araby" does the epiphany occur? **(b)** What does the narrator suddenly realize?

ARABY

## Conventions and Style

**Varying Syntax: Loose Sentences** Writers and poets often vary the **syntax**, or structure, of their sentences to achieve particular effects. For instance, Joyce uses loose sentences to add descriptive details and to give the narration a relaxed or conversational feel. In a **loose sentence**, the independent clause expressing the main idea comes first, followed by any modifying clauses or phrases.

Consider this loose sentence from paragraph 16 of "Araby."

> *I may have stood there for an hour, seeing nothing but the brown-clad figure cast by my imagination, touched discreetly by the lamplight at the curved neck, at the hand upon the railings and at the border below the dress.*

Joyce begins the sentence with an independent clause (underlined once), which expresses the main idea. Notice that he could end the thought there, and the sentence would still be complete. Instead, he continues with two long participial phrases (underlined twice), each containing one or more phrases of its own. The effect is to convey a richly detailed world—one whose setting seems to come to life and whose narrator seems to be recounting the story as it occurs to him.

Observe that Joyce varies his syntax by contrasting loose sentences with simpler, more direct sentences. For example, in paragraph 24, he follows a loose sentence with this: "I remained alone in the bare carriage." The terseness of this sentence, when contrasted with the preceding one, emphasizes the importance of the ideas it expresses.

TIP

**CLARIFICATION**

The modifying phrases in a loose sentence may include any of the following:

- participial phrases
- prepositional phrases
- infinitive phrases
- gerund phrases
- absolute phrases

Refer to the Grammar Handbook to learn more about these terms.

### Read It

1. Identify whether each of these sentences from "Araby" is *loose* or *not loose*.

   a. Her name sprang to my lips at moments in strange prayers and praises which I myself did not understand.

   b. When she addressed the first words to me I was so confused that I did not know what to answer.

   c. I had to endure the gossip of the tea table.

   d. She held one of the spikes, bowing her head toward me.

2. **Connect to Style** Reread this pair of sentences from "Araby": "My eyes were often full of tears (I could not tell why) and at times a flood from my heart seemed to pour itself out into my bosom. I thought little of the future." What effect does the contrast between the sentences' structures have? Discuss your answer with your group.

### Write It

**Notebook** Identify three additional examples of loose sentences in the story. Write the sentences, and note simpler sentences nearby that provide contrast. Then, write your own loose sentence, along with a contrasting sentence.

**STANDARDS**

**Reading Literature**

- Analyze the impact of the author's choices regarding how to develop and relate elements of a story or drama.
- Analyze how an author's choices concerning how to structure specific parts of a text contribute to its overall structure and meaning as well as its aesthetic impact.

**Language**

- Demonstrate command of the conventions of standard English grammar and usage when writing or speaking.
- Apply knowledge of language to understand how language functions in different contexts, to make effective choices for meaning or style, and to comprehend more fully when reading or listening.
- Vary syntax for effect, consulting references for guidance as needed; apply an understanding of syntax to the study of complex texts when reading.

# Writing to Sources

**Assignment**

Prepare to write a **compare-and-contrast essay**. Choose from the following options:

- [ ] **Comparison With Ernest Hemingway** Find a copy of "In Another Country" by Ernest Hemingway, and read it carefully. Then, write an essay comparing and contrasting the first-person narrators in "Araby" and "In Another Country."
- [ ] **Comparison With F. Scott Fitzgerald** Find a copy of "Winter Dreams" by F. Scott Fitzgerald, and read it carefully. Then, write an essay comparing and contrasting Dexter's epiphany with the epiphany of the narrator of "Araby." What has Joyce's narrator lost in the story's climactic scene? What has Dexter lost?
- [ ] **Comparison With Katherine Anne Porter** Find a copy of "The Circus" by Katherine Anne Porter, and read it carefully. Then, write an essay comparing and contrasting Miranda's epiphany with the epiphany of the narrator of "Araby." In what sense is each character moving closer to adulthood?

**Project Plan** Once you have selected and read your story, begin prewriting by jotting down your impressions of each character. In what way is each character "wounded?" In each story, what events trigger an epiphany, or a moment of sudden insight?

**Clarifying Ideas and Evidence** As you draft your essay, use your prewriting notes as a guide, addressing the details you listed for each character. Link these details to broader considerations about how one character's traits are similar to or different from the other's. Support your ideas with quotations from each story. Use a chart like this one to organize your ideas and evidence.

| NARRATOR 1 | NARRATOR 2 | EPIPHANY | EVIDENCE |
|---|---|---|---|
| | | | |

**Tying It Together** Review your draft, making sure that the sentences flow logically and that your ideas are well supported with details. Where evidence is lacking, review the stories to find relevant details to strengthen the support.

 EVIDENCE LOG

Before moving on to a new selection, go to your Evidence Log and record what you learned from "Araby."

STANDARDS

**Reading Literature**
Demonstrate knowledge of eighteenth-, nineteenth- and early twentieth-century foundational works of American literature, including how two or more texts from the same period treat similar themes or topics.

**Writing**
- Write informative/explanatory texts to examine and convey complex ideas, concepts, and information clearly and accurately through the effective selection, organization, and analysis of content.
- Draw evidence from literary or informational texts to support analysis, reflection, and research.
- Apply *grades 11–12 Reading standards* to literature.

POETRY COLLECTION 4

# The Explosion

# Old Love

## Concept Vocabulary

As you perform your first read of "The Explosion" and "Old Love," you will encounter these words.

| dimmed | prismatic | wavered |
|---|---|---|

**Base Words** Analyze an unfamiliar word to see whether it contains a base word you know. Then, use your knowledge of the base word, along with context, to find the meaning of the unfamiliar word.

**Unfamiliar Word:** *opalescent*

**Familiar Base Word:** *opal,* a type of gemstone whose surface has a rainbow-like appearance

**Context:** Just beneath the surface of the lake, **opalescent** fish darted past like shimmering water-colored ghosts.

**Conclusion:** The fish are likened to "shimmering" ghosts. *Opalescent* might mean "displaying rainbow-like colors, the way an opal does."

Apply your knowledge of base words and other vocabulary strategies to determine the meanings of unfamiliar words you encounter during your first read.

## First Read POETRY

Apply these strategies as you conduct your first read. You will have an opportunity to complete a close read after your first read.

NOTICE *who* or *what* is "speaking" the poem and whether the poem tells a story or describes a single moment.

ANNOTATE by marking vocabulary and key passages you want to revisit.

CONNECT ideas within the selection to what you already know and what you've already read.

RESPOND by completing the Comprehension Check.

First Read: NOTICE, ANNOTATE, CONNECT, RESPOND

STANDARDS

**Reading Literature**
By the end of grade 12, read and comprehend literature, including stories, dramas, and poems, at the high end of the grades 11–CCR text complexity band independently and proficiently.

**Language**
Determine or clarify the meaning of unknown and multiple-meaning words and phrases based on *grades 11–12 reading and content,* choosing flexibly from a range of strategies.

## About the Poets

**Philip Larkin** (1922–1985) was born in Coventry, England. He studied at the University of Oxford and published his first book of poetry in 1945. In 1955, Larkin moved to Yorkshire to become a librarian at the University of Hull. During his lifetime, Larkin's poetry was renowned for its cold, deflating tone and anti-romantic themes.

**Francesca Beard** (b. 1968) grew up in Penang, Malaysia. She became a London-based performance poet after working at a variety of professions. Beard has spent many years touring with her one-woman show called "Chinese Whispers." She has also spent significant time working as a workshop facilitator in creative writing and poetry.

## Backgrounds

### The Explosion

For centuries, men have worked in coal mines, picking with axes at seams of bitumen in order to earn enough to feed their families. Coal mines are dangerous places, and "coal towns" live in fear for their loved ones working thousands of feet below the ground. The workers know that they are in danger as they labor in the midst of the very elements, methane and coal dust, that can bring their lives to a sudden end.

### Old Love

As a performance poet, Francesca Beard writes poems that are meant to be both printed and performed on stage. She has stated that her poetry "is so much about audience. It is a very interactive art form. It always has an improvisational quality to it." Beard's work is often multidisciplinary and experimental.

POETRY

# The Explosion

Philip Larkin

On the day of the explosion
Shadows pointed towards the pithead:[1]
In the sun the slagheap[2] slept.

Down the lane came men in pitboots
Coughing oath-edged talk and pipe-smoke,
Shouldering off the freshened silence.

One chased after rabbits; lost them;
Came back with a nest of lark's eggs;
Showed them; lodged them in the grasses.

So they passed in beards and moleskins,[3]
Fathers, brothers, nicknames, laughter,
Through the tall gates standing open.

At noon, there came a tremor; cows
Stopped chewing for a second; sun,
Scarfed as in a heat-haze, **dimmed**.

*The dead go on before us, they*
*Are sitting in God's house in comfort,*
*We shall see them face to face—*

Plain as lettering in the chapels
It was said, and for a second
Wives saw men of the explosion

Larger than in life they managed—
Gold as on a coin, or walking
Somehow from the sun towards them,

One showing the eggs unbroken.

NOTES

Mark base words or indicate another strategy you used that helped you determine meaning.

**dimmed** (dihmd) *v.*

MEANING:

1. **pithead** *n.* entrance to a coal mine.
2. **slagheap** *n.* large mound of waste material dug up from a coal mine.
3. **moleskins** *n.* garments, especially pants, made of heavy cotton.



MEDIA CONNECTION

The Explosion

**Discuss It** How does listening to this audio recording of "The Explosion" add to your understanding of the lives of the British working class?

**Write your response before sharing your ideas.**

# Old Love

Francesca Beard

NOTES

Mark base words or indicate another strategy you used that helped you determine meaning.

**prismatic** (prihz MAT ihk) *adj.*

MEANING:

**wavered** (WAY vuhrd) *v.*

MEANING:

In the glance of a mirror, I saw a timid shape
standing in the beveled bit,
the thin **prismatic** strip on the edge of the frame
and thought it was a ghost of you.

What are you doing here?
You can't just appear, without warning,
like we were used to it being.
You seemed blurry, like the first and the last time.
In between, how huge you were.
The shadow you cast let much sleep beneath its shade.
You **wavered** in the air, vanishing.
How I wanted to hold out my hand,
so that your sad ghost
could crawl into a friendly cradle.
Of course it was nothing—a trick of the light
and a splinter in the eye
of a hair gummed across the heart.

No, you are frozen where you were that last time,
deaf and dumb,
a wax-work in the pin-hole museum,
while your tiny, passionate soul,
marooned in the middle of nowhere,
cries and stretches out its arms.

Meanwhile, on my own rock,
on the other side of the world,
I think of you, blind and stumbling in the dark,
while the rescuers throw the beams of their torches
into the wrong cave.

NOTES

## Comprehension Check

**Complete the following items after you finish your first read. Review and clarify details with your group.**

THE EXPLOSION

1. Who are the men in the poem?

2. Where do the tall gates in the poem lead?

3. What happens at noon?

OLD LOVE

1. What does the speaker think she sees?

2. What does the speaker want to offer to this vision?

3. What does the speaker say her vision really was?

## RESEARCH

**Research to Clarify** Choose at least one unfamiliar detail from one of the poems. Briefly research that detail. In what way does the information you learned shed light on an aspect of the poem?

## Close Read the Text

With your group, revisit sections of the text you marked during your first read. **Annotate** details that you notice. What **questions** do you have? What can you **conclude**?

## Analyze the Text

**CITE TEXTUAL EVIDENCE** to support your answers.

**Notebook** Complete the activities.

1. **Review and Clarify** With your group, reread the final stanza of "The Explosion." Discuss the idea that the men appear to the wives to be "larger than in life." What is the speaker suggesting about the impact of the explosion on those who survived?

2. **Present and Discuss** Now, work with your group to share the passages from "The Explosion" and "Old Love" that you found especially important. Take turns presenting your passages. Discuss what details you noticed, what questions you asked, and what conclusions you reached.

3. **Essential Question:** *Why are both vision and disillusion necessary?* What have these poems taught you about seeing things in a new way?

TIP

**GROUP DISCUSSION**

To help others understand your subjective thoughts about the poems, point out objective details from the text, and explain how they support your ideas.

LANGUAGE DEVELOPMENT

## Concept Vocabulary

**dimmed** **prismatic** **wavered**

**Why These Words?** The three concept vocabulary words are related. With your group, determine what the words have in common. Write your ideas, and add another word that fits the category.

### Practice

**Notebook** Confirm your understanding of these words from the text by using them in sentences. Then, read your sentences aloud to your group, but leave out the vocabulary words. Challenge your group members to use context clues to guess the missing words.

## Word Study

**Notebook** **Multiple-Meaning Words** Many words in English have multiple meanings, or more than one distinct definition. For example, the word *wavered*, which appears in line 11 of "Old Love," has a few different meanings. To determine which meaning a writer is using, consider context clues, or the surrounding words and phrases.

Write the meaning of *wavered* in "Old Love." Then, write two more definitions of the word. Consult a college-level dictionary as needed.

WORD NETWORK

Add interesting words related to seeing things new from the texts to your Word Network.

STANDARDS

**Reading Literature**

Determine the meaning of words and phrases as they are used in the text, including figurative and connotative meanings; analyze the impact of specific word choices on meaning and tone, including words with multiple meanings or language that is particularly fresh, engaging, or beautiful.

**Language**

- Determine or clarify the meaning of unknown and multiple-meaning words and phrases based on *grades 11–12 reading and content*, choosing flexibly from a range of strategies.
- Demonstrate understanding of figurative language, word relationships, and nuances in word meanings.

# Analyze Craft and Structure

**Impact of Word Choice** Both Larkin and Beard use imagery and sound devices in their poems to impart meaning in nonliteral ways. **Imagery** is the language that writers use to re-create sensory experiences and stir emotions. It is what helps you see, hear, feel, smell, and taste what an author is describing. **Sound devices** are patterns of similar sounds in nearby words, and their use enhances meaning. Types of sound devices include alliteration, consonance, and assonance.

- **Alliteration**—repeated initial consonant sounds in nearby words or syllables: "In the sun the slagheap slept."
- **Consonance**—repeated final consonant sounds in stressed syllables with dissimilar vowel sounds: "Down the lane came men. . . ."
- **Assonance**—repeated vowel sounds in stressed syllables with dissimilar consonant sounds: ". . . wavered in the air . . ."

## Practice

**CITE TEXTUAL EVIDENCE** to support your answers.

With your group, fill the chart with examples of imagery and sound devices in each poem. Then, respond to the questions that follow.

| "THE EXPLOSION," BY PHILIP LARKIN | | | |
|---|---|---|---|
| IMAGERY | ALLITERATION | CONSONANCE | ASSONANCE |
| *In the sun the slagheap slept.* (line 3) | | *Down the lane came men. . . .* (line 4) | |
| | | | |
| | | | |

| "OLD LOVE," BY FRANCESCA BEARD | | | |
|---|---|---|---|
| IMAGERY | ALLITERATION | CONSONANCE | ASSONANCE |
| *. . . a splinter in the eye . . .* (line 16) | | | *. . . wavered in the air . . .* (line 11) |
| | | | |
| | | | |

Notebook **Respond to these questions.**

1. Review the passages you gathered. Which examples of concrete imagery also feature a sound device?
2. Why do you think the poets employed the use of sound devices in these cases? What is the effect on the reader?

POETRY COLLECTION 4

## Conventions and Style

**Meter and Free Verse** Of the many choices poets make when writing poems, one of the most important is whether or not to use a standard **meter**, or rhythmical pattern. To determine if a poem uses a regular meter, scan each line, and mark stressed syllables with the symbol ( ʹ ) and unstressed syllable with the symbol ( ˘ ). The basic unit of meter is a **foot**, a group of one or more stressed and unstressed syllables.

- An **iamb** is one unstressed followed by one stressed syllable ( ˘ ʹ ).
- A **trochee** is one stressed followed by one unstressed syllable ( ʹ ˘ ).

Meter is described by its prevalent type of foot and number of feet per line. Three feet in a line is called *trimeter*; four feet, *tetrameter*; five feet, *pentameter*; six feet, *hexameter*. Thus, Larkin's poem is primarily trochaic tetrameter, with four stresses per line. This choice gives the poem a musical or chant-like quality.

Not all poems follow a regular meter, however. Some poets choose to write in **free verse**, or a style of poetry without a regular pattern of rhythm or rhyme. Beard uses free verse in "Old Love." This choice often reflects natural speech patterns.

STANDARDS

**Reading Literature**
Analyze how an author's choices concerning how to structure specific parts of a text contribute to its overall structure and meaning as well as its aesthetic impact.

### Read It

Work individually. Mark the stressed and unstressed syllables in the excerpts in this chart. Then, discuss with your group what makes "The Explosion" primarily trochaic tetrameter, and what makes "Old Love" free verse. Use words such as *meter, iamb,* and *trochee* in your explanations. Finally, consider the effect that the choice of metered or free verse creates.

| EXCERPT | EXPLANATION OF METER | EFFECT |
|---|---|---|
| The Explosion<br><br>So they passed in beards and moleskins, / Fathers, brothers, nicknames, laughter, / Through the tall gates standing open. | | |
| Old Love<br><br>Of course it was nothing—a trick of the light / and a splinter in the eye / of a hair gummed across the heart. | | |

### Write It

**Notebook** Write two passages of at least two lines each. In the first, use trochaic tetrameter. In the second, use free verse.

# Speaking and Listening

**Assignment**

These two poems offer nuanced perspectives on loss or absence. With your group, choose an activity and develop a **response to literature**. Choose from these options:

☐ **Panel Discussion** With your group, form a panel to discuss the themes of the two works. Consider these questions:

- For Larkin, do the "eggs all unbroken" represent genuine hope, an unattainable illusion, or a vision that is both inevitable and unattainable?
- How does Beard's vision of what is left after loss differ from Larkin's?
- How do the attitudes in the poems toward loss and its aftermath compare?

☐ **Poetry Reading** Each member of your group should write and present a poem using themes, techniques, or topics related to the Larkin and Beard poems. After each reading, have each group member take a turn leading a class discussion about the connections between members' poems and the poems by Larkin and Beard.

☐ **Multimedia Presentation** With your group, assemble a mixed media presentation of sound and images to accompany a reading of each poem. First, practice reading the poems. Then, present your reading, accompanied by the media, to the class. Afterwards, lead the class in discussing the relevance of the media to the poems and the effectiveness of the presentation.

**Discussion Plan** If you choose the panel discussion, make decisions about who the participants will be and which questions each student will discuss. Write out a list of at least five discussion questions and possible answers.

**Reading and Presentation Plan** Before you begin the poetry reading or multimedia presentation, make decisions about the order of the readers or speakers and the sound and images that might be needed. Create a written outline. Then, gather the items and materials that you will need. Use this chart to organize your ideas.

| READERS/SPEAKERS | SOUNDS | IMAGES |
|---|---|---|
| 1st | | |
| 2nd | | |
| 3rd | | |
| 4th | | |

EVIDENCE LOG

Before moving on to a new selection, go to your Evidence Log and record what you learned from "The Explosion" and "Old Love."

STANDARDS

**Speaking and Listening**

- Initiate and participate effectively in a range of collaborative discussions with diverse partners on *grades 11–12 topics, texts, and issues*, building on others' ideas and expressing their own clearly and persuasively.
- Come to discussions prepared, having read and researched material under study; explicitly draw on that preparation by referring to evidence from texts and other research on the topic or issue to stimulate a thoughtful, well-reasoned exchange of ideas.
- Propel conversations by posing and responding to questions that probe reasoning and evidence; ensure a hearing for a full range of positions on a topic or issue; clarify, verify, or challenge ideas and conclusions; and promote divergent and creative perspectives.
- Make strategic use of digital media in presentations to enhance understanding of findings, reasoning, and evidence and to add interest.

SOURCES

- TO HIS COY MISTRESS
- TO THE VIRGINS, TO MAKE MUCH OF TIME
- YOUTH'S THE SEASON MADE FOR JOYS
- *from the* DIVINE COMEDY: INFERNO
- THE SECOND COMING
- ARABY
- THE EXPLOSION
- OLD LOVE

# Present a Reflective Narrative

**Assignment**

You have read poems, listened to a reading, and read a short story about life-changing circumstances. Work with your group to plan and present a **reflective narrative** that completes the following sentence about a speaker, narrator, or character from this section:

**_________________'s world changed forever when . . .**

Determine the person and event on which you will focus. You may decide to speak from the perspective of that person or as an outside observer. Explain why and how the world changed.

## Plan With Your Group

**Analyze the Text** With your group, review the texts from this section, and choose a character, speaker, or narrator to use as the focus of your reflective narrative. Choose the event that changed his or her view of the world, and determine the distinct perspective that you will convey.

| TITLE | FOCUS OF REFLECTION |
|---|---|
| To His Coy Mistress<br>To the Virgins, to Make Much of Time<br>Youth's the Season Made for Joys | Speaker or Character:<br><br>Event: |
| *from the* Divine Comedy: Inferno<br>The Second Coming | Speaker or Character:<br><br>Event: |
| Araby | Narrator or Character:<br><br>Event: |
| The Explosion<br>Old Love | Speaker or Character:<br><br>Event: |

**Gather Evidence and Media Examples** Find specific details from the text you chose to make your presentation richer and more engaging. Each detail should reveal something meaningful about your speaker's view of the world, either before the event you are describing or after it.

STANDARDS

**Speaking and Listening**

Initiate and participate effectively in a range of collaborative discussions with diverse partners on *grades 11–12 topics, texts, and issues*, building on others' ideas and expressing their own clearly and persuasively.

**Organize Your Narrative** Have each member of your group prepare one minute of narrative. Be sure that members use different details to tell the story or to reflect thoughtfully on the events.

| MINUTE | DETAILS |
|---|---|
| 1 | |
| 2 | |

## Rehearse With Your Group

**Practice With Your Group** As you present your narrative, use this checklist to evaluate the effectiveness of your group's first run-through. Then, use your evaluation and the instructions here to guide your revision.

| CONTENT | COLLABORATION | PRESENTATION TECHNIQUES |
|---|---|---|
| ☐ All presenters respond to the prompt.<br>☐ Each presenter provides text evidence to support the narrative. | ☐ Presenters synthesize text evidence and comments from other group members.<br>☐ Presenters effectively build on one another's ideas. | ☐ Presenters speak clearly and convincingly.<br>☐ Presenters seem confident and well prepared. |

**Fine-Tune the Content** Does each speaker have adequate details that develop his or her part of the reflective narrative? If not, work as a group to locate more details.

**Improve Your Presentation Form** Make sure to stay within your time allotment. If necessary, revise language. Using precise descriptive words lets you communicate more precise information in less time.

**Brush Up on Your Presentation Techniques** Remember that you must speak clearly and with enough volume for the audience to hear. Keep your voice enthusiastic and lively.

## Present and Evaluate

As you present your narrative, work as a group. Support your teammates with your energetic response. As you watch other groups present, think about how well they meet the requirements on the checklist.

STANDARDS

**Speaking and Listening**
Present information, findings, and supporting evidence, conveying a clear and distinct perspective and a logical argument, such that listeners can follow the line of reasoning, alternative or opposing perspectives are addressed, and the organization, development, substance, and style are appropriate to purpose, audience, and a range of formal and informal tasks. Use appropriate contact, adequate volume, and pronunciation.

## OVERVIEW: INDEPENDENT LEARNING

ESSENTIAL QUESTION:

# Why are both vision and disillusion necessary?

How we develop a vision and deal with disillusion teaches us much about ourselves. In this section, you will complete your study of vision and disillusion by exploring an additional selection related to the topic. You'll then share what you learn with classmates. To choose a text, follow these steps.

**Look Back** Think about the selections you have already studied. What more do you want to know about the topics of vision and disillusion?

**Look Ahead** Preview the texts by reading the descriptions. Which one seems more interesting and appealing to you?

**Look Inside** Take a few minutes to scan the text you chose. Choose a different one if this text doesn't meet your needs.

## Independent Learning Strategies

Throughout your life, in school, in your community, and in your career, you will need to rely on yourself to learn and work on your own. Review these strategies and the actions you can take to practice them during Independent Learning. Add ideas of your own to each category.

| STRATEGY | ACTION PLAN |
|---|---|
| Create a schedule | • Understand your goals and deadlines.<br>• Make a plan for what to do each day.<br>• |
| Practice what you have learned | • Use first-read and close-read strategies to deepen your understanding.<br>• After you read, evaluate the usefulness of the evidence to help you understand the topic.<br>• Consider the quality and reliability of the source.<br>• |
| Take notes | • Record important ideas and information<br>• Review your notes before preparing to share with a group.<br>• |

Choose one selection. Selections are available online only.

CONTENTS

# First-Read Guide

**Tool Kit**
First-Read Guide and Model Annotation

**Use this page to record your first-read ideas.**

**Selection Title:** ______________________________

NOTICE

**NOTICE** new information or ideas you learn about the unit topic as you first read this text.

ANNOTATE

**ANNOTATE** by marking vocabulary and key passages you want to revisit.

NOTICE ANNOTATE First Read CONNECT RESPOND

**CONNECT** ideas within the selection to other knowledge and the selections you have read.

**RESPOND** by writing a brief summary of the selection.

CONNECT

RESPOND

STANDARD

**Reading** Read and comprehend complex literary and informational texts independently and proficiently.

# Close-Read Guide

**Tool Kit**
Close-Read Guide and Model Annotation

**Use this page to record your close-read ideas.**

**Selection Title:** ______________________________

## Close Read the Text

Revisit sections of the text you marked during your first read. Read these sections closely and **annotate** what you notice. Ask yourself **questions** about the text. What can you **conclude?** Write down your ideas.

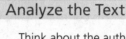

## Analyze the Text

Think about the author's choices of patterns, structure, techniques, and ideas included in the text. Select one and record your thoughts about what this choice conveys.

## QuickWrite

Pick a paragraph from the text that grabbed your interest. Explain the power of this passage.

STANDARD

**Reading** Read and comprehend complex literary and informational texts independently and proficiently.

EVIDENCE LOG

Go to your Evidence Log and record what you learned from the text you read.

# Share Your Independent Learning

## Prepare to Share

Why are both vision and disillusion necessary?

Even when you read or learn something independently, you can continue to grow by sharing what you have learned with others. Reflect on the text you explored independently and write notes about its connection to the unit. In your notes, consider why this text belongs in this unit.

## Learn From Your Classmates

**Discuss It** Share your ideas about the text you explored on your own. As you talk with your classmates, jot down ideas that you learn from them.

## Reflect

Review your notes, and mark the most important insight you gained from these writing and discussion activities. Explain how this idea adds to your understanding of the topics of vision and disillision.

STANDARDS

**Speaking and Listening**

Initiate and participate effectively in a range of collaborative discussions with diverse partners on *grades 11–12 topics, texts, and issues,* building on others' ideas and expressing their own clearly and persuasively.

## Review Notes for a Narrative

At the beginning of this unit, you responded to the following question:

> When can the way we look at things lead to growth—and when can it hold us back?

### EVIDENCE LOG

Review your Evidence Log and your QuickWrite from the beginning of the unit. Have your ideas changed?

| ☐ YES | ☐ NO |
|---|---|
| Identify at least three textual details that convinced you to change your mind. | Identify at least three textual details that reinforced your original response. |
| **1.** | **1.** |
| **2.** | **2.** |
| **3.** | **3.** |

Give one example of a time your viewpoint helped you grow: ____________

____________

Give one example of a time your viewpoint held you back: ____________

____________

**Evaluate the Strength of Your Evidence** Do you have enough evidence to develop your narrative? If not, make a plan.

☐ Do more research ☐ Talk with my classmates

☐ Reread a selection ☐ Ask an expert

☐ Other: ____________

**STANDARDS**

**Writing**

Engage and orient the reader by setting out a problem, situation, or observation and its significance, establishing one or multiple point(s) of view, and introducing a narrator and/or characters; create a smooth progression of experiences or events.

SOURCES

- WHOLE-CLASS SELECTIONS
- SMALL-GROUP SELECTIONS
- INDEPENDENT-LEARNING SELECTION

## PART 1

# Writing to Sources: Reflective Narrative

In this unit, you read a variety of texts in which writers responded to the world around them by seeing things in new ways. Sometimes, the new view was positive and enlightening. At other times, the new view was negative or reproachful. We need both visionaries and skeptics to show us how to view the world afresh.

### Assignment

Write a **reflective narrative** in which you respond to this question:

**When can the way we look at things lead to growth—and when can it hold us back?**

Consider the way external forces can change your personal point of view and engender a new way of looking at things. In a narrative based on your own experience, show how some of those transformations can be positive and others can be negative. Incorporate ideas from at least three of the texts in this unit. Conclude with a statement or section that reflects on what you have learned.

**Reread the Assignment** Review the assignment to be sure you fully understand it. The assignment may reference some of the academic words presented at the beginning of the unit. Be sure you understand each of the words here in order to complete the assignment correctly.

### Academic Vocabulary

| engender | transformation | incorporate |
|---|---|---|
| artifice | inexorable | |

**Review the Elements of a Narrative** Before you begin writing, read the Narrative Rubric. Once you have completed your first draft, check it against the rubric. If one or more of the elements is missing or not as strong as it could be, revise your narrative to add or strengthen that component.

WORD NETWORK

As you write and revise your narrative, use your Word Network to help vary your word choices.

STANDARDS

Writing

- Write narratives to develop real or imagined experiences or events using effective technique, well-chosen details, and well-structured event sequences.
- Write routinely over extended time frames and shorter time frames for a range of tasks, purposes, and audiences.

# Narrative Rubric

| | Focus and Organization | Evidence and Elaboration | Language Conventions |
|---|---|---|---|
| 4 | The narrative establishes and maintains a unique point of view.<br>Characters are developed in a way that suits the purpose and audience.<br>Events are in a clear sequence and combine to build toward a particular outcome.<br>The conclusion follows from and reflects on the rest of the narrative. | The narrative adeptly incorporates dialogue, reflection, and description.<br>Precise details give the reader a clear picture of events. | The narrative consistently uses standard English conventions of usage and mechanics.<br>Sentence structures are varied. |
| 3 | The narrative establishes and maintains a clear point of view.<br>Some characters are developed appropriately.<br>Events are in a clear sequence and mostly combine to build toward a particular outcome.<br>The conclusion follows from the narrative and includes some reflection. | Dialogue, description, and reflection move the narrative forward.<br>Some precise details give the reader a picture of events. | The narrative demonstrates accuracy in standard English conventions of usage and mechanics.<br>Sentence structures are varied in some parts of the narrative. |
| 2 | A point of view is maintained with occasional lapses.<br>Few characters are developed appropriately.<br>Events are mostly in sequence, but some events may not belong, and other clarifying events may be omitted.<br>The conclusion follows from the narrative. | Reflection moves the narrative forward; some dialogue or description may appear.<br>Some details give the reader a general picture of events. | The narrative demonstrates some accuracy in standard English conventions of usage and mechanics.<br>Sentence structures are rarely varied. |
| 1 | The point of view is not always clear.<br>Characters are not developed.<br>Events are not in a clear sequence, and clarifying events may be omitted.<br>The conclusion does not follow from the narrative, or there is no conclusion. | Dialogue and description do not appear, and reflection is minimal.<br>Few details are included, or details fail to give the reader a picture of events. | The narrative contains mistakes in standard English conventions of usage and mechanics.<br>Sentence structures are similar and monotonous. |

PART 2

# Speaking and Listening: Dramatic Reading

**Assignment**

After completing a final draft of your narrative, prepare a **dramatic reading** of your text.

Follow these steps to make your reading dramatic.

- Make a clean copy of your narrative. Which parts of the story are exciting, touching, or especially significant? Highlight the material you most want to emphasize for your audience. Think about how to use your voice, face, and body to stress those parts of your text.
- Practice your delivery, again keeping your audience in mind. Remember to make eye contact—it's hard to be dramatic if you are staring at your text.
- Use pauses, speak slowly and clearly, and vary your volume.

**Review the Rubric** The criteria by which your dramatic reading will be evaluated appear in this rubric. Review these criteria before presenting to ensure that you are prepared.

STANDARDS

**Speaking and Listening**
Present information, findings, and supporting evidence, conveying a clear and distinct perspective, such that listeners can follow the line of reasoning, alternative or opposing perspectives are addressed, and the organization, development, substance, and style are appropriate to purpose, audience, and a range of formal and informal tasks.

| | Content | Effectiveness | Presentation Techniques |
|---|---|---|---|
| 3 | The time and place of events is established in a clear and appealing way.<br><br>The narrative tells a fascinating, original personal story about positive and negative results of the way we look at things. | The speaker chooses reasonable parts of the text to emphasize or dramatize.<br><br>Listeners are engaged and interested. | The speaker maintains effective eye contact.<br><br>The speaker varies volume and pacing.<br><br>The speaker effectively uses body movement and facial expressions to emphasize key moments in the narrative. |
| 2 | The time and place of events is clearly established.<br><br>The narrative tells a personal story about positive and negative results of the way we look at things. | The speaker mostly chooses reasonable parts of the text to emphasize or dramatize.<br><br>Most listeners pay attention and seem interested. | The speaker mostly maintains effective eye contact.<br><br>The speaker occasionally varies volume or pacing.<br><br>The speaker occasionally uses body movement or facial expressions to emphasize key moments. |
| 1 | The time and place of events is confusing or never established.<br><br>The narrative tells a story, but the connection to the prompt or to broader themes is hard to find. | The speaker does not emphasize or dramatize particular parts of the text.<br><br>Listeners have difficulty paying attention or following the presentation. | The speaker fails to maintain effective eye contact.<br><br>The speaker speaks in a monotone.<br><br>The speaker does not use body movement or facial expressions to emphasize key moments. |

# Reflect on the Unit

Now that you've completed the unit, take a few moments to reflect on your learning. Use the questions below to think about where you succeeded, what skills and strategies helped you, and where you can continue to grow in the future.

## Reflect on the Unit Goals

Look back at the goals at the beginning of the unit. Use a different colored pen to rate yourself again. Think about readings and activities that contributed the most to the growth of your understanding. Record your thoughts.

## Reflect on the Learning Strategies

**Discuss It** Write a reflection on whether you were able to improve your learning based on your Action Plans. Think about what worked, what didn't, and what you might do to keep working on these strategies. Record your ideas before joining a class discussion.

## Reflect on the Text

Choose a selection that you found challenging, and explain what made it difficult.

Explain something that surprised you about a text in the unit.

Which activity taught you the most about "seeing things new"? What did you learn?

STANDARDS

**Speaking and Listening**

- Initiate and participate effectively in a range of collaborative discussions with diverse partners on *grades 11–12 topics, texts, and issues*, building on others' ideas and expressing their own clearly and persuasively.
- Come to discussions prepared, having read and researched material under study; explicitly draw on that preparation by referring to evidence from texts and other research on the topic or issue to stimulate a thoughtful, well-reasoned exchange of ideas.

UNIT 5

# Discovering the Self

## Individual, Nature, and Society

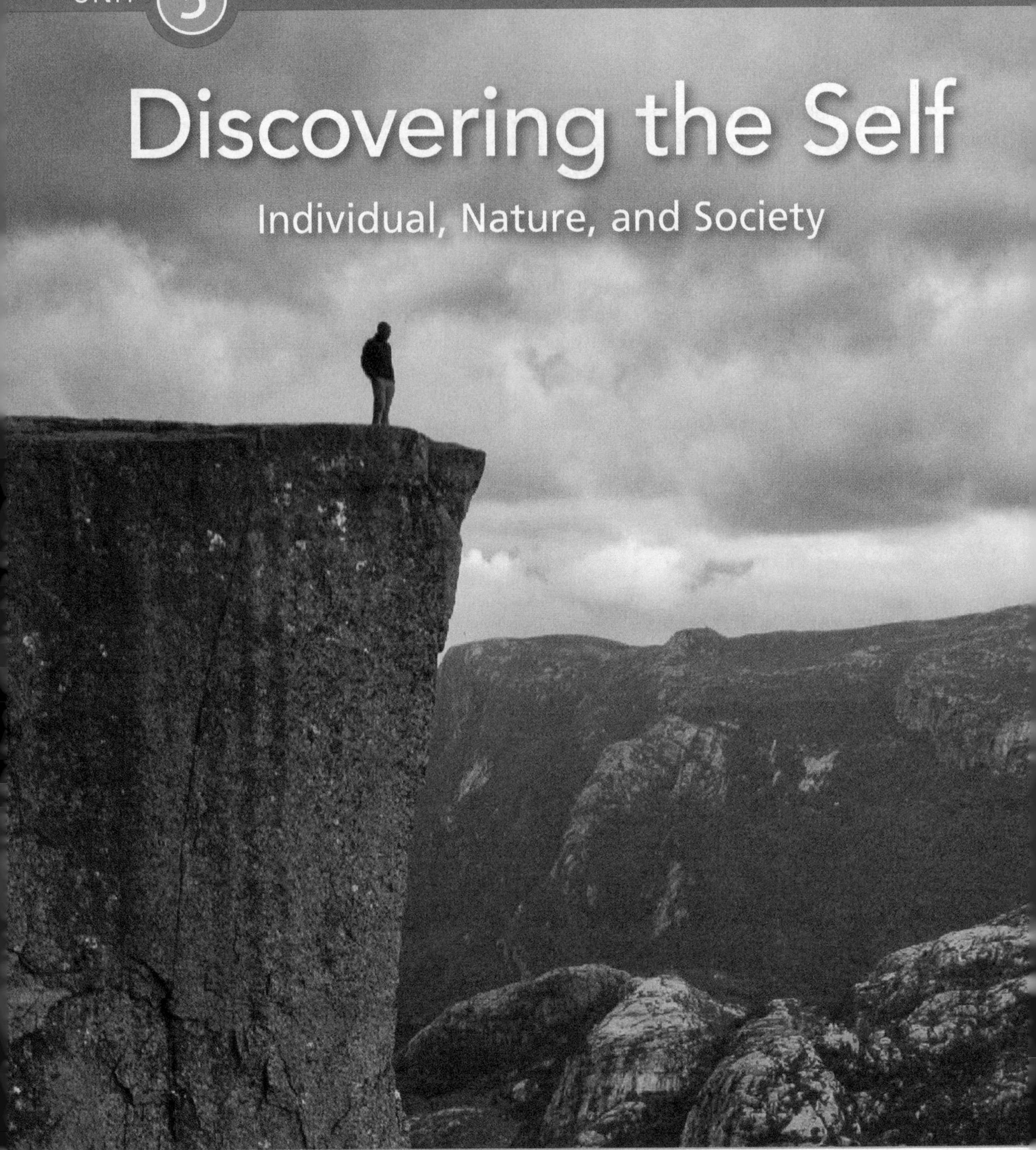

What Is the Self?

**Discuss It** If you could draw a map of the self, what would be its regions?

**Write your response before sharing your ideas.**

UNIT 5

## UNIT INTRODUCTION

ESSENTIAL QUESTION:

# How do we define ourselves?

LAUNCH TEXT
NARRATIVE MODEL
Early Dismissal
*Robin Wasserman*

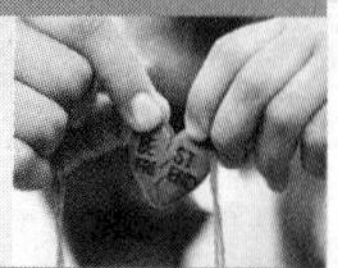

## WHOLE-CLASS LEARNING

HISTORICAL PERSPECTIVES

*Focus Period: 1798–1832*
An Era of Change

ANCHOR TEXT: POETRY COLLECTION 1

Lines Composed a Few Miles Above Tintern Abbey
*William Wordsworth*

*from* The Prelude
*William Wordsworth*

COMPARE

ANCHOR TEXT: POETRY COLLECTION 2

Ode to a Nightingale
*John Keats*

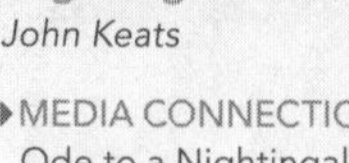

▸MEDIA CONNECTION: Ode to a Nightingale

Ode to the West Wind
*Percy Bysshe Shelley*

ANCHOR TEXT: NOVEL EXCERPT

*from* Frankenstein
*Mary Wollstonecraft Shelley*

PERFORMANCE TASK

WRITING FOCUS:
Write a Personal Narrative

## SMALL-GROUP LEARNING

NOVEL EXCERPT

*from* Mrs. Dalloway
*Virginia Woolf*

POETRY COLLECTION 3

Apostrophe to the Ocean
*from* Childe Harold's Pilgrimage
*George Gordon, Lord Byron*

The World Is Too Much With Us
*William Wordsworth*

London, 1802 *William Wordsworth*

NOVEL EXCERPT

The Madeleine
*from* Remembrance of Things Past
*Marcel Proust*

SCIENCE JOURNALISM

The Most Forgetful Man in the World
*from* Moonwalking With Einstein
*Joshua Foer*

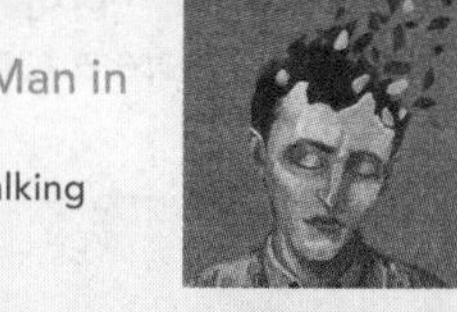

COMPARE

MEDIA: RADIO BROADCAST

When Memories Never Fade, the Past Can Poison the Present
*from* All Things Considered
*Alix Spiegel*

PERFORMANCE TASK

SPEAKING AND LISTENING FOCUS:
Present a Narrative

## INDEPENDENT LEARNING

NEWSPAPER ARTICLES

Seeing Narcissists Everywhere
*Douglas Quenqua*

A Year in a Word: Selfie
*Gautam Malkani*

ESSAY

*from* Time and Free Will
*Henri Bergson*

NOVEL EXCERPT

*from* The Portrait of a Lady
*Henry James*

PERFORMANCE-BASED ASSESSMENT PREP

Review Notes for a Personal Narrative

## PERFORMANCE-BASED ASSESSMENT

Narration: Personal Narrative and Elevator Introduction

PROMPT:

What types of experiences allow us to discover who we really are?

## Unit Goals

Throughout the unit, you will deepen your perspective on how we define ourselves by reading, writing, speaking, listening, and presenting. These goals will help you succeed on the Unit Performance-Based Assessment.

Rate how well you meet these goals right now. You will revisit your ratings later when you reflect on your growth during this unit.

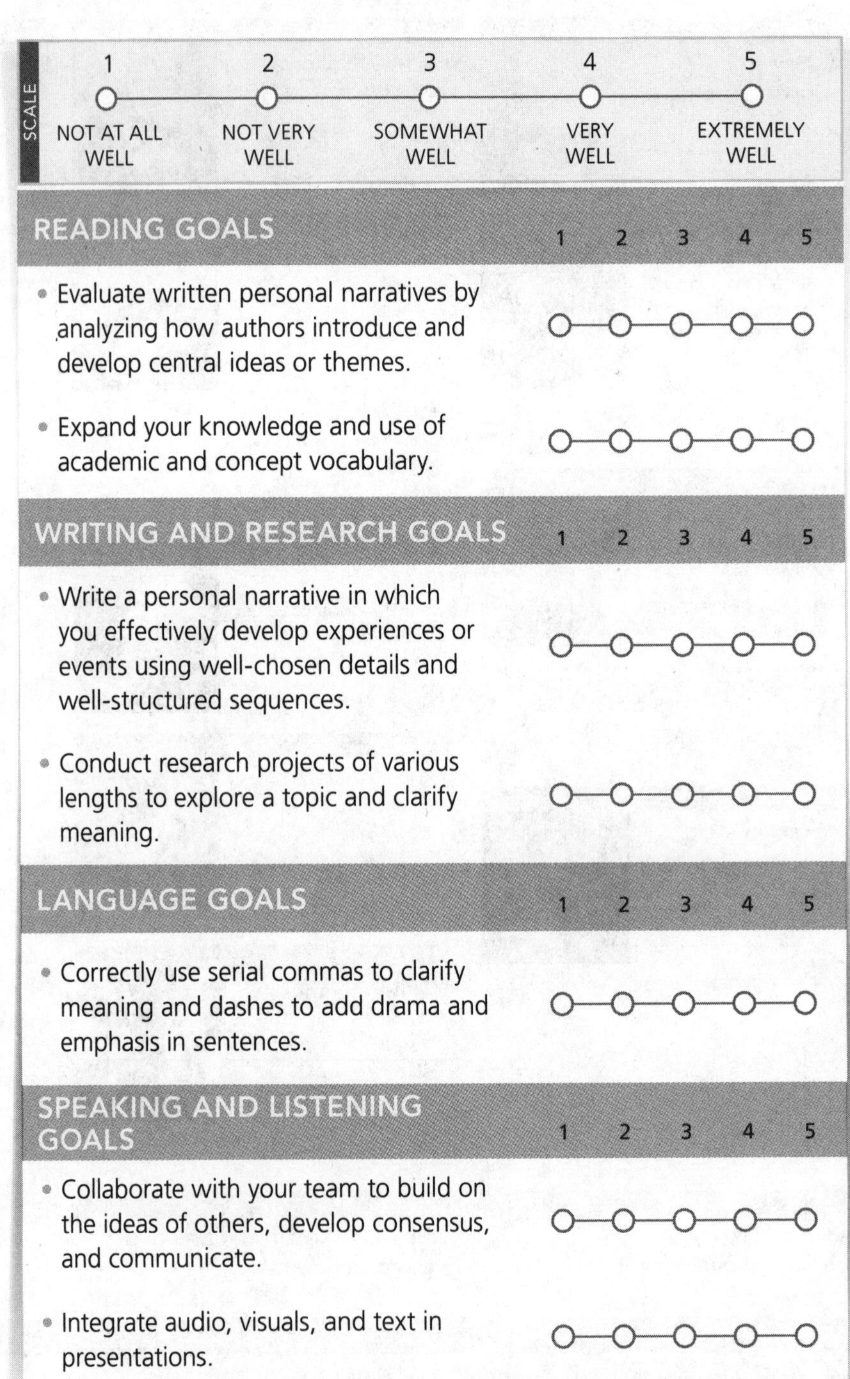

| SCALE | 1 | 2 | 3 | 4 | 5 |
|---|---|---|---|---|---|
| | NOT AT ALL WELL | NOT VERY WELL | SOMEWHAT WELL | VERY WELL | EXTREMELY WELL |

| READING GOALS | 1 | 2 | 3 | 4 | 5 |
|---|---|---|---|---|---|
| • Evaluate written personal narratives by analyzing how authors introduce and develop central ideas or themes. | O | O | O | O | O |
| • Expand your knowledge and use of academic and concept vocabulary. | O | O | O | O | O |

| WRITING AND RESEARCH GOALS | 1 | 2 | 3 | 4 | 5 |
|---|---|---|---|---|---|
| • Write a personal narrative in which you effectively develop experiences or events using well-chosen details and well-structured sequences. | O | O | O | O | O |
| • Conduct research projects of various lengths to explore a topic and clarify meaning. | O | O | O | O | O |

| LANGUAGE GOALS | 1 | 2 | 3 | 4 | 5 |
|---|---|---|---|---|---|
| • Correctly use serial commas to clarify meaning and dashes to add drama and emphasis in sentences. | O | O | O | O | O |

| SPEAKING AND LISTENING GOALS | 1 | 2 | 3 | 4 | 5 |
|---|---|---|---|---|---|
| • Collaborate with your team to build on the ideas of others, develop consensus, and communicate. | O | O | O | O | O |
| • Integrate audio, visuals, and text in presentations. | O | O | O | O | O |

STANDARDS

**Language**

Acquire and use accurately general academic and domain-specific words and phrases, sufficient for reading, writing, speaking, and listening at the college and career readiness level; demonstrate independence in gathering vocabulary knowledge when considering a word or phrase important to comprehension or expression.

# Academic Vocabulary: Personal Narrative

Academic terms appear in all subjects and can help you read, write, and discuss with more precision. Here are five academic words that will be useful to you in this unit as you analyze and write personal narratives.

**TIP**

**FOLLOW THROUGH**
Study the words in this chart, and highlight them or their forms wherever they appear in the unit.

**Complete the chart.**

1. Review each word, its root, and the mentor sentences.
2. Use the information and your own knowledge to predict the meaning of each word.
3. For each word, list at least two related words.
4. Refer to a dictionary or other resources if needed.

| WORD | MENTOR SENTENCES | PREDICT MEANING | RELATED WORDS |
|---|---|---|---|
| **inanimate**<br><br>ROOT:<br>***-anim-***<br>"spirit" | 1. A rock is an *inanimate* object.<br>2. I thought my sister put a real spider on my bed, then I realized I was screaming at an *inanimate* object. | | animate; animation |
| **infuse**<br><br>ROOT:<br>***-fus-***<br>"pour" | 1. This author is able to *infuse* her story with details that make her experiences come alive.<br>2. Your speech may be more enjoyable if you *infuse* it with a little humor. | | |
| **anachronism**<br><br>ROOT:<br>***-chron-***<br>"time" | 1. In today's high-tech world, a beeper is an *anachronism.*<br>2. Soon wired phones will be completely replaced by cell phones and will represent nothing more than an *anachronism.* | | |
| **repercussion**<br><br>ROOT:<br>***-cuss-***<br>"shake" | 1. One *repercussion* of my having stayed up all night was that I was exhausted all the next day.<br>2. Try to anticipate every *repercussion* of your choice before you make your final decision. | | |
| **revelation**<br><br>ROOT:<br>***-vel-***<br>"cover"; "veil" | 1. During the campaign, one *revelation* about the candidate's past actually boosted his popularity with voters.<br>2. In a good mystery story, the solution to the crime should be a *revelation,* but it should also be logical. | | |

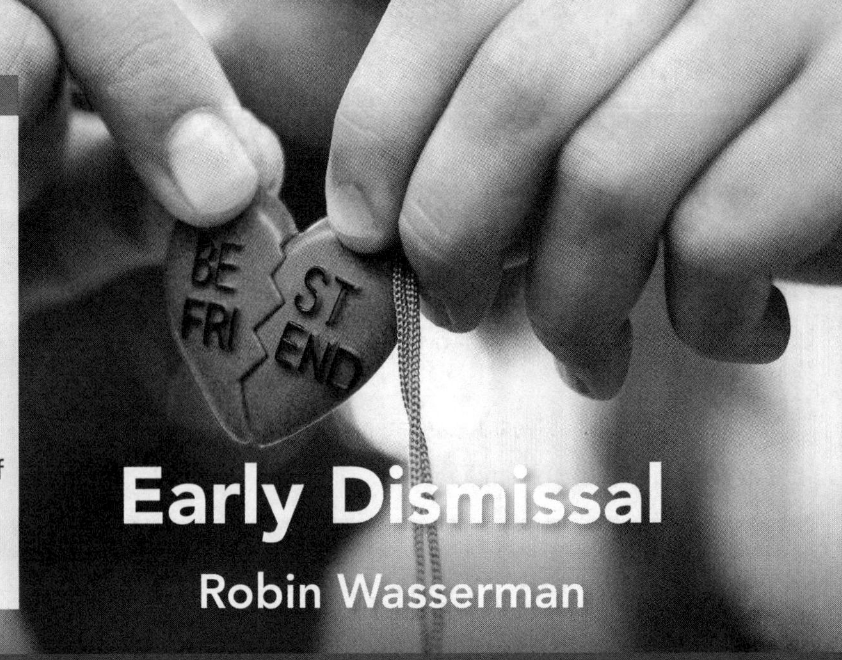


LAUNCH TEXT | NARRATIVE MODEL

This text is an example of a **personal narrative,** a type of writing in which an author tells a true story from his or her own life. You will write in this mode for the Performance-Based Assessment at the end of this unit.

**As you read,** look at the details the writer includes about herself and what she wants. How does her sense of self change throughout the story?

# Early Dismissal

Robin Wasserman

NOTES

1 When you're a rational, clear-eyed, culturally conversant, healthy, mature, and stable grown-up, there are certain fundamental facts you know about the world. One of which is that twelve-year-old girls come in only two varieties: the ones on the cusp of dumping their best friends and the ones who will be dumped. The corollary to this is that it would be rather inappropriate for any rational, clear-eyed, culturally conversant, healthy, mature, and stable grown-up to care. Much less still hold a grudge.

2 I was born to be a dumpee, the epitome of quiet and bookish, with oversized glasses stuck to my face since nursery school and an oversized helping of glee at any opportunity to be the teacher's pet. I was easily bored, easily charmed, and easily led, a ready-made sidekick to the school's resident (if relatively mild) wild child.

3 I was also, having been reared on a steady diet of *Anne of Green Gables,* well versed in the pursuit and cultivation of "kindred spirits," and desperate to get one of my own. Once I finally did, it was as if I morphed into a fifties cheerleader who'd just scored a varsity beau, obsessed with the trappings of my new status. Instead of letter jackets, fraternity pins, and promise rings, I coveted friendship bracelets, science project partnerships, manic sleepovers, and above all, the best friend necklace, which could be broken in two and worn by each of us as a badge of our unbreakable bond. But the reasoning behind it all was the same. These were talismans: proof to the world that I was no longer an *I,* but a *we.*

4 Don't get me wrong. I liked my best friend well enough—just not as much as I liked having a best friend, *any* best friend. I was a frightened child, not to mention an only child, and my best friend was my security blanket, the universe's guarantee that I would not face the future alone. She was also my mirror—a far more flattering mirror than the one hanging on the back of my bedroom door. Her

very existence was evidence that I couldn't possibly be *that* ugly, *that* awkward, *that* unlovable, because she was perfect, and she not only loved me, but loved me *best.*

NOTES

5 So you can imagine my surprise that sixth-grade day in the playground when, lurking in corners as I was wont to do, I overheard her casually tell some new group of admirers that, no, I wasn't her best friend, why would anyone ever think that?

6 That was it. No dramatic breakup scene. No slammed books, no rumor mongering, no cafeteria shunning, no mean girl antics whatsoever. Which was almost worse, because if I had become her worst enemy, it would at least have been an acknowledgment that I was once her best friend.

7 Instead, from that moment on, I was nothing.

8 It was the first time in my life it had occurred to me that kindred spirits might not last—that life, no matter how many talismans of attachment you accumulated, would be a constant struggle against being alone. There would eventually, at least after I'd crossed the social desert of junior high, be other best friends. Better ones. But much as I may have believed in those friendships, I have never again taken it for granted that they would last. In the real world, the Grown-Up world, people leave, people die—people sometimes just get bored and move on to another part of the playground. Anything can happen.

9 There are certain fundamental facts that twelve-year-old girls know, while grown-ups, even the wisest of us, have forgotten: the names of Magellan's ships, the difference between mitosis and meiosis, the formula to calculate the volume of a cube—and the fact that BFF is not meant to be ironic.

10 Knowing that no one's guaranteed to stick around has probably made me a better friend, and I'm certainly a better accessorizer now that I've left the ratty friendship bracelets and plastic necklaces behind.

11 But I'll admit: I liked believing in forever. ❧

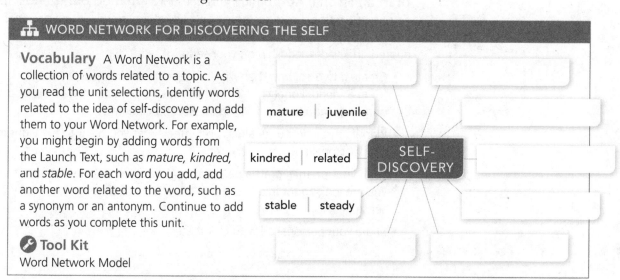

## WORD NETWORK FOR DISCOVERING THE SELF

**Vocabulary** A Word Network is a collection of words related to a topic. As you read the unit selections, identify words related to the idea of self-discovery and add them to your Word Network. For example, you might begin by adding words from the Launch Text, such as *mature, kindred,* and *stable*. For each word you add, add another word related to the word, such as a synonym or an antonym. Continue to add words as you complete this unit.

mature | juvenile

kindred | related

stable | steady

SELF-DISCOVERY

**Tool Kit**
Word Network Model

## Summary

Write a summary of "Early Dismissal." Remember that a **summary** is a concise, complete, objective overview of a text. It should contain neither opinion nor analysis.

## Launch Activity

**Draft a Personal Ad** Consider this question: **What do our friendships say about us and our sense of self?** With a partner, write a personal ad in which you list the qualities you look for in a friend and describe the desired effects of friendship on your sense of self.

- Create a two-column chart. In the first column, list qualities you look for in a friend. For each item in the first column, write the effect of that quality on your sense of self in the second column.
- Identify three or four qualities and effects that you want to highlight in your personal ad.
- With your partner, draft a personal ad that communicates the qualities you are looking for in a friend and the effects of those qualities on your sense of self.
- Share your personal ad with classmates.

## QuickWrite

Consider class discussions, presentations, the video, and the Launch Text as you think about the prompt. Record your first thoughts here.

PROMPT: **What types of experiences allow us to discover who we really are?**

### EVIDENCE LOG FOR DISCOVERING THE SELF

Review your QuickWrite. Summarize your initial position in one sentence to record in your Evidence Log. Then, record evidence from "Early Dismissal" that supports your initial position.

After each selection, you will continue to use your Evidence Log to record the evidence you gather and the connections you make. The graphic shows what your Evidence Log looks like.

Title of Text: ______ Date: ______

| CONNECTION TO PROMPT | TEXT EVIDENCE/DETAILS | ADDITIONAL NOTES/IDEAS |
|---|---|---|
| | | |

How does this text change or add to my thinking? Date: ______

**Tool Kit**
Evidence Log Model

ESSENTIAL QUESTION:

# How do we define ourselves?

As you read these selections, work with your whole class to explore ideas about self-definition.

**From Text to Topic** As we move through our lives, does our sense of self remain the same, or does it change in response to new experiences and knowledge? Is it possible to lose one's sense of self, and—if so—to find it again? The selections you will read present insights into the ways in which we understand and define ourselves.

## Whole-Class Learning Strategies

These learning strategies are key to success in school and will continue to be important in college and in your career.

Review these strategies and the actions you can take to practice them. Add ideas of your own for each step. Get ready to use these strategies during Whole-Class Learning.

| STRATEGY | ACTION PLAN |
|---|---|
| Listen actively | • Eliminate distractions. For example, put your cellphone away.<br>• Jot down brief notes on main ideas and points of confusion.<br>• |
| Clarify by asking questions | • If you're confused, other people probably are, too. Ask a question to help your whole class.<br>• Ask follow-up questions as needed; for example, if you do not understand the clarification or if you want to make an additional connection.<br>• |
| Monitor understanding | • Notice what information you already know, and be ready to build on it.<br>• Ask for help if you are struggling.<br>• |
| Interact and share ideas | • Share your ideas and answer questions, even if you are unsure.<br>• Build on the ideas of others by adding details or making a connection.<br>• |

# CONTENTS

HISTORICAL PERSPECTIVES

Focus Period: 1798–1832

## An Era of Change

During the late eighteenth century to the mid-nineteeth century, deep social unrest and rapid industrialization caused people to challenge previous assumptions about the individual's place in society.

COMPARE

ANCHOR TEXT: POETRY COLLECTION 1

## Lines Composed a Few Miles Above Tintern Abbey

*William Wordsworth*

## *from* The Prelude

*William Wordsworth*

By returning to the scene of memories, can we rediscover who we once were?

ANCHOR TEXT: POETRY COLLECTION 2

## Ode to a Nightingale *John Keats*

▸ MEDIA CONNECTION: Ode to a Nightingale

## Ode to the West Wind *Percy Bysshe Shelley*

Through art, the self can take flight.

ANCHOR TEXT: NOVEL EXCERPT

## *from* Frankenstein

*Mary Wollstonecraft Shelley*

Can love based on appearances truly be called love?

PERFORMANCE TASK

WRITING TO SOURCES

## Write a Personal Narrative

The Whole-Class readings illustrate the will and determination it takes to define yourself and the world around you. After reading the selections, you will write a mixed-mode personal narrative about how we find ourselves, lose ourselves, and learn to define ourselves all over again.

# An Era of Change

## Voices of the Period

*"I am sometimes a fox and sometimes a lion. The whole secret of government lies in knowing when to be the one or the other."*

*"History is the version of past events that people have decided to agree upon."*

*"Impossible is a word to be found only in the dictionary of fools."*

—Napoleon Bonaparte, military leader and emperor of France

*"As the component parts of all new machines may be said to be old[,] it is a nice discriminating judgment, which discovers that a particular arrangement will produce a new and desired effect. ... Therefore, the mechanic should sit down among levers, screws, wedges, wheels, etc. like a poet among the letters of the alphabet, considering them as the exhibition of his thoughts; in which a new arrangement transmits a new idea to the world."*

—Robert Fulton, inventor

*"If he ever had a friend, a dedicated friend from any rank of life, we protest that the name of him or her never reached us."*

—From an obituary on King George IV

## History of the Period

**At War with France** As the Romantic period opened in 1798, Britain had already been at war with France for five years. The war, which lasted more than twenty years, extended across five continents and cost Britain more than £1,650,000,000. It had a profound effect upon British society; by the early 1800s, approximately one in every four British men was in uniform.

In the ensuing conflict, two national heroes emerged for England. At sea, Lord Horatio Nelson shattered the French fleet at the Battle of Trafalgar (1805), ensuring that Britannia would rule the waves for the next century. Nelson, dying at his moment of triumph, passed immediately into legend. On land, the Duke of Wellington defeated Napoleon at Waterloo (1815).

With Napoleon in exile, the victors met at the conference known as the Congress of Vienna (1814–15) and tried to restore Europe to what it had been before the French Revolution. However, the ideas unleashed by that revolution and the earth-shaking changes of the Industrial Revolution were more powerful than any reactionary politician imagined.

**The Power of Steam** The revolution that had begun in the eighteenth century expanded in the nineteenth, as Britain surpassed all other nations in industrialization. Hand in hand with industrialization came population growth; the population of almost

## TIMELINE

1798

**1799: Egypt** Rosetta Stone, key to deciphering hieroglyphics, is discovered.

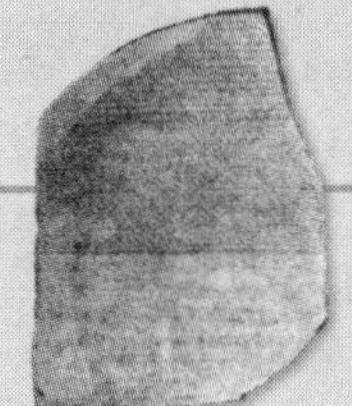

**1801:** Act of Union creates United Kingdom of Great Britain and Ireland.

**1801:** Union Jack becomes official flag of Great Britain and Ireland.

**1803: United States** Louisiana Territory is purchased from France.

**1804: France** Napoleon crowns himself emperor.

## Integration of Knowledge and Ideas

**Notebook** These paintings dramatize the way Romantic values challenged earlier beliefs. Which of the values described in the captions are still influential? Give examples from the world you live in today.

Seeking the Faraway

Wandering as a Rebel and an Outcast

Feeling Awe for Nature

Gaining Forbidden Knowledge

10 million in 1790 grew to more than 14 million in 1821. It was a young population, too, with an estimated 60 percent at 25 years old or younger.

Modernization of the textile industry had begun in England. By 1800, annual textile production had increased to 400,000 pieces, from about 50,000 just thirty years earlier. It was the textile industry that was at the forefront of change, moving the weaver from the spinning wheel in the kitchen to the enormous steam-driven looms on the factory floor.

Meanwhile, in the United States and England, steam was revolutionizing transportation. In 1807, Robert Fulton launched his steamboat, and in 1814, George Stephenson built a steam locomotive. Railroads changed the face of England, and steamships shrank oceans.

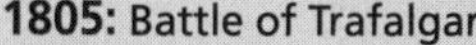
**1805:** Battle of Trafalgar

**1806: Western Europe** Official end of the Holy Roman Empire

**1806: Germany** Prussia declares war on France.

**1807: United States** Fulton's steamboat navigates Hudson River.

**1812: United States** War with Britain is declared.

1812

**Working and Living Conditions** Revolutions are about power, and the Industrial Revolution was about the application of power to work—the creation of machines that work while human beings feed and "tend" them. Unfortunately, the mills—and the cities that grew up around them—destroyed the spirits and bodies of many who came from the countryside looking for new opportunities. Economic progress exacted an enormous human price.

As Britain moved from being an agricultural to an industrial society, cities such as Manchester became smoky, crowded industrial centers in which men, women, and children toiled in factories, often for wages that barely allowed them to survive. While factory owners lived in splendor and a new middle class would begin to develop, workers often lived in squalor.

**Voice of the People** During this period—what we now call the Romantic period—all the attitudes and assumptions of eighteenth-century classicism and rationalism were dramatically challenged, in part by the social and political upheavals. The French Revolution had shaken the established order in the name of democratic ideals, while the Industrial Revolution boosted the growth of manufacturing but also brought poverty and suffering for those who worked (or failed to find work) in slum-ridden cities. Faith in science and reason, so characteristic of eighteenth-century thought, no longer applied in a world of tyranny and factories.

**The Reform Act of 1832** With industrialization, wealth no longer depended on land, and workers, separated from the land, realized that they would have to unite in political action. The Reform Bill of 1832, the product of democratic impulses and changing economic conditions, was a first step in extending the right to vote. It increased the voting rolls by 57 percent, but the working classes and some members of the lower middle classes were still unable to vote. In the spirit of reform, just a year later Parliament abolished slavery in the British Empire.

The Reform Bill of 1832 was another part of the peaceful revolution that was transforming England. Although it extended the right to vote to many males previously disqualified by lack of wealth, women still were denied suffrage. Nonetheless, the 1832 bill was a step in a long journey that, in the end, gave all citizens voting rights.

**A Changing Monarchy** The age of the Hanovers was about to come to an end. By 1811, George III was declared insane, and his son was named the Prince Regent (a regent substitutes for a ruler). The period became known as the Regency. The Regent's conduct gave the period its scandalous reputation.

In 1830, George IV was succeeded by his brother William, who had ten illegitimate children with his common-law wife but no legitimate heir. When William died in 1837, the daughter of his younger brother was next in the royal line. That daughter, Victoria, would become the queen and then the symbol of an era in which political reform and industrial might made England the most powerful country in the world.

## TIMELINE

**1812**

**1814:** George Stephenson constructs first successful steam locomotive.

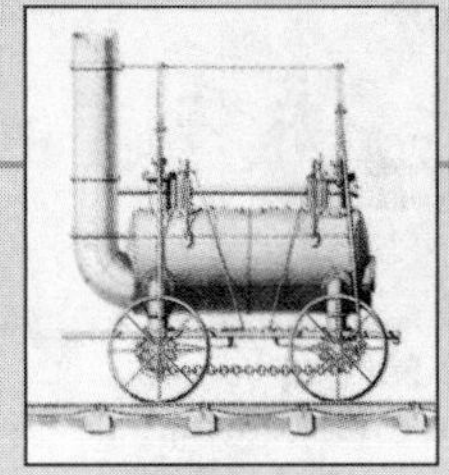

**1815: Belgium** Napoleon is defeated at Waterloo.

**1819:** Eleven protesters are killed at Peterloo when peacefully demonstrating for labor reform.

**1819:** First steamship crosses the Atlantic.

## Literature Selections

**Literature of the Focus Period** A number of the selections in this unit were written during the Focus Period. Most of them address ideas about the ways in which we define ourselves and how those definitions might change over time.

"Lines Composed a Few Miles Above Tintern Abbey," William Wordsworth

from *The Prelude*, William Wordsworth

"Ode to a Nightingale," John Keats

"Ode to the West Wind," Percy Bysshe Shelley

from *Frankenstein*, Mary Wollstonecraft Shelley

"Apostrophe to the Ocean," George Gordon, Lord Byron

"The World Is Too Much With Us," William Wordsworth

"London, 1802," William Wordsworth

**Connections Across Time** Of course, the search for self is a theme that writers continued to explore well past the Focus Period. The writers of the Romantic period have had a profound influence on the modern and contemporary writers included in this unit.

from *Mrs. Dalloway*, Virginia Woolf

"The Madeleine," Marcel Proust

"The Most Forgetful Man in the World," Joshua Foer

"When Memories Never Fade, the Past Can Poison the Present," Alix Spiegel

"Does Your Self Exist?" Steve Taylor

"Seeing Narcissists Everywhere," Douglas Quenqua

"A Year in a Word: Selfie," Gautam Malkani

from *Time and Free Will*, Henri Bergson

"The Soul with Boundaries," Fernando Pessoa

from *The Portrait of a Lady,* Henry James

ADDITIONAL FOCUS PERIOD LITERATURE

**Student Edition**

UNIT 3
"Ozymandias," Percy Bysshe Shelley

UNIT 4
"Kubla Khan," Samuel Taylor Coleridge

**1829:** Robert Peel establishes Metropolitan Police in London.

**1830:** Liverpool to Manchester railway opens.

**1832:** First Reform Act extends voting rights.

1832

POETRY COLLECTION 1

## Comparing Texts

In this lesson, you will compare poems by William Wordsworth with poems by John Keats and Percy Bysshe Shelley. First, you will complete the first-read and close-read activities for the Wordsworth poems. The work you do will help prepare you for your final comparison.

POETRY COLLECTION 2

POETRY COLLECTION 1

# Lines Composed a Few Miles Above Tintern Abbey

# *from* The Prelude

## Concept Vocabulary

You will encounter the following words as you read the poems by William Wordsworth. Before reading, note how familiar you are with each word. Then, rank the words in order from most familiar (1) to least familiar (6).

| WORD | YOUR RANKING |
|---|---|
| **tranquil** | |
| **sublime** | |
| **serene** | |
| **harmony** | |
| **bliss** | |
| **desire** | |

After completing the first read, come back to the concept vocabulary and review your rankings. Mark changes to your original rankings as needed.

## First Read POETRY

Apply these strategies as you conduct your first read. You will have an opportunity to complete the close-read notes after your first read.

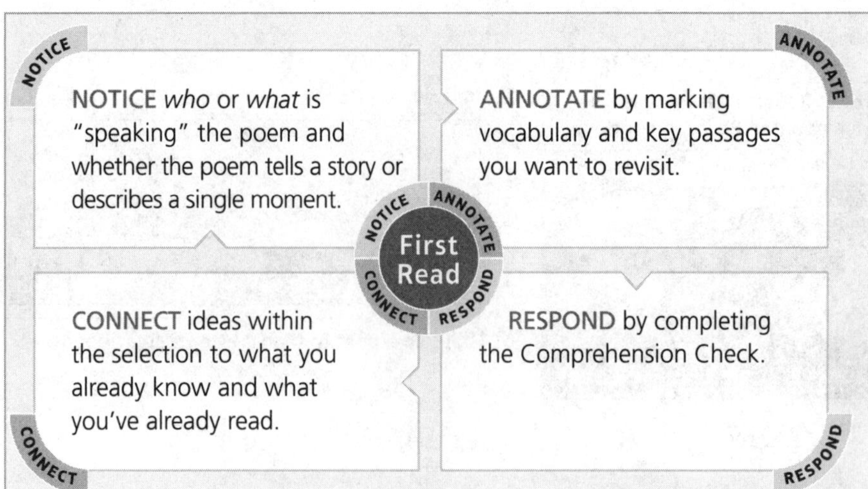
NOTICE
NOTICE *who* or *what* is "speaking" the poem and whether the poem tells a story or describes a single moment.
ANNOTATE
ANNOTATE by marking vocabulary and key passages you want to revisit.
First Read
NOTICE
ANNOTATE
CONNECT
RESPOND
CONNECT ideas within the selection to what you already know and what you've already read.
RESPOND by completing the Comprehension Check.
CONNECT
RESPOND

**Tool Kit**
First-Read Guide and Model Annotation

STANDARDS
**Reading Literature**
By the end of grade 12, read and comprehend literature, including stories, dramas, and poems, at the high end of the grades 11–CCR text complexity band independently and proficiently.

About the Poet

# William Wordsworth (1770–1850)

Writing poetry may seem like a quiet, meditative activity, a matter of words, not deeds—hardly the scene of upheavals and crises. Yet in 1798, when Wordsworth and his friend Samuel Taylor Coleridge published the first edition of *Lyrical Ballads*, a revolution shook the world of poetry. Together, Wordsworth and Coleridge rejected all the traditional assumptions about the proper style, words, and subject matter for a poem.

Gone were the flowery language, the wittily crafted figures of speech, the effusive praise, and the tragic complaints that had defined poetry in the past. In their place, Wordsworth offered an intensified presentation of ordinary life and nature using common language. Wordsworth's revolution took literature in a dramatic new direction, building the movement known as Romanticism.

Wordsworth's revolution was rooted in his early love for nature. Born in the beautiful Lake District of England, Wordsworth spent his youth roaming the countryside, and in later years, he found peace and reassurance there as well.

After graduating from Cambridge University in 1787, Wordsworth traveled through Europe, spending considerable time in France. There, he embraced the ideals of the newly born French Revolution—ideals that stressed social justice and individual rights.

Wordsworth's involvement with the Revolution ended abruptly, however, when he had to return home. Two months later, in 1793, England declared war on France, and the Revolution became increasingly violent. His dreams of liberty had been betrayed.

In 1798, Wordsworth published *Lyrical Ballads* with Coleridge. With the publication of this work, Wordsworth translated his revolutionary hopes from politics to literature. Eventually, Wordsworth's radical new approach to poetry gained acceptance. Meanwhile, a new generation of Romantics, more radical than Wordsworth and Coleridge, arose. Wordsworth's position was secure, however: We remember him as the father of English Romanticism.

## Backgrounds

### Lines Composed a Few Miles Above Tintern Abbey

This poem was written in 1798, during Wordsworth's second visit to the valley of the River Wye and the ruins of Tintern Abbey, once a great medieval church, in Wales. Wordsworth had passed through the region alone five years earlier. This time he brought his sister along to share the experience.

### *from* The Prelude

In 1790, Wordsworth witnessed the early, optimistic days of the French Revolution. The country seemed on the verge of achieving true freedom from outdated, oppressive feudal institutions. Caught up in the revolutionary fervor, Wordsworth felt he was seeing "France standing on the top of golden hours." The war between England and France (declared in 1793) and the violent turn taken by the French Revolution, known as the Reign of Terror (1793–1794), dashed Wordsworth's hopes.

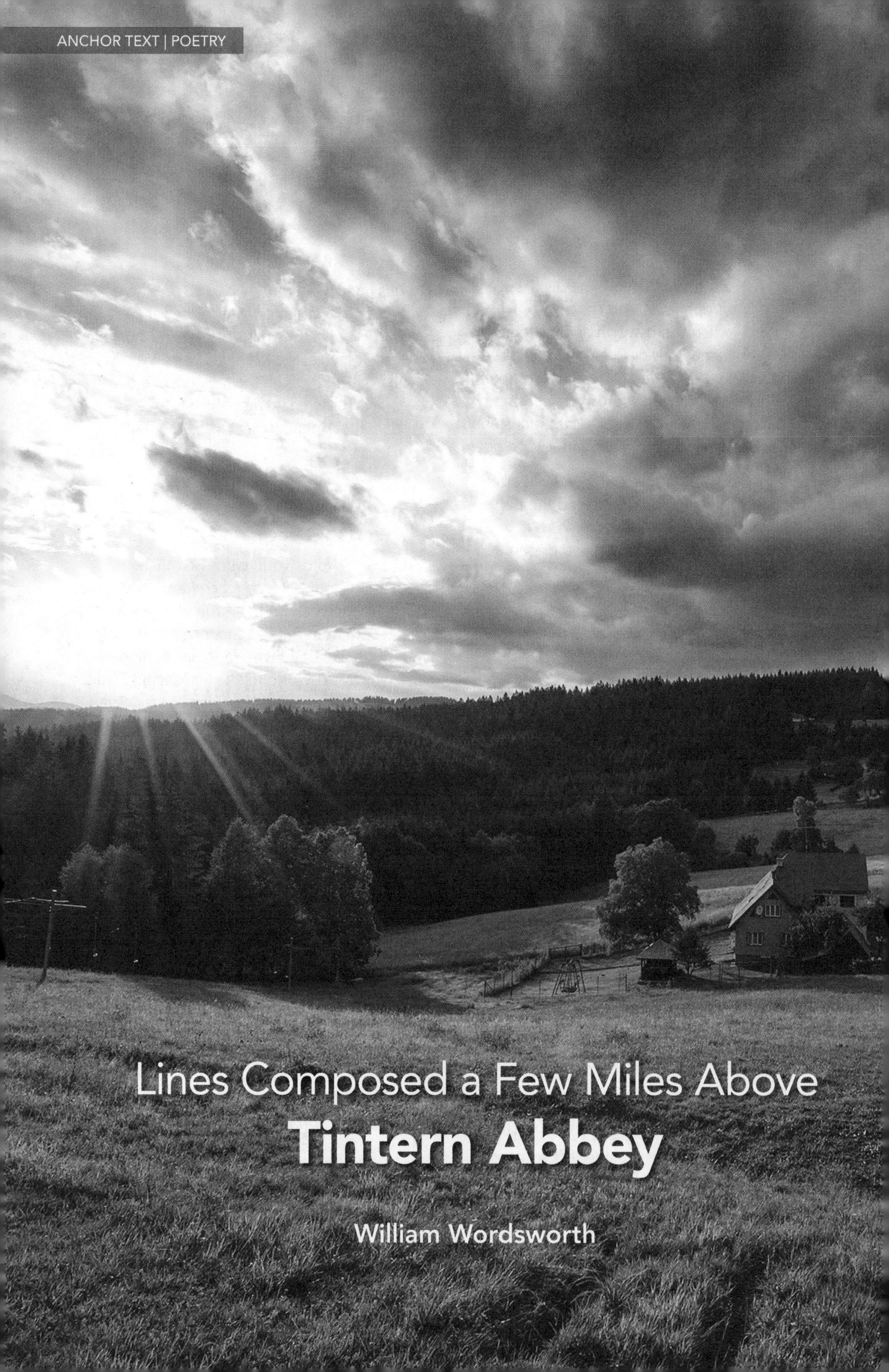

ANCHOR TEXT | POETRY

# Lines Composed a Few Miles Above **Tintern Abbey**

William Wordsworth

Five years have past; five summers, with the length
Of five long winters! and again I hear
These waters, rolling from their mountain springs
With a soft inland murmur. Once again
Do I behold these steep and lofty cliffs,
That on a wild secluded scene impress
Thoughts of more deep seclusion; and connect
The landscape with the quiet of the sky.
The day is come when I again repose
Here, under this dark sycamore, and view
These plots of cottage ground, these orchard tufts,
Which at this season, with their unripe fruits,
Are clad in one green hue, and lose themselves
'Mid groves and copses. Once again I see
These hedgerows, hardly hedgerows, little lines
Of sportive wood run wild: these pastoral farms,
Green to the very door; and wreaths of smoke
Sent up, in silence, from among the trees!
With some uncertain notice, as might seem
Of vagrant dwellers in the houseless woods,
Or of some hermit's cave, where by his fire
The hermit sits alone.

These beauteous forms,
Through a long absence, have not been to me
As is a landscape to a blind man's eye:
But oft, in lonely rooms, and 'mid the din
Of towns and cities, I have owed to them
In hours of weariness, sensations sweet,
Felt in the blood, and felt along the heart;
And passing even into my purer mind,
With **tranquil** restoration—feelings too
Of unremembered pleasure: such, perhaps,
As have no slight or trivial influence
On that best portion of a good man's life.
His little, nameless, unremembered, acts
Of kindness and of love. Nor less, I trust,
To them I may have owed another gift,
Of aspect more **sublime**; that blessed mood,
In which the burthen[1] of the mystery,
In which the heavy and the weary weight
Of all this unintelligible world
Is lightened—that **serene** and blessed mood,
In which the affections gently lead us on—
Until, the breath of this corporeal frame[2]
And even the motion of our human blood

NOTES

**CLOSE READ**

**ANNOTATE:** In lines 1–8, mark words that repeat the consonant sounds *m, s,* and *l.* (Read the lines aloud, if necessary.)

**QUESTION:** Why does the poet choose words with these repeated sounds?

**CONCLUDE:** In what ways do the sound qualities of the lines add to the mood and meaning of the opening scene?

**tranquil** (TRANG kwuhl) *adj.* peaceful; calm

**sublime** (suh BLYM) *adj.* magnificent; awe-inspiring

**serene** (suh REEN) *adj.* peaceful; calm

1. **burthen** burden.
2. **corporeal** (kawr PAWR ee uhl) **frame** body.

NOTES

**harmony** (HAHR muh nee) *n.* oneness; peacefulness

**CLOSE READ**

**ANNOTATE:** In lines 49–57, mark details that show the speaker addressing or describing the river as though it is a person.

**QUESTION:** Why does the speaker **personify** the river, or speak to and of it in human terms?

**CONCLUDE:** How does this use of personification suggest the intensity of the speaker's feelings?

Almost suspended, we are laid asleep
In body, and become a living soul:
While with an eye made quiet by the power
Of **harmony**, and the deep power of joy,
We see into the life of things.

If this
Be but a vain belief, yet, oh! how oft—
In darkness and amid the many shapes
Of joyless daylight; when the fretful stir
Unprofitable, and the fever of the world,
Have hung upon the beatings of my heart—
How oft, in spirit, have I turned to thee,
O sylvan[3] Wye! thou wanderer through the woods,
How often has my spirit turned to thee!

And now, with gleams of half-extinguished thought,
With many recognitions dim and faint,
And somewhat of a sad perplexity,
The picture of the mind revives again:
While here I stand, not only with the sense
Of present pleasure, but with pleasing thoughts
That in this moment there is life and food
For future years. And so I dare to hope,
Though changed, no doubt, from what I was when first
I came among these hills; when like a roe[4]
I bounded o'er the mountains, by the sides
Of the deep rivers, and the lonely streams,
Wherever nature led: more like a man
Flying from something that he dreads, than one
Who sought the thing he loved. For nature then
(The coarser pleasures of my boyish days,
And their glad animal movements all gone by)
To me was all in all—I cannot paint
What then I was. The sounding cataract
Haunted me like a passion; the tall rock,
The mountain, and the deep and gloomy wood,
Their colors and their forms, were then to me
An appetite; a feeling and a love,
That had no need of a remoter charm,
By thought supplied, nor any interest
Unborrowed from the eye. That time is past,
And all its aching joys are now no more,
And all its dizzy raptures. Not for this
Faint[5] I, nor mourn nor murmur; other gifts

3. **sylvan** (SIHL vuhn) *adj.* wooded.
4. **roe** type of deer.
5. **Faint** lose heart.

Have followed; for such loss, I would believe,
Abundant recompense. For I have learned
To look on nature, not as in the hour
Of thoughtless youth; but hearing oftentimes
The still, sad music of humanity,
Nor harsh nor grating, though of ample power
To chasten and subdue. And I have felt
A presence that disturbs me with the joy
Of elevated thoughts; a sense sublime
Of something far more deeply interfused,
Whose dwelling is the light of setting suns,
And the round ocean and the living air,
And the blue sky, and in the mind of man;
A motion and a spirit, that impels
All thinking things, all objects of all thought,
And rolls through all things. Therefore am I still
A lover of the meadows and the woods
And mountains; and of all that we behold
From this green earth; of all the mighty world
Of eye, and ear—both what they half create,
And what perceive; well pleased to recognize
In nature and the language of the sense,
The anchor of my purest thoughts, the nurse,
The guide, the guardian of my heart, and soul
Of all my moral being.

Nor perchance,
If I were not thus taught, should I the more
Suffer[6] my genial spirits[7] to decay;
For thou art with me here upon the banks
Of this fair river; thou my dearest Friend,[8]
My dear, dear Friend, and in thy voice I catch
The language of my former heart, and read
My former pleasures in the shooting lights
Of thy wild eyes. Oh! yet a little while
May I behold in thee what I was once,
My dear, dear Sister! and this prayer I make
Knowing that Nature never did betray
The heart that loved her; 'tis her privilege,
Through all the years of this our life, to lead
From joy to joy; for she can so inform
The mind that is within us, so impress
With quietness and beauty, and so feed
With lofty thoughts, that neither evil tongues,
Rash judgments, nor the sneers of selfish men,

6. **Suffer** allow.
7. **genial spirits** creative powers.
8. **Friend** his sister Dorothy.

NOTES

**CLOSE READ**

**ANNOTATE:** In lines 107–111, mark words that characterize the various roles "nature and the language of the senses" play in the speaker's life.

**QUESTION:** Why does the speaker use different terms to refer to the same thing?

**CONCLUDE:** What is the effect of these varied references?

NOTES

Nor greetings where no kindness is, nor all
The dreary intercourse of daily life,
Shall e'er prevail against us, or disturb
Our cheerful faith, that all which we behold
Is full of blessings. Therefore let the moon
Shine on thee in thy solitary walk;
And let the misty mountain winds be free
To blow against thee; and, in after years,
When these wild ecstasies shall be matured
Into a sober pleasure; when thy mind
Shall be a mansion for all lovely forms,
Thy memory be as a dwelling place
For all sweet sound and harmonies; oh! then,
If solitude, or fear, or pain, or grief,
Should be thy portion, with what healing thoughts
Of tender joy wilt thou remember me,
And these my exhortations! Nor, perchance—
If I should be where I no more can hear
Thy voice, nor catch from thy wild eyes these gleams
Of past existence—wilt thou then forget
That on the banks of this delightful stream
We stood together; and that I, so long
A worshipper of Nature, hither came
Unwearied in that service: rather say
With warmer love—oh! with far deeper zeal
Of holier love. Nor wilt thou then forget,
That after many wanderings, many years
Of absence, these steep woods and lofty cliffs,
And this green pastoral landscape, were to me
More dear, both for themselves and for thy sake!

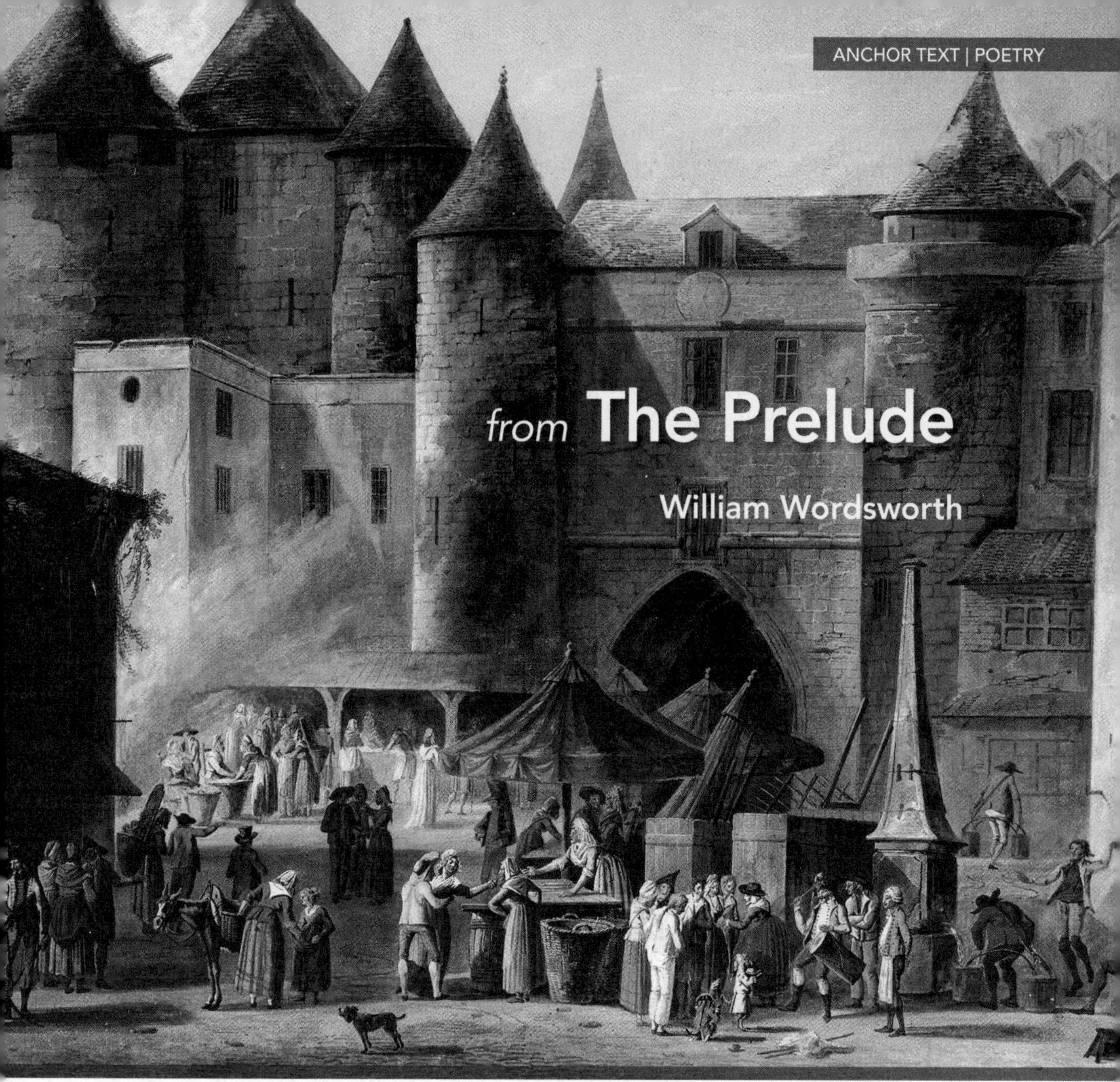

# *from* The Prelude

William Wordsworth

O pleasant exercise of hope and joy!
For mighty were the auxiliars which then stood
Upon our side, us who were strong in love!
**Bliss** was it in that dawn to be alive,
But to be young was very Heaven! O times,
In which the meager, stale, forbidding ways
Of custom, law, and statute, took at once
The attraction of a country in romance!
When Reason seemed the most to assert her rights
When most intent on making of herself
A prime enchantress—to assist the work,
Which then was going forward in her name!
Not favored spots alone, but the whole Earth,

NOTES

**bliss** (blihs) *n.* great happiness; ecstasy

NOTES

**CLOSE READ**

**ANNOTATE:** Mark three words in line 23 that repeat an initial consonant sound.

**QUESTION:** Why might the poet have chosen words with this sound relationship?

**CONCLUDE:** How does the repeated sound add to the meaning and impact of the line?

**desire** (dih ZYR) *n.* longing; strong wish or want

The beauty wore of promise—that which sets
(As at some moments might not be unfelt
Among the bowers of Paradise itself)
The budding rose above the rose full blown.
What temper at the prospect did not wake
To happiness unthought of? The inert
Were roused, and lively natures rapt away!
They who had fed their childhood upon dreams,
The play-fellows of fancy, who had made
All powers of swiftness, subtlety, and strength
Their ministers,—who in lordly wise had stirred
Among the grandest objects of the sense,
And dealt with whatsoever they found there
As if they had within some lurking right
To wield it;—they, too, who of gentle mood
Had watched all gentle motions, and to these
Had fitted their own thoughts, schemers more mild,
And in the region of their peaceful selves;—
Now was it that *both* found, the meek and lofty
Did both find helpers to their hearts' **desire**,
And stuff at hand, plastic as they could wish,—
Were called upon to exercise their skill,
Not in Utopia,—subterranean fields,—
Or some secreted island, Heaven knows where!
But in the very world, which is the world
Of all of us,—the place where, in the end,
We find our happiness, or not at all!

⌘ ⌘ ⌘

But now, become oppressors in their turn,
Frenchmen had changed a war of self-defense
For one of conquest, losing sight of all
Which they had struggled for: now mounted up,
Openly in the eye of earth and heaven,
The scale of liberty. I read her doom,
With anger vexed, with disappointment sore,
But not dismayed, nor taking to the shame
Of a false prophet. While resentment rose
Striving to hide, what nought could heal, the wounds
Of mortified presumption, I adhered
More firmly to old tenets, and, to prove
Their temper, strained them more: and thus, in heat
Of contest, did opinions every day
Grow into consequence, till round my mind
They clung, as if they were its life, nay more,
The very being of the immortal soul.

⌘ ⌘ ⌘

I summoned my best skill, and toiled, intent
To anatomize the frame of social life,
Yea, the whole body of society
Searched to its heart. Share with me, Friend! the wish
That some dramatic tale, endued with shapes
Livelier, and flinging out less guarded words
Than suit the work we fashion, might set forth
What then I learned, or think I learned, of truth,
And the errors into which I fell, betrayed
By present objects, and by reasonings false
From their beginnings, inasmuch as drawn
Out of a heart that had been turned aside
From Nature's way by outward accidents,
And which are thus confounded,[1] more and more
Misguided, and misguiding. So I fared,
Dragging all precepts, judgments, maxims, creeds,
Like culprits to the bar; calling the mind,
Suspiciously, to establish in plain day
Her titles and her honors; now believing,
Now disbelieving; endlessly perplexed
With impulse, motive, right and wrong, the ground
Of obligation, what the rule and whence
The sanction; till, demanding formal *proof,*
And seeking it in every thing, I lost
All feeling of conviction, and, in fine,
Sick, wearied out with contrarieties,
Yielded up moral questions in despair.

NOTES

1. **confounded** (kuhn FOWN dihd) *adj.* confused; mixed together indiscriminately; bewildered.

## Comprehension Check

**Complete the following items after you finish your first read.**

LINES COMPOSED A FEW MILES ABOVE TINTERN ABBEY

**1.** From what perspective does the speaker view Tintern Abbey?

**2.** When did the speaker first view the scene being described?

**3.** Who is the companion that accompanies the speaker in this poem?

**4.** What effects does the speaker believe that memories of the scene will have later in life, especially during difficult times?

*from* THE PRELUDE

**1.** To what does the phrase "pleasant exercise of hope and joy" in line 1 refer?

**2.** According to the speaker, where do the events described in lines 1–40 take place—Utopia, heaven, or the real world?

3. According to the speaker, in what ways did the war of self-defense change in a fundamental way?

4. With what emotions does the speaker react to the change that occurred in the actions of the leaders of the French Revolution?

## RESEARCH

**Research to Clarify** Choose at least one unfamiliar detail from one of the poems. Briefly research that detail. In what way does the information you learned shed light on an aspect of the poem?

**Research to Explore** Choose something that interested you from the poems, and formulate a research question. Write your question here.

POETRY COLLECTION 1

## Close Read the Text

1. This model, from lines 62–65 of "Lines Composed a Few Miles Above Tintern Abbey," shows two sample annotations, along with questions and conclusions. Close read the passage, and find another detail to annotate. Then, write a question and your conclusion.

Close Read: ANNOTATE, QUESTION, CONCLUDE

ANNOTATE: The speaker repeats a *p* sound.

QUESTION: What is the effect of this alliteration?

CONCLUDE: The alliteration connects and emphasizes the words "present" and "pleasure."

While here I stand, not only with the
sense
Of present pleasure, but with pleasing
thoughts
That in this moment there is life and food
For future years.

ANNOTATE: The speaker compares a moment to food.

QUESTION: What does this metaphor mean?

CONCLUDE: The speaker believes that happy memories can be nourishing.

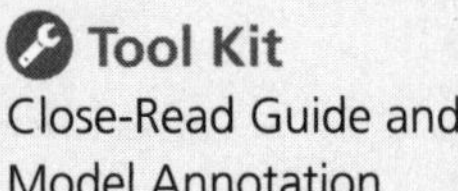

**Tool Kit**
Close-Read Guide and Model Annotation

2. For more practice, go back into the text, and complete the close-read notes.
3. Revisit a section of the text you found important during your first read. Read this section closely, and **annotate** what you notice. Ask yourself **questions** such as "Why did the author make this choice?" What can you **conclude**?

## Analyze the Text

**CITE TEXTUAL EVIDENCE** to support your answers.

Notebook **Respond to these questions.**

1. **Interpret** To what is the speaker referring in line 36 when he mentions "another gift" that this scene of Tintern Abbey has bestowed upon him?
2. (a) What wish for his sister does the speaker express in the last section of the poem about Tintern Abbey? (b) **Connect** How does this wish connect with Wordsworth's hopes in lines 62–65?
3. (a) **Interpret** In lines 69–70 of the excerpt from *The Prelude,* what does the speaker mean when he says his heart "had been turned aside / From Nature's way"? (b) **Analyze** At the end of the excerpt, how has the speaker resolved his conflict?
4. **Historical Perspectives** What does *The Prelude* reveal about the attitudes of observers toward the French Revolution?
5. **Essential Question:** *How do we define ourselves?* How do these two poems connect to the idea of defining oneself?

STANDARDS

**Reading Literature**

- Determine two or more themes or central ideas of a text and analyze their development over the course of the text, including how they interact and build on one another to produce a complex account; provide an objective summary of the text.
- Determine the meaning of words and phrases as they are used in the text, including figurative and connotative meanings; analyze the impact of specific word choices on meaning and tone, including words with multiple meanings or language that is particularly fresh, engaging, or beautiful.

## Analyze Craft and Structure

**Literary Movement: Romanticism** **Romanticism** was a late-eighteenth-century literary movement. Whereas earlier Neoclassical writers favored reason, wit, and elaborate, ornate language, the Romantics sought to create poetry that was more immediate, expressive, and personal.

**Romantic Philosophy** English Romanticism began with William Wordsworth. His poetry was driven by certain philosophical ideas and values.

- **Emphasis on the Self:** The Romantics valued the private self and its relationship to the natural world. Their poems emphasize responses to nature that lead to a deeper awareness of self.
- **Emphasis on Freedom:** The Romantics were influenced by the French and American revolutions. They valued freedom, rejected the aristocracy, and celebrated common folk.

**Romantic Aesthetic** The Romantics' aesthetic, or artistic, choices support their philosophical vision.

- **Ordinary Diction:** Wordsworth rejected clever, flowery, "poetic" diction in favor of language that sounds more like common speech. It elevates the common person over the aristocracy.
- **Sensory Language:** Romantics valued the experience of the self in the world. This led to their emphasis on sensory language, or words and phrases that evoke sense experiences and help the reader feel what the speaker feels.

### Practice

**CITE TEXTUAL EVIDENCE** to support your answers.

Reread "Lines Composed a Few Miles Above Tintern Abbey" and the excerpt from *The Prelude*.

Notebook **Respond to these questions.**

1. Use the chart to record examples of the characteristics of Romantic poetry in these works.

| | LINES COMPOSED . . . | THE PRELUDE |
|---|---|---|
| Emphasis on the Self | | |
| Emphasis on Freedom | | |
| Ordinary Diction | | |
| Sensory Language | | |

2. Choose one of the poems. Using the chart and your understanding of the poem, describe a theme expressed in the poem. Support your answer with evidence from the poem.

POETRY COLLECTION 1

# Concept Vocabulary

| tranquil | sublime | serene |
|---|---|---|
| harmony | bliss | desire |

**Why These Words?** These concept vocabulary words help the reader understand the speakers' spiritual and emotional responses to the events described in the two poems. One speaker feels *tranquil* and *sublime* as he views Tintern Abbey and the rustic scene around him. Likewise, the speaker in *The Prelude* feels *bliss*, or an overwhelming sense of well-being, when he considers the noble goals and actions of the early French revolutionaries.

1. What does the concept vocabulary convey about the nature of spiritual and emotional states?

2. What other words do you know that connect to this concept?

WORD NETWORK

Add interesting words related to self-discovery from the texts to your Word Network.

## Practice

Notebook Respond to these questions.

1. Would you want to look at *sublime* scenery on a vacation? Why or why not?
2. Is someone's strong *desire* to achieve success likely to result in inaction? Explain.
3. Would a noisy city night provide a *serene* environment that promotes a good night's sleep? Why or why not?
4. After seeing the damage that the tornado had done to their home, is it likely a family would be in a state of *bliss*? Explain.
5. How would you expect a *tranquil* lake to look?
6. Would a dilapidated building stand in *harmony* with a beautiful landscape surrounding it? Explain.

STANDARDS

**Reading Literature**
Analyze how an author's choices concerning how to structure specific parts of a text contribute to its overall structure and meaning as well as its aesthetic impact.

**Language**
• Consult general and specialized reference materials, both print and digital, to find the pronunciation of a word or determine or clarify its precise meaning, its part of speech, its etymology, or its standard usage.
• Demonstrate understanding of figurative language, word relationships, and nuances in word meanings.
• Analyze nuances in the meaning of words with similar denotations.

# Word Study

**Denotation and Nuance** Words have **denotations,** or literal dictionary definitions. Synonyms have the same denotation, but they may have slightly different **nuances,** or shades of meaning. For example, both *tranquil* and *serene* describe a calm emotional state, but *serene* is often used to suggest calm in the midst of difficulty or turbulence.

Poets use nuance to add depth and richness to their poems. Wordsworth reveals his thoughts and emotions through the use of carefully chosen words.

Use a print or online college-level dictionary or thesaurus to find synonyms of the concept vocabulary words. Explain how the nuances of each word differ from those of at least one of its synonyms.

## Conventions and Style

**Wordsworth's Poetic Structure** **Lyric poetry** expresses the personal thoughts and feelings of a single speaker. The earliest lyric poems were verses sung by the ancient Greeks to the accompaniment of a stringed instrument called a *lyre*. Though no longer sung, most lyric poems have a musical quality. William Wordsworth is credited with the invention of Romanticism, a literary movement for which the lyric poem was a perfect vehicle. Lyric poems may be rhymed or unrhymed, metered or free verse. Wordsworth's poems feature the following structural elements:

- **Variable Stanza Lengths:** Wordsworth's stanzas flow until an idea has been fully explored. A stanza break indicates the beginning of a new thought.
- **Simple Language:** Wordsworth intentionally abandoned the flowery or clever diction of earlier poetic generations. He uses simple diction, along with figurative language and sound devices.
- **Blank Verse:** Wordsworth wrote in **blank verse**, or unrhymed iambic pentameter. Blank verse consists of ten syllables per line arranged in five metrical feet, each consisting of an unstressed syllable followed by a stressed one. Although it is highly crafted, blank verse sounds like natural speech in English.
- **Fluid Line Breaks:** The end—or break—of a line is dictated by the meter and does not necessarily indicate the end of a thought. Often, Wordsworth uses **enjambment**, a technique in which the sentence continues beyond the end of one line onto the next.

**EVIDENCE LOG**

Before moving on to a new selection, go to your Evidence Log and record what you've learned from "Lines Composed a Few Miles Above Tintern Abbey" and the excerpt from *The Prelude*.

### Practice

1. Use the chart to identify examples of the structural elements Wordsworth uses in the two poems in this collection. Record line numbers where written examples are too long.

| STRUCTURAL ELEMENT | POEM | EXAMPLE |
|---|---|---|
| Fluid Stanzas | | |
| Simple Language | | |
| Blank Verse | | |
| Enjambment | | |

2. **Connect to Style** How does Wordsworth's use of fluid stanzas, blank verse, and enjambment contribute to the effect and meaning of the poems?

POETRY COLLECTION 1

## Comparing Texts

You will now read two poems from a second generation of Romantic poets. First, complete a first read and close read of the poems by Keats and Shelley. Then, compare the two poetry collections to analyze the similarities and differences in the ways the poets approach their subjects.

POETRY COLLECTION 2

POETRY COLLECTION 2

# Ode to a Nightingale

# Ode to the West Wind

## Concept Vocabulary

You will encounter the following words as you read the poems. Before reading, note how familiar you are with each word. Then, rank the words in order from most familiar (1) to least familiar (6).

| WORD | YOUR RANKING |
|---|---|
| **hemlock** | |
| **requiem** | |
| **corpse** | |
| **decaying** | |
| **dirge** | |
| **sepulcher** | |

After completing the first read, come back to the concept vocabulary and review your rankings. Mark changes to your original rankings as needed.

## First Read POETRY

Apply these strategies as you conduct your first read. You will have an opportunity to complete a close read after your first read.

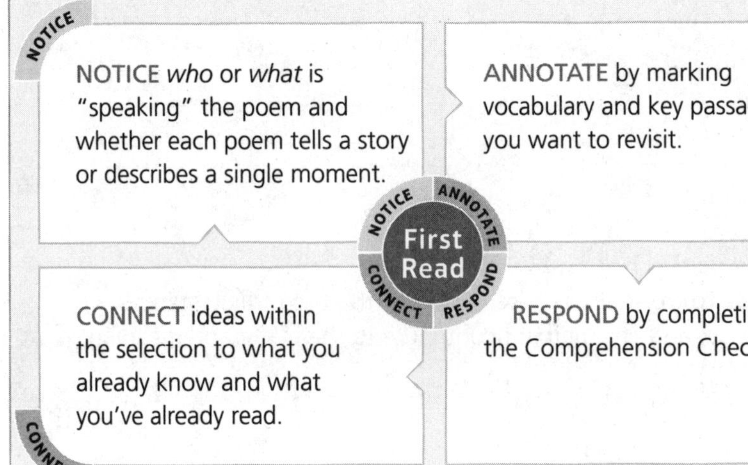

NOTICE
NOTICE *who* or *what* is "speaking" the poem and whether each poem tells a story or describes a single moment.
ANNOTATE
ANNOTATE by marking vocabulary and key passages you want to revisit.
NOTICE ANNOTATE First Read CONNECT RESPOND
CONNECT ideas within the selection to what you already know and what you've already read.
RESPOND by completing the Comprehension Check.
CONNECT
RESPOND


**Tool Kit**
First-Read Guide and Model Annotation

**STANDARDS**

**Reading Literature**

- Demonstrate knowledge of eighteenth-, nineteenth-, and early twentieth-century foundational works of American literature, including how two or more texts from the same period treat similar themes or topics.
- By the end of grade 12, read and comprehend literature, including stories, dramas, and poems, at the high end of the grades 11–CCR text complexity band independently and proficiently.

## About the Poets

**John Keats** (1795–1821) is considered one of the primary Romantic poets. Unlike his contemporaries Byron and Shelley, Keats was not an aristocrat. He was born to working-class Londoners. In 1815, Keats began studying medicine and eventually became an apothecary (pharmacist), but he soon abandoned that profession to become a poet. In 1818, Keats published *Endymion*, a long poem that the critics panned. Despite the critical rejection, Keats did not swerve from his new career. Keats soon after met the love of his life, Fanny Brawne, to whom he became engaged. Over a nine-month period, fired with creativity, he wrote the poems for which he is most famous, many of which are considered to be masterpieces. Sadly, Keats succumbed to tuberculosis at the age of twenty-five.

**Percy Bysshe Shelley** (1792–1822), another Romantic poet, was born to upper-class parents and raised on a country estate. He would have inherited a seat in Parliament but broke off relations with his father when he was expelled from Oxford after writing *The Necessity of Atheism*. Shelley began writing poetry seriously at age nineteen. Among his finest works are "Ode to the West Wind" and "To a Skylark." A friend of numerous writers, he married Mary Wollstonecraft Godwin, who, as Mary Shelley, wrote *Frankenstein.* Shelley drowned at sea while sailing a boat in a storm. He was twenty-nine years old.

## Backgrounds

### Ode to a Nightingale

Keats composed "Ode to a Nightingale" in 1819, while living in Hampstead with his friend Charles Brown. Brown wrote the following description about how the ode was composed: "In the spring of 1819 a nightingale had built her nest near my house. Keats felt a tranquil and continued joy in her song; and one morning he took his chair from the breakfast table to the grass plot under the plum tree, where he sat for two or three hours. When he came into the house, I perceived he had some scraps of paper in his hand, and these he was quietly thrusting behind the books. On inquiry, I found those scraps, four or five in number, contained his poetic feeling on the song of our nightingale."

### Ode to the West Wind

Shelley wrote "Ode to the West Wind" in 1819 near Florence, Italy. It was published the following year as part of a collection. When he wrote the poem, the Peterloo Massacre of August 1819 had recently taken place. In this massacre, in Manchester, England, cavalry disrupted a demonstration of some 70,000 people who were demanding parliamentary reform. Eleven people were killed, and as many as 500 were injured. Other poems Shelley wrote at the same time address political change, revolution, and the role of the poet, and some people see these themes in "Ode to the West Wind" as well.

ANCHOR TEXT | POETRY

# Ode to a Nightingale

John Keats

## I

My heart aches, and drowsy numbness pains
    My sense, as though of **hemlock** I had drunk,
Or emptied some dull opiate to the drains
    One minute past, and Lethe-wards[1] had sunk:
'Tis not through envy of thy happy lot,
    But being too happy in thine happiness,—
        That thou, light-wingèd Dryad[2] of the trees,
            In some melodious plot
    Of beechen green, and shadows numberless,
        Singest of summer in full-throated ease.

## II

O, for a draft[3] of vintage! that hath been
    Cooled a long age in the deep-delved earth,
Tasting of Flora[4] and the country green,
    Dance, and Provençal[5] song, and sunburnt mirth!
O for a beaker full of the warm South,
    Full of the true, the blushful Hippocrene,[6]
        With beaded bubbles winking at the brim,
            And purple-stained mouth;
    That I might drink, and leave the world unseen,
        And with thee fade away into the forest dim:

## III

Fade far away, dissolve, and quite forget
    What thou among the leaves hast never known,
The weariness, the fever, and the fret
    Here, where men sit and hear each other groan;
Where palsy shakes a few, sad, last gray hairs,
    Where youth grows pale, and specter-thin, and dies;[7]
        Where but to think is to be full of sorrow
            And leaden-eyed despairs,
    Where Beauty cannot keep her lustrous eyes,
        Or new Love pine at them beyond tomorrow.

NOTES

**hemlock** (HEHM lok) *n.* poisonous herb or a drink prepared from it

### CLOSE READ

**ANNOTATE:** In stanza III, mark details that suggest negative aspects of human life.

**QUESTION:** Why does the speaker emphasize these negative ideas?

**CONCLUDE:** Why might it be important to the speaker that the nightingale has "never known" about these aspects of human life?

---

1. **Lethe-wards** toward Lethe, the river of forgetfulness in Hades, the underworld, in classical mythology.
2. **Dryad** (DRY ad) in classical mythology, a wood nymph.
3. **draft** drink.
4. **Flora** in classical mythology, the goddess of flowers, or the flowers themselves.
5. **Provençal** (proh vuhn SAHL) pertaining to Provence, a region in southern France, renowned in the late Middle Ages for its troubadours, who composed and sang love songs.
6. **Hippocrene** (HIHP uh kreen) in classical mythology, the fountain of the Muses on Mount Helicon. From this fountain flowed the waters of inspiration.
7. **youth . . . dies** Keats is referring to his brother, Tom, who had died from tuberculosis the previous winter.

NOTES

## IV

Away! away! for I will fly to thee,
Not charioted by Bacchus[8] and his pards,
But on the viewless[9] wings of Poesy,[10]
Though the dull brain perplexes and retards:
Already with thee! tender is the night,
And haply[11] the Queen-Moon is on her throne,
Clustered around by all her starry Fays;[12]
But here there is no light,
Save what from heaven is with the breezes blown
Through verdurous[13] glooms and winding mossy ways.

## V

I cannot see what flowers are at my feet,
Nor what soft incense hangs upon the boughs,
But, in embalmed[14] darkness, guess each sweet
Wherewith the seasonable month endows
The grass, the thicket, and the fruit-tree wild;
White hawthorn, and the pastoral eglantine;[15]
Fast fading violets covered up in leaves;
And mid-May's eldest child,
The coming musk-rose, full of dewy wine,
The murmurous haunt of flies on summer eves.

## VI

Darkling[16] I listen; and, for many a time
I have been half in love with easeful Death,
Called him soft names in many a mused[17] rhyme,
To take into the air my quiet breath;
Now more than ever seems it rich to die,
To cease upon the midnight with no pain,
While thou art pouring forth thy soul abroad
In such an ecstasy!
Still wouldst thou sing, and I have ears in vain—
To thy high **requiem** become a sod.

**CLOSE READ**

**ANNOTATE:** Mark details in stanza VI that refer to death.

**QUESTION:** How does the speaker feel about death?

**CONCLUDE:** What insight about the speaker is revealed in this stanza?

**requiem** (REHK wee uhm) *n.* musical composition honoring the dead

8. **Bacchus** (BAK uhs) in classical mythology, the god of wine, who was often represented in a chariot drawn by leopards ("pards").
9. **viewless** invisible.
10. **Poesy** poetic fancy.
11. **haply** perhaps.
12. **Fays** fairies.
13. **verdurous** (VUR juhr uhs) *adj.* green-foliaged.
14. **embalmed** perfumed.
15. **eglantine** (EHG luhn tyn) sweetbrier or honeysuckle.
16. **Darkling** in the dark.
17. **mused** meditated.

## VII

Thou wast not born for death, immortal Bird!
No hungry generations tread thee down;
The voice I hear this passing night was heard
In ancient days by emperor and clown:
Perhaps the selfsame song that found a path
Through the sad heart of Ruth,[18] when, sick for home,
She stood in tears amid the alien corn;
The same that ofttimes hath
Charmed magic casements, opening on the foam
Of perilous seas, in fairylands forlorn.

## VIII

Forlorn! the very word is like a bell
To toll me back from thee to my sole self!
Adieu! the fancy cannot cheat so well
As she is famed[19] to do, deceiving elf.
Adieu! adieu! thy plaintive anthem fades
Past the near meadows, over the still stream,
Up the hillside; and now 'tis buried deep
In the next valley-glades:
Was it a vision, or a waking dream?
Fled is that music:—Do I wake or sleep?

18. **Ruth** in the bible (Ruth 2:1–23), a widow who left her home and went to Judah to work in the corn (wheat) fields.
19. **famed** reported.

NOTES

**CLOSE READ**

**ANNOTATE:** Mark the word that ends stanza VII and begins stanza VIII.

**QUESTION:** Why is this word so important to the speaker?

**CONCLUDE:** What effect does this word have on the speaker and on the reader?

MEDIA CONNECTION

Ode to a Nightingale

**Discuss It** How does listening to this audio recording add to your understanding of Keats's inspiration for writing the poem?

**Write your response before sharing your ideas.**

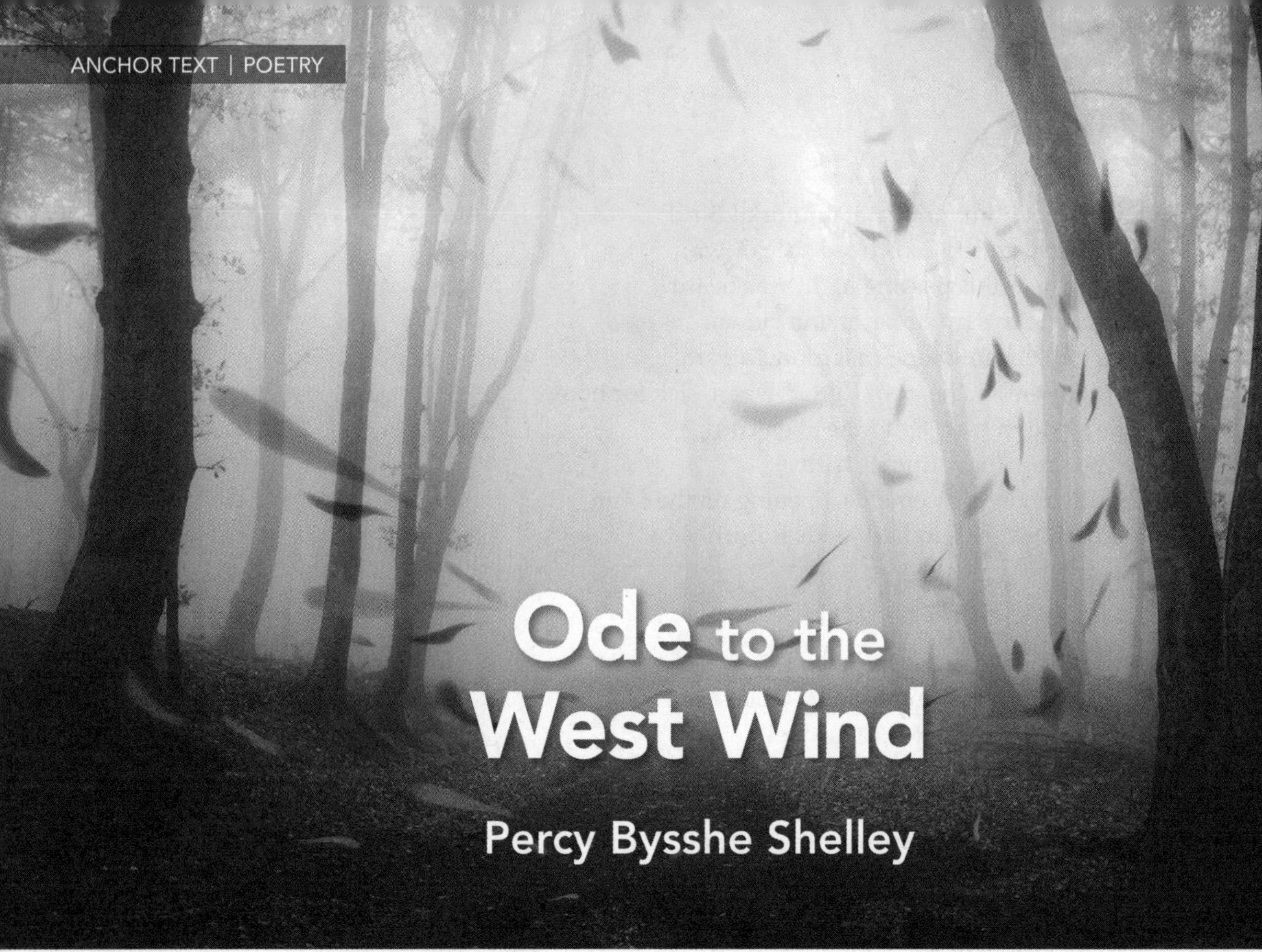

# Ode to the West Wind

Percy Bysshe Shelley

NOTES

**corpse** (kawrps) *n.* dead body

## I

O wild West Wind, thou breath of Autumn's being,
Thou, from whose unseen presence the leaves dead
Are driven, like ghosts from an enchanter fleeing,

Yellow, and black, and pale, and hectic red,
Pestilence-stricken multitudes: O thou,
Who chariotest to their dark and wintry bed

The wingèd seeds, where they lie cold and low,
Each like a **corpse** within its grave, until
Thine azure sister of the Spring[1] shall blow

Her clarion[2] o'er the dreaming earth, and fill
(Driving sweet buds like flocks to feed in air)
With loving hues and odors plain and hill:

Wild Spirit, which art moving everywhere;
Destroyer and preserver; hear, oh, hear!

1. **sister of the Spring** the wind prevailing during spring.
2. **clarion** *n.* trumpet producing clear, sharp tones.

## II

Thou on whose stream, 'mid the steep sky's commotion,
Loose clouds like earth's **decaying** leaves are shed,
Shook from the tangled boughs of Heaven and Ocean.

Angels[3] of rain and lightning: there are spread
On the blue surface of thine aery surge,
Like the bright hair uplifted from the head

Of some fierce Maenad,[4] even from the dim verge
Of the horizon to the zenith's height,
The locks of the approaching storm. Thou **dirge**

Of the dying year, to which this closing night
Will be the dome of a vast **sepulcher**,
Vaulted with all thy congregated might

Of vapors, from whose solid atmosphere
Black rain, and fire, and hail will burst: oh, hear!

## III

Thou who didst waken from his summer dreams
The blue Mediterranean, where he lay,
Lulled by the coil of his crystalline streams,

Beside a pumice[5] isle in Baiae's bay,[6]
And saw in sleep old palaces and towers
Quivering within the wave's intenser day,

All overgrown with azure moss and flowers
So sweet, the sense faints picturing them!
For whose path the Atlantic's level powers

Cleave themselves into chasms, while far below
The sea-blooms and the oozy woods which wear
The sapless foliage of the ocean, know

Thy voice, and suddenly grow gray with fear,
And tremble and despoil themselves: oh, hear!

NOTES

**decaying** (dih KAY ihng) *adj.* decomposing; rotting

**dirge** (durj) *n.* song of grief

**sepulcher** (SEHP uhl kuhr) *n.* tomb

**CLOSE READ**

**ANNOTATE:** Mark rhyming words at the ends of lines in part III.

**QUESTION:** What pattern of rhyme is the poet using in this poem?

**CONCLUDE:** How does this pattern of rhyme add to the poem's musical effect, power, and beauty?

3. **angels** messengers.
4. **Maenad** (MEE nad) priestess of Bacchus, the Greek and Roman god of wine and revelry.
5. **pumice** (PUHM ihs) *n.* volcanic rock.
6. **Baiae's** (BAY yeez) **bay** site of the ancient Roman resort near Naples, parts of which lie submerged.

NOTES

**CLOSE READ**

**ANNOTATE:** Mark details in part IV in which the speaker compares himself to something else.

**QUESTION:** Why does the speaker make these comparisons?

**CONCLUDE:** What conclusion can you draw about the speaker, based on these details?

## IV

If I were a dead leaf thou mightest bear;
If I were a swift cloud to fly with thee;
A wave to pant beneath thy power, and share

The impulse of thy strength, only less free
Than thou, O uncontrollable! If even
I were as in my boyhood, and could be

The comrade of thy wanderings over Heaven,
As then, when to outstrip thy skyey speed
Scarce seemed a vision; I would ne'er have striven

As thus with thee in prayer in my sore need.
Oh, lift me as a wave, a leaf, a cloud!
I fall upon the thorns of life! I bleed!

A heavy weight of hours has chained and bowed
One too like thee: tameless, and swift, and proud.

## V

Make me thy lyre,[7] even as the forest is:
What if my leaves are falling like its own!
The tumult of thy mighty harmonies

Will take from both a deep, autumnal tone,
Sweet though in sadness. Be thou, Spirit fierce,
My spirit! Be thou me, impetuous one!

Drive my dead thought over the universe
Like withered leaves to quicken a new birth!
And, by the incantation of this verse,

Scatter, as from an unextinguished hearth
Ashes and sparks, my words among mankind!
Be through my lips to unawakened earth

The trumpet of a prophecy! O Wind,
If Winter comes, can Spring be far behind?

---

7. **lyre** Aeolian (ee OH lee uhn) lyre, or wind harp, a stringed instrument that produces musical sounds when the wind passes over it.

## Comprehension Check

**Complete the following items after you finish your first read.**

ODE TO A NIGHTINGALE

**1.** What does the nightingale do at the end of stanza I?

**2.** What does the speaker of this poem want to forget?

**3.** What word is "like a bell" to the speaker in stanza VIII?

ODE TO THE WEST WIND

**1.** How does the poet end each of the final stanzas of parts I, II, and III?

**2.** In lines 61–62, what does the speaker want the wind's "Spirit" to become?

**3.** With what question does the poet end the poem?

## RESEARCH

**Research to Clarify** Choose at least one unfamiliar detail from one of the poems. Briefly research that detail. In what way does the information you learned shed light on an aspect of the poem?

**Research to Explore** Briefly research the Fireside Poets, a nineteenth-century group of American poets whose work was influenced by the British Romantics. Choose and read one of their poems—for instance, William Cullen Bryant's "To a Waterfowl." Consider similarities and differences in American and British approaches to similar themes or topics. You may wish to share your findings with the class.

POETRY COLLECTION 2

## Close Read the Text

1. This model, from lines 21–25 of "Ode to a Nightingale," shows two sample annotations, along with questions and conclusions. Close read the passage, and find another detail to annotate. Then, write a question and your conclusion.

Close Read: ANNOTATE · QUESTION · CONCLUDE

ANNOTATE: The speaker uses many words that start with *f*.

QUESTION: What does this alliteration show?

CONCLUDE: The alliteration connects what the speaker wants—to fade and forget—with what distresses him—fever and fret.

Fade far away, dissolve, and quite forget
What thou among the leaves hast never
known,
The weariness, the fever, and the fret
Here, where men sit and hear each other
groan;
Where palsy shakes a few, sad, last gray
hairs,

ANNOTATE: The speaker sets up a contrast between the world of the nightingale and the world of men.

QUESTION: What point is the speaker making?

CONCLUDE: The nightingale does not know the pain of weariness or old age.

2. For more practice, go back into the poems, and complete the close-read notes.
3. Revisit a section of one of the poems you found important during your first read. Read this section closely, and **annotate** what you notice. Ask yourself **questions** such as "Why did the poet make this choice?" What can you **conclude**?

**Tool Kit**
Close-Read Guide and Model Annotation

## Analyze the Text

**CITE TEXTUAL EVIDENCE** to support your answers.

Notebook **Respond to these questions.**

1. **Interpret** What does the speaker of "Ode to a Nightingale" mean when he says, "'Tis not through envy of thy happy lot, / But being too happy in thine happiness" (lines 5–6)?
2. (a) Describe the speaker's state of mind in lines 75–80 of "Ode to a Nightingale." (b) **Connect** How might you answer the final question posed in the poem?
3. **Interpret** What purpose do the images of death and dying in "Ode to the West Wind" serve?
4. **Essential Question:** *How do we define ourselves?* What have you learned about the nature of the self by reading these two poems?

STANDARDS

**Reading Literature**

- Determine two or more themes or central ideas of a text and analyze their development over the course of the text, including how they interact and build on one another to produce a complex account; provide an objective summary of the text.
- Analyze how an author's choices concerning how to structure specific parts of a text contribute to its overall structure and meaning as well as its aesthetic impact.

## Analyze Craft and Structure

**Literary Movement: Romanticism** The Romantic movement in England may be divided into two periods or "generations." The first generation comprises writers who were born in the 1770s and 1780s; this generation is represented by William Wordsworth, among others. The second generation writers were born in the 1790s; this generation includes John Keats and Percy Bysshe Shelley. All of these poets emphasized the importance of the self, heightened emotional expression, and the primacy of nature in their work. However, the younger generation departed from their elders in a few key ways:

- First-generation Romantics became disappointed with revolutionary political movements of their time. Second-generation writers retained their optimism regarding revolutionary politics.
- Second-generation poets idealized ancient Rome and Greece and their mythologies in a way that first-generation writers did not.

Although Wordsworth and other early Romantics often wrote poems that did not follow a specific form, the later poets were drawn to traditional forms, such as the Greek ode. An **ode** is a long poem with a serious theme and, traditionally, a formal, dignified tone. Odes pay respect to a person or thing that the speaker addresses directly.

Shelley and Keats use the ode form as well as other elements of Romantic poetry to develop **themes**, or insights into life and human nature.

### Practice

**CITE TEXTUAL EVIDENCE** to support your answers.

Notebook **Respond to these questions.**

1. What details in "Ode to a Nightingale" and "Ode to the West Wind" reflect characteristics of earlier Romantic poetry?
2. **(a)** Find two references to classical Greek and Roman mythology in "Ode to a Nightingale." **(b)** What purpose do these references serve?
3. Identify the elements of an ode evident in each of the two poems.

| | ODE TO A NIGHTINGALE | ODE TO THE WEST WIND |
|---|---|---|
| *Honors a Subject* | What subject? | What subject? |
| *Formal, Dignified Language* | What are some examples? | What are some examples? |
| *Serious Theme* | What is the theme? | What is the theme? |

4. **(a)** Which details or images in each poem connect to the theme of impermanence? **(b)** What message do the speakers of these poems convey about that idea?

POETRY COLLECTION 2

## Concept Vocabulary

| hemlock | requiem | corpse |
|---|---|---|
| decaying | dirge | sepulcher |

**Why These Words?** These concept vocabulary words all describe death and decay. For example, the speaker of "Ode to a Nightingale" describes his emotional state in this way: "My heart aches, and drowsy numbness pains / My sense, as though of *hemlock* I had drunk." The word *hemlock* conveys the idea that the speaker feels as if he has been drugged or poisoned. Later, the speaker uses the word *requiem* to say that he wishes to die while the nightingale sings a mournful song.

1. What impact does the concept vocabulary have on the moods of the poems?

2. What other words in the poems connect to the idea of death and decay?

### WORD NETWORK

Add interesting words related to self-discovery from the texts to your Word Network.

### Practice

Notebook

The concept vocabulary words appear in "Ode to a Nightingale" and "Ode to the West Wind."

1. Write a paragraph in which you use all of the concept words. Make sure the context conveys that you understand the meaning of each word.
2. Challenge yourself to think of a word or phrase that has an opposite or nearly opposite meaning to each of the concept words, and use it in a sentence. How is the mood of each sentence different from the mood of the paragraph you wrote in the preceding activity?

### STANDARDS

**Reading Literature**

- Determine two or more themes or central ideas of a text and analyze their development over the course of the text, including how they interact and build on one another to produce a complex account; provide an objective summary of the text.
- Determine the meaning of words and phrases as they are used in the text, including figurative and connotative meanings; analyze the impact of specific word choices on meaning and tone, including words with multiple meanings or language that is particularly fresh, engaging, or beautiful.

**Language**

- Consult general and specialized reference materials, both print and digital, to find the pronunciation of a word or determine or clarify its precise meaning, its part of speech, its etymology, or its standard usage.
- Demonstrate understanding of figurative language, word relationships, and nuances in word meanings.

## Word Study

**Latin Root: *-corp-*** The Latin root *-corp-* means "body." English words that employ this root often have to do with the human body or another kind of body. For example, in "Ode to the West Wind," the word *corpse* refers to a dead human body.

1. Use your understanding of the root *-corp-* and your prior knowledge to define the words *corporation* and *incorporate*.

2. Consult a thesaurus to find synonyms for the following words: *corporeal, corpulent, corps*. Then, use the synonyms you found to infer the meanings of the words.

# Conventions and Style

**Use of Symbolism** A **symbol** is a character, a place, an object, or an event that has its own meaning but also represents something else, often an abstract idea. Stock symbols have fixed meanings. For example, a red rose is a common symbol for love. Literary symbols, however, do not have fixed meanings. Instead, their meanings are shaped by the details of the work and are open to interpretation. Often, that interpretation illuminates the work's deeper message, or **theme**. To analyze a symbol in a poem, look carefully at any element that the poet emphasizes. It may be referred to in the title, repeatedly described, or addressed with special emotional intensity.

## Read It

1. Use this chart to gather details that suggest symbolic meanings in Keats's "Ode to a Nightingale" and Shelley's "Ode to the West Wind."

| | SIGNIFICANT DETAILS | SYMBOLIC MEANING(S) |
|---|---|---|
| Ode to a Nightingale | | |
| Ode to the West Wind | | |

2. **Connect to Style** Choose one of the symbols you analyzed. Which passage most clearly or powerfully suggests its symbolic meaning? Explain.

3. Describe how one of the symbols you analyzed gains deeper thematic meaning as it recurs throughout the poem.

## Write It

**Notebook** Write a short paragraph or poem in which you use at least one strong symbol. Your symbol may be a place, an object, an event, or even a character that you invest with deeper meaning through the use of details and description.

POETRY COLLECTION 1

POETRY COLLECTION 2

# Writing to Compare

You have read two poems from the early Romantic period and two from the later Romantic period. Deepen your understanding of all four poems by analyzing the influence of setting on the poems' themes and expressing your ideas in writing.

**Assignment**

The **historical context** of a poem is the social and cultural backdrop of the time period in which it is set or was written. The **setting** of a poem is the time and place in which the speaker speaks. In some works, historical context and setting are essentially the same. In other works, such as those set in the past or in an imagined world, they are different.

Write an **informative essay** in which you compare the historical contexts and settings of the early Romantic poems with those of the later Romantic poems. Explain how the historical contexts and settings help to advance one or more themes in each pair of poems.

## Prewriting

**Clarify Historical Contexts** Review information about the Romantic era provided in this unit. (See the Historical Perspectives feature, poets' biographies, and Literary Movement: Romanticism instruction). Note key facts in the charts.

| EARLY ROMANTIC PERIOD |
|---|
| |

| LATER ROMANTIC PERIOD |
|---|
| |

**STANDARDS**

**Reading Literature**
Determine two or more themes or central ideas of a text and analyze their development over the course of the text, including how they interact and build on one another to produce a complex account; provide an objective summary of the text.

**Writing**
- Write informative/explanatory texts to examine and convey complex ideas, concepts, and information clearly and accurately through the effective selection, organization, and analysis of content.
- Apply *grades 11–12 Reading standards* to literature.

Notebook **Analyze the Texts** Use a chart to identify the poems' themes and explore how setting contributes to their expression.

1. How are the settings of the two pairs of poems similar and different?
2. How do similar settings in each pair of poems contribute to similar themes?

| POEM | CENTRAL THEME(S) | DETAILS RELATED TO SETTING | CONNECTION TO THEME |
|---|---|---|---|
| Lines Composed . . . | | | |
| *from* The Prelude | | | |
| Ode to the West Wind | | | |
| Ode to a Nightingale | | | |

## Drafting

**Synthesize Ideas** Review your Prewriting notes. Decide how setting relates to the themes of Wordsworth's early Romantic poems and the themes of Keats's and Shelley's later Romantic works. Record your ideas using sentence frames like these:

In Wordsworth's early Romantic poems, ______________________________
______________________________________________________________

In Keats's and Shelley's later Romantic poems, _______________________
______________________________________________________________

Use your completed sentences as a working thesis.

**Organize Ideas** To compare both sets of poems, you will need to discuss each poem within each pair. Here is one way of organizing your essay.

**I.** Introduction

**II.** Early Romantic Poems

- A. "Tintern Abbey"
  1. settings
  2. related themes
- B. "Prelude"
  1. settings
  2. related themes

**III.** "Prelude"

- A. "Ode to a Nightingale"
  1. settings
  2. related themes
- B. "Ode to the West Wind"
  1. settings
  2. related themes

**Generate Content** Write each major heading of your outline at the top of a new page. Record your main ideas for each section, along with supporting evidence from the texts, on that page. Arrange the pages in order, and then use them to draft your essay.

## Review, Revise, and Edit

Once you have a complete draft, revise it for balance. Mark sections relating to each poem in a different color. If your organization is sound, the colored blocks should appear in a regular pattern and be of similar quantity. If you notice an imbalance, add or delete material as needed. Next, edit for precise language. Make sure you use appropriate literary terms such as *setting, theme, image,* and *symbol*. Finally, proofread to eliminate errors in grammar and mechanics.

EVIDENCE LOG

Before moving on to a new selection, go to your Evidence Log and record what you've learned from "Ode to a Nightingale" and "Ode to the West Wind."

About the Author

**Mary Wollstonecraft Shelley** (1797–1851) was born as Mary Godwin into a wealthy family and spent her early years in the company of the nineteenth century's most prominent literary figures. At age 16, she fell in love with Percy Bysshe Shelley, who would go on to become one of the century's major poets. Together, their lives knew almost nothing but tragedy. At age 29, Percy drowned in a boating accident. From that point Mary still carried on, writing her own books and promoting her late husband's poetry.

**Tool Kit**
First-Read Guide and Model Annotation

STANDARDS

**Reading Literature**
By the end of grade 12, read and comprehend literature, including stories, dramas, and poems, at the high end of the grades 11–CCR text complexity band independently and proficiently.

**Reading Informational Text**
- Delineate and evaluate the reasoning in seminal U.S. texts, including the application of constitutional principles and use of legal reasoning and the premises, purposes, and arguments in works of public advocacy.
- Analyze seventeenth-, eighteenth-, and nineteenth-century foundational U.S. documents of historical and literary significance for their themes, purposes, and rhetorical features.

# *from* Frankenstein

## Concept Vocabulary

You will encounter the following words as you read this excerpt from *Frankenstein*. Before reading, note how familiar you are with each word. Then, rank the words in order from most familiar (1) to least familiar (6).

| WORD | YOUR RANKING |
|---|---|
| **hideous** | |
| **odious** | |
| **despair** | |
| **dread** | |
| **consternation** | |
| **malicious** | |

After completing the first read, come back to the concept vocabulary and review your rankings. Mark changes to your original rankings as needed.

## First Read FICTION

Apply these strategies as you conduct your first read. You will have an opportunity to complete the close-read notes after your first read.

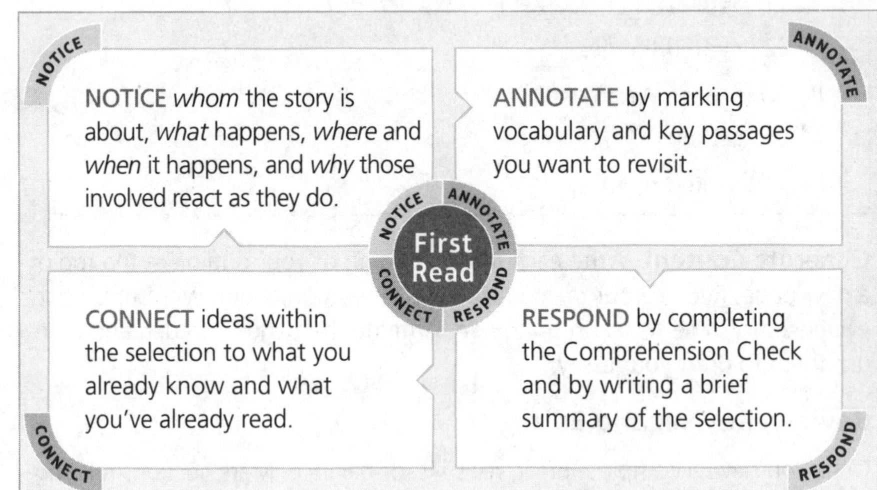

NOTICE
NOTICE *whom* the story is about, *what* happens, *where* and *when* it happens, and *why* those involved react as they do.
ANNOTATE
ANNOTATE by marking vocabulary and key passages you want to revisit.
First Read
NOTICE
ANNOTATE
CONNECT
RESPOND
CONNECT ideas within the selection to what you already know and what you've already read.
RESPOND by completing the Comprehension Check and by writing a brief summary of the selection.
CONNECT
RESPOND

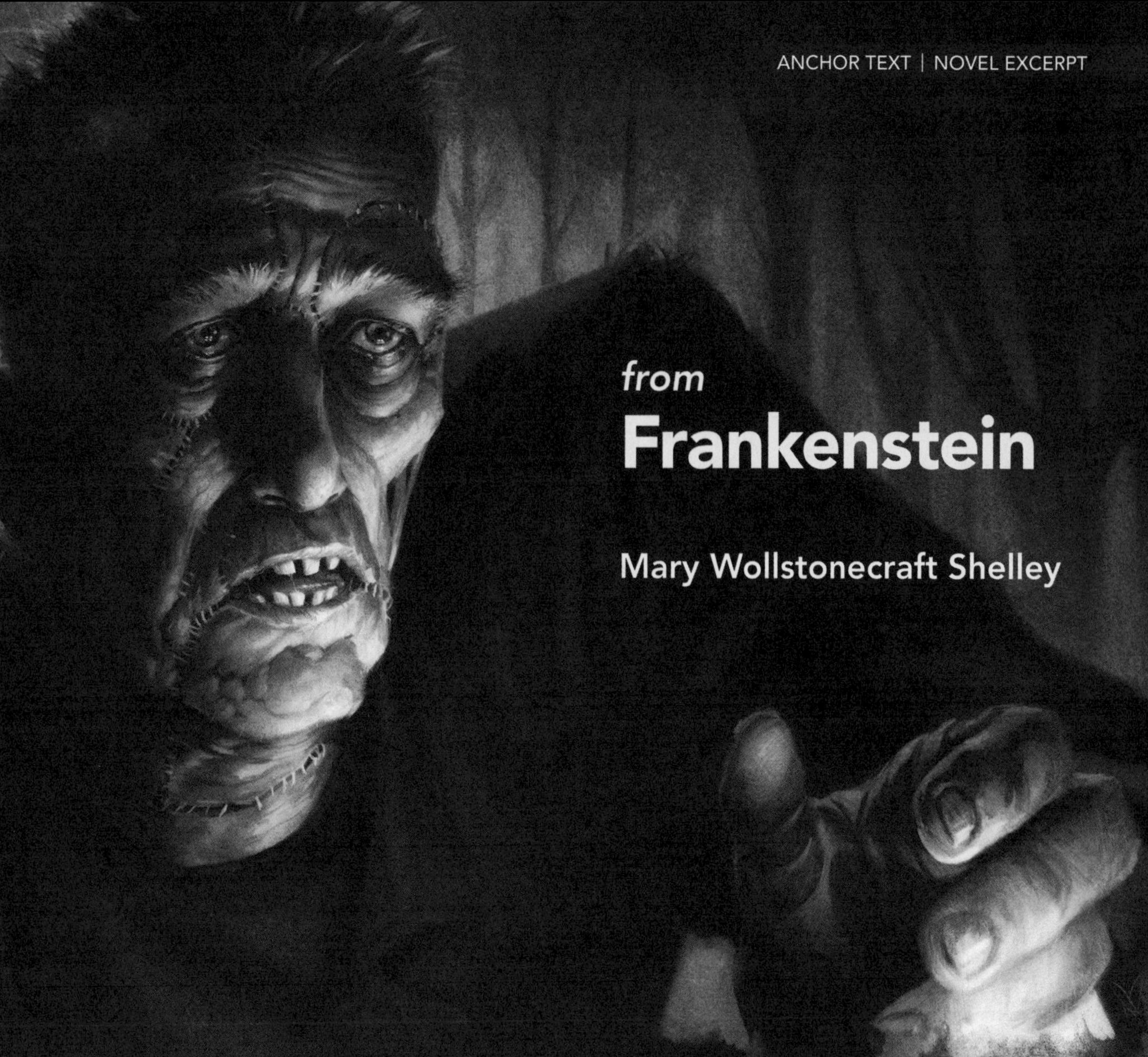

# *from* Frankenstein

Mary Wollstonecraft Shelley

## BACKGROUND

In *Frankenstein*, arguably the first modern science-fiction novel, a scientist named Victor von Frankenstein uses the body parts of corpses to create a living man. The Creature, as he is known, is the narrator of Chapter 15, the first section of this excerpt. At this point in the novel, after having fled to the woods, the Creature has returned to Dr. Frankenstein's home, where he describes his encounters with a family who lived in a small cottage near his hideout. Victor von Frankenstein narrates Chapter 17, the second section of this excerpt.

## Chapter 15

NOTES

1 "Such was the history of my beloved cottagers. It impressed me deeply. I learned, from the views of social life which it developed, to admire their virtues and to deprecate the vices of mankind.

2 "As yet I looked upon crime as a distant evil, benevolence and generosity were ever present before me, inciting within me a desire

NOTES

to become an actor in the busy scene where so many admirable qualities were called forth and displayed. But in giving an account of the progress of my intellect, I must not omit a circumstance which occurred in the beginning of the month of August of the same year.

3 "One night during my accustomed visit to the neighboring wood where I collected my own food and brought home firing for my protectors, I found on the ground a leathern portmanteau[1] containing several articles of dress and some books. I eagerly seized the prize and returned with it to my hovel. Fortunately the books were written in the language, the elements of which I had acquired at the cottage; they consisted of *Paradise Lost*, a volume of Plutarch's *Lives*, and the *Sorrows of Werter*. The possession of these treasures gave me extreme delight; I now continually studied and exercised my mind upon these histories, whilst my friends were employed in their ordinary occupations.

4 "I can hardly describe to you the effect of these books. They produced in me an infinity of new images and feelings, that sometimes raised me to ecstasy, but more frequently sunk me into the lowest dejection. In the *Sorrows of Werter*, besides the interest of its simple and affecting story, so many opinions are canvased; so many lights, thrown upon what had hitherto been to me obscure subjects that I found in it a never-ending source of speculation and astonishment. The gentle and domestic manners it described, combined with lofty sentiments and feelings, which had for their object something out of self, accorded well with my experience among my protectors and with the wants which were forever alive in my own bosom. But I thought Werter himself a more divine being than I had ever beheld or imagined; his character contained no pretension, but it sank deep. The disquisitions[2] upon death and suicide were calculated to fill me with wonder. I did not pretend to enter into the merits of the case, yet I inclined towards the opinions of the hero, whose extinction I wept, without precisely understanding it.

5 "As I read, however, I applied much personally to my own feelings and condition. I found myself similar yet at the same time strangely unlike to the beings concerning whom I read and to whose conversation I was a listener. I sympathized with and partly understood them, but I was unformed in mind; I was dependent on none and related to none. 'The path of my departure was free,' and there was none to lament my annihilation. My person was **hideous**; my stature, gigantic. What did this mean? Who was I? What was I? Whence did I come? What was my destination? These questions continually recurred, but I was unable to solve them.

**CLOSE READ**

**ANNOTATE:** Mark details in paragraphs 4 and 5 that relate to intense emotions. Mark other details that relate to the monster's physical appearance.

**QUESTION:** Why does the author stress the monster's extremes of feeling?

**CONCLUDE:** What do these details suggest about a contrast between the monster's inner being and his outer appearance?

**hideous** (HIHD ee uhs) *adj.* ugly or disgusting

1. **portmanteau** (pawrt man TOH) *n.* suitcase.
2. **disquisitions** (dihs kwuh ZIHSH uhnz) *n.* essays.

6 "The volume of Plutarch's *Lives* which I possessed contained the histories of the first founders of the ancient republics. This book had a far different effect upon me from the *Sorrows of Werter*. I learned from Werter's imaginations despondency and gloom, but Plutarch taught me high thoughts; he elevated me above the wretched sphere of my own reflections, to admire and love the heroes of past ages. Many things I read surpassed my understanding and experience. I had a very confused knowledge of kingdoms, wide extents of country, mighty rivers, and boundless seas. But I was perfectly unacquainted with towns and large assemblages of men. The cottage of my protectors had been the only school in which I had studied human nature, but this book developed new and mightier scenes of action. I read of men concerned in public affairs, governing or massacring their species. I felt the greatest ardor for virtue rise within me, and abhorrence for vice, as far as I understood the signification of those terms, relative as they were, as I applied them, to pleasure and pain alone. Induced by these feelings, I was of course led to admire peaceable lawgivers, Numa, Solon, and Lycurgus, in preference to Romulus and Theseus. The patriarchal lives of my protectors caused these impressions to take a firm hold on my mind; perhaps, if my first introduction to humanity had been made by a young soldier, burning for glory and slaughter, I should have been imbued with different sensations.

7 "But *Paradise Lost* excited different and far deeper emotions. I read it, as I had read the other volumes which had fallen into my hands, as a true history. It moved every feeling of wonder and awe that the picture of an omnipotent God warring with his creatures was capable of exciting. I often referred the several situations, as their similarity struck me, to my own. Like Adam, I was apparently united by no link to any other being in existence; but his state was far different from mine in every other respect. He had come forth from the hands of God a perfect creature, happy and prosperous, guarded by the especial care of his Creator; he was allowed to converse with and acquire knowledge from beings of a superior nature, but I was wretched, helpless, and alone. Many times I considered Satan as the fitter emblem of my condition, for often, like him, when I viewed the bliss of my protectors, the bitter gall of envy rose within me.

8 "Another circumstance strengthened and confirmed these feelings. Soon after my arrival in the hovel I discovered some papers in the pocket of the dress which I had taken from your laboratory. At first I had neglected them, but now that I was able to decipher the characters in which they were written, I began to study them with diligence. It was your journal of the four months that preceded my creation. You minutely described in these papers every step you took

NOTES

**CLOSE READ**

**ANNOTATE:** In paragraph 7, mark places in which the monster compares himself to Adam in the Bible and in John Milton's epic poem *Paradise Lost.*

**QUESTION:** What similarities does the Creature share with Adam?

**CONCLUDE:** What do the Creature's comparisons say about his view of himself?

NOTES

**odious** (OH dee uhs) *adj.* extremely unpleasant or repulsive

**despair** (dih SPAIR) *v.* abandon all hope

**dread** (drehd) *n.* state of great fear

in the progress of your work; this history was mingled with accounts of domestic occurrences. You doubtless recollect these papers. Here they are. Everything is related in them which bears reference to my accursed origin; the whole detail of that series of disgusting circumstances which produced it is set in view; the minutest description of my **odious** and loathsome person is given, in language which painted your own horrors and rendered mine indelible. I sickened as I read. 'Hateful day when I received life!' I exclaimed in agony. 'Accursed creator! Why did you form a monster so hideous that even YOU turned from me in disgust? God, in pity, made man beautiful and alluring, after his own image; but my form is a filthy type of yours, more horrid even from the very resemblance. Satan had his companions, fellow devils, to admire and encourage him, but I am solitary and abhorred.'

9 "These were the reflections of my hours of despondency and solitude; but when I contemplated the virtues of the cottagers, their amiable and benevolent dispositions, I persuaded myself that when they should become acquainted with my admiration of their virtues they would compassionate me and overlook my personal deformity. Could they turn from their door one, however monstrous, who solicited their compassion and friendship? I resolved, at least, not to **despair**, but in every way to fit myself for an interview with them which would decide my fate. I postponed this attempt for some months longer, for the importance attached to its success inspired me with a **dread** lest I should fail. Besides, I found that my understanding improved so much with every day's experience that I was unwilling to commence this undertaking until a few more months should have added to my sagacity.[3]

10 "Several changes, in the meantime, took place in the cottage. The presence of Safie diffused happiness among its inhabitants, and I also found that a greater degree of plenty reigned there. Felix and Agatha spent more time in amusement and conversation, and were assisted in their labors by servants. They did not appear rich, but they were contented and happy; their feelings were serene and peaceful, while mine became every day more tumultuous. Increase of knowledge only discovered to me more clearly what a wretched outcast I was. I cherished hope, it is true, but it vanished when I beheld my person reflected in water or my shadow in the moonshine, even as that frail image and that inconstant shade.

11 "I endeavored to crush these fears and to fortify myself for the trial which in a few months I resolved to undergo; and sometimes I allowed my thoughts, unchecked by reason, to ramble in the fields of Paradise, and dared to fancy amiable and lovely creatures

3. **sagacity** (suh GAS uh tee) *n.* wisdom.

sympathizing with my feelings and cheering my gloom; their angelic countenances breathed smiles of consolation. But it was all a dream; no Eve soothed my sorrows nor shared my thoughts; I was alone. I remembered Adam's supplication[4] to his Creator. But where was mine? He had abandoned me, and in the bitterness of my heart I cursed him.

12 "Autumn passed thus. I saw, with surprise and grief, the leaves decay and fall, and nature again assume the barren and bleak appearance it had worn when I first beheld the woods and the lovely moon. Yet I did not heed the bleakness of the weather; I was better fitted by my conformation for the endurance of cold than heat. But my chief delights were the sight of the flowers, the birds, and all the gay apparel of summer; when those deserted me, I turned with more attention towards the cottagers. Their happiness was not decreased by the absence of summer. They loved and sympathized with one another; and their joys, depending on each other, were not interrupted by the casualties that took place around them. The more I saw of them, the greater became my desire to claim their protection and kindness; my heart yearned to be known and loved by these amiable creatures; to see their sweet looks directed towards me with affection was the utmost limit of my ambition. I dared not think that they would turn them from me with disdain and horror. The poor that stopped at their door were never driven away. I asked, it is true, for greater treasures than a little food or rest: I required kindness and sympathy; but I did not believe myself utterly unworthy of it.

13 "The winter advanced, and an entire revolution of the seasons had taken place since I awoke into life. My attention at this time was solely directed towards my plan of introducing myself into the cottage of my protectors. I revolved many projects, but that on which I finally fixed was to enter the dwelling when the blind old man should be alone. I had sagacity enough to discover that the unnatural hideousness of my person was the chief object of horror with those who had formerly beheld me. My voice, although harsh, had nothing terrible in it; I thought, therefore, that if in the absence of his children I could gain the good will and mediation of the old De Lacey, I might by his means be tolerated by my younger protectors.

14 "One day, when the sun shone on the red leaves that strewed the ground and diffused cheerfulness, although it denied warmth, Safie, Agatha, and Felix departed on a long country walk, and the old man, at his own desire, was left alone in the cottage. When his children had departed, he took up his guitar and played several mournful but sweet airs, more sweet and mournful than I had ever heard him play before. At first his countenance was illuminated with pleasure, but as

NOTES

**CLOSE READ**

**ANNOTATE:** In paragraph 12, mark details that show the Creature's response to the beauty of nature.

**QUESTION:** Why does the author emphasize the Creature's love of beauty?

**CONCLUDE:** What does the Creature's delight in the summer suggest about his nature?

4. **supplication** *n.* plea.

NOTES

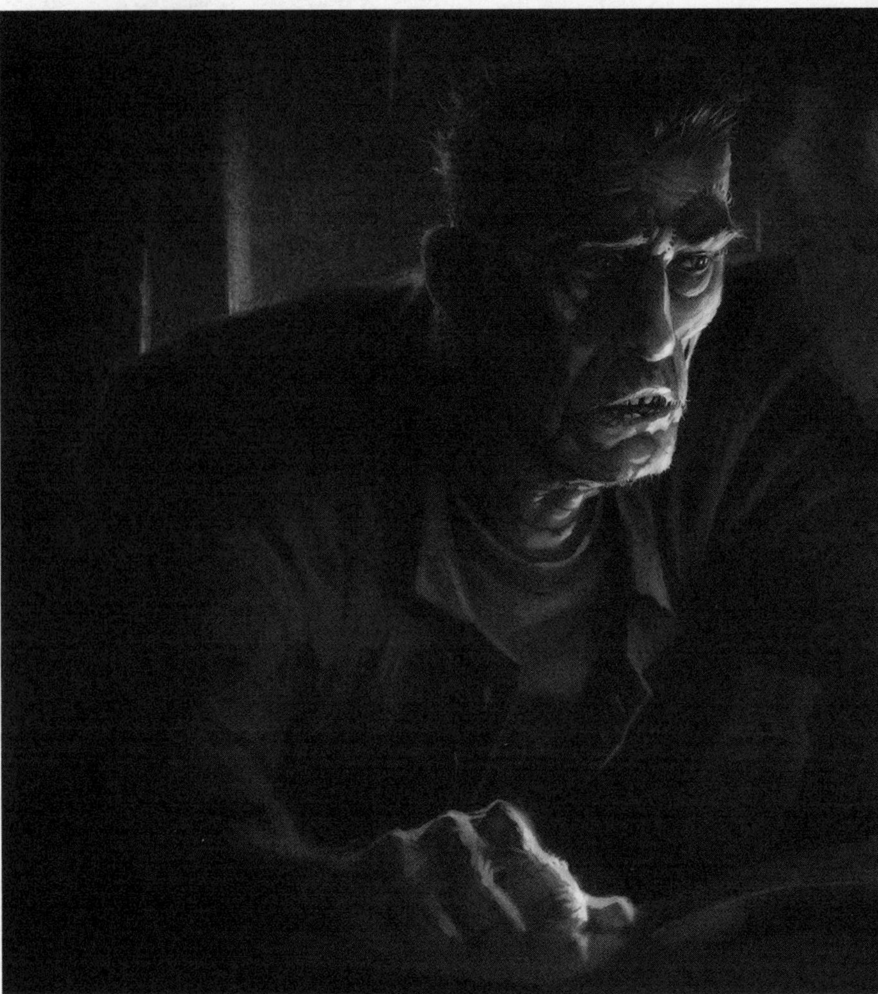

he continued, thoughtfulness and sadness succeeded; at length, laying aside the instrument, he sat absorbed in reflection.

15 "My heart beat quick; this was the hour and moment of trial, which would decide my hopes or realize my fears. The servants were gone to a neighboring fair. All was silent in and around the cottage; it was an excellent opportunity; yet, when I proceeded to execute my plan, my limbs failed me and I sank to the ground. Again I rose, and exerting all the firmness[5] of which I was master, removed the planks which I had placed before my hovel to conceal my retreat. The fresh air revived me, and with renewed determination I approached the door of their cottage.

16 "I knocked. 'Who is there?' said the old man. 'Come in.'

17 "I entered. 'Pardon this intrusion,' said I; 'I am a traveler in want of a little rest; you would greatly oblige me if you would allow me to remain a few minutes before the fire.'

18 "'Enter,' said De Lacey, 'and I will try in what manner I can to relieve your wants; but, unfortunately, my children are from home, and as I am blind, I am afraid I shall find it difficult to procure food for you.'

5. **firmness** *n.* courage; resolve.

NOTES

19 "'Do not trouble yourself, my kind host; I have food; it is warmth and rest only that I need.'

20 "I sat down, and a silence ensued. I knew that every minute was precious to me, yet I remained irresolute in what manner to commence the interview, when the old man addressed me. 'By your language, stranger, I suppose you are my countryman; are you French?'

21 "'No; but I was educated by a French family and understand that language only. I am now going to claim the protection of some friends, whom I sincerely love, and of whose favor I have some hopes.'

22 "'Are they Germans?'

23 "'No, they are French. But let us change the subject. I am an unfortunate and deserted creature, I look around and I have no relation or friend upon earth. These amiable people to whom I go have never seen me and know little of me. I am full of fears, for if I fail there, I am an outcast in the world forever.'

24 "'Do not despair. To be friendless is indeed to be unfortunate, but the hearts of men, when unprejudiced by any obvious self-interest, are full of brotherly love and charity. Rely, therefore, on your hopes; and if these friends are good and amiable, do not despair.'

NOTES

**CLOSE READ**

**ANNOTATE:** In paragraphs 25–27, mark the word that the Creature uses repeatedly to characterize the way in which he is seen by others.

**QUESTION:** What does this word mean, and what are its connotations?

**CONCLUDE:** Why do you think Shelley places such emphasis on this word?

25 "'They are kind—they are the most excellent creatures in the world; but, unfortunately, they are prejudiced against me. I have good dispositions; my life has been hitherto[6] harmless and in some degree beneficial; but a fatal prejudice clouds their eyes, and where they ought to see a feeling and kind friend, they behold only a detestable monster.'

26 "'That is indeed unfortunate; but if you are really blameless, cannot you undeceive them?'

27 "'I am about to undertake that task; and it is on that account that I feel so many overwhelming terrors. I tenderly love these friends; I have, unknown to them, been for many months in the habits of daily kindness towards them; but they believe that I wish to injure them, and it is that prejudice which I wish to overcome.'

28 "'Where do these friends reside?'

29 "'Near this spot.'

30 "The old man paused and then continued, 'If you will unreservedly confide to me the particulars of your tale, I perhaps may be of use in undeceiving them. I am blind and cannot judge of your countenance, but there is something in your words which persuades me that you are sincere. I am poor and an exile, but it will afford me true pleasure to be in any way serviceable to a human creature.'

31 "'Excellent man! I thank you and accept your generous offer. You raise me from the dust by this kindness; and I trust that, by your aid, I shall not be driven from the society and sympathy of your fellow creatures.'

32 "'Heaven forbid! Even if you were really criminal, for that can only drive you to desperation, and not instigate you to virtue. I also am unfortunate; I and my family have been condemned, although innocent; judge, therefore, if I do not feel for your misfortunes.'

33 "'How can I thank you, my best and only benefactor? From your lips first have I heard the voice of kindness directed towards me; I shall be forever grateful; and your present humanity assures me of success with those friends whom I am on the point of meeting.'

34 "'May I know the names and residence of those friends?'

35 "I paused. This, I thought, was the moment of decision, which was to rob me of or bestow happiness on me forever. I struggled vainly for firmness sufficient to answer him, but the effort destroyed all my remaining strength; I sank on the chair and sobbed aloud. At that moment I heard the steps of my younger protectors. I had not a moment to lose, but seizing the hand of the old man, I cried, 'Now is the time! Save and protect me! You and your family are the friends whom I seek. Do not you desert me in the hour of trial!'

36 "'Great God!' exclaimed the old man. 'Who are you?'

6. **hitherto** *adv.* until now.

37 "At that instant the cottage door was opened, and Felix, Safie, and Agatha entered. Who can describe their horror and **consternation** on beholding me? Agatha fainted, and Safie, unable to attend to her friend, rushed out of the cottage. Felix darted forward, and with supernatural force tore me from his father, to whose knees I clung, in a transport of fury, he dashed me to the ground and struck me violently with a stick. I could have torn him limb from limb, as the lion rends the antelope. But my heart sank within me as with bitter sickness, and I refrained. I saw him on the point of repeating his blow, when, overcome by pain and anguish, I quitted the cottage, and in the general tumult escaped unperceived to my hovel."

NOTES

**consternation** (kon stuhr NAY shuhn) *n.* sudden feeling of intense confusion; dismay

* * *

## Chapter 17

38 The being finished speaking and fixed his looks upon me in the expectation of a reply. But I was bewildered, perplexed, and unable to arrange my ideas sufficiently to understand the full extent of his proposition. He continued,

39 "You must create a female for me with whom I can live in the interchange of those sympathies necessary for my being. This you alone can do, and I demand it of you as a right which you must not refuse to concede."

40 The latter part of his tale had kindled anew in me the anger that had died away while he narrated his peaceful life among the cottagers, and as he said this I could no longer suppress the rage that burned within me.

41 "I do refuse it," I replied; "and no torture shall ever extort a consent from me. You may render me the most miserable of men, but you shall never make me base in my own eyes. Shall I create another like yourself, whose joint wickedness might desolate the world. Begone! I have answered you; you may torture me, but I will never consent."

42 "You are in the wrong," replied the fiend; "and instead of threatening, I am content to reason with you. I am **malicious** because I am miserable. Am I not shunned and hated by all mankind? You, my creator, would tear me to pieces and triumph; remember that, and tell me why I should pity man more than he pities me? You would not call it murder if you could precipitate me into one of those ice-rifts and destroy my frame, the work of your own hands. Shall I respect man when he condemns me? Let him live with me in the interchange of kindness, and instead of injury I would bestow every benefit upon him with tears of gratitude at his acceptance. But

### CLOSE READ

**ANNOTATE:** In paragraphs 41 and 42, mark details that relate to Victor Frankenstein's strong emotions. Mark other details that relate to the monster's logical reasoning.

**QUESTION:** Why does Shelley present Dr. Frankenstein as angry and emotional and the monster as reasoned and logical?

**CONCLUDE:** In what ways do these contrasts affect the reader's sympathies for one character or the other?

**malicious** (muh LIHSH uhs) *adj.* intending to do harm; evil

NOTES

**CLOSE READ**

**ANNOTATE:** In paragraph 44, mark the highlights of the Creature's plan for his future.

**QUESTION:** Why does the Creature think that his plan will end his misery?

**CONCLUDE:** Is the Creature deluding himself in thinking that he can escape from his own unhappiness?

that cannot be; the human senses are insurmountable barriers to our union. Yet mine shall not be the submission of abject slavery. I will revenge my injuries; if I cannot inspire love, I will cause fear, and chiefly towards you my archenemy, because my creator, do I swear inextinguishable hatred. Have a care; I will work at your destruction, nor finish until I desolate your heart, so that you shall curse the hour of your birth."

43 A fiendish rage animated him as he said this; his face was wrinkled into contortions too horrible for human eyes to behold; but presently he calmed himself and proceeded—

44 "I intended to reason. This passion is detrimental[7] to me, for you do not reflect that YOU are the cause of its excess. If any being felt emotions of benevolence towards me, I should return them a hundred and a hundredfold; for that one creature's sake I would make peace with the whole kind! But I now indulge in dreams of bliss that cannot be realized. What I ask of you is reasonable and moderate; I demand a creature of another sex, but as hideous as myself; the gratification is small, but it is all that I can receive, and it shall content me. It is true, we shall be monsters, cut off from all the world; but on that account we shall be more attached to one another. Our lives will not be happy, but they will be harmless and free from the misery I now feel. Oh! My creator, make me happy; let me feel gratitude towards you for one benefit! Let me see that I excite the sympathy of some existing thing; do not deny me my request!"

45 I was moved. I shuddered when I thought of the possible consequences of my consent, but I felt that there was some justice in his argument. His tale and the feelings he now expressed proved him to be a creature of fine sensations, and did I not as his maker owe him all the portion of happiness that it was in my power to bestow? He saw my change of feeling and continued,

46 "If you consent, neither you nor any other human being shall ever see us again; I will go to the vast wilds of South America. My food is not that of man; I do not destroy the lamb and the kid to glut my appetite; acorns and berries afford me sufficient nourishment. My companion will be of the same nature as myself and will be content with the same fare. We shall make our bed of dried leaves; the sun will shine on us as on man and will ripen our food. The picture I present to you is peaceful and human, and you must feel that you could deny it only in the wantonness of power and cruelty. Pitiless as you have been towards me, I now see compassion in your eyes; let me seize the favorable moment and persuade you to promise what I so ardently desire. "

47 "You propose," replied I, "to fly from the habitations of man, to dwell in those wilds where the beasts of the field will be your only companions. How can you, who long for the love and sympathy of man, persevere in this exile? You will return and again seek their kindness, and you will meet with their detestation; your evil passions

7. **detrimental** *adj.* harmful.

will be renewed, and you will then have a companion to aid you in the task of destruction. This may not be; cease to argue the point, for I cannot consent."

NOTES

48 "How inconstant are your feelings! But a moment ago you were moved by my representations, and why do you again harden yourself to my complaints? I swear to you, by the earth which I inhabit, and by you that made me, that with the companion you bestow I will quit the neighborhood of man and dwell, as it may chance, in the most savage of places. My evil passions will have fled, for I shall meet with sympathy! My life will flow quietly away, and in my dying moments I shall not curse my maker."

49 His words had a strange effect upon me. I compassionated him and sometimes felt a wish to console him, but when I looked upon him, when I saw the filthy mass that moved and talked, my heart sickened and my feelings were altered to those of horror and hatred. I tried to stifle these sensations; I thought that as I could not sympathize with him, I had no right to withhold from him the small portion of happiness which was yet in my power to bestow.

50 "You swear," I said, "to be harmless; but have you not already shown a degree of malice that should reasonably make me distrust you? May not even this be a feint[8] that will increase your triumph by affording a wider scope for your revenge?"

51 "How is this? I must not be trifled with, and I demand an answer. If I have no ties and no affections, hatred and vice must be my portion; the love of another will destroy the cause of my crimes, and I shall become a thing of whose existence everyone will be ignorant. My vices are the children of a forced solitude that I abhor, and my virtues will necessarily arise when I live in communion with an equal. I shall feel the affections of a sensitive being and become linked to the chain of existence and events from which I am now excluded."

52 I paused some time to reflect on all he had related and the various arguments which he had employed. I thought of the promise of virtues which he had displayed on the opening of his existence and the subsequent blight of all kindly feeling by the loathing and scorn which his protectors had manifested towards him. His power and threats were not omitted in my calculations; a creature who could exist in the ice caves of the glaciers and hide himself from pursuit among the ridges of inaccessible precipices was a being possessing faculties it would be vain to cope with. After a long pause of reflection I concluded that the justice due both to him and my fellow creatures demanded of me that I should comply with his request. Turning to him, therefore, I said, "I consent to your demand, on your solemn oath to quit Europe forever, and every other place in the neighborhood of man, as soon as I shall deliver into your hands a female who will accompany you in your exile."

8. **feint** (faynt) *n.* trick.

NOTES

**CLOSE READ**

**ANNOTATE:** In paragraphs 55 and 56, mark details that relate to the physical setting.

**QUESTION:** Why does the author provide this view of the scene through Victor's eyes?

**CONCLUDE:** What does this scene add to the reader's understanding of Victor's character?

53 "I swear," he cried, "by the sun, and by the blue sky of heaven, and by the fire of love that burns my heart, that if you grant my prayer, while they exist you shall never behold me again. Depart to your home and commence your labors; I shall watch their progress with unutterable anxiety; and fear not but that when you are ready I shall appear."

54 Saying this, he suddenly quitted me, fearful, perhaps, of any change in my sentiments. I saw him descend the mountain with greater speed than the flight of an eagle, and quickly lost among the undulations of the sea of ice.

55 His tale had occupied the whole day, and the sun was upon the verge of the horizon when he departed. I knew that I ought to hasten my descent towards the valley, as I should soon be encompassed in darkness, but my heart was heavy; my steps, slow. The labor of winding among the little paths of the mountain and fixing my feet firmly as I advanced perplexed me, occupied as I was by the emotions which the occurrences of the day had produced. Night was far advanced when I came to the halfway resting-place and seated myself beside the fountain. The stars shone at intervals as the clouds passed from over them; the dark pines rose before me, and every here and there a broken tree lay on the ground; it was a scene of wonderful solemnity and stirred strange thoughts within me. I wept bitterly, and clasping my hands in agony, I exclaimed, "Oh! Stars and clouds and winds, ye are all about to mock me; if ye really pity me, crush sensation and memory; let me become as nought; but if not, depart, depart, and leave me in darkness."

56 These were wild and miserable thoughts, but I cannot describe to you how the eternal twinkling of the stars weighed upon me and how I listened to every blast of wind as if it were a dull ugly siroc[9] on its way to consume me.

57 Morning dawned before I arrived at the village of Chamounix; I took no rest, but returned immediately to Geneva. Even in my own heart I could give no expression to my sensations—they weighed on me with a mountain's weight and their excess destroyed my agony beneath them. Thus I returned home, and entering the house, presented myself to the family. My haggard and wild appearance awoke intense alarm, but I answered no question, scarcely did I speak. I felt as if I were placed under a ban—as if I had no right to claim their sympathies—as if never more might I enjoy companionship with them. Yet even thus I loved them to adoration; and to save them, I resolved to dedicate myself to my most abhorred task. The prospect of such an occupation made every other circumstance of existence pass before me like a dream, and that thought only had to me the reality of life. ❧

9. **siroc** (suh ROK) *n.* hot, oppressive, dusty wind.

## Comprehension Check

**Complete the following items after you finish your first read.**

1. What does the Creature find in the pocket of a dress (lab coat) that he had taken from his creator's laboratory?

2. In his plan to gain favor with the cottagers, whom does the Creature intend to approach first, and under what conditions?

3. What is the response of the younger cottagers when they find the Creature in the cottage?

4. What demand does the Creature make in Chapter 17?

5. What does the Creature plan to do once his demand has been met?

6. **Notebook** Write a summary of this excerpt from *Frankenstein* to confirm your understanding of the text.

## RESEARCH

**Research to Explore** Shelley's *Frankenstein* touches on scientific, philosophical, and political ideas that were becoming increasingly important in both Europe and the United States during the 1800s. Find and read a copy of the Declaration of Independence, paying close attention to the opening lines of the Preamble. Then, consider similarities and differences between ideas the monster expresses in his plea to the doctor in Chapter 17 of *Frankenstein* and those the authors of the Declaration express in the Preamble. You may wish to share your observations with the class.

from FRANKENSTEIN

## Close Read the Text

1. This model, from paragraph 25 of the text, shows two sample annotations, along with questions and conclusions. Close read the passage, and find another detail to annotate. Then, write a question and your conclusion.

ANNOTATE · QUESTION · Close Read · CONCLUDE

**ANNOTATE:** The Creature describes himself in this passage.

**QUESTION:** What is interesting about his word choice?

**CONCLUDE:** The Creature is modest, using words such as *good* (instead of *great*) and "in some degree."

"'. . . unfortunately, they are prejudiced against me. I have good dispositions; my life has been hitherto harmless and in some degree beneficial; but a fatal prejudice clouds their eyes, and where they ought to see a feeling and kind friend, they behold only a detestable monster.'"

**ANNOTATE:** These are highly charged, negative terms.

**QUESTION:** Why does the Creature use such strong language?

**CONCLUDE:** These terms reflect the intensity of his suffering and anger.

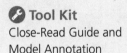

**Tool Kit**
Close-Read Guide and Model Annotation

2. For more practice, go back into the text, and complete the close-read notes.

3. Revisit a section of the text you found important during your first read. Read this section closely, and **annotate** what you notice. Ask yourself **questions** such as "Why did the author make this choice?" What can you **conclude**?

## Analyze the Text

**CITE TEXTUAL EVIDENCE** to support your answers.

**Notebook** Respond to these questions.

1. **Analyze** The Creature says that he is the most solitary being on Earth. What evidence does he cite to support this claim?

2. **(a)** How does Victor initially respond to the Creature's request for a companion? **(b) Evaluate** Is Victor's initial response fair? Explain.

3. **Evaluate** What are the strengths and weaknesses in the Creature's argument for a female companion? Explain.

4. **Historical Perspectives** Shelley published *Frankenstein* at a time when the Industrial Revolution was underway and modern medicine was beginning to change lives. In what way is *Frankenstein* a commentary on those scientific revolutions?

5. **Essential Question:** *How do we define ourselves?* What have you learned about the nature of the self from reading this text?

**STANDARDS**

**Reading Literature**
Analyze how an author's choices concerning how to structure specific parts of a text contribute to its overall structure and meaning as well as its aesthetic impact.

**Language**
Demonstrate understanding of figurative language, word relationships, and nuances in word meanings.

## Analyze Craft and Structure

**Literary Movement: Gothic Literature** *Frankenstein* is an example of **Gothic literature,** a style that grew popular during the Romantic period of the late eighteenth and early nineteenth centuries. Romanticism was a rejection of two central beliefs of the earlier Enlightenment period—that the ability to reason was the most important human trait, and that the world could be explained through reason. Romantic authors pushed literature in the opposite direction, emphasizing intense feeling and imagination over reason. Gothic literature extended the Romantic impulse into the darkest recesses of the human psyche by using the following elements:

- emphasis on imagination, freedom, and intense emotion—as opposed to reason, order, and restraint
- supernatural events that defy logic, including ghosts and monsters
- multiple narrators, plot lines, and themes within a single work
- dark, gloomy settings such as old castles, ruins, or wild natural locations
- cheerless, tormented characters
- mystery and terror as ways to provoke deeply emotional responses

Gothic writers produced many short stories and even poetry. However, Gothic style found its most successful expression in the **novel,** or book-length narrative.

### Practice

**CITE TEXTUAL EVIDENCE** to support your answers.

Notebook **Respond to these questions.**

1. (a) What supernatural characters and events does Shelley present in *Frankenstein*? (b) What ideas about life or human nature does Shelley explore with her use of the supernatural?
2. Record additional Gothic elements from the novel *Frankenstein* in the chart.

| GOTHIC ELEMENT | EXAMPLE IN FRANKENSTEIN |
|---|---|
| **Gloomy Settings** | |
| **Tormented Characters** | |
| **Intense Emotion** | |

3. In what ways are human reason and emotion at war with each other in each of the two chapters from *Frankenstein*?
4. Why do you think the Gothic style is still popular today in books and movies?

from FRANKENSTEIN

## Concept Vocabulary

| hideous | odious | despair |
|---|---|---|
| dread | consternation | malicious |

**Why These Words?** These concept words help to show the extreme sense of fear and gloom that the characters in *Frankenstein* feel. The monster describes himself as *hideous* and *odious*, two terms that vividly show his self-image. Both words go beyond the idea of being unattractive, conveying a sense of repulsion and disgust.

1. How do the concept vocabulary words heighten the mood of the story?

2. What other words in the selection connect to this concept?

WORD NETWORK

Add interesting words related to self-discovery from the text to your Word Network.

### Practice

Notebook **Respond to these questions.**

1. Under what conditions might a person *despair*?
2. Explain the difference between two dogs—one that is *malicious* and one that is not.
3. What is something you might find in the refrigerator that you would call *odious*?
4. Name a character in a story, movie, television show, or video game that you would describe as *hideous*.
5. When might you experience a sense of *dread* about an upcoming event?
6. When watching your team play an important game, what kind of event would bring on a sense of *consternation*?

## Word Study

**Latin Root: *-mal-*** The Latin root *-mal-*, which appears in the concept vocabulary word *malicious,* means "bad" or "evil." When it is used as a prefix, it may carry that same meaning, or it may mean "poorly" or "wrongly," as in *malformed*, meaning "poorly formed."

1. Write a definition of the word *malodorous* based on your understanding of the Latin root *-mal-*. Check your answer in a print or online college-level dictionary.

2. Identify and define two other words that have the root *-mal-*. Use a print or online college-level dictionary to check your work.

STANDARDS

**Language**

- Demonstrate command of the conventions of standard English grammar and usage when writing or speaking.
- Demonstrate command of the conventions of standard English capitalization, punctuation, and spelling when writing.
- Consult general and specialized reference materials both print and digital, to find the pronunciation of a word or determine or clarify its precise meaning, its part of speech, its etymology, or its standard usage.
- Verify the preliminary determination of the meaning of a word or phrase.

# Conventions and Style

**Commas in Elliptical Sentences** An **elliptical sentence** is a sentence in which a word or words that are understood are omitted. Writers may use elliptical sentences to mimic speech or to emphasize the close connection between adjacent, parallel phrases or clauses.

When punctuating an elliptical sentence in which a verb or verb phrase has been omitted, replace the understood word or words with a comma.

This chart shows examples of punctuation in elliptical sentences. The underlined words have been omitted and replaced with commas, but they are still understood.

| ORIGINAL SENTENCE | ELLIPTICAL SENTENCE |
|---|---|
| The Creature speaks loudly, and Victor <u>speaks</u> softly. | The Creature speaks loudly; Victor, softly. |
| Safie leaves the cottage immediately, and Agatha <u>leaves the cottage</u> soon after. | Safie leaves the cottage immediately; Agatha, soon after. |
| Plutarch's *Lives* excites in the Creature emotions that are moderate, but Milton's *Paradise Lost* <u>excites in the Creature emotions that are</u> far deeper. | Plutarch's *Lives* excites in the Creature emotions that are moderate; Milton's *Paradise Lost*, far deeper. |

Notice that, in each case, the ideas in the two clauses are closely related. Writing the sentence elliptically emphasizes the connection between the ideas. At the same time, it creates a rhythm that mimics natural speech.

## Read It

1. Read each of these elliptical sentences from the excerpt from *Frankenstein*. Mark the comma that indicates an omission. Write the word or words that are understood.
   a. In the *Sorrows of Werter*, . . . so many opinions are canvased; so many lights, thrown upon what had hitherto been to me obscure subjects. . . .
   b. My person was hideous; my stature, gigantic.
   c. I knew that I ought to hasten my descent towards the valley, as I should soon be encompassed in darkness, but my heart was heavy; my steps, slow.
2. **Connect to Style** Choose one of the elliptical sentences in item 1. Identify which sentence you have chosen. In your own words, explain the effect of the elliptical construction.

## Write It

**Notebook** Write a paragraph about *Frankenstein* in which you use at least one elliptical sentence.

*from* FRANKENSTEIN

## Writing to Sources

It is hard to read Shelley's *Frankenstein* without feeling sympathy for the Creature. One might want to ask: Is the monster the one who hungers for acceptance and friendship? Or is the real monster the one who withholds it?

### Assignment

Write a **personal narrative** in which you describe events that led to your achieving insight on your own identity or self-awareness of your place in the world. Connect the story you recount to the experiences of Frankenstein's creature. Include the following elements in your narrative:

- a description of the people involved and background information to engage and orient the reader
- a logical, clear sequence of events
- dialogue that reveals thoughts and perceptions
- connections between the experiences described and those of Frankenstein's creature

**Vocabulary and Conventions Connection** You may want to use some of the concept vocabulary words in your narrative. Try to include at least one elliptical sentence.

| hideous | odious | despair |
|---|---|---|
| dread | consternation | malicious |

## Reflect on Your Writing

After you have drafted your personal narrative, answer the following questions.

1. How did writing your own narrative change your understanding of the Creature in *Frankenstein*?

2. How could you revise your narrative to make it more effective?

3. **Why These Words?** The words you choose make a difference in your writing. Which words did you specifically choose to add power or clarity to your personal narrative?

STANDARDS

Writing

- Write narratives to develop real or imagined experiences or events using effective technique, well-chosen details, and well-structured event sequences.
- Engage and orient the reader by setting out a problem, situation, or observation, establishing one or multiple point(s) of view, and introducing a narrator and/or characters; create a smooth progression of experiences or events.
- Use narrative techniques, such as dialogue, pacing, description, reflection, and multiple plot lines, to develop experiences, events, and/or characters.

# Speaking and Listening

**Assignment**

*Frankenstein* has been adapted for movies, plays, graphic novels, and other formats. Create a **research presentation** that surveys the range of *Frankenstein* adaptations. Focus on three adaptations that you find appealing. Include digital media from each.

1. **Choose Your Adaptations** Use an Internet search to locate multiple adaptations of *Frankenstein*. Choose three very different versions of the story. Make sure at least one of your adaptations is a film, video, or television show. Include the following in your presentation:
   - the author, title, and date of each adaptation
   - a summary of each adaptation and a consideration of how it compares with Shelley's original in plot, characters, and format
   - digital media, such as photos, video clips, or audio
2. **Prepare Your Presentation** Pull together your information using presentation software or a combination of charts and media players. Practice your presentation before you present it to the class, using the evaluation guide as a reference.
3. **Present and Discuss** After you and your classmates have given your presentations, engage in a discussion. Compare the different versions of *Frankenstein* that classmates presented. Then, discuss questions such as:
   - What made each adaptation of *Frankenstein* special or different?
   - Which adaptation did the best job of enhancing the original meaning of *Frankenstein* or showing the story in a new light?
   - How did seeing all these adaptations of *Frankenstein* change your view of the original story?
4. **Evaluate the Presentation** Use a presentation evaluation guide like the one shown to analyze the presentations of your classmates.

PRESENTATION EVALUATION GUIDE

Rate each statement on a scale of 1 (not demonstrated) to 4 (demonstrated).

☐ The speaker presented the material clearly and in a logical sequence.

☐ The digital media material presented was appropriate and enhanced the meaning of the presentation.

☐ The speaker maintained good eye contact with the audience and used gestures and body language effectively.

☐ The speaker's tone and pace were appropriate and effective.

EVIDENCE LOG

Before moving on to a new selection, go to your Evidence Log and record what you learned from the excerpt from *Frankenstein*.

STANDARDS

Speaking and Listening

- Initiate and participate effectively in a range of collaborative discussions with diverse partners on *grades 11–12 topics, texts, and issues*, building on others' ideas and expressing their own clearly and persuasively.
- Integrate multiple sources of information presented in diverse formats and media in order to make informed decisions and solve problems, evaluating the credibility and accuracy of each source and noting any discrepancies among the data.
- Make strategic use of digital media in presentations to enhance understanding of findings, reasoning, and evidence and to add interest.

WRITING TO SOURCES

- LINES COMPOSED A FEW MILES ABOVE TINTERN ABBEY
- *from* THE PRELUDE
- ODE TO A NIGHTINGALE
- ODE TO THE WEST WIND
- *from* FRANKENSTEIN

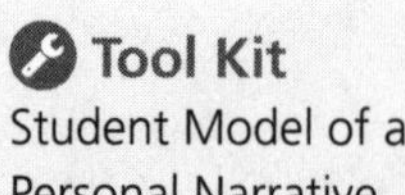

**Tool Kit**
Student Model of a Personal Narrative

ACADEMIC VOCABULARY

As you craft your narrative, consider using some of the academic vocabulary you learned in the beginning of the unit.

**inanimate**
**infuse**
**anachronism**
**repercussion**
**revelation**

STANDARDS

Writing

- Write narratives to develop real or imagined experiences or events using effective technique, well-chosen details, and well-structured event sequences.
- Write routinely over extended time frames and shorter time frames for a range of tasks, purposes, and audiences.

# Write a Personal Narrative

You have just read several poems and two excerpts from the novel *Frankenstein*. In the poems, the speakers relate experiences in which nature or world events contribute to their shifting senses of self. In the excerpts from *Frankenstein*, the Creature gains a sense of self but then grapples with that new understanding in the face of harsh rejection.

## Assignment

Use your knowledge of the poems and *Frankenstein* to explore your ideas about the self as an individual, in nature, or in society. Write a brief **personal narrative** that addresses this question:

**How does the world around us contribute to our sense of self?**

Write about a time you came to the realization that the world around us plays a role in shaping people's identities. Explain what lesson can be learned when a person loses and then finds himself or herself. Connect your ideas to specific examples from the poems and *Frankenstein*.

## Elements of Personal Narrative

A **personal narrative** tells a real story from the writer's life. As opposed to longer works, such as autobiographies or memoirs, personal narratives focus on just a few events.

Effective personal narratives often contain these elements:

- interesting people, with the main focus on the writer
- a setting with scenes and incidents in specific locations and concrete details, such as sights, sounds, and smells
- a sequence of events that clearly build on one another to create a coherent story
- conflict between people or between a person and another force
- a conclusion that reflects on an experience and the insights gained from it
- correct spelling and grammar, and accurate use of punctuation

**Model Personal Narrative** For a model of a well-crafted personal narrative, see the Launch Text, "Early Dismissal." Review the Launch Text for examples of the elements described above. You will look more closely at these elements as you prepare to write your own personal narrative.

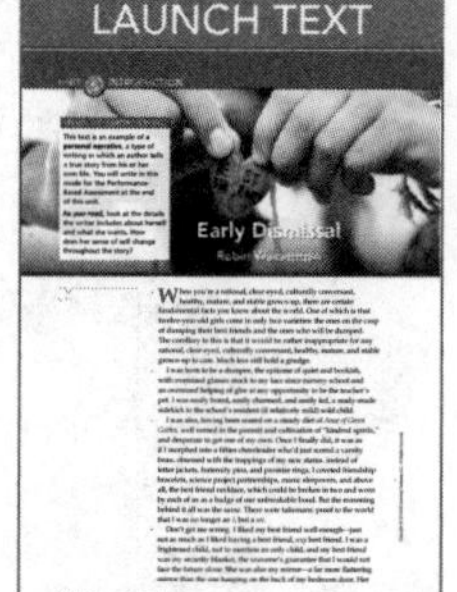

# Prewriting / Planning

## Choosing Your Topic

To choose a topic for your personal narrative, use one of these strategies:

- **Freewriting** Spend five minutes writing about experiences in your life that helped you understand something about yourself. Jot down as many ideas as you can. Then, look for connections between the people and places in the key events, and examine how they affected your sense of self.
- **Using Sentence Starters** Complete these sentences to generate ideas:
  - I learned something new about myself when ______________________________.
  - Under pressure, I ______________________________.
  - I found myself for the first time / again when ______________________________.
- **Narrowing Your Topic** Make your topic more specific by focusing on the one key point you want to convey. Narrow a general topic to focus on one key event that helps you to make that point.

| GENERAL TOPIC | NARROWED TOPIC | INSIGHT |
|---|---|---|
| camping with family in the woods | Camping was uncomfortable, and I was uneasy. | I thought I would be an outdoor adventurer, but I really like the comforts of home. |
| | | |

**Gather Details** The assignment asks you to share an incident from your own life and use that incident to illustrate how the world around us affects our sense of self. You need to support your ideas with details. To gather details, consider:

- discussing the event with those who shared it with you
- looking at diary entries, photographs, or video footage that relate to that incident or time period
- brainstorming detailed words and phrases that describe the people, places, and events.

**Connect Across Texts** The prompt asks you to connect your ideas to the poems in this unit and the excerpts from *Frankenstein*. Think about how an old abbey, a nightingale, and the west wind each affect the speakers of the poems. Think also about how living near the family affects the Creature in *Frankenstein*. Locate examples that show how the world around each of the speakers or characters affected his sense of self. Then, connect these examples to your own insights about how the world around you has affected your sense of self.

EVIDENCE LOG

Review your Evidence Log and identify key details you might want to cite in your personal narrative.

STANDARDS

**Writing**

- Engage and orient the reader by setting out a problem, situation, or observation and its significance, establishing one or multiple point(s) of view, and introducing a narrator and/or characters; create a smooth progression of experiences or events.
- Use precise words and phrases, telling details, and sensory language to convey a vivid picture of the experiences, events, setting, and/or characters.

## Drafting

Once you have chosen and narrowed your topic and thought about connections to the selections, it is time to start writing. Remember that you want to sequence events and ideas so that they create a unified whole, including a conclusion that flows naturally from the narrative. In this case, you will construct your narrative so that it shows how you gained a new appreciation or understanding of yourself.

**Shape Your Writing** As you start to write, it may be helpful to first jot down events and insights in the order in which they occurred. After you have written the highlights of the story, think about the best way to grab your readers' attention in the introduction.

| OPENING STRATEGY | EXAMPLE |
|---|---|
| **Introduce an Idea:** In the Launch Text, the author explains the topic of her essay in an engaging way. | *When you're a rational, clear-eyed, culturally conversant, healthy, mature, and stable grown-up, there are certain fundamental facts you know about the world. One of which is that twelve-year-old girls come in only two varieties: the ones on the cusp of dumping their best friends and the ones who will be dumped.* |
| **Introduce an Important Person:** Try opening with a description of an important person. | *Amelia seemed like the shyest girl on the playground, but when I noticed her smirking as she listened to our friends' conversation, I began to wonder what she was really thinking.* |
| **Focus on Setting:** Highlight the time and place. | *The first thing I noticed about our new apartment was the grime on the windowsills. The second thing was the smell—like old books that were rotting.* |
| **Begin With Dialogue:** Grab readers' attention with a line of dialogue. | *"Gabriel, didn't you hear me? I told you not to go in the woods alone!"* |

**Highlight the Conflict** Concentrate on descriptions and events that help you to sharpen the conflict.

**Flat:** I really liked having a best friend, someone I came first with.

**Vivid:** "Her very existence was evidence that I couldn't possibly be *that* ugly, *that* awkward, *that* unlovable, because she was perfect, and she not only loved me, but loved me *best.*" –"Early Dismissal"

**Provide a Conclusion** In the last part of your narrative, explain what you learned from the events you have described. Summarize your insights and connect them to broader ideas about how the world contributes to one's sense of self.

**Write a First Draft** Use your introduction, sequence of events, and conclusion to write your first draft. Make sure to introduce the topic and build the sequence of events so that they create a compelling whole. Explain your insights in the second half of your narrative, and provide a conclusion that reflects on the rest of the narrative.

STANDARDS

Writing

- Engage and orient the reader by setting out a problem, situation, or observation and its significance, establishing one or multiple point(s) of view, and introducing a narrator and/or characters; create a smooth progression of experiences or events.
- Use narrative techniques, such as dialogue, pacing, description, reflection, and multiple plot lines, to develop experiences, events, and/or characters.
- Use a variety of techniques to sequence events so that they build on one another to create a coherent whole and build toward a particular tone and outcome.
- Provide a conclusion that follows from and reflects on what is experienced, observed, or resolved over the course of the narrative.

LANGUAGE DEVELOPMENT: CONVENTIONS

# Spell Correctly

If you want readers to take your writing seriously, you need to take spelling seriously. Spelling errors can distract your readers from what you are saying or cause them to take your ideas less seriously. Pay particular attention in your writing to spelling rules that apply to words with prefixes or suffixes.

Review these spelling rules.

**Spelling With Prefixes** When a prefix is added to a base word, the spelling of the base remains the same.

un- + usual = unusual    over- + react = overreact

With some prefixes, the spelling of the prefix changes when joined to the base to make the pronunciation easier.

in- + mortal = immortal    com- + found = confound

**Spelling With Suffixes** When adding a suffix to a base word ending in *y* preceded by a consonant, change *y* to *i* unless the suffix begins with *i*.

defy + -ant = defiant    petty + ness = pettiness

try + -ing = trying    terrify + -ing = terrifying

For a base word ending in *e*, drop the *e* when adding a suffix beginning with a vowel.

move + -ing = moving    seize + -ure = seizure

SOME EXCEPTIONS: mileage, seeing, changeable

For a base word ending with a consonant + vowel + consonant in a stressed syllable, double the final consonant when adding a suffix that begins with a vowel.

trim + -er = trimmer    admit + -ed = admitted

SOME EXCEPTIONS: fixing, throwing, playable

TIP

**CLARIFICATION**
Although the spell-check function of most writing software will catch many spelling errors, it will miss commonly confused words such as *complement* and *compliment*. Read your draft carefully, and check a dictionary or usage guide for words that may be misused.

## Read It

Correct the misspellings in these sentences, and identify the rule you applied.

1. Our chess team had beginer's luck.
2. Her happyness made me happy, too.
3. Proveing that I was reliable was not easy.

## Write It

After you draft your essay, make sure words are spelled correctly. Focus on words with prefixes or suffixes, and make sure you are using the correct spelling. If you are unsure of the spelling of any word, consult a print or online college-level dictionary.

STANDARDS

**Language**
- Demonstrate command of the conventions of standard English capitalization, punctuation, and spelling when writing.
- Spell correctly.

## MAKING WRITING SOPHISTICATED

**Using Details** In order to bring your story to life, you should include **precise details**, details about characters and places that are especially revealing. The details should be specific and well chosen so that they help readers understand even more about the characters and places. Authors use details to help readers infer information about people and characters, rather than stating characteristics outright.

### Read It

This excerpt from the Launch Text shows how the use of precise and vivid details enlivens a narrative.

The author reveals that she got ideas about friendship from a classic children's book, allowing the reader to infer that she knows more about books than relationships.

The details list a fairly typical set of things that would interest a 12-year-old girl. The reader can infer that, like the 1950s cheerleader she contrasts herself with, the author wants mementos of affection to show the world.

LAUNCH TEXT

I was also, having been reared on a steady diet of *Anne of Green Gables*, well versed in the pursuit and cultivation of "kindred spirits," and desperate to get one of my own. Once I finally did, it was as if I morphed into a fifties cheerleader who'd just scored a varsity beau, obsessed with the trappings of my new status. Instead of letter jackets, fraternity pins, and promise rings, I coveted friendship bracelets, science project partnerships, manic sleepovers, and above all, the best friend necklace, which could be broken in two and worn by each of us as a badge of our unbreakable bond. But the reasoning behind it was all the same. These were talismans: proof to the world that I was no longer an *I*, but a *we*.

**Use Sensory Language** Good authors also use **sensory language,** words that appeal to the five senses, to help the reader better imagine the story. Notice how the following passage from the Launch Text appeals to readers' senses of sight and sound with the two underlined groups of words:

> *So you can imagine my surprise that sixth-grade day in the playground when, lurking in corners as I was wont to do, I overheard her casually tell some new group of admirers that, no, I wasn't her best friend, why would anyone ever think that?*

STANDARDS

**Writing**
Use precise words and phrases, telling details, and sensory language to convey a vivid picture of the experiences, events, setting, and/or characters.

College and Career Readiness

## Write It

Use a graphic organizer like this one to jot down details about a person, place, or event you describe in your personal narrative. Create a web for each person, place, or event that you feel needs additional detail.

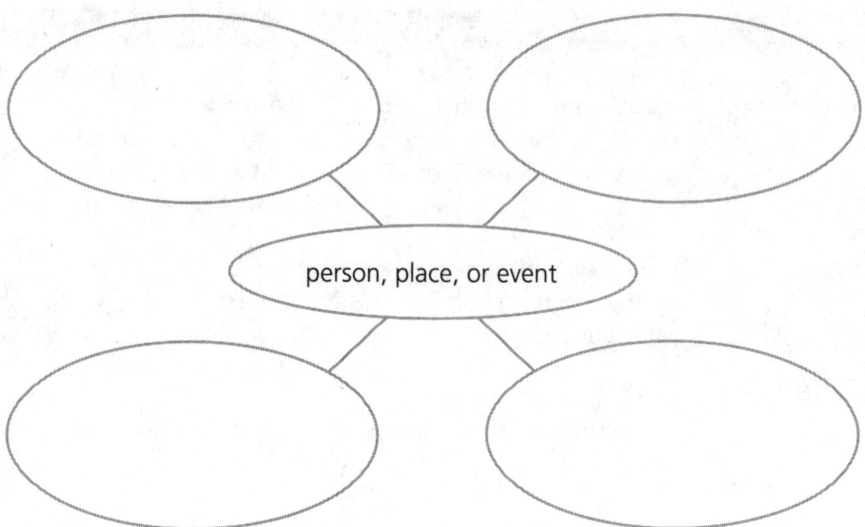


- Read over your draft, and consider where you might strengthen your writing by adding a telling detail or sensory language. Record your ideas here.

| PARAGRAPH | PERSON, PLACE, OR EVENT | NEW TELLING DETAIL |
|---|---|---|
| | | |
| | | |
| | | |
| | | |

You might find that some of the details you have listed above do not work in the context of the narrative. Discard them. When you add details, think about the effect that each will have on the reader. Ask yourself: Will this detail strengthen the reader's impression of this person or setting? Does the reader need to know this information to understand my ideas? Avoid adding unimportant details. They will distract readers and make your overall point harder to comprehend.

# Revising

## Evaluating Your Draft

Use the following checklist to evaluate the effectiveness of your first draft. Then, use your evaluation and the instruction on this page to guide your revision.

**WORD NETWORK**

Include interesting words from your Word Network in your personal narrative.

| FOCUS AND ORGANIZATION | DETAILS AND ELABORATION | CONVENTIONS |
| --- | --- | --- |
| ☐ Provides an engaging introduction<br>☐ Describes key people in the narrative<br>☐ Relates a problem or conflict<br>☐ Creates a smooth progression of events<br>☐ Concludes with a reflection on the significance of events | ☐ Includes precise details and sensory language to create a vivid picture of events and people<br>☐ Includes narrative elements such as dialogue and reflection<br>☐ Uses language that is appropriate for the audience and purpose | ☐ Attends to the norms and conventions of the discipline, especially correct spelling |

## Revising for Focus and Organization

**Progression of Events** Reread your narrative, paying attention to how the ideas and events are organized.

- Ask yourself: Is the conflict clear? Does each element build on what has come before? Where are there gaps that could confuse the reader? If the answer to any of these questions is no, add details about conflict, add details that flesh out the plot, or provide transitions to indicate causes and effects.

## Revising for Details and Elaboration

**Details** Sensory language brings the reader into your story. Have you provided sensory language that helps the reader see, hear, and feel the events? Using an ink or digital highlighter, go through your draft and mark words that appeal to the five senses. Then, decide if you need to add sensory details to more fully bring your story to life.

**Reflection** In your personal narrative, you are trying to make a point about how a person's sense of self is affected by the world around him or her.

- Ask yourself: Have you tied your ideas to the selections in the unit? Have you connected the experiences in your narrative to the larger theme of how the world affects each person's sense of self? If the answer to either question is no, take time to add details and explanations as needed.

**STANDARDS**

**Writing**

- Engage and orient the reader by setting out a problem, situation, or observation and its significance, establishing one or multiple point(s) of view, and introducing a narrator and/or characters; create a smooth progression of experiences or events.
- Use narrative techniques, such as dialogue, pacing, description, reflection, and multiple plot lines, to develop experiences, events, and/or characters.
- Use a variety of techniques to sequence events so that they build on one another to create a coherent whole and build toward a particular tone and outcome.
- Use precise words and phrases, telling details, and sensory language to convey a vivid picture of the experiences, events, setting, and/or characters.
- Provide a conclusion that follows from and reflects on what is experienced, observed, or resolved over the course of the narrative.

PEER REVIEW

Exchange papers with a classmate. Use the checklist to evaluate your classmate's narrative and provide supportive feedback.

1. Is the introduction engaging and clear?

   ☐ yes ☐ no If no, explain how the opening could be clearer or more interesting.

2. Do the events build on each other to form a coherent whole?

   ☐ yes ☐ no If no, what about the sequence did not work?

3. Does the author include thoughts, feelings, and reflections connecting the experience to larger ideas about the self and to the texts?

   ☐ yes ☐ no If no, write a brief note explaining what you thought was missing.

4. What is the strongest part of your classmate's narrative? Why?

## Editing and Proofreading

**Edit for Conventions** Reread your draft for accuracy and consistency. Correct errors in grammar and word usage. Check your narrative to make sure you spelled words with prefixes or suffixes correctly.

**Proofread for Accuracy** Read your draft carefully, looking for errors in spelling and punctuation. Double-check the capitalization of names and places. Common nouns name general categories and are lowercase. Proper nouns name specific people, places, or things and are capitalized.

## Publishing and Presenting

Create a final version of your narrative. If you feel comfortable sharing it, get together with a partner and reach each other's work. Discuss ways in which each narrative provides insight on how the world affects the development of personal identity.

## Reflecting

Think about what you learned while writing your narrative. What techniques did you learn that you could use when writing another nonfiction narrative? Would you change anything about how you present details about people and events? For example, you might write more about how the incident in your life ties to broader ideas of how the wider world affects our sense of self.

STANDARDS

**Writing**

Develop and strengthen writing as needed by planning, revising, editing, rewriting, or trying a new approach, focusing on addressing what is most significant for a specific purpose and audience.

**Language**

- Demonstrate command of the conventions of standard English grammar and usage when writing or speaking.
- Demonstrate command of the conventions of standard English capitalization, punctuation, and spelling when writing.
- Spell correctly.

ESSENTIAL QUESTION:

# How do we define ourselves?

To what extent is one's sense of self connected to memory and to the stories we tell about our lives? In this section, you will read selections that explore the connections between memory and selfhood. Then, you will work in a group to continue your exploration of selfhood.

## Small-Group Learning Strategies

Throughout your life, in school, in your community, and in your career, you will continue to develop strategies when you work in teams. Use these strategies during Small-Group Learning. Add ideas of your own for each step.

| STRATEGY | ACTION PLAN |
|---|---|
| Prepare | • Complete your assignments so that you are prepared for group work.<br>• Organize your thinking so you can contribute to your group's discussions.<br>• |
| Participate fully | • Make eye contact to signal that you are listening and taking in what is being said.<br>• Use text evidence when making a point.<br>• |
| Support others | • Build off ideas from others in your group.<br>• State the relationship of your ideas to those of others—for example, note whether you are supporting someone's idea, refuting it, or taking the discussion in a new direction.<br>• |
| Clarify | • Paraphrase the ideas of others to ensure that your understanding is correct.<br>• Ask follow-up questions.<br>• |

CONTENTS

## Working as a Team

1. **Take a Position** In your group, discuss the following question:

   What are some ways in which we can discover who we really are?

   As you take turns sharing your ideas, provide reasons that support them. After all group members have shared, discuss the process of recognizing your strengths and weaknesses, identifying your values, and setting your goals.

2. **List Your Rules** As a group, decide on the rules that you will follow as you work together. Samples are provided; add two more of your own. You may add or revise rules based on your experience together.
   - Everyone should participate in group discussions.
   - People should not interrupt.
   - ______________________________
   - ______________________________

3. **Apply the Rules** Practice working as a group. Share what you have learned about definitions of selfhood. Make sure each person in the group contributes. Take notes, and be prepared to share with the class one thing that you heard from another member of your group.

4. **Name Your Group** Choose a name that reflects the unit topic.

   Our group's name: ______________________________

5. **Create a Communication Plan** Decide how you want to communicate with one another. For example, you might use online collaboration tools, email, or instant messaging.

   Our group's decision: ______________________________

## Making a Schedule

First, find out the due dates for the Small-Group activities. Then, preview the texts and activities with your group, and make a schedule for completing the tasks.

| SELECTION | ACTIVITIES | DUE DATE |
|---|---|---|
| *from* Mrs. Dalloway | | |
| Apostrophe to the Ocean<br>The World Is Too Much With Us<br>London, 1802 | | |
| The Madeleine | | |
| The Most Forgetful Man in the World | | |
| When Memories Never Fade, the Past Can Poison the Present | | |

## Working on Group Projects

As your group works together, you'll find it more effective if each person has a specific role. Different projects require different roles. Before beginning a project, discuss the necessary roles and choose one for each group member. Here are some possible roles; add your own ideas.

**Project Manager:** monitors the schedule and keeps everyone on task
**Researcher:** organizes research activities
**Recorder:** takes notes during group meetings

About the Author

**Virginia Woolf** (1882–1941) was born into a wealthy and highly cultured household in London and spent much of her childhood immersed in books and learning. In her early twenties, she joined the Bloomsbury Group, a scholarly circle of writers and critics, many of whom went on to become major literary figures. It was in this group that she met the writer Leonard Woolf, her future husband. For much of her life, Woolf alternated between great bursts of creativity and bouts of intense depression. Her output included several essays seen as landmarks in feminist thought, as well as many groundbreaking novels told in her signature stream-of-consciousness style.

STANDARDS

**Reading Literature**

- By the end of grade 12, read and comprehend literature, including stories, dramas, and poems, at the high end of the grades 11–CCR text complexity band independently and proficiently.

**Language**

- Determine or clarify the meaning of unknown and multiple-meaning words and phrases based on *grades 11–12 reading and content*, choosing flexibly from a range of strategies.
- Identify and correctly use patterns of word changes that indicate different meanings or parts of speech.

# *from* Mrs. Dalloway

## Concept Vocabulary

You will encounter the following words as you read this excerpt from *Mrs. Dalloway.*

| solemnity | leaden | dejected |
|---|---|---|

**Familiar Word Parts** Separating a word into its parts can often help you identify its meaning. Those parts might include familiar base words, roots, prefixes, or suffixes.

**Base Words:** Look for the part of the word that contains the basic meaning. For example, you might break the word *unconditional* into *un-* + *condition* + *-al.* Being familiar with the word *condition* helps you to understand the meaning of *unconditional.*

**Suffixes:** The suffix *-al* in *unconditional* appears in words such as *natural, physical,* and *practical* and means "referring to" or "characterized by." Note that *condition* on its own is a noun, but when the prefix *-al* is attached, it becomes an adjective.

**Prefixes:** The prefix *un-* in *unconditional* means "not." You can apply the meaning of this prefix to the adjective *conditional.*

Apply your knowledge of familiar word parts and other vocabulary strategies to determine the meanings of unfamiliar words you encounter during your first read.

## First Read FICTION

Apply these strategies as you conduct your first read. You will have an opportunity to complete the close-read notes after your first read.

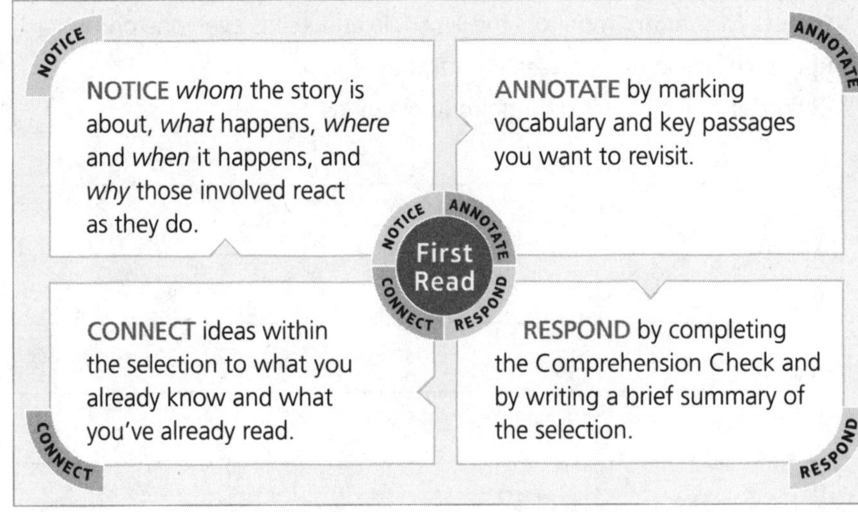
NOTICE
NOTICE *whom* the story is about, *what* happens, *where* and *when* it happens, and *why* those involved react as they do.
ANNOTATE
ANNOTATE by marking vocabulary and key passages you want to revisit.
First Read
CONNECT
CONNECT ideas within the selection to what you already know and what you've already read.
RESPOND
RESPOND by completing the Comprehension Check and by writing a brief summary of the selection.

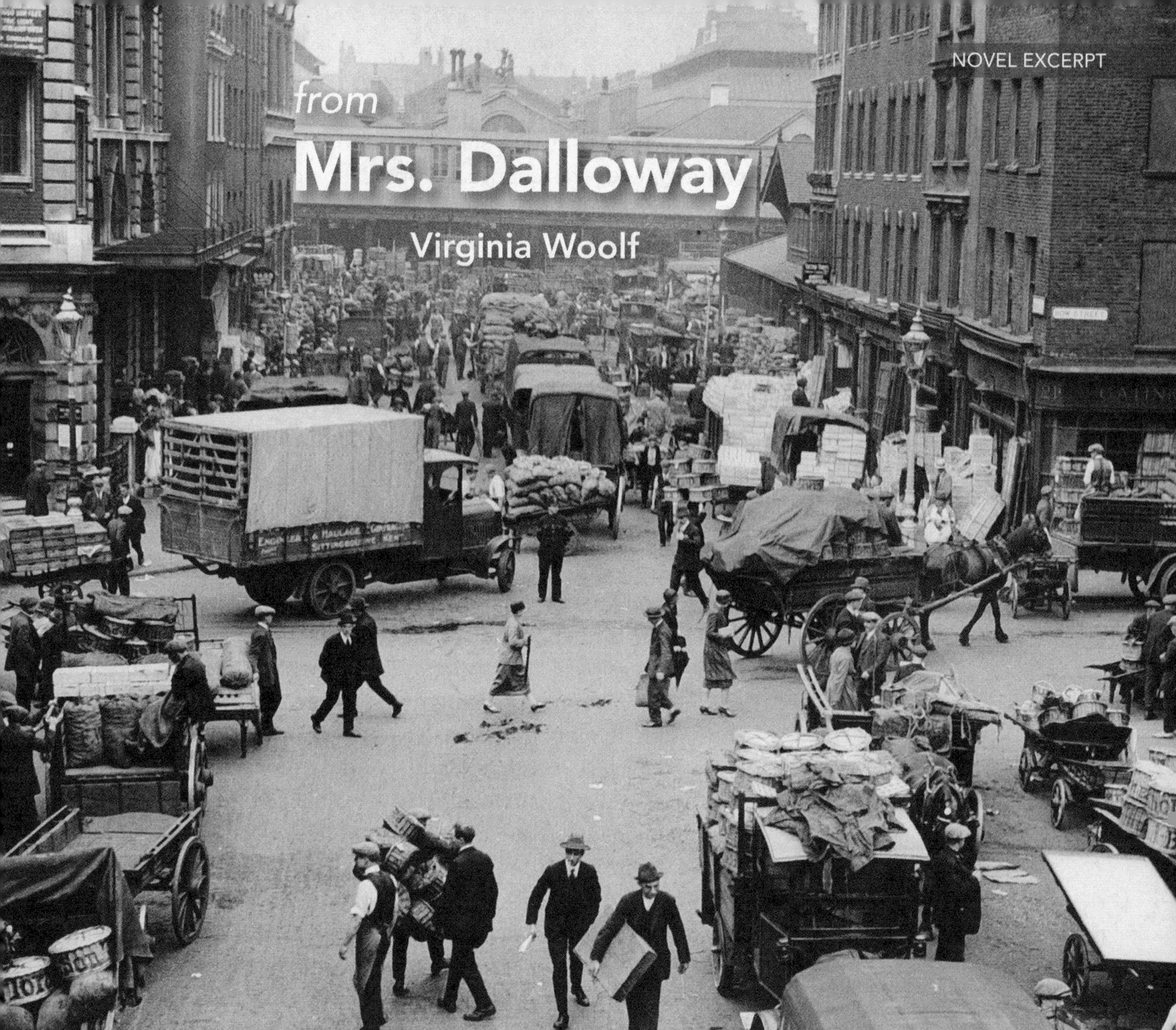

*from*

# Mrs. Dalloway

## Virginia Woolf

### BACKGROUND

*Mrs. Dalloway* depicts a single day in the lives of two people in London, England, in 1923. It frequently switches from the point of view of Clarissa Dalloway, a woman who spends the day preparing for a party, and Septimus Smith, a World War I veteran who suffers from mental illness. This excerpt is the opening scene of the book and is told from Mrs. Dalloway's perspective.

NOTES

1 Mrs. Dalloway said she would buy the flowers herself. For Lucy had her work cut out for her. The doors would be taken off their hinges; Rumpelmayer's men were coming. And then, thought Clarissa Dalloway, what a morning—fresh as if issued to children on a beach.

2 What a lark! What a plunge! For so it had always seemed to her, when, with a little squeak of the hinges, which she could hear now, she had burst open the French windows and plunged at Bourton into the open air. How fresh, how calm, stiller than this of course, the air was in the early morning; like the flap of a wave; the kiss of a wave; chill and sharp and yet (for a girl of eighteen as she then was)

NOTES

solemn, feeling as she did, standing there at the open window, that something awful was about to happen; looking at the flowers, at the trees with the smoke winding off them and the rooks[1] rising, falling; standing and looking until Peter Walsh said, "Musing among the vegetables?"—was that it?—"I prefer men to cauliflowers"—was that it? He must have said it at breakfast one morning when she had gone out on to the terrace—Peter Walsh. He would be back from India one of these days, June or July, she forgot which, for his letters were awfully dull; it was his sayings one remembered: his eyes, his pocket-knife, his smile, his grumpiness and, when millions of things had utterly vanished—how strange it was!—a few sayings like this about cabbages.

3 She stiffened a little on the kerb,[2] waiting for Durtnall's van to pass. A charming woman, Scrope Purvis thought her (knowing her as one does know people who live next door to one in Westminster); a touch of the bird about her, of the jay, blue-green, light, vivacious, though she was over fifty, and grown very white since her illness. There she perched, never seeing him, waiting to cross, very upright.

Mark familiar word parts or indicate another strategy you used that helped you determine meaning.

**solemnity** (suh LEHM nuh tee) *n.*

MEANING:

**leaden** (LEHD uhn) *adj.*

MEANING:

**dejected** (dih JEHK tihd) *adj.*

MEANING:

4 For having lived in Westminster—how many years now? over twenty.—one feels even in the midst of the traffic, or waking at night, Clarissa was positive, a particular hush, or **solemnity**; an indescribable pause; a suspense (but that might be her heart, affected, they said, by influenza) before Big Ben[3] strikes. There! Out it boomed. First a warning, musical; then the hour, irrevocable. The **leaden** circles dissolved in the air. Such fools we are, she thought, crossing Victoria Street. For Heaven only knows why one loves it so, how one sees it so, making it up, building it round one, tumbling it, creating it every moment afresh; but the veriest frumps,[4] the most **dejected** of miseries sitting on doorsteps (drink their downfall) do the same; can't be dealt with, she felt positive, by Acts of Parliament for that very reason: they love life. In people's eyes, in the swing, tramp, and trudge; in the bellow and the uproar; the carriages, motor cars, omnibuses,[5] vans, sandwich men shuffling and swinging; brass bands; barrel organs; in the triumph and the jingle and the strange high singing of some aeroplane overhead was what she loved; life; London; this moment of June. ❧

1. **rooks** crows.
2. **kerb** curb.
3. **Big Ben** tall clock tower that is one of London's most well-known landmarks.
4. **veriest frumps** most plain, unfashionable women.
5. **omnibuses** buses.

## Comprehension Check

**Complete the following items after you finish your first read. Review and clarify details with your group.**

1. What kind of day is it, and what is Mrs. Dalloway doing?

2. About whom does Mrs. Dalloway reminisce, and where is that person now?

3. What type of creature does Scrope Purvis think Mrs. Dalloway is like?

4. According to Mrs. Dalloway, what is it that all people do, even the "veriest frumps" among us?

5. What are Mrs. Dalloway's thoughts and mood as the scene ends?

6. **Notebook** Write a summary of this excerpt from *Mrs. Dalloway* to confirm your understanding of the text.

### RESEARCH

**Research to Clarify** Choose at least one unfamiliar detail from the text. Briefly research that detail. In what way does the information you learned shed light on an aspect of the story?

**Research to Explore** Research the Bloomsbury Group, the literary circle of which Virginia Woolf was a part. You may want to share your findings with your group.

*from* MRS. DALLOWAY

## Close Read the Text

With your group, revisit sections of the text you marked during your first read. **Annotate** details that you notice. What **questions** do you have? What can you **conclude**?

## Analyze the Text

**CITE TEXTUAL EVIDENCE** to support your answers.

**Notebook** Complete the activities.

1. **Review and Clarify** With your group, reread paragraph 2, and discuss Mrs. Dalloway's thoughts about Peter Walsh. What kinds of details does she remember? What do these comments suggest about the ability of one person to understand another?

2. **Present and Discuss** Now, work with your group to share the passages from the text that you found especially important. Take turns presenting your passages. Discuss what details you noticed, what questions you asked, and what conclusions you reached.

3. **Essential Question:** ***How do we define ourselves?*** What has this excerpt from *Mrs. Dalloway* taught you about how people define themselves? Discuss with your group.

LANGUAGE DEVELOPMENT

## Concept Vocabulary

| solemnity | leaden | dejected |
|---|---|---|

**Why These Words?** The three concept vocabulary words are related. With your group, determine what the words have in common. Write your ideas, and add another word that fits the category.

### Practice

**Notebook** Use each concept vocabulary word in a sentence about Woolf's word choice.

## Word Study

**Notebook** **Anglo-Saxon Suffix: *-en*** The Anglo-Saxon suffix *-en*, which appears in *leaden*, can have the literal meaning "made of." This suffix was used quite commonly in the past to form adjectives from nouns, but only a handful of those adjectives are still in use today. Moreover, those that do survive are more often used in a figurative, rather than literal, sense. Write the literal and figurative meanings of these words ending in *-en*: *leaden*, *wooden*, *brazen*. Consult a dictionary as needed.

**WORD NETWORK**

Add interesting words related to self-discovery from the text to your Word Network.

**STANDARDS**

**Reading Literature**

- Analyze the impact of the author's choices regarding how to develop and relate elements of a story or drama.
- Analyze how an author's choices concerning how to structure specific parts of a text contribute to its overall structure and meaning as well as its aesthetic impact.

**Language**

Identify and correctly use patterns of word changes that indicate different meanings or parts of speech.

# Analyze Craft and Structure

**Author's Choices: Modernist Structures Modernism** is an early-twentieth-century movement in all the arts that began as a means of expressing the sense of disillusionment that arose after the horrors of World War I. For Modernist writers, seamless narratives in which conflicts were fully resolved no longer represented reality. Instead, Modernists sought to reflect a painful, new understanding of a world that seemed disjointed and senseless. Modernist writers invented a variety of approaches, including the following, in an effort to express what it felt like to be alive in the twentieth century.

- **Stream-of-consciousness narration** is a technique that presents a spontaneous flow of seemingly random thoughts, feelings, and images as though they are coming directly from a character's mind. Transitional words and phrases are often omitted. Instead of being arranged in chronological order, the narration follows the character's branching currents of thought as they might naturally occur—a flow dictated by free association rather than conventional logic.
- **Nonlinear narratives** do not follow time order. They may contain flashbacks, dream sequences, or other devices that interrupt the chronological order of events.
- Modernist authors are interested in the **psychologies** of characters, the unconscious motivations for their choices. They explore how a character's unique experiences contribute to a separate, often alienated, sense of self.

In *Mrs. Dalloway,* Virginia Woolf, one of the key figures of the Modernist movement, uses these techniques to tell the story of Clarissa Dalloway as she goes about a single day.

Keep in mind that members of your group might have different impressions of Woolf's choices than you do. There's no right impression or conclusion, but talking out differing opinions and the reasons for them will help you clarify your thoughts and learn from one another.

## Practice

**CITE TEXTUAL EVIDENCE** to support your answers.

Work on your own to trace Modernist elements in the excerpt from *Mrs. Dalloway.* Then, discuss your observations with your group.

| MODERNIST TECHNIQUE | EXAMPLES |
|---|---|
| Stream-of-Consciousness Narration | |
| Nonlinear Structure | |
| Psychological Content | |

*from* MRS. DALLOWAY

## Conventions and Style

**Using Dashes for Effect** Writers may use a **dash (—)** to create a particular effect or to clarify the logical relationships among ideas. This chart shows several common uses for dashes.

| DASH USE | EXAMPLE |
|---|---|
| to indicate an abrupt change of thought | *"Jaime, answer your phone before I—never mind; the caller hung up."* |
| to set off a dramatic interrupting idea | *Idris took a deep breath—he was terrified of heights—and climbed the ladder.* |
| to indicate an unfinished thought | *Mrs. Wu had all she needed, and yet—* |
| to set off a list | *Miranda packed everything she needed for her trip—clothes, books, and her camera.* |
| to set off an appositive or modifier that is long or already punctuated | *Evanston—a small city just north of Chicago, Illinois—is known as a quiet place.* |
| to set off parenthetical material that is long or already punctuated | *The protagonist—whom most readers don't like but root for anyway—will likely solve the case at the end of the novel.* |

### Read It

1. Work individually. Read these sentences from *Mrs. Dalloway*. Identify the function of each dash.

   a. And then, thought Clarissa Dalloway, what a morning—fresh as if issued to children on a beach.

   b. He would be back from India one of these days, June or July, she forgot which, for his letters were awfully dull; it was his sayings one remembered: his eyes, his pocket-knife, his smile, his grumpiness and, when millions of things had utterly vanished—how strange it was!—a few sayings like this about cabbages.

2. **Connect to Style** What is the relationship between Woolf's use of dashes and stream-of-consciousness narration? Does Woolf's use of dashes enhance her narrative? Discuss your ideas with your group.

### Write It

**Notebook** Write a brief narrative about your day. Use stream-of-consciousness narration, and incorporate dashes to set off thoughts and ideas.

STANDARDS

**Language**

- Demonstrate command of the conventions of standard English capitalization, punctuation, and spelling when writing.
- Apply knowledge of language to understand how language functions in different contexts, to make effective choices for meaning or style, and to comprehend more fully when reading or listening.

# Speaking and Listening

**Assignment**

Create an **oral presentation** in response to this statement:

> In *Mrs. Dalloway*, Virginia Woolf chooses to emphasize the psychological lives, or subjective realities, of her characters rather than plot or action. In so doing, Woolf creates a nuanced, deep, and thoroughly modern portrayal of her characters.

Choose from one of the following options:

- ☐ Hold a **panel discussion.** Focus your discussion on the following question: *How does Woolf show the subjective reality of Clarissa Dalloway?* Work as a group to develop additional questions and answers relating to this key idea.
- ☐ Stage a **debate.** Divide into two teams and debate the following question: *Do you agree that Woolf's approach to the novel is "nuanced, deep, and thoroughly modern"?* Use textual evidence and your understanding of Modernism to support your points.
- ☐ Present a **response to literature**. Draft and present a formal response to the following question: *When compared to a more linear approach to character development, what are the advantages of Woolf's choices?* Work as a team to develop a response, and divide key points among group members.

**Panel Discussion Plan** Begin by assigning roles. Choose who will serve as a moderator, and who will participate as panelists. Work together to come up with discussion questions, and then work individually to find textual evidence and develop answers.

**Debate Plan** Divide the group evenly into two teams. One team will argue in support of the statement, and the other will argue against. Work in teams to find evidence to support your key points and to anticipate and prepare responses to the other team's counterarguments. Remember to defend your team's position, even if it is contrary to your personal opinion.

**Response to Literature Plan** A **response to literature** is a type of critical writing. Work as a team to develop a strong claim and to find details and examples from the text to support it. Develop an outline, and then assign a topic or paragraph to each group member. Assign presentation roles, and allow time to rehearse.

As each group gives its presentation, evaluate the clarity of ideas, logic, use of evidence, overall effectiveness. Rate each group on a scale of 1–4, with 4 being highly successful and 1 being less successful. Then, explain the reasons for your rating.

EVIDENCE LOG

Before moving on to a new selection, go to your Evidence Log and record what you learned from this excerpt from *Mrs. Dalloway.*

STANDARDS

**Speaking and Listening**

- Initiate and participate effectively in a range of collaborative discussions with diverse partners on grades 11–12 topics, texts, and issues, building on others' ideas and expressing their own clearly and persuasively.
- Come to discussions prepared, having read and researched material under study; explicitly draw on that preparation by referring to evidence from texts and other research on the topic or issue to stimulate a thoughtful, well-reasoned exchange of ideas.
- Work with peers to promote civil, democratic discussions and decision-making, set clear goals and deadlines, and establish individual roles as needed.

POETRY COLLECTION 3

# Apostrophe to the Ocean

# The World Is Too Much With Us

# London, 1802

## Concept Vocabulary

As you perform your first read of these three poems, you will encounter the following words.

| torrid | sordid | stagnant |
|---|---|---|

**Context Clues** If certain words are unfamiliar to you, try using **context clues**—other words and phrases that appear in a text—to help you determine their meanings. There are various types of context clues that you may encounter as you read.

**Definition:** The ballerina *pirouetted*, or whirled on the tips of her toes, as she danced.

**Synonym:** We listened to the music in *rapture*; I experienced pure bliss.

**Antonym:** Although the commentator's remarks sounded factual, they were later shown to be *erroneous*.

Apply your knowledge of context clues and other vocabulary strategies to determine the meanings of unfamiliar words you encounter during your first read.

## First Read POETRY

Apply these strategies as you conduct your first read. You will have an opportunity to complete a close read after your first read.

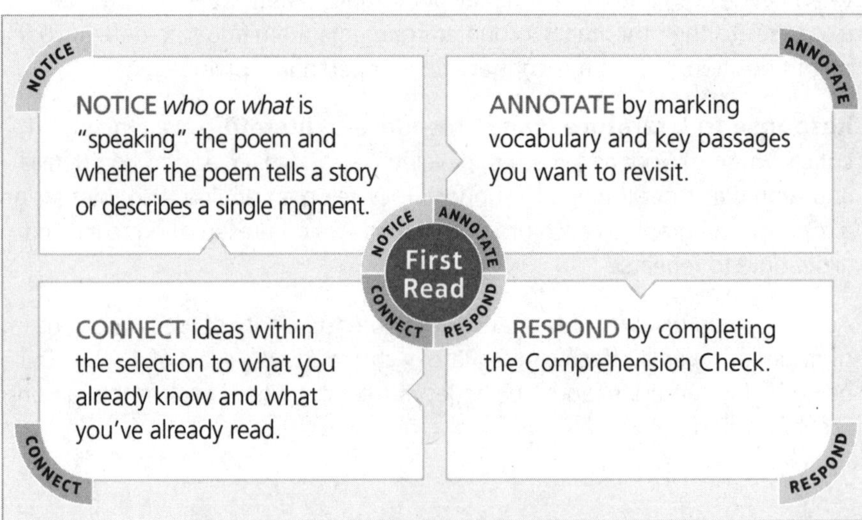
NOTICE
NOTICE *who* or *what* is "speaking" the poem and whether the poem tells a story or describes a single moment.
ANNOTATE
ANNOTATE by marking vocabulary and key passages you want to revisit.
First Read
CONNECT
CONNECT ideas within the selection to what you already know and what you've already read.
RESPOND
RESPOND by completing the Comprehension Check.

### STANDARDS

**Reading Literature**
By the end of grade 12, read and comprehend literature, including stories, dramas, and poems, at the high end of the grades 11–CCR text complexity band independently and proficiently.

**Language**
Determine or clarify the meaning of unknown and multiple-meaning words and phrases based on *grades 11–12 reading and content*, choosing flexibly from a range of strategies.

## About the Poets

**George Gordon, Lord Byron** (1788–1824) was one of the key figures among the English Romantic poets. He also wrote dramas and extensive letters. His poetry was very popular both within and outside of England, although critics often attacked it on moral grounds. Byron greatly influenced later generations of writers, as well as painters and composers. His dashing appearance and nonliterary exploits also added to his popular appeal. In one of his most famous nonliterary feats, Byron swam the tricky currents of the Hellespont, a roughly three-mile stretch of ocean that separates Europe from Asia in modern-day Turkey.

**William Wordsworth** (1770–1850), regarded by many scholars as the Father of English Romanticism, aimed to capture the voice of "the common man" in his poetry. His thinking was deeply influenced by his friend and colleague Samuel Taylor Coleridge, another critical figure in the Romantic movement. Together they wrote *Lyrical Ballads,* which is a landmark in the history of English Romanticism. Wordsworth's work was immensely popular in his lifetime and has remained so ever since. *To learn more about Wordsworth, see the biography that accompanies Poetry Collection 1 earlier in this unit.*

## Backgrounds

### Apostrophe to the Ocean

One of Byron's best-known works is *Childe Harold's Pilgrimage,* a long poem describing the travels and thoughts of Childe Harold, a pilgrim and outcast. The poem was extremely popular. "Apostrophe to the Ocean" is an excerpt from *Childe Harold's Pilgrimage*.

### The World Is Too Much With Us

"The World Is Too Much With Us" was written around 1802 and published in 1807 in *Poems, in Two Volumes*. Its form is that of the Petrarchan, or Italian, sonnet, composed of 14 lines. In that form, the last six lines (the sestet) "answer" the first eight lines (the octave).

### London, 1802

"London, 1802" was also published in 1807 in *Poems, in Two Volumes*. Wordsworth later wrote that the poem was "written immediately after my return from France and London, when I could not but be struck . . . with the vanity and parade of our own country . . . as contrasted with the quiet . . . in France." Wordsworth's contemporaries wrote bad reviews of the collection; Byron wrote that "Mr. W[ordsworth] ceases to please." Nevertheless, it contains some of the poet's best-known and most cherished work.

# Apostrophe to the Ocean

## *from* Childe Harold's Pilgrimage

George Gordon, Lord Byron

NOTES

There is a pleasure in the pathless woods,
There is a rapture on the lonely shore,
There is society, where none intrudes,
By the deep sea, and music in its roar;
I love not man the less, but nature more,
From these our interviews, in which I steal
From all I may be, or have been before,
To mingle with the universe, and feel
What I can ne'er express, yet cannot all conceal.

Roll on, thou deep and dark blue ocean—roll!
Ten thousand fleets sweep over thee in vain;
Man marks the earth with ruin—his control
Stops with the shore; upon the watery plain
The wrecks are all thy deed, nor doth remain
A shadow of man's ravage, save[1] his own,
When, for a moment, like a drop of rain,
He sinks into thy depths with bubbling groan,
Without a grave, unknelled, uncoffined, and unknown.

His steps are not upon thy paths—thy fields
Are not a spoil for him—thou dost arise
And shake him from thee; the vile strength he wields
For earth's destruction thou dost all despise,
Spurning him from thy bosom to the skies,
And send'st him, shivering in thy playful spray
And howling, to his gods, where haply[2] lies

1. **save** except.
2. **haply** perhaps.

His petty hope in some near port or bay,
And dashest him again to earth—there let him lay.[3]

The armaments which thunderstrike the walls
Of rock-built cities, bidding nations quake,
And monarchs tremble in their capitals,
The oak leviathans,[4] whose huge ribs make
Their clay creator[5] the vain title take
Of lord of thee, and arbiter of war—
These are thy toys, and, as the snowy flake,
They melt into thy yeast of waves, which mar
Alike the Armada's[6] pride or spoils of Trafalgar.[7]

Thy shores are empires, changed in all save thee—
Assyria, Greece, Rome, Carthage, what are they?
Thy waters washed them power while they were free,
And many a tyrant since; their shores obey
The stranger, slave, or savage: their decay
Has dried up realms to deserts—not so thou,
Unchangeable, save to thy wild waves' play.
Time writes no wrinkle on thine azure brow;
Such as creation's dawn beheld, thou rollest now.

Thou glorious mirror, where the Almighty's form
Glasses[8] itself in tempests: in all time,
Calm or convulsed—in breeze, or gale, or storm,
Icing the pole, or in the **torrid** clime
Dark-heaving—boundless, endless, and sublime;
The image of eternity, the throne
Of the Invisible; even from out thy slime
The monsters of the deep are made: each zone
Obeys thee; thou goest forth, dread, fathomless,[9] alone.

And I have loved thee, ocean! and my joy
Of youthful sports was on thy breast to be
Borne, like thy bubbles, onward; from a boy
I wantoned with thy breakers—they to me
Were a delight: and if the freshening sea
Made them a terror—'twas a pleasing fear,
For I was as it were a child of thee,
And trusted to thy billows far and near,
And laid my hand upon thy mane—as I do here.

3. **lay** A note on Byron's proof suggests that he intentionally made this grammatical error for the sake of the rhyme.
4. **leviathans** (luh VY uh thuhnz) originally, monstrous sea creatures, described in the Old Testament. Here the speaker is referring to "giant ships."
5. **clay creator** human beings.
6. **Armada's** refers to the Spanish Armada, defeated by the English in 1588.
7. **Trafalgar** battle in 1805 during which the French and Spanish fleets were defeated by the British fleet led by Lord Nelson.
8. **Glasses** mirrors.
9. **fathomless** (FATH uhm lihs) *adj.* too deep to be measured or understood.

NOTES

Mark context clues or indicate another strategy you used that helped you determine meaning.

**torrid** (TAWR ihd) *adj.*

MEANING:

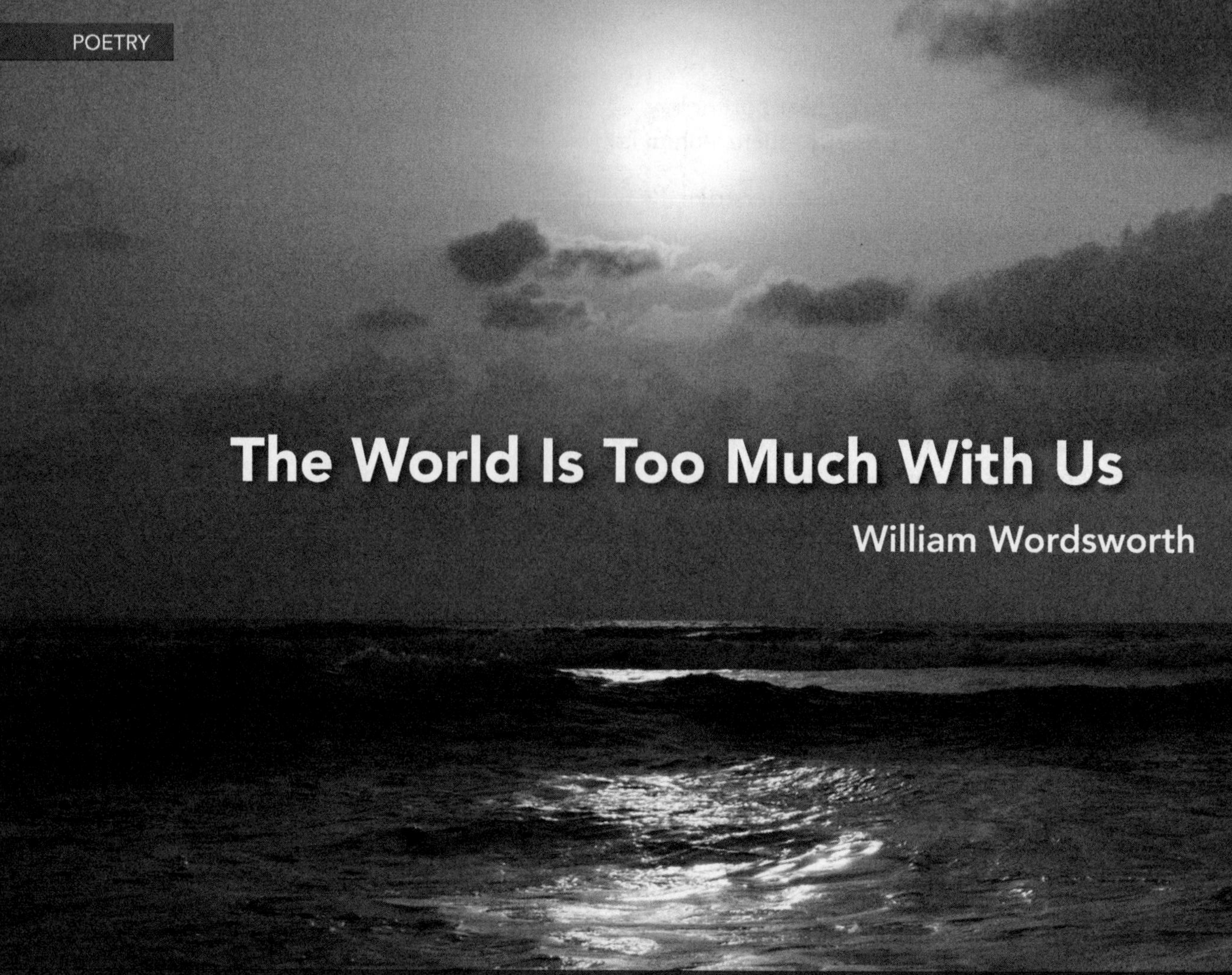

# The World Is Too Much With Us

William Wordsworth

NOTES

Mark context clues or indicate another strategy you used that helped you determine meaning.

**sordid** (SAWR dihd) *adj.*

MEANING:

The world is too much with us; late and soon,
Getting and spending, we lay waste our powers:
Little we see in Nature that is ours;
We have given our hearts away, a **sordid** boon![1]
This Sea that bares her bosom to the moon;
The winds that will be howling at all hours,
And are upgathered now like sleeping flowers;
For this, for everything, we are out of tune;
It moves us not.—Great God! I'd rather be
A Pagan suckled in a creed outworn;
So might I, standing on this pleasant lea,[2]
Have glimpses that would make me less forlorn;
Have sight of Proteus[3] rising from the sea;
Or hear old Triton[4] blow his wreathèd horn.

1. **boon** favor.
2. **lea** (lee) *n.* meadow.
3. **Proteus** (PROH tee uhs) in Greek mythology, a sea god who could change his appearance at will.
4. **Triton** in Greek mythology, a sea god with the head and upper body of a man and the tail of a fish.

# London, 1802

## William Wordsworth

Milton![1] thou should'st be living at this hour:
England hath need of thee: she is a fen[2]
Of **stagnant** waters: altar, sword, and pen,
Fireside, the heroic wealth of hall and bower,
Have forfeited their ancient English dower
Of inward happiness. We are selfish men;
Oh! raise us up, return to us again;
And give us manners, virtue, freedom, power.
Thy soul was like a Star, and dwelt apart:
Thou hadst a voice whose sound was like the sea:
Pure as the naked heavens, majestic, free,
So didst thou travel on life's common way,
In cheerful godliness; and yet thy heart
The lowliest duties on herself did lay.

NOTES

Mark context clues or indicate another strategy you used that helped you determine meaning.

**stagnant** (STAG nuhnt) *adj.*

MEANING:

1. **Milton** seventeenth-century English poet John Milton.
2. **fen** *n.* area of low, flat, marshy land.

## Comprehension Check

**Complete the following items after you finish your first read. Review and clarify details with your group.**

APOSTROPHE TO THE OCEAN

1. Whom or what does the speaker address in this poem?

2. According to the speaker, how is humankind's relationship with the ocean different from its relationship with the land?

3. What does the speaker say his relationship was with the ocean when he was a boy?

THE WORLD IS TOO MUCH WITH US

1. What activities cause people to exhaust their "powers"?

2. With what does the speaker say "we are out of tune"?

3. According to the speaker, what mythological figures would be visible in a "Pagan" era?

LONDON, 1802

1. Whom or what does the speaker address in this poem?

2. According to the speaker, what has contemporary England forfeited, or given up?

3. To what does the speaker compare Milton's voice?

## RESEARCH

**Research to Clarify** Choose at least one unfamiliar detail from one of the poems. Briefly research that detail. In what way does the information you learned shed light on an aspect of the poem?

**Research to Explore** Choose something that interested you from the poems, and perform brief research to learn more. For example, you may want to research the life of Lord Byron or discover more about London in the year 1802. Share your findings with your group.

POETRY COLLECTION 3

## Close Read the Text

With your group, revisit sections of the text you marked during your first read. **Annotate** details that you notice. What **questions** do you have? What can you **conclude**?

## Analyze the Text

**CITE TEXTUAL EVIDENCE** to support your answers.

**Notebook** Complete the activities.

1. **Review and Clarify** With your group, reread "The World Is Too Much With Us." What does the speaker mean when he says, "For this, for everything, we are out of tune"? What does this line suggest about humans' relationship with nature?

2. **Present and Discuss** Now, work with your group to share the passages from the poems that you found especially important. Take turns presenting your passages. Discuss what details you noticed, what questions you asked, and what conclusions you reached.

3. **Essential Question:** ***How do we define ourselves?*** What have these poems taught you about how people define themselves? Discuss with your group.

**TIP**

**GROUP DISCUSSION**
Keep in mind that poetry can often be interpreted on multiple levels. First, think about the literal meanings of the words and phrases the speakers use. Then, consider any figurative or connotative meanings.

LANGUAGE DEVELOPMENT

## Concept Vocabulary

**torrid** **sordid** **stagnant**

**Why These Words?** The three concept vocabulary words are related. With your group, determine what the words have in common. Write your ideas, and add another word that fits the category.

### Practice

**Notebook** Look up each word in a print or online college-level dictionary. Then, paraphrase each definition in your own words.

**WORD NETWORK**
Add interesting words related to self-discovery from the text to your Word Network.

## Word Study

**Notebook** **Cognates** When words share a common origin, they are called **cognates**. Often, their spellings and pronunciations have drifted apart over time, but their meanings remain related. For example, the word *motherly*, from Old English, and the word *maternal*, from Latin, are cognates. The source from which they derive is ancient, yet their meanings are still closely related.

The concept vocabulary word *torrid* comes from the Latin word *torridus*, meaning "dried with heat." Using your knowledge of cognates, infer whether *torrid* is cognate with the word *thirsty* or with the word *torment*. Explain your inference. Finally, use an etymological dictionary to verify your response.

**STANDARDS**

**Language**
- Determine or clarify the meaning of unknown and multiple-meaning words and phrases based on *grades 11–12 reading and content*, choosing flexibly from a range of strategies.
- Consult general and specialized reference materials, both print and digital, to find the pronunciation of a word or determine or clarify its precise meaning, its part of speech, its etymology, or its standard usage.
- Demonstrate understanding of figurative language, word relationships, and nuances in word meanings.

# Analyze Craft and Structure

**Figurative Language** Poetry often uses **figurative language,** or language not meant literally, to evoke emotions and state ideas in imaginative ways. Some common types of figurative language include simile, metaphor, personification, oxymoron, and apostrophe.

- A **simile** is a comparison of two unlike things using an explicit comparison word such as *like* or *as*.
  **Example:** The moon shines like a glowing ember in the night sky.
- A **metaphor** is a comparison of two unlike things that does not use an explicit comparison word such as *like* or *as*.
  **Example:** The moon is a glowing ember in the night sky.
- **Personification** is a figure of speech in which a nonhuman subject is given human qualities.
  **Example:** The moon smiles down from the night sky.
- An **oxymoron** is a figure of speech that juxtaposes two opposite or contradictory words.
  **Example:** The moon's dark brightness fills the night sky.
- An **apostrophe** is a direct address to either an absent person or an abstract or inanimate thing.
  **Example:** Oh, moon, you shine so beautifully against the night sky.

STANDARDS

**Reading Literature**
Determine the meaning of words and phrases as they are used in the text, including figurative and connotative meanings; analyze the impact of specific word choices on meaning and tone, including words with multiple meanings or language that is particularly fresh, engaging, or beautiful.

**Language**
- Demonstrate understanding of figurative language, word relationships, and nuances in word meanings.
- Interpret figures of speech in context and analyze their role in the text.

**CITE TEXTUAL EVIDENCE** to support your answers.

**Practice**

**Work together to identify examples of figurative language in these poems. Then, discuss how each example adds to the meaning or artistry of the poem.**

| POEM | LINE(S) | TYPE OF FIGURATIVE LANGUAGE |
|---|---|---|
| | | |
| | | |
| | | |
| | | |
| | | |
| | | |

POETRY COLLECTION 3

## Conventions and Style

**Archaic Diction** Word choice, or **diction,** is an essential aspect of a poem. **Archaic diction** refers to words and phrases that were once in standard usage but are no longer common. Both Byron and Wordsworth at times use archaic diction.

- Instead of the second-person pronoun *you*, both poets use the archaic *thou*. This pronoun becomes *thy* or *thine* when used possessively and *thee* when used as a direct or indirect object.
- Both poets use archaic verb forms. A second-person singular verb ends in *-st* ("Thou hadst a voice"); a third-person singular verb ends in *-th* ("England hath need of thee").

These pronoun and verb forms were already archaic when Byron and Wordsworth wrote these poems. However, the poets made the stylistic choice to use them to achieve a certain effect.

### Read It

1. Work individually to complete the chart. Mark each archaic pronoun or verb, and identify its form. Then, rewrite the line in contemporary English.

| LINE(S) | FORM OF PRONOUN/VERB | CONTEMPORARY ENGLISH |
|---|---|---|
| *The wrecks are all thy deed, nor doth remain / A shadow of man's ravage. . . .* | thy: second-person possessive pronoun; doth: third-person verb form | The wrecks are all your deed, nor does remain / A shadow of man's ravage. |
| *. . . the vile strength he wields / For earth's destruction thou dost all despise. . . .* | | |
| *Milton! thou should'st be living at this hour. . . .* | | |
| *Thy soul was like a Star, and dwelt apart. . . .* | | |
| *So didst thou travel on life's common way. . . .* | | |

2. **Connect to Style** After you have completed the chart, share your responses with your group. Discuss the effects of the poets' use of archaic diction. Consider how the use of modern revisions would either add to or detract from each poem's effect.

### Write It

**Notebook** Choose another passage from one of the poems, and rewrite it using contemporary English pronouns and verb forms.

STANDARDS

**Language**

- Demonstrate command of the conventions of standard English grammar and usage when writing or speaking.
- Apply the understanding that usage is a matter of convention, can change over time, and is sometimes contested.

# Research

### Assignment

Conduct a **historical investigative research report** that relates historical events of the period to the three poems you have read. Choose one of the following options:

- ☐ Plan and write a **report that compares** the importance of the ocean to empires and governments referred to in "Apostrophe to the Ocean." Include Britain as one of the empires, and explain the importance of the two battles mentioned in the poem: the defeat of the Spanish Armada (1588) and the Battle of Trafalgar (1805).
- ☐ Plan and write a **report that explains** Wordsworth's rejection of materialism in "The World Is Too Much With Us." Cite historical events to which Wordsworth may have been reacting or responding.
- ☐ Plan and write a **report that analyzes** Wordsworth's profound disppointment with French revolutionary politics, as explored in "London, 1802."

EVIDENCE LOG

Before moving on to a new selection, go to your Evidence Log and record what you learned from "Apostrophe to the Ocean," "The World Is Too Much With Us," and "London, 1802."

**Project Plan** Gather information from multiple authoritative print and digital sources. Authoritative sources are those that are widely acknowledged for their accuracy and reliability. They provide well-written and error-free content, and they openly cite their own sources. If they present ideas on which opinions differ, they say so. As you research, make sure to collect the information you will need to cite sources correctly using a standard format.

**Conduct Research** Use this chart to keep track of the kinds of information you are researching and the group member assigned to each kind. In addition, record the sources each person consults, and collect all the details needed for proper citation.

STANDARDS

**Writing**

- Conduct short as well as more sustained research projects to answer a question or solve a problem; narrow or broaden the inquiry when appropriate; synthesize multiple sources on the subject, demonstrating understanding of the subject under investigation.
- Gather relevant information from multiple authoritative print and digital sources, using advanced searches effectively; assess the strengths and limitations of each source in terms of the task, purpose, and audience; integrate information into the text selectively to maintain the flow of ideas, avoiding plagiarism and overreliance on any one source and following a standard format for citation including footnotes and endnotes.

| KIND OF INFORMATION | WHO IS RESPONSIBLE | SOURCE INFORMATION FOR CITATION |
|---|---|---|
| | | |
| | | |
| | | |
| | | |
| | | |

## About the Author

**Marcel Proust** (1871–1922) was the son of a wealthy Parisian doctor and his wife. As a child, the sickly, shy Marcel had trouble fitting in. Nevertheless, Proust served in the military and became a practicing lawyer as a young man. As time passed, Proust became increasingly withdrawn, and he devoted his time to writing. From an early age, Proust was determined not simply to be a successful writer, but to be the author of a truly "great" work. Locking himself up in a soundproof room, Proust eventually produced *Remembrance of Things Past*, which has been recognized as a truly "great" work.

# The Madeleine

## Concept Vocabulary

As you perform your first read of "The Madeleine," you will encounter the following words.

**innocuous** **illusory** **impalpable**

**Context Clues** If these words are unfamiliar to you, try using **context clues**—other words and phrases that appear in a text—to help you determine their meanings. Here are examples of common types of context clues.

**Definition:** Because of my **coulrophobia**, or intense fear of clowns, I avoid the circus at all costs.

**Elaborating Details:** The **abyss** was so dark and deep that she could not see the bottom.

**Antonyms:** The terseness of the second speaker stood in sharp contrast to the **prolixity** of the first.

Apply your knowledge of context clues and other vocabulary strategies to determine the meanings of unfamiliar words you encounter during your first read.

## First Read FICTION

Apply these strategies as you conduct your first read. You will have an opportunity to complete the close-read notes after your first read.

**NOTICE** *whom* the story is about, *what* happens, *where* and *when* it happens, and *why* the main characters react as they do.

**ANNOTATE** by marking vocabulary and key passages you want to revisit.

**CONNECT** ideas within the selection to what you already know and what you've already read.

**RESPOND** by completing the Comprehension Check and by writing a brief summary of the selection.

First Read: NOTICE, ANNOTATE, CONNECT, RESPOND

### STANDARDS

**Reading Literature**

By the end of grade 12, read and comprehend literature, including stories, dramas, and poems, at the high end of the grades 11-CCR text complexity band independently and proficiently.

**Language**

- Determine or clarify the meaning of unknown and multiple-meaning words and phrases based on *grades 11–12 reading and content*, choosing flexibly from a range of strategies.

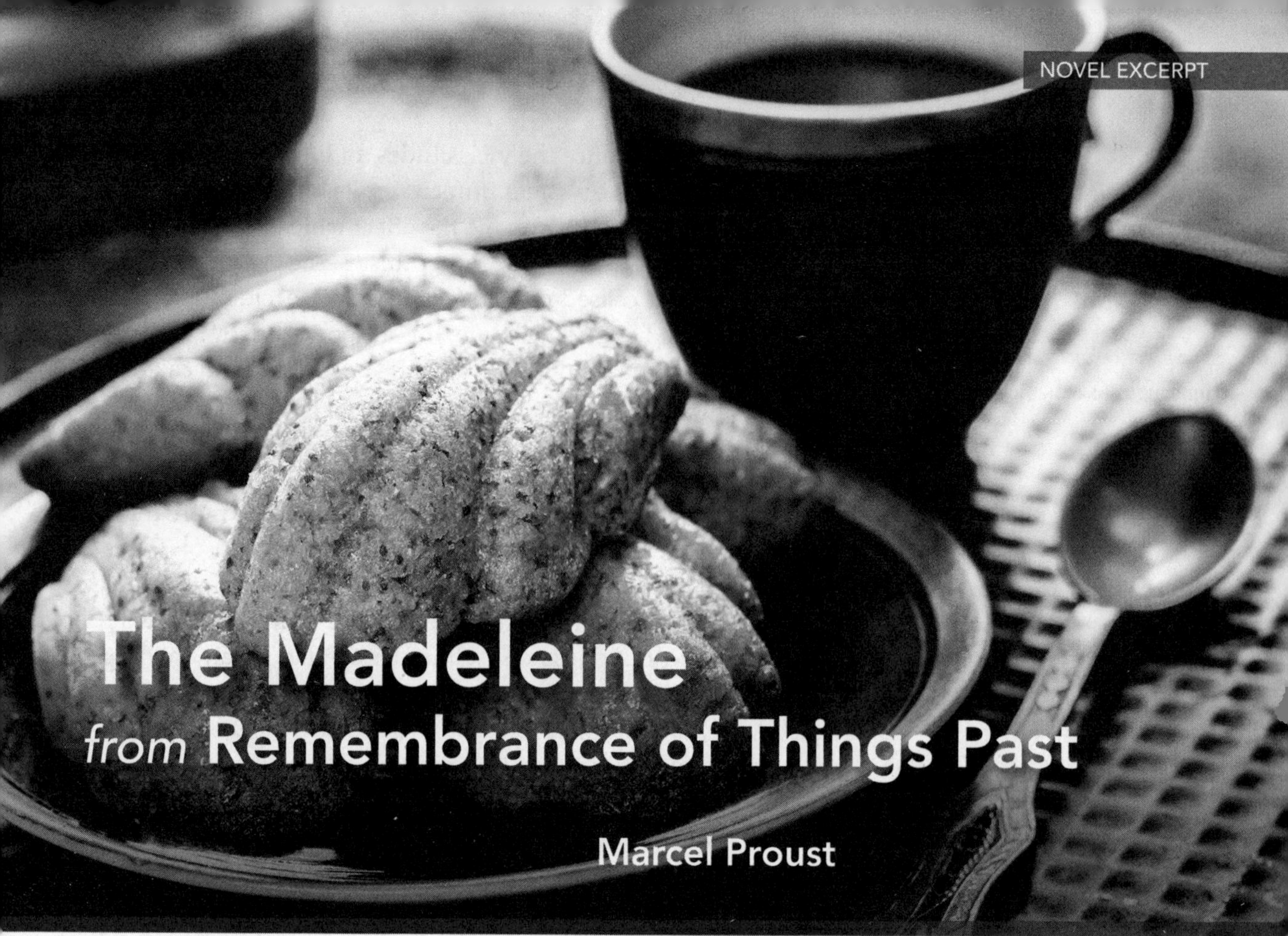


# The Madeleine
## *from* Remembrance of Things Past

Marcel Proust

BACKGROUND

The narrator muses about his current life and the difficulty in talking about the past with true accuracy. His prose seems fairly unfocused until he begins to reminisce about his days as a child in a small French town called Combray.

NOTES

1 Many years had elapsed during which nothing of Combray,[1] save what was comprised in the theater and the drama of my going to bed there, had any existence for me, when one day in winter, as I came home, my mother, seeing that I was cold, offered me some tea, a thing I did not ordinarily take. I declined at first, and then, for no particular reason, changed my mind. She sent out for one of those short, plump little cakes called "petites madeleines," which look as though they had been molded in the fluted scallop of a pilgrim's shell. And soon, mechanically, weary after a dull day with the prospect of a depressing morrow, I raised to my lips a spoonful of the tea in which I had soaked a morsel of the cake. No sooner had the warm liquid, and the crumbs with it, touched my palate than a shudder ran through my whole body, and I stopped, intent upon the extraordinary changes that were taking place. An exquisite pleasure had invaded my senses, but individual, detached, with no suggestion

1. **Combray** village where the narrator grew up.

NOTES

Mark context clues or indicate another strategy you used that helped you determine meaning.

**innocuous** (ih NOK yoo uhs) *adj.*

MEANING:

**illusory** (ih LOO suh ree) *adj.*

MEANING:

of its origin. And at once the vicissitudes[2] of life had become indifferent to me, its disasters **innocuous**, its brevity **illusory**—this new sensation having had on me the effect which love has of filling me with a precious essence; or rather this essence was not in me, it was myself. I had ceased now to feel mediocre, accidental, mortal. Whence could it have come to me, this all-powerful joy? I was conscious that it was connected with the taste of tea and cake, but that it infinitely transcended those savors, could not, indeed, be of the same nature as theirs. Whence did it come? What did it signify? How could I seize upon and define it?

2 I drink a second mouthful, in which I find nothing more than in the first, a third, which gives me rather less than the second. It is time to stop; the potion is losing its magic. It is plain that the object of my quest, the truth, lies not in the cup but in myself. The tea has called up in me, but does not itself understand, and can only repeat indefinitely, with a gradual loss of strength, the same testimony; which I, too, cannot interpret, though I hope at least to be able to call upon the tea for it again and to find it there presently, intact and at my disposal, for my final enlightenment. I put down my cup and examine my own mind. It is for it to discover the truth. But how? What an abyss of uncertainty whenever the mind feels that some part of it has strayed beyond its own borders; when it, the seeker, is at once the dark region through which it must go seeking, where all its equipment will avail it nothing. Seek? More than that: create. It is face to face with something which does not so far exist, to which it alone can give reality and substance, which it alone can bring into the light of day.

3 And I begin again to ask myself what it could have been, this unremembered state which brought with it no logical proof of its existence, but only the sense that it was a happy, that it was a real state in whose presence other states of consciousness melted and vanished. I decide to attempt to make it reappear. I retrace my thoughts to the moment at which I drank the first spoonful of tea. I find again the same state, illumined by no fresh light. I compel my mind to make one further effort, to follow and recapture once again the fleeting sensation. And that nothing may interrupt it in its course I shut out every obstacle, every extraneous idea, I stop my ears and inhibit all attention to the sounds which come from the next room. And then, feeling that my mind is growing fatigued without having any success to report, I compel it for a change to enjoy that distraction which I have just denied it, to think of other things, to rest and refresh itself before the supreme attempt. And then for the second time I clear an empty space in front of it. I place in position before my mind's eye the still recent taste of that first mouthful, and I feel something start within me, something that leaves its resting place and attempts to rise, something that has been embedded like an

2. **vicissitudez** (vih SIHS uh toodz) *n.* unpredictable changes in life, fortune, or circumstances.

anchor at a great depth; I do not know yet what it is, but I can feel it mounting slowly; I can measure the resistance, I can hear the echo of great spaces traversed.

4 Undoubtedly what is thus palpitating in the depths of my being must be the image, the visual memory which, being linked to that taste, has tried to follow it into my conscious mind. But its struggles are too far off, too much confused; scarcely can I perceive the colorless reflection in which are blended the uncapturable whirling medley of radiant hues, and I cannot distinguish its form, cannot invite it, as the one possible interpreter, to translate to me the evidence of its contemporary, its inseparable paramour,[3] the taste of cake soaked in tea; cannot ask it to inform me what special circumstance is in question, of what period in my past life.

5 Will it ultimately reach the clear surface of my consciousness, this memory, this old, dead moment which the magnetism of an identical moment has traveled so far to importune, to disturb, to raise up out of the very depths of my being? I cannot tell. Now that I feel nothing, it has stopped, has perhaps gone down again into its darkness, from which who can say whether it will ever rise? Ten times over I must essay[4] the task, must lean down over the abyss. And each time the natural laziness which deters us from every difficult enterprise, every work of importance, has urged me to leave the thing alone, to drink my tea and to think merely of the worries of today and of my hopes for tomorrow, which let themselves be pondered over without effort or distress of mind.

6 And suddenly the memory returns. The taste was that of the little crumb of madeleine which on Sunday mornings at Combray (because on those mornings I did not go out before church time), when I went to say good day to her in her bedroom, my aunt Leonie used to give me, dipping it first in her own cup of real or of lime-flower tea. The sight of the little madeleine had recalled nothing to my mind before I tasted it; perhaps because I had so often seen such things in the interval, without tasting them, on the trays in pastry-cooks' windows, that their image had dissociated itself from those Combray days to take its place among others more recent; perhaps because of those memories, so long abandoned and put out of mind, nothing now survived, everything was scattered; the forms of things, including that of the little scallop-shell of pastry, so richly sensual under its severe, religious folds, were either obliterated or had been so long dormant as to have lost the power of expansion which would have allowed them to resume their place in my consciousness. But when from a long-distant past nothing subsists, after the people are dead, after the things are broken and scattered, still, alone, more fragile, but with more vitality, more unsubstantial, more persistent, more faithful, the smell and taste of things remain poised a long time, like souls, ready to remind us, waiting and hoping for their moment, amid

3. **paramour** (PAR uh mawr) *n.* lover.
4. **essay** *v.* attempt.

NOTES

NOTES

Mark context clues or indicate another strategy you used that helped you determine meaning.

**impalpable** (ihm PAL puh buhl) *adj.*

MEANING:

the ruins of all the rest; and bear unfaltering, in the tiny and almost **impalpable** drop of their essence, the vast structure of recollection.

7 And once I had recognized the taste of the crumb of madeleine soaked in her decoction[5] of lime-flowers which my aunt used to give me (although I did not yet know and must long postpone the discovery of why this memory made me so happy) immediately the old gray house upon the street, where her room was, rose up like the scenery of a theater to attach itself to the little pavilion, opening on to the garden, which had been built out behind it for my parents (the isolated panel which until that moment had been all that I could see); and with the house the town, from morning to night and in all weathers, the Square where I was sent before luncheon, the streets along which I used to run errands, the country roads we took when it was fine. And just as the Japanese amuse themselves by filling a porcelain bowl with water and steeping in it little crumbs of paper which until then are without character or form, but, the moment they become wet, stretch themselves and bend, take on color and distinctive shape, become flowers or houses or people, permanent and recognizable, so in that moment all the flowers in our garden and in M. Swann's[6] park, and the waterlilies on the Vivonne[7] and the good folk of the village and their little dwellings and the parish church and the whole of Combray and of its surroundings, taking their proper shapes and growing solid, sprang into being, town and gardens alike, from my cup of tea. ❧

5. **decoction** (dih KOK shuhn) *n.* extract made from boiling down a substance.
6. **M. Swann** Monsieur (Mr.) Swann, friend of the narrator's family.
7. **Vivonne** river in Combray.

## Comprehension Check

**Complete the following items after you finish your first read. Review and clarify details with your group.**

1. What stirs a memory of the narrator's childhood in Combray?

2. What does the narrator feel when he experiences this memory?

3. Once the "essence" of the memory begins to fade, what does the narrator attempt to do?

4. What image sparks a feeling of joy to return to the narrator?

5. What comes to mind when the narrator begins to think of his aunt?

6. **Notebook** Write a summary of "The Madeleine" to confirm your understanding of the text.

## RESEARCH

**Research to Clarify** Choose at least one unfamiliar detail from the text. Briefly research that detail. In what way does the information you learned shed light on an aspect of the story?

**Research to Explore** Choose a detail from the text that interested you, and perform brief research to learn more about it. You might, for example, research the idea of an involuntary memory, which has been termed a "Proustian memory." Share your findings with your classmates.

THE MADELEINE

TIP

CLARIFICATION

The narrator and the author of this novel share the name Marcel. However, keep in mind that this is a work of fiction and that the remembrances of the narrator do not necessarily reflect the author's life story.

WORD NETWORK

Add interesting words related to self-discovery from the text to your Word Network.

STANDARDS

**Language**

- Identify and correctly use patterns of word changes that indicate different meanings or parts of speech.
- Verify the preliminary determination of the meaning of a word or phrase.

## Close Read the Text

With your group, revisit sections of the text you marked during your first read. **Annotate** details that you notice. What **questions** do you have? What can you **conclude**?

## Analyze the Text

**CITE TEXTUAL EVIDENCE** to support your answers.

Notebook Complete the activities.

1. **Review and Clarify** With your group, reread paragraph 2 of the excerpt. What do the narrator's repeated drinks suggest about how a person experiences memory?
2. **Present and Discuss** Work with your group to share the passages from the selection that you found especially important. Take turns presenting your passages. Discuss what details you noticed, what questions you asked, and what conclusions you reached.
3. **Essential Question:** ***How do we define ourselves?*** What has this story taught you about how people build their senses of self?

LANGUAGE DEVELOPMENT

## Concept Vocabulary

**innocuous** **illusory** **impalpable**

**Why These Words?** The three concept vocabulary words are related. With your group, determine what the words have in common. Write your ideas, and add another word that fits the category.

**Practice**

Notebook Use a dictionary or thesaurus to find and record at least two synonyms for each of the concept vocabulary words. Then, find the sentences in the selection that use each word, and rewrite them using the synonym that best fits the context.

## Word Study

Notebook **Latin Prefix: *in-*** The Latin prefix *in-* can mean either "not" or "into." In both cases, the prefix can take a variety of forms. Often, the *n* assimilates, or becomes more similar to, the first letter of the root or base word. For instance, in *impalpable*, the prefix *in-* becomes *im-* because the *m* sound better combines with the *p* sound. However, its meaning ("not") remains the same. Consider the words *incredible* and *import*. For each word, note whether the prefix means "not" or "in." Then, state whether the prefix has assimilated to better fit the root or base word.

# Analyze Craft and Structure

**Impact of Word Choice** People take in information about the world through the senses of sight, hearing, taste, touch, and smell. For this reason, literature makes heavy use of **sensory language,** or words and phrases that appeal to the senses. Sensory language creates word pictures, helping the reader to visualize and connect to what is happening in a text. In "The Madeleine," Marcel Proust uses sensory language to capture the sights, sounds, smells, tastes, and feelings associated with the narrator's experience and memories.

## Practice

**CITE TEXTUAL EVIDENCE** to support your answers.

1. Work independently to complete the chart. Identify passages from the text that appeal to the senses indicated. (Note that some passages may appeal to more than one sense.) Discuss your choices with your group, and consider the effects of each example.

| SENSE | EXAMPLE (S) |
|---|---|
| Sight | |
| Hearing | |
| Taste/Smell | |
| Touch | |

2. Cite an example of sensory language from the text that you feel is especially effective because it makes the narrator's experience more vivid, clarifies what the experience means to him, or both. Explain your choice. Then, discuss with your group.

**STANDARDS**

**Reading Literature**
Determine the meaning of words and phrases as they are used in the text, including figurative and connotative meanings; analyze the impact of specific word choices on meaning and tone, including words with multiple meanings or language that is particularly fresh, engaging, or beautiful.

**Language**
Demonstrate understanding of figurative language, word relationships, and nuances in word meanings.

THE MADELEINE

## Conventions and Style

**Rhetorical Devices** A **rhetorical device** is a special pattern of words or ideas that creates emphasis and stirs emotion. One rhetorical device that Proust uses in "The Madeleine" is anaphora. **Anaphora** is the deliberate repetition of the same sequence of words at the beginning of nearby phrases, clauses, or sentences.

**Example:** I do not know yet what it is, but I can feel it mounting slowly; I can measure the resistance; I can hear the echo of great spaces traversed.

Anaphora is effective for several reasons:

- It gives the text a rhythm that is pleasing to the ear.
- It emphasizes the relatedness of the ideas.
- It makes the text easier to grasp and remember.

### Read It

1. Mark the repeated word sequence in each passage from "The Madeleine."
   a. It is face to face with something which does not so far exist, to which it alone can give reality and substance, which it alone can bring into the light of day.
   b. I feel something start within me, something that leaves its resting place and attempts to rise, something that has been embedded like an anchor at a great depth. . . .
   c. I cannot distinguish its form, cannot invite it, as the one possible interpreter, to translate to me the evidence of its contemporary, its inseparable paramour, the taste of cake soaked in tea; cannot ask it to inform me what special circumstance is in question, of what period in my past life.
2. **Connect to Style** Find and mark an example of anaphora in paragraph 3 of "The Madeleine." Discuss with your group why it is particularly effective.

   **Notebook** After your discussion, explain in your own words how the use of anaphora helps enhance the style of the story and makes it more readable and enjoyable.

### Write It

Write a paragraph in which you comment on "The Madeleine." Include at least two examples of anaphora. Mark the examples, and identify the repeated word sequences.

TIP

**COLLABORATION**

If you or a group member is having trouble identifying anaphora or its effects, try reading the passage out loud and listening for the repeated words.

STANDARDS

**Reading Literature**
Analyze how an author's choices concerning how to structure specific parts of a text contribute to its overall structure and meaning as well as its aesthetic impact.

**Writing**
Write narratives to develop real or imagined experiences or events using effective technique, well-chosen details, and well-structured event sequences.

## Writing to Sources

**Assignment**

Write a **narrative** based on "The Madeleine" from Marcel Proust's *Remembrance of Things Past*. Keep in mind that a strong narrative includes well-drawn characters, a clear sequence of events, and effective use of narrative techniques, such as dialogue, description, and sensory language. Choose one of the following options with your group:

- ☐ Write a **narrative retelling** of the events of "The Madeleine" from another point of view. Create a third-person omniscient narrator—one who knows the thoughts and feelings of all the characters in your story—and describe what happens when Proust's narrator has tea with his mother. Include dialogue that reveals the narrator's thoughts and his mother's reactions.
- ☐ Write a **fictional diary entry** about a day Proust's narrator might have experienced as a child. Use first-person point of view to write about his life in Combray. Incorporate details from Proust's text, and include reflections on those experiences.
- ☐ Write an **extension** of the scene described in "The Madeleine." What do you think might happen next in the novel? Begin by summarizing the key events and details of the scene, and add a new conclusion that follows from and reflects on what the narrator experienced. Mimic Proust's tone and style.

**Project Plan** Each person in your group will write either a narrative retelling, a diary entry, or an extension of a scene, depending on which project your group chose. Begin by rereading "The Madeleine" individually and marking up the details you will include in your narrative. Then, use the chart to plan how you will adapt those details for your narrative. Finally, write your narrative. When you have finished, come together as a group. Take turns reading your narratives aloud, and discuss the different approaches you took to the same writing task. Then, come to consensus on one narrative to share with the larger class.

**EVIDENCE LOG**

Before moving on to a new selection, go to your Evidence Log and record what you learned from "The Madeleine."

| PASSAGE FROM "THE MADELEINE" | HOW I WILL ADAPT |
|---|---|
| | |
| | |
| | |
| | |

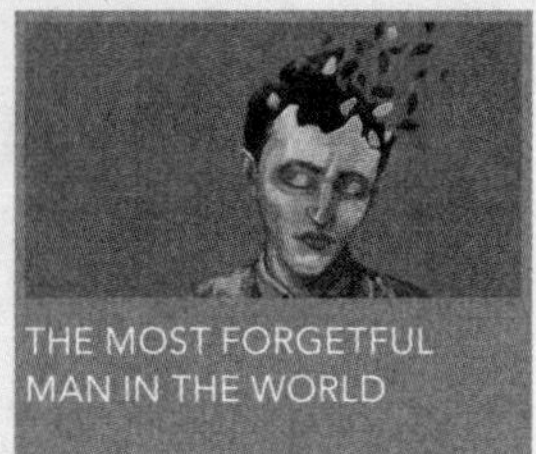


## Comparing Text to Media

In this lesson, you will compare an example of science journalism with a radio broadcast on a related topic. First, you will complete the first-read and close-read activities for "The Most Forgetful Man in the World." Your group work will help prepare you for the comparing task.

WHEN MEMORIES NEVER FADE, THE PAST CAN POISON THE PRESENT


### About the Author

**Joshua Foer** (b. 1982) is a freelance journalist who writes about hard science—research into the natural sciences that focuses on controlled experiments and mathematical models. Fascinated by the human mind, Foer entered and won the United States Memory Championship in 2006. He chronicled his year-long training for the event in the best-selling book *Moonwalking With Einstein: The Art and Science of Remembering Everything*.

# The Most Forgetful Man in the World

## Technical Vocabulary

As you perform your first read, you will encounter the following words.

**amnesia** **cognitive** **pathological**

**Context Clues** If these words are unfamiliar to you, try using various types of **context clues**—other words and phrases that appear in a text—to help you determine their meanings. Here is one example.

**Elaborating Details:** The factory spewed **noxious** chemicals that made people ill and poisoned the countryside.

Apply your knowledge of context clues and other vocabulary strategies to determine the meanings of unfamiliar words you encounter during your first read.

## First Read NONFICTION

Apply these strategies as you conduct your first read. You will have an opportunity to complete a close read after your first read.

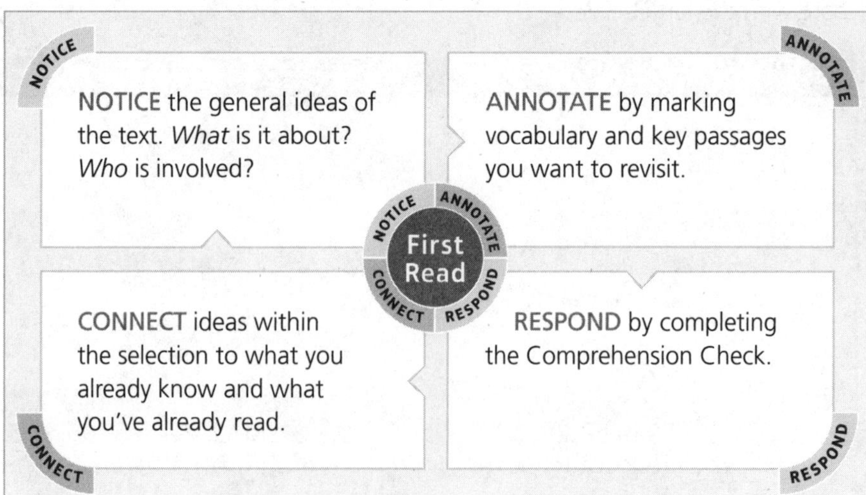

NOTICE the general ideas of the text. *What* is it about? *Who* is involved?
ANNOTATE by marking vocabulary and key passages you want to revisit.
CONNECT ideas within the selection to what you already know and what you've already read.
RESPOND by completing the Comprehension Check.
First Read
NOTICE
ANNOTATE
CONNECT
RESPOND


### STANDARDS

**Reading Informational Text**
By the end of grade 12, read and comprehend literary nonfiction at the high end of the grades 11–CCR text complexity band independently and proficiently.

**Language**
- Determine or clarify the meaning of unknown and multiple-meaning words and phrases based on *grades 11–12 reading and content*, choosing flexibly from a range of strategies.
- Use context as a clue to the meaning of a word or phrase.

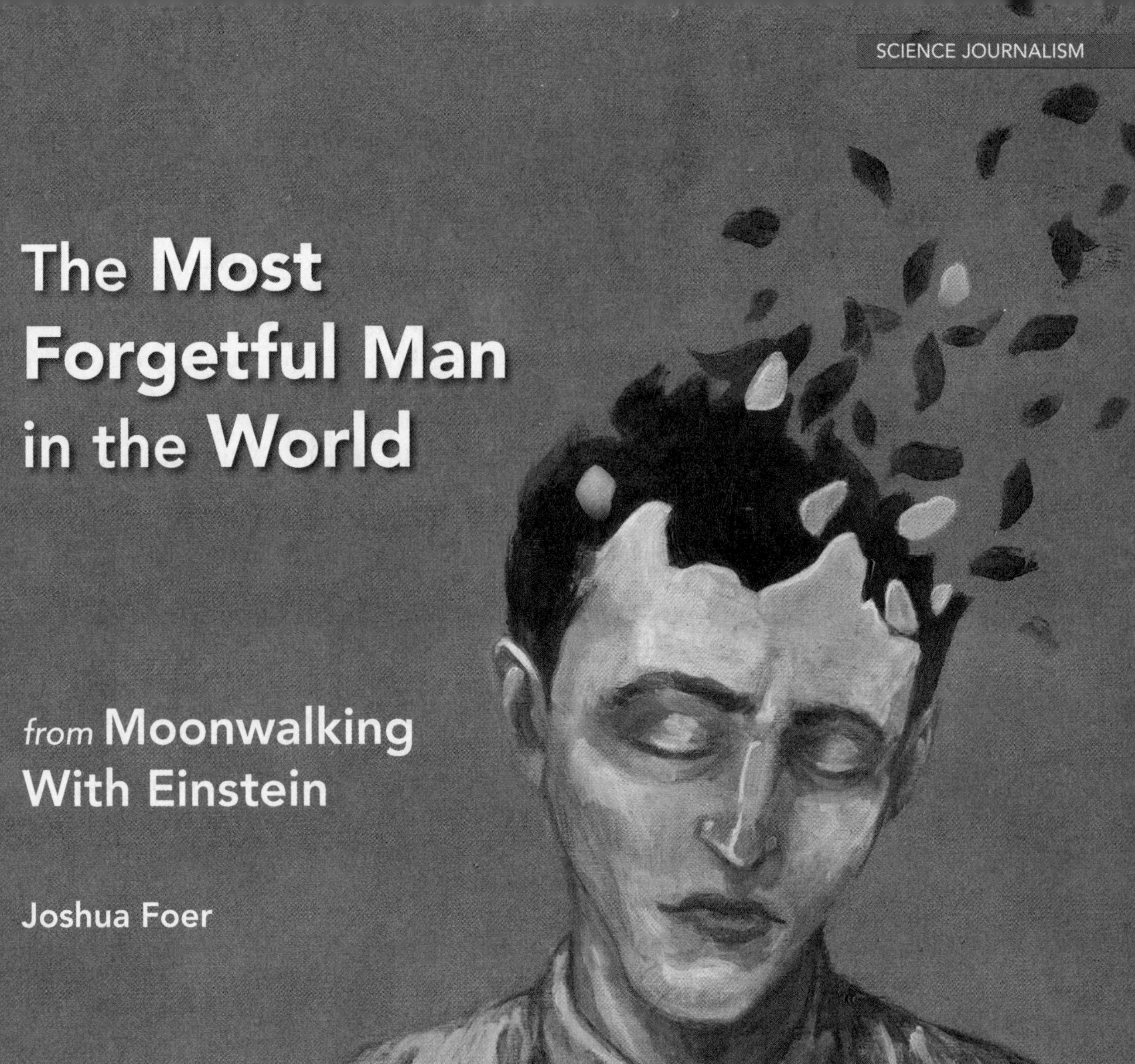

# The Most Forgetful Man in the World

## from Moonwalking With Einstein

Joshua Foer

BACKGROUND

Healthy human beings have both long-term and short-term, or working, memory. Working memory lasts only moments, such as the time between reading a phone number and writing it down. Long-term memory is anything one remembers once his or her attention has fully left it, and can last one's entire life.

1 Having met some of the best memories in the world, I decided that my next step would be to try to seek out the worst. What better way to try to begin to understand the nature and meaning of human memory than to investigate its absence? I went back to Google in search of Ben Pridmore's counterpart in the record books of forgetfulness, and dug up an article in *The Journal of Neuroscience* about an eighty-four-year-old retired lab technician called EP, whose memory extended back only as far as his most recent thought. He had one of the most severe cases of amnesia ever documented.

NOTES

Mark context clues or indicate another strategy you used that helped you determine meaning.

**amnesia** (am NEE zhuh) *n.*

MEANING:

NOTES

Mark context clues or indicate another strategy you used that helped you determine meaning.

**cognitive** (KOG nuh tihv) *adj.*

MEANING:

2 A few weeks after returning from Tallahassee, I phoned a neuroscientist and memory researcher named Larry Squire at the University of California, San Diego, and the San Diego VA Medical Center. Squire had been studying EP for over a decade, and agreed to bring me along on one of his visits to the bright bungalow in suburban San Diego where EP lives with his wife. We traveled there with Jen Frascino, the research coordinator in Squire's lab who visits EP regularly to administer **cognitive** tests. Even though Frascino has been to EP's home some two hundred times, he greets her as a total stranger every time.

3 EP is six-foot-two, with perfectly parted white hair and unusually long ears. He's personable, friendly, gracious. He laughs a lot. He seems at first like your average genial grandfather. Frascino, a tall, athletic blonde, sits down with me and Squire opposite EP at his dining room table and asks a series of questions that are meant to gauge his basic knowledge and common sense. She quizzes him about what continent Brazil is on, the number of weeks in a year, the boiling temperature of water. She wants to demonstrate what a battery of cognitive tests has already proved: EP has a working knowledge of the world. His IQ is 103, and his short-term memory is entirely unimpaired. He patiently answers the questions—all correctly—with roughly the same sense of bemusement I imagine I would have if a total stranger walked into my house and earnestly asked me if I knew the boiling point of water.

4 "What is the thing to do if you find an envelope in the street that is sealed, addressed, and has a stamp on it?" Frascino asks.

5 "Well, you'd put it in the mailbox. What else?" He chuckles and shoots me a knowing, sidelong glance, as if to say, "Do these people think I'm an idiot?" But sensing that the situation calls for politeness, he turns back to Fascino and adds, "But that's a really interesting question you've got there. Really interesting." He has no idea he's heard it many times before.

6 "Why do we cook food?"

7 "Because it's raw?" The word raw carries his voice clear across the tonal register, his bemusement giving away to incredulity.

8 I ask EP if he knows the name of the last president.

9 "I'm afraid it's slipped my mind. How strange."

10 "Does the name Bill Clinton sound familiar?"

11 "Of course I know Clinton! He's an old friend of mine, a scientist, a good guy. I worked with him, you know."

12 He sees my eyes widen in disbelief and stops himself.

13 "Unless, that is, there's another Clinton around that you're thinking of—"

14 "Well, you know, the last president was named Bill Clinton also."

15 "He was? I'll be—!" He slaps his thigh and chuckles, but doesn't seem all that embarrassed.

16 "Who's the last president you remember?"

NOTES

17 He takes a moment to search his brain. "Let's see. There was Franklin Roosevelt . . . "

18 "Ever heard of John F. Kennedy?"

19 "Kennedy? Hmm, I'm afraid I don't know him."

20 Frascino interjects with another question. "Why do we study history?"

21 "Well, we study history to know what happened in the past."

22 "But why do we want to know what happened in the past?"

23 "Because it's just interesting, frankly."

* * *

24 In November 1992, EP came down with what seemed like a mild case of the flu. For five days he lay in bed, feverish and lethargic, unsure of what was wrong, while inside his head a vicious virus known as herpes simplex was chewing its way through his brain, coring it like an apple. By the time the virus had run its course, two walnut-size chunks of brain matter in EP's medial temporal lobes had disappeared, and with them most of his memory.

25 The virus struck with freakish precision. The medial temporal lobes—there's one on each side of the brain—include the hippocampus and several adjacent regions that together perform the magical feat of turning our perceptions into long-term memories. Memories aren't actually stored in the hippocampus—they reside elsewhere, in the brain's corrugated outer layers, the neocortex—but the hippocampal area makes them stick. EP's hippocampus was destroyed, and without it he is like a camcorder without a working tape head. He sees, but he doesn't record.

26 EP has two types of amnesia—anterograde, which means he can't form new memories, and retrograde, which means he can't recall old memories either, at least not since about 1950. His childhood, his service in the merchant marine, World War II—all that is perfectly vivid. But as far as he knows, gas costs a quarter a gallon, and man never took that small step onto the moon.

27 Even though EP has been an amnesic for a decade and a half, and his condition has neither worsened nor improved, there's still much that Squire and his team hope to learn from him. A case like his, in which nature performs a cruel but perfect experiment, is, to put it crassly, a major boon to science. In a field in which so many basic questions are still unanswered, there is a limitless number of tests that can be performed on a mind like EP's. Indeed, there are only a handful of other individuals in the world in whom both hippocampi and the key adjacent structures have been so precisely notched out of an otherwise intact brain. Another severely amnesic case is Clive Wearing, a former music producer for the BBC who was struck by herpes encephalitis in 1985. Like EP's, his mind has become a sieve. Each time he greets his wife, it's as though he hasn't seen her in twenty years. He leaves her agonizing phone messages begging to

NOTES

be picked up from the nursing home where he lives. He also keeps an exhaustive diary that has become a tangible record of his daily anguish. But even the diary he finds hard to trust since—like every other object in his life—it is completely unfamiliar. Every time he opens it, it must feel like confronting a past life. It is filled with entries like this one:

> ~~8:31 A.M. Now I am really, completely awake.~~
> ~~9:06 A.M. Now I am perfectly, overwhelmingly awake.~~
> 9:34 A.M. Now I am superlatively, actually awake.

28 Those scratched-out entries suggest an awareness of his condition that EP, perhaps blissfully, lacks. From across the table, Squire asks EP how his memory is doing these days.

29 "It's fair. Hard to say it's real good or bad."

30 EP wears a metal medical alert bracelet around his left wrist. Even though it's obvious what it's for, I ask him anyway. He turns his wrist over and casually reads it.

31 "Hmm. It says memory loss."

32 EP doesn't even remember that he has a memory problem. That is something he discovers anew every moment. And since he forgets that he always forgets, every lost thought seems like just a casual slip—annoyance and nothing more—the same way it would to you or me.

When informed of the births of his grandchildren, EP's eyes welled up each time—and then he promptly forgot that they existed.

33 "There's nothing wrong with him in his mind. That's a blessing," his wife, Beverly, tells me later, while EP sits on the couch, out of earshot. "I suppose he must know something is wrong, but it doesn't come out in conversation or in his way of life. But underneath be must know. He just must."

34 When I hear those words, I'm stung by the realization of how much more than just memories have been lost. Even EP's own wife can no longer access his most basic emotions and thoughts. Which is not to say that he doesn't have emotions or thoughts. Moment to moment, he certainly does. When informed of the births of his grandchildren, EP's eyes welled up each time—and then he promptly forgot that they existed. But without the ability to compare today's feelings to yesterday's, he cannot tell any cohesive narrative about himself, or about those around him, which makes him incapable of providing even the most basic psychological sustenance to his family and friends. After all, EP can only remain truly interested in anyone or anything for as long as he can maintain his attention. Any rogue thought that distracts him effectively resets conversation. A meaningful relationship between two people cannot sustain itself only in the present tense.

35 Ever since his sickness, space for EP has existed only as far as he can see it. His social universe is only as large as the people in the room. He lives under a narrow spotlight, surrounded by darkness. On a typical morning, EP wakes up, has breakfast, and returns

to bed to listen to the radio. But back in bed, it's not always clear whether he's just had breakfast or just woken up. Often he'll have breakfast again, and return to bed to listen to some more radio. Some mornings he'll have breakfast for a third time. He watches TV, which can be very exciting from second to second, though shows with a clear beginning, middle, and end can pose a problem. He prefers the History Channel, or anything about World War II. He takes walks around the neighborhood, usually several times before lunch, and sometimes for as long as three quarters of an hour. He sits in the yard. He reads the newspaper, which must feel like stepping out of a time machine. Iraq? Internet? By the time EP gets to the end of a headline, he's usually forgotten how it began. Most of the time, after reading the weather, he just doodles on the paper, drawing mustaches on the photographs or tracing his spoon. When he sees home prices in the real estate section, he invariably announces his shock.

36 Without a memory, EP has fallen completely out of time. He has no stream of consciousness, just droplets that immediately evaporate. If you were to take the watch off his wrist—or, more cruelly, change the time—he'd be completely lost. Trapped in this limbo of an eternal present, between a past he can't remember and a future he can't contemplate, he lives a sedentary life, completely free from worry. "He's happy all the time. Very happy. I guess it's because he doesn't have any stress in his life," says his daughter Carol, who lives nearby. In his chronic forgetfulness, EP has achieved a kind of **pathological** enlightenment, a perverted vision of the Buddhist ideal of living entirely in the present.

37 "How old are you now?" Squire asks him.

38 "Let's see, fifty-nine or sixty. You got me," he says, raising his eyebrow contemplatively, as if he were making a calculation and not a guess. "My memory is not that perfect. It's pretty good, but sometimes people ask me questions that I just don't get. I'm sure you have that sometimes."

39 "Sure I do," says Squire kindly, even though EP's almost a quarter of a century off.

* * *

40 Without time, there would be no need for a memory. But without a memory, would there be such a thing as time? I don't mean time in the sense that, say, physicists speak of it: the fourth dimension, the independent variable, the quantity that dilates when you approach the speed of light. I mean psychological time, the tempo at which we experience life's passage. Time as a mental construct. Watching EP struggle to recount his own age, I recalled one of the stories Ed Cooke had told me about his research at the University of Paris when we met at the USA Memory Championship.

41 "I'm working on expanding subjective time so that it feels like I live longer," Ed had mumbled to me on the sidewalk outside the

NOTES

Mark context clues or indicate another strategy you used that helped you determine meaning.

**pathological** (path uh LOJ ih kuhl) *adj.*

MEANING:

NOTES

Con Ed headquarters. . . . "The idea is to avoid that feeling you have when you get to the end of the year and feel like, where . . . did that go?"

42 "And how are you going to do that?" I asked.

43 "By remembering more. By providing my life with more chronological landmarks. By making myself more aware of time's passage."

44 I told him that his plan reminded me of Dunbar, the pilot in Joseph Heller's *Catch-22* who reasons that since time flies when you're having fun, the surest way to slow life's passage is to make it as boring as possible.

45 Ed shrugged. "Quite the opposite. The more we pack our lives with memories, the slower time seems to fly."

46 Our subjective experience of time is highly variable. We all know that days can pass like weeks and months can feel like years, and that the opposite can be just as true: A month or year can zoom by in what feels like no time at all.

47 Our lives are structured by our memories of events. Event X happened just before the big Paris vacation. I was doing Y in the first summer after I learned to drive. Z happened the weekend after I landed my first job. We remember events by positioning them in time relative to other events. Just as we accumulate memories of facts by integrating them into a network, we accumulate life experiences by integrating them into a web of other chronological memories. The denser the web, the denser the experience of time.

48 It's a point well illustrated by Michel Siffre, a French chronobiologist (he studies the relationship between time and living organisms) who conducted one of the most extraordinary acts of self-experimentation in the history of science. In 1962, Siffre spent two months living in total isolation in a subterranean cave, without access to clock, calendar, or sun. Sleeping and eating only when his body told him to, he sought to discover how the natural rhythms of human life would be affected by living "beyond time."

49 Very quickly Siffre's memory deteriorated. In the dreary darkness, his days melded into one another and became one continuous, indistinguishable blob. Since there was nobody to talk to, and not much to do, there was nothing novel to impress itself upon his memory. There were no chronological landmarks by which he could measure the passage of time. At some point he stopped being able to remember what happened even the day before. His experience in isolation had turned him into EP. As time began to blur, he became effectively amnesic. Soon, his sleep patterns disintegrated. Some days he'd stay awake for thirty-six straight hours, other days for eight—without being able to tell the difference. When his support team on the surface finally called down to him on September 14, the day his experiment was scheduled to wrap up, it was only August 20 in his journal. He thought only a month had gone by. His experience of time's passage had compressed by a factor of two.

50 Monotony collapses time; novelty unfolds it. You can exercise daily and eat healthily and live a long life, while experiencing a short one. If you spend your life sitting in a cubicle and passing papers, one day is bound to blend unmemorably into the next—and disappear. That's why it's important to change routines regularly, and take vacations to exotic locales, and have as many new experiences as possible that can serve to anchor our memories. Creating new memories stretches out psychological time, and lengthens our perception of our lives.

51 William James first wrote about the curious warping and foreshortening of psychological time in his *Principles of Psychology* in 1890: "In youth we may have an absolutely new experience, subjective or objective, every hour of the day. Apprehension is vivid, retentiveness strong, and our recollections of that time, like those of a time spent in rapid and interesting travel, are of something intricate, multitudinous and long-drawn-out," he wrote. "But as each passing year converts some of this experience into automatic routine which we hardly note at all, the days and the weeks smooth themselves out in recollection to contentless units, and the years grow hollow and collapse." Life seems to speed up as we get older because life gets less memorable as we get older. "If to remember is to be human, then remembering more means being more human," said Ed.

52 There is perhaps a bit of Peter Pan to Ed's quest to make his life maximally memorable, but of all the things one could be obsessive about collecting, memories of one's own life don't seem like the most unreasonable. There's something even strangely rational about it. There's an old philosophical conundrum that often gets bandied about in introductory philosophy courses: In the nineteenth century, doctors began to wonder whether the general anesthetic they had been administering to patients might not actually put the patients to sleep so much as freeze their muscles and erase their memories of the surgery. If that were the case, could the doctors be said to have done anything wrong? Like the proverbial tree that falls without anyone hearing it, can an experience that isn't remembered be meaningfully said to have happened at all? Socrates thought the unexamined life was not worth living. How much more so the unremembered life? ❧

NOTES

## Comprehension Check

**Complete the following items after you finish your first read. Review and clarify details with your group.**

**1.** Why does the author interview EP?

**2.** How did EP lose his memory?

**3.** What experiment did Michel Siffre conduct? What was its outcome?

**4.** **Notebook** Confirm your understanding of the text by listing three obstacles that EP has faced.

## RESEARCH

**Research to Clarify** Choose at least one unfamiliar detail from the text. Briefly research that detail. In what way does the information you found shed light on an aspect of the selection?

**Research to Explore** Choose something from the text that interests you, and formulate a research question. Write your question here.

## Close Read the Text

With your group, revisit sections of the text you marked during your first read. **Annotate** details that you notice. What **questions** do you have? What can you **conclude**?

THE MOST FORGETFUL MAN IN THE WORLD

## Analyze the Text

**CITE TEXTUAL EVIDENCE** to support your answers.

**Notebook** Complete the activities.

1. **Review and Clarify** With your group, reread paragraph 34. Discuss the effects of memory loss. What point does the author suggest about the impact of memory on our lives and the lives of those around us?

2. **Present and Discuss** Now, work with your group to share the passages from the text that you found especially important. Take turns presenting your passages. Discuss what you noticed in the text, the questions you asked, and the conclusions you reached.

3. **Essential Question:** ***How do we define ourselves?*** What has this text taught you about the nature of personal identity? Discuss with your group.

**TIP**

**CLARIFICATION**

This text has a defined organization that the writer has emphasized with visual breaks. Identify the focus of each section, and consider how this organizational choice adds to the article's clarity and effectiveness.

LANGUAGE DEVELOPMENT

## Technical Vocabulary

**cognitive** **amnesia** **pathological**

**Why These Words?** The three technical vocabulary words from the text are related. With your group, determine what the words have in common. Write your ideas, and add another word that fits the category.

### Practice

**Notebook** Confirm your understanding of the technical vocabulary words by using them in sentences. Consult reference materials as needed, and use context clues that hint at meaning.

WORD NETWORK

Add interesting words related to self-discovery from the text to your Word Network.

## Word Study

**Greek Prefix: *a-*** The Greek prefix *a-* (which takes the form *an* before an *h* or a vowel) means "not" or "without." The word *amnesia* is formed from this prefix and the Greek root *-mne-* meaning "memory." The prefix appears in other scientific terms, as well. Using your knowledge of this prefix and the following notes, infer and record the meanings of *anhydrous*, *abiotic*, and *anaerobic*.

- A substance that is *hydrous* contains water.
- *Biotic* refers to living organisms.
- *Aerobic* processes take place in the presence of oxygen.

STANDARDS

**Language**

Identify and correctly use patterns of word changes that indicate different meanings or parts of speech.

THE MOST FORGETFUL MAN IN THE WORLD

# Analyze Craft and Structure

**Science Journalism** Nonfiction writing that reports on current scientific and technical news or research is called **science journalism.** Effective science journalism presents complex information in a way that captures its intricacies but also makes it clear and accessible to the general reading public. "The Most Forgetful Man in the World" illustrates several characteristics common to science journalism:

- It is written in a conversational tone, suited for general readers, despite its focus on a highly technical topic.
- It supports ideas through the inclusion of interviews, facts, the results of scientific studies, personal experiences, anecdotes, and data.
- It takes an in-depth look at a topic and seeks to inspire readers to reevaluate their own understanding of a concept. In this case, Foer explores memory from several angles, challenging readers to evolve their understanding of the concept as they read.
- It reveals a blend of **purposes**, or reasons for writing. There are three main *general purposes* for writing: to persuade, to inform/explain, and to entertain. However, the writer of any given text has a *specific purpose*—for example, to explain a particular topic, such as memory loss. Most writers, including Foer, write to fulfill a combination of purposes.

## Practice

**CITE TEXTUAL EVIDENCE** to support your answers.

Working as a group, analyze how Foer fulfills various purposes for writing in "The Most Forgetful Man in the World." Capture your observations in the chart.

| PURPOSE | PASSAGE THAT DEMONSTRATES PURPOSE |
|---|---|
| to entertain | |
| to inform or explain | |
| to persuade | |

**Notebook** Respond to these questions.

1. **(a)** What is Foer's general purpose for writing this text? **(b)** What is his specific purpose? Explain.
2. **(a)** How does Foer first define *memory*? **(b)** How does he refine and develop the discussion of *memory* over the course of the text?

**STANDARDS**

**Reading Informational Text**

- Determine the meaning of words and phrases as they are used in a text, including figurative, connotative, and technical meanings; analyze how an author uses and refines the meaning of a key term or terms over the course of a text.
- Determine an author's point of view or purpose in a text in which the rhetoric is particularly effective, analyzing how style and content contribute to the power, persuasiveness, or beauty of the text.

**Language**

Apply knowledge of language to understand how language functions in different contexts, to make effective choices for meaning or style, and to comprehend more fully when reading or listening.

## Conventions and Style

**Technical Writing and Audience** The form of communication known as **technical writing** refers to any type of writing that conveys complex information about how something works or how something is done. The owner's manual for a TV is technical writing, as is a lab report. Science, technology, and finance are the main fields in which you will likely find technical writing.

Technical writing presents unique challenges because a technical field may involve precise terminology that is unfamiliar to a general audience. Science journalism such as Foer's is not technical writing in its strictest sense, but it presents similar challenges. To make technical terms and concepts accessible, both technical writers and journalists may use these techniques:

- **definition**, or explaining what a technical term means literally: "EP has two types of amnesia—anterograde, *which means he can't form new memories, . . .* "
- **simile**, or a comparison of unlike things made with the help of an explicit comparison word such as *like* or *as*: ". . . a vicious virus known as herpes simplex was chewing its way through his brain, *coring it like an apple.*"
- **metaphor**, or a comparison of unlike things made without the help of an explicit comparison word such as *like* or *as*: "Trapped in this *limbo of an eternal present,* between a past he can't remember and a future he can't contemplate . . ."

**EVIDENCE LOG**

Before moving on to a new selection, go to your log and record what you learned from "The Most Forgetful Man in the World."

### Read It

Work individually. Use this chart to identify Foer's use of these techniques in "The Most Forgetful Man in the World." Then, discuss with your group how these techniques help Foer convey complex technical ideas to a general audience.

| DEFINITION | SIMILE | METAPHOR |
|---|---|---|
| paragraph 24: | paragraph 25: | paragraph 35: |
| paragraph 26: | paragraph 35: | paragraph 36: |

### Write It

**Notebook** Write a paragraph in which you explain how Foer conveys information clearly and completely in this text. Use examples of the techniques he employs.

THE MOST FORGETFUL MAN IN THE WORLD

## Comparing Text to Media

You have read a work of science journalism about memory loss. Now, listen to a radio broadcast that explores the opposite extreme of memory retention. After listening to this selection, you will evaluate the relative effects of the two conditions you have learned about.

WHEN MEMORIES NEVER FADE, THE PAST CAN POISON THE PRESENT

### About the Correspondent

**Alix Spiegel** was born in Baltimore, Maryland, and graduated from Oberlin College. She began her broadcasting career in 1995, serving as a founding producer of the public radio program *This American Life*. Spiegel has worked at National Public Radio's Science Desk for more than ten years, covering topics that concern human psychology. Her work has appeared in numerous publications, and she is the recipient of many broadcasting awards.

# When Memories Never Fade, the Past Can Poison the Present

## Media Vocabulary

These words will be useful to you as you analyze, discuss, and write about radio broadcasts.

| | |
|---|---|
| **host:** moderator or interviewer for a radio, television, or Web-based show | • Hosts prepare for interviews by researching and studying their subjects.<br>• Effective hosts are entertaining and informative. |
| **correspondent:** journalist employed by a media outlet to gather, report, or contribute news from a distant place | • Correspondents make sure their information is accurate and timely.<br>• They may provide print, digital, or audio materials, or a combination of all three. |
| **interviewee:** person who is questioned on a media broadcast | • Interviewees may be cooperative or uncooperative, depending on their role in a story.<br>• They may be experts on a topic, or they may share personal experiences. |

## First Review MEDIA: AUDIO

Apply these strategies as you complete your first review. You will have an opportunity to conduct a close review after your first review.

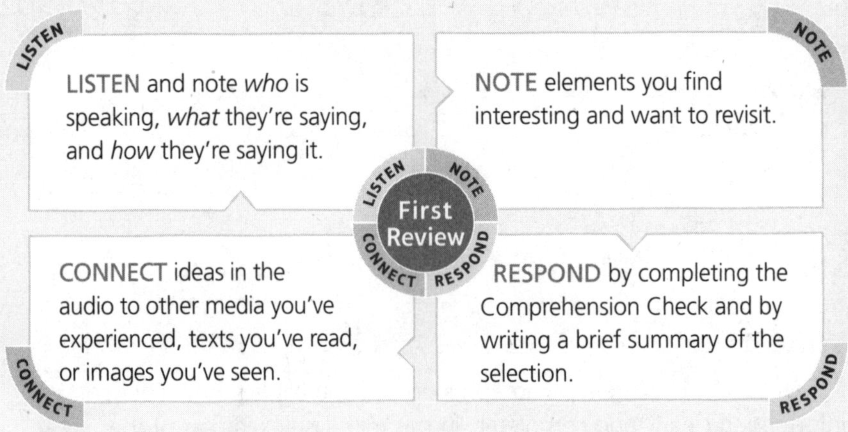


LISTEN and note *who* is speaking, *what* they're saying, and *how* they're saying it.

NOTE elements you find interesting and want to revisit.

CONNECT ideas in the audio to other media you've experienced, texts you've read, or images you've seen.

RESPOND by completing the Comprehension Check and by writing a brief summary of the selection.

**STANDARDS**

**Reading Informational Text**
By the end of grade 12, read and comprehend literary nonfiction at the high end of the grades 11–CCR text complexity band independently and proficiently.

**Language**
Acquire and use accurately general academic and domain-specific words and phrases, sufficient for reading, writing, speaking, and listening at the college and career readiness level; demonstrate independence in gathering vocabulary knowledge when considering a word or phrase important to comprehension or expression.

# When Memories Never Fade, the Past Can Poison the Present

Alix Spiegel

## BACKGROUND

*All Things Considered* is a news program on the American network National Public Radio (NPR). The program combines news, analysis, commentary, interviews, and special features. An incisive interviewer, the program's host, Robert Siegel, has 40 years of experience working in radio news. Among those interviewed for this feature are two people who possess highly superior autobiographical memory (HSAM): Alexandra Wolff and James McGaugh. Correspondent Alix Spiegel contributed the story.

NOTES

## Comprehension Check

**Complete the following items after you finish your first review. Review and clarify details with your group.**

1. According to Alix Spiegel, how is Alexandra Wolff different from other people?

2. What experience does Wolff remember from middle school?

3. What day does Wolff relive over and over?

4. What is different about people like Wolff?

5. **Notebook** Confirm your understanding of the radio broadcast by writing a brief summary of what you have learned.

## RESEARCH

**Research to Explore** Do some research on highly superior autobiographical memory (HSAM). Find statistics that reveal the effect of this anomaly on the lives of people who have HSAM. Consider sharing your findings with your group.

## Close Review

With your group, listen to the broadcast again, and revisit your first-review notes. Record any new observations that seem important. What **questions** do you have? What can you **conclude**?

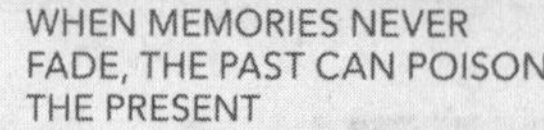
WHEN MEMORIES NEVER FADE, THE PAST CAN POISON THE PRESENT

## Analyze the Media

**CITE TEXTUAL EVIDENCE** to support your answers.

**Notebook** Complete the activities.

1. **Review and Clarify** Discuss key terms that Spiegel introduces in her feature. What does she mean when she says that "there are no fresh days, no clean slates without association" for people with highly superior autobiographical memory (HSAM)?

2. **Present and Discuss** Choose the part of the radio broadcast you found most interesting or powerful. Share your choice with the group, and discuss why you chose it. Explain what details you noticed, what questions you had, and what conclusions you reached.

3. **Review and Synthesize** With your group, review the entire broadcast. What does the broadcast add to your understanding of human memory and its connection to larger issues?

4. **Notebook** **Essential Question:** *How do we define ourselves?* How can the ability to remember everything affect a person's sense of self? Support your response with evidence from the broadcast.

### LANGUAGE DEVELOPMENT

## Media Vocabulary

**host** **correspondent** **interviewee**

Use the vocabulary words in your response to the questions.

1. Why is Spiegel's broadcast feature prefaced by Siegel's comments?

2. **(a)** What function does Spiegel serve in the broadcast?
   **(b)** How can you tell that she has prepared for the interview?

3. In what way do Alexandra Wolff and Bill Brown participate in the broadcast?

### STANDARDS

**Language**

Acquire and use accurately general academic and domain-specific words and phrases, sufficient for reading, writing, speaking, and listening at the college and career readiness level; demonstrate independence in gathering vocabulary knowledge when considering a word or phrase important to comprehension or expression.

THE MOST FORGETFUL MAN IN THE WORLD

WHEN MEMORIES NEVER FADE, THE PAST CAN POISON THE PRESENT

## Writing to Compare

You have explored two types of memory disorder by reading a piece of science journalism and listening to a radio broadcast. Now, deepen your understanding of the topic by analyzing what you have learned and expressing your ideas in writing.

**Assignment**

When you **evaluate** something, you assess or measure the degree to which it has a particular effect. Review what you have learned about anterograde and retrograde amnesia and highly superior autobiographical memory (HSAM). Then, write an **evaluative essay** in which you assess which disorder has a more profound effect on an individual's sense of self and relationship to society. Support your assessment with details and information from both the work of journalism and the radio broadcast.

### Prewriting

**Analyze Information** With your group, discuss how the text and the radio broadcast characterize the disorders. Use the chart to record facts, definitions, and images the two works use to show how the disorders affect people's lives.

| DISORDER | INTELLECTUAL EFFECTS | PHYSICAL EFFECTS | EMOTIONAL EFFECTS | SOCIAL EFFECTS |
|---|---|---|---|---|
| Total Anterograde and Retrograde Amnesia | | | | |
| Highly Superior Autobiographical Memory (HSAM) | | | | |

**Notebook** Respond to these questions.

1. How are the conditions similar? How are they different?
2. Which disorder seems to cause more suffering or disruption in a person's life? How so?

## Planning

**Discuss and Refine Ideas** Take an initial stand on the prompt for this assignment. Express your position, and discuss it with your group.

- Support your ideas with evidence from your Prewriting notes.
- Listen carefully to your peers' ideas, and then respond to them clearly and logically. Maintain a civil tone, and stay focused on the topic.
- After the discussion, consider what you learned. Has your initial stand been confirmed, or have you arrived at a new conclusion?

**Frame Your Argument** Write one sentence stating your central idea. Then, identify three supporting ideas. Think of each supporting idea as a "because" statement. For example, if your claim is that HSAM is the more devastating disorder, each supporting idea will be a reason that this is true. Record specific evidence from the texts you will use to bolster each supporting idea.

Central Idea: ______________________________

______________________________

Supporting Idea 1: ______________________________

______________________________

Evidence: ______________________________

Supporting Idea 2: ______________________________

______________________________

Evidence: ______________________________

Supporting Idea 3: ______________________________

______________________________

Evidence: ______________________________

EVIDENCE LOG

Before moving on to a new selection, go to your Evidence Log and record what you learned from "The Most Forgetful Man in the World" and "When Memories Never Fade, the Past Can Poison the Present."

## Drafting

**Write a Draft** Use your argument frame to draft your essay. Remember to include information from both the text and the broadcast to support your position. When appropriate, concede the negative aspects of the disorder you consider less disruptive.

### Review, Revise, and Edit

Once you have a complete draft, revise it for accuracy. Have you used precise language and accurate technical terms? Have you represented both disorders fully and thoughtfully? Have you omitted any information, or relied too heavily on minor facts? Swap drafts with group members, and proofread one another's work. Make the changes your peers recommend—and correct any other errors you find—to finalize your essay.

STANDARDS

**Reading Informational Text**
Integrate and evaluate multiple sources of information presented in different media or formats as well as in words in order to address a question or solve a problem.

**Writing**
- Write arguments to support claims in an analysis of substantive topics or texts, using valid reasoning and relevant and sufficient evidence.
- Introduce precise, knowledgeable claim(s), establish the significance of the claim(s), distinguish the claim(s) from alternate or opposing claims, and create an organization that logically sequences claim(s), counterclaims, reasons, and evidence.
- Apply *grades 11–12 Reading standards* to literary nonfiction.

SOURCES

- *from* MRS. DALLOWAY
- APOSTROPHE TO THE OCEAN
- THE WORLD IS TOO MUCH WITH US
- LONDON, 1802
- THE MADELEINE
- THE MOST FORGETFUL MAN IN THE WORLD
- WHEN MEMORIES NEVER FADE, THE PAST CAN POISON THE PRESENT

# Present a Narrative

**Assignment**

You have studied novel excerpts, poems, an excerpt from a science journalism text, and a radio broadcast about memory. Work with your group to plan and present a narrative in response to this question:

**What does it mean to find or lose oneself?**

Choose a character or person from one of the selections, and develop a **narrative** based on his or her experiences. Use details from the texts to develop your narrative. Remember to include a narrator, description, and a clear sequence of events. Then, present your narrative in front of the class.

## Plan With Your Group

**Analyze the Text** With your group, discuss the various ways in which the people and characters in these texts have found or lost themselves and how their experiences with memory have affected their senses of self. Use this chart to organize your ideas. Then, come to a consensus about which person or character you'd like to base your narrative on and why his or her story is so powerful.

| TITLE | DETAILS AND EXAMPLES |
|---|---|
| *from* Mrs. Dalloway | |
| Apostrophe to the Ocean<br>The World Is Too Much With Us<br>London, 1802 | |
| The Madeleine | |
| The Most Forgetful Man in the World | |
| When Memories Never Fade, the Past Can Poison the Present | |
| Our narrative will be based on ________________ because ________________________ | |

**Gather Details and Examples** Find specific details from the texts to support your narrative. Then, brainstorm for ways to integrate these details into a cohesive and engaging narrative. Consider whether you will directly quote or paraphrase your source material and how to blend this information into your original presentation. Allow each group member to make suggestions.

**Organize Your Narrative** Think about the sequence of events you will present in your narrative. Remember that most narratives begin with some exposition, feature a central conflict, and end with a satisfying conclusion. Decide if group members will take turns narrating a third-person account about the character or person you chose, or if you will assign roles and present your narrative as a drama, with one group member narrating the action.

## Rehearse With Your Group

**Practice With Your Group** Use this checklist to evaluate the effectiveness of your group's first run-through. Then, apply your findings and the instructions here to guide your revision.

| CONTENT | COLLABORATION | PRESENTATION TECHNIQUES |
|---|---|---|
| ☐ The narrative clearly responds to the question asked in the prompt.<br>☐ The narrative incorporates examples and details from the text. | ☐ Presenters work together to form a cohesive narrative with a clear sequence of events.<br>☐ Presenters build on each other's ideas in a clear and engaging way. | ☐ Presenters speak clearly and respond to one another.<br>☐ Presenters seem confident and well prepared. |

**Fine-Tune the Content** Does your narrative include adequate details and examples from your source text? If not, work as a group to find more and add them to the narrative.

**Improve Your Presentation Form** Make sure to stay within your time allotment. If necessary, summarize long descriptions or dialogue to get your main ideas across in a more succinct way.

**Brush Up on Your Presentation Techniques** Practice giving your presentation several times. Transitions between group members should be seamless. Try to memorize as much of your narrative as possible so you do not have to read from a piece of paper.

## Present and Evaluate

When you present as a group, make sure that each group member has taken into account each of the items on the checklist. As you watch the other groups present their narratives, evaluate how well they meet the same requirements.

STANDARDS

**Speaking and Listening**

- Initiate and participate effectively in a range of collaborative discussions with diverse partners on *grades 11–12 topics, texts, and issues*, building on others' ideas and expressing their own clearly and persuasively.
- Present information, findings, and supporting evidence, conveying a clear and distinct perspective and a logical argument, such that listeners can follow the line of reasoning, alternative or opposing perspectives are addressed, and the organization, development, substance, and style are appropriate to purpose, audience, and a range of formal and informal tasks. Use appropriate eye contact, adequate volume, and clear pronunciation.

## OVERVIEW: INDEPENDENT LEARNING

ESSENTIAL QUESTION:

# How do we define ourselves?

Ideas about what constitutes the "self" have changed over time. In what ways are modern ideas of selfhood different from those of the past? In this section, you will complete your study of perceptions of self by exploring an additional selection related to the topic. You will then share what you learn with classmates. To choose a text, follow these steps.

**Look Back** Think about the selections you have already studied. What more do you want to know about the topic of selfhood?

**Look Ahead** Preview the texts by reading the descriptions. Which one seems most interesting and appealing to you?

**Look Inside** Take a few minutes to scan the text you chose. Choose a different one if this text doesn't meet your needs.

## Independent Learning Strategies

Throughout your life, in school, in your community, and in your career, you will need to rely on yourself to learn and work on your own. Review these strategies and the actions you can take to practice them during Independent Learning. Add ideas of your own to each category.

| STRATEGY | ACTION PLAN |
|---|---|
| Create a schedule | • Understand your goals and deadlines.<br>• Make a plan for what to do each day.<br>• |
| Practice what you have learned | • Use first-read and close-read strategies to deepen your understanding.<br>• After you read, evaluate the usefulness of the evidence to help you understand the topic.<br>• Consider the quality and reliability of the source.<br>• |
| Take notes | • Record important ideas and information.<br>• Review your notes before preparing to share with a group.<br>• |

CONTENTS

Choose one selection. Selections are available online only.

NEWSPAPER ARTICLES

## Seeing Narcissists Everywhere

*Douglas Quenqua*

## A Year in a Word: Selfie

*Gautam Malkani*

Is there a difference between self-exploration and self-absorption?

ESSAY

## *from* Time and Free Will

*Henri Bergson*

Can you trust your own self?

NOVEL EXCERPT

## *from* The Portrait of a Lady

*Henry James*

Does it make sense to welcome hardships just to prove how strong and good you truly are?

PERFORMANCE-BASED ASSESSMENT PREP

## Review Notes for a Personal Narrative

Complete your Evidence Log for the unit by evaluating what you have learned and synthesizing the information you have recorded.

# First-Read Guide

**Tool Kit**
First-Read Guide and Model Annotation

Use this page to record your first-read ideas.

Selection Title: ______________________________

NOTICE

**NOTICE** new information or ideas you learn about the unit topic as you first read this text.

ANNOTATE

**ANNOTATE** by marking vocabulary and key passages you want to revisit.

NOTICE ANNOTATE First Read CONNECT RESPOND

**CONNECT** ideas within the selection to other knowledge and the selections you have read.

**RESPOND** by writing a brief summary of the selection.

CONNECT

RESPOND

STANDARD

**Reading** Read and comprehend complex literary and informational texts independently and proficiently.

# Close-Read Guide

**Tool Kit**
Close-Read Guide and Model Annotation

**Use this page to record your close-read ideas.**

**Selection Title:** ______________________________

## Close Read the Text

Revisit sections of the text you marked during your first read. Read these sections closely and **annotate** what you notice. Ask yourself **questions** about the text. What can you **conclude**? Write down your ideas.

## Analyze the Text

Think about the author's choices of patterns, structure, techniques, and ideas included in the text. Select one and record your thoughts about what this choice conveys.

## QuickWrite

Pick a paragraph from the text that grabbed your interest. Explain the power of this passage.

STANDARD

**Reading** Read and comprehend complex literary and informational texts independently and proficiently.

EVIDENCE LOG

Go to your Evidence Log and record what you learned from the text you read.

# Share Your Independent Learning

## Prepare to Share

How do we define ourselves?

Even when you read or learn something independently, you can continue to grow by sharing what you have learned with others. Reflect on the text you explored independently, and write notes about its connection to the unit. In your notes, consider why this text belongs in this unit.

## Learn From Your Classmates

**Discuss It** Share your ideas about the text you explored on your own. As you talk with your classmates, jot down ideas that you learn from them.

## Reflect

Review your notes, and underline the most important insight you gained from these writing and discussion activities. Explain how this idea adds to your understanding of the topic of how people define themselves.

STANDARDS

**Speaking and Listening**
Initiate and participate effectively in a range of collaborative discussions with diverse partners on *grades 11–12 topics, texts, and issues*, building on others' ideas and expressing their own clearly and persuasively.

# Review Notes for a Personal Narrative

At the beginning of this unit, you wrote about the following topic:

> **What types of experiences allow us to discover who we really are?**

EVIDENCE LOG

Review your Evidence Log and your QuickWrite from the beginning of the unit. Have your ideas changed?

| ☐ YES | ☐ NO |
|---|---|
| Identify at least three pieces of evidence that challenged your ideas. | Identify at least three pieces of evidence that supported your ideas. |
| **1.** | **1.** |
| **2.** | **2.** |
| **3.** | **3.** |

Develop your thoughts into a sentence that could be the theme of a narrative: *We learn most about who we really are when we*

______________________________

______________________________

Identify a character and an event that reflects your thematic idea and could be the kernel of a story:

______________________________

______________________________

**Evaluate the Strength of Your Ideas** Think about your own experiences with self-awareness. Write one positive and one negative experience you've had when trying to define yourself. List them here.

Positive experience: ______________________________

______________________________

Negative experience: ______________________________

______________________________

STANDARDS

**Writing**

Write narratives to develop real or imagined experiences or events using effective technique, well-chosen details, and well-structured event sequences.

SOURCES

- WHOLE-CLASS SELECTIONS
- SMALL-GROUP SELECTIONS
- INDEPENDENT-LEARNING SELECTION

## PART 1

# Writing to Sources: Personal Narrative

You have read a variety of texts that explore the development of a person's sense of self. Whether you experience an hour in the life of a character, as in *Mrs. Dalloway,* or watch as a speaker reveals deep feelings about nature and memory, as in "Lines Composed a Few Miles Above Tintern Abbey," you come away from the texts in this unit with a deeper understanding of what constitutes the "self."

**Assignment**

**Write a personal narrative in which you answer the following question:**

What types of experiences allow us to discover who we really are?

Think about one positive and one negative experience that helped you to develop a sense of self. Perhaps you came to some revelation while observing an object or a scene, as the Romantic poets did. Perhaps a conflict led to a change in your attitude. Record the experiences in narrative form, showing the repercussions of each event on your development. Infuse your narrative with sensory details that make your experiences come alive. Conclude with an explanation of how the experiences made you the person you are today.

**Reread the Assignment** Review the assignment to be sure you fully understand it. The assignment may reference some of the academic words presented at the beginning of the unit. Be sure you understand each of the words given below in order to complete the assignment correctly.

### Academic Vocabulary

| inanimate | anachronism | revelation |
|---|---|---|
| infuse | repercussion | |

**Review the Elements of a Personal Narrative** Before you begin writing, read the Narrative Rubric. Once you have completed your first draft, check it against the rubric. If one or more of the elements is missing or not as strong as it could be, revise your narrative to add or strengthen that component.

WORD NETWORK

As you write and revise your narrative, use your Word Network to help vary your word choices.

STANDARDS

**Writing**

- Write narratives to develop real or imagined experiences or events using effective technique, well-chosen details, and well-structured event sequences.
- Write routinely over extended time frames and shorter time frames for a range of tasks, purposes, and audiences.

# Narrative Rubric

| | Focus and Organization | Details and Elaboration | Language Conventions |
|---|---|---|---|
| 4 | The introduction engages the reader and reveals the focus of the narrative.<br>The narrative establishes and maintains a clear point of view.<br>Events are organized in a clear sequence and combine to build toward a particular outcome. At least two important events are clearly described.<br>The conclusion contains an engaging or original reflection on the significance of the events. | The narrative provides precise details that bring to life the setting, characters, and conflict.<br>The use of sensory language enriches the narrative. | The narrative intentionally uses standard English conventions of usage and mechanics.<br>The narrative contains no misspelled words. |
| 3 | The introduction is somewhat engaging and reveals the focus of the narrative.<br>The narrative establishes and maintains a point of view.<br>Events are organized in a clear sequence and mostly build toward a particular outcome. Two important events are described.<br>The conclusion contains a reflection on the significance of the events. | The narrative contains details that depict the setting, characters, and conflict.<br>The narrative makes use of some sensory details. | The narrative demonstrates accuracy in standard English conventions of usage and mechanics.<br>The narrative contains very few misspelled words. |
| 2 | The introduction reveals the focus of the narrative.<br>A point of view is maintained with occasional lapses.<br>Events are mostly in sequence, but the differentiation between events may be hard to follow. Two events are described.<br>The conclusion follows from the narrative but may not provide a reflection on the significance of events. | The narrative has few details that depict the setting, characters, and conflict.<br>Sensory details are used only sparingly; their effect is limited. | The narrative demonstrates some accuracy in standard English conventions of usage and mechanics.<br>The narrative suffers because of misspellings. |
| 1 | The introduction fails to reveal the focus of the narrative, or there is no introduction.<br>The point of view is not always clear.<br>Events are not organized in a clear sequence and are hard to follow. Two events are described minimally, or only one event is mentioned.<br>The conclusion does not follow from the narrative, or there is no conclusion. Little or no reflection is provided. | The narrative lacks details about the setting, characters, and conflict.<br>Few or no sensory details are used in the narrative. | The narrative contains mistakes in standard English conventions of usage and mechanics.<br>Misspellings are frequent, making the narrative difficult to read and understand. |

PART 2

# Speaking and Listening: Elevator Introduction

### Assignment

After completing a final draft of your narrative, condense the main ideas into a two-minute **elevator introduction**. In an elevator introduction, you tell significant details about yourself in a very short speech—the length of time you would spend riding up with someone in an elevator. Ask a classmate to record your speech in a video.

STANDARDS

**Speaking and Listening**

- Present information, findings, and supporting evidence, conveying a clear and distinct perspective, such that listeners can follow the line of reasoning, alternative or opposing perspectives are addressed, and the organization, development, substance, and style are appropriate to purpose, audience, and a range of formal and informal tasks.
- Make strategic use of digital media in presentations to enhance understanding of findings, reasoning, and evidence and to add interest.

Follow these steps to make your elevator introduction fascinating and understandable.

- Summarize your narrative, using key details from the two events you described. Include your explanation of how the events shaped your life.
- Decide how to use your voice to convey your feelings about the events.
- Practice your delivery, keeping in mind that your goal is to introduce yourself and intrigue your audience with your very short story.

**Review the Rubric** Before you deliver your elevator introduction, check your plans against this rubric. If one or more of the elements is missing or not as strong as it could be, revise your presentation.

| | Content | Use of Media | Presentation Techniques |
|---|---|---|---|
| 3 | The key events of the narrative are summarized in the elevator introduction.<br>The word choice is precise, lively, and engaging. | The video focuses on the speaker's face.<br>Sound is clear, and volume is appropriate. | The speaker looks at the camera.<br>The speaker effectively uses vocal changes to convey feelings. |
| 2 | Most of the key events of the narrative are included in the elevator speech.<br>The word choice is appropriate but could be more descriptive or engaging. | The video mostly focuses on the speaker's face.<br>Sound is mostly clear, and volume is usually appropriate. | The speaker looks at the camera from time to time.<br>The speaker occasionally uses vocal changes to convey feelings. |
| 1 | The narrative is poorly summarized, and the elevator introduction contains too few or too many details.<br>The word choice is uninteresting and unmemorable. | The focus of the video is erratic.<br>Sound and volume may vary. | The speaker seldom looks at the camera.<br>The speaker mumbles or speaks in a monotone. |

# Reflect on the Unit

Now that you've completed the unit, take a few moments to reflect on your learning. Use the questions below to think about where you succeeded, what skills and strategies helped you, and where you can continue to grow in the future.

## Reflect on the Unit Goals

Look back at the goals at the beginning of the unit. Use a different colored pen to rate yourself again. Think about readings and activities that contributed the most to the growth of your understanding. Record your thoughts.

## Reflect on the Learning Strategies

**Discuss It** Write a reflection on whether you were able to improve your learning based on your Action Plans. Think about what worked, what didn't, and what you might do to keep working on these strategies. Record your ideas before a class discussion.

## Reflect on the Text

Choose a selection that you found challenging, and explain what made it difficult.

Explain something that surprised you about a text in the unit.

Which activity taught you the most about discovering the self? What did you learn?

STANDARDS

**Speaking and Listening**

- Initiate and participate effectively in a range of collaborative discussions with diverse partners on *grades 11–12 topics, texts, and issues*, building on others' ideas and expressing their own clearly and persuasively.
- Come to discussions prepared, having read and researched material under study; explicitly draw on that preparation by referring to evidence from texts and other research on the topic or issue to stimulate a thoughtful, well-reasoned exchange of ideas.

# Finding a Home

## Nation, Exile, and Dominion

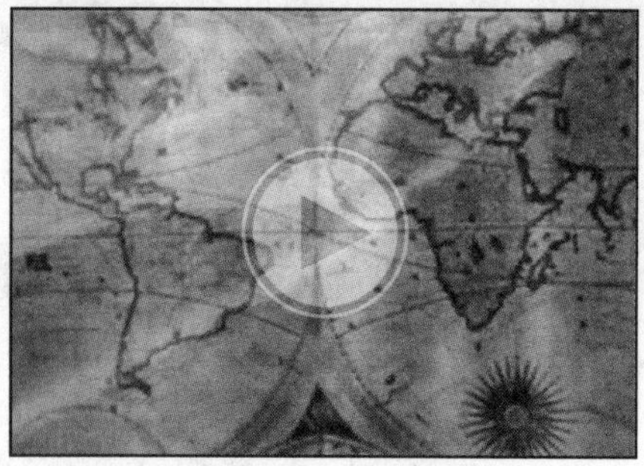

The British Empire Sets Its Sights West

**Discuss It** How do you define "home" when your nation is a global empire?

**Write your response before sharing your ideas.**

UNIT 6

## UNIT INTRODUCTION

ESSENTIAL QUESTION:

# What does it mean to call a place home?

LAUNCH TEXT
INFORMATIVE MODEL
Home Away From Home

## WHOLE-CLASS LEARNING

HISTORICAL PERSPECTIVES

*Focus Period: 1901–Present*
A Changing World

COMPARE

ANCHOR TEXT: ESSAY

Back to My Own Country: An Essay
*Andrea Levy*

ANCHOR TEXT: ESSAY

Shooting an Elephant
*George Orwell*

PERFORMANCE TASK

WRITING FOCUS:
Write an Informative Essay

## SMALL-GROUP LEARNING

COMPARE

HISTORY

*from* A History of the English Church and People
*Bede, translated by Leo Sherley-Price*

MEDIA: WEBSITE

*from* History of Jamaica
*Encyclopaedia Britannica*

POETRY COLLECTION 1

The Seafarer
*translated by Burton Raffel*

**MEDIA CONNECTION:**
The Seafarer

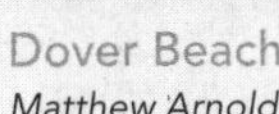

Dover Beach
*Matthew Arnold*

Escape From the Old Country
*Adrienne Su*

POETRY COLLECTION 2

The Widow at Windsor
*Rudyard Kipling*

From Lucy: Englan' Lady
*James Berry*

PERFORMANCE TASK

SPEAKING AND LISTENING FOCUS:
Present a Panel Discussion

## INDEPENDENT LEARNING

SPEECH | POETRY

St. Crispin's Day Speech
**from** Henry V, Act IV, Scene iii
*William Shakespeare*

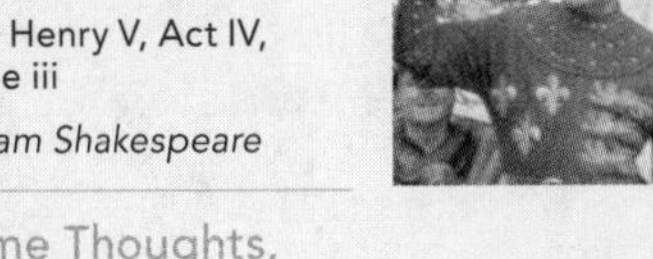

Home Thoughts, From Abroad
*Robert Browning*

NOVEL EXCERPT

*from* The Buried Giant
*Kazuo Ishiguro*

SHORT STORY

My Old Home
*Lu Hsun*

ESSAY

*from* Writing as an Act of Hope
*Isabel Allende*

PERFORMANCE-BASED ASSESSMENT PREP

Review Evidence for an Informative Essay

## PERFORMANCE-BASED ASSESSMENT

Informative Text: Essay and Media Presentation

PROMPT: In what ways is home both a place and a state of mind?

## Unit Goals

Throughout the unit, you will deepen your perspective of the meaning of home by reading, writing, speaking, listening, and presenting. These goals will help you succeed on the Unit Performance-Based Assessment.

Rate how well you meet these goals right now. You will revisit your ratings later when you reflect on your growth during this unit.

SCALE

| 1 | 2 | 3 | 4 | 5 |
|---|---|---|---|---|
| NOT AT ALL WELL | NOT VERY WELL | SOMEWHAT WELL | VERY WELL | EXTREMELY WELL |

| READING GOALS | 1 | 2 | 3 | 4 | 5 |
|---|---|---|---|---|---|
| • Evaluate written informative texts by analyzing how authors introduce and develop central ideas. | O | O | O | O | O |
| • Expand your knowledge and use of academic and concept vocabulary. | O | O | O | O | O |

| WRITING AND RESEARCH GOALS | 1 | 2 | 3 | 4 | 5 |
|---|---|---|---|---|---|
| • Write an informative essay in which you effectively convey complex ideas, concepts, and information. | O | O | O | O | O |
| • Conduct research projects of various lengths to explore a topic and clarify meaning. | O | O | O | O | O |

| LANGUAGE GOAL | 1 | 2 | 3 | 4 | 5 |
|---|---|---|---|---|---|
| • Correctly use appropriate and varied transitions to vary sentence structure and connect related ideas. | O | O | O | O | O |

| SPEAKING AND LISTENING GOALS | 1 | 2 | 3 | 4 | 5 |
|---|---|---|---|---|---|
| • Collaborate with your team to build on the ideas of others, develop consensus, and communicate. | O | O | O | O | O |
| • Integrate audio, visuals, and text in presentations. | O | O | O | O | O |

STANDARDS

**Language**

Acquire and use accurately general academic and domain-specific words and phrases, sufficient for reading, writing, speaking, and listening at the college and career readiness level; demonstrate independence in gathering vocabulary knowledge when considering a word or phrase important to comprehension or expression.

# Academic Vocabulary: Informative Text

Academic terms appear in in all subjects and can help you read, write, and discuss with more precision. Here are five academic words that will be useful to you in this unit as you analyze and write informative texts.

TIP

**FOLLOW THROUGH**

Study the words in this chart, and highlight them and their forms wherever they appear in the unit.

**Complete the chart.**

1. Review each word, its root, and the mentor sentences.
2. Use the information and your own knowledge to predict the meaning of each word.
3. For each word, list at least two related words.
4. Refer to a dictionary or other resources if needed.

| WORD | MENTOR SENTENCES | PREDICT MEANING | RELATED WORDS |
| --- | --- | --- | --- |
| **migrate**<br><br>ROOT:<br>***-migr-***<br>"move";<br>"shift" | **1.** Some animal species, including monarch butterflies, *migrate* thousands of miles every year.<br>**2.** With so many linked devices, it is easy to *migrate* documents from one environment to another. | | migration; migratory; immigrate; emigrate |
| **modify**<br><br>ROOT:<br>***-mod-***<br>"measure" | **1.** The weather forecast called for snow, so I had to *modify* my plans to bring shorts and sandals.<br>**2.** Your research may lead you to *modify* your thesis or even change it completely. | | |
| **requisite**<br><br>ROOT:<br>***-quis-***<br>"ask"; "seek" | **1.** To graduate on time, you must complete the *requisite* number of credits.<br>**2.** If you plan to be an expert in nineteenth–century British literature, that novel is *requisite* reading. | | |
| **reiterate**<br><br>ROOT:<br>***-iter-***<br>"again" | **1.** I plan to offer a new vision and will not just *reiterate* the same old ideas.<br>**2.** Olivia gets bored when I *reiterate* that story, but her little brother loves the repetition. | | |
| **implication**<br><br>ROOT:<br>***-plic- / -ply-***<br>"fold" | **1.** The council did not anticipate the *implication* of the new law, especially as it affects school funding.<br>**2.** One *implication* of her success as a medical student is that she'll be a great doctor. | | |

LAUNCH TEXT | INFORMATIVE MODEL

This selection is an example of an **informative text,** a type of writing in which the author examines concepts through the careful selection, organization, and analysis of information. You will write in this mode for the Performance-Based Assessment at the end of this unit.

**As you read,** look at how information is shared. Mark the text to help you answer this question: How does the writer introduce and develop a thesis about changing perspectives on the idea of "home"?

# Home Away From Home

NOTES

1 Leaving one's home to live elsewhere is one of humanity's oldest stories. Ever since people first began to settle in small villages, some of us have been pulled in the opposite direction, drawn toward life in new lands. Sometimes, we were fleeing danger; sometimes, by moving we faced new dangers. In all cases, our restlessness gave us new perspectives on the meaning of home. As Mark Twain wrote: "Broad, wholesome, charitable views of men and things cannot be acquired by vegetating in one little corner of the earth all one's lifetime."[1]

2 In the modern world, we are more mobile than ever. According to a United Nations report, there were nearly 191 million international immigrants worldwide in 2005. That represents about 3% of the world's population.[2] Despite these massive numbers, each person's experience of immigration can still feel unique and, often, challenging.

3 For example, new immigrants may struggle with language difficulties. Most people can speak and read the language of their country of origin. That sense of ease in a language may disappear in the adopted country. A language gap can make even ordinary chores a challenge. One might struggle to understand a receipt, to get on the right bus, or to read an ad. On a deeper level, language barriers may leave new immigrants feeling isolated, cut off from jobs, education, and even friendships.

4 Culture shock is another hurdle that new immigrants may face. Culture shock is a feeling of disorientation or alienation when one encounters the customs of another society. It can range from

1. Twain, Mark. *The Innocents Abroad.* Vol. 1, Bernard Tauchnitz, 1879, p. 333.
2. United Nations, Department of Economic and Social Affairs, Population Division. *International Migration Report 2006: A Global Assessment.* United Nations, 2009, pp. 5–6.

discomfort with new foods to a sense that certain behaviors are inappropriate. For example, in the United States it's considered proper to politely confront a co-worker with whom one is having problems. Asking a superior to intercede may be seen as a breach of trust or an inability to handle one's own problems. By contrast, in Japan, people generally avoid direct confrontation. An unhappy employee may readily ask a superior to speak to a co-worker on his or her behalf.

5 Gestures, facial expressions, and greetings can also be culturally specific. For example, in the United States, it is considered normal to smile at or say hello to a stranger one passes on the sidewalk. However, in Russia, most people do not smile at or greet strangers; they reserve outward signs of friendliness for friends and family.

6 Language and cultural barriers may make the prospect of feeling at home in a new country seem impossible to new immigrants. However, as the centuries have shown, human beings are resilient. We learn the languages of our adopted countries, often contributing words from the language we brought with us. We embrace or reshape the values of our adopted countries. Foods that were once foreign become part of the larger culture's culinary vocabulary. We build new senses of home. Perhaps, as our global mobility continues to increase, our sense of home will expand to include not just our immediate neighborhoods, but also the planet itself. ❧

NOTES

## WORD NETWORK FOR FINDING A HOME

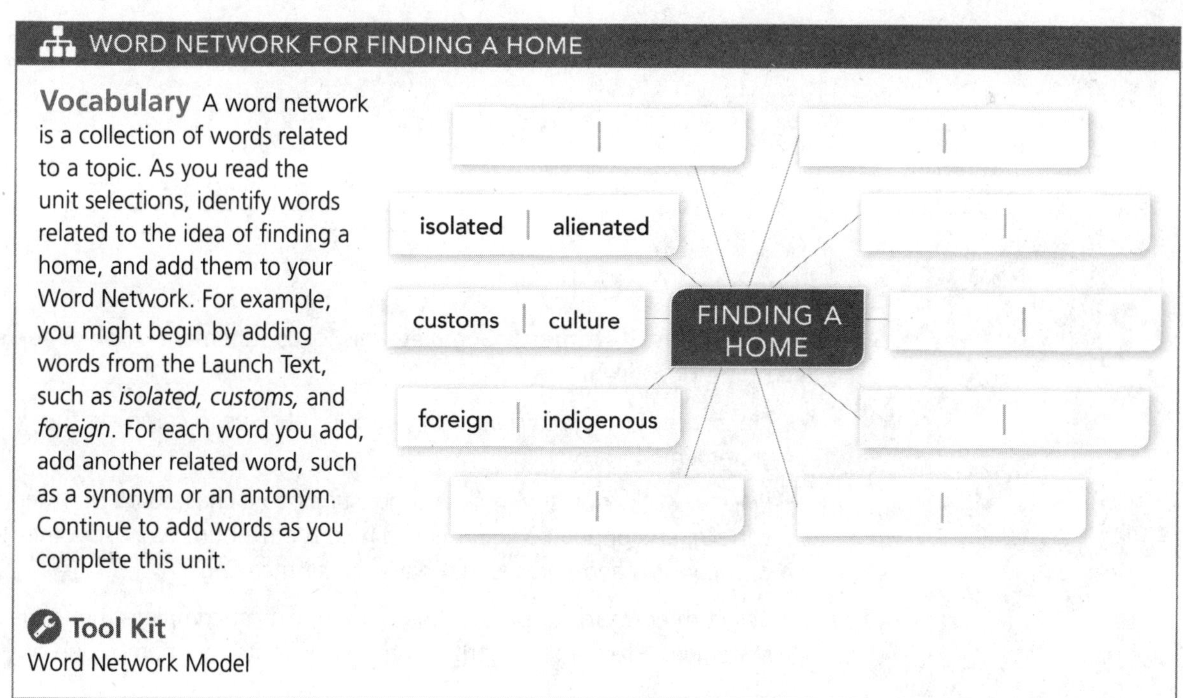


**Vocabulary** A word network is a collection of words related to a topic. As you read the unit selections, identify words related to the idea of finding a home, and add them to your Word Network. For example, you might begin by adding words from the Launch Text, such as *isolated, customs,* and *foreign*. For each word you add, add another related word, such as a synonym or an antonym. Continue to add words as you complete this unit.

**Tool Kit**
Word Network Model

## Summary

Write a summary of "Home Away from Home." Remember that a **summary** is a concise, complete, objective overview of a text. It should contain neither opinion nor analysis.

## Launch Activity

**Draft a Focus Statement** Complete this focus statement: A place feels like home because it is __________, __________, and __________.

- On a sticky note, record a set of words or phrases to complete the statement.
- Place all sticky notes with class suggestions on a chalkboard or other surface, and appoint a volunteer to read them aloud. Work together to group words and phrases that have similar meanings.
- Select three words or phrases that you think best complete the focus statement. Place a tally mark on each sticky note that names one of your choices.
- Find the three words or phrases that received the most votes. Decide as a class whether those three choices create a strong, convincing statement.

## QuickWrite

Consider class discussions, presentations, the video, and the Launch Text as you think about the prompt. Record your first thoughts here.

PROMPT: **In what ways is home both a place and a state of mind?**

### EVIDENCE LOG FOR FINDING A HOME

Review your QuickWrite. Summarize your initial position in one sentence to record in your Evidence Log. Then, record evidence from "Home Away From Home" that supports your initial position.

Prepare for the Performance-Based Assessment at the end of the unit by completing the Evidence Log after each selection.

**Tool Kit**
Evidence Log Model

Title of Text: ______ Date: ______

| CONNECTION TO PROMPT | TEXT EVIDENCE/DETAILS | ADDITIONAL NOTES/IDEAS |
| --- | --- | --- |
| | | |

How does this text change or add to my thinking? Date: ______

ESSENTIAL QUESTION:

# What does it mean to call a place home?

As you read these selections, work with your whole class to explore the idea of home.

**From Text to Topic** Is home simply the place that is most familiar to us or where our friends or family also live? Can we feel at home in a country where we are seen as different or as not belonging? As you read, consider the qualities that either make a place a home or keep it from being one.

## Whole-Class Learning Strategies

Throughout your life, in school, in your community, and in your career, you will continue to learn and work in large-group environments.

Review these strategies and the actions you can take to practice them. Add ideas of your own for each step. Get ready to use these strategies during Whole-Class Learning.

| STRATEGY | ACTION PLAN |
| --- | --- |
| Listen actively | • Eliminate distractions. For example, put your cellphone away.<br>• Jot down brief notes on main ideas and points of confusion.<br>• |
| Clarify by asking questions | • If you're confused, other people probably are, too. Ask a question to help your whole class.<br>• Ask follow-up questions as needed; for example, if you do not understand the clarification or if you want to make an additional connection.<br>• |
| Monitor understanding | • Notice what information you already know and be ready to build on it.<br>• Ask for help if you are struggling.<br>• |
| Interact and share ideas | • Share your ideas and answer questions, even if you are unsure.<br>• Build on the ideas of others by adding details or making a connection.<br>• |

HISTORICAL PERSPECTIVES

Focus Period: 1901–Present

## A Changing World

Cataclysmic events—two world wars, the Russian Revolution, and the collapse of the British Empire—fundamentally transformed England in the twentieth and twenty-first centuries. These events led writers—both those with traditional British ancestry and those who are the children of colonial subjects—to question what "home" really means.

COMPARE

ANCHOR TEXT: ESSAY

## Back to My Own Country: An Essay

*Andrea Levy*

How is an awkward trip on an English bus connected to the colonial history of Jamaica?

ANCHOR TEXT: ESSAY

## Shooting an Elephant

*George Orwell*

A rogue elephant presents a serious problem for a colonial policeman in Burma.

PERFORMANCE TASK

WRITING FOCUS

## Write an Informative Essay

The Whole-Class readings demonstrate how an individual's personal sense of home can be influenced by social issues, the passage of time, and even the strands of history. After reading, you will write an informative essay about how British colonialism complicated perceptions of home.

# A Changing World

## Voices of the Period

"*If we cast our glance back over the sixty-four years into which was encompassed the reign of Queen Victoria, we stand astonished, however familiar we may be with the facts, at the development of civilization which has taken place during that period. We stand astonished at the advance of culture, of wealth, of legislation, of education, of literature, of the arts and sciences, of locomotion by land and by sea, and of almost every department of human activity.*"

—Sir Wilfred Laurier, former British prime minister

"*At eleven o'clock this morning came to an end the cruelest and most terrible War that has ever scourged mankind. I hope we may say that thus, this fateful morning, came to an end all wars.*"

—David Lloyd George, former British prime minister

"*Only the dead have seen the end of war.*"

—George Santayana, philosopher

"*We shall defend our island, whatever the cost may be, we shall fight on the beaches, we shall fight on the landing grounds, we shall fight in the fields and in the streets, we shall fight in the hills; we shall never surrender.*"

—Winston Churchill, former British prime minister

## History of the Period

**The Victorian Era** When Queen Victoria died in 1901, she had reigned for more than six decades, longer than any British monarch until Queen Elizabeth II surpassed that mark in 2015. In the era that bears her name, Britain's old social and political order, which dated back to medieval times, was transformed into a modern democracy. When Victoria became queen in 1837, Great Britain was experiencing dramatic technological advances that had begun in the previous century. Rapid industrialization, the growth of cities, and political reforms were transforming Britain. At the same time, Britain became a worldwide empire. The period also witnessed the spread of poverty and great income inequality as well as advances in philosophy and science that threatened long-held beliefs. (Both Karl Marx's *The Communist Manifesto* and Charles Darwin's *On the Origin of Species* were published during this period.) Victorians could not escape the fact that on all fronts they were living "in an age of transition."

**An Empire Won** When Victoria celebrated her Diamond Jubilee in 1897, the British Empire stretched around the globe, making it the largest empire in history. Britain's flag flew over about a quarter of the earth's land, and the Royal Navy controlled all the oceans of the world. The right of one nation to control others, however, was not universally agreed upon either in Britain or in the many places subsumed into its empire. By 1922,

TIMELINE

1901

**1901:** Queen Victoria dies; Edward VII becomes king.

**1914:** Britain enters World War I.

**1917: Russia** Czar is overthrown; Bolsheviks, led by Lenin, seize power.

**1918:** Women over thirty achieve right to vote in Great Britain.

**1927: United States** Charles Lindbergh flies solo to Paris.

**1939: Europe** Hitler invades Poland; World War II begins.

**1940:** Winston Churchill becomes prime minister.

## Integration of Knowledge and Ideas

**Notebook** Compare the global political power of Britain in 1900 and today as shown on the two maps. Based on the list of Nobel Prize winners writing in English, what can you infer about the prevalence of the English language in former colonies?

**Nobel Prize Winners Writing in English**

| Year | Winner | Year | Winner |
|---|---|---|---|
| 1907 | Rudyard Kipling (Great Britain) | 1973 | Patrick White (Australia) |
| 1923 | William Butler Yeats (Ireland) | 1976 | Saul Bellow (United States) |
| 1925 | George Bernard Shaw (Great Britain) | 1983 | William Golding (Great Britain) |
| 1930 | Sinclair Lewis (United States) | 1986 | Wole Soyinka (Nigeria) |
| 1932 | John Galsworthy (Great Britain) | 1987 | Joseph Brodsky (United States) |
| 1936 | Eugene O'Neill (United States) | 1991 | Nadine Gordimer (South Africa) |
| 1938 | Pearl S. Buck (United States) | 1992 | Derek Walcott (St. Lucia) |
| 1948 | T. S. Eliot (Great Britain) | 1993 | Toni Morrison (United States) |
| 1949 | William Faulkner (United States) | 1995 | Seamus Heaney (Ireland) |
| 1950 | Bertrand Russell (Great Britain) | 2001 | V. S. Naipaul (Great Britain) |
| 1953 | Winston Churchill (Great Britain) | 2003 | J. M. Coetzee (South Africa) |
| 1954 | Ernest Hemingway (United States) | 2005 | Harold Pinter (Great Britain) |
| 1962 | John Steinbeck (United States) | 2007 | Doris Lessing (Great Britain) |
| 1969 | Samuel Beckett (Ireland) | 2013 | Alice Munro (Canada) |

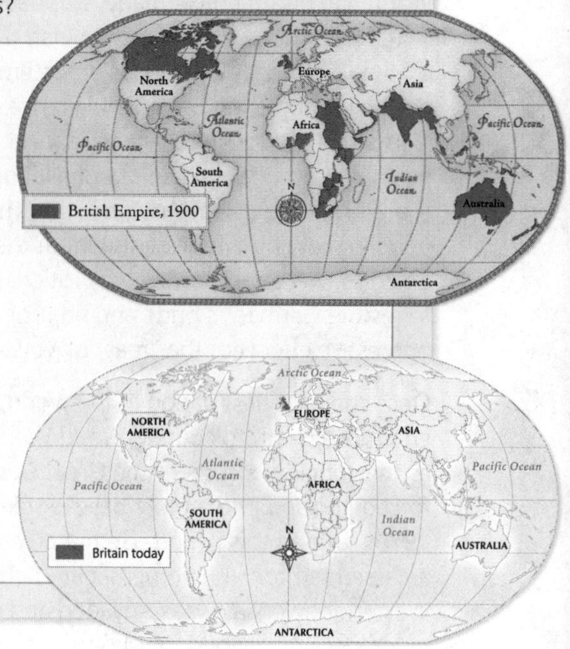


about one-fifth of the world's population was under British control.

**The War to End All Wars** On August 3, 1914, as Germany invaded Belgium, Sir Edward Grey, the British Foreign Secretary, looked over a darkening London and said, "The lamps are going out all over Europe; we shall not see them again in our lifetime." The next day, Britain declared war on Germany.

Many predicted the war would be brief. It was not. Instead, it lasted four long years. World War I cost Britain dearly—more than 700,000 British soldiers lost their lives. The war and its aftermath influenced much of what followed in the twentieth century.

In 1916, Irish nationalists, taking advantage of Britain's involvement in World War I, staged a rebellion against British rule. The rebellion failed, but its outcome deepened the ill feelings between Britain and Ireland.

In 1917, German authorities allowed Vladimir Lenin to return to Russia after a ten-year exile. There, he led the Bolshevik revolution, which transformed Russia from a czarist empire to a

**1941: United States** Japan bombs Pearl Harbor; United States enters World War II.

**1945: Japan** United States drops atomic bombs on Hiroshima and Nagasaki; World War II ends with Japanese surrender.

**1947: India** and **Pakistan** gain independence.

**1949: China** Mao Zedong establishes People's Republic.

**1955: United States** Martin Luther King, Jr., leads civil rights bus boycott.

1960

**1957: Russia** Sputnik I, first satellite, is launched.

Communist state, an event that would have far-reaching effects throughout the twentieth century and beyond.

The Treaty of Versailles, which followed World War I, had disarmed Germany, stripped it of valuable territory, and imposed harsh reparations on the German state. Zealous enforcement on the part of Great Britain and France led to Germany's economic collapse. Financial hardship, near-anarchy, and a sense of humiliation paved the way for the rise of Adolph Hitler. The German people, seething with resentment at their former enemies, were easily swayed by Hitler's promise to restore Germany's pride and rid it of the oppressive effects of the Treaty of Versailles.

Once the mightiest nation in the world, the enormous death toll during World War I as well as the crippling effects of the Great Depression forced England into a more passive role in the 1930s. During this period, Germany rearmed and amassed territory in Europe. Japan, perceiving Western powers as weak, invaded and occupied much of China. World War I, sometimes called "The war to end all wars," was the prelude to yet another global conflict.

**The Second World War** The aggression of Germany and Japan led inevitably to World War II. When Hitler's armies overran Europe, the English initially stood defiantly, but alone, shielded only by the English Channel and the Royal Air Force.

By the end of 1941, both Russia and the United States had entered the war. Finally, in 1945, after nearly six years of struggle, England emerged from the war victorious, battered, and impoverished—and soon to be without its empire as England's former colonies, one by one, became independent countries.

**A Time of Recovery** During the period of World War II know as the Blitz, in which the Germans bombed English cities over a period of 267 days, large sections of London were destroyed. From the ashes, a new London emerged. However, changes in other parts of the country were more problematic. The mill and mining country of the north was no longer the economic heart of the country as it had once been. Banking and technology, both concentrated in the south, took command. Over the following decades, the economic divide between the rusting north and the booming south only continued to grow.

**Pop Culture** After 1945, England's formerly conservative, somewhat rigid Victorian culture developed into a worldwide center of popular culture. From the Beatles to Carnaby Street, British culture swept the globe in "the swinging Sixties" and beyond.

**The New Face of Britain** In addition to an economic divide, postwar Britain felt the effects of racial and colonial divisions. When British citizens from the former colonies began to move to England, the nation became increasingly diverse. At the same time, an increase in the proportion of British students in universities contributed to innovation and new trends in British culture. The England that celebrated the Diamond Jubilee of Queen Elizabeth II in 2012 was a different nation from the England of Victoria's Diamond Jubilee 115 years earlier.

## TIMELINE

**1960**

**1961: Germany** Berlin Wall is built.

**1964: Vietnam** American involvement in Vietnam War grows.

**1969: United States** Apollo 11 lands on moon.

**1979:** Margaret Thatcher becomes first woman prime minister.

**1989: Germany** Berlin Wall comes down; reunification of East and West Germany follows.

## Literature Selections

**Literature of the Focus Period** A number of the selections in the unit were written during the Focus Period and pertain to perceptions of home as both a place and a state of mind.

"Back to My Own Country: An Essay," Andrea Levy

"Shooting an Elephant," George Orwell

from "History of Jamaica," Encyclopaedia Britannica

"Escape From the Old Country," Adrienne Su

"From Lucy: Englan' Lady," James Berry

from *The Buried Giant,* Kazuo Ishiguro

"My Old Home," Lu Hsun

from "Writing as an Act of Hope," Isabel Allende

**Connections Across Time** Reflections on the qualities of home as both a physical place and a psychological concept are age-old, as shown in literature of both the past and present.

from *A History of the English Church and People,* Bede

"The Seafarer," Burton Raffel, translator

"Dover Beach," Matthew Arnold

"The Widow at Windsor," Rudyard Kipling

"St. Crispin's Day," William Shakespeare

"Home Thoughts, From Abroad," Robert Browning

### ADDITIONAL FOCUS PERIOD LITERATURE

**Student Edition**

UNIT 1
"The Song of the Mud," Mary Borden
"Dulce et Decorum Est," Wilfred Owen
"Accidental Hero," Zadie Smith
"Defending Nonviolent Resistance," Mohandas Ghandi

UNIT 2
from "The Worms of the Earth Against the Lions," Barbara W. Tuchman
"Shakespeare's Sister," Virginia Woolf
"On Seeing England for the First Time," Jamaica Kincaid
"XXIII" from *Midsummer*, Derek Walcott
"The British"/"Who's Who," Benjamin Zephaniah

UNIT 3
from "The Naked Babe and the Cloak of Manliness," Cleanth Brooks
from "Macbeth," Frank Kermode
"Why Brownlee Left," Paul Muldoon
"The Lagoon," Joseph Conrad

UNIT 4
"The Second Coming," W. B. Yeats
"Araby," James Joyce
"The Explosion," Philip Larkin
"Old Love," Francesca Beard

UNIT 5
from *Mrs Dalloway*, Virginia Woolf
"The Madeleine," Marcel Proust
"The Most Forgetful Man in the World," Joshua Foer
from *Time and Free Will*, Henri Bergson
from *The Portrait of a Lady*, Henry James

**1991: Eastern Europe** Soviet Union is dissolved.

**2001: United States** Hijacked planes crash into the World Trade Center in New York, the Pentagon in Washington, D.C., and a field in rural Pennsylvania; thousands of lives are lost.

**2004:** United Kingdom's population surpasses 59 million.

**2012:** London hosts Olympic Games for the third time.

**2015:** Queen Elizabeth II becomes England's longest-reigning monarch.

Present

BACK TO MY OWN COUNTRY: AN ESSAY

## Comparing Texts

In this lesson, you will read and compare two essays. First, you will complete the first-read and close-read activities for the essay by Andrea Levy. The work you do on this selection will help prepare you for your final comparison.

SHOOTING AN ELEPHANT

**About the Author**

**Andrea Levy** (b. 1956) was born in London to parents who had emigrated from the Caribbean island of Jamaica. Her work—which includes novels, a short-story collection, and essays—is infused with questions about cultural identity and ethnicity in a post-colonial world. She is the winner of numerous awards, including the Orange Prize for Fiction and the Whitbread Award.

# Back to My Own Country: An Essay

## Concept Vocabulary

You will encounter the following words as you read "Back to My Own Country: An Essay." Before reading, note how familiar you are with each word. Then, rank the words in order from most familiar (1) to least familiar (6).

| WORD | YOUR RANKING |
|---|---|
| assimilate | |
| entitlement | |
| upbringing | |
| myriad | |
| indigenous | |
| hybrid | |

After completing the first read, come back to the concept vocabulary and review your rankings. Mark changes to your original rankings as needed.

## First Read NONFICTION

Apply these strategies as you conduct your first read. You will have an opportunity to complete the close-read notes after your first read.

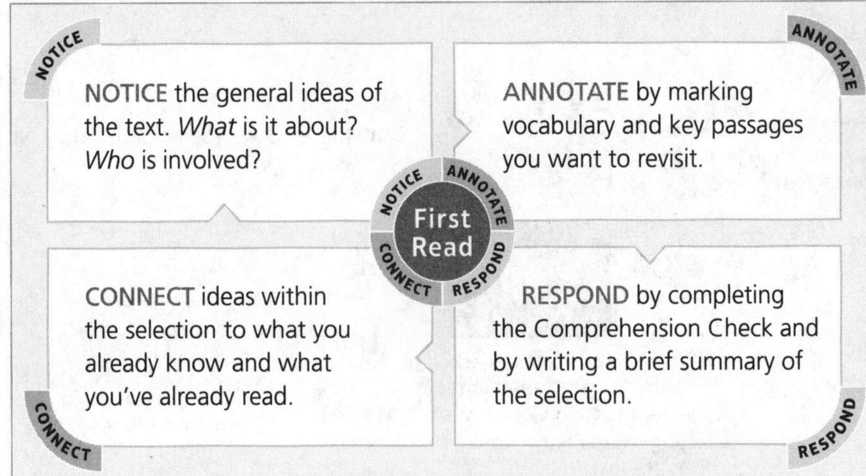

NOTICE
NOTICE the general ideas of the text. *What* is it about? *Who* is involved?
ANNOTATE
ANNOTATE by marking vocabulary and key passages you want to revisit.
First Read
NOTICE
ANNOTATE
CONNECT
RESPOND
CONNECT ideas within the selection to what you already know and what you've already read.
RESPOND by completing the Comprehension Check and by writing a brief summary of the selection.
CONNECT
RESPOND


**Tool Kit**
First-Read Guide and Model Annotation

**STANDARDS**

**Reading Informational Text**
By the end of grade 12, read and comprehend literary nonfiction at the high end of the grades 11–CCR text complexity band independently and proficiently.

# Back to My Own Country: An Essay

Andrea Levy

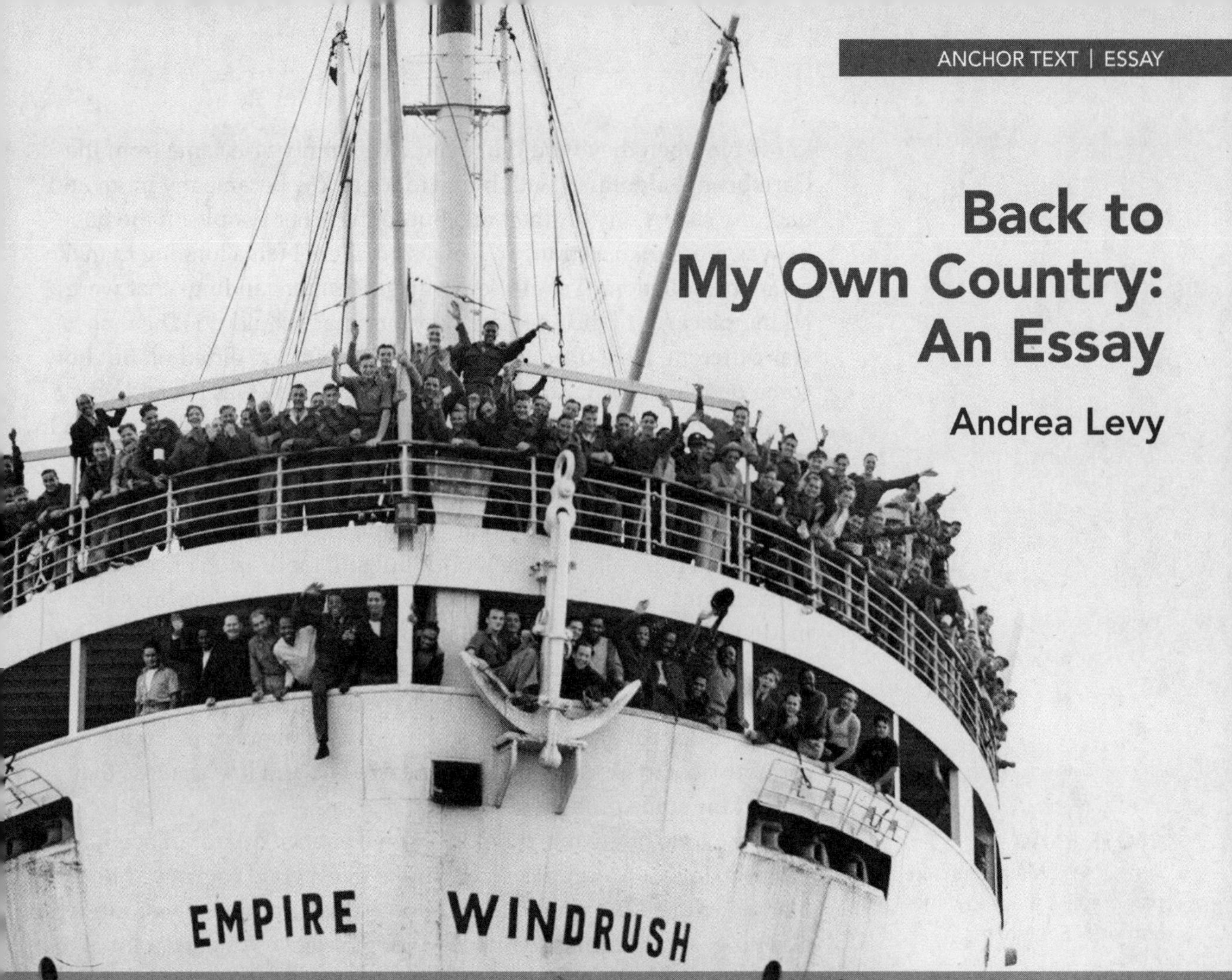


BACKGROUND

From the early 1500s to the late 1900s, Britain used its superior naval, technological, and economic power to colonize and control territories worldwide. At its peak, the British Empire covered more than 13 million square miles and included more than 450 million people. After World War II, independence movements transformed the empire. It was replaced with the British Commonwealth, an association of self-ruling nations, of which Jamaica is one.

1 I remember a journey I took on a London bus when I was a young girl. It was in the early nineteen sixties. The bus was full of people and one of them was a black man. That was not a common sight in those days. I could tell from his accent that, like my parents, he was from somewhere in the Caribbean. He was talkative, smiling politely at people and trying to engage them in chat. But all the other people on the bus were white and they were looking at him askance.[1] Nobody would be drawn into conversation; they clearly wanted nothing to do with him. But he carried on trying anyway.

2 I was embarrassed by him, but also overcome with pity for his hopeless attempt to be friendly on a London bus. I was sure that he was a nice man and that if those people on the bus could just get to

NOTES

**CLOSE READ**

**ANNOTATE:** Mark details in the first paragraph that describe the man from the Caribbean.

**QUESTION:** How do these details contrast with the description of the others on the bus?

**CONCLUDE:** With whom do the sympathies of the author lie in this anecdote? How can you tell?

1. **askance** (uh SKANS) *adv.* with suspicion or disapproval.

NOTES

know him then they would like him. My family also came from the Caribbean. I identified with him. He somehow became my mom and dad, my sisters, my brother, me. But to the other people on the bus he was more than a stranger, he was an alien. I felt a longing to make some introductions. I could sense the misunderstandings that were taking place, but I didn't know why, or what I could do. The man was different. He looked different and he sounded different. But how come people in England did not know him? Why was he, and why were all black people from Britain's old empire, so completely alien to them? This encounter is something I will never forget.

3 The same thing would not happen today in quite that way. Everyone is used to a mix of cultures and London buses are full of Londoners from all over the world. But still there are silences and gaps in our knowledge and understanding. What are the links that made Britain a natural destination for that Caribbean man on the bus, fifty years ago? How and why did Britain forge those links in the first place? These are questions that have come to fascinate me, because they reveal what amounts to a lost history for many of us. It was certainly lost to me for much of my early life, and it was a loss that caused me some problems.

**CLOSE READ**

**ANNOTATE:** Mark details in paragraph 4 that show the author's "Englishness."

**QUESTION:** How do these details contrast with the information she provides about her parents in paragraph 5?

**CONCLUDE:** What point is the author making by including these contrasting details after her bus anecdote?

4 At the time of my bus ride I lived on a council estate[2] in north London. I went to a local school. Spoke like a good cockney.[3] I played outside with all the white kids who lived around my way—rounders, skipping, and hide and seek. I ate a lot of sweets. Watched a lot of television: *Coronation Street, Emergency Ward 10.* Loved the Arsenal. Hated Tottenham Hotspur.[4] I lived the life of an ordinary London working-class girl.

5 But my parents had come to this country from Jamaica. And in the area of London where we lived, that made my family very odd. We were immigrants. Outsiders. My dad had been a passenger on the *Empire Windrush*[5] ship when it famously sailed into Tilbury in June 1948 and, according to many, changed the face of Britain for ever. My mom came to England on a Jamaica Banana Producer's boat. It sailed into West India dock on Guy Fawkes Night[6] in the same year, under a shower of fireworks that my mom believed were to welcome her.

6 My dad was an accounting clerk in Jamaica for, among other companies, Tate & Lyle. My mom was a teacher. They were middle class. They grew up in large houses. They even had servants. They came to Britain on British Empire passports in order to find more opportunities for work and advancement. But once here they struggled to find good housing. They had to live in one room for

2. **council estate** housing project.
3. **cockney** (KOK nee) *n.* someone from East London, with a distinctive accent.
4. **the Arsenal . . . Tottenham Hotspur** English sports teams.
5. ***Empire Windrush*** This ship brought thousands of Caribbean men and women to England after World War II, forming the foundation of the modern African Caribbean community in England.
6. **Guy Fawkes Night** Every year on November 5, people across the United Kingdom light fireworks and bonfires to celebrate the anniversary of Guy Fawkes's foiled attempt to blow up the Parliament in London in 1605.

many years. They had a period of being homeless and then living in halfway housing where my dad was not allowed to stay with his wife and his three children. Eventually they were housed in the council flat[7] in Highbury where I was born, and where I grew up.

NOTES

7 My dad did not have trouble finding work. He was employed by the Post Office. But my mom was not allowed to use her Jamaican teaching qualification to teach in England. She needed to retrain. So she took in sewing throughout my childhood. But she still nursed her dream of becoming a teacher again.

8 In England, the fabled Mother Country that they had learned so much about at school in Jamaica, my parents were poor and working class.

9 They believed that in order to get on in this country they should live quietly and not make a fuss. They should **assimilate** and be as respectable as they possibly could. Clean the front step every week. Go to church on Sundays. Keep their children well dressed and scrubbed behind the ears.

**assimilate** (uh SIHM uh layt) *v.* become like the majority in a region or country by adopting its customs, viewpoint, character, or attitude

10 On one occasion my mom did not have money to buy food for our dinner. None at all. She worried that she might be forced into the humiliation of asking someone, a neighbor perhaps, for a loan. She walked out into the street praying for a solution, and found a one-pound note lying on the pavement. In my mom's eyes that was not a stroke of luck, that was a strategy.

11 My parents believed that, with no real **entitlement** to anything, they must accept what this country was willing to give. They were, after all, immigrants. As long as they didn't do anything too unusual that might upset the people of England, then they could get on. My mom was desperate for my dad to lose his accent and stop saying "nah man" and "cha" in every sentence. They never discussed Jamaica with anyone. My mom would get embarrassed if she saw a black person drawing attention to themselves. It drew attention to her as well, and she hated that.

**entitlement** (ehn TY tuhl muhnt) *n.* expectation; right

12 My family is fair-skinned. In Jamaica this had had a big effect on my parents' **upbringing**, because of the class system, inherited from British colonial times, people took the color of your skin very seriously. My parents had grown up to believe themselves to be of a higher class than any darker-skinned person. This isolated them from other black Caribbeans who came to live here—they wanted nothing to do with them.

**upbringing** (UHP brihng ihng) *n.* care and training given to a child while growing up

13 My mom once told me how, back in Jamaica, her father would not let her play with children who were darker than her. She said wistfully, "But I had to, or I would have had no one to play with." So when she came to England she was pleased to be bringing her children up amongst white children. We would always have lighter-skinned children to play with. I was expected to isolate myself from darker-skinned people too, and it seemed perfectly normal to me that the color of your skin was one of the most important things

7. **flat** *n.* British English for "apartment".

NOTES

about you. White people of course never had to think about it. But if you were not white, well then, how black were you? I accepted all of this as logical. That was how I would be judged.

14 Light-skinned or not, still we were asked, "When are you going back to your own country?" "Why are you here?" "Why is your food so funny?" "Why does your hair stick up?" "Why do you smell?" The message was that our family was foreign and had no right to be here. When a member of the far-right group the National Front waved one of their leaflets in my face and started laughing, I felt I owed *them* some sort of apology. I wanted them to like me. It would be years before I realized I could be angry with them.

15 The racism I encountered was rarely violent, or extreme, but it was insidious and ever present and it had a profound effect on me. I hated myself. I was ashamed of my family, and embarrassed that they came from the Caribbean.

16 In my efforts to be as British as I could be, I was completely indifferent to Jamaica. None of my friends knew anything about the Caribbean. They didn't know where it was, or who lived there, or why. And they had no curiosity about it beyond asking why black people were in this country. It was too foreign and therefore not worth knowing.

17 As I got older my feeling of outsiderness became more marked, as did the feeling that nothing in my background—my class or my ethnicity—was really worth having. At art college I encountered middle-class people for the first time. Proper middle class—debutantes with ponies, that sort of thing. Keeping those origins of mine a secret became paramount. Few people at my college knew I lived on a council estate. Once, when given a lift home, I got my friends to drop me at the gate of a proper house. I walked up the path waving them off. Then as soon as they were out of view I walked back to my flat.

18 I got a degree in textile design and worked as a designer for about ten minutes before I realized it was not for me. After that I worked for a brief while as a shop assistant, a dresser at the BBC and the Royal Opera House, and a receptionist at a family-planning clinic.

**CLOSE READ**

**ANNOTATE:** Mark details in paragraph 19 that describe an incident that was a rude awakening for the author.

**QUESTION:** Why did this incident surprise her?

**CONCLUDE:** For what reason do you think the author has shared this anecdote with readers?

19 Then something happened. I was working part-time for a sex-education project for young people in Islington. One day the staff had to take part in a racism awareness course. We were asked to split into two groups, black and white. I walked over to the white side of the room. It was, ironically, where I felt most at home—all my friends, my boyfriend, my flatmates, were white. But my fellow workers had other ideas and I found myself being beckoned over by people on the black side. With some hesitation I crossed the floor. It was a rude awakening. It sent me to bed for a week.

20 By this time I was scared to call myself a black person. I didn't feel I had the right qualifications. Didn't you have to have grown up in a "black community"? Didn't you need to go to the Caribbean a lot? Didn't your parents need to be proud of being black? Didn't my

friends need to be black? My upbringing was so far removed from all of that, I felt sure I would be found out as an impostor. I was not part of the black experience, surely?

21 It was a life-changing moment.

22 Fortunately I had recently enrolled on an afternoon-a-week writing course at the City Lit in London, just as a hobby. Writing came to my rescue. The course had an emphasis on writing about what you know. So, nervously I began to explore what I knew—my family upbringing and background, and my complicated relationship with color. Thinking about what I knew, and exploring my background with words, began to open it up for me as never before. I soon came to realize that my experience of growing up in this country was part of what it meant to be black. All those agonies over skin shade. Those silences about where we had come from. The shame. The denial. In fact I came to see that every black person's life, no matter what it is, is part of the black experience. Because being black in a majority white country comes with a **myriad** of complications and contradictions. It was writing that helped me to understand that.

In fact, I came to see that every black person's life, no matter what it is, is part of the black experience.

NOTES

**myriad** (MIHR ee uhd) *n.* uncountably large number; variety

23 A few months into the course I had the urge to visit Jamaica for the very first time and stay with the family I had never met. I went for Christmas. It was an amazing experience. I discovered a family I had never really known I had. I realized that I meant something to people who lived on the other side of the world. I met my aunt and cousins and saw where my mom grew up. I realized for the first time that I had a background and an ancestry that was fascinating and worth exploring. Not only that, but I had the means to do it—through writing.

24 I am now happy to be called a black British writer, and the fiction I have written has all been about my Caribbean heritage in some way or another. It is a very rich seam for a writer and it is, quite simply, the reason that I write. Toni Morrison was once asked if she felt constrained by her being seen as a black writer. She replied: "Being a black woman writer is not a shallow place but a rich place to write from. It doesn't limit my imagination; it expands it." That is how I feel.

25 The more I began to delve into my Caribbean heritage the more interesting Britain's Caribbean story became for me. The story of the Caribbean is a white story, too, and one that goes back a long way. The region was right at the very heart of Europe's early experiments in colonizing the world. In the 1500s it was the Spanish who first exploited those newly found islands, displacing the **indigenous** people. The Dutch, the French, and the British came soon after. The island claimed earliest for Britain was Barbados, in 1625. But soon Britain was a major colonizer in the region. A whole string of islands became "British." Islands that for a long time were seen as

**indigenous** (ihn DIHJ uh nuhs) *adj.* native to a particular country or region

NOTES

our most lucrative overseas possessions. Sugar was the main crop, as important to Britain then as oil is today. It was planted, harvested, and processed by the slave labor of black Africans. That slave trade from West Africa to the Caribbean and the Americas was the largest forced migration in human history. Those islands soon became brutal island-factories helping to fuel and to fund the industrial revolution in Britain. Huge family fortunes were made. Major cities like Bristol, Liverpool, and London grew wealthy on the proceeds. The money that slavery in the Caribbean generated was reinvested in Britain's industry and infrastructure. Britain's empire grew as a result.

26 When British slavery finally ended in 1833, compensation was paid by the British Government. It amounted to twenty million pounds (many billions in today's money). It was paid to the slave owners for the loss of their property. They were seen as the injured party.

27 But there is more to those Caribbean islands than just the history of slavery. Many white people went, if not in chains, then under duress: indentured servants and poor people from all corners of Britain who were trying to escape hardship at home or to build a new life. Many were press-ganged sailors, or convict labor. There were Sephardic Jews from Iberia, merchants from the Middle East and, later, indentured laborers from India and China. A social mix was created like in no other place on Earth. Creole cultures developed with a wide range of skin colors that were elaborately classified (mulatto, quadroon, octoroon, and so on) as a divide-and-rule tactic by the

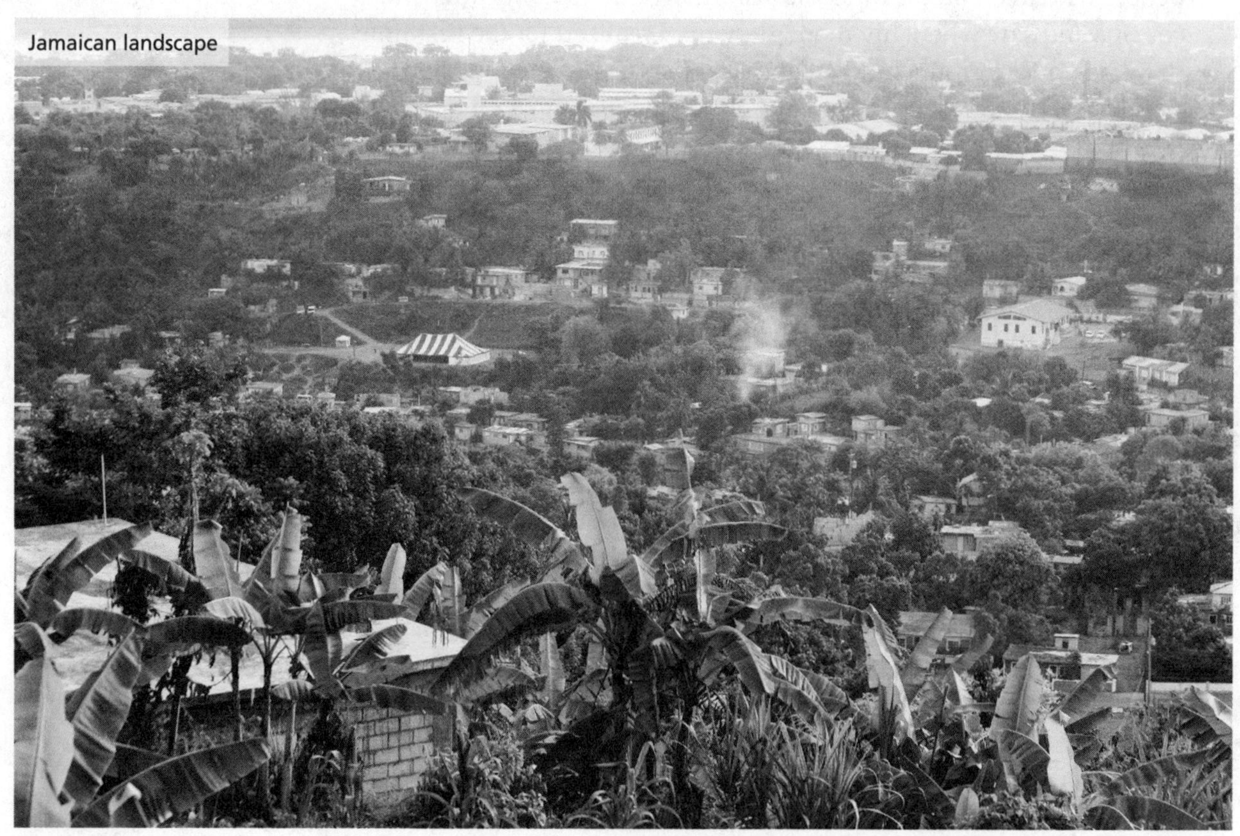
Jamaican landscape

British plantocracy.[8] Racial difference and racial value developed into a "science." After the end of slavery in the Caribbean the British continued to rule their islands through a policy of racial apartheid right up until they finally left in the nineteen sixties.

28 But all this happened three thousand miles away from Britain, and as a result it has been possible for it to quietly disappear from British mainstream history. This is the absence, the gap in knowledge, the amnesia of the British that made the black man on the bus such an alien. It is unthinkable that a book on American history could leave out plantation slavery in the southern states. But in British history books the equivalent is the case, or at least the importance of those centuries of British slavery in the Caribbean is underplayed. That British plantation slavery has no lasting legacy for this country is absurd, but it is a claim that is made implicitly by this silence. It was so very long ago, it seems to say, we don't need to dredge it up.

29 I remember what I was taught at school about Britain in the Caribbean. I had one lesson on the transatlantic slave trade. We looked at illustrations of slaves in ships. But that was all. I learned much more about William Wilberforce[9] and the campaign for the abolition of slavery than anything about the life of a slave. We know more about slavery in the American South than in the British Caribbean. We are familiar with the struggles of African Americans from the Civil War to the civil rights movement. But American slavery was different from Caribbean slavery. In the Caribbean, slaves far outnumbered the white owners, and that mix of isolation, fear, and dependency produced very different societies from those of the American South. America's story will not do for us. Our legacy of slavery is unique, and we need to understand what it is.

30 I wrote a novel, *The Long Song*, set in the time of slavery in the Caribbean, and when I was promoting the book I had numerous media interviews. On two separate occasions the interviewers—bright, university-educated people in each case—admitted to me that they had not known that Britain had used slaves in the Caribbean. Slavery they thought had only been in America. Going around the country doing readings I was surprised at the ignorance of people about where the islands were, or of how many of them there were. Many people I met believed all people from the Caribbean came from Jamaica.

31 And what of the period after slavery? What about the century of "racial apartheid" that grew up in the colonial era, the time when my mom and dad learned to know their racial place and to keep themselves separate? The history of the black people of the Caribbean is missing.

32 Apart from being an exotic holiday destination the islands have now become an irrelevance here. They are no longer wealthy. They

NOTES

**CLOSE READ**

**ANNOTATE:** Mark the sentences in paragraph 28 that show the main contrast the author sees between the teaching of American and British history.

**QUESTION:** Why is this contrast so surprising to the author?

**CONCLUDE:** What are the implications of this "silence" for British students studying their history?

8. **plantocracy** (plan TOK ruh see) *n.* plantation owners as a ruling class.
9. **William Wilberforce** English politician who fought for abolition of the slave trade.

NOTES

are not rich with natural resources. They no longer have the power they enjoyed when some of the most famous families in Britain were there. It is too easy to forget what happened and how it has affected our lives today. But it is as much a part of British history as the Norman Conquest, or the Tudors.[10]

33 No one would claim that out of Britain's many stories of empire the Caribbean is the most important. But it is one of the earliest, one of the longest in duration, and certainly one of the most unusual in terms of population mix and the creation of unique societies. In other parts of Britain's old empire, such as India or Africa, we can debate what fading legacy the British have left, whether it is railways, bureaucracies, or parliamentary systems. In the Caribbean the legacy is, in one sense, everything. Not just the towns, the cities, and the landscape, but the very people themselves; their origins, their ethnic mix, their **hybrid** cultures, all result from what the British did on those islands before they finally left them. And conversely, Britain growing to become a world power, its attitudes to race, and even how it sees itself today, these things are in no small part the legacy that the British Caribbean has left for modern Britain. "The very notion of Great Britain's 'greatness' is bound up with Empire," the cultural theorist Stuart Hall once wrote: "Euro-skepticism and little Englander nationalism[11] could hardly survive if people understood whose sugar flowed through English blood and rotted English teeth."

**hybrid** (HY brihd) *adj.* combined from different sources

34 What this means of course is that I, and my family, are products of Britain just as much as the white kids I grew up with in Highbury. Given Britain's history in the Caribbean it was almost inevitable that people like my dad and his fellow passengers on the *Windrush* would end up here. They belonged, whether Britain realized it or not. One of the consequences of having an empire, of being a cultural hub, is that the world ultimately comes to you. That's how hubs work.

**CLOSE READ**

**ANNOTATE:** Mark details in paragraph 35 that describe the "gift" of postwar immigration.

**QUESTION:** Why do you think the author chose the word *gift* as a way to represent the postwar history of immigration to Britain? What are the connotations of the word *gift*?

**CONCLUDE:** How would the impact of this paragraph change if the word *gift* were replaced with *benefit* or *asset*?

35 Britons of Caribbean heritage have been in this country in significant numbers for sixty-five years now. We are three or four generations on from the man on the London bus. Immigration to Britain since the end of the Second World War has been a final, unexpected gift to Britain from its old empire. The benefits that the labor and the enterprise of immigrants, like those from the Caribbean, have brought to Britain are incalculable. Their ideas, their creativity, and their ways of life have helped tum this country into a sophisticated multi-culture. This windfall of talent and variety is one of the great unforeseen benefits to Britain.

36 But there are still countless young Britons today of Afro-Caribbean descent who have as little understanding of their ancestry and have as little evidence of their worth as I did when I was growing up. And there are countless white Britons who are unaware of the

10. **the Norman Conquest, or the Tudors** The Norman Conquest was the takeover of England by invaders from northern France in 1066. The Tudors were highly successful kings and queens who ruled from the late 1400s to the early 1600s.
11. **Euro-skepticism and little Englander nationalism** political tendencies associated with mistrust of the European Union and of foreigners in general.

histories that bind us together. Britain made the Caribbean that my parents came from. It provided the people—black and white—who make up my ancestry. In return my ancestors, through their forced labor and their enterprise, contributed greatly to the development of modern Britain. My heritage is Britain's story, too. It is time to put the Caribbean back where it belongs—in the main narrative of British history. ❧

NOTES



## Comprehension Check

**Complete the following items after you finish your first read.**

1. According to Andrea Levy, why would the opening incident on the London bus not happen that way today?

2. What was the status of the author's parents when they were living in Jamaica? How did that status change when they got to England?

3. When Levy was growing up, why was she "indifferent to Jamaica"?

4. Why did the author resist being called "black"?

5. Why is Levy now happy to be called a black British writer—and to write about her Caribbean heritage?

6. **Notebook** Write a summary of "Back to My Own Country: An Essay" to confirm your understanding of the text.

### RESEARCH

**Research to Clarify** Choose at least one unfamiliar detail from the text. Briefly research that detail. In what way does the information you learned shed light on an aspect of the essay?

**Research to Explore** Conduct research on an aspect of the text you find interesting. For example, you might want to learn more about Andrea Levy's life in Britain and her literary achievements. Think about how your research findings enhance your understanding of the text.

BACK TO MY OWN COUNTRY: AN ESSAY

## Close Read the Text

1. This model, from paragraph 22 of the essay, shows two sample annotations, along with questions and conclusions. Close read the passage, and find another detail to annotate. Then, write a question and conclusion.

ANNOTATE QUESTION Close Read CONCLUDE

ANNOTATE: These short phrases come between elegant complex sentences.

QUESTION: Why does the author interrupt the flow of the passage with this series of short phrases?

CONCLUDE: They show that the author is sharing deep emotional thoughts instead of highly reasoned ideas.

I soon came to realize that my experience of growing up in this country was part of what it meant to be black. All those agonies over skin shade. Those silences about where we had come from. The shame. The denial. In fact I came to see that every black person's life, no matter what it is, is part of the black experience.

ANNOTATE: The author repeats the word *black* several times.

QUESTION: Why has the author chosen to emphasize this word?

CONCLUDE: After initially denying her ethnicity, the author now embraces it.

**Tool Kit**
Close-Read Guide and Model Annotation

2. For more practice, go back into the text, and complete the close-read notes.
3. Revisit a section of the text you found important during your first read. Read this section closely, and **annotate** what you notice. Ask yourself **questions** such as "Why did the author make this choice?" What can you **conclude**?

## Analyze the Text

**CITE TEXTUAL EVIDENCE** to support your answers.

**Notebook** **Respond to these questions.**

1. (a) What incident does the author describe at the beginning of the essay? (b) **Interpret** What role does this opening incident play in the essay?
2. (a) How did the author's family try to assimilate into the white culture? (b) **Make Inferences** What does this assimilation suggest about the family's beliefs about that culture?
3. **Historical Perspectives** In what way does the author's experience help you understand Britain's recent history?
4. **Essential Question: *What does it mean to call a place home?*** What have you learned about the concept of home from reading this essay?

STANDARDS

**Reading Informational Text**

- Cite strong and thorough textual evidence to support analysis of what the text says explicitly as well as inferences drawn from the text, including determining where the text leaves matters uncertain.
- Determine an author's point of view or purpose in a text in which the rhetoric is particularly effective, analyzing how style and content contribute to the power, persuasiveness, or beauty of the text.

# Analyze Craft and Structure

**Author's Point of View and Purpose** An **essay** is a short work of nonfiction that explores a specific topic and conveys a distinct **point of view:** the author's ideas, beliefs, and judgments about a specific topic. For example, in "Back to My Own Country: An Essay," Andrea Levy shares her point of view about growing up black in the predominantly white culture of 1960s London.

Once you have analyzed an author's point of view, the **author's purpose,** or reason for writing, becomes clearer. For example, you might determine that the writer is attempting to persuade, inform, or entertain readers. Most sophisticated writing, like Levy's, is driven by more than a single purpose. You can examine the ideas, opinions, and emotional tone of an essay and come to a conclusion about the author's specific reasons for writing.

## Practice

**CITE TEXTUAL EVIDENCE** to support your answers.

**Notebook Respond to these questions.**

1. Reread paragraphs 6–8 of "Back to My Own Country: An Essay." **(a)** What do these paragraphs describe? **(b)** What does this description and the author's reference in paragraph 8 to "England, the fabled Mother Country" reveal about Levy's point of view?
2. **(a)** Use the paragraphs from the text cited in the left column to determine the author's point of view about her subject.

| DETAILS FROM THE TEXT | AUTHOR'S POINT OF VIEW |
|---|---|
| The author encounters the man on the bus. (paragraphs 1 and 2) | |
| The author encounters middle-class people at college. (paragraph 17) | |
| The author begins writing about her background. (paragraph 22) | |
| The author visits Jamaica. (paragraph 23) | |

   **(b)** Use the details in the completed chart to describe how the author's point of view changes over time.
3. Judging from the details you have studied above, what might be the author's main purpose for writing this essay? Support your response with text evidence.

BACK TO MY OWN COUNTRY: AN ESSAY

# Concept Vocabulary

| assimilate | upbringing | indigenous |
|---|---|---|
| entitlement | myriad | hybrid |

**Why These Words?** These concept vocabulary words relate to encounters between cultures. For example, when the author's parents arrive in England from Jamaica, they try to *assimilate* into a new culture. During the author's *upbringing* in predominantly white London, she experiences a *myriad* of challenges due to her Afro-Caribbean heritage.

1. How does the concept vocabulary clarify the reader's understanding of the cultural conflicts Levy describes?

2. What other words in the essay connect to this concept?

## Practice

**Notebook** The concept words appear in "Back to My Own Country: An Essay."

1. Use each concept word in a sentence that demonstrates your understanding of the word's meaning.
2. Create sentence frames by rewriting your sentences, replacing the concept vocabulary word in each one with a blank. Share your sentence frames with a partner, and complete each other's sentences.

**WORD NETWORK**

Add interesting words related to finding a home from the text to your Word Network.

# Word Study

**Etymology and Usage: *myriad*** The word *myriad* originates from the Greek word *murioi*, which means "ten thousand" or, by extension, "uncountably many." *Myriad* may be used as either a noun ("a myriad of ideas") or an adjective ("myriad ideas"), although one of these uses is contested.

1. *Myriad* is used as a noun in paragraph 22 of Levy's essay. Rewrite the sentence from paragraph 22, using *myriad* as an adjective instead of as a noun.

2. Consult a reputable usage guide, such as *Merriam-Webster's Dictionary of English Usage,* to research which usage of *myriad* is contested. Explain your findings.

**STANDARDS**

**Reading Informational Text**
Determine an author's point of view or purpose in a text in which the rhetoric is particularly effective, analyzing how style and content contribute to the power, persuasiveness or beauty of the text.

**Language**
- Apply the understanding that usage is a matter of convention, can change over time, and is sometimes contested.
- Resolve issues of complex or contested usage, consulting references as needed.
- Apply knowledge of language to understand how language functions in different contexts, to make effective choices for meaning or style, and to comprehend more fully when reading or listening.

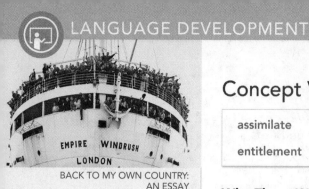

## Conventions and Style

**Voice and Development of Ideas** Authors use various techniques to convey a unique voice and develop ideas in their writing. For example, in "Back to My Own Country: An Essay," Andrea Levy uses **rhetorical questions**, or questions with obvious answers, to structure the development of her thoughts and cause the reader to identify with her position. Rhetorical questions can help readers feel personally and emotionally involved in a text by allowing them to see things from the author's perspective. Levy also uses **sentence fragments**, or groups of words that are punctuated like sentences but do not express a complete thought, in the essay. Sentence fragments can be used to create an informal tone, which enables readers to more closely identify with the author as a person.

The chart contains an example of each technique and the purpose it serves in the essay.

| TECHNIQUE | EXAMPLE | PURPOSE |
|---|---|---|
| Rhetorical question | *Why was he, and why were all black people . . . so completely alien to them?* (paragraph 2) | The author uses rhetorical questions to get readers' attention focused on issues she will then discuss. |
| Sentence fragments | *Watched a lot of television:* Coronation Street, Emergency Ward 10. *Loved the Arsenal. Hated Tottenham Hotspur.* (paragraph 4) | The author uses sentence fragments to create realistic, informal speech, enabling readers to regard her as a person, not an academic. |

### Read It

1. Reread this paragraph from "Back to My Own Country: An Essay."

   *And what of the period after slavery? What about the century of "racial apartheid" that grew up in the colonial era, the time when my mom and dad learned to know their racial place and to keep themselves separate? The history of the black people of the Caribbean is missing.*

   **a.** Identify and mark the rhetorical questions.

   **b.** What purpose do these questions serve in the paragraph?

2. What tone, or attitude, does the author convey through the use of this sentence fragment in paragraph 17: *Proper middle class—debutantes with ponies, that sort of thing.*

3. **Connect to Style** Reread paragraphs 20 and 22 of the essay. Mark the rhetorical questions and sentence fragments. Then, briefly describe the purpose each technique serves in the paragraph.

### Write It

**Notebook** Write a paragraph in which you describe someone you know or have read about who has assimilated into a new culture. Use at least one rhetorical question and one sentence fragment in your paragraph.

**PROCESS**
Analyzing the techniques an author uses to develop a unique voice is an important step in determining the effects of the author's style—how it contributes to the overall effectiveness or beauty of a text.

**EVIDENCE LOG**

Before moving on to a new selection, go to your Evidence Log and record what you've learned from "Back to My Own Country: An Essay."

## Comparing Texts

You will now read George Orwell's essay "Shooting an Elephant." After you have completed the first-read and close-read activities, you will compare the two essays in this section.

**About the Author**

**George Orwell** (1903–1950) is the pen name of Eric Arthur Blair, who was born in India to British parents working as civil servants. Though Orwell is recognized as a brilliant critic and essayist, he is best known for two of his novels, *Animal Farm* and *Nineteen Eighty-Four.* Both books explore the threat that totalitarianism posed to twentieth-century society. In *Nineteen Eighty-Four*, he showed how a government with total control over people's lives could distort information to the point where words no longer have meaning.

**Tool Kit**
First-Read Guide and Model Annotation

**STANDARDS**
**Reading Informational Text**
By the end of grade 12, read and comprehend literary nonfiction at the high end of the grades 11–CCR text complexity band independently and proficiently.

# Shooting an Elephant

## Concept Vocabulary

You will encounter the following words as you read "Shooting an Elephant." Before reading, note how familiar you are with each word. Then, rank the words in order from most familiar (1) to least familiar (6).

| WORD | YOUR RANKING |
|---|---|
| **imperialism** | |
| **supplant** | |
| **despotic** | |
| **conventionalized** | |
| **resolute** | |
| **pretext** | |

After completing your first read, come back to the concept vocabulary and review your rankings. Mark changes to your original rankings as needed.

## First Read NONFICTION

Apply these strategies as you conduct your first read. You will have an opportunity to complete the close-read notes after your first read.

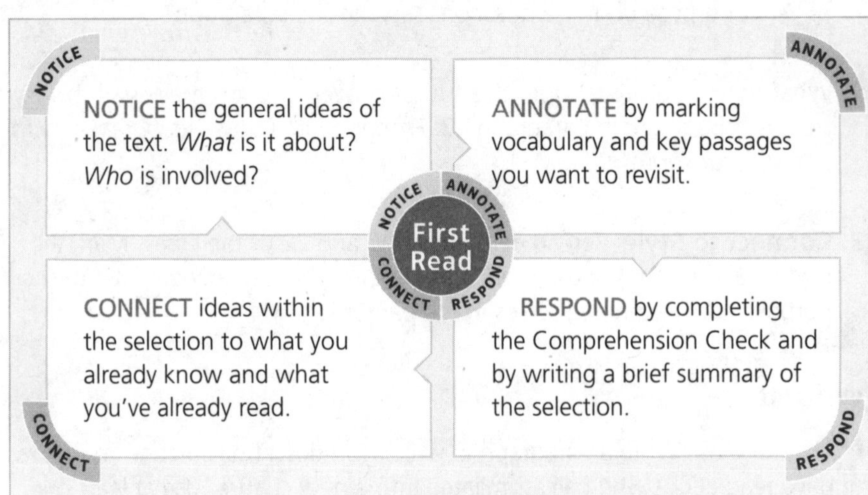

NOTICE
NOTICE the general ideas of the text. *What* is it about? *Who* is involved?
ANNOTATE
ANNOTATE by marking vocabulary and key passages you want to revisit.
First Read
NOTICE
ANNOTATE
CONNECT
RESPOND
CONNECT
CONNECT ideas within the selection to what you already know and what you've already read.
RESPOND
RESPOND by completing the Comprehension Check and by writing a brief summary of the selection.

# Shooting an Elephant

George Orwell

## BACKGROUND

Seeking more territory for its rapidly expanding empire, Great Britain launched three wars during the nineteenth century to conquer Burma, which is a region in southeast Asia now known as Myanmar. The Burmese never fully accepted British rule, and they finally achieved independence in 1948. This essay was written in 1936, during the time that the British Raj, or rule, controlled Burma with an iron fist.

1 In Moulmein, in lower Burma, I was hated by large numbers of people—the only time in my life that I have been important enough for this to happen to me. I was subdivisional police officer of the town, and in an aimless, petty kind of way anti-European feeling was very bitter. No one had the guts to raise a riot, but if a European woman went through the bazaars alone somebody would probably spit betel juice over her dress. As a police officer I was an obvious target and was baited whenever it seemed safe to do so. When a nimble Burman tripped me up on the football field and the referee (another Burman) looked the other way, the crowd yelled with hideous laughter. This happened more than once. In the end the sneering yellow faces of young men that met me everywhere, the insults hooted after me when I was at a safe distance, got badly on my nerves. The young Buddhist priests were the worst of all. There were several thousands of them in the town and none of them seemed to have anything to do except stand on street corners and jeer at Europeans.

2 All this was perplexing and upsetting. For at that time I had already made up my mind that imperialism was an evil thing and the sooner I chucked up my job and got out of it the better. Theoretically—and secretly, of course—I was all for the Burmese and all against their oppressors, the British. As for the job I was doing, I hated it more bitterly than I can perhaps make clear. In a

NOTES

**CLOSE READ**

**ANNOTATE:** In paragraph 1, mark words Orwell uses to describe the way Burmese people feel about Europeans.

**QUESTION:** What does Orwell's word choice reveal about the situation and setting?

**CONCLUDE:** Why do you think Orwell chooses to begin the essay with this information?

**imperialism** (ihm PEER ee uhl ihz uhm) *n.* policy of one nation's taking control over another in order to exploit its people and resources for its own benefit

NOTES

**CLOSE READ**

**ANNOTATE:** In paragraph 2, mark sentences that show Orwell's feelings about the British and Burmese.

**QUESTION:** What does the use of descriptions such as *oppressors* and *evil-spirited little beasts* show about Orwell's conflicting feelings?

**CONCLUDE:** Why does the author choose to be so brutally honest about his thoughts?

**supplant** (suh PLANT) *v.* replace one thing with another

**despotic** (dehs POT ihk) *adj.* in an oppressive manner typical of a tyrant or dictator

job like that you see the dirty work of Empire at close quarters. The wretched prisoners huddling in the stinking cages of the lockups, the gray, cowed faces of the long-term convicts, the scarred buttocks of the men who had been flogged with bamboos—all these oppressed me with an intolerable sense of guilt. But I could get nothing into perspective. I was young and ill educated and I had had to think out my problems in the utter silence that is imposed on every Englishman in the East. I did not even know that the British Empire is dying, still less did I know that it is a great deal better than the younger empires that are going to **supplant** it. All I knew was that I was stuck between my hatred of the empire I served and my rage against the evil-spirited little beasts who tried to make my job impossible. With one part of my mind I thought of the British Raj[1] as an unbreakable tyranny, as something clamped down, *in saecula saeculorum*,[2] upon the will of prostrate peoples; with another part I thought that the greatest joy in the world would be to drive a bayonet into a Buddhist priest's guts. Feelings like these are the normal byproducts of imperialism; ask any Anglo-Indian official, if you can catch him off duty.

3 One day something happened which in a roundabout way was enlightening. It was a tiny incident in itself, but it gave me a better glimpse than I had had before of the real nature of imperialism—the real motives for which **despotic** governments act. Early one morning the subinspector at a police station the other end of the town rang me up on the phone and said that an elephant was ravaging the bazaar. Would I please come and do something about it? I did not know what I could do, but I wanted to see what was happening and I got onto a pony and started out. I took my rifle, an old .44 Winchester and much too small to kill an elephant, but I thought the noise might be useful *in terrorem*.[3] Various Burmans stopped me on the way and told me about the elephant's doings. It was not, of course, a wild elephant, but a tame one which had gone "must."[4] It had been chained up, as tame elephants always are when their attack of "must" is due, but on the previous night it had broken its chain and escaped. Its mahout,[5] the only person who could manage it when it was in that state, had set out in pursuit, but had taken the wrong direction and was now twelve hours' journey away, and in the morning the elephant had suddenly reappeared in the town. The Burmese population had no weapons and were quite helpless against it. It had already destroyed somebody's bamboo hut, killed a cow, and raided some fruit stalls and devoured the stock; also it had met the municipal rubbish van and, when the driver jumped out and took to his heels, had turned the van over and inflicted violences upon it.

4 The Burmese subinspector and some Indian constables were waiting for me in the quarter where the elephant had been seen. It was a very

1. **Raj** (rahj) rule.
2. ***in saecula saeculorum*** (ihn SEE koo luh see koo LAWR uhm) "forever and ever" (Latin).
3. ***in terrorem*** "for terror" (Latin).
4. **must** into a dangerous, frenzied state.
5. **mahout** (muh HOOT) *n.* elephant keeper and rider.

poor quarter, a labyrinth of squalid bamboo huts, thatched with palm leaf, winding all over a steep hillside. I remember that it was a cloudy, stuffy morning at the beginning of the rains. We began questioning the people as to where the elephant had gone and, as usual, failed to get any definite information. That is invariably the case in the East; a story always sounds clear enough at a distance, but the nearer you get to the scene of events the vaguer it becomes. Some of the people said that the elephant had gone in one direction, some said that he had gone in another, some professed not even to have heard of any elephant. I had almost made up my mind that the whole story was a pack of lies, when we heard yells a little distance away. There was a loud scandalized cry of "Go away, child! Go away this instant!" and an old woman with a switch in her hand came round the corner of a hut, violently shooing away a crowd of naked children. Some more women followed, clicking their tongues and exclaiming; evidently there was something that the children ought not to have seen. I rounded the hut and saw a man's dead body sprawling in the mud. He was an Indian, a black Dravidian[6] coolie,[7] almost naked, and he could not have been dead many minutes. The people said that the elephant had come suddenly upon him round the corner of the hut, caught him with its trunk, put its foot on his back and ground him into the earth. This was the rainy season and the ground was soft, and his face had scored a trench a foot deep and a couple of yards long. He was lying on his belly with arms crucified and head sharply twisted to one side. His face was coated with mud, the eyes wide open, the teeth bared and grinning with an expression of unendurable agony. (Never tell me, by the way, that the dead look peaceful. Most of the corpses I have seen looked devilish.) The friction of the great beast's foot had stripped the skin from his back as neatly as one skins a rabbit. As soon as I saw the dead man I sent an orderly to a friend's house nearby to borrow an elephant rifle. I had already sent back the pony, not wanting it to go mad with fright and throw me if it smelled the elephant.

5 The orderly came back in a few minutes with a rifle and five cartridges, and meanwhile some Burmans had arrived and told us that the elephant was in the paddy fields[8] below, only a few hundred yards away. As I started forward practically the whole population of the quarter flocked out of the houses and followed me. They had seen the rifle and were all shouting excitedly that I was going to shoot the elephant. They had not shown much interest in the elephant when he was merely ravaging their homes, but it was different now that he was going to be shot. It was a bit of fun to them, as it would be to an English crowd; besides they wanted the meat. It made me vaguely uneasy. I had no intention of shooting the elephant—I had merely sent for the rifle to defend myself if necessary—and it is always unnerving to have a crowd following you. I marched down the hill,

NOTES

**CLOSE READ**

**ANNOTATE:** In paragraph 4, mark details that describe the events that are taking place.

**QUESTION:** Does a policeman encountering conflicting stories of an event seem unusual to you? Why or why not?

**CONCLUDE:** What do the author's descriptions reveal about the gulf between Orwell, the British policeman, and the Burmese people he's meant to protect?

6. **Dravidian** (druh VIHD ee uhn) belonging to a group of people inhabiting southern India.
7. **coolie** *n.* laborer; an offensive term that is no longer used.
8. **paddy fields** rice fields.

NOTES

looking and feeling a fool, with the rifle over my shoulder and an ever-growing army of people jostling at my heels. At the bottom, when you got away from the huts, there was a metaled road[9] and beyond that a miry waste of paddy fields a thousand yards across, not yet plowed but soggy from the first rains and dotted with coarse grass. The elephant was standing eight yards from the road, his left side toward us. He took not the slightest notice of the crowd's approach. He was tearing up bunches of grass, beating them against his knees to clean them, and stuffing them into his mouth.

6 I had halted on the road. As soon as I saw the elephant I knew with perfect certainty that I ought not to shoot him. It is a serious matter to shoot a working elephant—it is comparable to destroying a huge and costly piece of machinery—and obviously one ought not to do it if it can possibly be avoided. And at that distance, peacefully eating, the elephant looked no more dangerous than a cow. I thought then and I think now that his attack of "must" was already passing off; in which case he would merely wander harmlessly about until the mahout came back and caught him. Moreover, I did not in the least want to shoot him. I decided that I would watch him for a little while to make sure that he did not turn savage again, and then go home.

**CLOSE READ**

**ANNOTATE:** In paragraph 7, mark adjectives that Orwell uses to describe his mission.

**QUESTION:** How do these adjectives reflect the way Orwell seem to feel about his role?

**CONCLUDE:** Why does Orwell seem to lack firm conviction regarding any action he might take?

7 But at that moment I glanced round at the crowd that had followed me. It was an immense crowd, two thousand at the least and growing every minute. It blocked the road for a long distance on either side. I looked at the sea of yellow faces above the garish clothes—faces all happy and excited over this bit of fun, all certain that the elephant was going to be shot. They were watching me as they would watch a conjurer about to perform a trick. They did not like me, but with the magical rifle in my hands I was momentarily worth watching. And suddenly I realized that I should have to shoot the elephant after all. The people expected it of me and I had got to do it; I could feel their two thousand wills pressing me forward, irresistibly. And it was at this moment, as I stood there with the rifle in my hands, that I first grasped the hollowness, the futility of the white man's dominion in the East. Here was I, the white man with his gun, standing in front of the unarmed native crowd—seemingly the leading actor of the piece; but in reality I was only an absurd puppet pushed to and fro by the will of those yellow faces behind. I perceived in this moment that when the white man turns tyrant it is his own freedom that he destroys. He becomes a sort of hollow, posing dummy, the **conventionalized** figure of a sahib.[10] For it is the condition of his rule that he shall spend his life in trying to impress the "natives," and so in every crisis he has got to do what the "natives" expect of him. He wears a mask, and his face grows to fit it. I had got to shoot the elephant. I had committed myself to doing it when I sent for the rifle. A sahib has got to act like a sahib; he has got to appear **resolute**, to know his own mind and do definite things. To come all that way, rifle

**conventionalized** (kuhn VEHN shuhn uh lyzd) *adj.* turned into something predictable and expected

**resolute** (REHZ uh loot) *adj.* determined; firm

9. **metaled road** road in which the pavement is reinforced with metal strips.
10. **sahib** (SAH ihb) form of address for a European gentleman on the Indian subcontinent.

in hand, with two thousand people marching at my heels, and then to trail feebly away, having done nothing—no, that was impossible. The crowd would laugh at me. And my whole life, every white man's life in the East, was one long struggle not to be laughed at.

8 But I did not want to shoot the elephant. I watched him beating his bunch of grass against his knees with that preoccupied grandmotherly air that elephants have. It seemed to me that it would be murder to shoot him. At that age I was not squeamish about killing animals, but I had never shot an elephant and never wanted to. (Somehow it always seems worse to kill a *large* animal.) Besides, there was the beast's owner to be considered. Alive, the elephant was worth at least a hundred pounds, dead, he would only be worth the value of his tusks, five pounds, possibly. But I had got to act quickly. I turned to some experienced-looking Burmans who had been there when we arrived, and asked them how the elephant had been behaving. They all said the same thing: he took no notice of you if you left him alone, but he might charge if you went too close to him.

9 It was perfectly clear to me what I ought to do. I ought to walk up to within, say, twenty-five yards of the elephant and test his behavior. If he charged, I could shoot; if he took no notice of me, it would be safe to leave him until the mahout came back. But also I knew that I was going to do no such thing. I was a poor shot with a rifle and the ground was soft mud into which one would sink at every step. If the elephant charged and I missed him, I should have about as much chance as a toad under a steamroller. But even then I was not thinking particularly of my own skin, only of the watchful yellow faces behind. For at that moment, with the crowd watching me, I was not afraid in the ordinary sense, as I would have been if I had been alone. A white man mustn't be frightened in front of "natives"; and so, in general, he isn't frightened. The sole thought in my mind was that if anything went wrong those two thousand Burmans would see me pursued, caught, trampled on, and reduced to a grinning corpse like that Indian up the hill. And if that happened it was quite probable that some of them would laugh. That would never do. There was only one alternative. I shoved the cartridges into the magazine and lay down on the road to get a better aim.

10 The crowd grew very still, and a deep, low, happy sigh, as of people who see the theater curtain go up at last, breathed from innumerable throats. They were going to have their bit of fun, after all. The rifle was a beautiful German thing with cross-hair sights. I did not then know that in shooting an elephant one would shoot to cut an imaginary bar running from ear hole to ear hole. I ought, therefore, as the elephant was sideways on, to have aimed straight at his ear-hole; actually I aimed several inches in front of this, thinking the brain would be further forward.

11 When I pulled the trigger I did not hear the bang or feel the kick—one never does when a shot goes home—but I heard the devilish roar of glee that went up from the crowd. In that instant, in

NOTES

**CLOSE READ**

**ANNOTATE:** In paragraph 9, mark the details of Orwell's plan.

**QUESTION:** How do the details and practicality of Orwell's initial plan contrast with what he knows he's going to end up doing?

**CONCLUDE:** What larger observation about life does Orwell seem to be making by sharing this information?

NOTES

too short a time, one would have thought, even for the bullet to get there, a mysterious, terrible change had come over the elephant. He neither stirred nor fell, but every line of his body had altered. He looked suddenly stricken, shrunken, immensely old, as though the frightful impact of the bullet had paralyzed him without knocking him down. At last, after what seemed a long time—it might have been five seconds, I dare say—he sagged flabbily to his knees. His mouth slobbered. An enormous senility[11] seemed to have settled upon him. One could have imagined him thousands of years old. I fired again into the same spot. At the second shot he did not collapse but climbed with desperate slowness to his feet and stood weakly upright, with legs sagging and head drooping. I fired a third time. That was the shot that did for him. You could see the agony of it jolt his whole body and knock the last remnant of strength from his legs. But in falling he seemed for a moment to rise, for as his hind legs collapsed beneath him he seemed to tower upward like a huge rock toppling, his trunk reaching skyward like a tree. He trumpeted, for the first and only time. And then down he came, his belly toward me, with a crash that seemed to shake the ground even where I lay.

12 I got up. The Burmans were already racing past me across the mud. It was obvious that the elephant would never rise again, but he was not dead. He was breathing very rhythmically with long rattling gasps, his great mound of a side painfully rising and falling. His mouth was wide open—I could see far down into caverns of pale pink throat. I waited a long time for him to die, but his breathing did not weaken. Finally I fired my two remaining shots into the spot where I thought his heart must be. The thick blood welled out of him like red velvet, but still he did not die. His body did not even jerk when the shots hit him, the tortured breathing continued without a pause. He was dying, very slowly and in great agony, but in some world remote from me where not even a bullet could damage him further. I felt that I had got to put an end to that dreadful noise. It seemed dreadful to see the great beast lying there, powerless to move and yet powerless to die, and not even to be able to finish him. I sent back for my small rifle and poured shot after shot into his heart and down his throat. They seemed to make no impression. The tortured gasps continued as steadily as the ticking of a clock.

13 In the end I could not stand it any longer and went away. I heard later that it took him half an hour to die. Burmans were bringing dahs[12] and baskets even before I left, and I was told they had stripped his body almost to the bones by the afternoon.

14 Afterward, of course, there were endless discussions about the shooting of the elephant. The owner was furious, but he was only an Indian and could do nothing. Besides, legally I had done the right thing, for a mad elephant has to be killed, like a mad dog, if its owner fails to control it. Among the Europeans opinion was divided.

**CLOSE READ**

**ANNOTATE:** In paragraph 14, mark people's responses to the killing of the elephant.

**QUESTION:** Why does Orwell include these varying points of view in the final paragraph of the essay?

**CONCLUDE:** What idea about life does the final sentence of the essay suggest?

11. **senility** (suh NIHL uh tee) *n.* mental deterioration due to old age.
12. **dahs** (dahz) knives.

The older men said I was right, the younger men said it was a shame to shoot an elephant for killing a coolie, because an elephant was worth more than any Coringhee[13] coolie. And afterward I was very glad that the coolie had been killed; it put me legally in the right and it gave me a sufficient pretext for shooting the elephant. I often wondered whether any of the others grasped that I had done it solely to avoid looking a fool. ❧

NOTES

**pretext** (PREE tehkst) *n.* plausible but false reason

13. **Coringhee** (kawr IHNG gee) Southern Indian.

## Comprehension Check

**Complete the following items after you finish your first read.**

**1.** Why is Orwell asked to shoot the elephant?

**2.** How does Orwell's position force him into a situation that he would rather avoid?

**3.** What does the situation with the elephant make Orwell realize about the British imperialist mission in Burma?

**4.** What is the value of the elephant?

**5.** Why does Orwell finally decide to shoot the elephant despite its gentle appearance?

**6.** **Notebook** Write a summary of "Shooting an Elephant" to confirm your understanding of the text.

### RESEARCH

**Research to Clarify** Choose at least one unfamiliar detail from the text. Briefly research that detail. In what way does the information you learned shed light on an aspect of the essay?

SHOOTING AN ELEPHANT

## Close Read the Text

1. This model, from paragraph 7 of the essay, shows two sample annotations, along with questions and conclusions. Close read the passage, and find another detail to annotate. Then, write a question and conclusion.

Close Read — ANNOTATE, QUESTION, CONCLUDE

**ANNOTATE:** This passage features repetition, assonance, and alliteration.

**QUESTION:** Why has Orwell chosen to use devices such as these?

**CONCLUDE:** The use of poetic devices makes this passage rhythmic and memorable.

A sahib has got to act like a sahib; he has got to appear resolute, to know his own mind and do definite things. To come all that way, rifle in hand, with two thousand people marching at my heels, and then to trail feebly away, having done nothing—no, that was impossible. The crowd would laugh at me.

**ANNOTATE:** This sentence uses monosyllabic words; it sounds terse.

**QUESTION:** Why has Orwell chosen to follow long, complex sentences with this simple construction?

**CONCLUDE:** The change in style breaks the rhythm and gives emphasis to the sentence.

**Tool Kit**
Close-Read Guide and Model Annotation

2. For more practice, go back into the text, and complete the close-read notes.
3. Revisit a section of the text you found important during your first read. Read this section closely, and **annotate** what you notice. Ask yourself **questions** such as "Why did the author make this choice?" What can you **conclude?**

## Analyze the Text

**CITE TEXTUAL EVIDENCE** to support your answers.

**Notebook** **Respond to these questions.**

1. **Interpret** Orwell describes several ways in which the Burmese disrespect him. Does he blame them for treating him this way? Explain.
2. (a) How does Orwell feel about the British Empire and imperialism?
   (b) **Draw Conclusions** How do Orwell's feelings about the Empire affect his feelings about himself as a police officer?
3. **Make a Judgment** Ultimately, what reason does Orwell give for killing the elephant? How legitimate do you find his reason? Explain.
4. **Historical Perspectives** Orwell speaks of the British Empire as being in a state of decay. How true does Orwell's statement prove to be?
5. **Essential Question:** ***What does it mean to call a place home?*** What have you learned about the nature of home by reading this text?

**STANDARDS**

**Reading Informational Text**
Analyze a complex set of ideas or sequence of events and explain how specific individuals, ideas, or events interact and develop over the course of the text.

## Analyze Craft and Structure

**Situational Irony** George Orwell's "Shooting an Elephant" is a complex autobiographical essay that examines an event that took place in colonial Burma. Orwell's analysis of the situation is dependent on the narrative he tells about himself as a young man. To fully appreciate the essay and its nuances, look for ways in which the narrative element leads to **situational irony.** This is a circumstance in which the outcome of events is significantly different from what either participants in the story or readers expected. To prepare for your analysis, look for the following:

| | QUESTIONS FOR ANALYSIS |
|---|---|
| Characters' Actions | What causes people to act and speak as they do? Are any actions surprising or contrary to expectations? |
| Characters' Relationships | What sorts of relationships exist between Orwell and the other people he describes? Are these relationships typical or surprising? |
| Characters' Attitudes | How does the author feel about his situation or circumstance? In what ways is his attitude surprising, given his job title? |

### Practice

**CITE TEXTUAL EVIDENCE** to support your answers.

Notebook **Respond to these questions.**

1. Explain the situational irony in the statement "I was all for the Burmese and all against their oppressors, the British."
2. In the chart, list examples of situational irony from "Shooting an Elephant."

| SITUATIONAL IRONY IN "SHOOTING AN ELEPHANT" | |
|---|---|
| EXAMPLE | EXPLANATION |
| | |
| | |
| | |
| | |

3. How does Orwell's ironic style help convey the central idea of the essay?
4. Suppose Orwell needed to write an official police report of the incident. How might his report have differed from the account he wrote in "Shooting an Elephant"? Explain.

SHOOTING AN ELEPHANT

# Concept Vocabulary

| | | |
|---|---|---|
| **imperialism** | **supplant** | **despotic** |
| **conventionalized** | **resolute** | **pretext** |

**Why These Words?** These concept vocabulary words relate to the idea of political struggles, such as those the Burmese faced during the time of British rule.

1. How do the concept vocabulary words sharpen the description of political conflict that is depicted in the essay?

2. What other words in the selection connect to this concept?

## Practice

**Notebook** The concept vocabulary words appear in "Shooting an Elephant."

1. Write a fill-in-the-blank sentence for each concept vocabulary word. Be sure the context clearly shows the meaning of the word. Then, trade sentences with a partner, and complete the sentences with the appropriate word.
2. Consider the sentences that you read. Which concept vocabulary words were hardest to identify? Explain.

WORD NETWORK

Add interesting words related to finding a home from the text to your Word Network.

# Word Study

**Word Origins and Connotation** The word *imperialism* comes from the Latin word *imperium*, meaning "command" or "empire." The word *despotic* comes from the Greek word *despotēs*, meaning "master" or "lord." These words both have negative **connotations**, or associations.

1. Write whether each of the following words from the selection has a positive or negative connotation: *perplexing, oppressors, imposed, tyranny, prostrate*. Now, find each word in a dictionary, and determine from which Latin or Greek word it comes.

2. Choose three more words from "Shooting an Elephant," and tell whether they have positive or negative connotations. Verify your determinations using a college-level dictionary.

STANDARDS

**Reading Informational Text**
Determine an author's point of view or purpose in a text in which the rhetoric is particularly effective, analyzing how style and content contribute to the power, persuasiveness or beauty of the text.

**Language**
- Apply knowledge of language to understand how language functions in different contexts, to make effective choices for meaning or style, and to comprehend more fully when reading or listening.
- Demonstrate understanding of figurative language, word relationships, and nuances in word meanings.

## Conventions and Style

**Formal and Informal Language** In "Shooting an Elephant," Orwell explores a bitter conflict between cultures that both sides are reluctant to recognize openly. To capture this contradictory situation, Orwell takes on a **tone,** or attitude toward the subject or audience, that itself is contradictory. In one instant, he may be highly informal and adopt a joking tone, yet in the next, he may use terms that create a serious, formal, and solemn tone.

| FORMAL | INFORMAL |
|---|---|
| *With one part of my mind I thought of the British Raj as an unbreakable tyranny, as something clamped down,* in saecula saeculorum, *upon the will of prostrate peoples. . . .* (paragraph 2) | *. . . with another part [of my mind] I thought that the greatest joy in the world would be to drive a bayonet into a Buddhist priest's guts.* (paragraph 2) |
| *All this was perplexing and upsetting.* (paragraph 2) | *. . . the sooner I chucked up my job and got out of it the better.* (paragraph 2) |
| *. . . he has got to appear resolute, to know his own mind and do definite things.* (paragraph 7) | *. . . I had done it solely to avoid looking a fool.* (paragraph 14) |

### Read It

1. Reread paragraphs 2 and 3 of "Shooting an Elephant." Identify examples of formal and informal language.
2. **Connect to Style** Reread paragraph 4 of "Shooting an Elephant." Identify examples of formal and informal language. What effect does the change from formal to informal language have?

### Write It

In the example, the original formal sentence has been rewritten in an informal style.

EXAMPLE

**Formal:** As it were, the man responded with an overabundance of colorful and vulgar verbiage in which he called into question my basic integrity as a public police official.

**Informal:** The guy came back with a bunch of nasty hogwash in which he trashed me as a crooked cop.

**Notebook** Using the example as a model, rewrite each sentence (the first from "Shooting an Elephant") in the manner described.

1. **From formal to informal:** It is a serious matter to shoot a working elephant—it is comparable to destroying a huge and costly piece of machinery—and obviously one ought not to do it if it can possibly be avoided.
2. **From informal to formal:** After that little adventure, I had a few laughs with my buddy to blow off steam before heading home to mull the whole thing over.

BACK TO MY OWN COUNTRY: AN ESSAY

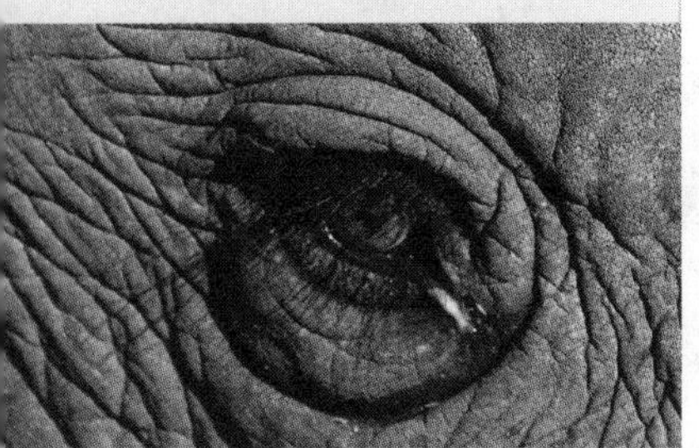
SHOOTING AN ELEPHANT

# Writing to Compare

You have read two essays that explore cultural tensions: "Back to My Own Country: An Essay," by Andrea Levy, and "Shooting an Elephant," by George Orwell. Both essayists base their discussions about broad cultural issues on personal experiences. Yet, each writer's **voice**—or personality on the page—is distinctive. A writer's voice is shaped by many elements, including **tone,** the writer's attitude toward his or her subject; **diction,** the types of words and phrases the writer uses; and **sentence structure,** the way a writer casts thoughts into language. Now, deepen your understanding of both texts by analyzing the authors' choices, and comparing and contrasting the essays in writing

### Assignment

Write a **comparison-and-contrast essay** in which you analyze the two works. Focus on the authors' voices and the structures of the stories they tell. Draw conclusions about what each essay does particularly well.

STANDARDS

**Reading Informational Text**

- Analyze a complex set of ideas or sequence of events and explain how specific individuals, ideas, or events interact and develop over the course of the text.
- Analyze and evaluate the effectiveness of the structure an author uses in his or her exposition or argument, including whether the structure makes points clear, convincing, and engaging.

## Prewriting

**Analyze the Texts** Compare and contrast the authors' choices regarding language, structure, and content. Use these questions to guide your analysis:

- **Text structure:** From what key memory or episode does each essay spring? In what order does the author present information? How does each author connect a specific event to larger ideas?
- **Timeframe:** What is the chronological scope of the essay? How does such a scope of time—long or short—help express a central idea?
- **Voice:** Is the voice formal, or casual? What is the tone? How do words, phrases, and sentences create that tone?

| | BACK TO MY OWN COUNTRY | SHOOTING AN ELEPHANT |
|---|---|---|
| Text Structure | | |
| Timeframe | | |
| Voice | | |

**Notebook** Respond to these questions.

1. What is your response to each author's voice? Does it evoke sympathy, respect, concern, a sense of camaraderie—or something else?
2. Which elements of each text keep the reader most engaged? Why?

## Drafting

**Write a Thesis Statement** In a compare-and-contrast essay, the thesis statement should indicate the major similarities and major differences of the two works being compared. Draft a thesis statement consisting of two or three sentences. State how "Back to My Own Country" and "Shooting an Elephant" are similar, and how they are different. Use compare and contrast key words such as those underlined in the frame below.

**Thesis frame:**

Both "Back to My Own Country" and "Shooting an Elephant" ______________________________________________
______________________________________________.

However, Levy's essay ______________________________,
whereas Orwell's ______________________________

**Choose a Structure** Decide how you want to organize your essay. Consider using one of the following two formats.

| BLOCK ORGANIZATION | POINT-BY-POINT ORGANIZATION |
|---|---|
| **I. "Back to My Own Country: An Essay"**<br>**A. text structure**<br>**B. timeframe**<br>**C. voice**<br>**II. "Shooting an Elephant"**<br>**A. text structure**<br>**B. timeframe**<br>**C. voice** | **I. Text structure**<br>**A. "Back to My Own Country: An Essay"**<br>**B. "Shooting an Elephant"**<br>**II. Timeframe**<br>**A. "Back to My Own Country: An Essay"**<br>**B. "Shooting an Elephant"**<br>**III. Voice**<br>**A. "Back to My Own Country: An Essay"**<br>**B. "Shooting an Elephant"** |

**Use Clear Transitions** When writing a compare-and-contrast essay, you will need to pivot from one subject or work to another. Use transition words and phrases such as those shown here to help your reader follow your logic.

| COMPARISON | CONTRAST |
|---|---|
| *in addition, likewise, in the same way, similarly* | *however, on the other hand, in a different way, to the contrary* |

## Review, Revise, and Edit

Focus on your introduction and conclusion. Does your introduction present a clear central idea and help your reader know what will follow? Does your conclusion state what each essay does particularly well? After you fine-tune the content of your essay, carefully edit for grammatical accuracy, and then proofread to eliminate errors in spelling and mechanics.

EVIDENCE LOG

Before moving on to a new selection, go to your log and record what you learned from "Shooting an Elephant."

STANDARDS

**Writing**

- Write informative/explanatory texts to examine and convey complex ideas, concepts, and information clearly and accurately through the effective selection, organization, and analysis of content.
- Introduce a topic; organize complex ideas, concepts, and information so that each new element builds on that which precedes it to create a unified whole; include formatting, graphics, and multimedia when useful to aiding comprehension.
- Use appropriate and varied transitions and syntax to link the major sections of the text, create cohesion, and clarify the relationships among complex ideas and concepts.
- Provide a concluding statement or section that follows from and supports the information or explanation presented.
- Apply *grades 11–12 Reading standards* to literary nonfiction.

WRITING TO SOURCES

- BACK TO MY OWN COUNTRY: AN ESSAY
- SHOOTING AN ELEPHANT

# Write an Informative Essay

You have read two essays that discuss what it is like to live in a place where you are not accepted. In "Back to My Own Country: An Essay," Andrea Levy writes of being raised by Jamaican parents in England, where her Caribbean ancestry and her working class home set her apart. In "Shooting an Elephant," George Orwell writes about being a British officer in Burma, where he is hated and jeered by the Burmese, though he privately sympathizes with their plight. Now, use your knowledge of the topic to write an informative essay about perceptions of home.

**Tool Kit**
Student Model of an Informative Essay

### Assignment

Think about how Andrea Levy and George Orwell both define and wrestle with their relationships to Britain. Conduct research to write an **informative essay** in response to this question:

**How did British colonialism complicate the idea of home?**

ACADEMIC VOCABULARY

As you craft your informative essay, consider using some of the academic vocabulary you learned in the beginning of the unit.

**migrate**
**modify**
**requisite**
**reiterate**
**implication**

## Elements of an Informative Essay

An **informative essay** presents and interprets information gathered through the extensive study of a subject. An effective informative essay includes these elements:

- a clear thesis statement
- significant facts from a variety of reliable, credited sources
- definitions, quotations, and summaries that support the thesis
- an effective organization of complex ideas in which elements build to create a coherent whole
- appropriate transitions that show connections among ideas
- precise language and effective techniques to clarify ideas and manage the complexity of the topic
- proper documentation and listing of sources; footnotes in which sources are cited
- a conclusion that follows from and supports the rest of the paper
- correct grammar, a formal style, and an objective tone

**Model Informative Essay** For a model of a well-crafted Informative Essay, see the Launch Text, "Home Away From Home."

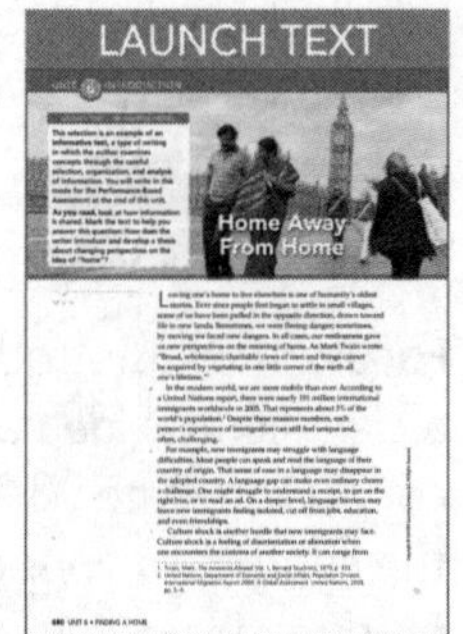


Challenge yourself to find all of the elements of effective informative writing in the essay. You will have the opportunity to review these elements as you start to write your own essay.

STANDARDS
Writing
- Write informative/explanatory texts to examine and convey complex ideas, concepts, and information clearly and accurately through the effective selection, organization, and analysis of content.
- Write routinely over extended time frames and shorter time frames for a range of tasks, purposes, and audiences.

# Prewriting / Planning

**Conduct Research** Now that you have read the selections and thought about Levy's and Orwell's complex relationships with the idea of home, use the prompt question to guide your research. As you conduct research, keep the following strategies in mind:

- Use both print and electronic sources. Be sure your sources are reliable.
- Online, look for sources that have *.gov* or *.edu* in their addresses.
- When possible, use **primary sources**—firsthand or original accounts, such as diaries, journals, or newspaper articles.
- You may also use **media resources**, such as documentaries, television programs, and podcasts.

**Gather Evidence** As you research, think of related questions that can help guide and focus your search. For example, you might ask, "What was the nature and structure of British rule in Burma?" if you decided you needed more information to understand Orwell's complicated feelings toward Britain.

Take notes as you find and connect relevant information, and keep a reference list of every source you use.

- Create a source card that includes each source's author, title, publisher, and date of publication. Then, create a note card for each fact, idea, or quotation you discover. Write the general topic at the top.
- Next, write the fact, idea, or quotation, followed by a keyword, such as the author's name, that links the information with its source.
- For Internet sources, record the name and address of the site, and the date you accessed it. For print sources, note the page numbers on which you found information.

**Source Card**

[Twain]

Twain, Mark. *The Innocents Abroad.* Vol. 1, Bernard Tauchnitz, 1879.

**Note Card**

[quote about home/traveling]

"Broad, wholesome, charitable views of men and things cannot be acquired by vegetating in one little corner of the earth all one's lifetime."

Source: Twain, p. 333.

EVIDENCE LOG

Review your Evidence Log and identify key details you may want to cite in your research report.

**Connect Across Texts** As you write your informative essay, review Levy's and Orwell's impressions of the countries in which they lived, both of which had a complicated historical relationship with Britain. Think about how living in Burma affected Orwell's ideas about England, and how visiting Jamaica affected Levy's perceptions of home. Connect these examples to your own ideas and evidence. Remember to paraphrase or quote with precision, making sure to credit each source accurately.

STANDARDS

**Writing**

Conduct short as well as more sustained research projects to answer a question or solve a problem; narrow or broaden the inquiry when appropriate; synthesize multiple sources on the subject, demonstrating understanding of the subject under investigation.

## ENRICHING WRITING WITH RESEARCH

**Provide Appropriate Citations** When you write informative texts, you must cite the sources of the information you use. Note that you must provide a citation for someone else's ideas even when you state these ideas using your own words.

In the body of your paper, provide references to the source material you used. Follow the format your teacher recommends, such as Modern Language Association (MLA style) or American Psychological Association (APA) style. Use either footnotes on each page or endnotes at the end of your paper.

If you do not give credit for the information you use, you are **plagiarizing,** which is presenting someone else's work as your own. It is important to note that even if plagiarism is done unintentionally, it nonetheless renders a work invalid.

### Read It

In your informative essay, give credit for ideas, concepts, or theories presented by other writers, including:

- Any facts or statistics that are not common knowledge.
- Direct quotations of spoken or written words.
- Paraphrases of spoken or written words.

This excerpt from the Launch Text shows how the writer uses a footnote to identify the source of a key piece of evidence.

LAUNCH TEXT

In the modern world, we are more mobile than ever. According to a United Nations report, there were nearly 191 million international immigrants worldwide in 2005. That represents about 3% of the world's population.[1] Despite these massive numbers, each person's experience of immigration can still feel unique and, often, challenging.

1. United Nations, Department of Economic and Social Affairs, Population Division. *International Migration Report 2006: A Global Assessment.* United Nations, 2009, pp. 5–6.

STANDARDS

**Writing**

Gather relevant information from multiple authoritative print and digital sources, using advanced searches effectively; assess the strengths and limitations of each source in terms of the task, purpose, and audience; integrate information into the text selectively to maintain the flow of ideas, avoiding plagiarism and overreliance on any one source and following a standard format for citation.

College and Career Readiness

## Write It

Review your informative essay, and mark all the sentences that contain information you gathered from research. If a fact is common knowledge, it does not need to be cited. However, you must cite opinions and ideas that are *not* common knowledge. This chart shows the difference between common knowledge and facts that should be cited.

| COMMON KNOWLEDGE |
|---|
| • Jamaica is an island in the Caribbean Sea. |
| • Much of the Jamaican population is descended from enslaved African people. |
| **FACTS TO BE CITED** |
| • Some British people resented Jamaican immigrants when they began arriving in England after World War II.<br>Source: Phillips, Mike. "Windrush—the Passengers." *BBC*, 10 Mar. 2011, www.bbc.co.uk/history/british/modern/windrush_01.shtml. Accessed 11 Apr. 2017. |
| • Today, more than half of the British people believe immigrants "make their country stronger because of their work and talents."<br>Source: "A Fragile Rebound for EU Image on Eve of European Parliament Elections." *Pew Research Center: Global Attitudes and Trends*, 12 May 2014, www.pewglobal.org/2014/05/12/chapter-3-most-support-limiting-immigration. |

Be sure that all citations include the author, date of publication, title of article or page, and title of publication or website. Confirm the specifics of the citation style you will be using. For instance, MLA (8th ed.) style requires the URL of a Web page, but it leaves the date that you accessed the Web page optional.

Use a chart like this as you decide which information in your essay should be cited.

| COMMON KNOWLEDGE |
|---|
| |
| |
| **FACTS OR OPINIONS TO BE CITED** |
| |
| |
| |

**Use Footnotes or Endnotes** Footnotes are numbered and credit the sources that will also be listed in the Works Cited section or Bibliography at the end of the paper. As shown in the earlier example from the Launch Text, footnotes appear on the page on which the information is referenced. Endnotes serve the same function, but they appear at the end of the paper.

## Drafting

**Develop a Thesis Statement** Review your research notes, and write a thesis statement that reflects your conclusions about the material you have collected. An effective thesis statement should have the following qualities:

- It should be the result of careful study and reflection.
- It should make a direct claim in response to the prompt.
- It should be specific and indicate the ideas you intend to develop.

**Choose an Organizational Structure** Using your thesis statement and the information you have gathered, choose an organizational structure for your informative essay. The chart shows five possible structures.

| METHOD | |
|---|---|
| Part-to-Whole Order | Examine how categories affect a larger subject. This works well for an analysis of social issues and for historical topics. |
| Cause and Effect | Analyze the causes and effects of an event. |
| Problem/Solution | Identify a specific problem and explain how it was or was not solved. |
| Order of Importance | Present your information and explanations from most to least important or from least to most important. |
| Comparison and Contrast | Present the similarities and differences between two subjects. This is useful if you are comparing two people's or groups of people's experiences. |

After deciding on an organizational structure, create an outline that places ideas and evidence in a logical sequence. Decide whether to use formatting, such as headings, subheadings, or lists, to clarify that structure. Also, consider whether the use of images will help convey your ideas and plan where you might add them.

**Write a Strong Introduction and Conclusion** Use your opening paragraph to introduce your analysis of Orwell's and Levy's attitudes toward and feelings about their countries during an era of British colonialism. In the conclusion, restate the thesis in such a way that readers will be able to easily connect it to the evidence that you have presented. Also, provide a fresh or original insight about your thesis: Leave readers with something to think about.

**Write a First Draft** Use your introduction, conclusion, and notes to write your first draft. Remember to introduce your thesis and use a variety of evidence, details, quotations, and examples to support your ideas. As you write, make sure that the relationship among complex ideas, concepts, and information is clear. Use a variety of transitions to connect those ideas. Then, write a conclusion that follows from your thesis and supports the information you presented.

STANDARDS

**Writing**

- Introduce a topic; organize complex ideas, concepts, and information so that each new element builds on that which precedes it to create a unified whole; include formatting, graphics, and multimedia when useful to aiding comprehension.
- Develop the topic thoroughly by selecting the most significant and relevant facts, extended definitions, concrete details, quotations, or other information and examples appropriate to the audience's knowledge of the topic.
- Provide a concluding statement or section that follows from and supports the information or explanation presented.

LANGUAGE DEVELOPMENT: AUTHOR'S STYLE

# Create a Coherent Whole: Use Transitions

As you write your draft, use a variety of appropriate **transitions**, words and phrases that connect and show relationships among ideas. These will help the reader understand your informative essay and follow the evidence that supports your thesis.

## Read It

These sentences from the Launch Text use transitions to show the relationships among ideas.

- *For example, in the United States it is considered normal to smile at or say hello to a stranger one passes on the sidewalk.* (connects detail to concept)
- *However, as the centuries have shown, human beings are resilient.* (shows contrast)
- *On a deeper level, language barriers may leave new immigrants feeling isolated, cut off from jobs, education, and even friendships.* (shows intensity)

Read the Launch Text to find other examples of transitions.

## Write It

As you write, use transitions to link your sentences, paragraphs, and sections. Read your paper aloud, listening for how the ideas connect. Sudden shifts may indicate that a transition is needed. Refer to the chart for example transitional expressions.

| TRANSITIONAL WORDS AND PHRASES | | | |
|---|---|---|---|
| above all | besides | however | on the other hand |
| accordingly | clearly | in other words | otherwise |
| alternatively | consequently | instead | particularly |
| although | for example | likewise | similarly |
| as a result | for that reason | on a deeper level | therefore |
| as well as | furthermore | on the contrary | usually |

STANDARDS

**Writing**
Use appropriate and varied transitions and sentence structures to link the major sections of the text, create cohesion, and clarify the relationships among complex ideas and concepts.

# Revising

## Evaluating Your Draft

Use the following checklist to evaluate the effectiveness of your first draft. Then, use your evaluation and the instruction on this page to guide your revision.

| FOCUS AND ORGANIZATION | EVIDENCE AND ELABORATION | CONVENTIONS |
|---|---|---|
| ☐ Provides a clear thesis statement.<br>☐ Includes effective organization of complex ideas.<br>☐ Uses facts and evidence from a variety of reliable, credited sources.<br>☐ Provides a logical text structure and clear transitions among ideas.<br>☐ Concludes with a summary of thesis and evidence. | ☐ Includes specific details, facts, and quotations to support thesis.<br>☐ Provides adequate support for each major idea.<br>☐ Uses precise language that is appropriate for the audience and purpose.<br>☐ Establishes a formal, objective tone. | ☐ Attends to the norms and conventions of the discipline, especially regarding crediting sources properly. |

## Revising for Focus and Organization

**Internal Logic** Reread your essay, paying attention to whether the ideas flow logically from paragraph to paragraph. Rearrange paragraphs or sections that do not build in a logical way. Do you need to add transitions to help readers see connections you want to emphasize? If so, add transitional words and phrases.

## Revising for Evidence and Elaboration

**Thesis Support** Review your essay to be sure you have included specific details to support your thesis. Do you have facts, quotations, examples, or other types of evidence for each of your major points? If not, review your notes to find and add more relevant information.

**Precise Language** Reread the draft of your essay, looking for sections that are vague. Revise these sections to include precise, domain-specific words and phrases. To help readers understand difficult concepts or make connections between specific pieces of information, you might consider using figures of speech, such as analogies (extended comparisons of unlike things) and similes (comparisons of unlike things, using explicit comparison words such as *like* or *as*).

**Tone** Analyze your draft to ensure it has a formal, objective tone appropriate for informative writing. Avoid slang words and contractions, and add missing words to incomplete sentences so that you do not have any sentence fragments. Be sure that you have remained neutral, or objective, throughout your essay. Edit any passages that reveal bias or opinion.

WORD NETWORK

Include interesting words from your Word Network in your informative essay.

STANDARDS

**Writing**

- Use precise language, domain-specific vocabulary, and techniques such as metaphor, simile, and analogy to manage the complexity of the topic.
- Establish and maintain a formal style and objective tone while attending to the norms and conventions of the discipline which they are writing.

PEER REVIEW

Exchange papers with a classmate. Use the checklist to evaluate your classmate's informative essay and provide supportive feedback.

1. Is the thesis clear?

☐ yes ☐ no If no, explain what confused you.

2. Is the text organized logically?

☐ yes ☐ no If no, what about the organization does not work?

3. Does the paper fully support the thesis by citing information from research?

☐ yes ☐ no If no, write a brief note explaining what you thought was missing.

4. What is the strongest part of your classmate's essay? Why?

## Editing and Proofreading

**Edit for Conventions** Reread your draft for accuracy and consistency. Correct errors in grammar and word usage. Use a style guide if you need help crediting your sources correctly.

**Proofread for Accuracy** Read your draft carefully, looking for errors in spelling and punctuation. Double-check that your transitions give readers an accurate and thorough understanding of the relationships among facts, details, and ideas.

## Publishing and Presenting

Create a final version of your essay. Share it with a small group so that your classmates can read it and make comments. In turn, review and comment on your classmates' work. Together, determine what your different essays convey about how time or distance sharpen our perceptions of home. Listen and respond respectfully to comments about your work.

## Reflecting

Think about what you learned while writing your informative essay. What techniques did you learn that you could use when writing another informative text? How could you improve the process? What methods for narrowing your focus and conducting research were most helpful?

STANDARDS

**Writing**
Develop and strengthen writing as needed by planning, revising, editing, rewriting, or trying a new approach, focusing on addressing what is most significant for a specific purpose and audience.

**Language**
- Demonstrate command of the conventions of standard English grammar and usage when writing or speaking.
- Demonstrate command of the conventions of standard English capitalization, punctuation, and spelling when writing.
- Spell correctly.

ESSENTIAL QUESTION:

# What does it mean to call a place home?

As you read these selections, work with your group to explore the idea of home.

**From Text to Topic** When we think of home, is it a country, a city or town, a house or an apartment, or even a single room that is clearest in our minds and feelings? Is home a group of people, or is it a place? As you read, consider the different ideas of home each selection conveys.

## Small-Group Learning Strategies

Throughout your life, in school, in your community, and in your career, you will continue to develop strategies when you work in teams. Use these strategies during Small-Group Learning. Add ideas of your own at each step.

| STRATEGY | ACTION PLAN |
|---|---|
| Prepare | • Complete your assignments so that you are prepared for group work.<br>• Take notes on your reading so you can contribute to your group's discussions.<br>• |
| Participate fully | • Make eye contact to signal that you are listening and taking in what is being said.<br>• Use text evidence when making a point.<br>• |
| Support others | • Build off ideas from others in your group.<br>• State the relationship of your points to the points of others—whether you are supporting someone's point, refuting it, or taking the conversation in a new direction.<br>• |
| Clarify | • Paraphrase the ideas of others to ensure that your understanding is correct.<br>• Ask follow-up questions.<br>• |

## CONTENTS

COMPARE

## Working as a Team

1. **Take a Position** In your group, discuss the following question:

   Which is more important: an external home or an internal sense of home?

   As you take turns sharing your positions, be sure to provide reasons for your choice. After all group members have shared, discuss some of the personal attributes that might help someone develop an internal sense of home.

2. **List Your Rules** As a group, decide on the rules that you will follow as you work together. Samples are provided; add two more of your own. You may add or revise rules based on your experience together.

   - Everyone should participate in group discussions.
   - People should not interrupt.
   - ______________________________
   - ______________________________

3. **Apply the Rules** Practice working as a group. Share what you have learned about what defines a home. Make sure each person in the group contributes. Take notes and be prepared to share with the class one thing that you heard from another member of your group.

4. **Name Your Group** Choose a name that reflects the unit topic.

   Our group's name: ______________________________

5. **Create a Communication Plan** Decide how you want to communicate with one another. For example, you might use online collaboration tools, email, or instant messaging.

   Our group's decision: ______________________________

## Making a Schedule

First, find out the due dates for the small-group activities. Then, preview the texts and activities with your group, and make a schedule for completing the tasks.

| SELECTION | ACTIVITIES | DUE DATE |
|---|---|---|
| *from* A History of the English Church and People | | |
| *from* History of Jamaica | | |
| The Seafarer<br>Dover Beach<br>Escape From the Old Country | | |
| The Widow at Windsor<br>From Lucy: Englan' Lady | | |

## Working on Group Projects

As your group works together, you'll find it more effective if each person has a specific role. Different projects require different roles. Before beginning a project, discuss the necessary roles, and choose one for each group member. Here are some possible roles; add your own ideas.

**Project Manager:** monitors the schedule and keeps everyone on task

**Researcher:** organizes research activities

**Recorder:** takes notes during group meetings

______________________________

______________________________

______________________________

______________________________

______________________________

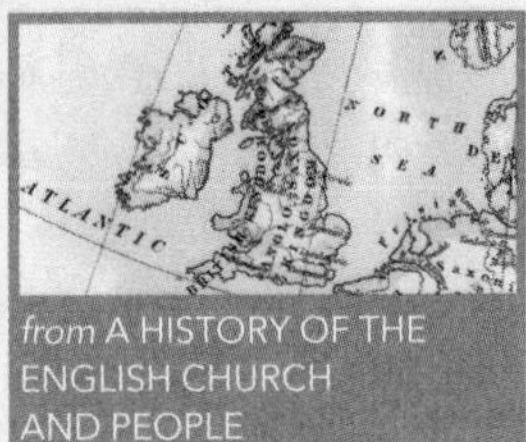

*from* A HISTORY OF THE ENGLISH CHURCH AND PEOPLE

## Comparing Text to Media

In this lesson, you will compare an eighth-century history with a modern-day encyclopedia entry. First, you will complete the first-read and close-read activities for the excerpt from *A History of the English Church and People*. The work you do with your group on this title will help prepare you for the comparing task.

*from* HISTORY OF JAMAICA

### About the Author

**Bede** (673–735) was born near the Monastery of St. Peter and St. Paul at Jarrow in Northumbria, now northeast England. He was sent to live in the monastery at the age of seven, was ordained a deacon at nineteen, and became a priest at thirty. Bede rarely left the monastery and followed a strict daily schedule of prayer, study, teaching, and writing. During his lifetime, he completed more than 60 books on religious and scientific topics, most of which have survived to the current day.

# *from* A History of the English Church and People

## Concept Vocabulary

As you perform your first read, you will encounter these words.

**breadth** **abounding** **innumerable**

**Familiar Word Parts** To find the meaning of an unfamiliar word, look for familiar word parts, such as roots, prefixes, or suffixes.

**Unfamiliar Word:** It extends 800 miles northward . . . except where a number of **promontories** stretch farther. . . .

**Familiar Word Parts:** The prefix *pro-*, as in *propel* and *project*, often means "forward." The root *-mont-* looks as though it is related to the words *mount* and *mountain*.

**Possible Meaning:** *Promontories,* then, may be tall land formations that jut forward in some way.

Apply your knowledge of familiar word parts and other vocabulary strategies to determine the meanings of unfamiliar words you encounter during your first read.

## First Read NONFICTION

Apply these strategies as you conduct your first read. You will have an opportunity to complete a close read after your first read.

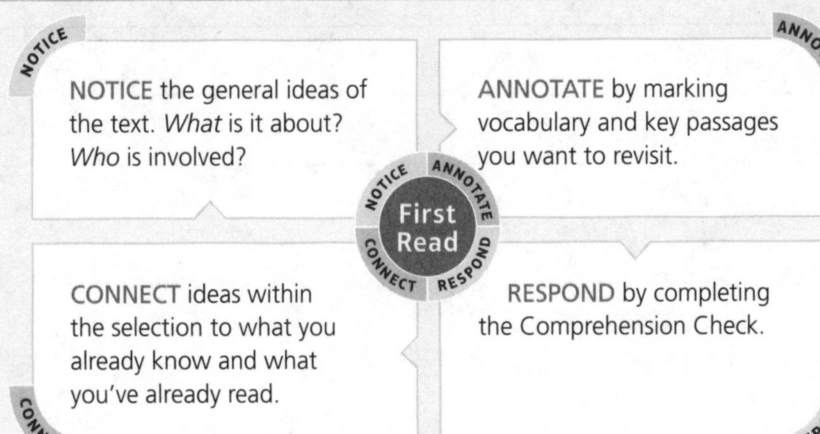

NOTICE
NOTICE the general ideas of the text. *What* is it about? *Who* is involved?
ANNOTATE
ANNOTATE by marking vocabulary and key passages you want to revisit.
NOTICE ANNOTATE First Read CONNECT RESPOND
CONNECT ideas within the selection to what you already know and what you've already read.
RESPOND by completing the Comprehension Check.
CONNECT
RESPOND


### STANDARDS

**Reading Informational Text**
By the end of grade 12, read and comprehend literary nonfiction at the high end of the grades 11–CCR text complexity band independently and proficiently.

**Language**
Identify and correctly use patterns of word changes that indicate different meanings or parts of speech.

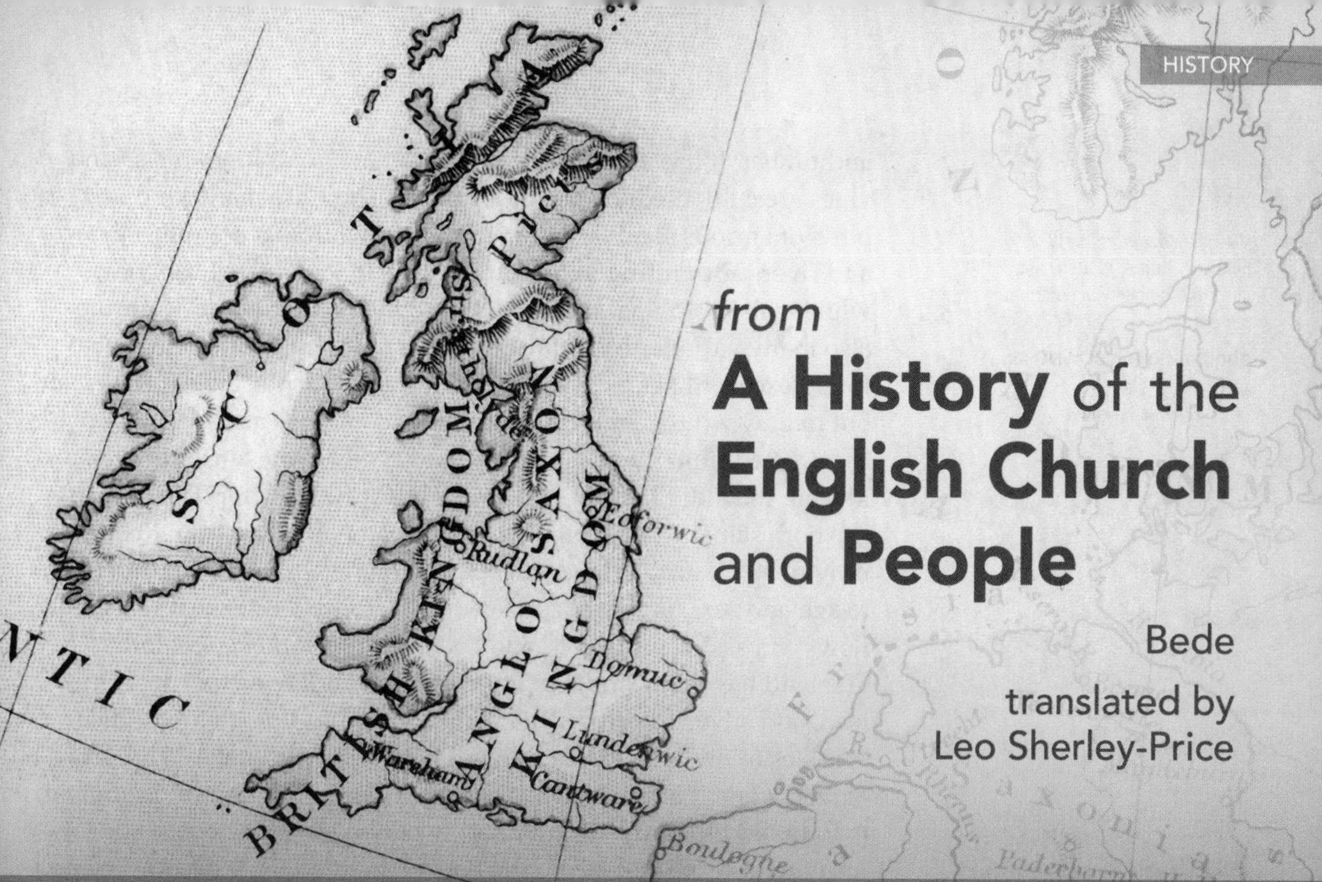


# from A History of the English Church and People

Bede

translated by Leo Sherley-Price

BACKGROUND

Although the majority of people in Bede's day were illiterate, and written records were scarce, Bede had access to books and documents, as well as contact with other learned monks, through his monastery. Using these sources, he was able to write a history of Britain. Bede hoped to reach a larger world of readers for his work—the Church to which he belonged and the Roman civilization in which it participated. Bede wrote his account of Britain for such readers, starting with the basics.

## The Situation of Britain and Ireland: Their Earliest Inhabitants

1 Britain, formerly known as Albion, is an island in the ocean, facing between north and west, and lying at a considerable distance from the coasts of Germany, Gaul, and Spain, which together form the greater part of Europe. It extends 800 miles northwards, and is 200 in **breadth**, except where a number of promontories stretch farther, the coastline round which extends to 3,675 miles. To the south lies Belgic Gaul,[1] from the nearest shore of which travelers can see the city known as Rutubi Portus, which the English have corrupted to Reptacestir.[2] The distance from there across the sea to Gessoriacum,[3] the nearest coast of the Morini, is 50 miles or, as some write it, 450 furlongs.[4] On the opposite side of Britain, which lies open to the boundless ocean, lie the isles of the Orcades.[5] Britain is rich in grain

NOTES

Mark familiar word parts or indicate another strategy you used that helped you determine meaning.

**breadth** (brehdth) *n.*

1. **Belgic Gaul** France.
2. **Reptacestir** Richborough, part of the city of Sandwich.
3. **Gessoriacum** Boulogne, France.
4. **furlongs** *n.* units for measuring distance; a furlong is equal to one eighth of a mile.
5. **Orcades** Orkney Isles.

NOTES

Mark familiar word parts or indicate another strategy you used that helped you determine meaning.

**abounding** (uh BOWND ihng) *adj.*

**innumerable** (ih NOO muhr uh buhl) *adj.*

and timber; it has good pasturage for cattle and draft animals,[6] and vines are cultivated in various localities. There are many land and sea birds of various species, and it is well known for its plentiful springs and rivers **abounding** in fish. There are salmon and eel fisheries, while seals, dolphins, and sometimes whales are caught. There are also many varieties of shellfish, such as mussels, in which are often found excellent pearls of several colors: red, purple, violet, and green, but mainly white. Cockles[7] are abundant, and a beautiful scarlet dye is extracted from them, which remains unfaded by sunshine or rain; indeed, the older the cloth, the more beautiful its color. The country has both salt and hot springs, and the waters flowing from them provide hot baths, in which the people bathe separately according to age and sex. As Saint Basil says: "Water receives its heat when it flows across certain metals, and becomes hot, and even scalding." The land has rich veins of many metals, including copper, iron, lead, and silver. There is also much black jet[8] of fine quality, which sparkles in firelight. When burned, it drives away snakes, and, like amber, when it is warmed by friction, it clings to whatever is applied to it. In old times, the country had twenty-eight noble cities, and **innumerable** castles, all of which were guarded by walls, towers, and barred gates.

2 Since Britain lies far north toward the pole, the nights are short in summer, and at midnight it is hard to tell whether the evening twilight still lingers or whether dawn is approaching; for in these northern latitudes the sun does not remain long below the horizon at night. Consequently both summer days and winter nights are long, and when the sun withdraws southwards, the winter nights last eighteen hours. In Armenia,[9] Macedonia,[10] and Italy, and other countries of that latitude, the longest day lasts only fifteen hours and the shortest nine.

3 At the present time there are in Britain, in harmony with the five books of the divine law, five languages and four nations—English, British, Scots, and Picts. Each of these have their own language, but all are united in their study of God's truth by the fifth, Latin, which has become a common medium through the study of the scriptures. The original inhabitants of the island were the Britons, from whom it takes its name, and who, according to tradition, crossed into Britain from Armorica,[11] and occupied the southern parts. When they had spread northwards and possessed the greater part of the islands, it is said that some Picts from Scythia[12] put to sea in a few long ships and were driven by storms around the coasts of Britain, arriving at

6. **draft animals** animals used for pulling loads.
7. **Cockles** *n.* edible shellfish with two heart-shaped shells.
8. **jet** *n.* type of coal.
9. **Armenia** region between the Black and the Caspian seas, now divided between the nations of Armenia and Turkey.
10. **Macedonia** region in the eastern Mediterranean, now divided among Greece, Bulgaria, Albania, Serbia, Kosovo, and the Republic of Macedonia.
11. **Armorica** Brittany, France.
12. **Scythia** ancient region in southeastern Europe.

length on the north coast of Ireland. Here they found the nation of the Scots, from whom they asked permission to settle, but their request was refused. Ireland is the largest island after Britain, and lies to the west. It is shorter than Britain to the north, but extends far beyond it to the south towards the northern coasts of Spain, although a wide sea separates them. These Pictish seafarers, as I have said, asked for a grant of land to make a settlement. The Scots replied that there was not room for them both, but said: "We can give you good advice. There is another island not far to the east, which we often see in the distance on clear days. Go and settle there if you wish; should you meet resistance, we will come to your help." So the Picts crossed into Britain, and began to settle in the north of the island, since the Britons were in possession of the south. Having no women with them, these Picts asked wives of the Scots, who consented on condition that, when any dispute arose, they should choose a king from the female royal line rather than the male. This custom continues among the Picts to this day. As time went on, Britain received a third nation, that of the Scots, who migrated from Ireland under their chieftain Reuda, and by a combination of force and treaty, obtained from the Picts the settlements that they still hold. From the name of this chieftain, they are still known as Dalreudians, for in their tongue *dal* means a division.

4 Ireland is broader than Britain, and its mild and healthy climate is superior. Snow rarely lies longer than three days, so that there is no need to store hay in summer for winter use or to build stables for beasts. There are no reptiles, and no snake can exist there, for although often brought over from Britain, as soon as the ship nears land, they breathe its scented air and die. In fact, almost everything in this isle enjoys immunity to poison, and I have heard that folk suffering from snakebite have drunk water in which scrapings from the leaves of books from Ireland had been steeped, and that this remedy checked the spreading poison and reduced the swelling. The island abounds in milk and honey, and there is no lack of vines, fish, and birds, while deer and goats are widely hunted. It is the original home of the Scots, who, as already mentioned, later migrated and joined the Britons and Picts in Britain. There is a very extensive arm of the sea, which originally formed the boundary between the Britons and the Picts. This runs inland from the west for a great distance as far as the strongly fortified British city of Alcuith.[13] It was to the northern shores of this firth[14] that the Scots came and established their new homeland. ❧

NOTES

13. **Alcuith** Dumbarton, Scotland.
14. **firth** *n.* narrow arm of the sea.

## Comprehension Check

**Complete the following items after you finish your first read. Review and clarify details with your group.**

1. How does Britain's latitude, or distance from the equator, affect the lengths of days and nights throughout the year?

2. Into what nations is Britain divided at the time Bede is writing his history?

3. According to Bede, how does Latin unite Britain?

4. What claim does Bede make about reptiles in Ireland?

5. **Notebook** Summarize the history by writing a list of the most important characteristics of Britain that Bede describes.

## RESEARCH

**Research to Clarify** Choose at least one unfamiliar detail from the text. Briefly research that detail. In what way does the information you learned shed light on an aspect of Bede's history?

**Research to Explore** Choose something that interested you from the text, and formulate a research question. Write your question here.

## Close Read the Text

With your group, revisit sections of the text you marked during your first read. **Annotate** details that you notice. What **questions** do you have? What can you **conclude**?

## Analyze the Text

**Notebook** Complete the activities.

1. **Review and Clarify** With your group, reread paragraph 3. What techniques does Bede use to present information? Discuss the effect that each technique has on readers.
2. **Present and Discuss** Now, work with your group to share passages from the text that you found especially important. Take turns presenting your examples. Discuss what details you noticed, what questions you asked, and what conclusions you reached.
3. **Essential Question:** ***What does it mean to call a place home?*** What has this text taught you about the meaning of home? Discuss.

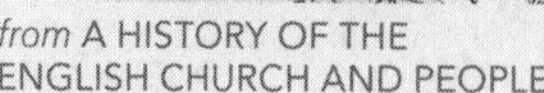

*from* A HISTORY OF THE ENGLISH CHURCH AND PEOPLE

TIP

**GROUP DISCUSSION**

When talking about selections with long paragraphs, it can be helpful to mark key words or phrases as a group. You can then refer to these marks to quickly locate details you wish to discuss in depth.

LANGUAGE DEVELOPMENT

## Concept Vocabulary

**breadth** **abounding** **innumerable**

**Why These Words?** The three concept vocabulary words are related. With your group, determine what the words have in common. Discuss your ideas, and add another word that fits this category.

### Practice

**Notebook** Confirm your understanding of the concept vocabulary words by using them to write a short paragraph about a place you once visited. Make sure to use each word at least once. If you are unsure about the exact meaning of a word, look it up in a college-level dictionary.

WORD NETWORK

Add interesting words related to finding a home from the text to your Word Network.

## Word Study

**Anglo-Saxon Suffix: *-th*** The Anglo-Saxon suffix *-th* is used to form nouns from adjectives. Sometimes, the length or quality of the vowel in the base word changes when *-th* is added. For example, consider these pairs: *wide/width, long/length, broad/breadth*. In other cases, the vowel is unaffected, as in *warm/warmth*.

1. Using this knowledge, infer the most notable characteristic of the animal known as the *sloth*.
2. What adjective is the base of the noun *health?* Use a dictionary to verify your deduction.

STANDARDS

**Language**

- Identify and correctly use patterns of word changes that indicate different meanings or parts of speech.
- Consult general and specialized reference materials, both print and digital, to find the pronunciation of a word or determine or clarify its precise meaning, its part of speech, its etymology, or its standard usage.

*from* A HISTORY OF THE ENGLISH CHURCH AND PEOPLE

# Analyze Craft and Structure

**Elements of Historical Writing** Historical writing tells the story of past events using reliable evidence, such as eyewitness reports and documents. Because historical writing aims to inform readers, historians such as Bede use various techniques to present information clearly.

- Statements of fact
- Varying patterns of organization, such as descriptions of geography or chronological listings of events, tailored to clarify complex topics
- Hierarchical structures that show how each part relates to a larger whole; a **hierarchy** is the formal ranking of elements within a group, such as Bede's description of the nations within Britain.
- Repetition of main ideas to emphasize key points.

Bede, however, lived at a time when even educated people were more superstitious and less informed than they are today. Also, as occurs in any era, his biases and beliefs affected his accounts. In Bede's historical writing, therefore, you will also find the following elements:

- Statements that reflect superstition, rumor, or incorrect information
- Statements of personal religious belief

## Practice

**CITE TEXTUAL EVIDENCE** to support your answers.

As a group, complete this chart to note examples of Bede's approach to historical writing in the excerpt from *A History of the English Church and People.*

| ELEMENT | EXAMPLES |
|---|---|
| facts | |
| superstitions | |
| personal beliefs | |

**Notebook Respond to these questions.**

1. **(a)** What patterns of organization does Bede use in the first paragraph of the selection? **(b)** What topics are described, using each pattern?
2. What central idea about Britain's geography does Bede emphasize through the use of hierarchical structures?
3. What aspects of Bede's writing reinforce a positive impression of Britain?

**STANDARDS**

**Reading informational Text**

- Cite strong and thorough textual evidence to support analysis of what the text says explicitly as well as inferences drawn from the text, including determining where the text leaves matters uncertain.
- Analyze and evaluate the effectiveness of the structure an author uses in his or her exposition or argument, including whether the structure makes points clear, convincing, and engaging.

**Language**

- Apply the understanding that usage is a matter of convention, can change over time, and is sometimes contested.
- Resolve issues of complex or contested usage, consulting references as needed.
- Demonstrate command of the conventions of standard English capitalization, punctuation, and spelling when writing.

## Conventions and Style

**Punctuation in Series** Writers can use punctuation to clarify the relationships between words and phrases within a sentence. For example, commas are used along with a conjunction to join two independent clauses. Commas are also used to separate items in a series.

Many writers use the **serial comma** (also known as the **Oxford comma**) immediately before the coordinating conjunction (usually *and, or,* or *nor*) in a series of three or more terms. The serial comma is a matter of style, not a universal rule of English punctuation. Some newspapers and other sources do not require the use of serial commas.

This sentence from the excerpt from *A History of the English Church and People* shows an example of a series punctuated with a serial comma.

> *There are salmon and eel fisheries, while seals, dolphins, and sometimes whales are caught.* (paragraph 1)

You may need to consult a style guide or other reference when deciding whether or not to use serial commas in your writing. Teachers, editors, or publishers for whom you are writing will provide information about their preferred style.

TIP

**CLARIFICATION**

Serial commas can increase the clarity of your writing. Consider this sentence without a serial comma: "The reporter interviewed Marcel, a librarian and a tennis player." Did the reporter interview one person, Marcel, who happens to be a librarian and a tennis player? Or did she interview three separate people? Consistent use of the serial comma eliminates this ambiguity.

### Read It

Work individually. Use this chart to identify the words separated by serial commas in the first two examples. Then, fill in the rest of the chart with two additional examples of serial commas in Bede's writing.

| EXAMPLE | WORDS SEPARATED BY SERIAL COMMA |
|---|---|
| *The land has rich veins of many metals, including copper, iron, lead, and silver.* (paragraph 1) | |
| *In Armenia, Macedonia, and Italy, and other countries of that latitude, the longest day lasts only fifteen hours and the shortest nine.* (paragraph 2) | |
| | |
| | |

### Write It

**Notebook** Write a paragraph in which you describe the most interesting details you learned about Britain by reading Bede's history. Include at least two sets of items in a series. Consult a reference source recommended by your school or teacher to determine whether or not to use serial commas.

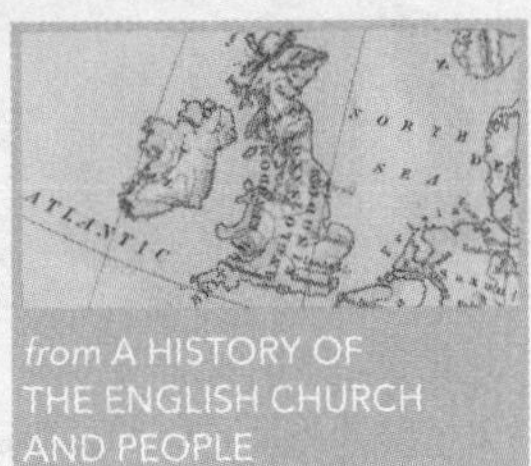


## Comparing Text to Media

The encyclopedia entry you are about to read comes from the *Encyclopaedia Britannica* website. After exploring and reading this selection, you will compare Bede's historical writing about Britain with contemporary historians' writing about Jamaica.

### About the Source

The **Encyclopaedia Britannica** first appeared in 1768 and has been revised and enhanced through 15 editions. It was the product of a printer and bookseller, an engraver, and an editor, all three of Scotland. Although encyclopedias had been written since antiquity, the *Britannica* was conceived during the Scottish Enlightenment, a time of intellectual fervor, and its creators envisioned a new type of source. Existing encyclopedias in English listed topics briefly and alphabetically, somewhat like a dictionary, so related topics did not appear together. The *Britannica,* by contrast, integrated related topics into essays that were then alphabetized. The encyclopedia retains that format even today.

# *from* History of Jamaica

## Media Vocabulary

These words will be useful to you as you analyze, discuss, and write about encyclopedia articles.

| | |
|---|---|
| **entry:** main article in an encyclopedia; it may be divided into a series of *subentries* | • Entries in an encyclopedia are usually arranged alphabetically.<br>• A subentry focuses on an aspect of a larger topic. Subentries are not alphabetized; they are placed where they are most relevant to the text. |
| **cross-reference:** note directing readers to another part of the text | • Cross-references direct readers to other entries with more information about a topic.<br>• Some encyclopedias limit cross-references in order to improve readability. Readers use the complete index to locate relevant material. |
| **hyperlink:** interactive word or passage of an online text that links to additional information | • Some hyperlinks provide concise information, such as word definitions or biographical information.<br>• Other hyperlinks take readers to other encyclopedia entries or subentries. |

## First Review INTERACTIVE MEDIA

Apply these strategies as you conduct your first review. You will have an opportunity to complete a close review after your first review.

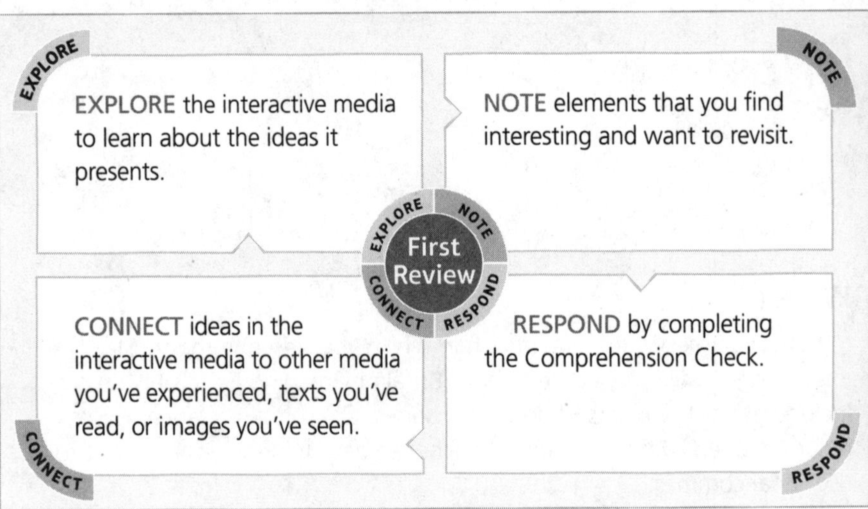

EXPLORE
EXPLORE the interactive media to learn about the ideas it presents.
NOTE
NOTE elements that you find interesting and want to revisit.
EXPLORE NOTE First Review CONNECT RESPOND
CONNECT ideas in the interactive media to other media you've experienced, texts you've read, or images you've seen.
RESPOND by completing the Comprehension Check.
CONNECT
RESPOND


### STANDARDS

**Reading Informational Text**
By the end of grade 12, read and comprehend literary nonfiction at the high end of the grades 11–CCR text complexity band independently and proficiently.

**Language**
Acquire and use accurately general academic and domain-specific words and phrases, sufficient for reading, writing, speaking, and listening at the college and career readiness level; demonstrate independence in gathering vocabulary knowledge when considering a word or phrase important to comprehension or expression.

# *from* History of Jamaica

Encyclopaedia Britannica

## BACKGROUND

Jamaica is the third-largest island in the Caribbean Sea and the West Indies. In 1962, Jamaica attained independence from the United Kingdom and became a constitutional monarchy. Culturally, Jamaica is known as the home of the musical genres of ska and reggae, and it has an extensive local tradition of poetry and the visual arts. The capital city is Kingston.

NOTES

## Comprehension Check

**Complete the following items after you finish your first review. Review and clarify details with your group.**

1. How did the British gain control of Jamaica?

2. Who were Maroons, and what roles did they play in Jamaica's history?

3. How did one agricultural resource come to dominate the Jamaican economy in the eighteenth century, and how was it eventually replaced?

4. What steps led to the development of full self-government in Jamaica?

5. **Notebook** Create a timeline to summarize the history of Jamaica described in this encyclopedia entry.

### RESEARCH

**Research to Clarify** Choose at least one unfamiliar detail from the selection. Briefly research that detail. In what way does the information you learned shed light on an aspect of Jamaica's history?

**Research to Explore** Choose something that interested you from the selection, and formulate a research question. Write your question here.

## Close Review

With your group, revisit the article and your first-review notes. Record any new observations that seem important. What **questions** do you have? What can you **conclude**?

*from* HISTORY OF JAMAICA

## Analyze the Media

**CITE TEXTUAL EVIDENCE** to support your answers.

**Notebook** Complete the activities.

1. **Review and Clarify** With your group, reread the section about the Crown Colony. What changes are explained? What major causes of change are identified?
2. **Present and Discuss** Now, work with your group to share passages or features from the selection that you found especially important. Take turns presenting your responses. Discuss what details you noticed, what questions you asked, and what conclusions you reached.
3. **Essential Question:** ***What does it mean to call a place home?*** What has this article taught you about the relationship between people and place? Discuss with your group.

TIP

**GROUP DISCUSSION**

Keep in mind that discussions of social and political events, either historical or current, should be conducted in the same civil and thoughtful manner as any other group discussion. Listen attentively to the input of each group member. Provide evidence for your own conclusions, and ask questions to clarify the statements of others.

LANGUAGE DEVELOPMENT

## Media Vocabulary

**entry** **cross-reference** **hyperlink**

Respond to the following questions, and share your responses with your group.

1. What process would you use to look up a country other than Jamaica in an online encyclopedia? How would detailed information about that country be organized?
2. Where might cross-references be used to bring online readers to additional information? Explain the reasons for your choices.
3. What purpose do subentries and cross-references serve?

**STANDARDS**

**Language**

Acquire and use accurately general academic and domain-specific words and phrases, sufficient for reading, writing, speaking, and listening at the college and career readiness level; demonstrate independence in gathering vocabulary knowledge when considering a word or phrase important to comprehension or expression.

from A HISTORY OF THE ENGLISH CHURCH AND PEOPLE

from HISTORY OF JAMAICA

# Writing to Compare

You have read two texts that describe the history of a nation: an excerpt from Bede's *A History of the English Church and People* and a portion of the *Encyclopaedia Britannica* article "History of Jamaica." Both selections provide information on their subjects, but in very different ways. Deepen your understanding of historical writing by comparing and contrasting the texts and expressing your ideas in writing.

**Assignment**

Informative texts share factual material with readers. At the same time, they reveal something about the writers themselves and the historical context—the time and place—in which the writers live. Write a **compare-and-contrast essay** in which you explain how Bede's history of England and the *Encylopaedia Britannica's* history of Jamaica are similar and different. Focus your analysis on the differences. What accounts for them? What do they reveal about the writers'—or the readers'—values and worldviews? What do they say about the era in which each text was produced?

## Prewriting

**Analyze the Texts** With your group, discuss the texts' similarities and differences. Start by generating five questions about elements of historical writing that are used in the two texts. For example, you might ask what categories of information are included and how the information is organized. List your questions. Then, as a group, work to answer them. As you analyze and discuss the texts, use follow-up questions to deepen each other's responses.

| ASKING FOLLOW-UP QUESTIONS | |
|---|---|
| When you want a speaker to ... | Use a question like this: |
| Restate and clarify an idea | When you say ______, do you mean that ______? |
| Be more specific | What is one example of ______? |
| Make logical connections | Since you claim that ______, does it follow that ______? |
| Offer more support | What evidence suggests that ______ is true? |

**Notebook** After you have completed your group discussion, answer these questions on your own.

1. What do the texts' differences suggest about their eras and audiences? What kinds of information or reading experiences might a member of each audience expect?

2. What underlying values or worldviews are suggested by your answer to question 1?

**STANDARDS**

**Reading Informational Text**
- Cite strong and thorough textual evidence to support analysis of what the text says explicitly as well as inferences drawn from the text, including determining where the text leaves matters uncertain.
- Integrate and evaluate multiple sources of information presented in different media or formats as well as in words in order to address a question or solve a problem.

**Writing**
- Write informative/explanatory texts to examine and convey complex ideas, concepts, and information clearly and accurately through the effective selection, organization, and analysis of content.
- Apply *grades 11–12 Reading standards* to literary nonfiction.

## Drafting

**Draw Conclusions** With your group, review the features of historical texts you identified in each selection. Discuss what those details suggest about the era in which each text was written. What kinds of information were considered useful or interesting? What were writers trying to deliver, and how did they do so? Write some conclusions here.

1. ______________________________

2. ______________________________

3. ______________________________

4. ______________________________

**Locate Supporting Information** Find and record evidence from the texts—quotations, descriptions, or other details—that supports or illustrates each conclusion. If all group members are working with the same list of conclusions, have each person locate evidence to support a different one. Share what you found with the group. Discuss the strength of each piece of evidence, and make changes as needed.

**Evidence to Support Conclusions**

1. ______________________________
______________________________

2. ______________________________
______________________________

3. ______________________________
______________________________

4. ______________________________
______________________________

**EVIDENCE LOG**

Before moving on to a new selection, go to your Evidence Log and record what you've learned from the excerpts from *A History of the English Church and People* and "History of Jamaica."

**Write a Draft** Decide on a structure for your essay. Which general ideas, or conclusions, will you focus on? Will you present your conclusions first, and then offer evidence? Or will you tell how the texts are similar and different, and then offer your conclusions? Once you decide, write your first draft.

## Review, Revise, and Edit

Read your draft aloud to your group. Ask for feedback, and listen to it with an open mind. Use your peers' ideas—and your own—to revise your draft. Make sure you have included ample support for each conclusion you draw. After revising, finalize your essay by editing and proofreading thoroughly.

POETRY COLLECTION 1

# The Seafarer

# Dover Beach

# Escape From the Old Country

## Concept Vocabulary

As you perform your first read of these three poems, you will encounter the following words.

| desolation | fervent | blanch |
|---|---|---|

**Context Clues** If these words are unfamiliar to you, try using **context clues**—other words and phrases that appear in a text—to help determine their meanings. There are various types of context clues that you may encounter as you read. Here are three examples.

**Restatement:** Evan thought the acrobats made only a **semblance** of enjoying their routine; clearly, it was just for show.

**Synonym or Definition:** Whitney couldn't help drifting off into a **reverie**, or daydream, during her history class.

**Contrast of Ideas:** Just an hour after the raging storm was over, the air was utterly **tranquil**.

Apply your knowledge of context clues and other vocabulary strategies to determine the meanings of unfamiliar words you encounter during your first read.

## First Read POETRY

Apply these strategies as you conduct your first read. You will have an opportunity to complete a close read after your first read.

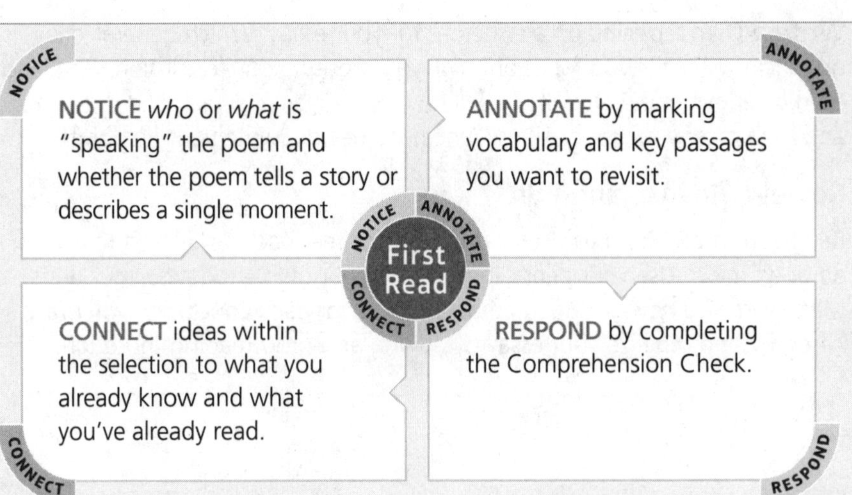
NOTICE
NOTICE *who* or *what* is "speaking" the poem and whether the poem tells a story or describes a single moment.
ANNOTATE
ANNOTATE by marking vocabulary and key passages you want to revisit.
First Read
CONNECT
CONNECT ideas within the selection to what you already know and what you've already read.
RESPOND
RESPOND by completing the Comprehension Check.

STANDARDS

**Reading Literature**

- By the end of grade 12, read and comprehend literature, including stories, dramas, and poems, at the high end of the grades 11–CCR text complexity band independently and proficiently.

**Language**

- Use context as a clue to the meaning of a word or phrase.
- Determine or clarify the meaning of unknown and multiple-meaning words and phrases based on *grades 11–12 reading and content*, choosing flexibly from a range of strategies.

## About the Poets

**Burton Raffel** (1928–2015) was a poet and translator who published more than 100 books in his lifetime, including poetry, fiction, literary theory, and, especially, translations. Among his translations, he is best known for *Beowulf*, an Anglo-Saxon classic, but he also translated the Middle English *The Canterbury Tales*, by Geoffrey Chaucer; the Spanish *Don Quixote*, by Miguel de Cervantes; and the Italian *Divine Comedy*, by Dante Alighieri.

**Matthew Arnold** (1822–1888) was a poet and essayist. As a professor at Oxford, Arnold became the first professor to lecture in English rather than Latin. His essays established literary criticism as a distinct genre of writing, and they greatly influenced later critics. His poetry was influential as well; the work of William Butler Yeats and Sylvia Plath, among others, was shaped in part by Arnold's style.

**Adrienne Su** (b. 1967) was raised in Atlanta, Georgia. She graduated from Radcliffe College at Harvard University and received a Master of Fine Arts from the University of Virginia. She has published three books of poetry and teaches at Dickinson College in Carlisle, Pennsylvania. She says that "writing goes best for me when it's woven into everyday life."

## Backgrounds

### The Seafarer

"The Seafarer" is a poem written in Anglo-Saxon (Old English), the language that was spoken in Britain before the arrival of the Normans in 1066. The Anglo-Saxons took ocean voyages, often lasting for months at a time, on wooden vessels that were powered by both oars and sails and were similar to Viking ships.

### Dover Beach

"Dover Beach" is one of Matthew Arnold's best-known poems. In it, he wrestles with the topic of psychological isolation, a common theme in his work, linking it with what he felt was the shrinking faith of his time. References to "Dover Beach" can be seen in many books, poems, songs, and movies, including *Armies of the Night*, by Norman Mailer; *A Darkling Plain*, by Philip Reeve; music by both the rock band Rush and the classical composer Samuel Barber; and a poem by the former Poet Laureate Billy Collins.

### Escape From the Old Country

"Escape From the Old Country" is a poem from Su's collection *Sanctuary*, published in 2006. It is about being the child of parents who immigrated to the United States from China. Like much of Su's work, the poem illuminates what it means to be a member of a community, whether it be a family, a neighborhood, or an ethnic group.

# The Seafarer

translated by Burton Raffel

NOTES

This tale is true, and mine. It tells
How the sea took me, swept me back
And forth in sorrow and fear and pain,
Showed me suffering in a hundred ships,
In a thousand ports, and in me. It tells
Of smashing surf when I sweated in the cold
Of an anxious watch, perched in the bow
As it dashed under cliffs. My feet were cast
In icy bands, bound with frost.
With frozen chains, and hardship groaned
Around my heart. Hunger tore
At my sea-weary soul. No man sheltered
On the quiet fairness of earth can feel
How wretched I was, drifting through winter
On an ice-cold sea, whirled in sorrow,
Alone in a world blown clear of love,
Hung with icicles. The hailstorms flew.
The only sound was the roaring sea,
The freezing waves. The song of the swan
Might serve for pleasure, the cry of the sea-fowl,
The death-noise of birds instead of laughter,
The mewing of gulls instead of mead.[1]
Storms beat on the rocky cliffs and were echoed
By icy-feathered terns and the eagle's screams;
No kinsman could offer comfort there,
To a soul left drowning in **desolation**.
And who could believe, knowing but
The passion of cities, swelled proud with wine
And no taste of misfortune, how often, how wearily,
I put myself back on the paths of the sea.
Night would blacken; it would snow from the north;
Frost bound the earth and hail would fall,
The coldest seeds. And how my heart
Would begin to beat, knowing once more
The salt waves tossing and the towering sea!
The time for journeys would come and my soul
Called me eagerly out, sent me over
The horizon, seeking foreigners' homes.
But there isn't a man on earth so proud,
So born to greatness, so bold with his youth,
Grown so brave, or so graced by God,
That he feels no fear as the sails unfurl,
Wondering what Fate has willed and will do.
No harps ring in his heart, no rewards,
No passion for women, no worldly pleasures,
Nothing, only the ocean's heave;

Mark context clues or indicate another strategy you used that helped you determine meaning.

**desolation** (deh suh LAY shuhn) *n.*

MEANING:

1. **mead** *n.* liquor made from fermented honey and water.

NOTES

But longing wraps itself around him.
Orchards blossom, the towns bloom,
Fields grow lovely as the world springs fresh,
And all these admonish that willing mind
Leaping to journeys, always set
In thoughts traveling on a quickening tide.
So summer's sentinel, the cuckoo, sings
In his murmuring voice, and our hearts mourn
As he urges. Who could understand,
In ignorant ease, what we others suffer
As the paths of exile stretch endlessly on?
And yet my heart wanders away,
My soul roams with the sea, the whales'
Home, wandering to the widest corners
Of the world, returning ravenous with desire,
Flying solitary, screaming, exciting me
To the open ocean, breaking oaths
On the curve of a wave.
Thus the joys of God
Are **fervent** with life, where life itself
Fades quickly into the earth. The wealth
Of the world neither reaches to Heaven nor remains.
No man has ever faced the dawn
Certain which of Fate's three threats
Would fall: illness, or age, or an enemy's
Sword, snatching the life from his soul.
The praise the living pour on the dead
Flowers from reputation: plant
An earthly life of profit reaped
Even from hatred and rancor, of bravery
Flung in the devil's face, and death
Can only bring you earthly praise
And a song to celebrate a place
With the angels, life eternally blessed
In the hosts of Heaven.
The days are gone
When the kingdoms of earth flourished in glory;
Now there are no rulers, no emperors,
No givers of gold, as once there were,
When wonderful things were worked among them
And they lived in lordly magnificence.
Those powers have vanished, those pleasures are dead.
The weakest survives and the world continues,
Kept spinning by toil. All glory is tarnished.
The world's honor ages and shrinks,
Bent like the men who mold it. Their faces
**Blanch** as time advances, their beards
Wither and they mourn the memory of friends.

Mark context clues or indicate another strategy you used that helped you determine meaning.

**fervent** (FUR vuhnt) *adj.*

MEANING:

Mark context clues or indicate another strategy you used that helped you determine meaning.

**blanch** (blanch) *v.*

MEANING:

The sons of princes, sown in the dust.
The soul stripped of its flesh knows nothing
Of sweetness or sour, feels no pain,
Bends neither its hand nor its brain. A brother
Opens his palms and pours down gold.
On his kinsman's grave, strewing his coffin
With treasures intended for Heaven, but nothing
Golden shakes the wrath of God
For a soul overflowing with sin, and nothing
Hidden on earth rises to Heaven.
        We all fear God. He turns the earth,
He set it swinging firmly in space,
Gave life to the world and light to the sky.
Death leaps at the fools who forget their God.
He who lives humbly has angels from Heaven
To carry him courage and strength and belief.
A man must conquer pride, not kill it,
Be firm with his fellows, chaste for himself,
Treat all the world as the world deserves,
With love or with hate but never with harm,
Though an enemy seek to scorch him in hell,
Or set the flames of a funeral pyre
Under his lord. Fate is stronger
And God mightier than any man's mind.
Our thoughts should turn to where our home is,
Consider the ways of coming there,
Then strive for sure permission for us
To rise to that eternal joy,
That life born in the love of God
And the hope of Heaven. Praise the Holy
Grace of Him who honored us,
Eternal, unchanging creator of earth. Amen.



NOTES

MEDIA CONNECTION

The Seafarer

**Discuss It**

In what ways is the cellist's relationship to the cello similar to or different from the sailor's relationship to the sea in "The Seafarer"?

Write your response before sharing your ideas.

# Dover Beach

Matthew Arnold

The sea is calm tonight.
The tide is full, the moon lies fair
Upon the straits;[1] on the French coast the light
Gleams and is gone; the cliffs of England stand,
Glimmering and vast, out in the tranquil bay.
Come to the window, sweet is the night air!

Only, from the long line of spray
Where the sea meets the moon-blanched land,
Listen! you hear the grating roar
Of pebbles which the waves draw back, and fling,
At their return, up the high strand,[2]
Begin, and cease, and then again begin,
With tremulous cadence slow, and bring
The eternal note of sadness in.

Sophocles[3] long ago
Heard it on the Aegean,[4] and it brought
Into his mind the turbid ebb and flow
Of human misery; we
Find also in the sound a thought,
Hearing it by this distant northern sea.

The Sea of Faith
Was once, too, at the full, and round earth's shore
Lay like the folds of a bright girdle furled.
But now I only hear
Its melancholy, long, withdrawing roar,
Retreating, to the breath
Of the night wind, down the vast edges drear
And naked shingles[5] of the world.

Ah, love, let us be true
To one another! for the world, which seems
To lie before us like a land of dreams,
So various, so beautiful, so new,
Hath really neither joy, nor love, nor light,
Nor certitude, nor peace, nor help for pain;
And we are here as on a darkling[6] plain
Swept with confused alarms of struggle and flight,
Where ignorant armies clash by night.

NOTES

1. **straits** Straits of Dover, between England and France.
2. **strand** shore.
3. **Sophocles** (SOF uh kleez) Greek tragic dramatist (c. 496–406 B.C.).
4. **Aegean** (ee JEE uhn) arm of the Mediterranean Sea between Greece and Turkey.
5. **shingles** *n.* beaches covered with large, coarse, waterworn gravel.
6. **darkling** *adj.* in the dark.

# Escape From the Old Country

Adrienne Su

I never had to make one,
no sickening weeks by ocean,

no waiting for the aerogrammes[1]
that gradually ceased to come.

Spent the babysitting money
on novels, shoes, and movies,

yet the neighborhood stayed empty.
It had nothing to do with a journey

not undertaken, not with dialect,
nor with a land that waited

to be rediscovered, then rejected.
As acid rain collected

above the suburban hills, I tried
to imagine being nothing, tried

to be able to claim, "I have
no culture," and be believed.

Yet the land occupies the person
even as the semblance of freedom

invites a kind of recklessness.
Tradition, unobserved, unasked,

hangs on tight; ancestors roam
into reverie, interfering at the most

awkward moments, first flirtations,
in doorways and dressing rooms—

But of course. Here in America,
no one escapes. In the end, each traveler

returns to the town where, everyone
knew, she hadn't even been born.

NOTES

* **aerogrammes** (AIR uh gramz) *n.* letters sent by air.

## Comprehension Check

**Complete the following items after you finish your first read. Review and clarify details with your group.**

THE SEAFARER

1. According to the speaker, what tale does this poem relate?

2. What does the speaker say all men feel when they see the sails of a ship unfurl?

3. According to the speaker, what has happened to the world's honor?

DOVER BEACH

1. As the poem begins, what scene does the speaker describe?

2. For the speaker, what sound seems to have an "eternal" sadness?

3. In the final stanza, what does the speaker say the world lacks?

ESCAPE FROM THE OLD COUNTRY

1. What type of journey has the speaker never had to take?

2. What does the speaker try to imagine being?

3. According to the speaker, what does tradition do?

## RESEARCH

**Research to Clarify** Choose at least one unfamiliar detail from one of the poems. Briefly research that detail. In what way does the information you learned shed light on an aspect of the poem?

**Research to Explore** Conduct research on Anglo-Saxon seafaring as described in the poem "The Seafarer." Discuss your findings with your group.

POETRY COLLECTION 1

# Close Read the Text

With your group, revisit sections of the text you marked during your first read. **Annotate** details that you notice. What **questions** do you have? What can you **conclude**?

# Analyze the Text

**CITE TEXTUAL EVIDENCE** to support your answers.

**Notebook** Complete the activities.

1. **Review and Clarify** With your group, reread lines 101–108 of "The Seafarer." What single line summarizes this passage? In what way is this line significant?

2. **Present and Discuss** Now, work with your group to share the passages from the poems that you found especially important. Take turns presenting your passages. Discuss what details you noticed, what questions you asked, and what conclusions you reached.

3. **Essential Question:** *What does it mean to call a place home?* What have these poems taught you about the meaning of *home*? Discuss.

**TIP**

**GROUP DISCUSSION**

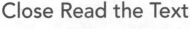

Although it is not necessary for group members to agree about a subject, it can be helpful to seek common ground, especially as you begin a discussion. Find aspects of the poems on which your group can agree. Then, discuss your differences of opinion.

LANGUAGE DEVELOPMENT

# Concept Vocabulary

desolation | fervent | blanch

**Why These Words?** The three concept vocabulary words are related. With your group, determine what the words have in common. Write your ideas, and add another word that fits this category.

## Practice

**Notebook** Use each of the concept vocabulary words in a sentence. Include context clues that hint at each word's meaning.

**WORD NETWORK**

Add interesting words related to finding a home from the text to your Word Network.

# Word Study

**Latin Root: *-sol-*** In "The Seafarer," the speaker refers to a "soul left drowning in desolation." The word *desolation* contains the Latin root *-sol-*, meaning "alone."

Reread lines 58–64 of "The Seafarer." Mark a word that contains the root *-sol-*, and write its meaning. Then, challenge yourself to think of other words containing this root, and write the words here. Use a print or online dictionary to verify your answers.

**STANDARDS**

**Reading Literature**
Determine two or more themes or central ideas of a text and analyze their development over the course of the text, including how they interact and build on one another to produce a complex account; provide an objective summary of the text.

**Language**
Verify the preliminary determination of the meaning of a word or phrase.

## Analyze Craft and Structure

**Development of Theme** A **theme** is the central idea, message, or insight that a literary work reveals. Themes can either be universal or specific.

- A **universal theme** is a message about life that is expressed in the literature of all cultures and time periods. Some common universal themes include those that express the importance of courage, the power of love, or the danger of greed. These themes continue to appear in literature throughout the world.
- A **culturally specific theme** relates meaningfully to some cultures but not others. For example, alienation may be a universal theme, but alienation from a dominant culture is a theme that people in minority cultures experience exclusively. A culturally specific theme might also rely on a work's **historical context**, or the time period in which it was written.

Poems usually have a single subject, but they can express more than one theme. In those cases, the themes often connect or build on one another. For example, "The Seafarer," "Dover Beach," and "Escape From the Old Country" each develop multiple themes, but they all share one subject: exile.

TIP

**GROUP DISCUSSION**

Keep in mind that a work of literature may contain multiple themes. Other members of your group may interpret the same events in a story or poem differently and find other themes. As long as you can offer sufficient textual support for a theme, it should be considered a valid interpretation.

### Practice

**CITE TEXTUAL EVIDENCE** to support your answers.

As a group, use this chart to analyze specific details about each poem's subject and to identify their universal and culturally specific themes.

| POEM | MEANINGFUL DETAILS | THEMES—UNIVERSAL or SPECIFIC? | HOW THE THEMES CONNECT |
|---|---|---|---|
| The Seafarer | | | |
| Dover Beach | | | |
| Escape From the Old Country | | | |

POETRY COLLECTION 1

## STANDARDS

**Reading Literature**
Analyze the impact of the author's choices regarding how to develop and relate elements of a story or drama.

**Language**
Apply knowledge of language to understand how language functions in different contexts, to make effective choices for meaning or style, and to comprehend more fully when reading or listening.

# Conventions and Style

**Forms of Address** In a literary work, **point of view** is the perspective, or vantage point, from which a story is told. Point of view is determined by what type of voice is telling the story. In a poem that uses first-person point of view, such as "The Seafarer," the speaker provides description and commentary from his or her own perspective, and readers see the world of the poem through the speaker's eyes. In addition to a speaker, a poem might feature a specific audience. Poets leave clues that help readers determine who the audience may be.

- A speaker uses **direct address** to speak directly to an audience. Speakers may name a specific person to whom they are talking, or they might use pronouns such as "you" and "we" to invite readers to think of themselves as part of the audience.
- A speaker may address an **implied audience**, or an audience that is hinted at but not explicitly revealed. If a poem has an implied audience, readers need to use clues to determine whom the speaker is addressing.

## Read It

Working individually, use this chart to analyze forms of address in the poems. When you finish, gather as a group and discuss your responses.

| POEM | DETAILS RELATED TO AUDIENCE | DIRECT ADDRESS or IMPLIED AUDIENCE? | WHO OR WHAT IS THE AUDIENCE? |
|---|---|---|---|
| The Seafarer | | | |
| Dover Beach | | | |
| Escape From the Old Country | | | |

## Write It

**Notebook** Draft a short poem about your hometown. Use first-person point of view, and keep a specific audience in mind as you write. Decide whether to use direct address or to leave clues about an implied audience.

# Speaking and Listening

**Assignment**

Work with your group to plan and create a **podcast** that informs listeners. Choose one of the following topics:

- [ ] Plan and produce a podcast in which group members contribute **informative presentations** about different meanings of exile. With your group, find references that allow you to consider questions such as:
  - How is the word *exile* defined, and how is it used in literature?
  - What examples of exile exist in literature, including examples from classical Greek and Roman literature to contemporary works by authors such as Pablo Neruda and Salman Rushdie?
- [ ] Plan and produce a podcast of **descriptive analysis** about the development of poetry, from the Anglo-Saxon classic "The Seafarer" to the nineteenth-century poem "Dover Beach" to the contemporary work "Escape From the Old Country." Consider what has changed about poetry's styles and themes—and what has not.
- [ ] Plan and produce a podcast of a **roundtable discussion** in which the group discusses the ocean as a metaphor in poetry:
  - the ocean as a mother figure and the source of all life on Earth
  - the ocean as an unstoppable force that cannot be resisted
  - the ocean as the vast unknown

EVIDENCE LOG

Before moving on to a new selection, go to your Evidence Log and record what you learned from "The Seafarer," "Dover Beach," and "Escape From the Old Country."

### Conduct Research

Once your group has agreed on a focus for your podcast, set forth the outline for the podcast, and begin to gather details that will provide clear and distinct perspectives on your topic. Use a chart to keep track of the kinds of information you are researching and the group member assigned to each task. Also, record the sources each person consults. Work together to integrate information from each person's sources into a cohesive podcast.

| KIND OF INFORMATION | WHO IS RESPONSIBLE | SOURCE(S) CONSULTED |
|---|---|---|
| | | |
| | | |
| | | |
| | | |

**Produce and Present** Once you are satisfied with the content of your podcast, work as a group to produce it. Assign roles, and rehearse before recording. Speakers should enunciate clearly and adapt their tone, volume, and pacing to suit the content and audience. Those recording should ensure that the podcast is free from outside noise and that the speakers' voices are clearly captured. Then, play the podcast for your class, and answer questions your audience may have.

STANDARDS

**Speaking and Listening**
Present information, findings, and supporting evidence, conveying a clear and distinct perspective and a logical argument, such that listeners can follow the line of reasoning, alternative or opposing perspectives are addressed, and the organization, development, substance, and style are appropriate to purpose, audience, and a range of formal and informal tasks.

POETRY COLLECTION 2

# The Widow at Windsor

# From Lucy: Englan' Lady

## Concept Vocabulary

As you perform your first read of "The Widow at Windsor" and "From Lucy: Englan' Lady," you will encounter the following words.

| cavalry | stores | rank |
|---|---|---|

**Context Clues** If these words are unfamiliar to you, try using **context clues**—words and phrases that appear in nearby text—to help you determine their meanings. There are various types of context clues that you may encounter as you read.

**Synonyms:** The **rectitude,** or virtue, of the queen's decisions earned the people's respect.

**Antonyms:** The queen refused to tolerate dishonesty. The **rectitude** of her decisions, therefore, appealed to everyone in the realm.

**Example:** From her first decree—that all of the nation's children be guaranteed an education—the queen's decisions were known for their **rectitude.**

Apply your knowledge of context clues and other vocabulary strategies to determine the meanings of unfamiliar words you encounter during your first read.

## First Read POETRY

Apply these strategies as you conduct your first read. You will have an opportunity to complete a close read after your first read.

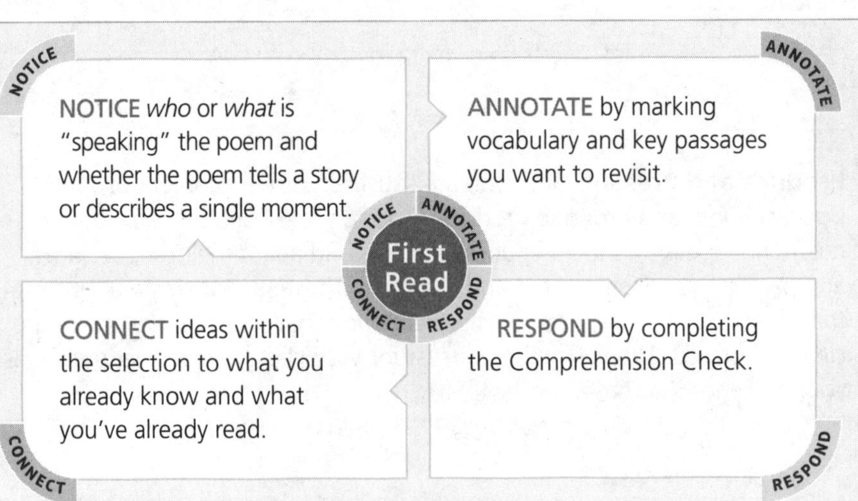
NOTICE
NOTICE *who* or *what* is "speaking" the poem and whether the poem tells a story or describes a single moment.
ANNOTATE
ANNOTATE by marking vocabulary and key passages you want to revisit.
First Read
NOTICE
ANNOTATE
CONNECT
RESPOND
CONNECT ideas within the selection to what you already know and what you've already read.
RESPOND by completing the Comprehension Check.
CONNECT
RESPOND

### STANDARDS

**Reading Literature**
By the end of grade 12, read and comprehend literature, including stories, dramas, and poems, at the high end of the grades 11–CCR text complexity band independently and proficiently.

**Language**
- Determine or clarify the meaning of unknown and multiple-meaning words and phrases based on *grades 11–12 reading and content*, choosing flexibly from a range of strategies.
- Use context as a clue to the meaning of a word or phrase.

## About the Poets

**Rudyard Kipling** (1865–1936) was born to British parents in colonial India. He attended school in England but returned to India in 1882 and took a job with a newspaper. Kipling published a number of witty poems and stories while there, and when he returned to England in 1889 he was a celebrity. The popularity of his works, such as the poems "Gunga Din" (1890) and "If—" (1910), the short-story collection *The Jungle Book* (1894), and the novels *Captains Courageous* (1897) and *Kim* (1901), made Kipling the highest-paid author of his time. In 1907, he became the first English author to receive the Nobel Prize in Literature.

**James Berry** (b. 1924) spent his childhood in a coastal village in Jamaica, where he started writing stories and poems while still in school. He moved to London after World War II and continued to write while working there. Berry published his first collection of poems, *Fractured Circles*, in 1979. Two years later, he became the first West Indian to win the Poetry Society's National Poetry Competition. Berry's other awards and honors include the Signal Poetry Award in 1989 for *When I Dance* and the Order of the British Empire in 1990.

## Backgrounds

### The Widow at Windsor

Queen Victoria was the queen of England from 1837 to 1901. During her reign, the British Empire reached the height of its power as the most influential colonial ruler in the world. Her long reign during this time of vigorous expansion and prosperity resulted in the period becoming known as the Victorian Age. By the last decade of the nineteenth century, however, cracks in the strength of the British Empire were beginning to show.

### From Lucy: Englan' Lady

"From Lucy: Englan' Lady" is part of a group of poems that James Berry wrote in the Caribbean Creole language and in the voice of Lucy, a Jamaican immigrant woman living in London, England. According to the poet, most people who came to Britain in the 1950s had a natural respect for the Royal Family, which wields ceremonial authority and often represents Britain to the rest of the world.

POETRY

# The Widow at Windsor

Rudyard Kipling

NOTES

Mark context clues or indicate another strategy you used that helped you determine meaning.

**cavalry** (KAV uhl ree) *adj.*

MEANING:

**stores** (stawrz) *n.*

MEANING:

'Ave you 'eard o' the Widow at Windsor[1]
With a hairy gold crown on 'er 'ead?
She 'as ships on the foam—she 'as millions at 'ome,
An' she pays us poor beggars in red.
(Ow, poor beggars in red!)
There's 'er nick[2] on the **cavalry** 'orses,
There's 'er mark on the medical
**stores**—An' 'er troops you'll find with a fair wind be'ind
That takes us to various wars.

1. **the Widow at Windsor** Queen Victoria. She spent the rest of her life in mourning at Windsor Palace after the death of her husband, Prince Albert.
2. **nick** mark.

(Poor beggars!—barbarious wars!)
Then 'ere's to the Widow at Windsor,
An' 'ere's to the stores an' the guns,
The men an' the 'orses what makes up the forces
O' Missis Victorier's sons.
(Poor beggars! Victorier's sons!)

Walk wide o' the Widow at Windsor,
For 'alf o' Creation she owns:
We'ave bought 'er the same with the sword an' the flame,
An' we've salted it down with our bones.
(Poor beggars!—it's blue with our bones!)
Hands off o' the sons o' the widow,
Hands off o' the goods in 'er shop.
For the kings must come down an' the emperors frown
When the Widow at Windsor says "Stop!"
(Poor beggars!—we're sent to say "Stop!")
Then 'ere's to the Lodge o' the Widow,
From the Pole to the Tropics it runs—
To the Lodge that we tile with the **rank** an' the file,
An' open in form with the guns.
(Poor beggars!—it's always they guns!)

We 'ave 'eard o' the Widow at Windsor,
It's safest to leave 'er alone:
For 'er sentries we stand by the sea an' the land
Wherever the bugles are blown.
(Poor beggars!—an' don't we get blown!)
Take 'old o' the Wings o' the Mornin',
An' flop round the earth till you're dead;
But you won't get away from the tune that they play
To the bloomin' old rag over'ead.
(Poor beggars!—it's 'ot over'ead!)
Then 'ere's to the sons o' the Widow,
Wherever, 'owever they roam.
'Ere's all they desire, an' if they require
A speedy return to their 'ome.
(Poor beggars!—they'll never see 'ome!)

NOTES

Mark context clues or indicate another strategy you used that helped you determine meaning.

**rank** (rangk) *n.*

MEANING:

# From Lucy: Englan' Lady

James Berry

NOTES

You ask me 'bout the lady. Me dear,
old center here still shine
with Queen.[1] She affec' the place
like the sun: not comin' out oft'n
an' when it happ'n everybody's out
smilin' as she wave a han'
like a seagull flyin' slow slow.

An' you know she come from
dust free rooms an' velvet
an' diamond. She make you feel
this on-an'-on[2] town, London,
where long long time deeper than mind.[3]
An' han's after han's[4] die away,
makin' streets, putt'n' up bricks,
a piece of brass, a piece of wood
an' plantin' trees: an' it give
a car a halfday job gett'n' through.

An' Leela, darlin', no, I never
meet the Queen in flesh. Yet
sometimes, deep deep, I sorry for her.

1. **Queen** Queen Elizabeth II, who became heir to the throne in 1952 at the age of 25.
2. **on-an'-on** extraordinary.
3. **deeper . . . mind** more than can be comprehended.
4. **han's after han's** many generations.

Everybody expec' a show
from her, like she a space touris'
on earth. An' darlin', unless
you can go home an' scratch up[5]
you' husban', it mus' be hard
strain keepin' good graces for
all hypocrite faces.

Anyhow, me dear, you know what
ole time people say,
"Bird sing sweet for its nest."[6]

NOTES

5. **scratch up** lose your temper at.
6. **"Bird . . . nest"** Jamaican proverb, referring to the nightingale's habit of singing loudest near its nest. It means, "Those closest to home are the most contented."

## Comprehension Check

**Complete the following items after you finish your first read. Review and clarify details with your group.**

THE WIDOW AT WINDSOR

1. According to the speaker, on what two things can you find the queen's mark?

2. In his parenthetical statements, how does the speaker repeatedly identify himself and other members of the British military?

FROM LUCY: ENGLAN' LADY

1. According to the speaker, what does everybody do when the queen comes out?

2. What does the speaker say everybody expects from the queen?

## RESEARCH

**Research to Clarify** Choose at least one unfamiliar detail from one of the poems. Briefly research that detail. In what way does the information you found shed light on an aspect of the poem?

POETRY COLLECTION 2

## Close Read the Text

With your group, revisit sections of the text you marked during your first read. **Annotate** details that you notice. What **questions** do you have? What can you **conclude**?

TIP

**GROUP DISCUSSION**

As you discuss the poems, stay on task, and avoid digressing into discussions that are off-topic. Also avoid side conversations. Make sure that everyone is involved in the discussion and that every meeting of your group is productive.

## Analyze the Text

**CITE TEXTUAL EVIDENCE** to support your answers.

**Notebook** Complete the activities.

1. **Review and Clarify** With your group, reread the second stanza of "The Widow at Windsor." Discuss how the lines enclosed in parentheses affect your understanding of the poem. What does the speaker suggest about the costs of being a world power?

2. **Present and Discuss** Now, work with your group to share the passages from the poems that you found especially important. Take turns presenting your passages. Discuss what details you noticed, what questions you asked, and what conclusions you reached.

3. **Essential Question:** *What does it mean to call a place home?* What have these poems taught you about the meaning of home? Discuss with your group.

LANGUAGE DEVELOPMENT

## Concept Vocabulary

**cavalry** **stores** **rank**

**Why These Words?** The three concept vocabulary words are related. With your group, determine what the words have in common. Write your ideas, and add another word that fits the category.

### Practice

**Notebook** Confirm your understanding of each concept vocabulary word by using it in a sentence. Be sure to consult reference materials, if necessary, and to use context clues that hint at each word's meaning.

WORD NETWORK

Add interesting words related to finding a home from the texts to your Word Network.

## Word Study

**Notebook** **Multiple-Meaning Words** Many words in English have more than one definition. For example, the words *stores* and *rank*, which appear in "The Widow at Windsor," have several meanings. Write the meanings of *stores* and *rank* as Kipling uses them in the poem. Then, write two more definitions for each word. Use a college-level dictionary, if necessary. Finally, identify three other multiple-meaning words in the poems. Record the words, and write two definitions for each.

STANDARDS

**Reading Literature**
Analyze how an author's choices concerning how to structure specific parts of a text contribute to its overall structure and meaning as well as its aesthetic impact.

**Language**
• Determine or clarify the meaning of unknown and multiple-meaning words and phrases based on *grades 11–12 reading and content*, choosing flexibly from a range of strategies.
• Demonstrate understanding of figurative language, word relationships, and nuances in word meanings.

# Analyze Craft and Structure

**Author's Choices: Structure** "The Widow at Windsor" and "From Lucy: Englan' Lady" are **dramatic monologues**, poems in which a distinct *persona*, or fictional self created by the poet, expresses his or her ideas about a topic to a silent listener. It is, in essence, a one-sided poetic conversation. The form developed during the Victorian era, and author George Thornbury coined the term in 1857. Dramatic monologues rely on two main elements to develop key ideas and themes:

- a speaker, who describes or discusses a situation, revealing clues to his or her character and using a distinctive tone
- a silent listener, or one whose responses are implied

In some dramatic monologues, the speaker may refer to but not directly describe what the silent listener says or does. Using details the speaker does provide, the reader infers that the silent listener has reacted, gestured, asked a question, or otherwise responded.

TIP

**CLARIFICATION**

As you discuss the poems, remember that a dramatic monologue presents one side of a conversation. The speaker has a specific listener, which affects what he or she says and how he or says it.

## Practice

**CITE TEXTUAL EVIDENCE** to support your answers.

Use this chart to record details about each dramatic monologue. Then, analyze those details to determine a theme, or deeper insight, each poem conveys. Discuss your findings and interpretations with your group.

| THE WIDOW AT WINDSOR | |
|---|---|
| Speaker's Situation (Include details about the listener.) | |
| Speaker's Character | |
| Speaker's Tone, or Emotional Attitude | |
| Possible Theme | |
| **FROM LUCY: ENGLAN' LADY** | |
| Speaker's Situation (Include details about the listener.) | |
| Speaker's Character | |
| Speaker's Tone, or Emotional Attitude | |
| Possible Theme | |

POETRY COLLECTION 2

TIP

**PROCESS**

Take turns with your group members reading the poems aloud. Listen and identify examples of added or omitted sounds that you hear.

## Conventions and Style

**Dialect** The form of a language spoken by people who live in a particular place or belong to a particular group is a **dialect**. The grammar, syntax, vocabulary, and pronunciation found in a particular dialect varies from what is considered the standard form of a language. In literature, authors use dialect for several reasons, including the following:

- to develop character, mood, and setting
- to add authenticity and freshness to a literary work

Authors employ many different techniques to convey dialect. One common technique is the use of apostrophes to indicate missing sounds or dropped letters. Both Kipling and Berry use this technique, and others, to convey two very different dialects.

| EXAMPLE OF DIALECT | HOW THE AUTHOR CONVEYS DIALECT |
|---|---|
| The Widow at Windsor<br>(Poor beggars! <u>Victorier's</u> sons!) | The author uses a nonstandard spelling. |
| From Lucy: Englan' Lady<br>Anyhow, <u>me</u> dear, you know what | The author uses nonstandard pronouns. |

### Read It

Work individually. Use this chart to analyze examples of dialect that Kipling and Berry use in their poems. Identify another example of dialect in each poem, and explain how the author conveys dialect in the example. Try to identify a technique that is not shown in the examples provided. Then, discuss with your group the effect the use of dialect has on each poem.

| POEM | EXAMPLE OF DIALECT | HOW THE AUTHOR CONVEYS DIALECT |
|---|---|---|
| The Widow at Windsor | | |
| From Lucy: Englan' Lady | | |

### Write It

**Notebook** Write a poem in which you convey the dialect of the region in which you live or another dialect with which you are familiar. Think about how the dialect is unique and how you will capture those elements in writing before you write your poem.

**STANDARDS**

**Reading Literature**
Determine the meaning of words and phrases as they are used in the text, including figurative and connotative meanings; analyze the impact of specific word choices on meaning and tone, including words with multiple meanings or language that is particularly fresh, engaging, or beautiful.

**Writing**
- Write informative/ explanatory texts to examine and convey complex ideas, concepts, and information clearly and accurately through the effective selection, organization, and analysis of content.
- Establish and maintain a formal style and objective tone while attending to the norms and conventions of the discipline in which they are writing.

**Language**
Apply knowledge of language to understand how language functions in different contexts, to make effective choices for meaning or style, and to comprehend more fully when reading or listening.

# Writing to Sources

## Assignment

With your group, write a **formal analysis** of the key features of dramatic monologues, and consider what makes the form powerful or effective. Use examples from the "The Widow at Windsor" and "From Lucy: Englan' Lady" in your analysis. You may also locate other dramatic monologues, such as those by Robert Browning, to use as examples. Assume that your audience is unfamiliar with the poems you are citing, and provide clear explanations of their content and language. As you write, maintain an appropriately formal academic style and tone. After you have completed the writing, present your work to the class. Choose from among the following topics:

- ☐ an **overview** of the most important features of dramatic monologues
- ☐ an **explanation** of how the use of dialect in dramatic monologues contributes to the development of character, musicality, and meaning
- ☐ a **compare-and-contrast analysis** of Kipling's and Berry's poems, highlighting key similarities and differences between them

**Plan Your Project** List the tasks you will need to complete to fulfill the assignment. Decide how you will organize the work. Then, appoint individual group members to each task.

**Gather Examples** Identify text evidence that helps support your formal analysis. Remember that you can use examples from other poems to illustrate key features and support your ideas.

| THE WIDOW AT WINDSOR | FROM LUCY: ENGLAN' LADY |
|---|---|
| **Omitting Letters/Sounds**<br>**'Ave (have)** you **'eard (heard) o' (of)** the Widow at Windsor | **Omitting Letters/Sounds**<br>like the sun: not **comin' (coming)** out out **oft'n (often)** |
| **Adding Letters/Sounds**<br>(Poor beggars! **Victorier's (Victoria's)** sons!) | **Repeating Words**<br>where **long long** time deeper than mind |

**Review and Revise** Once you have finished drafting your analysis, check to make sure that the organization is clear and that you have supported your key ideas. When you feel comfortable with both, work on your style and tone. Consider whether any words or phrases are too casual or emotional. Make any revisions needed, and then proofread your analysis to ensure it is free from errors in grammar, spelling, and punctuation.

**EVIDENCE LOG**

Before moving on to a new selection, go to your Evidence Log and record what you learned from "The Widow at Windsor" and "From Lucy: Englan' Lady."

SOURCES

- *from* A HISTORY OF THE ENGLISH CHURCH AND PEOPLE
- *from* HISTORY OF JAMAICA
- THE SEAFARER
- DOVER BEACH
- ESCAPE FROM THE OLD COUNTRY
- THE WIDOW AT WINDSOR
- FROM LUCY: ENGLAN' LADY

# Present a Panel Discussion

**Assignment**

You have read a variety of texts in which a sense of place is key. Work with your group to hold an informative **panel discussion** on this question:

**What makes a place important enough to write about?**

Capture your discussion on video to share with others.

## Plan With Your Group

**Analyze the Text** With your group, choose three texts from this section, and then work individually to analyze how each writer conveys a strong sense of place. What key characteristics of each place do the writers communicate? In what ways does each writer show that the place is important to a society, to a smaller group, or to an individual? Use the chart to identify details that help you build your analysis.

| TITLE (choose three) | DETAILS AND DESCRIPTIONS |
|---|---|
| *from* A History of the English Church and People | |
| *from* History of Jamaica | |
| The Seafarer | |
| Dover Beach | |
| Escape From the Old Country | |
| The Widow at Windsor | |
| From Lucy: Englan' Lady | |

**Gather Evidence and Examples** Reconvene with your group to share your analysis and identify the strongest ideas. Combine your ideas into a master chart, or take notes or use note cards to capture them. Go back into the text as needed to provide more specific support for your analysis.

STANDARDS

**Speaking and Listening**

- Initiate and participate effectively in a range of collaborative discussions with diverse partners on *grades 11–12 topics, texts, and issues,* building on others' ideas and expressing their own clearly and persuasively.
- Propel conversations by posing and responding to questions that probe reasoning and evidence; ensure a hearing for a full range of positions on a topic or issue; clarify, verify, or challenge ideas and conclusions; and promote divergent and creative perspectives.

**Organize Your Presentation** Meet with your group to determine how you will present the information you gathered. Choose a moderator, who will write and present the questions to be answered by each panel member in turn. The moderator may also help facilitate smooth transitions between speakers during the discussion. Divide the texts you chose among the remaining group members. Work individually to brainstorm responses to the moderator's questions, using details from your assigned text. Invite a classmate from outside the group to video-record your discussion.

## Rehearse With Your Group

**Practice with Your Group** As you deliver your portion of the presentation, use this checklist to evaluate the effectiveness of your group's first run-through. Then, use your evaluation and these instructions to guide changes you make to the content or presentation.

| CONTENT | USE OF MEDIA | PRESENTATION TECHNIQUES |
|---|---|---|
| ☐ The responses from each speaker clearly answer the questions asked.<br>☐ Ideas are supported with evidence from the texts. | ☐ Equipment functions properly.<br>☐ Focus moves smoothly from speaker to speaker. | ☐ The speaker uses formal language appropriately.<br>☐ The speaker uses eye contact and speaks clearly.<br>☐ The interaction between speakers and moderator is smooth. |

**Fine-Tune the Content** If necessary, find additional examples from the texts to support your ideas.

**Improve Your Use of Media** Watch the playback, and give your recorder feedback. Make sure that the sound is audible so that viewers can easily hear what is being asked and answered.

**Brush-Up on Your Presentation Techniques** Remember that you are speaking directly to the moderator and other group members in addition to your viewing audience. Take care to make eye contact with your group members rather than stare into the camera.

## Present and Evaluate

When presenting your discussion, try to ensure that all speakers have equal time to share their ideas. As you watch other group's videos, evaluate how well each discussion meets the requirements on the checklist.

STANDARDS

**Speaking and Listening**

- Present information, findings, and supporting evidence, conveying a clear and distinct perspective and a logical argument, such that listeners can follow the line of reasoning, alternative or opposing perspectives are addressed, and the organization, development, substance, and style are appropriate to purpose, audience, and a range of formal and informal tasks.
- Make strategic use of digital media in presentations to enhance understanding of findings, reasoning, and evidence and to add interest.
- Adapt speech to a variety of contexts and tasks, demonstrating a command of formal English when indicated or appropriate.

ESSENTIAL QUESTION:

# What does it mean to call a place home?

As we venture away from home, the memories we bring with us may be detailed or vague, accurate or distorted. In this section, you will complete your study of what it means to call a place a home by exploring an additional selection related to the topic. You'll then share what you learn with classmates. To choose a text, follow these steps.

**Look Back** Think about the selections you have already studied. What more do you want to know about the topic of what it means to call a place a home?

**Look Ahead** Preview the texts by reading the descriptions. Which one seems most interesting and appealing to you?

**Look Inside** Take a few minutes to scan the text you chose. Choose a different one if this text doesn't meet your needs.

## Independent Learning Strategies

Throughout your life, in school, in your community, and in your career, you will need to rely on yourself to learn and work on your own. Review these strategies and the actions you can take to practice them during Independent Learning. Add ideas of your own to each category.

| STRATEGY | ACTION PLAN |
|---|---|
| Create a schedule | • Understand your goals and deadlines.<br>• Make a plan for what to do each day.<br>• |
| Practice what you have learned | • Use first-read and close-read strategies to deepen your understanding.<br>• After you read, evaluate the usefulness of the evidence to help you understand the topic.<br>• After reading, consult reference sources for background information that can help you clarify meaning.<br>• |
| Take notes | • Record important ideas and information.<br>• Review your notes before preparing to share with a group.<br>• |

CONTENTS

Choose one selection. Selections are available online only.

SPEECH | POETRY

## St. Crispin's Day Speech

*from* Henry V, Act IV, Scene iii

*William Shakespeare*

## Home Thoughts, From Abroad

*Robert Browning*

When we are facing danger or are far away, thoughts of home can be sweet.

NOVEL EXCERPT

## *from* The Buried Giant

*Kazuo Ishiguro*

In sixth-century England, where ogres still roam the land, what is home like?

SHORT STORY

## My Old Home

*Lu Hsun*

Was the old house—the old home—always like this?

ESSAY

## *from* Writing as an Act of Hope

*Isabel Allende*

Is it possible to write the past back into existence?

PERFORMANCE-BASED ASSESSMENT PREP

## Review Evidence for an Informative Essay

Complete your Evidence Log for the unit by evaluating what you have learned and synthesizing the information you have recorded.

## First-Read Guide

**Tool Kit**
First-Read Guide and Model Annotation

**Use this page to record your first-read ideas.**

**Selection Title:** ______________________________

NOTICE

**NOTICE** new information or ideas you learn about the unit topic as you first read this text.

ANNOTATE

**ANNOTATE** by marking vocabulary and key passages you want to revisit.

NOTICE ANNOTATE First Read CONNECT RESPOND

**CONNECT** ideas within the selection to other knowledge and the selections you have read.

**RESPOND** by writing a brief summary of the selection.

CONNECT

RESPOND

STANDARD

**Reading** Read and comprehend complex literary and informational texts independently and proficiently.

# Close-Read Guide

**Tool Kit**
Close-Read Guide and Model Annotation

**Use this page to record your close-read ideas.**

**Selection Title:** ___

## Close Read the Text

Revisit sections of the text you marked during your first read. Read these sections closely and **annotate** what you notice. Ask yourself **questions** about the text. What can you **conclude?** Write down your ideas.

## Analyze the Text

Think about the author's choices of patterns, structure, techniques, and ideas included in the text. Select one, and record your thoughts about what this choice conveys.

## QuickWrite

Pick a paragraph or stanza from the text that grabbed your interest. Explain the power of this passage.

STANDARD

**Reading** Read and comprehend complex literary and informational texts independently and proficiently.

## Share Your Independent Learning

**Prepare to Share**

What does it mean to call a place home?

Even when you read or learn something independently, you can continue to grow by sharing what you have learned with others. Reflect on the text you explored independently, and write notes about its connection to the unit. In your notes, consider why this text belongs in this unit.

EVIDENCE LOG

Go to your Evidence Log and record what you learned from the text you read.

**Learn From Your Classmates**

**Discuss It** Share your ideas about the text you explored on your own. As you talk with your classmates, jot down ideas that you learn from them.

**Reflect**

Review your notes, and mark the most important insight you gained from these writing and discussion activities. Explain how this idea adds to your understanding of the topic of finding a home.

STANDARDS

**Speaking and Listening**
Initiate and participate effectively in a range of collaborative discussions with diverse partners on *grades 11–12 topics, texts, and issues*, building on others' ideas and expressing their own clearly and persuasively.

# Review Evidence for an Informative Essay

At the beginning of this unit, you responded to the following question:

**In what ways is home both a place and a state of mind?**

EVIDENCE LOG

Review your Evidence Log and your QuickWrite from the beginning of the unit. Has your response to the question changed?

| ☐ YES | ☐ NO |
|---|---|
| Identify at least three pieces of evidence that caused your ideas to change or grow. | Identify at least three pieces of evidence that supported your initial response. |
| **1.** | **1.** |
| **2.** | **2.** |
| **3.** | **3.** |

Write a thesis statement in response to the question: ____________________

____________________

____________________

Identify research strategies to develop the topic: ____________________

____________________

____________________

**Evaluate the Strength of Your Evidence** Consider your informative essay. Do you have facts to support your thesis? Do you use quotations from primary and secondary sources? If not, make a plan.

☐ Do more research

☐ Talk with my classmates

☐ Reread a selection

☐ Ask an expert

☐ Other: ____________________

STANDARDS

**Writing**

Introduce a topic or thesis statement; organize complex ideas, concepts, and information to make important connections and distinctions; include formatting, graphics, and multimedia when useful to aiding comprehension.

SOURCES

- WHOLE-CLASS SELECTIONS
- SMALL-GROUP SELECTIONS
- INDEPENDENT-LEARNING SELECTION

## PART 1

# Writing to Sources: Informative Essay

The texts in this unit share a theme of finding home at a time when the definition of home was changing. As borders altered, populations moved, and the concept of nationalism evolved, writers recorded these changes and examined what the idea of home means in a world full of such dramatic shifts.

**Assignment**

Write an **informative essay** in which you explain different perspectives on the concept of home. In your essay, explore this question:

In what ways is home both a place and a state of mind?

Integrate evidence from the texts you have read or watched and the research you have conducted in this unit to develop your ideas. Begin with a clear thesis statement that reflects your insights into the source texts. Finish with a conclusion in which you reiterate the significance of the question and reflect on its implications for individuals, families, and communities.

**Reread the Assignment** Review the assignment to be sure you fully understand it. The assignment may reference some of the academic words presented at the beginning of the unit. Be sure you understand each of the words in order to complete the assignment correctly.

### Academic Vocabulary

| migrate | requisite | implication |
|---|---|---|
| modify | reiterate | |

**Review the Elements of an Informative Essay** Before you begin writing, read the Informative Text Rubric. Once you have completed your first draft, check it against the rubric. If one or more of the elements is missing or not as strong as it could be, revise your essay to add or strengthen that component.

WORD NETWORK

As you write and revise your informative essay, use your Word Network to help vary your word choices.

STANDARDS

Writing

- Write informative/explanatory texts to examine and convey complex ideas, concepts, information clearly and accurately through the effective selection, organization, and analysis of content.
- Write routinely over extended time frames and shorter time frames for a range of tasks, purposes, and audiences.

# Informative Text Rubric

| | Focus and Organization | Evidence and Elaboration | Language Conventions |
|---|---|---|---|
| 4 | The introduction is engaging and reveals the topic in a way that appeals to a reader.<br><br>Facts, details, and examples progress logically, and transition words and phrases link and separate ideas.<br><br>The conclusion leaves a strong impression on the reader. | Ideas are supported with specific and relevant examples from research and the texts.<br><br>The tone of the essay is formal and objective.<br><br>Vocabulary is used strategically and appropriately for the audience and purpose. | The essay intentionally uses standard English conventions of usage and mechanics. |
| 3 | The introduction is engaging and clearly reveals the topic.<br><br>Facts, details, and examples progress logically, and transition words appear frequently.<br><br>The conclusion follows from the rest of the essay. | Ideas are supported with relevant examples from research and the texts.<br><br>The tone of the essay is mostly formal and objective.<br><br>Vocabulary is generally appropriate for the audience and purpose. | The essay demonstrates accuracy in standard English conventions of usage and mechanics. |
| 2 | The introduction states the topic.<br><br>Facts, details and examples progress somewhat logically, and transition words may be used.<br><br>The conclusion restates the main ideas. | Many ideas are supported with examples from research and the texts.<br><br>The tone of the essay is occasionally formal and objective.<br><br>Vocabulary is somewhat appropriate for the audience and purpose. | The essay demonstrates some accuracy in standard English conventions of usage and mechanics. |
| 1 | The introduction does not clearly state the topic, or there is no introduction.<br><br>Facts, details, and examples do not progress logically, and sentences seem disconnected.<br><br>The conclusion does not follow from the essay, or there is no conclusion. | Ideas are not supported with examples from research and the texts, or examples are irrelevant.<br><br>The tone of the essay is informal.<br><br>Vocabulary is limited or ineffective. | The essay contains mistakes in standard English conventions of usage and mechanics. |

PART 2

# Speaking and Listening: Media Presentation

**Assignment**

**Use your informative essay as the basis for a media presentation. Enhance your presentation with images to add interest and aid comprehension.**

STANDARDS

**Speaking and Listening**

- Present information, findings, and supporting evidence, conveying a clear and distinct perspective, such that listeners can follow the line of reasoning, alternative or opposing perspectives are addressed, and the organization, development, substance, and style are appropriate to purpose, audience, and a range of formal and informal tasks.
- Make strategic use of digital media in presentations to enhance understanding of findings, reasoning, and evidence and to add interest.

Follow these steps to make your presentation memorable:

- Reread your informative essay, and note concepts that could be illuminated or expanded upon through the use of images.
- Create or locate a few key images to use as slides or posters for your presentation.
- During your presentation, speak clearly, and adapt your volume, pacing, and tone to suit both your audience and the content you are sharing.

**Review the Rubric** Before you deliver your presentation, check your plans against this rubric. If one or more of the elements is missing or not as strong as it could be, revise your presentation.

| | Content | Use of Media | Presentation Technique |
|---|---|---|---|
| 3 | The presentation clearly and compellingly responds to the question in the prompt.<br><br>The presentation contains a clear introduction and conclusion, with interesting and relevant examples from research and the texts. | The images supplement but do not overwhelm the presentation.<br><br>The images chosen are relevant, minimal but powerful, and enhance the presentation. | The speaker maintains effective eye contact.<br><br>The speaker presents with energy and enthusiasm. |
| 2 | The presentation clearly responds to the question in the prompt.<br><br>The presentation contains an introduction and conclusion with some examples in support. | The images supplement but may sometimes overwhelm or distract from the presentation.<br><br>Most images chosen are relevant, but there may be too many or too few images. | The speaker mostly maintains effective eye contact.<br><br>The speaker presents with some level of energy and enthusiasm. |
| 1 | The presentation does not respond to the prompt.<br><br>An introduction or conclusion may be lacking, and some examples may lack relevance. | The images overwhelm or do not add information to the presentation.<br><br>The images may be irrelevant, and there may be too many or too few images. | The speaker does not establish eye contact.<br><br>The speaker presents without energy or enthusiasm. |

# Reflect on the Unit

Now that you've completed the unit, take a few moments to reflect on your learning. Use the questions below to think about where you succeeded, what skills and strategies helped you, and where you can continue to grow in the future.

## Reflect on the Unit Goals

Look back at the goals at the beginning of the unit. Use a different colored pen to rate yourself again. Think about readings and activities that contributed the most to the growth of your understanding. Record your thoughts.

## Reflect on the Learning Strategies

**Discuss It** Write a reflection on whether you were able to improve your learning based on your Action Plans. Think about what worked, what didn't, and what you might do to keep working on these strategies. Record your ideas before joining a class discussion.

## Reflect on the Text

Choose a selection that you found challenging, and explain what made it difficult.

Explain something that surprised you about a text in the unit.

Which activity taught you the most about what it means to call a place home? What did you learn?

STANDARDS

**Speaking and Listening**

- Come to discussions prepared, having read and researched material under study; explicitly draw on that preparation by referring to evidence from texts and other research on the topic or issue to stimulate a thoughtful, well-reasoned exchange of ideas.
- Initiate and participate effectively in a range of collaborative discussions with diverse partners on *grades 11–12 topics, texts, and issues,* building on others' ideas and expressing their own clearly and persuasively.

# RESOURCES

## CONTENTS

### TOOL KIT



### GLOSSARY



### INDEXES



### ACKNOWLEDGMENTS

# Marking the Text: Strategies and Tips for Annotation

When you close read a text, you read for comprehension and then reread to unlock layers of meaning and to analyze a writer's style and techniques. Marking a text as you read it enables you to participate more fully in the close-reading process.

Following are some strategies for text mark-ups, along with samples of how the strategies can be applied. These mark-ups are suggestions; you and your teacher may want to use other mark-up strategies.

| | |
|---|---|
| * | Key Idea |
| ! | I love it! |
| ? | I have questions |
| ◯ | Unfamiliar or important word |
| ---- | Context Clues |

## Suggested Mark-Up Notations

| WHAT I NOTICE | HOW TO MARK UP | QUESTIONS TO ASK |
|---|---|---|
| Key Ideas and Details | • Highlight key ideas or claims.<br>• Underline supporting details or evidence. | • What does the text say? What does it leave unsaid?<br>• What inferences do you need to make?<br>• What details lead you to make your inferences? |
| Word Choice | • Circle unfamiliar words.<br>• Put a dotted line under context clues, if any exist.<br>• Put an exclamation point beside especially rich or poetic passages. | • What inferences about word meaning can you make?<br>• What tone and mood are created by word choice?<br>• What alternate word choices might the author have made? |
| Text Structure | • Highlight passages that show key details supporting the main idea.<br>• Use arrows to indicate how sentences and paragraphs work together to build ideas.<br>• Use a right-facing arrow to indicate foreshadowing.<br>• Use a left-facing arrow to indicate flashback. | • Is the text logically structured?<br>• What emotional impact do the structural choices create? |
| Author's Craft | • Circle or highlight instances of repetition, either of words, phrases, consonants, or vowel sounds.<br>• Mark rhythmic beats in poetry using checkmarks and slashes.<br>• Underline instances of symbolism or figurative language. | • Does the author's style enrich or detract from the reading experience?<br>• What levels of meaning are created by the author's techniques? |

In a first read, work to get a sense of the main idea of a text. Look for key details and ideas that help you understand what the author conveys to you. Mark passages which prompt a strong response from you.

Here is how one reader marked up this text.

- * Key Idea
- ! I love it!
- ? I have questions
- ⬭ Unfamiliar or important word
- ---- Context Clues

NOTES

MODEL

INFORMATIONAL TEXT

# *from* Classifying the Stars

**Cecilia H. Payne**

1 Sunlight and starlight are composed of waves of various lengths, which the eye, even aided by a telescope, is unable to separate. We must use more than a telescope. In order to sort out the component colors, the light must be dispersed by a prism, or split up by some other means. For instance, sunbeams passing through rain drops, are transformed into the myriad-tinted rainbow. The familiar rainbow spanning the sky is Nature's most glorious demonstration that light is composed of many colors.

2 The very beginning of our knowledge of the nature of a star dates back to 1672, when Isaac Newton gave to the world the results of his experiments on passing sunlight through a prism. To describe the beautiful band of rainbow tints, produced when sunlight was dispersed by his three-cornered piece of glass, he took from the Latin the word *spectrum*, meaning an appearance. The rainbow is the spectrum of the Sun. . . .

3 In 1814, more than a century after Newton, the spectrum of the Sun was obtained in such purity that an amazing detail was seen and studied by the German optician, Fraunhofer. He saw that the multiple spectral tints, ranging from delicate violet to deep red, were crossed by hundreds of fine dark lines. In other words, there were narrow gaps in the spectrum where certain shades were wholly blotted out. We must remember that the word spectrum is applied not only to sunlight, but also to the light of any glowing substance when its rays are sorted out by a prism or a grating.

MODEL

# First-Read Guide

You may want to use a guide like this to organize your thoughts after you read. Here is how a reader completed a First-Read Guide.

**Use this page to record your first-read ideas.**

**Selection Title:** Classifying the Stars

NOTICE

**NOTICE** new information or ideas you learned about the unit topic as you first read this text.

Light = different waves of colors. (Spectrum)

Newton - the first person to observe these waves using a prism.

Faunhofer saw gaps in the spectrum.

ANNOTATE

**ANNOTATE** by marking vocabulary and key passages you want to revisit.

Vocabulary

myriad

grating

component colors

Different light types = different lengths

Isaac Newton also worked theories of gravity.

Multiple spectral tints? "colors of various appearance"

Key Passage:
Paragraph 3 shows that Fraunhofer discovered more about the nature of light spectrums: he saw the spaces in between the tints.

NOTICE ANNOTATE First Read CONNECT RESPOND

**CONNECT** ideas within the selection to other knowledge and the selections you have read.

I remember learning about prisms in science class.

Double rainbows! My favorite. How are they made?

**RESPOND** by writing a brief summary of the selection.

Science allows us to see things not visible to the naked eye. What we see as sunlight is really a spectrum of colors. By using tools, such as prisms, we can see the components of sunlight and other light. They appear as single colors or as multiple colors separated by gaps of no color. White light contains a rainbow of colors.

CONNECT

RESPOND

# CLOSE READING

In a close read, go back into the text to study it in greater detail. Take the time to analyze not only the author's ideas but the way that those ideas are conveyed. Consider the genre of the text, the author's word choice, the writer's unique style, and the message of the text.

Here is how one reader close read this text.

* * Key Idea
* ! I love it!
* ? I have questions
* ◯ Unfamiliar or important word
* ---- Context Clues

MODEL

INFORMATIONAL TEXT

## *from* Classifying the Stars

**Cecilia H. Payne**

NOTES

- explanation of sunlight and starlight
- What is light and where do the colors come from?
- This paragraph is about Newton and the prism.
- What discoveries helped us understand light?
- Fraunhofer and gaps in spectrum

1 Sunlight and starlight are composed of waves of various lengths, which the eye, even aided by a telescope, is unable to separate. We must use more than a telescope. In order to sort out the component colors, the light must be dispersed by a prism, or split up by some other means. For instance, sunbeams passing through rain drops, are transformed into the myriad-tinted rainbow. The familiar rainbow spanning the sky is Nature's most glorious demonstration that light is composed of many colors.

2 The very beginning of our knowledge of the nature of a star dates back to 1672, when Isaac Newton gave to the world the results of his experiments on passing sunlight through a prism. To describe the beautiful band of rainbow tints, produced when sunlight was dispersed by his three-cornered piece of glass, he took from the Latin the word *spectrum*, meaning an appearance. The rainbow is the spectrum of the Sun. . . .

3 In 1814, more than a century after Newton, the spectrum of the Sun was obtained in such purity that an amazing detail was seen and studied by the German optician, Fraunhofer. He saw that the multiple spectral tints, ranging from delicate violet to deep red, were crossed by hundreds of fine dark lines. In other words, there were narrow gaps in the spectrum where certain shades were wholly blotted out. We must remember that the word spectrum is applied not only to sunlight, but also to the light of any glowing substance when its rays are sorted out by a prism or a grating.

MODEL

# Close-Read Guide

You can use the Close-Read Guide to help you dig deeper into the text. Here is how a reader completed a Close-Read Guide.

**Use this page to record your close-read ideas.**

Selection Title: Classifying the Stars

## Close Read the Text

Revisit sections of the text you marked during your first read. Read these sections closely and **annotate** what you notice. Ask yourself **questions** about the text. What can you **conclude?** Write down your ideas.

ANNOTATE QUESTION Close Read CONCLUDE

Paragraph 3: Light is composed of waves of various lengths. Prisms let us see different colors in light. This is called the spectrum. Fraunhofer proved that there are gaps in the spectrum, where certain shades are blotted out.

More than one researcher studied this and each built off the ideas that were already discovered.

## Analyze the Text

Think about the author's choices of patterns, structure, techniques, and ideas included in the text. Select one, and record your thoughts about what this choice conveys.

The author showed the development of human knowledge of the spectrum chronologically. Helped me see how ideas were built upon earlier understandings. Used dates and "more than a century after Newton" to show time.

## QuickWrite

Pick a paragraph from the text that grabbed your interest. Explain the power of this passage.

The first paragraph grabbed my attention, specifically the sentence "The familiar rainbow spanning the sky is Nature's most glorious demonstration that light is composed of many colors." The paragraph began as a straightforward scientific explanation. When I read the word "glorious," I had to stop and deeply consider what was being said. It is a word loaded with personal feelings. With that one word, the author let the reader know what was important to her.

NOTES

# Analyzing Legal Meanings and Reasoning

Reading historical and legal texts requires careful analysis of both the vocabulary and the logical flow of ideas that support a conclusion.

## Understanding Legal Meanings

The language of historical and legal documents is formal, precise, and technical. Many words in these texts have specific meanings that you need to understand in order to follow the flow of ideas. For example, the second amendment to the U.S. Constitution states that "A well regulated Militia being necessary to the security of a free State, the right of the people to keep and bear Arms shall not be infringed." To understand this amendment, it is important to know that in this context *militia* means "armed forces," *bear* means "carry," and *infringed* means "denied." To understand legal meanings:

- Use your knowledge of word roots to help you understand unfamiliar words. Many legal terms use familiar Greek or Latin roots, prefixes, or suffixes.
- Do not assume that you know a word's legal meaning: Use a dictionary to check the meanings of key words to be certain that you are applying the correct meaning.
- Paraphrase the text to aid comprehension. Replace difficult words with synonyms to make sure you follow the logic of the argument.

## Delineating Legal Reasoning

Works of public advocacy, such as court decisions, political proclamations, proposed laws, or constitutional amendments, use careful reasoning to support conclusions. These strategies can help you understand the legal reasoning in an argument:

- State the **purpose** of the document in your own words to help you focus on the writer's primary goal.
- Look for the line of reasoning that supports the **arguments** presented. To be valid and persuasive, key arguments should be backed up by clearly stated logical analysis. Be aware of persuasive techniques, such as citing facts and statistics, referring to expert testimonials, and using emotional language with strong connotations.
- Identify the **premises,** or evidence, upon which a decision rests. In legal texts, premises often include **precedents,** which are earlier examples that must be followed or specifically overturned. Legal reasoning is usually based on the decisions of earlier trials. Be sure you understand precedents in order to identify how the court arrived at the current decision.

MODEL

Note the strategies used to evaluate legal meanings and reasoning in this Supreme Court decision from 1954 regarding the legality of segregated, "separate but equal" schools for students of different races.

LEGAL TEXT

## from *Brown v. Board of Education of Topeka,* Opinion of the Supreme Court by Chief Justice Earl Warren

We come then to the question presented: Does segregation of children in public schools solely on the basis of race, even though the physical facilities and other "tangible" factors may be equal, deprive the children of the minority group of equal educational opportunities? We believe that it does.

In *Sweatt v. Painter*, in finding that a segregated law school for Negroes could not provide them equal educational opportunities, this Court relied in large part on "those qualities which are incapable of objective measurement but which make for greatness in a law school." In *McLaurin v. Oklahoma State Regents*, the Court, in requiring that a Negro admitted to a white graduate school be treated like all other students, again resorted to intangible considerations: ". . . his ability to study, to engage in discussions and exchange views with other students, and, in general, to learn his profession." Such considerations apply with added force to children in grade and high schools. To separate them from others of similar age and qualifications solely because of their race generates a feeling of inferiority as to their status in the community that may affect their hearts and minds in a way unlikely ever to be undone. The effect of this separation on their educational opportunities was well stated by a finding in the Kansas case by a court which nevertheless felt compelled to rule against the Negro plaintiffs: Segregation of white and colored children in public schools has a detrimental effect upon the colored children. The impact is greater when it has the sanction of the law, for the policy of separating the races is usually interpreted as denoting the inferiority of the negro group. A sense of inferiority affects the motivation of a child to learn. Segregation with the sanction of law, therefore, has a tendency to [retard] the educational and mental development of negro children and to deprive them of some of the benefits they would receive in a racially integrated school system. Whatever may have been the extent of psychological knowledge at the time of *Plessy v. Ferguson*, this finding is amply supported by modern authority. Any language in *Plessy v. Ferguson* contrary to this finding is rejected.

We conclude that, in the field of public education, the doctrine of "separate but equal" has no place. Separate educational facilities are inherently unequal.

**Use Word Roots** The word *tangible* comes from the Latin root meaning "to touch." In this decision, the court contrasts tangible, measurable features with intangible features that are difficult to measure.

**Identify the Premises** The court cites two precedents: earlier cases relating to unequal education opportunities for black students.

**Paraphrase the Text** Here's one way you might break down the ideas in this sentence when you paraphrase: Segregating students just because of their race makes them feel as if they are less valued by our society. This separation can have a permanent negative influence on their character.

**Line of Reasoning** The conclusion makes the **purpose** of the decision clear: to overturn the precedent established by *Plessy v.* Ferguson. The **argument** describes the reasons the Court no longer considers the reasoning in that earlier case to be valid.

## Argument

When you think of the word *argument*, you might think of a disagreement between two people, but an argument is more than that. An argument is a logical way of presenting a belief, conclusion, or stance. A good argument is supported with reasoning and evidence.

Argument writing can be used for many purposes, such as to change a reader's point of view or opinion or to bring about an action or a response from a reader.

### Elements of an Argumentative Text

An **argument** is a logical way of presenting a viewpoint, belief, or stand on an issue. A well-written argument may convince the reader, change the reader's mind, or motivate the reader to take a certain action.

An effective argument contains these elements:

- a precise claim
- consideration of counterclaims, or opposing positions, and a discussion of their strengths and weaknesses
- logical organization that makes clear connections among claim, counterclaim, reasons, and evidence
- valid reasoning and evidence
- a concluding statement or section that logically completes the argument
- formal and objective language and tone
- error-free grammar, including accurate use of transitions

MODEL

ARGUMENT: SCORE 1

## Community Service Should be a Requirement for High School Graduation

Volunteering is a great idea for high school students. Those who don't volunteer are missing out.

> The claim is not clearly stated in the introduction.

You can learn a lot at your volunteer job. It might not seem like a big deal at the time, but the things you learn and do can be useful. You might volunteer somewhere with a  spreadsheet. Everyone needs to know how to use a spreadsheet! That's going to be a useful again really soon.

Their lots of reasons to get involved. One of them is to become a better student in school. Also, to feel better about yourself and not act out so much.

> The argument contains mistakes in standard English conventions of usage and mechanics.

So, volunteering helps you learn and get better at lots of things, not just what you are doing at your volunteer job. It's good not just to learn reading and writing and math and science all the time—the usual stuff we study in school. That's how volunteering can help you out.

> The vocabulary used is limited and ineffective, and the tone is informal.

Students today are really busy and they can't add anything more to they're busy schedules. But I think they can add a little more if it doesn't take too much time. Especially if it is important like volunteering.

> The writer does not acknowledge counterclaims.

High school students who volunteer get involved with the real world outside school, and that means a lot. They have a chance to do something that can make a difference in the world. This helps them learn things that maybe they can't learn in school, like, how to be kind and jenerous and care about making the world a better place.

Volunteering in high school is a great idea. Everybody should do it. There are lots of different ways to volunteer. You can even do it on weekends with your friends.

MODEL

ARGUMENT: SCORE 2

## Community Service Should be a Requirement for High School Graduation

High school students should have to volunteer before they can graduate. It makes sense because it is helpful to them and others. Some students would volunteer anyway even if it wasn't required, but some wouldn't. If they have to do it for graduation then they won't miss out.

The introduction establishes the claim.

Their lots of reasons to get involved. One is to be a better student in school. Researchers have done studies to see the connection between community service and doing well in school. One study showed that most schools with programs said grades went up most of the time for kids that volunteered. Another study said elementary and middle school kids got better at problem-solving and were more interested in school. One study said students showed more responsibility. Another researcher discovered that kids who been volunteering have better self-esteem. They also have fewer problems.

The tone of the argument is occasionally formal and objective.

Volunteering helps you learn and improve at lots of things, not just what you are doing at your volunteer job. One thing you might get better at is being a nicer person, like having more patience and listening well to others. Because you might need those skills when you are volunteering at a senior center or a preschool.

Some people say that volunteering in high school should NOT be required for graduation. They say students already have too much to do and they can't add anything more to they're schedules. But they can add a little more if it doesn't take too much time. Especially if it is important like volunteering.

The writer briefly acknowledges and refutes counterclaims.

Why should students be forced to do something, even if it is good? Well, that's just the way it is. When you force students to do something that is good, you are doing them a favor. Like forcing them to eat their vegetables or do their homework. The kids might not like it at first but what do you want to bet they are happy about it later on. That's the point.

The writers relies too much on weak anecdotal evidence.

Volunteering should be required for all high school students before they graduate. That's not just because they can do a lot of good in the world, but also because doing community service will help them in lots of ways.

The conclusion offers some insight into the claim and restates some information.

MODEL

ARGUMENT: SCORE 3

## Community Service Should be a Requirement for High School Graduation

Requiring community service for high school graduation is an excellent idea that offers benefits not only to the community but to the student as well. Making it a requirement ensures that all students will be able to get in on the act.

The claim is established in the introduction but is not as clear as it could be.

Volunteering is a great way to build skills. It might not seem like a big deal at the time, but the experience you gain is very likely to be useful in the future. For example, while tracking, sorting, and distributing donations at an afterschool program, a volunteer might learn how to use a spreadsheet. That's going to come in handy very quickly, both in and out of school.

Participating in service learning can help you do better in school. ("Service learning" is when community service is part of a class curriculum.) For example, one study found that most schools with service learning programs reported grade point averages of participating students improved 76 percent of the time. Another study showed improved problem-solving skills and increased interest in academics among elementary and middle school students.

The tone of the argument is mostly formal and objective.

A study showed that middle and high school students who participated in quality service learning projects showed more personal and social responsibility. Another study found that students were more likely to help each other and be kind to each other, and care about doing their best. Studies also show better self-esteem and fewer behavioral problems in students who have been involved with service learning.

The writer does not transition very well into new topics.

Despite all this, many people say that volunteering in high school should NOT be a requirement for graduation. They point out that students today are already over-stressed and over-scheduled. There simply isn't room for anything more.

The writer uses some transitional phrases.

The writer gives a reason for the counterclaim, but does not provide firm examples.

True! But community service doesn't have to take up a lot of time. It might be possible for a group of time-stressed students to use class-time to organize a fundraiser, or to squeeze their service into a single "marathon" weekend. It's all a question of priorities.

In short, volunteering is a great way for students to help others, and reap benefits for themselves as well. Making it a requirement ensures that all students have the chance to grow through involvement with their communities. Volunteering opens doors and offers life-long benefits, and high school is the perfect time to get started!

The conclusion restates the claim and provides additional detail.

MODEL

ARGUMENT: SCORE 4

## Community Service Should be a Requirement for High School Graduation

Every high school student should be required to do community service in order to graduate. Volunteering offers life-long benefits that will prepare all students for adulthood.

The introduction establishes the writer's claim in a clear and compelling way.

First and foremost, studies show that participating in service learning —when community service is part of a class curriculum—often helps students do better in school. For example, a study conducted by Leeward County found that 83 percent of schools with service learning programs reported grade point averages of participating students improved 76 percent of the time. Another study, conducted by Hilliard Research, showed improved problem-solving skills and increased interest in academics among elementary and middle school students who participated in service learning.

The writer uses a variety of sentence transitions.

Sources of evidence are comprehensive and contain relevant information.

But it's not just academic performance that can improve through volunteering: There are social and psychological benefits as well. For example, a student survey showed that students who participated in quality service learning projects showed more personal and social responsibility. Another survey found that students involved in service learning were more likely to be kind to each other, and care about doing their best. Studies also show better self-esteem and fewer behavioral problems in students who have been involved with service learning.

Despite all this, there are still many who say that volunteering in high school should NOT be a requirement for graduation. They point out that students today are already over-stressed and over-scheduled. What's more, requiring community service for graduation would be particularly hard on athletes and low-income students who work after school to help their families make ends meet.

Counterclaims are clearly acknowledged and refuted.

Good points, but community service does not have to take up vast quantities of time. It might be possible for a group of time-stressed students to use class-time to organize a fundraiser, or to compress their service into a single "marathon" weekend. Showing students that helping others is something to make time for is an important lesson.

In short, volunteering encourages engagement: It shows students that their actions matter, and that they have the power—and responsibility—to make the world a better place. What could be a more important lesson than that?

The conclusion offers fresh insight into the claim.

## Argument Rubric

| | Focus and Organization | Evidence and Elaboration | Conventions |
|---|---|---|---|
| 4 | The introduction engages the reader and establishes a claim in a compelling way.<br>The argument includes valid reasons and evidence that address and support the claim while clearly acknowledging counterclaims.<br>The ideas progress logically, and transitions make connections among ideas clear.<br>The conclusion offers fresh insight into the claim. | The sources of evidence are comprehensive and specific and contain relevant information.<br>The tone of the argument is always formal and objective.<br>The vocabulary is always appropriate for the audience and purpose. | The argument intentionally uses standard English conventions of usage and mechanics. |
| 3 | The introduction engages the reader and establishes the claim.<br>The argument includes reasons and evidence that address and support my claim while acknowledging counterclaims.<br>The ideas progress logically, and some transitions are used to help make connections among ideas clear.<br>The conclusion restates the claim and important information. | The sources of evidence contain relevant information.<br>The tone of the argument is mostly formal and objective.<br>The vocabulary is generally appropriate for the audience and purpose. | The argument demonstrates general accuracy in standard English conventions of usage and mechanics. |
| 2 | The introduction establishes a claim.<br>The argument includes some reasons and evidence that address and support the claim while briefly acknowledging counterclaims.<br>The ideas progress somewhat logically. A few sentence transitions are used that connect readers to the argument.<br>The conclusion offers some insight into the claim and restates information. | The sources of evidence contain some relevant information.<br>The tone of the argument is occasionally formal and objective.<br>The vocabulary is somewhat appropriate for the audience and purpose. | The argument demonstrates some accuracy in standard English conventions of usage and mechanics. |
| 1 | The introduction does not clearly state the claim.<br>The argument does not include reasons or evidence for the claim. No counterclaims are acknowledged.<br>The ideas do not progress logically. Transitions are not included to connect ideas.<br>The conclusion does not restate any information that is important. | Reliable and relevant evidence is not included.<br>The vocabulary used is limited or ineffective.<br>The tone of the argument is not objective or formal. | The argument contains mistakes in standard English conventions of usage and mechanics. |

## Informative/Explanatory Texts

Informative and explanatory writing should rely on facts to inform or explain. Informative writing serves several purposes: to increase readers' knowledge of a subject, to help readers better understand a procedure or process, or to provide readers with an enhanced comprehension of a concept. It should also feature a clear introduction, body, and conclusion.

### Elements of Informative/Explanatory Texts

**Informative/explanatory texts** present facts, details, data, and other kinds of evidence to give information about a topic. Readers turn to informational and explanatory texts when they wish to learn about a specific idea, concept, or subject area, or if they want to learn how to do something.

An effective informative/explanatory text contains these elements:

- a topic sentence or thesis statement that introduces the concept or subject
- relevant facts, examples, and details that expand upon a topic
- definitions, quotations, and/or graphics that support the information given
- headings (if desired) to separate sections of the essay
- a structure that presents information in a direct, clear manner
- clear transitions that link sections of the essay
- precise words and technical vocabulary where appropriate
- formal and object language and tone
- a conclusion that supports the information given and provides fresh insights

MODEL

INFORMATIVE: SCORE 1

## How Technology is Changing the Way We Work

Lot's of people work on computers. So, technology is everywhere. If you feel comfortable using computers and all kinds of other technology, your going to be a head at work, for sure.

They're new Devices and Apps out there every day. Each different job has its own gadgets and programs and apps that you have to learn. Every day their more new apps and devices, they can do all kinds of things.

In the past, people only worked at the office. They didn't get to work at home. Now, if you have a smart phone, you can check your email wherever. You can work at home on a computer. You can work in cafés or wherever. Also on a tablet. If you wanted to, you can be working all the time. But that will be a drag!

Technology is now an important part of almost every job. You also have to have a website. You have to have a social media page. Maybe if your business is doing really well you could afford to hire someone to take care of all that stuff—but it would be better if you knew how to do it yourself.

Technology brings people together and helps them work. It could be someone next to you or someone even on the other side of the world. You can connect with them using email. You can send a text. You could have a conference or video call.

Working from home is cheaper for the worker and boss. They can get stuff done during the day like going to the post office or the library, or picking up their kids at school. This is all thanks to technology.

Lots of jobs today are in technology. Way more than before! That's why it's a good idea to take classes and learn about something in technology, because then you will be able to find a job.

There are apps to find houses for sale, find restaurants, learn new recipes, keep track of how much you exercise, and all kinds of other things, like playing games and tuning your guitar. And there are apps to help you work. It's hard to imagine how people would manage to work now without this kind of technology to help them.

The writer's opening statement does not adequately introduce the thesis, and there are numerous spelling mistakes.

The writer's word choice often does not support the proper tone the essay ought to have.

The essay's sentences are often not purposeful, varied, or well-controlled.

The writer does not include a concluding statement.

MODEL

INFORMATIVE: SCORE 2

## How Technology is Changing the Way We Work

Technology affects the way we work, in every kind of job and industry. Each different job has its own gadgets and programs and apps that you have to learn. Every day there are more new apps and devices that can do all kinds of things.

The writer's opening does not clearly introduce the thesis.

In the past, people went to the office to work. That's not always true today. Now if you have a smart phone, you can check your email wherever you are. You can work at home on a desktop computer. You can work on a laptop in a café or wherever. Or a tablet. Technology makes it so people can work all the time.

It doesn't matter whether the person is on the other side of the world—technology brings you together. Theirs email. Theirs text messaging. You have conference calls. You've got video calling. All these things let people work together wherever they are. And don't forget, today people can access files from the cloud. That helps them work from whatever device they want. More than one person can work on the same file.

The essay is somewhat lacking in organizational structure.

Different kinds of work places and schedules are becoming more common and normal. Working from home has benefits businesses. It means cost savings. It means higher productivity. It means higher job satisfaction. They can get stuff done during the day like going to the post office or the bank, or picking up their kids at school. That is very convenient.

The essay has many interesting details, but some do not relate specifically to the topic.

It's also true that lots and lots of jobs today are in technology, or related to technology in some way. Way more than before! That's why it's a good idea to get a degree or take classes and learn about something in technology, because it seems like that's where all the new jobs are. Software designers make a really good salary, and so do other tech-related jobs.

The writer's word choice is overly informal.

Technology is now an important part of almost every job. It's no longer enough to be just a photographer or whatever. You have to get a social media page. You have to be able to use the latest tech gadgets. You can't just take pictures.

The writer's sentences are disjointed and ineffective.

In todays world, technology is changing how we work. You have to be able to feel comfortable with technology in order to survive at work. Even if you really don't like technology, you don't really have a choice. So, get used to it!

The conclusion follows logically but is not mature and is overly informal.

MODEL

INFORMATIVE: SCORE 3

## How Technology Is Changing the Way We Work

Technology has been changing how we work for a long time, but the pace of change has gotten dramatically faster. No industry or job is exempt. Powerful computing technology and Internet connectivity affects all sectors of the economy. It doesn't matter what job you're talking about: Technology is transforming the way people work. It's an exciting time to be entering the workforce!

### The Office Is Everywhere

Technology is rapidly changing not just *how* but *where, when,* and *with whom* we work. It used to be that work was something that happened only at the office. All kinds of different work places and schedules are becoming much more common and normal. According to a study, telecommuting (working from home) rose 79 percent between 2005 and 2012. Working from home has benefits for both the employee and employer. It means cost savings for both, increased productivity, and higher job satisfaction.

### The Cloud

Cloud and other data storage and sharing options mean that workers have access to information whenever they want, wherever they are. Whether it's one person who wants the convenience of being able to work on a file from several devices (and locations), or several people who are working on something together, the ability to store data in the cloud and access it from anywhere is a huge change in the way we work. It's almost like all being in the same office, working on the same computer.

### Tech Industries and Jobs

Technology is changing the way we work in part by making technology itself such an important element in almost every profession. Therefore, you can see it's no longer good enough to be just a photographer or contractor. You have to know something about technology to do your job, market yourself, and track your performance. No matter what jobs someone does they have to be tech-savvy to be able to use their devices to connect and interact with each other across the globe.

### Conclusion

In todays world, technology is quickly and continuously changing how we work, what we do, where and when we do it. In order to do well and thrive, everyone has to be a little bit of a tech geek. So, get used to technology being a part of your work life. And get used to change. Because, in a constantly changing technological world, change is going to be one of the few things that stays the same!

The thesis is introduced but is buried in the introduction.

The writer uses headings to help make the organization of ideas clear.

Statistics support the writer's claim.

The writer uses some transitions and sentence connections, but more would be helpful.

There are a few errors in spelling and punctuation but they do not detract from the effectiveness of the essay.

The conclusion sums up the main ideas of the essay and links to the opening statements.

MODEL

INFORMATIVE: SCORE 4

## How Technology Is Changing the Way We Work

While advances in technology have been changing how we work for hundreds of years, the pace of change has accelerated dramatically in the past two decades. With powerful computing technology and Internet connectivity affecting all sectors of the economy, no industry or profession is exempt. It doesn't matter whether you're talking about financial advisors, architects, or farmers: Technology is transforming the way people work.

### The Office Is Everywhere

Technology is rapidly revolutionizing not just *how* but *where, when,* and *with whom* we work. It used to be that work was something that happened strictly at the office. In fact, non-traditional work places are becoming much more common. According to one study, telecommuting rose 79 percent between 2005 and 2012. Working from home has proven benefits for both the employee and employer, including cost savings for both, increased productivity, and job satisfaction.

### Working with the Cloud

Another important technological advancement that is impacting how we work is the development of cloud computing. Whether it's one person who wants the convenience of being able to work from several devices, or several people who are working together from different locations, the ability to store data in the cloud and access it from anywhere is a huge change in the way we work. Over long distances, coworkers can not only *communicate* with each other, they can *collaborate*, in real time, by sharing and accessing files through the. Only five years ago, this kind of instant access was impossible.

### Tech Industries and Jobs

Technology is changing the way we work is by making technology itself an important element in almost every job. It's no longer good enough to be just a photographer or contractor: you have to know something about technology to perform, market, and track your work. No matter what job someone is doing, he or she has to be tech-savvy to be able to use their devices to connect and interact.

### Conclusion

In today's world, technology is quickly and continuously changing what work we do, and how, where, when, and with whom we do it. Comfort with new technology—and with rapid technological change—is a prerequisite for success, no matter where your interests lie, or what kind of job you are looking to find. It's a brave new technological world of work, and it's changing every day!

The opening paragraph ends with a thesis, which is strong and clear.

The writer makes an effort to be thoughtful and engage the reader.

Headings help ensure that the organizing structure of the essay is clear and effective.

The sentences in the essay are purposeful and varied.

The progression of ideas in the essay is logical and well-controlled.

The writer's word choice contributes to the clarity of the essay and shows awareness of the essay's purpose and tone.

# Informative/Explanatory Rubric

| | Focus and Organization | Evidence and Elaboration | Conventions |
|---|---|---|---|
| 4 | The introduction engages the reader and states a thesis in a compelling way.<br>The essay includes a clear introduction, body, and conclusion.<br>The conclusion summarizes ideas and offers fresh insight into the thesis. | The essay includes specific reasons, details, facts, and quotations from selections and outside resources to support the thesis.<br>The tone of the essay is always formal and objective.<br>The language is always precise and appropriate for the audience and purpose. | The essay uses standard English conventions of usage and mechanics.<br>The essay contains no spelling errors. |
| 3 | The introduction engages the reader and sets forth the thesis.<br>The essay includes an introduction, body, and conclusion.<br>The conclusion summarizes ideas and supports the thesis. | The essay includes some specific reasons, details, facts, and quotations from selections and outside resources to support the thesis.<br>The tone of the essay is mostly formal and objective.<br>The language is generally precise and appropriate for the audience and purpose. | The essay demonstrates general accuracy in standard English conventions of usage and mechanics.<br>The essay contains few spelling errors. |
| 2 | The introduction sets forth the thesis.<br>The essay includes an introduction, body, and conclusion, but one or more parts are weak.<br>The conclusion partially summarizes ideas but may not provide strong support of the thesis. | The essay includes a few reasons, details, facts, and quotations from selections and outside resources to support the thesis.<br>The tone of the essay is occasionally formal and objective.<br>The language is somewhat precise and appropriate for the audience and purpose. | The essay demonstrates some accuracy in standard English conventions of usage and mechanics.<br>The essay contains some spelling errors. |
| 1 | The introduction does not state the thesis clearly.<br>The essay does not include an introduction, body, and conclusion.<br>The conclusion does not summarize ideas and may not relate to the thesis. | Reliable and relevant evidence is not included.<br>The tone of the essay is not objective or formal.<br>The language used is imprecise and not appropriate for the audience and purpose. | The essay contains mistakes in standard English conventions of usage and mechanics.<br>The essay contains many spelling errors. |

## Narration

Narrative writing conveys experience, either real or imaginary, and uses time to provide structure. It can be used to inform, instruct, persuade, or entertain. Whenever writers tell a story, they are using narrative writing. Most types of narrative writing share certain elements, such as characters, setting, a sequence of events, and, often, a theme.

### Elements of a Narrative Text

A **narrative** is any type of writing that tells a story, whether it is fiction, nonfiction, poetry, or drama.

An effective nonfiction narrative usually contains these elements:

- an engaging beginning in which characters and setting are established
- characters who participate in the story events
- a well-structured, logical sequence of events
- details that show time and place
- effective story elements such as dialogue, description, and reflection
- the narrator's thoughts, feelings, or views about the significance of events
- use of language that brings the characters and setting to life

An effective fictional narrative usually contains these elements:

- an engaging beginning in which characters, setting, or a main conflict is introduced
- a main character and supporting characters who participate in the story events
- a narrator who relates the events of the plot from a particular point of view
- details that show time and place
- conflict that is resolved in the course of the narrative
- narrative techniques such as dialogue, description, and suspense
- use of language that vividly brings to life characters and events

MODEL

NARRATIVE: SCORE 1

## Getting Away With It

That night, Luanne made two mistakes.

She ran in the house.

The McTweedys were rich and had a huge place and there was an expensive rug.

She was sad in her room remembering what happened:

She was carrying a tray of glasses back to the kitchen and spilled on the carpet. She tried to put furniture over it. Then she ran in the rain.

Luanne should have come clean. She would of said I'm sorry, Mrs. Mc Tweedy, I spilled punch on ur carpet.

She knew getting away with it felt crummy for some reason. it was wrong and she also didn't want to get in trouble.

The phone rings.

"Oh, hello?"

"It's Mrs. Tweedy's!" said her mom. "You forgot to get paid!"

Luanne felt relieve. She was going to do the right thing.

The introduction is interesting but is not built upon.

The chronology and situation are unclear.

The narrative contains mistakes in standard English conventions of usage and mechanics.

The name of the character does not remain consistent.

The conclusion reveals what will happen but is not interesting.

MODEL

NARRATIVE: SCORE 2

## Getting Away With It

That night, Luanne made two fatal mistakes: ruining a rug, and thinking she could get away with it.

She ran in the house.

The McTweedys hired her to be a waiter at their party. They were rich and had a huge place and there was an expensive rug.

She was sad in her room remembering what happened:

Luanne was wearing black pants and a white shirt. She was carrying a tray of glasses back to the kitchen. One spilled on the carpet. She tried to put furniture to cover up the stain. She ran away in the rain.

Luanne should have come clean right away. But what would she have said? I'm sorry, Mrs. McTweedy, but I spilled punch all over your expensive carpet.

Luanne imagined getting away with it. But getting away with it felt crummy for some reason. She knew it was wrong somehow, but she also didn't want to get in trouble.

The phone rang.

"Oh, hello, how was the party?"

Luanne felt like throwing up.

"Mrs. McTweedy's on the phone!" her mom sang out. "She said you forgot your check!"

Luanne felt relieved. But she already made up her mind to do the right thing.

The introduction establishes a clear context.

The writer has made some mistakes in spelling, grammar, and punctuation.

The chronology is sometimes unclear.

Narrative techniques, such as the use of dialogue, are used at times.

The conclusion tells what will happen but is not interesting.

MODEL

NARRATIVE: SCORE 3

## Getting Away With It

That night, Luanne made two fatal mistakes: (1) ruining a priceless Persian rug, and (2) thinking she could get away with it.

She bursted in the front door breathless.

"How was it?" called her mom.

The McTweedys had hired her to serve drinks at their fundraiser. Henry and Estelle McTweedy loved having parties. They were rich and had a huge apartment filled with rare books, art, and tapestries from all over the world.

"Luanne? Are you alright?"

"Just tired, Mom."

Actually she was face-planted on her bed, replaying the scene over and over just in case she could change it.

It was like a movie: A girl in black trousers and a crisp white shirt carrying a tray of empty glasses back to the kitchen. Then the girl's horrified expression as she realizes that one of the glasses was not quite as empty as she'd thought and was dripping onto the carpet. The girl frantically moving furniture to cover up the stain. The girl running out of the apartment into the hard rain.

Luanne kicked herself. She should have come clean right away. But what would she have said? I'm sorry, Mrs. McTweedy, but I spilled punch all over your expensive carpet.

Luanne imagined getting away with it. But getting away with it felt crummy for some reason. She knew it was wrong somehow, but she also didn't want to get in trouble.

The phone was ringing. Luanne froze.

"Oh, hello there, Mrs. McTweedy! How was the party?"

Luanne felt felt like throwing up.

"Mrs. McTweedy's on the phone!" her mom sang out. "She said you forgot your check!"

Luanne felt relief. It was nothing at all! Although she'd already made up her mind to come clean. Because she had to do the right thing.

She walked into the kitchen. And then she explained the whole thing to both her mom and Mrs. McTweedy.

The story's introduction establishes a clear context and point of view.

Descriptive details, sensory language, and precise words and phrases help to bring the narrative to life.

The writer mostly attends to the norms and conventions of usage and punctuation, but sometimes makes mistakes.

The writer has effectively used dialogue in her story.

The conclusion follows logically but is not memorable.

MODEL

NARRATIVE: SCORE 4

## Getting Away With It

That night, Luanne made two fatal mistakes: (1) ruining a priceless Persian rug, and (2) thinking she could get away with it.

She'd burst in the front door breathless.

"How was it?" called her mother from the kitchen.

The McTweedys had hired Luanne to serve drinks at their fundraiser. Henry and Estelle McTweedy loved entertaining. They loved traveling, and the opera, and the finer things in life. They had a huge apartment filled with rare books, art, and tapestries from all over the world.

"Luanne? Are you alright?"

"Just tired, Mom."

Actually she was face-down on her bed, replaying the humiliating scene over and over just in case she could make it come out differently.

It was like a movie: A girl in black trousers and a crisp white shirt carrying a tray of empty glasses back to the kitchen. Cut to the girl's horrified expression as she realizes that one of the glasses —not quite as empty as she'd thought—was dripping its lurid contents onto the carpet. Close in on the girl's frantic attempts to move furniture over the stain. Montage of images showing the girl running out of the apartment into the pounding rain. Fade to Black.

Luanne could kick herself. She should have come clean right away. But what would she have said? *I'm sorry, Mrs. McTweedy, but I spilled punch all over your irreplaceable carpet.*

Luanne imagined getting away with it. If she got away with it, she'd be a person who got away with things. For the rest of her life, no matter what, she'd be a person who got away with things. And if something good happened to her, she'd feel like she didn't deserve it.

Somewhere in the house, a phone was ringing. Luanne froze and listened in.

"Oh, hello there, Estelle! How was the party?"

Luanne felt cold, then hot. Her skin prickled. She was sweating. She felt like throwing up.

"Mrs. McTweedy's on the phone!" Luanne's mother sang out. "She wants to tell you that you forgot your check!"

Luanne felt a surge a relief wash over her—it was nothing, nothing at all!—but she'd already made up her mind to come clean. Not because owning up to it was so Right, but because getting away with it was so wrong. Which made it right.

Luanne padded into the kitchen. "Don't hang up," she told her mother.

The writer provides an introduction that establishes a clear context and point of view.

The writer has used descriptive details, sensory language, and precise words and phrases.

The writer's use of movie terminology is clever and memorable.

The narrative presents a clear chronological sequence of events.

The writer effectively uses narrative techniques, such as dialogue.

The story's conclusion is abrupt but fitting. It reveals a critical decision that resolves the conflict.

## Narrative Rubric

| | Focus and Organization | Development of Ideas/ Elaboration | Conventions |
|---|---|---|---|
| 4 | The introduction establishes a clear context and point of view.<br>Events are presented in a clear sequence, building to a climax, then moving toward the conclusion.<br>The conclusion follows from and reflects on the events and experiences in the narrative. | Narrative techniques such as dialogue, pacing, and description are used effectively to develop characters, events, and setting.<br>Descriptive details, sensory language, and precise words and phrases are used to convey the experiences in the narrative and to help the reader imagine the characters and setting.<br>Voice is established through word choice, sentence structure, and tone. | The narrative uses standard English conventions of usage and mechanics. Deviations from standard English are intentional and serve the purpose of the narrative.<br>Rules of spelling and punctuation are followed. |
| 3 | The introduction gives the reader some context and sets the point of view.<br>Events are presented logically, though there are some jumps in time.<br>The conclusion logically ends the story, but provides only some reflection on the experiences related in the story. | Narrative techniques such as dialogue, pacing, and description are used occasionally.<br>Descriptive details, sensory language, and precise words and phrases are used occasionally.<br>Voice is established through word choice, sentence structure, and tone occasionally, though not evenly. | The narrative mostly uses standard English conventions of usage and mechanics, though there are some errors.<br>There are few errors in spelling and punctuation. |
| 2 | The introduction provides some description of a place. The point of view can be unclear at times.<br>Transitions between events are occasionally unclear.<br>The conclusion comes abruptly and provides only a small amount of reflection on the experiences related in the narrative. | Narrative techniques such as dialogue, pacing, and description are used sparingly.<br>The story contains few examples of descriptive details and sensory language.<br>Voice is not established for characters, so that it becomes difficult to determine who is speaking. | The narrative contains some errors in standard English conventions of usage and mechanics.<br>There are many errors in spelling and punctuation. |
| 1 | The introduction fails to set a scene or is omitted altogether. The point of view is not always clear.<br>The events are not in a clear sequence, and events that would clarify the narrative may not appear.<br>The conclusion does not follow from the narrative or is omitted altogether. | Narrative techniques such as dialogue, pacing, and description are not used.<br>Descriptive details are vague or missing. No sensory language is included.<br>Voice has not been developed. | The text contains mistakes in standard English conventions of usage and mechanics.<br>Rules of spelling and punctuation have not been followed. |

## Conducting Research

We are lucky to live in an age when information is accessible and plentiful. However, not all information is equally useful, or even accurate. Strong research skills will help you locate and evaluate information.

### Narrowing or Broadening a Topic

The first step of any research project is determining your topic. Consider the scope of your project and choose a topic that is narrow enough to address completely and effectively. If you can name your topic in just one or two words, it is probably too broad. Topics such as Shakespeare, jazz, or science fiction are too broad to cover in a single report. Narrow a broad topic into smaller subcategories.

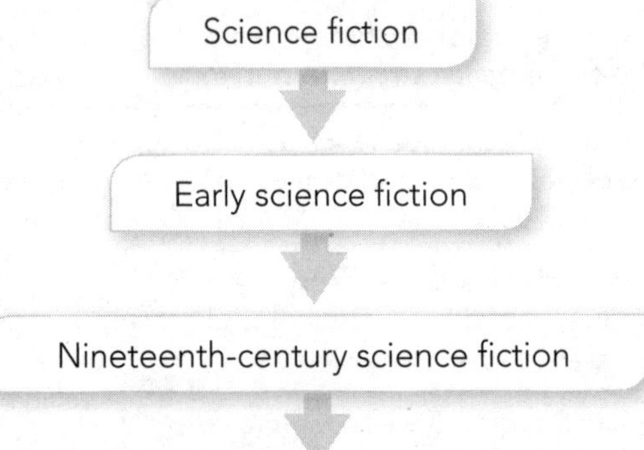


Nineteenth-century science fiction that predicted the future accurately

When you begin to research a topic, pay attention to the amount of information available. If you feel overwhelmed by the number of relevant sources, you may need to narrow your topic further.

If there isn't enough information available as your research, you might need to broaden your topic. A topic is too narrow when it can be thoroughly presented in less space than the required size of your assignment. It might also be too narrow if you can find little or no information in library and media sources, so consider broadening your topic to include other related ideas.

### Generating Research Questions

Use research questions to focus your research. Specific questions can help you avoid time-wasting digressions. For example, instead of simply hunting for information about Mark Twain, you might ask, "What jobs did Mark Twain have, other than being a writer?" or "Which of Twain's books was most popular during his lifetime?"

In a research report, your research question often becomes your thesis statement, or may lead up to it. The question will also help you focus your research into a comprehensive but flexible search plan, as well as prevent you from gathering unnecessary details. As your research teaches you more about your topic, you may find it necessary to refocus your original question.

## Consulting Print and Digital Sources

Effective research combines information from several sources, and does not rely too heavily on a single source. The creativity and originality of your research depends on how you combine ideas from multiple sources. Plan to consult a variety of resources, such as the following:

- **Primary and Secondary Sources:** To get a thorough view of your topic, use primary sources (firsthand or original accounts, such as interview transcripts, eyewitness reports, and newspaper articles) and secondary sources (accounts, created after an event occurred, such as encyclopedia entries).
- **Print and Digital Resources:** The Internet allows fast access to data, but print resources are often edited more carefully. Use both print and digital resources in order to guarantee the accuracy of your findings.
- **Media Resources:** You can find valuable information in media resources such as documentaries, television programs, podcasts, and museum exhibitions. Consider attending public lectures given by experts to gain an even more in-depth view of your topic.
- **Original Research:** Depending on your topic, you may wish to conduct original research to include among your sources. For example, you might interview experts or eyewitnesses, or conduct a survey of people in your community.

### Using Online Encyclopedias

Online encyclopedias are often written by anonymous contributors who are not required to fact-check information. These sites can be very useful as a launching point for research, but should not be considered accurate. Look for footnotes, endnotes, or hyperlinks that support facts with reliable sources that have been carefully checked by editors.

**Evaluating Sources** It is important to evaluate the credibility, validity, and accuracy of any information you find, as well as its appropriateness for your purpose and audience. You may find the information you need to answer your research question in specialized and authoritative sources, such as almanacs (for social, cultural, and natural statistics), government publications (for law, government programs, and subjects such as agriculture), and information services. Also, consider consumer, workplace, and public documents.

Ask yourself questions such as these to evaluate these additional sources:

- **Authority:** Is the author well known? What are the author's credentials? Does the source include references to other reliable sources? Does the author's tone win your confidence? Why or why not?
- **Bias:** Does the author have any obvious biases? What is the author's purpose for writing? Who is the target audience?
- **Currency:** When was the work created? Has it been revised? Is there more current information available?

# RESEARCH



## Using Search Terms

Finding information on the Internet can be both easy and challenging. Type a word or phrase into a general search engine and you will probably get hundreds—or thousands—of results. However, those results are not guaranteed to be relevant or accurate.

These strategies can help you find information from the Internet:

- Create a list of keywords that apply to your topic before you begin using a search engine. Consult a thesaurus to expand your list.
- Enter six to eight keywords.
- Choose precise nouns. Most search engines ignore articles and prepositions. Verbs may be used in multiple contexts, leading to sources that are not relevant. Use modifiers, such as adjectives, when necessary to specify a category.
- Use quotation marks to focus a search. Place a phrase in quotation marks to find pages that include exactly that phrase. Add several phrases in quotation marks to narrow your results.
- Spell carefully. Many search engines autocorrect spelling, but they cannot produce accurate results for all spelling errors.
- Scan search results before you click them. The first result isn't always the most relevant. Read the text and consider the domain before make a choice.
- Utilize more than one search engine.

### Evaluating Internet Domains

Not everything you read on the Internet is true, so you have to evaluate sources carefully. The last three letters of an Internet URL identify the Website's domain, which can help you evaluate the information of the site.

- **.gov**—Government sites are sponsored by a branch of the United States federal government, such as the Census Bureau, Supreme Court, or Congress. These sites are considered reliable.
- **.edu**—Education domains include schools from kindergartens to universities. Information from an educational research center or department is likely to be carefully checked. However, education domains can also include student pages that are not edited or monitored.
- **.org**—Organizations are nonprofit groups and usually maintain a high level of credibility. Keep in mind that some organizations may express strong biases.
- **.com** and **.net**—Commercial sites exist to make a profit. Information may be biased to show a product or service in a good light. The company may be providing information to encourage sales or promote a positive image.

## Taking Notes

Take notes as you locate and connect useful information from multiple sources, and keep a reference list of every source you use. This will help you make distinctions between the relative value and significance of specific data, facts, and ideas.

For long-term research projects, create source cards and notecards to keep track of information gathered from multiple resources.

**Source Cards**
Create a card that identifies each source.

- For print materials, list the author, title, publisher, date of publication, and relevant page numbers.
- For Internet sources, record the name and Web address of the site, and the date you accessed the information.
- For media sources, list the title, person, or group credited with creating the media, and the year of production.

**Source Card** [A]

Marsh, Peter. *Eye to Eye: How People Interact.* Salem House Publishers, 1988.

**Notecard**

Gestures vary from culture to culture. The American "OK" symbol (thumb and forefinger) is considered insulting in Greece and Turkey.

Source Card: A, p. 54.

**Notecards**
Create a separate notecard for each item of information.

- Include the fact or idea, the letter of the related source card, and the specific page(s) on which the fact or idea appears.
- Use quotation marks around words and phrases taken directly from print or media resources.
- Mark particularly useful or relevant details using your own annotation method, such as stars, underlining, or colored highlighting.

**Quote Accurately** Responsible research begins with the first note you take. Be sure to quote and paraphrase your sources accurately so you can identify these sources later. In your notes, circle all quotations and paraphrases to distinguish them from your own comments. When photocopying from a source, include the copyright information. When printing out information from an online source, include the Web address.

## Reviewing Research Findings

While conducting research, you will need to review your findings, checking that you have collected enough accurate and appropriate information.

### Considering Audience and Purpose

Always keep your audience in mind as you gather information, since different audiences may have very different needs. For example, if you are writing an in-depth analysis of a text that your entire class has read together and you are writing for your audience, you will not need to gather background information that has been thoroughly discussed in class. However, if you are writing the same analysis for a national student magazine, you cannot assume that all of your readers have the same background information. You will need to provide facts from reliable sources to help orient these readers to your subject. When considering whether or not your research will satisfy your audience, ask yourself:

- Who am I writing for?
- Have I collected enough information to explain my topic to this audience?
- Are there details in my research that I can omit because they are already familiar to my audience?

Your purpose for writing will also influence your review of research. If you are researching a question to satisfy your own curiosity, you can stop researching when you feel you understand the answer completely. If you are writing a research report that will be graded, you need to consider the criteria of the assignment. When considering whether or not you have enough information, ask yourself:

- What is my purpose for writing?
- Will the information I have gathered be enough to achieve my purpose?
- If I need more information, where might I find it?

### Synthesizing Sources

Effective research writing does not merely present facts and details; it synthesizes—gathers, orders, and interprets—them. These strategies will help you synthesize information effectively:

- Review your notes and look for connections and patterns among the details you have collected.
- Arrange notes or notecards in different ways to help you decide how to best combine related details and present them in a logical way.
- Pay close attention to details that support one other, emphasizing the same main idea.
- Also look for details that challenge each other, highlighting ideas about which there is no single, or consensus, opinion. You might decide to conduct additional research to help you decide which side of the issue has more support.

## Types of Evidence

When reviewing your research, also consider the kinds of evidence you have collected. The strongest writing contains a variety of evidence effectively. This chart describes three of the most common types of evidence: statistical, testimonial, and anecdotal.

| TYPE OF EVIDENCE | DESCRIPTION | EXAMPLE |
|---|---|---|
| **Statistical evidence** includes facts and other numerical data used to support a claim or explain a topic. | Examples of statistical evidence include historical dates and information, quantitative analyses, poll results, and quantitative descriptions. | "Although it went on to become a hugely popular novel, the first edition of William Goldman's book sold fewer than 3,000 copies." |
| **Testimonial evidence** includes any ideas or opinions presented by others, especially experts in a field. | Firsthand testimonies present ideas from eyewitnesses to events or subjects being discussed. | "The ground rose and fell like an ocean at ebb tide."<br>—Fred J. Hewitt, eyewitness to the 1906 San Francisco earthquake |
| | Secondary testimonies include commentaries on events by people who were not involved. You might quote a well-known literary critic when discussing a writer's most famous novel, or a prominent historian when discussing the effects of an important event | Gladys Hansen insists that "there was plenty of water in hydrants throughout [San Francisco] . . . The problem was this fire got away." |
| **Anecdotal evidence** presents one person's view of the world, often by describing specific events or incidents. | Compelling research should not rely solely on this form of evidence, but it can be very useful for adding personal insights and refuting inaccurate generalizations. An individual's experience can be used with other forms of evidence to present complete and persuasive support. | Although many critics claim the novel is universally beloved, at least one reader "threw the book against a wall because it made me so angry." |

## Incorporating Research Into Writing

### Avoiding Plagiarism

Plagiarism is the unethical presentation of someone else's ideas as your own. You must cite sources for direct quotations, paraphrased information, or facts that are specific to a single source. When you are drafting and revising, circle any words or ideas that are not your own. Follow the instructions on pages R34 and R35 to correctly cite those passages.

**Review for Plagiarism** Always take time to review your writing for unintentional plagiarism. Read what you have written and take note of any phrases or sentences that do not have your personal writing voice. Compare those passages with your resource materials. You might have copied them without remembering the exact source. Add a correct citation to give credit to the original author. If you cannot find the questionable phrase in your notes, revise it to ensure that your final report reflects your own thinking and not someone else's work.

### Quoting and Paraphrasing

When including ideas from research into your writing, you will decide to quote directly or paraphrase.

**Direct Quotation** Use the author's exact words when they are interesting or persuasive. You might decide to include direct quotations for these reasons:

- to share an especially clear and relevant statement
- to reference a historically significant passage
- to show that an expert agrees with your position
- to present an argument that you will counter in your writing.

Include complete quotations, without deleting or changing words. If you need to omit words for space or clarity, use ellipsis points to indicate the omission. Enclose direct quotations in quotation marks and indicate the author's name.

**Paraphrase** A paraphrase restates an author's ideas in your own words. Be careful to paraphrase accurately. Beware of making sweeping generalizations in a paraphrase that were not made by the original author. You may use some words from the original source, but a legitimate paraphrase does more than simply rearrange an author's phrases, or replace a few words with synonyms.

| | |
|---|---|
| **Original Text** | "*The Tempest* was written as a farewell to art and the artist's life, just before the completion of his forty-ninth year, and everything in the play bespeaks the touch of autumn." Brandes, Georg. "Analogies Between *The Tempest* and *A Midsummer Night's Dream*." *The Tempest*, by William Shakespeare, William Heinemann, 1904, p. 668. |
| **Patchwork Plagiarism**<br>phrases from the original are rearranged, but too closely follows the original text. | A farewell to art, Shakespeare's play, *The Tempest*, was finished just before the completion of his forty-ninth year. The artist's life was to end within three years. The touch of autumn is apparent in nearly everything in the play. |
| **Good Paraphrase** | Images of autumn occur throughout *The Tempest*, which Shakespeare wrote as a way of saying goodbye to both his craft and his own life. |

## Maintaining the Flow of Ideas

Effective research writing is much more that just a list of facts. Be sure to maintain the flow of ideas by connecting research information to your own ideas. Instead of simply stating a piece of evidence, use transition words and phrases to explain the connection between information you found from outside resources and your own ideas and purpose for writing. The following transitions can be used to introduce, compare, contrast, and clarify.

### Useful Transitions

**When providing examples:**

for example   for instance   to illustrate   in [name of resource], [author]

**When comparing and contrasting ideas or information:**

in the same way   similarly   however   on the other hand

**When clarifying ideas or opinions:**

in other words   that is   to explain   to put it another way

Choosing an effective organizational structure for your writing will help you create a logical flow of ideas. Once you have established a clear organizational structure, insert facts and details from your research in appropriate places to provide evidence and support for your writing.

| ORGANIZATIONAL STRUCTURE | USES |
|---|---|
| **Chronological order** presents information in the sequence in which it happens. | historical topics; science experiments; analysis of narratives |
| **Part-to-whole order** examines how several categories affect a larger subject. | analysis of social issues; historical topics |
| **Order of importance** presents information in order of increasing or decreasing importance. | persuasive arguments; supporting a bold or challenging thesis |
| **Comparison-and-contrast organization** outlines the similarities and differences of a given topic. | addressing two or more subjects |

## Formats for Citing Sources

In research writing, cite your sources. In the body of your paper, provide a footnote, an endnote, or a parenthetical citation, identifying the sources of facts, opinions, or quotations. At the end of your paper, provide a bibliography or a Works Cited list, a list of all the sources referred to in your research. Follow an established format, such as Modern Language Association (MLA) style.

**Parenthetical Citations (MLA Style)** A parenthetical citation briefly identifies the source from which you have taken a specific quotation, factual claim, or opinion. It refers readers to one of the entries on your Works Cited list. A parenthetical citation has the following features:

- It appears in parentheses.
- It identifies the source by the last name of the author, editor, or translator, or by the title (for a lengthy title, list the first word only).
- It provides a page reference, the page(s) of the source on which the information cited can be found.

A parenthetical citation generally falls outside a closing quotation mark but within the final punctuation of a clause or sentence. For a long quotation set off from the rest of your text, place the citation at the end of the excerpt without any punctuation following.

**Sample Parenthetical Citations**

It makes sense that baleen whales such as the blue whale, the bowhead whale, the humpback whale, and the sei whale (to name just a few) grow to immense sizes (Carwardine et al. 19–21). The blue whale has grooves running from under its chin to partway along the length of its underbelly. As in some other whales, these grooves expand and allow even more food and water to be taken in (Ellis 18–21).

Authors' last names

Page numbers where information can be found

**Works Cited List (MLA Style)** A Works Cited list must contain accurate information to enable a reader to locate each source you cite. The basic components of an entry are as follows:

- name of the author, editor, translator, and/or group responsible for the work
- title of the work
- publisher
- date of publication

For print materials, the information for a citation generally appears on the copyright and title pages. For the format of a Works Cited list, consult the examples on this page and in the MLA Style for Listing Sources chart.

**Sample Works Cited List (MLA 8th Edition)**

Carwardine, Mark, et al. *The Nature Company Guides: Whales, Dolphins, and Porpoises.* Time-Life, 1998.

"Discovering Whales." *Whales on the Net.* Whales in Danger, 1998, www.whales.org.au/discover/index.html. Accessed 11 Apr. 2017.

Neruda, Pablo. "Ode to Spring." *Odes to Opposites,* translated by Ken Krabbenhoft, edited and illustrated by Ferris Cook, Little, 1995, p. 16.

*The Saga of the Volsungs*. Translated by Jesse L. Byock, Penguin, 1990.

List an anonymous work by title.

List both the title of the work and the collection in which it is found.

**Works Cited List or Bibliography?**

A Works Cited list includes only those sources you paraphrased or quoted directly in your research paper. By contrast, a bibliography lists all the sources you consulted during research—even those you did not cite.

## MLA (8th Edition) Style for Listing Sources

| | |
|---|---|
| **Book with one author** | Pyles, Thomas. *The Origins and Development of the English Language.* 2nd ed., Harcourt Brace Jovanovich, 1971.<br>[Indicate the edition or version number when relevant.] |
| **Book with two authors** | Pyles, Thomas, and John Algeo. *The Origins and Development of the English Language.* 5th ed., Cengage Learning, 2004. |
| **Book with three or more authors** | Donald, Robert B., et al. *Writing Clear Essays.* Prentice Hall, 1983. |
| **Book with an editor** | Truth, Sojourner. *Narrative of Sojourner Truth.* Edited by Margaret Washington, Vintage Books, 1993. |
| **Introduction to a work in a published edition** | Washington, Margaret. Introduction. *Narrative of Sojourner Truth,* by Sojourner Truth, edited by Washington, Vintage Books, 1993, pp. v–xi. |
| **Single work in an anthology** | Hawthorne, Nathaniel. "Young Goodman Brown." *Literature: An Introduction to Reading and Writing,* edited by Edgar V. Roberts and Henry E. Jacobs, 5th ed., Prentice Hall, 1998, pp. 376–385.<br>[Indicate pages for the entire selection.] |
| **Signed article from an encyclopedia** | Askeland, Donald R. "Welding." *World Book Encyclopedia,* vol. 21, World Book, 1991, p. 58. |
| **Signed article in a weekly magazine** | Wallace, Charles. "A Vodacious Deal." *Time,* 14 Feb. 2000, p. 63. |
| **Signed article in a monthly magazine** | Gustaitis, Joseph. "The Sticky History of Chewing Gum." *American History,* Oct. 1998, pp. 30–38. |
| **Newspaper article** | Thurow, Roger. "South Africans Who Fought for Sanctions Now Scrap for Investors." *Wall Street Journal,* 11 Feb. 2000, pp. A1+.<br>[For a multipage article that does not appear on consecutive pages, write only the first page number on which it appears, followed by the plus sign.] |
| **Unsigned editorial or story** | "Selective Silence." Editorial. *Wall Street Journal,* 11 Feb. 2000, p. A14.<br>[If the editorial or story is signed, begin with the author's name.] |
| **Signed pamphlet or brochure** | [Treat the pamphlet as though it were a book.] |
| **Work from a library subscription service** | Ertman, Earl L. "Nefertiti's Eyes." *Archaeology,* Mar.–Apr. 2008, pp. 28–32. *Kids Search,* EBSCO, New York Public Library. Accessed 7 Jan. 2017.<br>[Indicating the date you accessed the information is optional but recommended.] |
| **Filmstrips, slide programs, videocassettes, DVDs, and other audiovisual media** | *The Diary of Anne Frank.* 1959. Directed by George Stevens, performances by Millie Perkins, Shelley Winters, Joseph Schildkraut, Lou Jacobi, and Richard Beymer, Twentieth Century Fox, 2004.<br>[Indicating the original release date after the title is optional but recommended.] |
| **CD-ROM (with multiple publishers)** | Simms, James, editor. *Romeo and Juliet.* By William Shakespeare, Attica Cybernetics / BBC Education / Harper, 1995. |
| **Radio or television program transcript** | "Washington's Crossing of the Delaware." *Weekend Edition Sunday,* National Public Radio, 23 Dec. 2013. Transcript. |
| **Web page** | "Fun Facts About Gum." ICGA, 2005–2017, www.gumassociation.org/index.cfm/facts-figures/fun-facts-about-gum. Accessed 19 Feb. 2017.<br>[Indicating the date you accessed the information is optional but recommended.] |
| **Personal interview** | Smith, Jane. Personal interview, 10 Feb. 2017. |

All examples follow the style given in the MLA Handbook, 8th edition, published in 2016.

MODEL

## Evidence Log

Unit Title: Discovery

Perfomance-Based Assessment Prompt:
Do all discoveries benefit humanity?

My initial thoughts:
Yes - all knowledge moves us forward.

As you read multiple texts about a topic, your thinking may change. Use an Evidence Log like this one to record your thoughts, to track details you might use in later writing or discussion, and to make further connections.

Here is a sample to show how one reader's ideas deepened as she read two texts.

Title of Text: Classifying the Stars Date: Sept. 17

| CONNECTION TO THE PROMPT | TEXT EVIDENCE/DETAILS | ADDITIONAL NOTES/IDEAS |
|---|---|---|
| Newton shared his discoveries and then other scientists built on his discoveries. | Paragraph 2: "Isaac Newton gave to the world the results of his experiments on passing sunlight through a prism." Paragraph 3: "In 1814 . . . the German optician, Fraunhofer . . . saw that the multiple spectral tints . . . were crossed by hundreds of fine dark lines." | It's not always clear how a discovery might benefit humanity in the future. |

How does this text change or add to my thinking? This confirms what I think. Date: Sept. 20

Title of Text: Cell Phone Mania Date: Sept. 21

| CONNECTION TO THE PROMPT | TEXT EVIDENCE/DETAILS | ADDITIONAL NOTES/IDEAS |
|---|---|---|
| Cell phones have made some forms of communication easier, but people don't talk to each other as much as they did in the past. | Paragraph 7: "Over 80% of young adults state that texting is their primary method of communicating with friends. This contrasts with older adults who state that they prefer a phone call." | Is it good that we don't talk to each other as much?<br><br>Look for article about social media to learn more about this question. |

How does this text change or add to my thinking? Date: Sept. 25
Maybe there are some downsides to discoveries. I still think that knowledge moves us forward, but there are sometimes unintended negative effects.

MODEL

## Word Network

A word network is a collection of words related to a topic. As you read the selections in a unit, identify interesting theme-related words and build your vocabulary by adding them to your Word Network.

Use your Word Network as a resource for your discussions and writings. Here is an example:

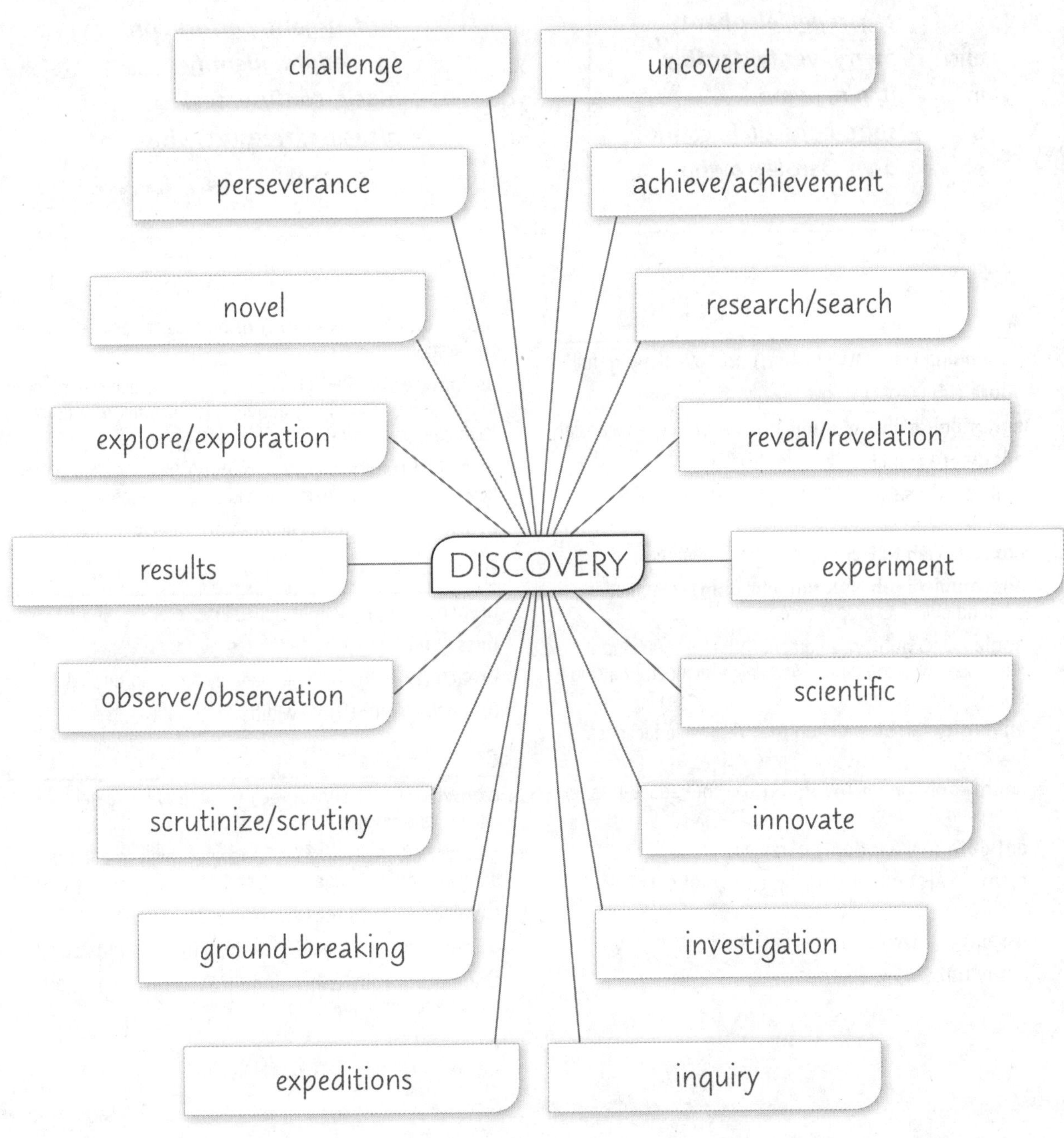


TOOL KIT: PROGRAM RESOURCES

# ACADEMIC / CONCEPT VOCABULARY

Academic vocabulary appears in **blue type**.

## Pronunciation Key

| Symbol | Sample Words | Symbol | Sample Words |
|---|---|---|---|
| a | ***at, catapult, Alabama*** | oo | ***boot, soup, crucial*** |
| ah | ***father, charms, argue*** | ow | ***now, stout, flounder*** |
| ai | ***care, various, hair*** | oy | ***boy, toil, oyster*** |
| aw | ***law, maraud, caution*** | s | ***say, nice, press*** |
| awr | ***pour, organism, forewarn*** | sh | ***she, abolition, motion*** |
| ay | ***ape, sails, implication*** | u | ***full, put, book*** |
| ee | ***even, teeth, really*** | uh | ***ago, focus, contemplation*** |
| eh | ***ten, repel, elephant*** | ur | ***bird, urgent. perforation*** |
| ehr | ***merry, verify, terribly*** | y | ***by, delight, identify*** |
| ih | ***it, pin, hymn*** | yoo | ***music, confuse, few*** |
| o | ***shot, hopscotch, condo*** | zh | ***pleasure, treasure, vision*** |
| oh | ***own, parole, rowboat*** | | |



## A

**abounding** (uh BOWND ihng) *adj.* overflowing; full of

**adore** (uh DAWR) *v.* love greatly

**agitation** (aj uh TAY shuhn) *n.* state of nervous anxiety

**allegiance** (uh LEE juhns) *n.* loyalty

**ambassadors** (am BAS uh duhrz) *n.* special representatives to other countries

**amnesia** (am NEE zhuh) *n.* loss of memory

**anachronism** (uh NAK ruh nihz uhm) *n.* something occuring out of its proper time

**angle** (ANG guhl) *n.* in graphic art, measurement of how much space, horizontal and vertical, is included in a single visual

**animosity** (an uh MOS uh tee) *n.* hostile feelings; hatred

**annotation** (an uh TAY shuhn) *n.* note added to a text to explain

**antidote** (AN tuh doht) *n.* remedy

**artifice** (AHR tuh fihs) *n.* sly, clever, artful trick or strategy

**assault** (uh SAWLT) *n.* military attack

**assay** (uh SAY) *v.* analyze

**assertion** (uh SUR shuhn) *n.* positive statement; formal declaration

**assimilate** (uh SIHM uh layt) *v.* become like the majority in a region or country by adopting its customs, viewpoint, character, or attitude

**audience reaction** (AW dee uhns) (ree AK shuhn) *n.* how viewers or listeners respond to a performance

**avaricious** (av uh RIHSH uhs) *adj.* greedy

## B

**blanch** (blanch) *v.* make pale; lose color

**bliss** (blihs) *n.* great happiness; ecstasy

**breach** (breech) *n.* hole made by breaking through

**breadth** (brehdth) *n.* width

## C

**captivity** (kap TIHV uh tee) *n.* state of being held against one's will

**catalyst** (KAT uh lihst) *n.* person or thing creating or bringing about change

**cavalry** (KAV uhl ree) *n.* soldiers on horseback

**chafed** (chayft) *v.* made sore from rubbing; irritated

**cinematography** (sihn uh muh TOG ruh fee) *n.* art and science of filmmaking

**cognitive** (KOG nuh tihv) *adj.* having to do with knowing; dealing with awareness

**composition** (KOM puh ZIHSH uhn) *n.* arrangement of the parts of an image, whether drawn or recorded in some other visual format

**consternation** (kon stuhr NAY shuhn) *n.* sudden feeling of intense confusion; dismay

**contradictory** (kon truh DIHK tuhr ee) *adj.* saying the opposite; in disagreement

**conventionalized** (kuhn VEHN shuhn uh lyzd) *adj.* turned into something predictable and expected

**converged** (kuhn VURJD) *v.* came together

**conviction** (kuhn VIHK shuhn) *n.* state of being convinced; firm belief

**corpse** (kawrps) *n.* dead body

**correspondent** (kawr uh SPON duhnt) *n.* journalist employed by a media outlet to gather, report, or contribute news from a distant place

**counterfeit** (KOWN tuhr fiht) *n.* false imitation

**cover design** (KUHV uhr) (dih ZYN) *n.* visual art created by an illustrator, photographer, or graphic artist for the cover of a book or other printed material

**credible** (KREHD uh buhl) *adj.* believable

**cross-reference** (KRAWS rehf ruhns) *n.* note directing readers to another part of the text

## D

**decaying** (dih KAY ihng) *adj.* decomposing; rotting

**dejected** (dih JEHK tihd) *adj.* depressed; saddened

**delivery** (dih LIHV uhr ee) *n.* way in which speakers, such as actors or poets, say their words; giving up or handing over

**demagogue** (DEHM uh gawg) *n.* leader who stirs people's emotions by appealing to emotion or prejudice to gain power

**desire** (dih ZYR) *n.* longing; strong wish or want

**desolation** (dehs uh LAY shuhn) *n.* lonely sorrow; condition of being ruined or deserted

**despair** (dih SPAIR) *v.* abandon all hope

**despotic** (dehs POT ihk) *adj.* in an oppressive manner typical of a tyrant or dictator

**devise** (dih VYZ) *v.* plan; think out

**diligent** (DIHL uh juhnt) *adj.* conscientious and hard-working

**dimmed** (dihmd) *v.* became less bright

**dirge** (durj) *n.* song of grief

**discreet** (dihs KREET) *adj.* careful about what one says or does; prudent

**diverse** (dih VURS) *adj.* varied; made up of many different elements

**dominions** (duh MIHN yuhnz) *n.* governed territories or countries

**dread** (drehd) *n.* state of great fear

**dreadful** (DREHD fuhl) *adj.* inspiring fear or awe

## E

**edict** (EE dihkt) *n.* formal order issued by authority

**editing** (EHD iht ihng) *n.* process of selecting, correcting, and sequencing the written, visual, and audio elements of a media production

**embedded video** (ehm BEHD ihd) (VIHD ee oh) *n.* video that has been placed within the HTML code of a Web page

**embrace** (ehm BRAYS) *v.* accept or adopt eagerly

**eminent** (EHM uh nuhnt) *adj.* rising above others in rank or achievement

**engender** (ehn JEHN duhr) *v.* create; produce; cause

**enrages** (ehn RAY juhz) *v.* causes become very angry

**entitlement** (ehn TY tuhl muhnt) *n.* expectation; right

**entry** (EHN tree) *n.* main article in an encyclopedia; it may be divided into a series of *subentries*

**entwining** (ehn TWYN ihng) *v.* twisting or knotting together; encircling

**equivocate** (ih KWIHV uh kayt) *v.* speak in a way that hides the truth

**eternally** (ih TUR nuh lee) *adv.* lasting forever

## F

**faction** (FAK shuhn) *n.* partisan conflict within an organization or a country; dissension

**fancy** (FAN see) *n.* taste for something; fondness

**fellowships** (FEHL oh shihps) *n.* groups of people who share interests

**fervent** (FUR vuhnt) *adj.* passionate; intense-feeling

**flout** (flowt) *v.* break a rule or law without hiding it or showing shame

**foully** (FOWL lee) *adv.* wrongly; in an evil way

## G

**gesture** (JEHS chuhr) *n.* movement of part of the body, especially the hands, that conveys meaning

**gifted** (GIHF tihd) *adj.* having a natural talent

**gorge** (gawrj) *v.* fill by eating greedily

**gruesome** (GROO suhm) *adj.* horrible; ghastly

## H

**harmony** (HAHR muh nee) *n.* oneness; peacefulness

**headings** (HEHD ihngz) *n.* entries that describe the information recorded in the columns of a document such as a spreadsheet

**hemlock** (HEHM lok) *n.* poisonous herb or a drink prepared from it

**hideous** (HIHD ee uhs) *adj.* ugly or disgusting

**honor** (ON uhr) *v.* respect greatly

**host** (hohst) *n.* moderator or interviewer for a radio, television, or Web-based show

**hybrid** (HY brihd) *adj.* combined from different sources

**hyperlink** (HY puhr lihngk) *n.* interactive word or passage of an online text that links to additional information

## I

**idiosyncratic** (ihd ee oh sihn KRAT ihk) *adj.* peculiar

**illusory** (ih LOO suhr ee) *adj.* misleading; unreal

**impalpable** (ihm PAL puh buhl) *adj.* unable to be felt by touching; hard to understand

**imperial** (ihm PEER ee uhl) *adj.* of or related to an empire or emperor; of superior quality

**imperialism** (ihm PIHR ee uhl ihz uhm) *n.* policy of one nation's taking control over another in order to exploit its people and resources for its own benefit

**impertinent** (ihm PURT uhn uhnt) *adj.* rude; out of place

**implication** (ihm pluh KAY shuhn) *n.* indirect suggestion; hint

**inanimate** (ihn AN uh miht) *adj.* not alive; seeming to be lifeless

**incensed** (ihn SEHNST) *v.* made angry

**incorporate** (ihn KAWR puh rayt) *v.* combine; merge

**indigenous** (ihn DIHJ uh nuhs) *adj.* native to a particular country or region

**inexorable** (ihn EHK suhr uh buhl) *adj.* unable to be altered or changed

**infuse** (ihn FYOOZ) *v.* put into; fill

**innocuous** (ih NOK yoo uhs) *adj.* harmless

**innumerable** (ih NOO muhr uh buhl) *adj.* too many to count

**integrity** (ihn TEHG ruh tee) *n.* moral uprightness

**interviewee** (ihn tuhr vyoo EE) *n.* person who is questioned on a media broadcast

**intolerable** (ihn TOL uhr uh buhl) *adj.* hard to endure; unbearable

## J

**justify** (JUHS tuh fy) *v.* give good reason for; show to be right

**jutted** (JUHT ihd) *v.* stuck out

## L

**lair** (lair) *n.* den; hiding place

**laity** (LAY uh tee) *n.* people of religious faith who are not members of the clergy

**languish** (LANG gwihsh) *v.* grow tired or weak; droop

**laudable** (LAWD uh buhl) *adj.* praiseworthy

**leaden** (LEHD uhn) *adj.* heavy; hard to lift; dull and gloomy

**lighting/color** (LY tihng) (KUHL ur) *n.* in graphic art, use of light and dark shades

**loathsome** (LOHTH suhm) *adj.* disgusting; detestable

## M

**malevolence** (muh LEHV uh luhns) *n.* desire to do evil

**malice** (MAL ihs) *n.* desire to hurt another person

**malicious** (muh LIHSH uhs) *adj.* intending to do harm; evil

**migrate** (MY grayt) *v.* move from one place to settle in another; move with the seasons

**mime** (mym) *n.* theatrical technique of portraying characters and actions wordlessly, using movement only

**modify** (MOD uh fy) *v.* partly change

**myriad** (MIHR ee uhd) *n.* uncountably large number; variety

## N

**navigation** (nav uh GAY shuhn) *n.* moving from place to place on a website or on the Internet to find information

## O

**odious** (OH dee uhs) *adj.* extremely unpleasant or repulsive

## P

**pacing** (PAY sihng) *n.* tempo or overall sense of the speed at which a theatrical production takes place

**palette** (PAL iht) *n.* range of colors and shades used by an illustrator

**panel** (PAN uhl) *n.* individual scene in a graphic novel, often framed by a border

**pathological** (path uh LOJ ih kuhl) *adj.* dealing with disease

**perception** (puhr SEHP shuhn) *n.* act of making an observation

**pernicious** (puhr NIHSH uhs) *adj.* harmful, often in a way that is not readily noticed

**personable** (PUR suh nuh buhl) *adj.* having a pleasant manner

**perspective** (puhr SPEHK tihv) *n.* in graphic novels, the point of view of an image, which may be *close up, middle distance,* or *long distance*

**perturbation** (puhr tuhr BAY shuhn) *n.* disturbance

**prescribe** (prih SKRYB) *v.* set down as a direction; order medicine or treatment

**presume** (prih ZOOM) *v.* assume; take for granted without proof

**pretext** (PREE tehkst) *n.* plausible but false reason

**prime** (prym) *n.* youth; young adulthood

**prismatic** (prihz MAT ihk) *adj.* like a prism; varied in color

**pristine** (prihs TEEN) *adj.* original; unspoiled

**privileged** (PRIHV lihjd) *adj.* given special advantages

**proclamation** (prok luh MAY shuhn) *n.* something that is proclaimed, or announced officially

**profanation** (prof uh NAY shuhn) *n.* act of disrespecting sacred ideas, persons, or things

**proficient** (pruh FIHSH uhnt) *adj.* skilled; expert

**provoke** (pruh VOHK) *v.* make angry; cause

**purge** (purj) *n.* ousting; removal

**purport** (puhr PAWRT) *v.* claim or profess, often falsely

**putrid** (PYOO trihd) *adj.* decaying; rotton and smelly

## R

**rancors** (RANG kuhrz) *n.* angry feelings

**rank** (rangk) *n.* row or line of soldiers

**realism** and **stylization** (REE uh lihz uhm) (sty luh ZAY shuhn) *n.* In art, realism portrays images as they actually appear; stylization presents images that are exaggerated, distorted, or otherwise altered to show an imagined vision.

**rebellious** (rih BEHL yuhs) *adj.* acting against authority

**reiterate** (ree IHT uh rayt) *v.* say or do several times; repeat

**repercussion** (ree puhr KUHSH uhn) *n.* effect of or reaction to some event

**requiem** (REHK wee uhm) *n.* musical composition honoring the dead

**requisite** (REHK wuh ziht) *adj.* required; necessary; essential

**resolute** (REHZ uh loot) *adj.* determined; firm

**revelation** (rehv uh LAY shuhn) *n.* something made known, disclosed, or discovered

**revolt** (rih VOHLT) *n.* attempt to overthrow a lawful ruler

**rows** and **columns** (rohz) (KOL uhmz) *n.* how information is organized in a speadsheet

## S

**sacrilegious** (sak ruh LIHJ uhs) *adj.* treating a religious object, person, or belief with disrespect

**sanctity** (SANGK tuh tee) *n.* holiness; goodness

**season** (SEE zuhn) *n.* special time

**sepulcher** (SEHP uhl kuhr) *n.* tomb

**serene** (suh REEN) *adj.* peaceful; calm

**sincerity** (sihn SEHR uh tee) *n.* truthfulness; good faith

**slide show** (slyd) (shoh) *n.* presentation based on or supplemented by a series of still images

**solemnity** (suh LEHM nuh tee) *n.* solemn feeling; seriousness

**sordid** (SAWR dihd) *adj.* dirty; filthy

**sound effects** (sownd) (ih FEHKTS) *n.* recorded sounds that are neither speech nor music

**sport** (spawrt) *v.* amuse

**stagnant** (STAG nuhnt) *adj.* lacking motion or current

**stalked** (stawkt) *v.* pursued stealthily; hunted

**statistics** (stuh TIHS tihks) *n.* numerical facts or data that have been assembled or tabulated

**stealthy** (STEHL thee) *adj.* slow and secretive

**stores** (stawrz) *n.* supplies

**subjugation** (suhb juh GAY shuhn) *n.* conquest

**sublime** (suh BLYM) *adj.* magnificent; awe-inspiring

**succeed** (suhk SEED) *v.* come after

**superimposition** (soo puhr ihm puh ZIHSH uhn) *n.* placement of one image on top of another to create a new image or effect

**supplant** (suh PLANT) *v.* replace one thing with another

## T

**taste** (tayst) *n.* liking for something; fondness

**tedious** (TEE dee uhs) *adj.* boring; long and tiring

**tenacious** (tih NAY shuhs) *adj.* stubborn; persistent

**theoretical** (thee uh REHT uh kuhl) *adj.* based on theory; not proven

**toil** (toyl) *n.* hard work

**torrid** (TAWR ihd) *adj.* very hot; burning

**tranquil** (TRANG kwuhl) *adj.* peaceful; calm

**transformation** (trans fuhr MAY shuhn) *n.* act of changing in form or appearance

**treacherous** (TREHCH uhr uhs) *adj.* guilty of deception or betrayal

**treasons** (TREE zuhnz) *n.* crimes of helping the enemies of one's country

**typography** (ty POG ruh fee) *n.* size and style of type used for books and other printed materials

## U

**unambiguous** (uhn am BIHG yoo uhs) *adj.* not confused; clear; definite

**upbringing** (UHP brihng ihng) *n.* care and training given to a child while growing up

**usurper** (yoo SURP uhr) *n.* person who takes control without the proper authority

## V

**valiantly** (VAL yuhnt lee) *adv.* courageously

**vile** (vyl) *adj.* disgusting

**virtuous** (VUR choo uhs) *adj.* having high moral standards

## W

**wavered** (WAY vuhrd) *v.* flickered; fluttered

**writhing** (RY thihng) *adj.* making twisting or turning motions

# VOCABULARIO ACADÉMICO/ VOCABULARIO DE CONCEPTOS

El vocabulario académico está en **letra azul.**

## A

**abounding / abundante** *adj.* rebosante; lleno

**adore / adorar** *v.* amar enormemente

**agitation / agitación** *s.* estado de anxiedad y nerviosismo

**allegiance / lealtad** *s.* fidelidad

**ambassadors / embajadores** *s.* representantes en otro países

**amnesia / amnesia** *s.* pérdida de la memoria

**anachronism / anacronismo** *s.* algo que no ocurre en su propio tiempo o época

**angle / ángulo** *s.* en las artes gráficas, medida de cuánto espacio, tanto horizontal como vertical, se incluye en una ilustración

**animosity / animosidad** *s.* hostilidad; odio

**annotation / anotación** *s.* nota explicativa que se agrega a un texto

**antidote / antídoto** *s.* remedio

**artifice / artificio** *s.* recurso o estrategia ingeniosa y, a veces, taimada

**assault / asalto** *s.* ataque militar

**assay / evaluar** *v.* analizar

**assertion / aseveración** *s.* enunciado positivo; declaración formal

**assimilate / asimilarse** *v.* volverse similar a la mayoría de las personas que habitan una región o país adoptando sus costumbres, puntos de vista, carácter o actitud

**audience reaction / reacción de la audiencia** *s.* la manera en que los espectadores u oyentes responden a una actuación

**avaricious / avaro** *adj.* codicioso

## B

**blanch / blanquear** *v.* hacer que algo tome un color más pálido, o que pierda el color

**bliss / dicha** *s.* gran felicidad, éxtasis

**breach / brecha** *s.* grieta o agujero que se hace en una pared o edificio

**breadth / anchura** *s.* ancho, amplitud

## C

**captivity / cautiverio** *s.* estado en el cual se está retenido contra la propia voluntad

**catalyst / catalizador** *s.* persona o cosa que crea o produce un cambio

**cavalry / caballería** *s.* ejército de soldados a caballo

**chafed / irritado** *adj.* sensibilizado a causa de haberlo frotado o raspado mucho

**cinematography / cinematografía** *s.* arte y ciencia de hacer y procesar películas

**cognitive / cognitivo** *adj.* relativo al conocimiento o con la concientización

**composition / composición** *s.* arreglo o disposición de las partes de una imagen, ya sea dibujada o grabada en algún tipo de soporte visual

**consternation / consternación** *s.* sentimiento repentino de gran confusión; desaliento

**contradictory / contradictorio** *adj.* que expresa lo opuesto; que está en desacuerdo

**conventionalized / convencional** *adj.* algo predecible o de esperarse

**converged / convergió** *v.* se juntó o reunió

**conviction / convicción** *s.* seguridad, certeza; creencia firme

**corpse / cadáver** *s.* cuerpo muerto

**correspondent / corresponsal** *s.* empleado de un medio de comunicación encargado de reunir, informar o enviar noticias desde un lugar distante

**counterfeit / falsificación** *s.* imitación ilegítima

**cover design / diseño de tapa** *s.* arte creado por un ilustrador, un fotógrafo o un artista gráfico para la tapa de un libro u otro tipo de material impreso

**credible / verosímil** *adj.* creíble

**cross-reference / referencia cruzada** *s.* referencia que remite a otra parte del mismo texto

## D

**decaying / descompuesto** *adj.* que se está pudriendo o echando a perder

**dejected / desalentado** *adj.* deprimido; entristecido

**delivery / presentación oral** *s.* la manera en la que un hablante, por ejemplo un estudiante, hace una exposición o un discurso

**delivery / reparto** *s.* entrega en mano o a domicilio

**demagogue / demagogo** *s.* líder que despierta emociones en la gente apelando a sus prejuicios para aumentar su poder

**desire / deseo** *s.* anhelo; inclinación o atracción profunda hacia algo o alguien

**desolation / desolación** *s.* pena solitaria; estado o sentimiento de ruina y abandono

**despair / desesperación** *s.* sentir que ya no se tiene ninguna esperanza

**despotic / despótico** *adj.* se dice de lo que se hace de manera opresiva, propia de un déspota o tirano

**devise / concebir** *v.* planear, idear

diligent / diligente *adj.* cuidadoso y laborioso

dimmed / atenuado *adj.* que se hizo menos brillante o colorido

dirge / endecha *s.* canción lúgubre o de mucho dolor

discreet / discreto *adj.* cauto, prudente

diverse / diverso *adj.* diferente

dominions / dominios *s.* países o territorios que se gobiernan

dread / terror *s.* miedo muy profundo

dreadful / aterrador *adj.* que produce miedo o sobrecogimiento

## E

**edict / edicto** *s.* ordenanza emitida por una autoridad

**editing / edición** *s.* proceso mediante el cual se seleccionan, corrigen y organizan los elementos escritos, visuales y sonoros de una producción de medios de comunicación

**embedded video / video integrado** *s.* video que se ha insertado en el código HTML de una página web

**embrace / acoger** *v.* aceptar o adoptar con los brazos abiertos

**eminent / eminente** *adj.* distinguido; famoso; notable

**engender / engendrar** *v.* crear; producir; causar

**enrages / enfurece** *v.* provoca un enfado o enojo muy grande

**entitlement / privilegio** *s.* derecho; beneficio

**entry / entrada** *s.* cada artículo de una enciclopedia; puede dividirse en una serie de *entradas secundarias*

**entwining / enroscar** *v.* enrollar o entramar dos o más cosas; envolver o rodear

**equivocate / ser equívoco** *v.* hablar de una manera que oculta la verdad

**eternally / eternamente** *adv.* para siempre

## F

**faction / facción** *s.* cada uno de los grupos que participa en un conflicto dentro de una organización o país; disensión, desacuerdo

**fancy / inclinación** *s.* gusto o debilidad por algo o alguien

**fellowships / hermandades** *s.* grupos de personas que comparten intereses

**fervent / ferviente** *adj.* apasionado; de sentimientos intensos

**flout / inclumplir** *v.* desobedecer una regla o ley sin ocultarlo ni mostrarse avergonzado por ello

**font / tipo** *s.* conjunto de caracteres tipográficos del mismo tamaño y estilo

**foully / vilmente** *adv.* ofensivamente, maliciosamente; de manera malvada

## G

**gesture / gesto** *s.* movimiento de una parte del cuerpo

**gifted / dotado** *adj.* que tiene un talento natural

**gorge / atracarse** *v.* comer con avidez

**gruesome / repelente** *adj.* horrible; espeluznante

## H

**harmony / armonía** *s.* unidad; paz

**headings / encabezados** *s.* títulos que describen la información que se incluye en las columnas de un documento como una hoja de cálculo

**hemlock / cicuta** *s.* hierba venenosa; la bebida que se prepara con ella

**hideous / horroroso** *adj.* muy feo, espantoso

**honor / honrar** *v.* respetar mucho

**host / conductor** *s.* moderador o entrevistador de un programa de radio, televisión o virtual

**hybrid / híbrido** *adj.* se dice del producto de la combinación de distintas fuentes

**hyperlink / hipervínculo** *s.* referencia cruzada que les da a los lectores más información sobre una palabra que está resaltada

## I

**idiosyncratic / idiosincrático** *adj.* peculiar

**illusory / ilusorio** *adj.* irreal; engañoso

**impalpable / impalpable** *adj.* que no se puede percibir por vía del tacto; difícil de entender

**imperial / imperial** *adj.* relacionado con un imperio o un emperador; de calidad superior

**imperialism / imperialismo** *s.* la política de un país que controla a otro para explotar a su pueblo y sus recursos para beneficio propio

**impertinent / impertinente** *adj.* grosero; fuera de lugar

**implication / implicación** *s.* sugerencia indirecta; pista

**inanimate / inanimado** *adj.* que no está vivo; falto de alma o vida

**incensed / enfurecido** *adj.* enojado, furioso

**incorporate / incorporar** *v.* combinar; fusionar

**indigenous / indígena** *adj.* nativo de un país o región en particular

**inexorable / inexorable** *adj.* que no puede alterarse ni cambiar

**infuse / infundir** *v.* inculcar; inspirar

**innocuous / inocuo** *adj.* que no hace daño

**innumerable / innumerables** *adj.* que son demasiados para poder contarlos

**integrity / integridad** *s.* corrección moral

**interviewee / entrevistado** *s.* persona a la que se le están haciendo preguntas en un medio de comunicación

**intolerable / intolerable** *adj.* difícil de aguantar; insoportable

## J

**justify / justificar** *v.* dar buenas razones; demostrar que se tiene razón

**jutted / sobresaliente** *adj.* que se distingue

## L

**lair / guarida** *s.* madriguera; lugar donde ocultarse

**laity / laicado** *s.* conjunto de personas que comparten una fe religiosa pero que no son miembros del clero

**languish / languidecer** *v.* cansarse o debilitarse; desfallecer

**laudable / loable** *adj.* que merece ser alabado o felicitado

**leaden / plúmbeo** *adj.* pesado; difícil del alzar; aburrido y plomizo

**lighting/color / sombreado** *s.* en las artes gráficas, el uso de sombras claras y oscuras

**loathsome / repugnante** *adj.* asqueroso, desagradable

## M

**malevolence / malevolencia** *s.* deseo de hacer el mal

**malice / malicia** *s.* deseo de herir a otra persona

**malicious / malicioso** *adj.* se dice de algo o alguien que tiene el propósito de herir

**manifest / lista de embarque** *s.* documento que detalla información sobre un barco, un avión u otro tipo de vehículo

**menu / menú** *s.* lista de opciones o mandos de una computadora entre los cuales se puede escoger

**migrate / migrar** *v.* trasladarse de un lugar para asentarse en otro; mudarse según las estaciones del año

**mime / mímica** *s.* técnica teatral con la que se sugieren acciones, personajes y emociones sin utilizar palabras

**modify / modificar** *v.* cambiar parcialmente

**myriad / miríada** *s.* una cantidad tan grande que resulta incontable; variedad

## N

**navigation / navegación** *s.* ir de un lugar a otro en una página web o en Internet buscando información

## O

**odious / odioso** *adj.* extremadamente desagradable o repulsivo

## P

**pacing / tempo** *s.* ritmo al que se desarrolla una obra teatral

**palette / paleta** *s.* rango de colores que utiliza un ilustrador

**panel / viñeta** *s.* escena de una novela gráfica, por lo general enmarcada por una línea

**pathological / patológico** *adj.* relacionado con alguna enfermedad

**perception / apreciación** *s.* el acto de hacer una observación

**pernicious / pernicioso** *adj.* dañino, generalmente de una manera que tarda en notarse

**personable / afable** *adj.* de maneras y trato agradables

**perspective / perspectiva** *s.* en las artes, la ilusión de profundidad; en las novelas gráficas, el punto de vista de una imagen, que puede ser un primer plano, un plano medio o un plano general

**perturbation / perturbación** *s.* disturbio

**prescribe / prescribir** *v.* indicar una dirección o camino a seguir; recetar un medicamento o tratamiento

**presume / presuponer** *v.* asumir; dar algo por sentado

**pretext / pretexto** *s.* excusa falsa

**prime / plenitud** *s.* juventud; primera edad adulta

**prismatic / prismático** *adj.* con la forma de un prisma; de colores variados

**pristine / prístino** *adj.* antiguo, original; inmaculado

**privileged / privilegiado** *adj.* que recibe ciertas ventajas o tratamientos especiales

**proclamation / proclama** *s.* anuncio oficial

**profanation / profanación** *s.* acto de faltarle el repecto a cosas, ideas o personas que se consideran sagradas

**proficient / competente** *adj.* capaz; diestro; experto en algo

**provoke / provocar** *v.* hacer enojar; producir o causar algo

**purge / purga** *s.* expulsión; eliminación

**purport / pretender** *v.* reclamar; asegurar o sostener una idea

**putrid / pútrido** *adj.* descompuesto; podrido y apestoso

## R

**rancors / rencores** *s.* sentimientos de ira o enojo

**rank / rango** *s.* hilera o fila de soldados

**realism** and **stylization / realismo** y **estilización** *s.* en las representaciones artísticas el realismo, o arte realista, es como una fotografía, mientras que la estilización, o arte estilizado, es como una caricatura

**rebellious / rebelde** *adj.* que actúa en contra de la autoridad

**reiterate / reiterar** *v.* decir o hacer algo varias veces; repetir

**repercussion / repercusión** *s.* efecto o reacción ante algún hecho

**requiem / requiem** *s.* composición musical en honor de los muertos

**requisite / requerido** *adj.* necesario; esencial

**resolute / resuelto** *adj.* de carácter firme, decidido

**revelation / revelación** *s.* algo que se devela o descubre; manifestación de algo que estaba oculto

**revolt / revuelta** *s.* intento de derrocar a un gobernante legítimamente elegido

**rows** and **columns / hileras y columnas** *s.* el modo en que se organiza la información en una hoja de cálculo

## S

**sacrilegious / sacrílego** *adj.* se dice de un modo irrespetuoso de tratar a un objeto, persona o creencia religiosa

**sanctity / santidad** *s.* calidad de santo; beatitud

**season / estación** *s.* tiempo o época particular

**sepulcher / sepulcro** *s.* tumba

**serene / sereno** *adj.* calmo, pacífico

**sincerity / sinceridad** *s.* veracidad; de buena fe

**slide show / pase de diapositivas** *s.* prepresentación basada total o parcialmente en el uso de una serie de imágenes fijas

**solemnity / solemnidad** *s.* seriedad; formalidad

**sordid / sórdido** *adj.* sucio; mugriento

**sound effects / efecto de sonido** s. sonidos grabados que no son ni voz ni música

**sport / broma** *s.* chiste; algo dicho o hecho con ánimo juguetón

**stagnant / estancado** *adj.* que no se mueve o fluye; quieto

**stalked / acosó** *v.* persiguió obsesivamente

**statistics / estadísticas** *s.* información o datos numéricos que se han agrupado o tabulado

**stealthy / furtivo** *adj.* lento y secreto

**stores / reservas** *s.* provisiones

**stylization / estilización** *s.* el acto de procurar darle a algo o alguien una determinada apariencia

**subjugation / subyugación** *s.* conquista

**sublime / sublime** *adj.* magnífico, asombroso

**succeed / lograr** *v.* conseguir lo que se ha intentado hacer

**superimposition / sobreimposición** *s.* la acción de imprimir una imagen encima de otra ya existente con el fin de lograr un efecto determinado

**supplant / suplantar** *v.* reemplazar una cosa por otra

## T

**taste / gusto** *s.* aprecio o debilidad por algo

**tedious / tedioso** *adj.* aburrido; largo y cansado

**tenacious / tenaz** *adj.* terco; persistente

**theoretical / teórico** *adj.* que se basa en la teoría; que no está probado

**toil / esfuerzo** *s.* trabajo duro o difícil

**torrid / tórrido** *adj.* muy caluroso; ardiente

**tranquil / sosegado** *adj.* calmo, tranquilo

**transformation / transformación** *s.* el acto de cambiar de forma o apariencia

**treacherous / traicionero** *adj.* culpable de engañar o traicionar

**treasons / traiciones** *s.* delitos de deslealtad como, por ejemplo, ayudar a los enemigos del propio país

**typography** and **font / tipografía** y **tipo** *s.* tamaño y estilo del conjunto de caracteres tipográficos que se utilizan en los libros y otros materiales impresos

## U

**unambiguous / inequívoco** *adj.* que no es confuso; claro, definido

**upbringing / crianza** *s.* el cuidado y la educación que se le da a un niño cuando está creciendo

**usurper / usurpador** *s.* persona que toma el control sin la debida autoridad

## V

**valiantly / valerosamente** *adv.* con valor y coraje

**vile / vil** *adj.* canalla, infame

**virtuous / virtuoso** *adj.* moralmente puro; recto

## W

**wavered / titilante** *adj.* que parpadea o titila

**writhing / retorciéndose** *v.* que se contorsiona o contrae, por lo general a causa de un dolor

# LITERARY TERMS HANDBOOK

**ALLITERATION** ***Alliteration*** is the repetition of initial consonant sounds in accented syllables.

**Example:** a **m**elody of **m**ur**m**uring **m**en

Alliteration is used to emphasize and to link words, as well as to create musical sounds.

**ALLUSION** ***Allusion*** is a reference to a well-known person, place, event, literary work, or work of art.

**AMPLIFICATION** ***Amplification*** is a stylistic device in which the writer expands an idea, and adds depth and detail, by repetition or elaboration.

**ANALOGY** An ***analogy*** is an extended comparison of relationships. It is based on the idea or insight that the relationship between one pair of things is like the relationship between another pair. Unlike a metaphor, another form of comparison, an analogy involves an explicit comparison, often using the word *like* or *as*.

**ANAPHORA** ***Anaphora*** is a rhetorical device that involves the deliberate repetition of the same sequence of words at the beginning of nearby phrases, clauses, or sentences.

**ANGLO-SAXON POETRY** The rhythmic poetry composed in the Old English language before A.D. 1100 is known as ***Anglo-Saxon poetry.*** It generally has four accented syllables and an indefinite number of unaccented syllables in each line. Each line is divided in half by a *caesura*, or pause, and the halves are linked by the alliteration of two or three of the accented syllables.

Anglo-Saxon poetry was sung or chanted to the accompaniment of a primitive harp; it was not written, but was passed down orally.

**APOSTROPHE** An ***apostrophe*** is a figure of speech in which a speaker directly addresses an absent person or a personified quality, object, or idea.

**ARCHETYPE** An ***archetype*** is a pattern found in literary works across time and place. For more information, see *Archetypal Literary Elements.*

**ARCHAIC DICTION** ***Archaic diction*** refers to words and phrases that were once in standard usage but are no longer common.

**ARCHETYPAL LITERARY ELEMENTS** ***Archetypal literary elements*** are patterns in literature found around the world. For instance, the occurrence of events in threes is an archetypal element of fairy tales. Certain character types, such as mysterious guides, are also archetypal elements of traditional stories. According to some critics, these elements express in symbolic form truths about the human mind.

**ARGUMENT** An ***argument*** is writing or speech that attempts to convince a reader to think or act in a particular way. An argument is a logical way of presenting a belief, conclusion, or stance. A good argument is supported with reasoning and evidence.

**ASSONANCE** ***Assonance*** is the repetition of vowel sounds in stressed syllables containing dissimilar consonant sounds, as in this line from Robert Browning's "Andrea del Sarto," in which the **long e** sound is repeated:
Ah, but man's r**ea**ch should exc**ee**d his grasp."

**BLANK VERSE** ***Blank verse*** is unrhymed poetry usually written in iambic pentameter (see Meter). Occasional variations in rhythm are introduced in blank verse to create emphasis, variety, and naturalness of sound. Because blank verse sounds much like ordinary spoken English, it is often used in drama, as by Shakespeare, and in poetry.

**CARPE DIEM** A Latin phrase, ***carpe diem*** means "seize the day" or "make the most of passing time." Many great literary works have been written with the *carpe diem* theme.

**CHARACTER** The personality that takes part in the action of a literary work is known as a character. Characters can be classified in different ways. A character who plays an important role is called a ***major character.*** A character who does not is called a ***minor character.*** A character who plays the central role in a story is called the ***protagonist.*** A character who opposes the protagonist is called the ***antagonist.*** A ***round character*** has many aspects to his or her personality. A ***flat character*** is defined by only a few qualities. A character who changes is called ***dynamic;*** a character who does not change is called ***static.***

**CHARACTERIZATION** ***Characterization*** is the act of creating and developing a character. A writer uses ***direct characterization*** when he or she describes a character's traits explicitly. Writers also use ***indirect characterization.*** A character's traits can be revealed indirectly in what he or she says, thinks, or does; in a description of his or her appearance; or in the statements, thoughts, or actions of other characters.

**CLIMAX** The ***climax*** is the high point of interest or suspense in a literary work. Often, the climax is also the crisis in the plot, the point at which the protagonist changes his or her understanding or situation. Sometimes, the climax coincides with the ***resolution,*** the point at which the central conflict is ended.

**COMIC RELIEF** Playwrights of tragedies often create one or two humorous characters and scenes to lighten the overall tense mood of the work. These characters and scenes provide ***comic relief*** in an otherwise suspenseful or tense production.

**COMPRESSION** ***Compression*** is the pressing together of disparate ideas or images and creates a density and complexity of meaning.

**CONCEIT** A ***conceit*** is an unusual and surprising comparison between two very different things. This special kind of metaphor or complicated analogy is often the basis for a whole poem. During the Elizabethan Age, sonnets commonly included Petrarchan conceits. ***Petrarchan conceits*** make extravagant claims about the beloved's beauty or the speaker's suffering, with comparisons to divine beings, powerful natural forces, and objects that contain a given quality in the highest degree. Seventeenth-century ***metaphysical*** poets used elaborate, unusual, and highly intellectual conceits.

**CONFLICT** A ***conflict*** is a struggle between opposing forces. Sometimes, this struggle is internal, or within a character. At other times, the struggle is external, or between the character and some outside force. The outside force may be another character, nature, or some element of society such as a custom or a political institution. Often, the conflict in a work combines several of these possibilities.

**CONNOTATION** ***Connotation*** refers to the associations that a word calls to mind in addition to its dictionary meaning. For example, the words *home* and *domicile* have the same dictionary meaning. However, the first word has positive connotations of warmth and security, whereas the second does not.

**CONSONANCE** ***Consonance*** is the repetition of final consonant sounds in stressed syllables containing dissimilar vowel sounds, as in this excerpt from Coleridge's "The Rime of the Ancient Mariner:"

a frightful fie**nd** / Doth close behi**nd** him tread.

**COUPLET** A ***couplet*** is a pair of rhyming lines written in the same meter. A ***heroic couplet*** is a rhymed pair of iambic pentameter lines. In a ***closed couplet,*** the meaning and syntax are completed within the two lines, as in this example from Alexander Pope's "Essay on Criticism":

True ease in writing comes from art, not chance,
As those move easiest who have learned to dance.

Shakespearean sonnets usually end with heroic couplets.

**CULTURALLY SPECIFIC THEME** A ***culturally specific theme*** relates meaningfully to some cultures but not others.

**DENOTATION** ***Denotation*** is the objective meaning of a word—that to which the word refers, independent of other associations that the word calls to mind. Dictionaries list the denotative meanings of words.

**DIALECT** ***Dialect*** is the form of a language spoken by people in a particular region or group. Dialects differ from one another in grammar, vocabulary, and pronunciation.

**DIALOGUE** ***Dialogue*** is a conversation between characters. Writers use dialogue to reveal character, to present events, to add variety to narratives, and to interest readers. Dialogue in a story is usually set off by quotation marks and paragraphing. Dialogue in a play script generally follows the name of the speaker.

**DIARY** A ***diary*** is a personal record of daily events, usually written in prose. Most diaries are not written for publication; sometimes, however, interesting diaries written by influential people are published.

**DICTION** ***Diction*** is a writer's word choice. It can be a major determinant of the writer's style. Diction can be described as formal or informal, abstract or concrete, plain or ornate, ordinary or technical.

**DRAMA** A ***drama*** is a story written to be performed by actors. It may consist of one or more large sections, called acts, which are made up of any number of smaller sections, called scenes.

Drama originated in the religious rituals and symbolic reenactments of primitive peoples. The ancient Greeks, who developed drama into a sophisticated art form, created such dramatic forms as tragedy and comedy.

The first dramas in England were the miracle plays and morality plays of the Middle Ages. Miracle plays told biblical stories. Morality plays, such as *Everyman,* were allegories dealing with personified virtues and vices. The English Renaissance saw a flowering of drama in England, culminating in the works of William Shakespeare, who wrote many of the world's greatest comedies, tragedies, histories, and romances. During the Neoclassical Age, English drama turned to satirical comedies of manners that probed the virtues of upper-class society. In the Romantic and Victorian ages, a few good verse plays were written, including Percy Bysshe Shelley's *The Cenci* and *Prometheus Unbound.* The end of the nineteenth and beginning of the twentieth centuries saw a resurgence of the drama in England and throughout the English-speaking world. Great plays of the Modern period include works by Bernard Shaw, Christopher Fry, T. S. Eliot, Harold Pinter, and Samuel Beckett.

**DRAMATIC MONOLOGUE** A ***dramatic monologue*** is a poem in which an imaginary character speaks to a silent listener.

**ENJAMBMENT** ***Enjambment***, or a run-on line, is a poetic structure in which both the grammatical structure and sense continue past the end of the line.

**EPIC** An ***epic*** is a long narrative poem about the adventures of gods or of an ***epic hero***.

***Epic conventions*** are traditional characteristics of epic poems, including an opening statement of the theme; an appeal for supernatural help in telling the story (an invocation); a beginning ***in medias res*** (Latin: "in the middle of things"); catalogs of people and things; accounts of past events; and descriptive phrases.

**EPIGRAM** An ***epigram*** is a brief statement in prose or in verse. The concluding couplet in an English sonnet may be epigrammatic. An essay may be written in an epigrammatic style.

**EPIPHANY** ***Epiphany*** is a sudden revelation or flash of insight in which a character recognizes a truth.

**EPITAPH** An ***epitaph*** is an inscription written on a tomb or burial place. In literature, epitaphs include serious or humorous lines written as if intended for such use, like the epitaph in Thomas Gray's "Elegy Written in a Country Churchyard."

**ESSAY** An ***essay*** is a short nonfiction work about a particular subject. Essays can be classified as formal or informal, personal or impersonal. They can also be classified according to purpose, such as cause-and-effect, satirical, or reflective. Modes of discourse, such as explanatory, descriptive, persuasive, or narrative, are other means of classifying essays.

**EXPLANATORY ESSAY** An ***explanatory essay*** describes and provides detail about a process or concept.

**FICTION** ***Fiction*** is prose writing about imaginary characters and events. Some writers of fiction base their stories on real events, whereas others rely solely on their imaginations.

**FIGURATIVE LANGUAGE** Figurative language is writing or speech not meant to be interpreted literally. Poets and other writers use figurative language to paint vivid word pictures, to make their writing emotionally intense and concentrated, and to state their ideas in new and unusual ways. Among the figures of speech making up figurative language are hyperbole, irony, metaphor, metonymy, oxymoron, paradox, personification, simile, and synecdoche.

See also the entries for individual figures of speech.

**FOLKLORE** The stories, legends, myths, ballads, riddles, sayings, and other traditional works produced orally by illiterate or semiliterate peoples are known as ***folklore.*** Folklore influences written literature in many ways.

**FOOT** The basic unit of meter, a ***foot*** is a group of one or more stressed and unstressed syllables.

**FREE VERSE** ***Free verse*** is poetry not written in a regular, rhythmical pattern, or meter. Instead of having metrical feet and lines, free verse has a rhythm that suits its meaning and that uses the sounds of spoken language in lines of different lengths. Free verse has been widely used in twentieth-century poetry.

**GOTHIC** ***Gothic*** is a term used to describe literary works that make extensive use of primitive, medieval, wild, mysterious, or natural elements. Gothic novels often depict horrifying events set in gloomy castles.

**HYPERBOLE** ***Hyperbole*** is a deliberate exaggeration or overstatement.

**IMAGE** An ***image*** is a word or phrase that appeals to one or more of the senses—sight, hearing, touch, taste, or smell.

**IMAGERY** ***Imagery*** is the descriptive language used in literature to recreate sensory experiences. Imagery enriches writing by making it more vivid, setting a tone, suggesting emotions, and guiding readers' reactions.

**IRONY** ***Irony*** is the general name given to literary techniques that involve surprising, interesting, or amusing contradictions. In ***verbal irony,*** words are used to suggest the opposite of their usual meaning. In ***dramatic irony,*** there is a contradiction between what a character thinks and what the reader or audience knows to be true. In ***irony of situation,*** an event occurs that directly contradicts expectations.

**LYRIC POEM** A ***lyric poem*** is a poem expressing the observations and feelings of a single speaker. Unlike a narrative poem, it presents an experience or a single effect, but it does not tell a full story. Types of lyric poems include the elegy, the ode, and the sonnet.

**METAPHOR** A ***metaphor*** is a figure of speech in which one thing is spoken of as though it were something else, as in "death, that long sleep." Through this identification of dissimilar things, a comparison is suggested or implied.

An ***extended metaphor*** is developed at length and involves several points of comparison. A mixed metaphor occurs when two metaphors are jumbled together, as in "The thorns of life rained down on him."

A ***dead metaphor*** is one that has been so overused that its original metaphorical impact has been lost. Examples of dead metaphors include "the foot of the bed" and "toe the line."

**METAPHYSICAL POETRY** The term ***metaphysical poetry*** describes the works of such seventeenth-century English poets as Richard Crashaw, John Donne, George Herbert, and Andrew Marvell. Characteristic features of metaphysical poetry include intellectual playfulness, argument, paradoxes, irony, elaborate and unusual conceits, incongruity, and the rhythms of ordinary speech.

**METER** ***Meter*** is the rhythmical pattern of a poem. This pattern is determined by the number and types of stresses, or beats, in each line. To describe the meter of a poem, you must scan its lines. Scanning involves marking the stressed and unstressed syllables, as follows:

Í wĕen | thát, whĕn | thĕ gráve's | dărk wáll
Dĭd fírst | hĕr fórm | rĕtáin,
Thĕy thóught | thĕir héarts | cóuld nĕ'er | rĕcáll
Thĕ líght | ŏf jóy | ăgáin.

—Emily Brontë, "Song"

As you can see, each stressed syllable is marked with a slanted line (´) and each unstressed syllable with a horseshoe symbol (˘). The stresses are then divided by vertical lines into groups called *feet*. The following types of feet are common in English poetry:

1. ***Iamb:*** a foot with one unstressed syllable followed by one stressed syllable, as in the word *afraid*
2. ***Trochee:*** a foot with one stressed syllable followed by one unstressed syllable, as in the word *heather*
3. ***Anapest:*** a foot with two unstressed syllables followed by one stressed syllable, as in the word *disembark*
4. ***Dactyl:*** a foot with one stressed syllable followed by two unstressed syllables, as in the word *solitude*
5. ***Spondee:*** a foot with two stressed syllables, as in the word *workday*
6. ***Pyrrhic:*** a foot with two unstressed syllables, as in the last foot of the word *unspeak | ably*
7. ***Amphibrach:*** a foot with an unstressed syllable, one stressed syllable, and another unstressed syllable, as in the word *another*
8. ***Amphimacer:*** a foot with a stressed syllable, one unstressed syllable, and another stressed syllable, as in "up and down"

A line of poetry is described as ***iambic, trochaic, anapestic,*** or ***dactylic*** according to the kind of foot that appears most often in the line. Lines are also described in terms of the number of feet that occur in them, as follows:

1. ***Monometer:*** verse written in one-foot lines:

   Sound the Flute!
   Now it's mute.
   Birds delight
   Day and Night.
   —William Blake, "Spring"

2. ***Dimeter:*** verse written in two-foot lines:

   O Rose | thou art sick.
   The invis | ible worm.
   That flies | in the night
   In the how | ling storm:
   Has found | out thy bed
   Of crim | son joy : . . .
   —William Blake, "The Sick Rose"

3. ***Trimeter:*** verse written in three-foot lines:

   I went | to the Gard | en of Love
   And saw | what I nev | er had seen:
   A Chap | el was built | in the midst,
   Where I used | to play | on the green.
   —William Blake, "The Garden of Love"

4. ***Tetrameter:*** verse written in four-foot lines:

   I wand |er thro' | each chart | er'd street
   Near where | the chart | er'd Thames | does flow
   And mark | in ev | ery face | I meet
   Marks of | weakness, | marks of | woe.
   —William Blake, "London"

A six-foot line is called a ***hexameter.*** A line with seven feet is a ***heptameter.***

A complete description of the meter of a line tells both how many feet there are in the line and what kind of foot is most common. Thus, the stanza from Emily Brontë's poem, quoted at the beginning of this entry, would be described as being made up of alternating iambic tetrameter and iambic trimeter lines. Poetry that does not have a regular meter is called ***free verse.***

**MODERNISM** ***Modernism*** describes an international movement in the arts during the early twentieth century. Modernists rejected old forms and experimented with the new. Literary Modernists—such as James Joyce, W. B. Yeats, and T. S. Eliot—used images as symbols. They presented human experiences in fragments, rather than as a coherent whole, which led to new experiments in the forms of poetry and fiction.

**MONOLOGUE** A ***monologue*** is a speech or performance given entirely by one person or by one character.

**NARRATION** ***Narration*** is writing that tells a story. The act of telling a story is also called *narration*. The ***narrative,*** or story, is told by a character or speaker called the ***narrator.*** Biographies, autobiographies, journals, reports, novels, short stories, plays, narrative poems, anecdotes, fables, parables, myths, legends, folk tales, ballads, and epic poems are all narratives, or types of narration.

**NARRATIVE POEM** A ***narrative poem*** is a poem that tells a story in verse. Three traditional types of narrative poems include ballads, epics, and metrical romances.

**NONFICTION** ***Nonfiction*** is prose writing that presents and explains ideas or tells about real places, objects or events. To be classified as nonfiction, a work must be true.

**NONLINEAR STRUCTURES** A ***nonlinear structure*** does not follow chronological order. It may contain flashbacks, dream sequences, or other devices that interrupt the chronological flow of events.

**NOVEL** A ***novel*** is an extended work of fiction that often has a complicated plot, many major and minor characters, a unifying theme, and several settings. Novels can be grouped in many ways, based on the historical periods in which they are written (such as Victorian), on the subjects and themes that they treat (such as Gothic or regional), on the techniques used in them (such as stream of consciousness), or on their part in literary movements (such as Naturalism or Realism).

A ***novella*** is not as long as a novel but is longer than a short story.

**ODE** An ***ode*** is a long, formal lyric poem with a serious theme. It may have a traditional structure with stanzas grouped in threes, called the ***strophe,*** the ***antistrophe,*** and the ***epode.*** Odes often honor people, commemorate events, or respond to natural scenes.

**ORAL TRADITION** ***Oral tradition*** is the body of songs, stories, and poems preserved by being passed from generation to generation by word of mouth. Folk epics, ballads, myths, legends, folk tales, folk songs, proverbs, and nursery rhymes are all products of the oral tradition.

**OXYMORON** An ***oxymoron*** is a figure of speech that fuses two contradictory ideas, such as "freezing fire" or "happy grief," thus suggesting a paradox in just a few words.

**PARADOX** A ***paradox*** is a statement that seems to be contradictory but that actually presents a truth. In Shakespeare's *Hamlet*, for example, Hamlet's line "I must be cruel to be kind" is a paradox.

Because a paradox is surprising, or even shocking, it draws the reader's attention to what is being said.

**PARALLELISM** ***Parallelism*** is the presentation of similar ideas, in sequence, using the same grammatical structure.

**PERIPHRASIS** ***Periphrasis*** is a literary device in which writers use descriptive and inventive substitutes to make simple names and terms more colorful and imaginative.

**PERSONIFICATION** ***Personification*** is a figure of speech in which a nonhuman subject is given human characteristics.

Effective personification of things or ideas makes their qualities seem unified, like the characteristics of a person, and their relationship with the reader seem closer.

**PERSUASION** ***Persuasion*** is writing or speech that attempts to convince a reader to think or act in a particular way. Persuasion is used in advertising, in editorials, in sermons, and in political speeches. An ***argument*** is a logical way of presenting a belief, conclusion, or stance. A good argument is supported with reasoning and evidence.

**PLOT** ***Plot*** is the sequence of events in a literary work. The two primary elements of any plot are characters and a conflict. Most plots can be analyzed into many or all of the following parts:

1. The ***exposition*** introduces the setting, the characters, and the basic situation.
2. The ***inciting incident*** introduces the central conflict and develops the rising action.
3. During the ***development,*** or rising action, the conflict runs its course and usually intensifies.
4. At the ***climax,*** the conflict reaches a high point of interest or suspense.
5. The ***denouement,*** or ***falling action,*** ties up loose ends that remain after the climax of the conflict.
6. At the ***resolution,*** the story is resolved and an insight is revealed.

There are many variations on the standard plot structure. Some stories begin ***in medias res*** ("in the middle of things"), after the inciting incident has already occurred. In some stories, the expository material appears toward the middle, in flashbacks. In many stories, there is no denouement. Occasionally, the conflict is left unresolved.

**POETRY** ***Poetry*** is one of the three major types, or genres, of literature, the others being prose and drama. Poetry defies simple definition because there is no single characteristic that is found in all poems and not found in all nonpoems.

Often, poems are divided into lines and stanzas. Poems such as sonnets, odes, villanelles, and sestinas are governed by rules regarding the number of lines, the number and placement of stressed syllables in each line, and the rhyme scheme. In the case of villanelles and sestinas, the repetition of words at the ends of lines or of entire lines is required. Most poems make use of highly concise, musical, and emotionally charged language. Many also use imagery, figurative language, and devices of sound, like rhyme.

Types of poetry include ***narrative poetry*** (ballads, epics, and metrical romances); ***dramatic poetry*** (dramatic monologues and dramatic dialogues); ***lyrics*** (sonnets, odes, elegies, and love poems); and ***concrete poetry*** (a poem presented on the page in a shape that suggests its subject).

**POINT OF VIEW** The perspective, or vantage point, from which a story is told is its ***point of view.*** If a character within the story narrates, then it is told from the ***first-person point of view.*** If a voice from outside the story tells it, then the story is told from the ***third-person point of view.*** If the knowledge of the storyteller is limited to the internal states of one character, then the storyteller has a ***limited point of view.*** If the storyteller's knowledge extends to the internal states of all the characters, then the storyteller has an ***omniscient point of view.***

**PROSE** ***Prose*** is the ordinary form of written language and one of the three major types of literature. Most writing that is not poetry, drama, or song is considered prose. Prose occurs in two major forms: fiction and nonfiction.

**REALISM** ***Realism*** is the presentation in art of details from actual life. During the last part of the nineteenth century and the first part of the twentieth, Realism enjoyed considerable popularity among writers in the English-speaking world. Novels often dealt with grim social realities and presented realistic portrayals of the psychological states of characters.

**RHETORICAL DEVICES** ***Rhetorical devices*** are special patterns of words and ideas that create emphasis and stir emotion, especially in speeches or other oral presentations. ***Parallelism,*** for example, is the repetition of a grammatical structure in order to create a rhythm and make words more memorable. Other common rhetorical devices include: ***analogy,*** drawing comparisons between two unlike things, ***charged language,*** words that appeal to the emotions, ***concession,*** an acknowledgement of the opposition's argument, ***humor,*** using language and details that make characters or situations funny, ***paradox,*** a statement that seems to contradict but presents a truth, ***restatement,*** expressing the same idea in different words, ***rhetorical questions,*** questions with obvious answers, and ***tone,*** the author's attitude toward the audience.

**RHYME** ***Rhyme*** is the repetition of sounds at the ends of words. ***End rhyme*** occurs when rhyming words appear at the ends of lines. ***Internal rhyme*** occurs when rhyming words fall within a line. ***Exact rhyme*** is the use of identical rhyming sounds, as in *love* and *dove*. ***Approximate,*** or ***slant, rhyme*** is the use of sounds that are similar but not identical, as in *prove* and *glove*.

**ROMANTICISM** ***Romanticism*** was a literary and artistic movement of the eighteenth and nineteenth centuries. In reaction to Neoclassicism, the Romantics emphasized imagination, fancy, freedom, emotion, wildness, the beauty of the untamed natural world, the rights of the individual, the nobility of the common man, and the attractiveness of pastoral life. Important figures in the Romantic Movement included William Wordsworth, Samuel Taylor Coleridge, Percy Bysshe Shelley, John Keats, and George Gordon, Lord Byron.

**SATIRE** ***Satire*** is writing that ridicules or holds up to contempt the faults of individuals or groups. Satires include Jonathan Swift's prose work *Gulliver's Travels* and Alexander Pope's poem "The Rape of the Lock." Although a satire is often humorous, its purpose is not simply to make readers laugh but also to correct the flaws and shortcomings that it points out.

**SENSORY LANGUAGE** ***Sensory language*** is writing or speech that appeals to one or more of the five senses.

**SETTING** The ***setting*** is the time and place of the action of a literary work. A setting can provide a backdrop for the action. It can be the force that the protagonist strugles against, and thus the source of the central conflict. It can also be used to create an atmosphere. In many works, the setting symbolizes a point that the author wishes to emphasize.

**SHORT STORY** A ***short story*** is a brief work of fiction. The short story resembles the longer novel, but it generally has a simpler plot and setting. In addition, a short story tends to reveal character at a crucial moment, rather than to develop it through many incidents.

**SIMILE** A ***simile*** is a figure of speech that compares two apparently dissimilar things using *like* or *as*.

By comparing apparently dissimilar things, the writer of a simile surprises the reader into an appreciation of the hidden similarities of the things being compared.

**SOCIAL COMMENTARY** ***Social commentary*** is writing that offers insight into society, its values, and its customs.

**SOLILOQUY** A ***soliloquy*** is a long speech in a play or in a prose work made by a character who is alone, and thus reveals private thoughts and feelings to the audience or reader.

**SONNET** A sonnet is a fourteen-line lyric poem with a single theme. Sonnets are usually written in iambic pentameter. The ***Petrarchan,*** or ***Italian sonnet,*** is divided into two parts, an eight-line octave and a six-line sestet. The octave rhymes ***abba abba,*** while the sestet generally rhymes ***cde cde*** or uses some combination of ***cd*** rhymes. The octave raises a question, states a problem, or presents a brief narrative, and the sestet answers the question, solves the problem, or comments on the narrative.

The ***Shakespearean,*** or ***English, sonnet*** has three four-line quatrains plus a concluding two-line couplet. The rhyme scheme of such a sonnet is usually ***abab cdcd efef gg.*** Each of the three quatrains usually explores a different variation of the main theme. Then, the couplet presents a summarizing or concluding statement.

The ***Spenserian*** sonnet has three quatrains and a couplet, but the quatrains are joined by linking rhymes like those of an Italian sonnet. The rhyme scheme of this type of sonnet is ***abab bcbc cdcd ee.***

**SOUND DEVICES** ***Sound devices*** are groups of words that have particular sound relationships to one another. Types of sound devices include ***alliteration, consonance,*** and ***assonance.***

**SPEAKER** The ***speaker*** is the imaginary voice assumed by the writer of a poem; the character who "says" the poem. For example, the title of William Blake's poem "The Chimney Sweeper" identifies the speaker, a child who gives an account of his life. This character is often not identified by name but may be identified otherwise.

Recognizing the speaker and thinking about his or her characteristics are often central to interpreting a lyric poem. For example, the title of William Blake's poem "The Chimney Sweeper" identifies the speaker, a child who gives an account of his life. In this poem the speaker's acceptance of his oppressive life is offered for the reader's evaluation.

**STANZA** A ***stanza*** is a group of lines in a poem, which is seen as a unit. Many poems are divided into stanzas that are separated by spaces. Stanzas often function like paragraphs in prose. Each stanza states and develops one main idea.

Stanzas are commonly named according to the number of lines found in them, as follows:

1. ***Couplet:*** a two-line stanza
2. ***Tercet:*** a three-line stanza
3. ***Quatrain:*** a four-line stanza
4. ***Cinquain:*** a five-line stanza
5. ***Sestet:*** a six-line stanza
6. ***Heptastich:*** a seven-line stanza
7. ***Octave:*** an eight-line stanza

**STREAM OF CONSCIOUSNESS** ***Stream of consciousness*** is a narrative technique that presents thoughts as if they were coming directly from a character's mind. Instead of being arranged in chronological order, the events are presented from the character's point of view, mixed in with the character's thoughts just as they might spontaneously occur.

**STYLE** ***Style*** is a writer's typical way of writing. Determinants of a writer's style include formality, use of figurative language, use of rhythm, typical grammatical patterns, typical sentence lengths, and typical methods of organization.

**SYMBOL** A ***symbol*** is a sign, word, phrase, image, or other object that stands for or represents something else. Thus, a flag can symbolize a country, a spoken word can symbolize an object, a fine car can symbolize wealth, and so on. In literary criticism, a distinction is often made between traditional or conventional symbols—those that are part of our general cultural inheritance—and ***personal symbols***—those that are created by particular authors for use in particular works.

Conventional symbolism is often based on elements of nature. For example, youth is often symbolized by greenery or springtime, middle age by summer, and old age by autumn or winter. Conventional symbols are also borrowed from religion and politics. For example, a cross may be a symbol of Christianity, or the color red may be a symbol of Marxist ideology.

**SYNECDOCHE** ***Synecdoche*** is a figure of speech in which a part of something is used to stand for the whole.

**SYNTAX** ***Syntax*** is the way words are organized—for example, their order is a sentence or phrase.

**THEME** ***Theme*** is the central idea, concern, or purpose in a literary work. In an essay, the theme might be directly stated in what is known as a thesis statement. In a serious literary work, the theme is usually expressed indirectly rather than directly. A light work, one written strictly for entertainment, may not have a theme.

**TONE** ***Tone*** is the writer's attitude toward the reader and toward the subject. It may be formal or informal, friendly or distant, personal or pompous.

**TRAGEDY** ***Tragedy*** is a type of drama or literature that shows the downfall or destruction of a noble or outstanding person, traditionally one who possesses a character weakness called a ***tragic flaw.*** Macbeth, for example, is a brave and noble figure led astray by ambition. The ***tragic hero*** is caught up in a sequence of events that inevitably results in disaster. Because the protagonist is neither a wicked villain nor an innocent victim, the audience reacts with mixed emotions—both pity and fear, according to the Greek philosopher Aristotle, who defined tragedy in the *Poetics*. The outcome of a tragedy, in which the protagonist is isolated from society, contrasts with the happy resolution of a comedy, in which the protagonist makes peace with society.

**UNDERSTATEMENT** In an ***understatement***, the literal meaning of the statement falls short of what is meant.

**UNIVERSAL THEME** A ***universal theme*** is a message that is expressed regularly in the literature of many different cultures and time periods.

**VOICE** The ***voice*** of a writer is his or her "sound" on the page. It is based on elements such as word choice, sound devices, pace, and attitude.

# MANUAL DE TÉRMINOS LITERARIOS

**ALITERACIÓN** La ***aliteración*** es la repetición de los sonidos consonantes iniciales de las sílabas acentuadas.

**Ejemplo:** el **r**uido con que **r**ueda la **r**onca tempestad

La aliteración se usa para dar énfasis y asociar palabras, así como para crear efectos de musicalidad.

**ALUSIÓN** Una ***alusión*** es una referencia a una persona, lugar, hecho, obra literaria u obra de arte muy conocida.

**AMPLIFICACIÓN** La ***amplificación*** es un recurso estilístico en el cual el autor expande una idea, la profundiza y detalla, por medio de la repetición o la elaboración.

**ANALOGÍA** Una ***analogía*** es una comparación entre relaciones. Se basa en la idea o concepción de que la relación entre un par de cosas es semejante a la relación entre otro par de cosas. A diferencia de la metáfora—otra forma de comparación—una analogía presenta la comparación explícitamente, a menudo utilizando las expresiones *como* o *tal como.*

**ANÁFORA** La ***anáfora*** es una figura retórica que conlleva la repetición deliberada de la misma secuencia de palabras al comienzo de frases, cláusulas u oraciones cercanas.

**POESÍA ANGLOSAJONA** Se llama ***poesía anglosajona*** a la poesía rítmica compuesta en inglés antiguo antes del siglo XII. Por lo general consiste en versos de cuatro sílabas acentuadas y un número indefinido de sílabas no acentuadas. Cada verso está dividido en dos por una *cesura,* o pausa, y las mitades están unidas por la aliteración de dos o tres de las sílabas acentuadas. La poesía anglosajona se cantaba o recitaba con el acompañamiento de un arpa primitiva. No se escribía, sino que se transmitía oralmente.

**APÓSTROFE** El ***apóstrofe*** es una figura retórica en la que el hablante se dirige directamente a una persona ausente o a una idea, objeto o cualidad personificada.

**ARQUETIPO** Un ***arquetipo*** es un patrón que se encuentra en las obras literarias de distintas épocas y lugares. Para más información ver *Elementos literarios arquetípicos.*

**DICCIÓN ARCAICA** La ***dicción arcaica*** se refiere a las palabras y frases que eran de uso estándar en otra época, pero que ya no son comunes.

**ELEMENTOS LITERARIOS ARQUETÍPICOS** Los ***elementos literarios arquetípicos*** son patrones que se encuentran en la literatura de todas las latitudes del mundo. Por ejemplo, la ocurrencia de sucesos en secuencias de a tres es un elemento arquetípico de los cuentos de hadas. Algunos personajes, tales como el guía misterioso, también son elementos arquetípicos de los relatos tradicionales. Según algunos críticos, estos elementos expresan de manera simbólica ciertas verdades sobre la mentalidad humana.

**ARGUMENTO** Un ***argumento*** es un escrito o discurso que trata de convencer al lector para que piense o actúe de cierta manera. Un argumento es una manera lógica de presentar una creencia, una conclusión o una postura. Un buen argumento se respalda con razonamientos y pruebas.

**ASONANCIA** La ***asonancia*** es la repetición de los sonidos vocálicos de sílabas acentuadas con distintas consonantes, como en este verso del poema "Andrea del Sarto" de Robert Browning en el que se repite el sonido largo de la *e* inglesa:
Ah, but man's r**ea**ch should exc**ee**d his grasp.

**VERSO BLANCO** El ***verso blanco*** es poesía escrita por lo general en pentámetros yámbicos sin rima (ver Metro). En el verso blanco a veces se introducen variaciones rítmicas para enfatizar, o para lograr una mayor variedad y naturalidad sonora. Como el verso blanco suena de manera muy parecida al inglés que se habla normalmente, suele usarse en obras dramáticas, como lo hizo Shakespeare, y en poesía.

**CARPE DIEM** La expresión latina ***carpe diem*** significa "vive el día" o "aprovecha el momento", pues la vida es fugaz. Muchas grandes obras literarias tienen por tema el *carpe diem*.

**PERSONAJE** Un ***personaje*** es una persona o animal que participa de la acción en una obra literaria. Los personajes pueden clasificarse de distinta manera. A los personajes que representan un papel importante se los llama ***personajes principales***. A los personajes que no representan papeles importantes se los llama ***personajes secundarios***. Un personaje que representa el papel central de una historia recibe el nombre de ***protagonista***. Un personaje que se opone al protagonista recibe el nombre de ***antagonista***. Un ***personaje chato o plano*** muestra solo unos pocos rasgos. Un personaje que cambia es un ***personaje dinámico***. Un personaje que no cambia es un ***personaje estático***.

**CARACTERIZACIÓN** La ***caracterización*** es el acto de crear y desarrollar un personaje. En una ***caracterización directa***, el autor presenta explícitamente las características de un personaje. Los autores también puede recurrir a una ***caracterización indirecta***. Las características de un personaje se puede revelar indirectamente a través de lo que el personaje dice o hace; a través de la descripción de su apariencia física; o a través de las afirmaciones, pensamientos y acciones de otros personajes.

**CLÍMAX** El ***clímax*** de una obra literaria es el punto de mayor interés o suspenso. Con frecuencia, el clímax coincide con el momento crítico de la trama, el punto en el que cambia la situación o la percepción del protagonista. A veces, el clímax coincide con el ***desenlace***, el momento en el que termina o se resuelve el conflicto central.

**ALIVIO CÓMICO** Los autores de tragedias suelen crear uno o dos personajes o escenas cómicas para relajar el tono tenso de la obra. Estos personajes o escenas dotan de ***alivio cómico*** a una producción que está, por lo demás, llena de suspenso.

**COMPRESIÓN** La ***compresión*** consiste en juntar varias ideas o imágenes distintas, con el fin de crear una mayor densidad y complejidad de sentido.

**CONCEPTO** Como recurso literario, el ***concepto*** es una comparación extraña y sorprendente entre dos cosas muy distintas. Este tipo especial de metáfora o de analogía compleja a menudo constituye la base de todo un poema. Durante la época isabelina, los sonetos solían incluir el tipo de concepto llamado "petrarquista". El ***concepto petrarquista*** expresa algo extravagante o extremo sobre la belleza de la amada o sobre el sufrimiento del hablante, a través de comparaciones con seres divinos, fuerzas naturales poderosas u objetos que poseen en el más alto grado alguna cualidad determinada. Los poetas ***metafísicos*** del siglo XVII usaban conceptos altamente elaborados, extraños e intelectuales.

**CONFLICTO** Un ***conflicto*** es una lucha entre fuerzas opuestas. A veces, esta lucha es interna, es decir, que se da en la interioridad de un personaje. Otras veces, la lucha es externa, es decir, entre el personaje y alguna fuerza exterior. La fuerza exterior puede ser otro personaje, la naturaleza o algún elemento de la sociedad, tal como una costumbre o una institución política. A menudo, en una misma obra se combinan varios conflictos de distinto tipo.

**CONNOTACIÓN** La ***connotación*** de una palabra es el conjunto de ideas que se asocian a ella, además del significado que da el diccionario. Por ejemplo, las palabras *hogar* y *domicilio* tienen, según el diccionario, el mismo significado. Sin embargo, la primera tiene connotaciones positivas de calidez y seguridad, mientras que la segunda no.

**CONSONANCIA** La ***consonancia*** es la repetición de los sonidos consonantes finales de sílabas acentuadas con distintos sonidos vocálicos, como en este fragmento de la balada "The Rime of the Ancient Mariner" de Coleridge:
a frightful fie**nd** / Doth close behi**nd** him tread.

**PAREADO** Un ***dístico*** o ***pareado*** es un par de versos rimados escritos en el mismo metro. Un ***dístico heroico*** es un par de pentámetros yámbicos rimados. En un ***dístico cerrado,*** el significado y la sintaxis se completan en esos dos versos, como en este ejemplo de "Essay on Criticism" de Alexander Pope:

True ease in writing comes from art, not chance,
As those move easiest who have learned to dance.

Los sonetos shakesperianos suelen terminar con dísticos heroicos.

**TEMA CULTURALMENTE ESPECÍFICO** Un ***tema culturalmente específico*** es aquel que se relaciona de manera significativa con determinadas culturas.

**DENOTACIÓN** La ***denotación*** de una palabra es su significado objetivo —es decir, aquello a lo que la palabra se refiere—, independientemente de las otras asociaciones que la palabra pueda suscitar. Los diccionarios dan los significados denotativos de las palabras.

**DIALECTO** El ***dialecto*** es la forma de un lenguaje hablado por la gente en una región o por un grupo particular. Los dialectos difieren entre sí en la gramática, el vocabulario y la pronunciación.

**DIÁLOGO** Un ***diálogo*** es una conversación entre personajes. Los escritores usan el diálogo para revelar las características de los personajes, para presentar sucesos, para dar variedad al relato y para despertar el interés de los lectores. En un relato, el diálogo por lo general se presenta entre comillas o en párrafos. En un guión u obra de teatro, el diálogo por lo general sigue al nombre de los interlocutores.

**DIARIO** Un ***diario*** es un registro personal de hechos cotidianos, y se suele escribir en prosa. La mayoría de los diarios no se escriben para ser publicados; a veces, sin embargo, los diarios particularmente interesantes o escritos por personas reconocidas, sí se publican.

**DICCIÓN** La ***dicción*** es la elección de palabras que hace el autor. Puede ser uno de los elementos más determinantes del estilo. La dicción puede describirse como formal o informal, abstracta o concreta, llana o elaborada, común o técnica.

**DRAMA** Un ***drama*** es una historia escrita para ser representada por actores. Puede consistir en una o más secciones de cierta extensión, llamadas actos, formadas a su vez por cierto número de secciones más pequeñas, llamadas escenas.

El drama se originó en los rituales religiosos y en las reconstrucciones simbólicas de los pueblos primitivos. Los habitantes de la antigua Grecia, que desarrollaron el drama hasta transformarlo en una sofisticada forma artística crearon géneros dramáticos tales como la tragedia y la comedia.

Los primeros dramas que se representaron en Inglaterra fueron los misterios y moralidades medievales. Los misterios eran dramas que representaban pasajes bíblicos. Las moralidades, como la titulada *Everyman*, eran alegorías en las que los personajes eran personificaciones de vicios y virtudes. El Renacimiento inglés fue testigo de un florecimiento del drama que culminó en las obras de William Shakespeare, quien escribió muchas de las comedias, tragedias, cuentos y poemas más celebrados del mundo. Durante el Neoclasicismo, el drama inglés privilegió las sátiras de costumbres, especialmente de las clases más acomodadas de la sociedad. Durante el Romanticismo y la época victoriana se escribieron algunos dramas en verso de real valor, como *Los Cenci* y *Prometeo liberado*, de Percy Bysshe Shelley. El final del siglo XIX y el principio del XX vio un resurgimiento del drama, tanto en Inglaterra como en todo el mundo anglohablante. Entre los grandes dramas de la modernidad se encuentran los de Bernard Shaw, Christopher Fry, T.S. Eliot, Harold Pinter y Samuel Beckett.

**MONÓLOGO DRAMÁTICO** Un ***monólogo dramático*** es un poema en el cual un personaje imaginario le habla a otro que lo escucha en silencio.

**ENCABALGAMIENTO** El ***encabalgamiento*** es una estructura poética en la que tanto la estructura gramatical como el sentido continúa de un verso al siguiente.

**POEMA ÉPICO** Un ***poema épico*** es un poema narrativo extenso sobre las aventuras de dioses o de un ***héroe épico***.

Las ***convenciones de la épica*** son las características tradicionales de los poemas épicos, tales como un enunciado inicial presentando el tema; la apelación (o "invocación") a un ser sobrenatural para ayudar al poeta a relatar los hechos; un comienzo ***in medias res*** (en latín: "en la mitad de las cosas"); los catálogos de pueblos y de cosas; el relato de hechos pasados; y las frases descriptivas.

**EPIGRAMA** Un ***epigrama*** es un enunciado breve en prosa o en verso. El pareado final de un soneto inglés bien puede ser epigramático. Un ensayo también puede estar escrito en un estilo epigramático.

**EPIFANÍA** Una ***epifanía*** es una revelación repentina o un súbito entendimiento mediante el cual un personaje reconoce la verdad.

**EPITAFIO** Un ***epitafio*** es una inscripción grabada en una tumba o lugar funerario. En la literatura, los epitafios pueden ser unas líneas serias o humorísticas que se pretende que tendrán esa función, como es el caso del epitafio incluido en la elegía de Thomas Grey.

**ENSAYO** Un ***ensayo*** es una obra breve de no-ficción sobre un tema en particular. Los ensayos pueden clasificarse en formales e informales, y personales o impersonales. También pueden clasificarse según su propósito, como por ejemplo: de causa y efecto, satírico o reflexivo. Otra manera de clasificar los ensayos es por el tipo de discurso; así, un ensayo puede ser explicativo, descriptivo, persuasivo o narrativo.

**ENSAYO EXPLICATIVO** Un ***ensayo explicativo*** ofrece detalles sobre un proceso o concepto.

**FICCIÓN** Una obra de ***ficción*** es un escrito en prosa que cuenta algo sobre personajes y hechos imaginarios. Algunos escritores basan sus relatos de ficción en hechos reales, mientras que otros parten exclusivamente de su imaginación.

**LENGUAJE FIGURADO** El ***lenguaje figurado*** es un escrito o discurso que no se debe interpretar literalmente. Los poetas y otros escritores usan el lenguaje figurado para representar algo de manera más vívida, para hacer que sus escritos resulten emocionalmente intensos y concentrados, y para expresar sus ideas de maneras nuevas y poco habituales. Entre las figuras retóricas que conforman el lenguaje figurado están la hipérbole, la ironía, la metáfora, la metonimia, el oxímoron, la paradoja, la personificación, el símil y la sinécdoque.

Ver también las entradas sobre algunas figuras retóricas en particular.

**FOLKLORE** Los relatos, leyendas, mitos, baladas, adivinanzas, dichos y otros géneros propios de la tradición oral constituyen el ***folklore***. Algunas de esas obras fueron compuestas por personas analfabetas o semianalfabetas. El folklore influye de distintas maneras en la literatura escrita.

**PIE** Un ***pie*** es la unidad básica de la métrica, y se compone de un grupo de una o más sílabas, ya sean acentuadas o no acentuadas.

**VERSO LIBRE** El ***verso libre*** es una forma poética en la que no se sigue un patrón regular de metro ni de rima. En vez de tener pies y versos, el verso libre tiene el ritmo que corresponde a su sentido y que recurre a los sonidos del lenguaje hablado en versos de distinta extensión. El verso libre ha sido ampliamente cultivado en la poesía del siglo XX.

**GÓTICO** Se llama ***gótico*** al estilo literario que hace un uso constante de elementos primitivos, medievales, salvajes, misteriosos o naturales. La novela gótica a menudo describe hechos horripilantes que tienen lugar en castillos tenebrosos.

**HIPÉRBOLE** Una ***hipérbole*** es una exageración o magnificación deliberada.

**IMAGEN** Una ***imagen*** es una palabra o frase que apela a uno o más sentidos; es decir, a la vista, el oído, el tacto, el gusto o el olfato.

**IMÁGENES** Se llama ***imágenes*** al lenguaje descriptivo que se usa en la literatura para recrear experiencias sensoriales. Las imágenes enriquecen la escritura al hacerla más vívida, sentar el tono, sugerir emociones y guiar las reacciones de los lectores.

**IRONÍA** ***Ironía*** es un término general para distintas técnicas literarias que implican contradicciones sorprendentes, interesantes o divertidas. En una ***ironía verbal***, las palabras se usan para sugerir lo opuesto a su sentido habitual. En la ***ironía dramática*** hay una contradicción entre lo que un personaje piensa y lo que el lector o la audiencia sabe que es verdad. En una ***ironía situacional***, ocurre un suceso que contradice directamente las expectativas.

**POEMA LÍRICO** Un ***poema lírico*** es un poema que expresa los pensamientos, observaciones y sentimientos de un único hablante. A diferencia del poema narrativo, el poema lírico propone una experiencia o un efecto único, sin contar toda la historia. Los poemas líricos pueden ser de distintos tipos, tales como la elegía, la oda y el soneto.

**METÁFORA** Una ***metáfora*** es una figura literaria en la que se habla de algo como si fuera otra cosa, como por ejemplo en "la muerte, ese largo sueño". A través de la identificación de cosas disímiles, se sugiere o implica una comparación.

Una ***metáfora extendida*** se desarrolla extensamente y los puntos que se comparan son varios. Una ***metáfora mixta*** ocurre cuando dos metáforas se unen, como en "le llovieron encima las espinas de la vida". Una ***metáfora muerta*** es una metáfora que ya se ha utilizado demasiado, por lo que su impacto metafórico ha desaparecido. Es el caso de metáforas como "el pie de la cama" o "los dientes del tenedor".

**POESÍA METAFÍSICA** El término ***poesía metafísica*** describe las obras de poetas ingleses del siglo XVII tales como Richard Crashaw, John Donne, George Herbert y Andrew Marvell. Los rasgos más característicos de la poesía metafísica son: el juego intelectual, la argumentación, las paradojas y los ritmos del habla cotidiana.

**METRO** El ***metro*** de un poema es el patrón rítmico que sigue. Este patrón está determinado por el número y tipo de sílabas acentuadas en cada verso. Para describir el metro de un poema hay que escandir los versos. Escandir significa marcar las sílabas acentuadas y no acentuadas.

Í wĕen | thát, whĕn | thé grăve's | dárk wăll
Dĭd fírst | hĕr fórm | rĕtaín,
Thĕy thóught | thĕir heárts | cŏuld ne'ér | rĕcáll
Thĕ líght | ŏf jóy | ăgaín.

—Emily Brontë, "Song"

Como puedes ver, cada sílaba acentuada se marca con un (´), y cada sílaba no acentuada se marca con un (˘). Las sílabas acentuadas e inacentuadas se dividen luego con líneas verticales (|) en grupos llamados *pies*. En la poesía en inglés algunos de los pies más frecuentes son:

1. el ***yambo***: un pie con una sílaba no acentuada seguida por una sílaba acentuada, como en la palabra *afraid*.
2. el ***troqueo***: un pie con una sílaba acentuada seguida por una sílaba no acentuada, como en la palabra *heather*.
3. el ***anapesto***: un pie con dos sílabas no acentuadas seguidas por un acento fuerte, como en la palabra *disembark*.
4. el ***dáctilo***: un pie con un acento fuerte seguido por dos sílabas no acentuadas, como en la palabra *solitude*.
5. el ***espondeo***: un pie con dos acentos fuertes, como en la palabra *workday*.

6. el ***pírrico***: un pie con dos sílabas no acentuadas, como las del último pie de la palabra *unspeak | ably.*

7. el ***anfíbraco***: un pie con una sílaba no acentuada, una sílaba acentuada y otra inacentuada, como en la palabra *another.*

8. el ***anfímacro***: un pie con una sílaba acentuada, una no acentuada y otra acentuada, como en *up and down.*

Según el tipo de pie más frecuente en ellos, los versos de un poema se describen como ***yámbicos, trocaicos, anapésticos*** o ***dactílicos.*** Los versos también se describen según el número de pies que los forman. Por ejemplo:

1. ***monómetro:*** verso de un solo pie

   Soúnd thĕ Flúte!
   Nóẃ ĭt's múte.
   Bírds dĕlíght
   Dáy ănd Níght.
   —William Blake, "Spring"

2. ***dímetro:*** verso de dos pies

   Ŏ Róse | thŏu árt síck.
   Thĕ ĭnvís | ĭblĕ wórm.
   Thăt flíes | ĭn thĕ níght
   Ĭn thĕ hów | lĭng stórm:
   Hăs fóund | óut thy̆ béd
   Ŏf crím | sŏn jóy : . . .
   —William Blake, "The Sick Rose"

3. ***trímetro:*** verso de tres pies

   Ĭ wént | tŏ thĕ Gárd | ĕn ŏf Lóve
   Ănd sáw | whăt Ĭ név | ĕr hăd séen:
   Ă Chăp | eĭ wăs búilt | ĭn thĕ mídst,
   Whĕre Ĭ uséd | tŏ pláy | ŏn thĕ gréen.
   —William Blake, "The Garden of Love"

4. ***tetrámetro:*** verso de cuatro pies

   Ĭ wánd |ĕr thró | eăch chárt | ĕr'd stréet
   Neár whĕre | thĕ chárt | ĕr'd Thámes | dŏes flów
   Ănd márk | ĭn év | ĕry̆ fáce | Ĭ méet
   Márks ŏf | wéaknĕss, | márks ŏf | wóe.
   —William Blake, "London"

Un verso de seis pies es un ***hexámetro.*** Un verso de siete pies es un ***heptámetro.***

La descripción completa del metro de un verso incluye el número de pies en cada verso y qué tipo de pie prevalece. Por lo tanto, la estrofa del poema de Emily Brontë citada al comienzo de esta entrada, debería describirse como formada por tetrámetros yámbicos que alternan con trímetros yámbicos. La poesía que no sigue un metro regular se dice que está escrita en ***verso libre***.

**MODERNISMO NORTEAMERICANO** El ***modernismo norteamericano*** es parte de un movimiento artístico internacional que se desarrolló a principios del siglo XX. Los modernistas rechazaron las formas tradicionales y experimentaron con nuevas formas. Los escritores modernistas, tales como James Joyce, W.B. Yeats y T.S. Eliot, usaron imágenes como símbolos y representaron las experiencias humanas de forma fragmentaria, en vez de como un todo coherente, lo que llevó a nuevos experimentos formales tanto en la poesía como en la ficción.

**MONÓLOGO** Un ***monólogo*** es un discurso o representación a cargo de una sola persona o de un solo personaje.

**NARRACIÓN** Una ***narración*** es un escrito que cuenta una historia. El acto de contar una historia también se llama *narración*. La ***narración***, o historia, es contada por un personaje o hablante llamado ***el narrador***. Las biografías, autobiografías, diarios, informes, novelas, cuentos, obras de teatro, poemas narrativos, anécdotas, fábulas, parábolas, mitos, leyendas, cuentos folklóricos, baladas y poemas épicos son todas obras narrativas de distinto tipo.

**POEMA NARRATIVO** Un ***poema narrativo*** es un poema que cuenta una historia en verso. Hay tres tipos de poemas narrativos tradicionales: las baladas, los poemas épicos y los romances en verso.

**NO-FICCIÓN** La ***no-ficción*** es un escrito en prosa que presenta y explica ideas o cuenta algo acerca de personas, lugares, ideas o hechos reales. Para ser clasificado como no-ficción un escrito debe ser verdadero.

**ESTRUCTURA NO LINEAL** La ***estructura no lineal*** no sigue un orden cronológico. Puede contener escenas retrospectivas (*flashbacks*), sueños u otros recursos que interrumpen la cronología de sucesos.

**NOVELA** Una ***novela*** es una obra extensa de ficción que suele tener una trama complicada, como personajes principales y secundarios, un tema unificador y varias ambientaciones. Las novelas pueden agruparse de distintas maneras, según el período histórico en el que fueron escritas (como la novela victoriana), en los temas que trata (como la novela gótica o la novela regional), en las técnicas que usa (como el fluir de la conciencia), o como parte de un movimiento literario (como el naturalismo o el realismo).

La ***novela corta*** tiene una extensión menor que la novela y mayor que el cuento.

**ODA** Una ***oda*** es un poema lírico extenso sobre un tema grave. Puede tener una estructura tradicional, con estrofas agrupadas de a tres: llamadas ***estrofa***, ***antistrofa*** y ***epodo***. Las odas a menudo son en honor de una persona o conmemoran eventos, o se presentan como respuesta a una escena de la naturaleza.

**TRADICIÓN ORAL** La ***tradición oral*** es el conjunto de canciones, cuentos y poemas que perduran en la memoria de un pueblo y que se han transmitido de boca en boca de una generación a otra. La épica, las baladas, los mitos, las leyendas, los cuentos folklóricos, las canciones populares, los proverbios y las canciones de cuna son todos productos de la tradición oral.

**OXÍMORON** Un ***oxímoron*** es una figura retórica que une dos ideas contrarias, como en las frases "el fuego helado" o "la alegre pena", que sugieren una paradoja en unas pocas palabras.

**PARADOJA** Una ***paradoja*** es un enunciado que parece ser contradictorio pero que en realidad presenta una verdad. Por ejemplo, en *Hamlet*, de Shakespeare, el verso "Debo ser cruel para ser rey" es una paradoja. Como la paradoja suele ser sorprendente e incluso chocante, llama la atención del lector hacia lo que se está diciendo.

**PARALELISMO** Un ***paralelismo*** es la presentación en secuencia de ideas similares, usando la misma estructura gramatical.

**PERÍFRASIS** La ***perífrasis*** es un recurso literario en el que los escritores usan sustitutos descriptivos y originales para hacer que algunos nombres y términos resulten más coloridos e imaginativos.

**PERSONIFICACIÓN** La ***personificación*** es una figura retórica en la que se dota a una instancia no humana de rasgos y actitudes humanas. La personificación efectiva de cosas o ideas hace que sus cualidades aparezcan unificadas, como las características de una persona, y que su relación con el lector parezca más cercana.

**PERSUASIÓN** La ***persuasión*** es un recurso escrito u oral por el que se intenta convencer al lector de que piense o actúe de determinada manera. La persuasión se utiliza en la publicidad, en los editoriales, en sermones y en los discursos políticos. Un ***argumento*** es una manera lógica de presentar una creencia, una conclusión o una postura. Un buen argumento se respalda con razones y evidencias.

**TRAMA o ARGUMENTO** La ***trama*** o ***argumento*** es la secuencia de los hechos que se suceden en una obra literaria. Dos elementos claves de la trama son los personajes y el conflicto central. La mayoría de las tramas pueden dividirse en las siguientes partes:

1. La ***exposición*** introduce la ambientación, los personajes y la situación básica.
2. El ***suceso desencadenante*** introduce el conflicto central e inicia el desarrollo.
3. Durante el ***desarrollo***, el conflicto sigue su curso y, por lo general, se intensifica.
4. En el ***clímax***, el conflicto alcanza su punto de tensión o suspenso más alto.
5. En el ***desenlace*** se atan los cabos sueltos que quedan una vez que el conflicto ha llegado al clímax.
6. En la ***resolución,*** se resuelve el conflicto y se revela algún tipo de percepción o idea general.

Hay muchas variaciones posibles de la estructura estándar de la trama. Algunos relatos comienzan ***in medias res*** ("en la mitad de las cosas"), cuando el suceso desencadenante ya ha ocurrido. En algunos relatos, el material expositivo aparece hacia la mitad de la obra, en forma de escenas retrospectivas, o *flashbacks*. En muchos casos, el relato no llega a ningún desenlace. También puede suceder que el conflicto quede sin resolver.

**POESÍA** La ***poesía*** es uno de los tres géneros literarios más importantes. Los otros dos son la prosa y el drama. La poesía no se presta a una definición sencilla porque no hay un solo rasgo que se encuentre en todos los poemas y que a su vez no se encuentre en ningún otro género.

A menudo, los poemas se dividen en versos y estrofas. Los poemas tales como los sonetos, las odas, las villanelles y las sextinas se basan en reglas que determinan el número de versos, el número y ubicación de las sílabas acentuadas de cada verso, y el esquema de rima. En el caso de las villanelles y las sextinas, también se exige la repetición de versos enteros o de palabras al final de ciertos versos. La mayoría de los poemas usan un lenguaje muy conciso, musical y emocionalmente cargado. Muchos también recurren al uso de imágenes, de lenguaje figurado y de recursos sonoros tales como la rima.

Entre los distintos tipos de poesía se pueden mencionar: la ***poesía narrativa*** (las baladas, la poesía épica, los romances en verso); la ***poesía dramática*** (los monólogos y diálogos dramáticos); la ***poesía lírica*** (sonetos, odas, elegías y la poesía amorosa); y la ***poesía concreta*** (un poema que dibuja en la página una forma o figura que coincide o se relaciona con su tema).

**PUNTO DE VISTA** La perspectiva desde el cual se narra una historia es el ***punto de vista.*** Cuando quien cuenta la historia es uno de los personajes, se dice que la historia está narrada desde el ***punto de vista de la primera persona.*** Cuando quien narra la historia es una voz exterior al relato, entonces el relato está escrito desde el ***punto de vista de la tercera persona.*** Si el conocimiento de la voz que narra la historia se limita a los estados interiores de un solo personaje, entonces el narrador tiene un ***punto de vista limitado***. Si el conocimiento del narrador abarca los estados de ánimo de todos los personajes, entonces el narrador tiene un ***punto de vista omnisciente.***

**PROSA** La ***prosa*** es la forma común del lenguaje escrito y uno de los tres tipos de literatura más importantes. La mayoría de los escritos que no son poesía, ni drama, ni canciones, se consideran prosa. La prosa puede ser de dos formas: de ficción y de no-ficción.

**REALISMO** El ***realismo*** es la representación artística de detalles de la vida real. Durante la última parte del siglo XIX y la primera parte del XX, el realismo gozó de una considerable popularidad entre los escritores del mundo anglohablante. Las novelas de esa época a menudo tratan las realidades sociales más tristes y presentan retratos realistas de los estados psicológicos de los personajes.

**FIGURAS RETÓRICAS** Las ***figuras retóricas*** son patrones especiales de palabras e ideas que dan énfasis y producen emoción, especialmente cuando se usan en discursos y otras presentaciones orales. El ***paralelismo***, por ejemplo, es la repetición de una estructura gramatical con el propósito de crear un ritmo y hacer que las palabras resulten más memorables. Otras figuras retóricas muy frecuentes son: la ***analogía***, que establece una comparación entre dos cosas diferentes; el ***lenguaje emocionalmente cargado***, en el que las palabras apelan a las emociones; la ***concesión,*** en la que se reconoce el argumento del oponente; el ***humor,*** en el que se utiliza un tipo de lenguaje y de detalles que hacen que los personajes o las situaciones resulten cómicos; la ***paradoja,*** un enunciado que parece contradecirse, pero que presenta cierta verdad; la ***reafirmación***, en la que se expresa la misma idea con distintas palabras; las ***preguntas retóricas***, que son preguntas cuyas respuestas son obvias; y el ***tono***, es decir, la actitud del autor hacia la audiencia.

**RIMA** La ***rima*** es la repetición de los sonidos finales de las palabras. Se llama ***rima de final de verso*** a la rima entre las palabras finales de dos o más versos. La ***rima interna*** se produce cuando una de las palabras que riman está situada en el interior de un verso. En la ***rima perfecta (o consonante)*** todas las vocales y las consonantes a partir de la vocal acentuada son iguales, como en *love* y *dove*. Se llama ***rima falsa*** o ***aproximada*** a la que se da entre palabras que suenan de modo parecido pero no idéntico, como en *prove* y *glove.*

**ROMANTICISMO** El ***Romanticismo*** fue un movimiento artístico y literario que se desarrolló durante los siglos XVIII y XIX. En reacción al Neoclasicismo, los románticos dieron prioridad a la imaginación, la fantasía, la libertad, la emoción, la vida salvaje, la belleza del mundo natural, los derechos de los individuos, la nobleza del individuo común y los atractivos de la vida campestre. Entre las figuras más importantes del Romanticismo en lengua inglesa podemos nombrar a William Wordsworth, Samuel Taylor Coleridge, Percy Bysshe Shelley, John Keats y George Gordon (Lord Byron).

**SÁTIRA** Una ***sátira*** es una obra literaria que ridiculiza las fallas de ciertos individuos o grupos. La obra en prosa de Jonathan Swift, *Gulliver's Travels*, y el poema de Alexander Pope, "The Rape of the Lock", son algunos ejemplos de sátira. Aunque las sátiras a menudo son humorísticas, su propósito no es simplemente hacer reír a los lectores, sino también corregir los fallos y defectos que critica.

**LENGUAJE SENSORIAL** El ***lenguaje sensorial*** es un escrito o discurso que incluye detalles que apelan a uno o más de los cinco sentidos.

**AMBIENTACIÓN** La ***ambientación*** de una obra literaria es la época y el lugar en el que se desarrolla la acción. La ambientación a veces proporciona el telón de fondo de la acción. Puede ser una fuerza que el protagonista debe enfrentar y, por lo tanto, la fuente del conflicto central. También puede usarse para crear una atmósfera. En muchas obras, la ambientación simboliza algo en lo que el autor quiere hacer hincapié.

**CUENTO** Un ***cuento*** es una obra breve de ficción. El cuento se parece a la novela, que es más extensa, pero por lo general tiene una trama y una ambientación más simples. Además, un cuento tiende a dar cuenta de un personaje en un momento crucial, más que a desarrollarlo a través de muchas peripecias.

**SÍMIL** Un ***símil*** es una figura retórica en la que se usa las palabras *como* o *tal como* para establecer una comparación entre dos cosas aparentemente disímiles. Al comparar cosas aparentemente diferentes, el autor del símil sorprende al lector haciéndole apreciar las ocultas similitudes de las cosas que se están comparando.

**COMENTARIO SOCIAL** El ***comentario social*** es un escrito que presenta alguna apreciación acerca de la sociedad, sus valores y sus costumbres.

**SOLILOQUIO** Un ***soliloquio*** es un largo parlamento en una obra de teatro o escrito en prosa, en el que un personaje, solo en escena, le revela sus pensamientos y sentimientos más íntimos a la audiencia o al lector.

**SONETO** Un ***soneto*** es un poema lírico de catorce versos sobre un solo tema. Por lo general los sonetos están escritos en pentámetros yámbicos. El ***soneto italiano o petrarquista*** se divide en dos partes, una octava (ocho versos) y una sextina (seis versos). La octava rima ***abba abba***, mientras que la sextina por lo general rima ***cde cde,*** o sigue alguna combinación de rimas ***cd.*** La octava propone una pregunta, plantea un problema, o presenta un breve relato, y la sextina responde la pregunta, resuelve el problema o comenta el relato.

El ***soneto inglés o shakesperiano*** consiste en tres cuartetos (estrofas de cuatro versos) y un pareado final (estrofa de dos versos). Por lo general la rima sigue el esquema ***abab cdcd efef gg.*** Cada uno de los cuartetos por lo general explora una variación distinta del mismo tema. Luego el pareado presenta un enunciado que resume o propone una conclusión.

El ***soneto spenseriano*** está compuesto por tres cuartetos y un pareado, pero los cuartetos están unidos por la rima, como los del soneto italiano. El esquema de rima de este tipo de soneto es ***abab bcbc cdcd ee.***

**RECURSOS SONOROS** Los ***recursos sonoros*** son grupos de palabras que se relacionan entre sí por ciertos sonidos. Entre los recursos sonoros se encuentran la ***aliteración,*** la ***consonancia*** y la ***asonancia.***

**HABLANTE** El ***hablante*** es la voz imaginaria que asume el escritor en un poema; es el personaje en cuya boca está el poema. Este personaje por lo general no se identifica con un nombre, pero puede identificarse de alguna otra manera.

Reconocer al hablante y pensar en sus características a menudo resulta crucial para comprender el poema. Por ejemplo, el título del poema de William Blake "The

Chimney Sweeper" identifica al hablante, un niño que cuenta su vida. En este poema la aceptación por parte del hablante del carácter opresivo de su vida se somete a la evaluación del lector.

**ESTROFA** Una ***estrofa*** es un grupo de dos o más versos que forman una unidad. Muchos poemas se dividen en estrofas separadas por espacios. Las estrofas a menudo funcionan como los párrafos en la prosa. Cada estrofa presenta y desarrolla una idea principal.

Las estrofas por lo general reciben su nombre del número de versos que las componen. Por ejemplo:

1. un ***dístico*** o ***pareado*** es una estrofa de dos versos
2. un ***terceto*** es una estrofa de tres versos
3. un ***cuarteto*** o una ***cuarteta*** son estrofas de cuatro versos
4. una ***quintilla*** es una estrofa de cinco versos
5. una ***sextina*** es una estrofa de seis versos
6. una ***séptima*** es una estrofa de siete versos
7. una ***octava*** es una estrofa de ocho versos.

**FLUIR DE LA CONCIENCIA** El ***fluir de la conciencia*** es una técnica narrativa que presenta los pensamientos como si vinieran directamente de la mente del personaje. En vez de presentar los hechos en orden cronológico, se los presenta desde el punto de vista del personaje, juntos con los pensamientos del personaje, exactamente como si se sucedieran espontáneamente.

**ESTILO** El ***estilo*** es la manera particular en que escribe un autor. Los elementos que determinan el estilo son: el lenguaje formal, el uso del lenguaje figurado, el ritmo, los patrones gramaticales más usados, la extensión de las oraciones y los métodos en los que por lo general organiza su material.

**SÍMBOLO** Un ***símbolo*** es un signo, palabra, frase, imagen u otro objeto que representa otra cosa. Por ejemplo, una bandera puede simbolizar un país, una palabra puede simbolizar un objeto, un auto caro puede simbolizar riqueza, etc. La crítica literaria suele hacer una distinción entre los símbolos tradicionales o convencionales —aquellos que son parte de nuestro legado cultural— y los ***símbolos personales***; es decir, aquellos que los autores crean y usan en sus propias obras.

El simbolismo convencional a menudo se basa en elementos de la naturaleza. Por ejemplo, un prado o la primavera simboliza la juventud; el verano representa la adultez; y el otoño y el invierno simbolizan la edad avanzada. Los símbolos convencionales también pueden tomarse de las religiones y la política. Por ejemplo, una cruz puede simbolizar la cristiandad, el color rojo puede ser el símbolo de la ideología marxista.

**SINÉCDOQUE** La ***sinécdoque*** es una figura retórica en la cual una parte de algo se usa para representar el todo.

**SINTAXIS** La ***sintaxis*** es la manera en que se organizan las palabras, por ejemplo, el orden en que aparecen en una oración o frase.

**TEMA** El ***tema*** es la idea o propósito o preocupación central que plantea una obra literaria. En un ensayo, el tema puede expresarse directamente en lo que se conoce como "enunciado de tesis". En una obra literaria seria, el tema por lo general se expresa indirecta, más que directamente. Una obra ligera, escrita exclusivamente para entretener, puede no tener ningún tema.

**TONO** El ***tono*** de una obra literaria es la actitud del escritor hacia su tema y sus lectores. El tono puede ser formal o informal, amistoso o distante, personal o pomposo.

**TRAGEDIA** Una ***tragedia*** es una obra literaria, por lo general una obra de teatro, que termina en la caída o destrucción de un ser noble o importante, un personaje que por lo general tiene una debilidad de carácter que se conoce con el nombre de ***error trágico***. Macbeth, por ejemplo, es una figura noble y valiente cegada por la ambición. El ***héroe trágico*** se ve arrastrado por una secuencia de sucesos que inevitablemente conducirán al desastre. Como el protagonista no es ni un malvado villano ni una víctima inocente, la audiencia reacciona con emociones encontradas, con miedo y con compasión, según el filósofo griego Aristóteles, quien definió la tragedia en su *Poética*. El desenlace de una tragedia, en el que el protagonista queda aislado de la sociedad, contrasta con el desenlace de la comedia, en el que el protagonista se reconcilia con la sociedad.

**LÍTOTE** En un ***lítote,*** el enunciado no expresa todo lo que se quiere dar a entender.

**TEMA UNIVERSAL** Un ***tema universal*** es un mensaje que se encuentra con frecuencia en la literatura de muchas culturas distintas y a través de distintos períodos de la historia.

**VOZ** La ***voz*** de un escritor es la manera en que "suena" en la página. La voz se basa en elementos tales como la elección del vocabulario, los recursos sonoros, el ritmo y la actitud.

# GRAMMAR HANDBOOK

## PARTS OF SPEECH

Every English word, depending on its meaning and its use in a sentence, can be identified as one of the eight parts of speech. These are nouns, pronouns, verbs, adjectives, adverbs, prepositions, conjunctions, and interjections. Understanding the parts of speech will help you learn the rules of English grammar and usage.

**Nouns** A **noun** names a person, place, or thing. A **common noun** names any one of a class of persons, places, or things. A **proper noun** names a specific person, place, or thing.

| Common Noun | Proper Noun |
|---|---|
| writer, country, novel | Charles Dickens, Great Britain, *Hard Times* |

**Pronouns** A **pronoun** is a word that stands for one or more nouns. The word to which a pronoun refers (whose place it takes) is the **antecedent** of the pronoun.

A **personal pronoun** refers to the person speaking (first person); the person spoken to (second person); or the person, place, or thing spoken about (third person).

| | Singular | Plural |
|---|---|---|
| **First Person** | I, me, my, mine | we, us, our, ours |
| **Second Person** | you, your, yours | you, your, yours |
| **Third Person** | he, him, his, she, her, hers, it, its | they, them, their, theirs |

A **reflexive pronoun** reflects the action of a verb back on its subject. It indicates that the person or thing performing the action also is receiving the action.

I keep *myself* fit by taking a walk every day.

An **intensive pronoun** adds emphasis to a noun or pronoun.

It took the work of the president *himself* to pass the law.

A **demonstrative** pronoun points out a specific person(s), place(s), or thing(s).

this, that, these, those

A **relative pronoun** begins a subordinate clause and connects it to another idea in the sentence.

that, which, who, whom, whose

An **interrogative pronoun** begins a question.

what, which, who, whom, whose

An **indefinite pronoun** refers to a person, place, or thing that may or may not be specifically named.

all, another, any, both, each, everyone,
few, most, none, no one, somebody

**Verbs** A **verb** expresses action or the existence of a state or condition.

An **action verb** tells what action someone or something is performing.

gather, read, work, jump, imagine, analyze, conclude

A **linking verb** connects the subject with another word that identifies or describes the subject. The most common linking verb is *be*.

appear, be, become, feel, look, remain, seem, smell, sound, stay, taste

A **helping verb,** or **auxiliary verb,** is added to a main verb to make a verb phrase.

be, do, have, should, can, could, may, might, must, will, would

**Adjectives** An **adjective** modifies a noun or pronoun by describing it or giving it a more specific meaning. An adjective answers the questions:

| | |
|---|---|
| What kind? | *purple* hat, *happy* face, *loud* sound |
| Which one? | *this* bowl |
| How many? | *three* cars |
| How much? | *enough* food |

The articles *the, a,* and *an* are adjectives.

A **proper adjective** is an adjective derived from a proper noun.

French, Shakespearean

**Adverbs** An **adverb** modifies a verb, an adjective, or another adverb by telling *where, when, how,* or *to what extent.*

will answer *soon, extremely* sad, calls *more* often

**Prepositions** A **preposition** relates a noun or pronoun that appears with it to another word in the sentence.

Dad made a meal *for* us. We talked *till* dusk. Bo missed school *because of* his illness.

**Conjunctions** A **conjunction** connects words or groups of words. A **coordinating conjunction** joins words or groups of words of equal rank.

bread *and* cheese, brief *but* powerful

**Correlative conjunctions** are used in pairs to connect words or groups of words of equal importance.

*both* Luis *and* Rosa, *neither* you *nor* I

## PARTS OF SPEECH continued

**Subordinating conjunctions** indicate the connection between two ideas by placing one below the other in rank or importance. A subordinating conjunction introduces a subordinate, or dependent, clause.

We will miss her *if* she leaves. Hank shrieked *when* he slipped on the ice.

**Interjections** An **interjection** expresses feeling or emotion. It is not related to other words in the sentence.

ah, hey, ouch, well, yippee

## PHRASES AND CLAUSES

**Phrases** A **phrase** is a group of words that does not have both a subject and a verb and that functions as one part of speech. A phrase expresses an idea but cannot stand alone.

**Prepositional Phrases** A **prepositional phrase** is a group of words that begins with a preposition and ends with a noun or pronoun that is the **object of the preposition.**

before dawn as a result of the rain

An **adjective phrase** is a prepositional phrase that modifies a noun or pronoun.

Eliza appreciates the beauty **of a well-crafted poem.**

An **adverb phrase** is a prepositional phrase that modifies a verb, an adjective, or an adverb.

She reads Spenser's sonnets **with great pleasure.**

**Appositive Phrases** An **appositive** is a noun or pronoun placed next to another noun or pronoun to add information about it. An **appositive phrase** consists of an appositive and its modifiers.

Mr. Roth, **my music teacher**, is sick.

**Verbal Phrases** A **verbal** is a verb form that functions as a different part of speech (not as a verb) in a sentence. **Participles, gerunds,** and **infinitives** are verbals.

A **verbal phrase** includes a verbal and any modifiers or complements it may have. Verbal phrases may function as nouns, as adjectives, or as adverbs.

A **participle** is a verb form that can act as an adjective. Present participles end in *-ing;* past participles of regular verbs end in *-ed.*

A **participial phrase** consists of a participle and its modifiers or complements. The entire phrase acts as an adjective.

Jenna's backpack, **loaded with equipment,** was heavy.

**Barking incessantly,** the dogs chased the squirrels out of sight.

A **gerund** is a verb form that ends in *-ing* and is used as a noun.

A **gerund phrase** consists of a gerund with any modifiers or complements, all acting together as a noun.

**Taking photographs of wildlife** is her main hobby. [acts as subject]

We always enjoy **listening to live music.** [acts as object]

An **infinitive** is a verb form, usually preceded by *to,* that can act as a noun, an adjective, or an adverb.

An **infinitive phrase** consists of an infinitive and its modifiers or complements, and sometimes its subject, all acting together as a single part of speech.

She tries **to get out into the wilderness often.** [acts as a noun; direct object of *tries*]

The Tigers are the team **to beat.** [acts as an adjective; describes *team*]

I drove twenty miles **to witness the event.** [acts as an adverb; tells why I drove]

**Clauses** A **clause** is a group of words with its own subject and verb.

**Independent Clauses** An independent clause can stand by itself as a complete sentence.

George Orwell wrote with extraordinary insight.

**Subordinate Clauses** A subordinate clause, also called a dependent clause, cannot stand by itself as a complete sentence. Subordinate clauses always appear connected in some way with one or more independent clauses.

George Orwell, **who wrote with extraordinary insight,** produced many politically relevant works.

An **adjective clause** is a subordinate clause that acts as an adjective. It modifies a noun or a pronoun by telling *what kind* or *which one.* Also called relative clauses, adjective clauses usually begin with a **relative pronoun:** *who, which, that, whom, or whose.*

"The Lamb" is the poem **that I memorized for class.**

An **adverb clause** is a subordinate clause that, like an adverb, modifies a verb, an adjective, or an adverb. An adverb clause tells *where, when, in what way, to what extent, under what condition,* or *why.*

The students will read another poetry collection **if their schedule allows.**

**When I recited the poem,** Mr. Lopez was impressed.

A **noun clause** is a subordinate clause that acts as a noun.

William Blake survived on **whatever he made as an engraver.**

## SENTENCE STRUCTURE

**Subject and Predicate** A **sentence** is a group of words that expresses a complete thought. A sentence has two main parts: a *subject* and a *predicate*.

A **fragment** is a group of words that does not express a complete thought. It lacks an independent clause.

The **subject** tells *whom* or *what* the sentence is about. The **predicate** tells what the subject of the sentence does or is.

A subject or a predicate can consist of a single word or of many words. All the words in the subject make up the **complete subject.** All the words in the predicate make up the **complete predicate.**

**Complete Subject** **Complete Predicate**
Both of those girls | have already read *Macbeth*.

The **simple subject** is the essential noun, pronoun, or group of words acting as a noun that cannot be left out of the complete subject. The **simple predicate** is the essential verb or verb phrase that cannot be left out of the complete predicate.

**Both** of those girls | **have** already **read** *Macbeth*.
[Simple subject: *Both;* simple predicate: *have read*]

A **compound subject** is two or more subjects that have the same verb and are joined by a conjunction.

**Neither the horse nor the driver** looked tired.

A **compound predicate** is two or more verbs that have the same subject and are joined by a conjunction.

She **sneezed and coughed** throughout the trip.

**Complements** A **complement** is a word or word group that completes the meaning of the subject or verb in a sentence. There are four kinds of complements: *direct objects, indirect objects, objective complements,* and *subject complements.*

A **direct object** is a noun, a pronoun, or a group of words acting as a noun that receives the action of a transitive verb.

We watched the **liftoff**.
She drove **Zach** to the launch site.

An **indirect object** is a noun or pronoun that appears with a direct object and names the person or thing to which or for which something is done.

He sold the **family** a mirror. [The direct object is *mirror.*]

An **objective complement** is an adjective or noun that appears with a direct object and describes or renames it.

The decision made her **unhappy**.
[The direct object is *her.*]
Many consider Shakespeare the greatest **playwright.** [The direct object is *Shakespeare.*]

A **subject complement** follows a linking verb and tells something about the subject. There are two kinds: *predicate nominatives* and *predicate adjectives.*

A **predicate nominative** is a noun or pronoun that follows a linking verb and identifies or renames the subject.

"A Modest Proposal" is a **pamphlet.**

A **predicate adjective** is an adjective that follows a linking verb and describes the subject of the sentence.

"A Modest Proposal" is **satirical.**

### Classifying Sentences by Structure

Sentences can be classified according to the kind and number of clauses they contain. The four basic sentence structures are *simple, compound, complex,* and *compound-complex.*

A **simple sentence** consists of one independent clause.

Terrence enjoys modern British literature.

A **compound sentence** consists of two or more independent clauses. The clauses are joined by a conjunction or a semicolon.

Terrence enjoys modern British literature, but his brother prefers the classics.

A **complex sentence** consists of one independent clause and one or more subordinate clauses.

Terrence, who reads voraciously, enjoys modern British literature.

A **compound-complex sentence** consists of two or more independent clauses and one or more subordinate clauses.

Terrence, who reads voraciously, enjoys modern British literature, but his brother prefers the classics.

### Classifying Sentences by Function

Sentences can be classified according to their function or purpose. The four types are *declarative, interrogative, imperative,* and *exclamatory.*

A **declarative sentence** states an idea and ends with a period.

An **interrogative sentence** asks a question and ends with a question mark.

An **imperative sentence** gives an order or a direction and ends with either a period or an exclamation mark.

An **exclamatory sentence** conveys a strong emotion and ends with an exclamation mark.

## PARAGRAPH STRUCTURE

An effective paragraph is organized around one **main idea,** which is often stated in a **topic sentence.** The other sentences support the main idea. To give the paragraph **unity,** make sure the connection between each sentence and the main idea is clear.

### Unnecessary Shift in Person

Do not change needlessly from one grammatical person to another. Keep the person consistent in your sentences.

**Max** went to the bakery, but **you** can't buy mints there. [shift from third person to second person]

**Max** went to the bakery, but **he** can't buy mints there. [consistent]

### Unnecessary Shift in Voice

Do not change needlessly from active voice to passive voice in your use of verbs.

Elena and I **searched** the trail for evidence, but no clues **were found.** [shift from active voice to passive voice]

Elena and I **searched** the trail for evidence, but we **found** no clues. [consistent]

## AGREEMENT

### Subject and Verb Agreement

A singular subject must have a singular verb. A plural subject must have a plural verb.

**Dr. Boone uses** a telescope to view the night sky.

The **students use** a telescope to view the night sky.

A verb always agrees with its subject, not its object.

*Incorrect:* The best part of the show were the jugglers.

*Correct:* The best part of the show was the jugglers.

A phrase or clause that comes between a subject and verb does not affect subject-verb agreement.

His **theory**, as well as his claims, **lacks** support.

Two subjects joined by *and* usually take a plural verb.

The **dog** and the **cat are** healthy.

Two singular subjects joined by *or* or *nor* take a singular verb.

The **dog** or the **cat is** hiding.

Two plural subjects joined by *or* or *nor* take a plural verb.

The **dogs** or the **cats are** coming home with us.

When a singular and a plural subject are joined by *or* or *nor,* the verb agrees with the closer subject.

Either the **dogs** or the **cat is** behind the door.

Either the **cat** or the **dogs are** behind the door.

### Pronoun and Antecedent Agreement

Pronouns must agree with their antecedents in number and gender. Use singular pronouns with singular antecedents and plural pronouns with plural antecedents.

**Doris Lessing** uses **her** writing to challenge ideas about women's roles.

**Writers** often use **their** skills to promote social change.

Use a singular pronoun when the antecedent is a singular indefinite pronoun such as *anybody, each, either, everybody, neither, no one, one, or someone.*

Judge **each** of the articles on **its** merits.

Use a plural pronoun when the antecedent is a plural indefinite pronoun such as *both, few, many,* or *several.*

**Both** of the articles have **their** flaws.

The indefinite pronouns *all, any, more, most, none,* and *some* can be singular or plural depending on the number of the word to which they refer.

**Most** of the *books* are in **their** proper places.

**Most** of the *book* has been torn from **its** binding.

## USING VERBS

### Principal Parts of Regular and Irregular Verbs

A verb has four principal parts:

| Present | Present Participle | Past | Past Participle |
|---|---|---|---|
| learn | learning | learned | learned |
| discuss | discussing | discussed | discussed |
| stand | standing | stood | stood |
| begin | beginning | began | begun |

**Regular verbs** such as *learn* and *discuss* form the past and past participle by adding *-ed* to the present form. **Irregular verbs** such as *stand* and *begin* form the past and past participle in other ways. If you are in doubt about the principal parts of an irregular verb, check a dictionary.

### The Tenses of Verbs

The different tenses of verbs indicate the time an action or condition occurs.

The **present tense** expresses an action that happens regularly or states a current condition or a general truth.

Tourists **flock** to the site yearly.

Daily exercise **is** good for your heallth.

The **past tense** expresses a completed action or a condition that is no longer true.

The squirrel **dropped** the nut and **ran** up the tree.

I **was** very tired last night by 9:00.

The **future tense** indicates an action that will happen in the future or a condition that will be true.

The Glazers **will visit** us tomorrow.

They **will be** glad to arrive from their long journey.

The **present perfect tense** expresses an action that happened at an indefinite time in the past or an action that began in the past and continues into the present.

Someone **has cleaned** the trash from the park.

The puppy **has been** under the bed all day.

The **past perfect tense** shows an action that was completed before another action in the past.

Gerard **had revised** his essay before he turned it in.

The **future perfect tense** indicates an action that will have been completed before another action takes place.

Mimi **will have painted** the kitchen by the time we finish the shutters.

## USING MODIFIERS

### Degrees of Comparison

Adjectives and adverbs take different forms to show the three degrees of comparison: the *positive*, the *comparative*, and the *superlative*.

| Positive | Comparative | Superlative |
|---|---|---|
| fast | faster | fastest |
| crafty | craftier | craftiest |
| abruptly | more abruptly | most abruptly |
| badly | worse | worst |

### Using Comparative and Superlative Adjectives and Adverbs

Use comparative adjectives and adverbs to compare two things. Use superlative adjectives and adverbs to compare three or more things.

This season's weather was **drier** than last year's.

This season has been one of the **driest** on record.

Jake practices **more often** than Jamal.

Of everyone in the band, Jake practices **most often.**

## USING PRONOUNS

### Pronoun Case

The **case** of a pronoun is the form it takes to show its function in a sentence. There are three pronoun cases: *nominative*, *objective*, and *possessive*.

| Nominative | Objective | Possessive |
|---|---|---|
| I, you, he, she, it, we, you, they | me, you, him, her, it, us, you, them | my, your, yours, his, her, hers, its, our, ours, their, theirs |

Use the **nominative case** when a pronoun functions as a *subject* or as a *predicate nominative.*

**They** are going to the movies. [subject]

The biggest movie fan is **she.** [predicate nominative]

Use the **objective case** for a pronoun acting as a *direct object*, an *indirect object*, or the *object of a preposition.*

The ending of the play surprised **me.** [direct object]

Mary gave **us** two tickets to the play. [indirect object]

The audience cheered for **him.** [object of preposition]

Use the **possessive case** to show ownership.

The red suitcase is **hers.**

**Diction** The words you choose contribute to the overall effectiveness of your writing. **Diction** refers to word choice and to the clearness and correctness of those words. You can improve one aspect of your diction by choosing carefully between commonly confused words, such as the pairs listed below.

**accept, except**

*Accept* is a verb that means "to receive" or "to agree to." *Except* is a preposition that means "other than" or "leaving out."

Please **accept** my offer to buy you lunch this weekend.

He is busy every day **except** the weekends.

**affect, effect**

*Affect* is normally a verb meaning "to influence" or "to bring about a change in." *Effect* is usually a noun meaning "result."

The distractions outside **affect** Steven's ability to concentrate.

The teacher's remedies had a positive **effect** on Steven's ability to concentrate.

**among, between**

*Among* is usually used with three or more items, and it emphasizes collective relationships or indicates distribution. *Between* is generally used with only two items, but it can be used with more than two if the emphasis is on individual (one-to-one) relationships within the group.

I had to choose a snack **among** the various vegetables.

He handed out the booklets **among** the conference participants.

Our school is **between** a park and an old barn.

The tournament included matches **between** France, Spain, Mexico, and the United States.

**amount, number**

*Amount* refers to overall quantity and is mainly used with mass nouns (those that can't be counted). *Number* refers to individual items that can be counted.

The **amount** of attention that great writers have paid to Shakespeare is remarkable.

A **number** of important English writers have been fascinated by the legend of King Arthur.

**assure, ensure, insure**

*Assure* means "to convince [someone of something]; to guarantee." *Ensure* means "to make certain [that something happens]." *Insure* means "to arrange for payment in case of loss."

The attorney **assured** us we'd win the case.

The rules **ensure** that no one gets treated unfairly.

Many professional musicians **insure** their valuable instruments.

**bad, badly**

Use the adjective *bad* before a noun or after linking verbs such as *feel, look,* and *seem*. Use *badly* whenever an adverb is required.

The situation may seem **bad**, but it will improve over time.

Though our team played **badly** today, we will focus on practicing for the next match.

**beside, besides**

*Beside* means "at the side of" or "close to." *Besides* means "in addition to."

The stapler sits **beside** the pencil sharpener in our classroom.

**Besides** being very clean, the classroom is also very organized.

**can, may**

The helping verb *can* generally refers to the ability to do something. The helping verb *may* generally refers to permission to do something.

I **can** run one mile in six minutes.

**May** we have a race during recess?

**complement, compliment**

The verb *complement* means "to enhance"; the verb *compliment* means "to praise."

Online exercises **complement** the textbook lessons.

Ms. Lewis **complimented** our team on our excellent debate.

**compose, comprise**

*Compose* means "to make up; constitute." *Comprise* means "to include or contain." Remember that the whole comprises its parts or is composed of its parts, and the parts compose the whole.

The assignment **comprises** three different tasks.

The assignment is **composed** of three different tasks.

Three different tasks **compose** the assignment.

**different from, different than**

*Different from* is generally preferred over *different than*, but *different than* can be used before a clause. Always use *different from* before a noun or pronoun.

Your point of view is so **different from** mine.

His idea was so **different from** [or **different than**] what we had expected.

**farther, further**

Use *farther* to refer to distance. Use *further* to mean "to a greater degree or extent" or "additional."

Chiang has traveled **farther** than anybody else in the class.

If I want **further** details about his travels, I can read his blog.

**fewer, less**

Use *fewer* for things that can be counted. Use *less* for amounts or quantities that cannot be counted. *Fewer* must be followed by a plural noun.

**Fewer** students drive to school since the weather improved.

There is **less** noise outside in the mornings.

**good, well**

Use the adjective *good* before a noun or after a linking verb. Use *well* whenever an adverb is required, such as when modifying a verb.

I feel **good** after sleeping for eight hours.

I did **well** on my test, and my soccer team played **well** in that afternoon's game. It was a **good** day!

**its, it's**

The word *its* with no apostrophe is a possessive pronoun. The word *it's* is a contraction of "it is."

Angelica will try to fix the computer and **its** keyboard.

**It's** a difficult job, but she can do it.

**lay, lie**

*Lay* is a transitive verb meaning "to set or put something down." Its principal parts are *lay, laying, laid, laid. Lie* is an intransitive verb meaning "to recline" or "to exist in a certain place." Its principal parts are *lie, lying, lay, lain.*

Please **lay** that box down and help me with the sofa.

When we are done moving, I am going to **lie** down.

My hometown **lies** sixty miles north of here.

**like, as**

*Like* is a preposition that usually means "similar to" and precedes a noun or pronoun. The conjunction *as* means "in the way that" and usually precedes a clause.

**Like** the other students, I was prepared for a quiz.

**As** I said yesterday, we expect to finish before noon.

Use **such as,** not **like,** before a series of examples.

Foods **such as** apples, nuts, and pretzels make good snacks.

**of, have**

Do not use *of* in place of *have* after auxiliary verbs such as *would, could, should, may, might,* or *must.* The contraction of *have* is formed by adding *-ve* after these verbs.

I **would have** stayed after school today, but I had to help cook at home.

Mom **must've** called while I was still in the gym.

**principal, principle**

*Principal* can be an adjective meaning "main; most important." It can also be a noun meaning "chief officer of a school." *Principle* is a noun meaning "moral rule" or "fundamental truth."

His strange behavior was the **principal** reason for our concern.

Democratic **principles** form the basis of our country's laws.

**raise, rise**

*Raise* is a transitive verb that usually takes a direct object. *Rise* is intransitive and never takes a direct object.

Iliana and Josef **raise** the flag every morning.

They **rise** from their seats and volunteer immediately whenever help is needed.

**than, then**

The conjunction *than* is used to connect the two parts of a comparison. The adverb *then* usually refers to time.

My backpack is heavier **than** hers.

I will finish my homework and **then** meet my friends at the park.

**that, which, who**

Use the relative pronoun *that* to refer to things or people. Use *which* only for things and *who* only for people.

*That* introduces a restrictive phrase or clause, that is, one that is essential to the meaning of the sentence. *Which* introduces a nonrestrictive phrase or clause—one that adds information but could be deleted from the sentence—and is preceded by a comma.

Ben ran to the park **that** just reopened.

The park, **which** just reopened, has many attractions.

The man **who** built the park loves to see people smiling.

**when, where, why**

Do not use *when, where,* or *why* directly after a linking verb, such as *is*. Reword the sentence.

*Incorrect:* The morning is when he left for the beach.

*Correct:* He left for the beach in the morning.

**who, whom**

In formal writing, use *who* only as a subject in clauses and sentences. Use *whom* only as the object of a verb or of a preposition.

**Who** paid for the tickets?

**Whom** should I pay for the tickets?

I can't recall to **whom** I gave the money for the tickets.

**your, you're**

*Your* is a possessive pronoun expressing ownership. *You're* is the contraction of "you are."

Have you finished writing **your** informative essay?

**You're** supposed to turn it in tomorrow. If **you're** late, **your** grade will be affected.

## Capitalization

### First Words

Capitalize the first word of a sentence.

**S**tories about knights and their deeds interest me.

Capitalize the first word of direct speech.

**S**haron asked, "**D**o you like stories about knights?"

Capitalize the first word of a quotation that is a complete sentence.

**E**instein said, "**A**nyone who has never made a mistake has never tried anything new."

### Proper Nouns and Proper Adjectives

Capitalize all proper nouns, including geographical names, historical events and periods, and names of organizations.

**T**hames **R**iver    **J**ohn **K**eats    the **R**enaissance
**U**nited **N**ations    **W**orld **W**ar II    **S**ierra **N**evada

Capitalize all proper adjectives.

**S**hakespearean play    **B**ritish invaision
**A**merican citizen    **L**atin **A**merican literature

### Academic Course Names

Capitalize course names only if they are language courses, are followed by a number, or are preceded by a proper noun or adjective.

**S**panish    **H**onors **C**hemistry    **H**istory 101
**g**eology    **a**lgebra    **s**ocial **s**tudies

### Titles

Capitalize personal titles when followed by the person's name.

**M**s. Hughes    **D**r. Perez    **K**ing George

Capitalize titles showing family relationships when they are followed by a specific person's name, unless they are preceded by a possessive noun or pronoun.

**U**ncle Oscar    Mangan's **s**ister    his **a**unt Tessa

Capitalize the first word and all other key words in the titles of books, stories, songs, and other works of art.

*Frankenstein*    "**S**hooting an **E**lephant"

## Punctuation

### End Marks

Use a **period** to end a declarative sentence or an imperative sentence.

We are studying the structure of sonnets.
Read the biography of Mary Shelley.

Use periods with initials and abbreviations.

D. H. Lawrence    Mrs. Browning
Mt. Everest    Maple St.

Use a **question mark** to end an interrogative sentence.

What is Macbeth's fatal flaw?

Use an **exclamation mark** after an exclamatory sentence or a forceful imperative sentence.

That's a beautiful painting!    Let me go now!

### Commas

Use a **comma** before a coordinating conjunction to separate two independent clauses in a compound sentence.

The game was very close, but we were victorious.

Use commas to separate three or more words, phrases, or clauses in a series.

William Blake was a writer, artist, and printer.

Use commas to separate coordinate adjectives.

It was a witty, amusing novel.

Use a comma after an introductory word, phrase, or clause.

When the novelist finished his book, he celebrated with his family.

Use commas to set off nonessential expressions.

Old English, of course, requires translation.

Use commas with places and dates.

Coventry, England    September 1, 1939

### Semicolons

Use a **semicolon** to join closely related independent clauses that are not already joined by a conjunction.

Tanya likes to write poetry; Heather prefers prose.

Use semicolons to avoid confusion when items in a series contain commas.

They traveled to London, England; Madrid, Spain; and Rome, Italy.

### Colons

Use a **colon** before a list of items following an independent clause.

Notable Victorian poets include the following: Tennyson, Arnold, Housman, and Hopkins.

Use a colon to introduce information that summarizes or explains the independent clause before it.

She just wanted to do one thing: rest.
Malcolm loves volunteering: He reads to sick children every Saturday afternoon.

### Quotation Marks

Use **quotation marks** to enclose a direct quotation.

"Short stories," Ms. Hildebrand said, "should have rich, well-developed characters."

An **indirect quotation** does not require quotation marks.

Ms. Hildebrand said that short stories should have well-developed characters.

Use quotation marks around the titles of short written works, episodes in a series, songs, and works mentioned as parts of collections.

"The Lagoon"    "Boswell Meets Johnson"

**Italics**

Italicize the titles of long written works, movies, television and radio shows, lengthy works of music, paintings, and sculptures.

*Howards End*　*60 Minutes*　*Guernica*

For handwritten material, you can use underlining instead of italics.

The Princess Bride　Mona Lisa

**Dashes**

Use **dashes** to indicate an abrupt change of thought, a dramatic interrupting idea, or a summary statement.

I read the entire first act of *Macbeth*—you won't believe what happens next.

The director—what's her name again?—attended the movie premiere.

**Hyphens**

Use a **hyphen** with certain numbers, after certain prefixes, with two or more words used as one word, and with a compound modifier that comes before a noun.

seventy-two
self-esteem
president-elect
five-year contract

**Parentheses**

Use **parentheses** to set off asides and explanations when the material is not essential or when it consists of one or more sentences. When the sentence in parentheses interrupts the larger sentence, it does not have a capital letter or a period.

He listened intently (it was too dark to see who was speaking) to try to identify the voices.

When a sentence in parentheses falls between two other complete sentences, it should start with a capital letter and end with a period.

The quarterback threw three touchdown passes. (We knew he could do it.) Our team won the game by two points.

**Apostrophes**

Add an **apostrophe** and an *s* to show the possessive case of most singular nouns and of plural nouns that do not end in *-s* or *-es*.

Blake's poems　the mice's whiskers

Names ending in *s* form their possessives in the same way, except for classical and biblical names, which add only an apostrophe to form the possessive.

Dickens's　Hercules'

Add an apostrophe to show the possessive case of plural nouns ending in *-s* and *-es*.

the girls' songs　the Ortizes' car

Use an apostrophe in a contraction to indicate the position of the missing letter or letters.

She's never read a Coleridge poem she didn't like.

**Brackets**

Use **brackets** to enclose clarifying information inserted within a quotation.

Columbus's journal entry from October 21, 1492, begins as follows: "At 10 o'clock, we arrived at a cape of the island [San Salvador], and anchored, the other vessels in company."

**Ellipses**

Use three ellipsis points, also known as an **ellipsis,** to indicate where you have omitted words from quoted material.

Wollestonecraft wrote, "The education of women has of late been more attended to than formerly; yet they are still . . . ridiculed or pitied. . . ."

In the example above, the four dots at the end of the sentence are the three ellipsis points plus the period from the original sentence.

Use an ellipsis to indicate a pause or interruption in speech.

"When he told me the news," said the coach, "I was . . . I was shocked . . . completely shocked."

## Spelling

**Spelling Rules**

Learning the rules of English spelling will help you make **generalizations** about how to spell words.

**Word Parts**

The three word parts that can combine to form a word are roots, prefixes, and suffixes. Many of these word parts come from the Greek, Latin, and Anglo-Saxon languages.

The **root word** carries a word's basic meaning.

| Root and Origin | Meaning | Examples |
|---|---|---|
| -leg- (-log-) [Gr.] | to say, speak | *legal, logic* |
| -pon- (-pos-) [L.] | to put, place | *postpone, deposit* |

A **prefix** is one or more syllables added to the beginning of a word that alter the meaning of the root.

| Prefix and Origin | Meaning | Example |
|---|---|---|
| anti- [Gr.] | against | *antipathy* |
| inter- [L.] | between | *international* |
| mis- [A.S.] | wrong | *misplace* |

A **suffix** is a letter or group of letters added to the end of a root word that changes the word's meaning or part of speech.

| Suffix and Origin | Meaning and Example | Part of Speech |
|---|---|---|
| -ful [A.S.] | full of: *scornful* | adjective |
| -ity [L.] | state of being: *adversity* | noun |
| -ize (-ise) [Gr.] | to make: *idolize* | verb |
| -ly [A.S.] | in a manner: *calmly* | adverb |

**Rules for Adding Suffixes to Root Words**

When adding a suffix to a root word ending in *y* preceded by a consonant, change *y* to *i* unless the suffix begins with *i*.

ply + -able = pliable  happy + -ness = happiness
defy + -ing = defying  cry + -ing = crying

For a root word ending in *e*, drop the *e* when adding a suffix beginning with a vowel.

drive + -ing = driving  move + -able = movable
SOME EXCEPTIONS: traceable, seeing, dyeing

For root words ending with a consonant + vowel + consonant in a stressed syllable, double the final consonant when adding a suffix that begins with a vowel.

mud + -y = muddy  submit + -ed = submitted
SOME EXCEPTIONS: mixing, fixed

**Rules for Adding Prefixes to Root Words**

When a prefix is added to a root word, the spelling of the root remains the same.

un- + certain = uncertain  mis- + spell = misspell

With some prefixes, the spelling of the prefix changes when joined to the root to make the pronunciation easier.

in- + mortal = immortal  ad- + vert = avert

**Orthographic Patterns**

Certain letter combinations in English make certain sounds. For instance, *ph* sounds like *f*, *eigh* usually makes a long *a* sound, and the *k* before an *n* is often silent.

**ph**armacy  n**eigh**bor  **k**nowledge

Understanding **orthographic patterns** such as these can help you improve your spelling.

**Forming Plurals**

The plural form of most nouns is formed by adding *-s* to the singular.

computers  gadgets  Washingtons

For words ending in *s, ss, x, z, sh,* or *ch,* add *-es.*

circus**es**  tax**es**  wish**es**  bench**es**

For words ending in *y* or *o* preceded by a vowel, add *-s.*

key**s**  patio**s**

For words ending in *y* preceded by a consonant, change the *y* to an *i* and add *-es.*

cit**ies**  enem**ies**  troph**ies**

For most words ending in *o* preceded by a consonant, add *-es.*

echo**es**  tomato**es**

Some words form the plural in irregular ways.

women  oxen  children  teeth  deer

**Foreign Words Used in English**

Some words used in English are actually foreign words that have been adopted. Learning to spell these words requires memorization. When in doubt, check a dictionary.

sushi  enchilada  au pair  fiancé
laissez faire  croissant

# INDEX OF SKILLS

## Analyzing Text

## Assessment



## Language Conventions

## Research



## Speaking and Listening



## Vocabulary

## Writing

# INDEX OF AUTHORS AND TITLES

The following authors and titles appear in the print and online versions of *myPerspectives*.

# ADDITIONAL SELECTIONS: AUTHOR AND TITLE INDEX

The following authors and titles appear in the Interactive Student Edition only.

## Acknowledgments

The following selections appear in Grade 12 of *myPerspectives.* Some selections appear online only.

**A.M. Heath & Co. Ltd.** *Shooting an Elephant and Other Essays* by George Orwell (Copyright ©George Orwell, 1946) Reproduced by permission of Bill Hamilton as the Literary Executor of the Estate of the Late Sonia Brownell Orwell.

**BBC News Online.** "How did Harry Patch become an unlikely WW1 Hero?" from BBC, used with permission.

**BBC Worldwide Americas, Inc.** "How did Harry Patch become an unlikely WW1 Hero?" from Faulks on Fiction, episode one ©BBC Worldwide Learning; Queen Elizabeth I's Speech Before Her Troops ©BBC Worldwide Learning; The Medieval Age and The Canterbury Tales ©BBC Worldwide Learning; Introduction to *Macbeth* ©BBC Worldwide Learning; Macbeth's Early Motivation ©BBC Worldwide Learning; The Darkness in Macbeth's Human Characters ©BBC Worldwide Learning; Philip Larkin reads "The Explosion" ©BBC Worldwide Learning; The British Empire Sets Its Sights West ©BBC Worldwide Learning.

**Beard, Francesca.** "Old Love" by Francesca Beard. Used with permission of the author.

**Brandt & Hochman Literary Agents Inc.** "The Assignment of My Life" by Ruth Gruber, from *The Moment: Wild, Poignant, Life-Changing Stories from 125 Writers and Artists Famous & Obscure*, edited by Larry Smith. Used with permission of Brandt & Hochman Literary Agents on behalf of the author's estate; "Back to My Own Country: An Essay" from *Six Stories and an Essay* by Andrea Levy. Copyright 2014 by Andrea Levy. Used by permission of Brandt & Hochman Literary Agents, Inc. Any copying or distribution of this text is expressly forbidden. All rights reserved.

**Candlewick Press.** *Beowulf.* Copyright © 1999, 2000, 2007 by Gareth Hinds. Reproduced by permission of the publisher, Candlewick Press, Somerville, MA.

**Carmen Balcells Agencia Literaria.** Isabel Allende, "Writing as an Act of Hope" ©Isabel Allende, 1989.

**Clark, Kevin.** "The Seafarer" used by permission of Kevin Clark.

**Classical Comics Ltd.** from *Macbeth: The Graphic Novel* ©Classical Comics.

**Columbia University Press.** From *The Pillow Book* by Sei Shonagon, translated by Ivan Morris. Copyright ©1992 Columbia University Press. Reprinted with permission of the publisher.

**Conville and Walsh Literary Agency.** "The Most Forgetful Man in the World", from *Moonwalking with Einstein: The Art and Science of Remembering Everything* by Joshua Foer, copyright ©2011 by Joshua Foer. Used by permission of Conville and Walsh Literary Agency.

**Cort, Julia.** "NOVA: Sleep" by Julia Cort. Used with permission.

**Crown Copyright Officer.** Passenger Manifest for the M.V. Empire Windrush, Courtesy of National Archives.

**Curtis Brown, Ltd. (UK).** "Pericles' Funeral Oration" reproduced with permission of Curtis Brown Book Group Ltd, London on behalf of The Beneficiaries of the Estate of Rex Warner ©1972; *The Canterbury Tales*: "The Prologue" reproduced with permission of Curtis Brown Book Group Ltd, London on behalf of The Estate of Nevill Coghill ©1951.

**Encyclopedia Britannica, Inc.** "Jamaica" reprinted with permission from *Encyclopædia Britannica,* ©2015 by Encyclopædia Britannica, Inc.

**Faber & Faber, Ltd. (UK).** "The Explosion" from *Collected Poems* by Philip Larkin. Used with permission of Faber & Faber Ltd.; "Midsummer" from *The Poetry of Derek Walcott,* 1948–2013 by Derek Walcott, selected by Glyn Maxwell. Copyright ©2014 by Derek Walcott. Reprinted by permission of Faber & Faber Ltd.; "Why Brownee Left" from *Poems*: 1968–1998 by Paul Muldoon. Copyright ©2001 by Paul Muldoon. Reprinted by permission of Faber & Faber Ltd.

**Farrar, Straus and Giroux.** "The Explosion" from *The Complete Poems of Philip Larkin* by Philip Larkin, edited by Archie Burnett. Copyright ©2012 by The Estate of Philip Larkin. CAUTION: Users are warned that this work is protected under copyright laws and downloading is strictly prohibited. The right to reproduce or transfer the work via any medium must be secured with Farrar, Straus and Giroux, LLC; "Why Brownee Left" from *Poems*: 1968–1998 by Paul Muldoon. Copyright ©2001 by Paul Muldoon. Reprinted by permission of Farrar, Straus and Giroux, LLC. CAUTION: Users are warned that this work is protected under copyright laws and downloading is strictly prohibited. The right to reproduce or transfer the work via any medium must be secured with Farrar, Straus and Giroux, LLC.; Excerpt from "Midsummer" from *The Poetry of Derek Walcott*, 1948-2013 by Derek Walcott, selected by Glyn Maxwell. Copyright ©2014 by Derek Walcott. Reprinted by permission of Farrar, Straus and Giroux, LLC. CAUTION: Users are warned that this work is protected under copyright laws and downloading is strictly prohibited. The right to reproduce or transfer the work via any medium must be secured with Farrar, Straus and Giroux, LLC.; Excerpts from "Macbeth" from *Shakespeare's Language 2000* by Frank Kermode. Copyright ©2000 by Frank Kermode. Reprinted by permission of Farrar, Straus and Giroux, LLC. CAUTION: Users are warned that this work is protected under copyright laws and downloading is strictly prohibited. The right to reproduce or transfer the work via any medium must be secured with Farrar, Straus and Giroux, LLC.

**Financial Times Ltd.** "A Year in a Word: Selfie." *Financial Times*, December 27, 2013.

**Guardian News and Media Limited.** "Occupy LSX May Be Gone, but the Movement Won't Be Forgotten," Copyright Guardian New & Media Ltd 2015; Copyright Guardian News & Media Ltd 2015; Copyright Guardian News & Media Ltd 2015.

**Hinds, Gareth.** *Beowulf.* Copyright ©1999, 2000, 2007 by Gareth Hinds. Reproduced by permission of the publisher, Candlewick Press, Somerville, MA.

**Houghton Mifflin Harcourt.** "Shakespeare's Sister" from *A Room of One's Own* by Virginia Woolf. Copyright 1929 by Houghton Mifflin Harcourt Publishing Company and renewed 1957 by Leonard Woolf. Reprinted by permission of Houghton Mifflin Harcourt Publishing Company. All rights reserved; "Shooting an Elephant" from *A Collection of Essays* by George Orwell. Copyright ©1950 by Sonia Brownell Orwell and renewed 1978 by Sonia Pitt-Rivers. Reprinted by permission of Houghton Mifflin Harcourt Publishing Company. All rights reserved; Excerpt from *Mrs. Dalloway* by Virginia Woolf. Copyright 1925 by Houghton Mifflin Publishing Company. Copyright renewed 1953 by Leonard Woolf. Reprinted by permission of

Houghton Mifflin Harcourt Publishing Company. All rights reserved; Excerpt from "The Naked Babe and the Cloak of Manliness" from *The Well Wrought Urn* by Cleanth Brooks. Copyright ©1947 and renewed 1975 by Cleanth Brooks. Reprinted by permission of Houghton Mifflin Harcourt Publishing Company. All rights reserved.

**International Creative Management (ICM).** Excerpt(s) from *The Buried Giant: A Novel* by Kazuo Ishiguro, copyright ©2015 by Kazuo Ishiguro. Used by permission of International Creative Management.

**Kenrick, Douglas.** "Do You Understand the Joys of Nature?" by Douglas Kenrick, from *Psychology Today*, September 4, 2011. Used with permission of the author.

**Kunapipi.** From "An Interview with Bejamin Zephaniah" by Eric Doumerc, from *Kunapipi*, Vol. 26, I. 1 (2004). Reprinted with permission.

**LibriVox.** *The Tragedy of Macbeth*, Act V, Scene i, Courtesy of LibriVox.

**Manic D Press.** "Escape from the Old Country" by Adrienne Su, from *Sanctuary* (Manic D Press: San Francisco) ©2006 Adrienne Su. Reprinted with permission from publishers.

**Méliès, Georges.** *Le Voyage De Gulliver À Lilliput Et Chez Les Géants, Gulliver's Travels Among the Lilliputians and the Giants* (1902).

**MIT News Office.** "Does Time Pass: Philosopher Brad Skow's new book says it does — but not in the way you may think." by Peter Dizikes, from MIT News Office, January 28, 2015. Reprinted with permission of MIT News.

**Neti Neti Media.** What Is the Self? ©Science and Nonduality.

**NPR (National Public Radio).** "When Memories Never Fade, the Past Can Poison the Present," ©2013 National Public Radio, Inc. News report was originally broadcast on NPR's All Things Considered on December 2, 2013, and is used with the permission of NPR. Any unauthorized duplication is strictly prohibited

**PARS International Corporation.** "Seeing Narcissists Everywhere," from *The New York Times*, August 7, 2013 ©2013 The New York Times. All rights reserved. Used by permission and protected by the Copyright Laws of the United States. The printing, copying, redistribution, or retransmission of this Content without express written permission is prohibited.

**Penguin Books, Ltd. (UK).** "The Most Forgetful Man in the World," from *Moonwalking with Einstein: The Art and Science of Remembering Everything* by Joshua Foer, copyright ©2011 by Joshua Foer. Reproduced by permission of Penguin Books Ltd.; From *Bede: Ecclesiastical History of the English People.* 'The History' translated by Leo Sherley-Price and revised by R. E. Latham, translation of the minor works, new Introduction and Notes by D. H. Farmer (Penguin Classics 1955, Revised edition 1968, 1990). Translation copyright ©Leo Sherley-Price, 1955, 1968. Translation of 'Ecclesiastical History of the English People' copyright ©Leo Sherley-Price, 1955, 1968. Introduction copyright ©D. H. Farmer, 1990. Translation of 'Bede's Letter to Egbert' and Cuthbert's Letter on the Illness and Death of the Venerable Bede' copyright ©D. H. Farmer, 1990. Reproduced by permission of Penguin Books Ltd.; "Accidental Hero," From *Changing My Mind* by Zadie Smith. Copyright ©2009 by Zadie Smith. Reproduced by permission of Penguin Books Ltd.; "Shooting an Elephant," from *Shooting an Elephant and Other Essays* by George Orwell (Penguin Books, 2009). Copyright ©George Orwell, 1950. Reproduced by permission of Penguin Books Ltd.; "The Prologue," from *The Canterbury Tales* by Geoffrey Chaucer, translated by Nevill Coghill (Penguin Classics 1951, Fourth revised edition 1977). Copyright 1951 by Nevill Coghill. Copyright ©The Estate of Nevill Coghill, 1958, 1960, 1975, 1977. Reproduced by permission of Penguin Books Ltd.; "Pericles' Funeral Oration," from *The History of the Peloponnesian War* by Thucydides, translated by Rex Warner, with an introduction and notes by M.I. Finley (Penguin Classics 1954, Revised edition 1972). Translation copyright ©Rex Warner, 1954. Introduction and Appendices copyright ©M. I. Finley, 1972. Reproduced by permission of Penguin Books Ltd.; "The British," from *Wicked World* by Benjamin Zephaniah (Puffin, 2000) Text copyright ©Benjamin Zephaniah, 2000 Illustrations copyright ©Sarah Symonds, 2000. Reproduced by permission of Penguin Books Ltd.; "Who's Who," from *Talking Turkeys* by Benjamin Zephaniah (Viking, 1994) Copyright ©Benjamin Zephaniah, 1994. Reproduced by permission of Penguin Books Ltd.

**Penguin Group (Canada).** "Accidental Hero," from *Changing My Mind* by Zadie Smith. Copyright ©2009 Zadie Smith. Reprinted by permission of Penguin Canada, a division of Penguin Random House Canada Limited.

**Penguin Publishing Group.** "Accidental Hero," from *Changing My Mind: Occasional Essays* by Zadie Smith, copyright ©2009 by Zadie Smith. Used by permission of Penguin Press, an imprint of Penguin Publishing Group, a division of Penguin Random House LLC.; "The Most Forgetful Man in the World," from *Moonwalking with Einstein: The Art and Science of Remembering Everything* by Joshua Foer, copyright ©2011 by Joshua Foer. Used by permission of Penguin Press, an imprint of Penguin Publishing Group, a division of Penguin Random House LLC.; From *Beowulf*, translated by Burton Raffel, copyright ©1963, renewed ©1991 by Burton Raffel. Used by permission of New American Library, an imprint of Penguin Publishing Group, a division of Penguin Random House LLC.

**Peters Fraser & Dunlop.** "From Lucy: Lovely Englan' Lady" from *Lucy's Letter & Loving* by James Berry, reprinted by permission of Peters Fraser & Dunlop on behalf of James Berry.

**Peters, Fraser and Dunlop Group.** "Shakespeare's Language: Macbeth." Extract from *Shakespeare's Language* by Frank Kermode reprinted by permission of Peters Fraser & Dunlop Limited on behalf of the Estate of Frank Kermode.

**Princeton University Press.** "Ode to a Nightingale" by John Keats. Department of Rare Books and Special Collections. Princeton University Library.

**PsychCentral.com.** "What's Your Time Perspective?" from PsychCentral, http://psychcentral.com/lib/whats-your-time-perspective/. Copyright 2015 Psych Central.com. All rights reserved. Reprinted here with permission.

**Random House, Inc.** Excerpt(s) from *A Distant Mirror: The Calamitous 14th Century* by Barbara W. Tuchman, copyright ©1978 by Barbara W. Tuchman. Used by permission of Alfred A. Knopf, an imprint of the Knopf Doubleday Publishing Group, a division of Penguin Random House LLC. All rights reserved; Excerpt(s) from *The Buried Giant: A Novel* by Kazuo Ishiguro, copyright ©2015 by Kazuo Ishiguro. Used by permission of Alfred A. Knopf, an imprint of the Knopf Doubleday Publishing Group, a division of Penguin Random House LLC. All rights reserved; Excerpt(s) from *The Making of the*

*English Working Class* by E.P. Thompson, copyright © 1963 by E.P. Thompson. Used by permission of Pantheon Books, an imprint of the Knopf Doubleday Publishing Group, a division of Penguin Random House LLC. All rights reserved. Any third party use of this material, outside of this publication, is prohibited. Interested parties must apply directly to Penguin Random House LLC for permission.

**Russell & Volkening, Inc.** from "The Worms of the Earth Against the Lions," from *A Distant Mirror* reprinted by the permission of Russell & Volkening as agents for the author. Copyright ©1978 by Barbara Tuchman.

**Scientific American.** "The New Psychology of Leadership" reproduced with permission. Copyright ©2007 Scientific American, a division of Nature America, Inc. All rights reserved.

**Simon & Schuster, Inc.** "The Second Coming" reprinted with the permission of Scribner, a Division of Simon & Schuster, Inc. from *The Collected Works of W. B. Yeats, Volume I: The Poems*, Revised by W. B. Yeats, edited by Richard J. Finneran. Copyright ©1924 by The Macmillan Company, renewed 1952 by Bertha Georgie Yeats. All rights reserved.

**The English and Media Centre.** Patience Agbabi: Prologue from the Canterbury Tales: The Slam Remix, filmed at the emagazine Conference 2013 is reproduced by kind permission of the English and Media Centre.

**The Society of Authors (UK).** "Mrs. Dalloway" by Virginia Woolf, used with permission of The Society of Authors as the literary representative of the Estate of Virginia Woolf; "Shakespeare's Sister" from *A Room of One's Own* by Virginia Woolf. Used with permission of The Society of Authors.

**Tinder Press.** "Back to My Own Country: An Essay" by Andrea Levy, from *Six Stories & an Essay*. Copyright ©2014 Andrea Levy. Reproduced by permission of Headline Publishing Group; "Back to My Own Country: An Essay" by Andrea Levy, from *Six Stories & an Essay*. Copyright ©2014 Andrea Levy. Reproduced by permission of Headline Publishing Group.

**United Agents.** "The British" from WICKED WORLD by Benjamin Zephaniah (Puffin, 2000) Text copyright ©Benjamin Zephaniah, 2000. Used by permission of United Artists; "Who's Who" from *Talking Turkeys* by Benjamin Zephaniah (Viking, 1994). Copyright ©Benjamin Zephaniah, 1994. Used with permission of United Agents.

**University of Chicago Press.** Excerpt from *Oedipus the King* by Sophocles, D. Grene, trans., from *The Complete Greek Tragedies*, R. Lattimore and D. Grene, eds. Used with permission of The University of Chicago Press.

**Victoria R.M. Brown.** "How Proust Can Change Your Life" ©Victoria R.M. Brown. Big Think.

**W. W. Norton & Co.** "*The Inferno*: Canto XXXIV," from *The Divine Comedy* by Dante Allghieri, translated by John Ciardi. Copyright 1954, 1957, 1959, 1960, 1961, 1965, 1967, 1970 by the Ciardi Family Publishing Trust. Used by permission of W.W. Norton & Company, Inc.; "My Old Home" from *Selected Stories of Lu Hsun* by Lu Hsun, translated by Yang Xianyi and Gladys Yang. Copyright ©1960. Used by permission of W.W. Norton & Company, Inc.

**WGBH Media Library & Archives.** From NOVA ScienceNow, "Sleep," ©1996-2015 WGBH Educational Foundation.

**Wylie Agency.** "On Seeing England for the First Time" by Jamaica Kincaid, originally published in *Harper's*. Copyright ©1991 by Jamaica Kincaid, used by permission of The Wylie Agency, Inc.

**Yale University Press.** "Battle of Maldon" from *Poems and Prose from the Old English* by Burton Raffel. Copyright ©1998. Used with permission of the publisher, Yale University Press; "The Seafarer" from *Poems and Prose from the Old English* by Burton Raffel. Copyright ©1998. Used with permission of the publisher, Yale University Press.

# Credits

**vi** Mikkelwilliam/Getty Images;viii Olivier Martel/akg-images; **x** World History Archive/Alamy; **2** Mikkelwilliam/Getty Images; **3** (BC) Matt Cardy/ Getty Images, (BL) F.106r The Coronation of Emperor Charlemagne (742–814) by Pope Leo III (c.750–816) at St. Peters, Rome in 800, Grandes Chroniques de France, 1375–79 (vellum), French School, (14th century)/Bibliotheque Municipale, Castres, France/Bridgeman Art Library, (BR) Elizabeth I - (1533–1603) The Warrior Queen (gouache on paper), Doughty, C.L. (1913–85)/Private Collection/Look and Learn/Bridgeman Art Library, (C) Universal History Archive/UIG/Getty Images, (CL) Images from The Odyssey (c) 2010 by Gareth Hinds appear courtesy of the publisher, Candlewick Press.,(CR) UpperCut Images/Getty Images, (T) Steven Day/AP Images; (TC) Gabriel Metsu/akg-images,(TR) Hulton-Deutsch Collection/Corbis; **6** Steven Day/AP Images; 11(B) Images from The Odyssey (c) 2010 by Gareth Hinds appear courtesy of the publisher, Candlewick Press., (T) f.106r The Coronation of Emperor Charlemagne (742–814) by Pope Leo III (c.750–816) at St. Peters, Rome in 800, Grandes Chroniques de France, 1375–79 (vellum), French School, (14th century)/Bibliotheque Municipale, Castres, France/ Bridgeman Art Library; **12**(C) f.106r The Coronation of Emperor Charlemagne (742–814) by Pope Leo III (c.750–816) at St. Peters, Rome in 800, Grandes Chroniques de France, 1375–79 (vellum), French School, (14th century)/Bibliotheque Municipale, Castres, France/ Bridgeman Art Library, (L) Robana/British Library Board/Art Resource, New York, (R) Christophe Boisvieux/Corbis; 13(BL) Michael Nicholson/ Corbis, (BR) The British Library Board;**14**(L) Z.Radovan/BPL/Lebrecht Music & Arts/Lebrecht Music & Arts/Corbis, (R) Werner Forman/Corbis; **15**(L) North Wind Picture Archives/Alamy, (R) North Wind Picture Archives; **16** Burton Raffel; **17** Perart/Shutterstock; 50-60 Images from The Odyssey (c) 2010 by Gareth Hinds appear courtesy of the publisher, Candlewick Press.; **62** Steven Day/AP Images; **71**(B) Matt Cardy/Getty Images, (BCL) Everett Historical/Shutterstock; (C) Universal History Archive/UIG/Getty Images, (T) Gabriel Metsu/akg-images, (TCL) Joint Services Command and Staff College, Defence Academy of the United Kingdom; **74**(L) Gabriel Metsu/akg-images, (R) Universal History Archive/UIG/Getty Images; **75**(B) H. D. Falkenstein/Glow Images, (T) William Dobson/akg-images; **76** Gabriel Metsu/akg-images; **78** Joint Services Command and Staff College, Defence Academy of the United Kingdom; **84**(L) Gabriel Metsu/akg-images, (R) Universal History Archive/UIG/Getty Images; **85** Mary Evans/Robert Hunt Library/AGE Fotostock; **86** Universal History Archive/UIG/Getty Images; **88** Everett Historical/Shutterstock; **97** Matt Cardy/Getty Images; **99** Matt Cardy/Getty Images; Baden-Powell in the Uniform of the South African Constabulary, Standing by His Charger by John Edward Chapman 'Chester' Mathews (Major) The Scout Association; **112** Olivier Martel/akg-images; **113** (BC) Mubus7/ Shutterstock, (BR) Guzel Studio/Shutterstock, (C) Michael Nicholson/ Corbis, (CR) Gregory James Van Raalte/Shutterstock, (T) Pictorial Press Ltd/Alamy, (TC) Bob Thomas/Popperfoto/Getty Images, (TL) Heritage Image Partnership Ltd/Alamy, (TR) Anky/Shutterstock; **116** Pictorial Press Ltd/Alamy; **121**(B) Patience Agbabi Prologue to the Canterbury Tales, The Slam Remix, filmed at the emagazine Conference 2013 is reproduced by kind permission of the English and Media Centre, (T) Heritage Image Partnership Ltd/Alamy; **122** (L) Pawelkowalczyk/Fotolia, (R) Heritage Image Partnership Ltd/Alamy; **123** (C) Lordprice Collection/Alamy,(L) J.D. Dallet/AGE Fotostock, (R) The Print Collector/Alamy; **124** (C) Fototehnik/ Fotolia, (L) Prisma Archivo/Alamy, (R) Album/Prisma/Newscom; **125**(L) Pictures From History/The Image Works, (R) GFC Collection/Alamy; **126** Stapleton Collection/Corbis; **160-164** Patience Agbabi Prologue to the Canterbury Tales, The Slam Remix, filmed at the emagazine Conference 2013 is reproduced by kind permission of the English and Media Centre; **175** (B) Courtesy of The National Archives, U.K.,(C) Mubus7/ Shutterstock,(T) Bob Thomas/Popperfoto/Getty Images; (TC) Michael Nicholson/Corbis; **178** Bob Child/AP Images; **179** Bob Thomas/ Popperfoto/Getty Images; **182** Mary Evans Picture Library/Alamy; **186**, 188 Bob Thomas/Popperfoto/Getty Images;**190** Lebrecht Music and Arts Photo Library/Alamy; **191** Michael Nicholson/Corbis; **194** Michael Nicholson/Corbis; **196** Michael Nicholson/Corbis; **198** Mubus7/ Shutterstock; **199**(B) Album/Alonso & Marful/Newscom, (T) Cosima Scavolini/ZUMApress/Newscom; **200** Mubus7/Shutterstock; **209** David Levenson/Simon Dack/Keystone/Hulton Archive/Getty Images; **218, 222** Courtesy of The National Archives, U.K.; **219, 220** National Archives; **236** World History Archive/Alamy; **237**(BL) Everett Collection, (C) Hugo Philpott/Epa/Newscom, (CL) Everett Collection, (CR) Matej Michelizza/ istock/Getty Images, (T) Everett Collection, (TC) Ambrozinio/Shutterstock, (TL) Georgios Kollidas/Shutterstock, (TR) Netfalls - Remy Musser/ Shutterstock; **240** Everett Collection; **245** (BCL) Ronald Grant Archive/ Mary Evans Picture Library, (BL) Mary Evans/Ronald Grant/Everett Collection, (BR) Everett Collection, (CL) Mary Evans/Ronald Grant/Everett Collection, (CR) Everett Collection, (TCL) AF archive/Alamy; TL Everett Collection, (TR) Georgios Kollidas/Shutterstock; **246** (C) Ivy Close Images/ AGE Fotostock, (L) Georgios Kollidas/Shutterstock, (R) Marco Andras/ AGE Fotostock, (BL) Songquan Deng/123RF; **247**(BR) Georgios Kollidas/ Shutterstock, (T) Pavila/Shutterstock; **248** (C) Stocksnapper/Shutterstock, (L) Everett Historical/Shutterstock, (R) J.L. Kraemer/Blue Lantern Studio/ Corbis; **249** (L) North Wind Picture Archives/Alamy, (R) Dea/A Dagli Orti/ AGE Fotostock; **250** English School/Getty Images; **251** (B) Peter Phipp/ Britain On View/Getty Images, (R) Rafael Ben-Ari/Chameleons Eye/ Newscom; **251** (T) Moviestore collection Ltd / Alamy, (L) Everett Collection; **253** Moviestore collection Ltd / Alamy; **254** © PjrTravel / Alamy; **255** Everett Collection; **258, 280, 296** Georgios Kollidas/ Shutterstock; **259** Mary Evans/Playboy Productions Inc. Ronald Grant/ Everett Collection; **260, 266, 273, 277, 278** Everett Collection; **281** AF archive/Alamy; **285** Everett Collection; **293** AF archive/Alamy; **294** AF archive/Alamy; **306** Columbia Pictures/Album/Newscom; **297, 311, 312, 315, 331, 332, 335, 34, 350,** Mary Evans/Ronald Grant/Everett Collection; **314, 334** Georgios Kollidas/Shutterstock; **319** Everett Collection; **344** Mary Evans/Columbia Pictures/Ronald Grant/Everett Collection; **351** (C) English School/Getty Images, (B) Rafael Ben-Ari/Chameleons Eye/ Newscom, (T) Peter Phipp/Britain On View/Getty Images; **352** (B) PjrTravel/Alamy, (T) Mary Evans/Ronald Grant/Everett Collection; **354**(B) The Weinstein Company/Everett Collection, (R) Everett Collection, (T) Moviestore collection Ltd / Alamy, (TL) Everett Collection; **355** Mary Evans/Ronald Grant/Everett Collection; **357, 358, 360** Everett Collection; **369**(B) Hugo Philpott/Epa/Newscom, (T) Ambrozinio/Shutterstock; **372** Ambrozinio/Shutterstock; **373**(B) Print Collector/Hulton Archive/Getty Images, (C) Mary Osbaldeston, Lady Wrothe (1678–before 1721), Dahl, Michael (1656–1743)/Killerton, Devon, UK/National Trust Photographic Library/Bridgeman Art Library, (T) Georgios Kollidas/Shutterstock; **374** Ambrozinio/Shutterstock; **376** Pressmaster/Shutterstock; **377** Apichart Meesri/Shutterstock; **384** Hugo Philpott/Epa/Newscom; **385**(B) Martin Godwin/Hulton Archive/Getty Images, (T) Fox Photos/ Hulton Archive/Getty Images; **386** Hugo Philpott/Epa/Newscom; **390** Dominic Dibbs/Alamy; **412** Philipp Igumnov/Flickr/Photos/Woodcum/ Moment/Getty Images; **413** (BC) Inferno, Canto 21 The demons threaten Virgil, illustration from 'The Divine Comedy' by Dante Alighieri, **1885** (digitally coloured engraving), Dore, Gustave (1832–83) (after)/ Private Collection/Costa/Leemage/Bridgeman Art Library, (BL) Gulliver's Travels, from 'Treasure', **1966** (gouache on paper), Mendoza, Philip (1898–1973)/Private Collection/Look and Learn/Bridgeman Art Library, (BR) Hung Chung Chih/Shutterstock, (C) Thomas Zsebok/Shutterstock, (CL) Drop of Light/Shutterstock, (CR) Patjo/Shutterstock, T Bettmann/ Corbis, (TC) Lovers in a Punt (oil on board), Burgess, John-Bagnold (1830–97)/Private Collection/Arthur Ackermann Ltd., London/Bridgeman Art Library, (TL) GL Archive/Alamy, (TR) Timewatch Images/Alamy; **416** Bettmann/Corbis; **421** (B) Georges Méliès, BC Gulliver's Travels, from 'Treasure', 1966 (gouache on paper), Mendoza, Philip (1898–1973)/ Private Collection/Look and Learn/Bridgeman Art Library, (BC) Gulliver's Travels, from 'Treasure', 1966 (gouache on paper), Mendoza, Philip (1898–1973)/Private Collection/Look and Learn/Bridgeman Art Library, (T) GL Archive/Alamy, (TC) Drop of Light/Shutterstock; **422** (L) World History Archive/Alamy, (R) Stocktrek Images, Inc./Alamy; **423** (BC) North Wind Picture Archives/Alamy, (BL) GL Archive/Alamy, (BR) James Brittain/ Bridgeman Art Library; **424**(C) Md3d/Fotolia, (L) Fox Photos/Hulton Archive/Getty Images, (R) North Wind Picture Archives/Alamy; **425** (L) ClassicStock/Alamy, (R) Photos 12/Alamy; **426** Drop of Light/ Shutterstock; 427 Culture Club/Hulton Archive/Getty Images; **428, 432, 434, 436** Drop of Light/Shutterstock; **430** Audran Gosling/Shutterstock; **438** Gulliver's Travels, from 'Treasure', 1966 (gouache on paper), Mendoza, Philip (1898–1973)/Private Collection/Look and Learn/

Bridgeman Art Library; **438** Gulliver's Travels, from 'Treasure', 1966 (gouache on paper), Mendoza, Philip (1898–1973)/Private Collection/ Look and Learn/Bridgeman Art Library; **439** Apic/Hulton Fine Art Collection/Getty Images; **441, 446, 448, 450, 452** (L), **459**(R) Gulliver's Travels, from 'Treasure', 1966 (gouache on paper), Mendoza, Philip (1898–1973)/Private Collection/Look and Learn/Bridgeman Art Library; 452(R), **454, 457, 459** (B) Georges Méliès; **455** (L) The Advertising Archives/Alamy, (R) Arthur Rackham/Lebrecht; **456** (L) Josse Collection/ Collection Christophel/Everett Collection, (R) Lebrecht; **469** Jo Millington/ Shutterstock, (B) Prussia Art/Shutterstock, (BC) Mariusz Niedzwiedzki/ Shutterstock, (C) Inferno, Canto 21 The demons threaten Virgil, illustration from 'The Divine Comedy' by Dante Alighieri, 1885 (digitally coloured engraving), Dore, Gustave (1832–83) (after)/Private Collection / Costa/Leemage/Bridgeman Art Library, (T) Lovers in a Punt (oil on board), Burgess, JohnBagnold (1830–97)/Private Collection/ Arthur Ackermann Ltd., London/Bridgeman Art Library, (TC) Thomas Zsebok/Shutterstock; **472**(BL) Culture Club/Contributor/Getty Images, (TL) Lovers in a Punt (oil on board), Burgess, John-Bagnold (1830–97)/Private Collection/Arthur Ackermann Ltd., London/Bridgeman Art Library, (TR) Thomas Zsebok/Shutterstock; **473, 477, 479, 480**(L) Lovers in a Punt (oil on board), Burgess, John-Bagnold (1830–97)/Private Collection/Arthur Ackermann Ltd., London/Bridgeman Art Library; **480** (R) Thomas Zsebok/Shutterstock; **481**(B) Kean Collection/Archive Photos/Getty Images, (T) Universal History Archive/Getty Images; **482** Thomas Zsebok/Shutterstock; 483 Pingu2004/Fotolia; **490, 492** Inferno, Canto 21 The demons threaten Virgil, illustration from 'The Divine Comedy' by Dante Alighieri, 1885 (digitally coloured engraving), Dore, Gustave (1832–83) (after)/Private Collection /Costa/Leemage/ Bridgeman Art Library; **491**(B) Dea Picture Library/De Agostini/Getty Images, (T) Stock Montage/Archive Photos/Getty Images; **498** Clive Rees Photography/Moment/Getty Images; **504** Culture Club/Hulton Archive/ Getty Images; **505**(L),**512**(L), **514**(L) Jo Millington/Shutterstock; **505**(R),**512** (R), **514** (R) Mariusz Niedzwiedzki/Shutterstock; **516, 518, 519** Prussia Art/Shutterstock; **517**(B) Jason Larkin,(T) Photoshot/Newscom; **520** Prill/Shutterstock; **538** Paul Zizka/All Canada Photos/Getty Images, **539** (BC) Nataliya Arzamasova/Shutterstock, (BL) Vitaly Ilyasov/Fotolia, (BR) Masson/Shutterstock, (C) Dudarev Mikhail/Shutterstock, (CL) Honza Krej/Shutterstock, (CR) Usamedeniz/Fotolia, (T) Melissa Ross/ Moment Open/Getty Images, (TC) Popperfoto/Getty Images, (TL) Glasshouse Images/Alamy, (TR) Blue Iris/Shutterstock; **542** Melissa Ross/ Moment Open/Getty Images; **547**(BC) Vitaly Ilyasov/Fotolia, (T) Glasshouse Images/Alamy, (TC) Honza Krej/Shutterstock; **548**(C) Ayzek/123RF, (L) Dieter Hawlan/123RF, (R) Gianni Dagli Orti/The Art Archive at Art Resource, New York; **549**(BL) Glasshouse Images/Alamy, (BR) Bettmann/Corbis, (CL) Igor Zh./Shutterstock, (CR) The Orrery'. c.1766 (oil on canvas), Wright of Derby, Joseph (1734–97)/Derby Museum and Art Gallery, UK/Bridgeman Art Library, (TL) Active Museum/Alamy, (TR) Berlin/Bpk/Art Resource, New York; **550**(C) North Wind Picture Archives/Alamy, (L) HodagMedia/Shutterstock, (R) North Wind Picture Archives/Alamy; **551**(L) Guildhall Library & Art Gallery/ Heritage Images/Getty Images, (R) Mary Evans Picture Library/Alamy; **552**(L), **554, 556, 568**(L) Honza Krej/Shutterstock; **552** (R), **568** (R), **570, 573** Vitaly Ilyasov/Fotolia; **553** Georgios Kollidas/Shutterstock; **559** Leemage/Corbis, **569** (B) The Print Collector/Hulton Archive/Getty Images, (T) Corbis; **574** Andreiuc88/Shutterstock; **584** Dea Picture Library/DeAgostini/Getty Images; **604** Melissa Ross/Moment Open/Getty Images; **613**(B) Ssilver/123RF,(BC) Fanatic Studio/Getty Images, (C) Nataliya Arzamasova/Shutterstock, (T) Popperfoto/Getty Images, (TC) Dudarev Mikhail/Shutterstock; **616** Culture Club/Hulton Archive/Getty Images; **617, 620, 622** Popperfoto/Getty Images; **624, 626** Dudarev Mikhail/Shutterstock; **625** (B) Georgios Kollidas/Shutterstock, (T) Hulton Archive/Getty Images; **628** Margo_black/Shutterstock; **636** Apic/ Hulton Archive/Getty Images; **637, 642, 644** Nataliya Arzamasova/ Shutterstock; **646**(BL) Manuel Silvestri/Polaris/Newscom, (R) Ssilver/123RF, (TL) Fanatic Studio/Getty Images; **647, 655, 656, 658**(L), **662**(T) Fanatic Studio/Getty Images; **658**(R), **659, 661, 662** (B) Ssilver/123RF; **676** Carlos Cazalis/Corbis; **677** (BC) Nodff/Shutterstock, (BL) Jonathan Pledger/Shutterstock, BR Yi Lu/Viewstock/Corbis; (C) Martin Moxter/imageBROKER/Corbis, (CL) Daily Herald Archive/SSPL/ Getty Images, (T) Anthony Hatley/Alamy, (TC) North Wind Picture Archives/Alamy; (TL) Robert Maass/Corbis; (TR) Samuel Goldwyn/Everett Collection; **680** Anthony Hatley/Alamy; **685**(B) Jonathan Pledger/ Shutterstock, (C) Daily Herald Archive/SSPL/Getty Images, (T) Robert Maass/Corbis; **686**(C) Akademie/Alamy, (L) Interfoto/Alamy, (R) Everett Collection Historical/Alamy; **687** (C) Marka/Alamy, (L) Everett Historical/Shutterstock, (R) Bettmann/Corbis; **688**(C) Homer Sykes/Alamy, (L) NASA, (R) Robert Maass/Corbis; **689** (L) PCN Photography/Alamy, (R) Luca Teuchmann/WireImage/Getty Images; **690**(BL) David Levenson/Getty Images, (TL) Daily Herald Archive/SSPL/Getty Images, (TR) Jonathan Pledger/Shutterstock; **691, 700, 702, 704, 716** Daily Herald Archive/SSPL/Getty Images; **696** Peeter Viisimaa/Ocean/Corbis; **704**(BL) Ullstein Bild/Getty Images,(TR) Jonathan Pledger/Shutterstock; **705, 712, 714** Jonathan Pledger/Shutterstock; **718** Anthony Hatley/Alamy; **727**(BC) The Print Collector/Print Collector/Getty Images, (C) Nodff/Shutterstock, (T) North Wind Picture Archives/Alamy, (TC) Martin Moxter/Image Broker/Corbis; **730**(BL) Hulton Archive/Getty Images, (TL) North Wind Picture Archives/Alamy, (TR) Martin Moxter/Image Broker/Corbis; **731, 735, 737, 738** (L), 742T North Wind Picture Archives/Alamy; **738**(R), **739, 741, 742** (B) Martin Moxter/Image Broker/Corbis; **744, 746** Nodff/ Shutterstock; **745**(B) © Guy Freeman, (C) Hulton Archive/Getty Images, (T) Burton Raffel; **750** Oks88/Shutterstock; **752** Mike_expert/ Shutterstock; **758** The Print Collector/Print Collector/Getty Images; **759** (C) Rischgitz/Hulton Archive/Getty Images, (B) Foto © gezett; **760** The Print Collector/Print Collector/Getty Images; **762** Trinity Mirror/Mirrorpix/ Alamy.

## Credits for Images in Interactive Student Edition Only

### Unit 1

© Mary Evans Picture Library; Alessandro0770/Alamy; Bettmann/Corbis; Colin McPherson/Corbis; Elizabeth I, Armada Portrait, c.1588 (oil on panel), Gower, George (1540–96) (attr. to)/Woburn Abbey, Bedfordshire, UK/Bridgeman Images; Hulton-Deutsch Collection/Corbis; James Mackay/Alamy; North Wind Picture Archives/AP Images; Raymond Lynde, Nurse Edith Cavell, oil on canvas, Norfolk Museums Service (Norwich Castle Museum & Art Gallery); Baden-Powell in the Uniform of the South African Constabulary, Standing by His Charger by John Edward Chapman 'Chester' Mathews (Major) The Scout Association; Dan Llywelyn Hall; Eileen Tweedy/The Art Archive at Art Resource, NY; Imperial War Museum/The Art Archive at Art Resource, NY; National Army Museum/The Art Archive at Art Resource, NY; PjrStudio/Alamy; Portrait of Harry Patch, 2009 (oil on canvas), Llywelyn Hall, Dan (b.1980)/Victoria Art Gallery, Bath and North East Somerset Council/Bridgeman Art Library; Private Collection The Stapleton Collection/Bridgeman Art Library; Seapix/Alamy; Wellcome Library, London.

### Unit 2

1000 Words/Shutterstock; A katz/Shutterstock; Everett Collection/Shutterstock; Ian Gavan/ZUMA Press/Newscom; JeniFoto/Shutterstock; Justin Williams/REX/Newscom; Lebrecht Music and Arts Photo Library/Alamy; Lfi/Zumapress/Newscom; North Wind Picture Archives/Alamy; North Wind Picture Archives/AP Images; Tal Cohen/Photoshot/Newscom; Trinity Mirror/Mirrorpix/Alamy

### Unit 3

© John H. McDonald; © Jon Haward; © Nigel Dobbyn; Agsandrew/Shutterstock; Gary Erskine; Georgios Kollidas/Shutterstock; Hulton Archive/Getty Images; Hulton-Deutsch Collection/Corbis; Jane Collingwood; Northy Sona Sladeckova/Shutterstock; Oliver Morris/Archive Photos/Getty Images; Peter Dizikes; Szabkovphoto/Shutterstock; The Print Collector/Hulton Archive/Getty Images; TuanBesar/Alamy; Vera Zinkova/Shutterstock; YoONSpY/Shutterstock

### Unit 4

David Levenson/Hulton Archive/Getty Images; Duncan1890/Istock/Getty Images; Japan: Sei Shonagon (c. 966–1017) Japanese author and court lady of the middle Heian Era, is best known as the author of The Pillow Book 'Makura no Soshi'/Pictures from History/Bridgeman Images; Mike Coppola/Getty Images; Stock Montage/Archive Photos/Getty Images; Sundari/Shutterstock; UniversalImagesGroup/Getty Images; O'Keeffe, Georgia (1887–1986) © ARS, NY From the Faraway, Nearby, 1937. Oil on canvas, H. 36, W. 40–1/8 inches (91.2 x 102 cm.). Alfred Stieglitz Collection, 1959 (59.204.2). Photo: Malcom Varon.

### Unit 5

Ann Ronan Pictures/Print Collector/Getty Images; David Levenson/Getty Images; Ilya S.Savenok/Getty Images; Jesus Colon; Monkey Business/Fotolia; STF/AFP/Getty Images

### Unit 6

Bettmann/Corbis; Christie's Images/Corbis; David Oxberry/AGE Fotostock; Tiziana Fabi/AFP/Getty Images